D1665604

Published by:
Kluwer Law International B.V.
PO Box 316
2400 AH Alphen aan den Rijn
The Netherlands
E-mail: lrs-sales@wolterskluwer.com
Website: www.wolterskluwer.com/en/solutions/kluwerlawinternational

Sold and distributed by:
Wolters Kluwer Legal & Regulatory U.S.
7201 McKinney Circle
Frederick, MD 21704
United States of America
E-mail: customer.service@wolterskluwer.com

ISBN 978-94-035-1026-2

e-Book: ISBN 978-94-035-1046-0
web-PDF: ISBN 978-94-035-1056-9

Platforms in EU VAT Law

A Legal Analysis of the Supply of Goods

Christina Pollak

Platforms in EU VAT Law

EUCOTAX Series on European Taxation

VOLUME 70

Series Editors

Prof. Dr Peter H.J. Essers, Fiscal Institute Tilburg/Center for Company Law, Tilburg University

Prof. Dr Eric C.C.M. Kemmeren, Fiscal Institute Tilburg/Center for Company Law, Tilburg University

Prof. Dr Dr h.c. Michael Lang, WU (Vienna University of Economics and Business)

Introduction

EUCOTAX (European Universities Cooperating on Taxes) is a network of tax institutes currently consisting of eleven universities: WU (Vienna University of Economics and Business) in Austria, Katholieke Universiteit Leuven in Belgium, Corvinus University of Budapest, Hungary, Université Paris-I Panthéon-Sorbonne in France, Universität Osnabrück in Germany, Libera, Università Internazionale di Studi Sociali in Rome (and Università degli Studi di Bologna for the research part), in Italy, Fiscaal Instituut Tilburg at Tilburg University in the Netherlands, Universidad de Barcelona in Spain, Uppsala University in Sweden, Queen Mary and Westfield College at the University of London in the United Kingdom, and Georgetown University in Washington DC, United States of America. The network aims at initiating and coordinating both comparative education in taxation, through the organization of activities such as winter courses and guest lectures, and comparative research in the field, by means of joint research projects, international conferences and exchange of researchers between various countries.

Contents/Subjects

The EUCOTAX series covers a wide range of topics in European tax law. For example tax treaties, EC case law, tax planning, exchange of information and VAT. The series is well-known for its high-quality research and practical solutions.

Objective

The series aims to provide insights on new developments in European taxation.

Readership

Practitioners and academics dealing with European tax law.

Frequency of Publication

2-3 new volumes published each year.

The titles published in this series are listed at the end of this volume.

Table of Contents

xi

List of Figures

List of Tables

List of Abbreviations

AG	Advocate General at the European Court of Justice
Apr.	April
Art.	article(s)
AT	Austria, Austrian
Aug.	August
B2B	business to business: transactions conducted between two taxable persons for VAT purposes
BEPS	Base Erosion and Profit Shifting
BFH	Bundesfinanzhof (German Federal Tax Court)
BGH	Bundesgerichtshof (German Federal Court of Justice)
C2B	consumer to business: transactions conducted between a non-taxable and a taxable person for VAT purposes
C2C	consumer to consumer: transactions conducted between two non-taxable persons for VAT purposes
CFR	Charter of Fundamental Rights of the European Union
ch.	chapter(s)
CJEU	Court of Justice of the European Union
DAC 7	Council Directive (EU) 2021/514 of 22 March 2021 Amending Directive 2011/16/EU on Administrative Cooperation in the Field of Taxation
Dec.	December
DStR	Deutsches Steuerrecht
e.g.	*exempli gratia*: meaning 'for example'
EC	European Community
e-commerce	electronic commerce
EEA	European Economic Area
e-retailer	electronic retailer

et seq.	et sequens: and the following (page/paragraph)
et seqq.	et sequential: and the following (pages/paragraphs)
EU	European Union
EuGH	Europäischer Gerichtshof: German-language version of the European Court of Justice
EU-OSS	European Union One-Stop-Shop
EUR	Euro(s)
Euratom	European Atomic Energy Community
EY	Ernst & Young
Feb.	February
FG	Finanzgericht (German Tax Court)
First VAT Directive	First Council Directive 67/227/EEC of 11 April 1967 on the Harmonisation of Legislation of Member States Concerning Turnover Taxes
GST	Goods and Services Tax
HU	Hungary, Hungarian
i.e.	*id est*: meaning 'that is to say'
IBFD	International Bureau of Fiscal Documentation
IOSS	Import One-Stop-Shop
Jan.	January
Jul.	July
Jun.	June
Mar.	March
MOSS	Mini-One-Stop-Shop
MwStR	Mehrwertsteuerrecht
no.	number(s)
Non-EU-OSS	Non-European Union One-Stop-Shop
Nov.	November
NWB	Neue Wirtschaftsbriefe
Oct.	October
OECD	Organisation for Economic Co-operation and Development
OSS	One-Stop-Shop
ÖStZ	Österreichische Steuerzeitung
p.	page
pp.	pages
para.	paragraph
paras	paragraphs
pt.	point(s)
RU	Russia, Russian
s.	section(s)
Sep.	September

Sixth VAT Directive	Sixth Council Directive 77/388/EEC of 17 May 1977 on the Harmonization of the Laws of the Member States Relating to Turnover Taxes – Common System of Value Added Tax: Uniform Basis of Assessment
SME	Small- and Medium-Sized Enterprises
SSRN	Social Science Research Network
SWI	Steuer und Wirtschaft International
SWK	Steuer- und WirtschaftsKartei
TAG	Technical Advisory Group
taxud	Taxation and Customs Union Directorate-General
TEU	Treaty on European Union
TFEU	Treaty on the Functioning of the European Union
the Court	Court of Justice of the European Union
UCC	Regulation (EU) No 952/2013 of the European Parliament and of the Council of 9 October 2013 Laying Down the Union Customs Code
UCC-DA	Commission Delegated Regulation (EU) 2015/2446 of 28 July 2015 Supplementing Regulation (EU) No 952/2013 of the European Parliament and of the Council as Regards Detailed Rules Concerning Certain Provisions of the Union Customs Code
UCC-IR	Commission Implementing Regulation (EU) 2015/2447 of 24 November 2015 Laying Down Detailed Rules for Implementing Certain Provisions of Regulation (EU) No 952/2013 of the European Parliament and of the Council Laying Down the Union Customs Code
US	United States
VAT	value added tax
VAT Directive	Council Directive 2006/112/EC of 28 November 2006 on the common system of value added tax
VAT Implementing Regulation	Council Implementing Regulation (EU) No 282/2011 of 15 March 2011 Laying Down Implementing Measures for Directive 2006/112/EC on the Common System of Value Added Tax
VAT-ID	Value Added Tax Identification
WCO	World Customs Organisation

Acknowledgements

This book was written during my work as a KPMG Research Project Assistant at the Institute for Austrian and International Tax Law and was accepted as a doctoral thesis at the Vienna University of Economics and Business in the summer semester of 2022. It takes into account the legislation, cases, and literature published up until April 2022.

I would like to take this opportunity to thank all of the people who have supported me in writing this dissertation. I sincerely thank the doctoral committee of this book, Karoline Spies, Claus Staringer, and Caroline Heber for their patience, support, and valuable input throughout the progress. Special thanks must be appointed to the primary supervisor of this book, Karoline Spies, for her thorough feedback as well as academic guidance not only on this book but also on all of my projects in the last years. I sincerely want to thank you for being my academic mentor but most of all for sharing your passion for VAT with me. Additionally, I would also like to thank Georg Kofler, Michael Lang, Alexander Rust, and Josef Schuch for their support and guidance on my academic journey in the last years. A big thank you also to my dear friends at the institute who have kept on challenging my thinking with critical and interesting input and discussions in the course of our joint publications, conferences, and VAT coffees.

Additionally, the finalisation of this book would not have been possible without the support from KPMG. I want to thank Esther Freitag who has always given me the confidence not to give up even in difficult phases and to consistently pursue my goal. Special thanks also go to Klaudia Nadlinger who was, with her comprehensive knowledge and practical input, a decisive support. A big thank you also to Alfred Mühlberger for having my back and filling in for me when it was most necessary.

Moreover, I would also like to extend my deepest gratitude to my family for their unconditional support, faith, and continuous encouragement for my education during the last years. Finally, I am extremely grateful for my dear Devid who stood by my side throughout this process and who repeatedly took the indispensable little things of everyday life off my hands to ensure that I got through this intensive time well.

Chapter 1

Setting the Scene

1.1   BACKGROUND

The taxation of the digital economy has been a major challenge for governments and tax administrations. Due to globalisation and digitalisation, the economic market for goods and services has expanded. Suppliers transitioned their attention from a local market to a global market. This market expansion concerns not only goods that are imported from throughout the world into the EU but also services. One priority for tax authorities must be to establish a fair and uniform taxation for the suppliers. This applies both to taxes on income and especially to the VAT. VAT is an important instrument for taxing the turnover of the platform economy at the place of consumption. In order to ensure fair and equitable taxation for all parties, the enforcement of tax obligations and correct determination by the Member States must be ensured. The tax obligations of the platform economy should not be based on tax arbitrariness nor be dependent on where the supplier is established.

In general, the VAT system was developed in analogue times and is still linked to territorial circumstances. Thereby, especially the determination of the place of supply is decisive in determining the place of taxation. In the case of transactions involving physical objects that are sold 'online', it is rather easy to determine two locations, i.e., the place from where the goods come and the place where the goods are delivered. This is mainly because, in cross-border business processes, the physical goods are at least theoretically subject to investigation by the customs authorities. Nevertheless, in the past years, especially the importation from third countries and supplies by third country suppliers have resulted in VAT revenue losses within the EU. This was mainly caused by two reasons. The first is the small-consignment exemption for imports of

EUR 22 or below as determined by the Member States.[1] Studies show that a considerable amount of VAT was lost due to the small-consignment exemption because of fraudulent behaviour or misdeclarations of suppliers.[2] Second, it was difficult to get third country suppliers to comply with the European VAT rules and to register and pay the VAT due which led to a distortion of competition in favour of third country suppliers.[3] Since a lot of the sales to EU customers are enabled through digital platforms, the platforms hold all of the information necessary for the correct taxation of the supplied goods. With the goal of countering the missing information of the European tax authorities and to fight the VAT fraud within the EU, European rules for platforms have been introduced.

As of July 2021, platforms became liable for the VAT on supplies of imported low-value goods and on supplies of goods by third country suppliers supplied throughout their medium.[4] At the same time, the import exemption for small consignments was abolished. The objective of these extensive changes was to make the VAT system resilient to fraud, simplify compliance obligations, enforce the principle of neutrality, and reduce distortion of competition.[5] The amendments should secure that non-European businesses become more compliant with the EU compliance rules.

Against this background, it is timely to comprehensively study the VAT treatment of digital platforms, updated in light of recent developments. Thereby, a study of the scope and consequences of the new rules would be particularly useful while taking into consideration the case law of the CJEU when necessary and the literature provided in academia. This research analyses the legislative changes and identifies their weaknesses, their opportunities, and possible limits for the Member States' implementation.

1. *See* a report from the European Commission of 2014 in which the European Commission argued that the small-consignment exemption causes distortions of competition and should therefore be abandoned; *see* European Commission, *Proposal for a Council Directive Amending Directive 2006/112/EC and Directive 2009/132/EC as Regards Certain Value Added Tax Obligations for Supplies of Services and Distance Sales of Goods*, COM(2016) 757 final 2 (1 Dec. 2016), https://ec.europa.eu/transparency/regdoc/rep/1/2016/EN/COM-2016-757-F1-EN-MAIN-PART-1.PDF (last visited 28 Jan. 2021).
2. *See* the study conducted by EY on behalf of the European Commission: European Commission, *Assessment of the Application and Impact of the VAT Exemption for Importation of Small Consignments*, Specific Contract No 7 TAXUD/2013/DE/334 Based on Framework Contract No Taxud/2012/CC/117, Final Report 70 (May 2015), https://ec.europa.eu/taxation_customs/sites /taxation/files/docs/body/lvcr-study.pdf (last visited 2 Feb. 2021); *see* also Steven Pope et al., *Import Value De Minimis Level in Selected Economies as Cause of Undervaluation of Imported Goods*, 8 World Customs Journal (2014).
3. European Commission, *Proposal for a Council Directive Amending Directive 2006/112/EC and Directive 2009/132/EC as Regards Certain Value Added Tax Obligations for Supplies of Services and Distance Sales of Goods*, *supra* note 1, at 2.
4. *See* Article 14a of the Council Directive 2006/112/EC of 28 November 2006 on the common system of value added tax, OJ L 347/1 (2006).
5. European Commission, *Proposal for a Council Directive Amending Directive 2006/112/EC and Directive 2009/132/EC as Regards Certain Value Added Tax Obligations for Supplies of Services and Distance Sales of Goods*, *supra* note 1, at 2.

1.2   JUSTIFICATION OF THE TOPIC

1.2.1   State of the Field

The VAT treatment of different business models conducted with the help of the Internet has been discussed from different angles in literature over the past years. The rapid development of the Internet and the new business opportunities provided thereof are pushing the existing European VAT system to a limit as the basic structure of the European VAT system was introduced in the 1970s with the Sixth Directive.[6] Since then, the European VAT system has undergone several legislative changes; the biggest reform is the introduction of the VAT Directive currently in force.[7] Still, it is challenging to apply the VAT rules in force to the new forms of supplies on the Internet. Therefore, subsequent partial changes to the VAT Directive have been introduced. The issue of digital sales and platforms has not only been on the legislative agenda of the EU but also the OECD published an extensive report on the collection of VAT for sales through platforms in 2019.[8]

The research undergone in this area can be clustered into four different subtopics that will be shortly discussed in the following: (i) the supply of online services, (ii) the question of whether data should be considered as consideration in VAT terms, (iii) questions originating from the platform economy which include: (a) the blurred line of taxable persons for the supply of goods or services over such platforms and (b) the question of the VAT treatment of the service offered by platforms and, finally, (iv) the amendments of the VAT treatment of platforms due to the e-commerce package.[9]

The first amendment of the VAT system to counter issues resulting from the digitalisation was undertaken regarding the supply of online services (i) with the introduction of a separate VAT system for electronically supplied services.[10] With this legislative change, the place of supply rules have been amended in order to implement the principle of destination. Since 2015, any electronically supplied service provided to a consumer (B2C) is to be taxed at the place of residence of the consumer. Hand in hand with this amendment, the MOSS system was introduced with the goal of limiting the compliance burdens for businesses.[11] The challenges evolving from digital supplies of

---

6. Sixth Council Directive 77/388/EEC of 17 May 1977 on the Harmonization of the Laws of the Member States Relating to Turnover Taxes – Common System of Value Added Tax: Uniform Basis of Assessment, OJ L 145 (1977).
7. Council Directive 2006/112/EC of 28 November 2006 on the Common System of Value Added Tax, OJ L 347/1 (2006).
8. See OECD, *The Role of Digital Platforms in the Collection of VAT/GST on Online Sales* (Mar. 2019), http://www.oecd.org/tax/consumption/the-role-of-digital-platforms-in-the-collection-of-vat-gst -on-online-sales.pdf (last visited 24 Jul. 2020).
9. The undergone research on the amendments of the VAT treatment of platforms due to the e-commerce package (iv) will be discussed in the subsequent s. 1.2.2 Research Objectives.
10. Council Directive 2008/8/EC of 12 February 2008 Amending Directive 2006/112/EC as Regards the Place of Supply of Services, OJ L 44/11 (2008); *see also* Marie Lamensch, *Tax Assessment in a Digital Context: A Critical Analysis of the 2015 EU Rules*, in *Value Added Tax and the Digital Economy* (Marie Lamensch et al. eds., Wolters Kluwer 2016).
11. Council Directive 2008/8/EC of 12 February 2008 Amending Directive 2006/112/EC as Regards the Place of Supply of Services; Commission Implementing Regulation (EU) No 815/2012 of 13

services have been discussed and analysed in depth by Lamensch who also gave suggestions on how to reform the EU VAT framework.[12]

With the rise of social media, one issue has been widely discussed especially in German literature: (ii) the question of whether 'free' online services should be taxable. Examples of these free online services are search engines, social media platforms, and mobile apps. Although the services are free of monetary charge for the consumer, the consumer agrees that the service providers may use the generated users' data. This data is used by the service provider not only to improve the services but also, e.g., for personalised advertisement. Therefore, in academia, the widely discussed question arose of whether the data provided by the consumer could be qualified as 'consideration' and consequently might lead to a taxable transaction by the platform.[13]

September 2012 Laying down Detailed Rules for the Application of Council Regulation (EU) No 904/2010, as Regards Special Schemes for Non-Established Taxable Persons Supplying Telecommunications, Broadcasting or Electronic Services to Non-Taxable Persons, OJ L 249 (2012); Council Regulation (EU) No 967/2012 of 9 October 2012 Amending Implementing Regulation (EU) No 282/2011 as Regards the Special Schemes for Non-Established Taxable Persons Supplying Telecommunications Services, Broadcasting Services or Electronic Services to Non-Taxable Persons, OJ L 290 (2012); *see also* European Commission, *Guide to the VAT Mini One Stop Shop* (23 Oct. 2013), https://ec.europa.eu/taxation_customs/business/vat/tele communications-broadcasting-electronic-services/sites/default/files/taxud-2013-01228-02-01-en-ori-00-en.pdf (last visited 19 Jul. 2021); European Commission, *Explanatory Notes on the EU VAT Changes to the Place of Supply of Telecommunications, Broadcasting and Electronic Services That Enter into Force in 2015* (3 Apr. 2014), https://ec.europa.eu/taxation_customs/sites/taxation/files/resources/documents/taxation/vat/how_vat_works/telecom/explanatory_notes _2015_en.pdf (last visited 2 Feb. 2021); Ine Lejeune & Sophie Claessens, *The VAT One Stop Shop System: An Efficient Way to Collect VAT on Digital Supplies into the EU Consumer Market?*, in *Value Added Tax and the Digital Economy* (Marie Lamensch et al. eds., Wolters Kluwer 2016); Panos Thliveros, *EU OSS & MOSS: A Solution to the Challenges of the Digital Economy?*, in *Taxation in a Global Digital Economy* (Ina Kerschner & Maryte Somare eds., Linde Verlag 2017).

12. Marie Lamensch, *European Value Added Tax in the Digital Era: A Critical Analysis and Proposals for Reform* 253 et seqq. (IBFD 2015).

13. *See* the authors, who support that this is a taxable transaction: David Dietsch, *Umsatzsteuerpflicht von kostenlosen sozialen Netzwerken*, MwStR (2017); Tina Ehrke-Rabel et al., *Umsatzsteuer in einer digitalisierten Welt* 33 et seqq. (ifst-Schrift 2020); Tina Ehrke-Rabel & Sebastian Pfeiffer, *Umsatzsteuerbarer Leistungsaustausch durch 'entgeltlose' digitale Dienstleistungen*, SWK (2017); Nevada Melan & Sebastian Pfeiffer, *Bezahlen mit Rechten, nicht mit Daten: Weitere offene Fragen zur Umsatzsteuerpflicht 'kostenloser' Internetdienste und Smartphone-Apps*, DStR (2017); Nevada Melan & Bertram Wecke, *Umsatzsteuerpflicht von 'kostenlosen' Internetdiensten und Smartphone-Apps*, DStR (2015); Nevada Melan & Bertram Wecke, *Einzelfragen der Umsatzsteuerpflicht 'kostenloser' Internetdienste und Smartphone-Apps*, DStR (2015); Stephan Filtzinger, *Sektorales oder generelles Reverse-Charge? – Reformbedarf bei der Steuerschuldverlagerung*, in *100 Jahre Umsatzsteuer in Deutschland 1918-2018: Festschrift* 708 (Umsatzsteuer-Forum e.V. ed., Otto Schmidt 2018); Sebastian Pfeiffer, *VAT on 'Free' Electronic Services?*, 27 International VAT Monitor (2016); Sebastian Pfeiffer, *Comment on 'Free' Internet Services*, in *CJEU – Recent Developments in Value Added Tax 2017* (Michael Lang et al. eds., Linde Verlag 2018). *See* the authors, who disagree with this approach: Katharina Artinger, *Taxing Consumption in the Digital Age: Challenges for European VAT* 212 et seq. (Nomos 2020); Dietmar Aigner et al., *Digitale Leistungen ohne Geldzahlung im Internet*, SWK (2017); Joachim Englisch, *'Kostenlose' Online-Dienstleistungen: tauschähnlicher Umsatz?*, 66 Umsatzsteuer-Rundschau (2017); Hans-Martin Grambeck, *Keine Umsatzsteuerpflicht bei kostenlosen Internetdiensten und Smartphone-Apps*, DStR 2026 et seqq. (2015); Nicole Looks & Benjamin Bergau, *Tauschähnlicher Umsatz mit Nutzerdaten – Kein Stück vom Kuchen*, MwStR (2016). Michael Tumpel, *Umsatzsteuer bei 'unentgeltlichen' Onlinediensten*, in *Digitalisierung im Konzernsteuerrecht* (Sabine Kirchmayr et al. eds., Linde Verlag 2018). *See* also the discussion on the question of

Furthermore, among the discussed issues are several questions arising from (iii) the platform economy where non-taxable persons act as suppliers. Within these new business models, the tax authorities are confronted with the issue of regarding when suppliers of goods or services become taxable persons according to Article 9 VAT Directive which is one of the prerequisites for being liable to pay VAT (a). The question under which conditions a person becomes a taxable person has been discussed in several cases in the CJEU[14] but never in the context of platform economy suppliers. Several authors have elaborated on this question in academia.[15] Moreover, the European Commission has also tried to draw a line for when suppliers become taxable persons within the sharing economy.[16] Recently, the VAT treatment of the supplies provided by platforms has caused discussions (b). The main question of this discussion is how the services provided by a digital platform should be qualified and whether they are two distinct supplies, i.e., one being the supply of the good or service provided by the underlying supplier and the other one being the intermediation provided by the platform. Additionally, the follow-up question of what kind of service is provided by the platform has been analysed by scholars.[17]

---

whether third-party payments by the person to whom the data is sold could be the basis for the consideration: Florian Zawodsky, *Value Added Taxation in the Digital Economy*, British Tax Review (2018); Giorgio Beretta, *European VAT and the Sharing Economy* 124 et seqq. (Kluwer Law International 2019).

14. Case C-230/94, *Enkler v Finanzamt Homburg*, 26 Sep. 1996, ECLI:EU:C:1996:352; Joined Cases C-180/10 and C-181/10, *Jarosław Słaby v Minister Finansów (C-180/10) and Emilian Kuć and Halina Jeziorska-Kuć v Dyrektor Izby Skarbowej w Warszawie (C-181/10)*, 15 Sep. 2011, ECLI:EU:C:2011:589; Case C-263/11, *Ainars Redlihs v Valsts ieņemumu dienests*, 19 Jul. 2012, ECLI:EU:C:2012:497; Case C-219/12, *Finanzamt Freistadt Rohrbach Urfahr v Unabhängiger Finanzsenat Außenstelle Linz*, 20 Jun. 2013, ECLI:EU:C:2013:413.

15. *See*, e.g., Giorgio Beretta, *supra* note 13, at 75 et seqq.; Nevia Čičin-Šain, *Taxing Uber*, in *Uber – Brave New Service or Unfair Competition: Legal Analysis of the Nature of Uber Services* 187 et seq. (Jasenko Marin et al. eds., Springer International Publishing 2020); Tina Ehrke-Rabel et al., *supra* note 13, at 58 et seqq.; Ivo Grlica, *How the Sharing Economy Is Challenging the EU VAT System*, 28 International VAT Monitor 127 (2017); Marie Lamensch, *The Scope of the EU VAT System: Traditional Digital Economy Related Questions*, in *CJEU – Recent Developments in Value Added Tax 2017* (Michael Lang et al. eds., Linde Verlag 2018); Katerina Pantazatou, *Taxation of the Sharing Economy in the European Union*, in *The Cambridge Handbook of the Law of the Sharing Economy* (Nestor M. Davidson et al. eds., Oxford University Press 2018); Desiree Auer et al., *Umsatzsteuer im Rahmen der digitalen Transformation*, taxlex (2019).

16. *See* VAT Committee, *VAT Treatment of Sharing Economy*, Working Paper No. 878, tax-ud.c.1(2015)4370160 (22 Sep. 2015), https://circabc.europa.eu/sd/a/878e0591-80c9-4c58-baf3-b9fda1094338/878%20-%20VAT%20treatment%20of%20sharing%20economy.pdf (last visited 19 Jul. 2021); *see also* VAT Committee, *VAT Treatment of Crowdfunding*, Working Paper No. 836, taxud.c.1(2015)576037 (6 Feb. 2015), https://circabc.europa.eu/sd/a/c9b4bb6f-3313-4c5d-8b4c-c8bbaf0c175a/836%20-%20VAT%20treatment%20of%20Crowd%20funding.pdf (last visited 19 Jul. 2021).

17. *See*, e.g., Selina Siller & Annika Streicher, *Online Beherbungsplattformen: Leistung des Vermieters und Leistung der Plattform als einheitliche Leistung?*, taxlex (2020); Selina Siller & Annika Streicher, *Online-Beherbungsplattformen: Zwischen elektronisch erbrachter Dienstleistung und Margenbesteuerung*, taxlex (2020); Lily Zechner, *How to Treat the Ride-Hailing Company Uber for VAT Purposes*, 30 International VAT Monitor (2019); Lily Zechner, *Ist Uber auch aus Sicht des Umsatzsteuerrechts Beförderungsdienstleister?*, 29 SWI (2019); Lily Zechner, *Internetplattformen und umsatzsteuerrechtliche Leistungszurechnung am Beispiel Airbnb*, ÖStZ (2020).

1.2.2 Research Objectives

Although the amendments of the e-commerce package that include the introduction of Article 14a of the VAT Directive were already published in 2017, the research in this area is rather limited up until now. The published works mainly describe the amendments and changes due to the introduction of the new rules for platforms[18] or pick up certain specific subquestions linked to Article 14a of the VAT Directive.[19] It is surprising that, despite the novelty and significance of the changes, no work in the international literature has yet devoted itself comprehensively and in detail to the systematics of the changes for platforms based on the e-commerce package. Connecting the dots, so to speak, between these recent developments, an evolution of the VAT obligations regarding platforms can be observed that will, in the near future, demand the legislators', the tax authorities', the platforms', and academia's attention.

This research is intended to remedy the fact that there is no comprehensive in-depth analysis of Article 14a of the VAT Directive in the European literature. This

---

18. *See* in general on the amendments on the European level, e.g., Aleksandra Bal, *The Changing Landscape of the EU VAT: Digital VAT Package and Definitive VAT System*, 59 European Taxation 77 (2019); Aleksandra Bal, *Managing EU VAT Risks for Platform Business Models*, 72 Bulletin for International Taxation, s. 3.4 (2018); Stephen Dale & Venise Vincent, *The European Union's Approach to VAT and E-Commerce*, 6 World Journal of VAT/GST Law 60 (2017); Lukas Franke & Julia Tumpel, *Aus für Mehrwertsteuerbetrug im Onlinehandel?*, SWK (2018); Anne Janssen, *The Problematic Combination of EU Harmonized and Domestic Legislation Regarding VAT Platform Liability*, 32 International VAT Monitor, s. 2 (2021); Marie Lamensch, *Adoption of the E-Commerce VAT Package: The Road Ahead Is Still a Rocky One*, 27 EC Tax Review (2018); Marie Lamensch, *Rendering Platforms Liable to Collect and Pay VAT on B2C Imports: A Silver Bullet?*, 29 International VAT Monitor (2018); Marie Lamensch & Rebecca Millar, *The Role of Marketplaces in Taxing B2C Supplies*, in *CJEU – Recent Developments in Value Added Tax 2018* (Michael Lang et al. eds., Linde Verlag 2019); Marie Lamensch et al., *New EU VAT-Related Obligations for E-Commerce Platforms Worldwide: A Qualitative Impact Assessment*, 13 World Tax Journal (2021); Marta Papis-Almansa, *VAT and Electronic Commerce: The New Rules as a Means for Simplification, Combatting Fraud and Creating a More Level Playing Field?*, 20 ERA Forum (2019); Jordi Sol, *EU VAT E-Commerce Package – Trust in MOSS and in Electronic Interfaces as Collection Methods*, 32 International VAT Monitor (2021); Patrick Wille, *New VAT Rules on E-Commerce*, 32 International VAT Monitor (2021); *see* also the comparisons between the EU system and the US system Aleksandra Bal, *Taxation of Digital Supplies in the European Union and United States – What Can They Learn from Each Other?*, 55 European Taxation (2015); Elvire Tardivon-Lorizon & Amanda Z Quenette, *Indirect Taxation of E-Commerce – Significant Recent Changes in the United States and the European Union*, 29 International VAT Monitor (2018); *see* also, on the implementation in Germany, e.g., Aleksandra Bal, *Germany: New VAT Compliance Obligations for Online Platforms*, 28 EC Tax Review 115 (2019); Stefanie Becker, *Bericht aus Brüssel – Umsetzung der Neuregelungen im E-Commerce ab 1.1.2021*, MwStR (2019); Andreas Erdbrügger, *Änderung der EU-Umsatzsteuervorschriften für den E-Commerce ab 2019 bzw. 2021*, DStR (2018); Tina Ehrke-Rabel et al., *supra* note 13, at 107 et seqq.; *see* also, on the implementation in Austria, e.g., Stefan Hammerl & Lily Zechner, *SWK-Spezial Plattformhaftung* (Linde Verlag 2020); Christina Pollak & Karoline Spies, *Die umsatzsteuerlichen Änderungen bei Warenverkäufen über Plattformen: Online-Plattformen als Steuerschuldner*, ecolex (2021); Christine Weinzierl, *SWK-Spezial E-Commerce Paket 2021* 72 et seqq. (Linde Verlag 2021); *see* also, on the implementation in the UK, Aleksandra Bal, *Managing EU VAT Risks for Platform Business Models*, *supra*.
19. *See*, e.g., Sergio Messina, *VAT E-Commerce Package: Customs Bugs in the System? Analysis of the Issues Undermining the New Import VAT Platform Collecting Model*, 13 World Tax Journal (2021).

book aims to comprehensively examine the challenges that digital platforms are facing due to the changes introduced by the e-commerce package. The book will concentrate on EU law sidesteps into national implementations when necessary. Thus, the book will comprehensively discuss the amendments for platforms in both width and depth. Therefore, the importance of the book lies in the identification of the various changes and in the scope and legal consequences of the newly introduced legislative provisions. The identification of the scope of the legislative provisions will form the basis for the subsequent legal analysis. The aim is to critically analyse and discuss the strengths and weaknesses of the new provision in Article 14a of the VAT Directive from a legal and practical point of view. The book will not only concentrate on theoretical explanations but will also try to identify practical issues that will often form the basis for the underlying theoretical discussions. The book aims to be a significant step towards a more comprehensive study of the VAT challenges for digital platforms and thrives on updating the debate. In addition, the book should critically examine the latest developments in this area and thus contribute to further academic and legal policy discussions on this topic.

1.3   LEGAL FRAMEWORK

1.3.1   Sources of EU Law

In general, EU law can be divided into three different sources: primary, secondary, and tertiary law.[20] Primary law is the cornerstone of EU law and at the top of the hierarchy. Therefore, primary law is the fundament of EU law, and secondary and tertiary law must not infringe primary law. Primary law is constituted of treaties, namely the TEU and TFEU, including their protocols and the Euratom Treaty.[21] Moreover, according to Article 6 (1) of the TEU, primary law also includes the Charter of Fundamental Rights of the European Union.[22] Finally, the general principles are also primary law.[23] For VAT law, especially the fundamental freedoms in the TFEU[24] and the fundamental rights of

---

20. *See,* for a detailed overview of the sources of EU law, Koen Lenaerts & Piet Van Nuffel, *Constitutional Law of the European Union* 703 (Robert Bray ed., Sweet & Maxwell 2005); *see* also Rita Szudoczky, *The Sources of EU Law and Their Relationships: Lessons for the Field of Taxation: Primary Law, Secondary Law, Fundamental Freedoms and State Aid Rules,* s. 2 and for a detailed overview of the hierarchy s. 5 (IBFD 2014).
21. Consolidated Version of the Treaty on European Union, OJ C 326 (2012); Consolidated Version of the Treaty on the Functioning of the European Union, OJ C 326 (2012); Consolidated Version of the Treaty Establishing the European Atomic Energy Community, OJ C 327 (2012).
22. Charter of Fundamental Rights of the European Union, OJ C 326 (2012).
23. *See* Article 6 (3) of the TFEU; *see* critically Paul P. Craig & Gráinne De Búrca, *EU Law: Text, Cases, and Materials* 142 (Oxford University Press 7th ed. 2020), who argue that the general principles are in the hierarchy of EU law below the Treaties; *see* also the critical discussion of the application of principles in tax law by Frans Vanistendael, *The Role of (Legal) Principles in EU Tax Law, in Principles of Law: Function, Status and Impact in EU Tax Law* (Cécile Brokelind ed., IBFD 2014).
24. The fundamental freedoms are stipulated in Articles 26 (internal market), 45-48 (persons), 49-55 (establishment) 56-62 (services), and 63-66 (capital and payments) of the TFEU.

the CFR are of high relevance. Moreover, general principles such as the principle of proportionality, legal certainty and the general prohibition of abuse impact VAT law.[25]

Secondary law is the law adopted by the institutions of the European Union. For the introduction of secondary EU law, Article 288 of the TFEU stipulates different acts: regulations, directives, decisions, recommendations, and opinions. Secondary law must be in line with primary law. In VAT law, the legal instrument of a directive has been predominantly implemented.[26] Due to the implementation of the VAT law in the form of a directive, the VAT Directive must be transposed into domestic law and is, in general, not directly applicable (as opposed to primary law and regulations).[27]

Finally, the EU legislator can introduce EU tertiary law based on Article 290 (1) of the TFEU for delegation acts and Article 291 (2) of the TFEU for implementing acts. For both tertiary acts, a secondary law must exist in order for them to become effective. Tertiary law must be in line with primary law as well as secondary law. Pursuant to Article 397 of the VAT Directive, the Council has the power to adopt, based on a proposal of the European Commission, implementing measures in VAT law. The Council has made use of this power by the introduction of the (directly applicable) VAT Implementing Regulation.[28]

1.3.2   Other Legal Instruments in VAT

Additionally to the described primary, secondary, and tertiary laws, also other legal opinions, guidelines, and explanations are available. This additional material can only be qualified as an interpretational aid. The only official body allowed to interpret legally binding EU law is the CJEU. The opinions, guidelines, and explanations by the

---

25. Karoline Spies, *Permanent Establishments in Value Added Tax: The Role of Establishments in International B2B Trade in Services Under VAT/GST Law* 7 (IBFD 2020).

26. The implementation of the VAT Directive (and its preceding directives) was based on Article 113 of the TFEU (and the corresponding articles of the preceding treaties).

27. For directives to have a direct effect, the following three criteria must be met: (i) the provision of the directive must be sufficiently clear and precise, (ii) the provision of the directive must be unconditional, and (iii) the period for implementation of the directive must have expired; *see* Joined Cases C-6/90 and C-9/90, *Andrea Francovich and Danila Bonifaci and others v Italian Republic*, 19 Nov. 1991, ECLI:EU:C:1991:428, para. 11; Case C-226/07, *Flughafen Köln/Bonn GmbH v Hauptzollamt Köln*, 17 Jul. 2008, ECLI:EU:C:2008:429, paras 22 et seq.; Joined Cases C-152/07 to C-154/07, *Arcor AG & Co. KG (C-152/07), Communication Services TELE2 GmbH (C-153/07) and Firma 01051 Telekom GmbH (C-154/07) v Bundesrepublik Deutschland*, 17 Jul. 2008, ECLI:EU:C:2008:426, paras. 39 et seqq.; Joined Cases C-471/07 and C-472/07, *Association générale de l'industrie du médicament (AGIM) ASBL and Others (C-471/07 and C-472/07), Janssen Cilag SA (C-471/07) and Sanofi-Aventis Belgium SA (C-472/07) v Belgian State*, 14 Jan. 2010, ECLI:EU:C:2010:9, paras. 25 et seqq.; *see* also Paul P. Craig & Gráinne De Búrca, *supra* note 23, at 235 et seqq.

28. Council Implementing Regulation (EU) No 282/2011 of 15 March 2011 Laying down Implementing Measures for Directive 2006/112/EC on the Common System of Value Added Tax, OJ L 77/1 (2011); for further information on the legal qualification of the VAT Implementing Regulation, *see* Karoline Spies, *supra* note 25, at 10 et seqq.

VAT Committee, the European Commission, and the VAT Expert Group qualify as 'soft law' and are therefore not binding.[29]

One of these instruments are the guidelines of the VAT Committee.[30] According to Article 398 (4) of the VAT Directive, the VAT Committee 'shall examine questions raised by its chairman, on his own initiative or at the request of the representative of a Member State, which concern the application of Community provisions on VAT'.[31] The published guidelines are not legally binding and only have an advisory function for actors interpreting and applying the VAT Directive.[32] Up to date, it seems that the CJEU has not yet decided any case against the VAT guidelines[33] and recently even cites them.[34]

Another interpretational aid to the VAT Directive are the explanatory notes and guidelines by the European Commission that were published recently when amendments to the VAT Directive were introduced.[35] The explanatory notes by the European

---

29. *See*, on the term 'soft law' in VAT law Juliane Kokott, *Das Steuerrecht der Europäischen Union*, para. 36 (C.H. Beck 2018); *see* also Marie Lamensch, *The Use of Soft Law by the European VAT Legislator, and What the CJEU Makes of It, in CJEU – Recent Developments in Value Added Tax 2015* (Linde Verlag 2016); Marie Lamensch, *Soft Law and EU VAT: From Informal to Inclusive Governance?*, 5 World Journal of VAT/GST Law (2016). *See* also, on the legal qualification of the VAT/GST Guidelines and other reports by the OECD s. 2.3.3 The OECD Proposal's Influence on the Interpretation of the EU E-Commerce Package.

30. *See*, for further information on the guidelines of the VAT Committee Kokott, *supra* note 29, para. 37; Lamensch, *The Use of Soft Law*, *supra* note 29, at 29 et seqq.; Lamensch, *Soft Law and EU VAT*, *supra* note 29, at 13 et seqq.

31. Currently, it is under discussion whether the power of the VAT Committee should be extended to become a comitology committee and thereby oversee the adoption of implementing acts by the European Commission; *see* European Commission, *Communication from the Commission to the European Parliament and the Council an Action Plan for Fair and Simple Taxation Supporting the Recovery Strategy*, COM/2020/312 final, para. 19 (15.7.2020), https://eur-lex.europa.eu/resource.html?uri = cellar:e8467e73-c74b-11ea-adf7-01aa75ed71a1.0003.02/DOC_1&format = PDF (last visited 19 Jan. 2021); *see* also VAT Committee, *Conferring Implementing Powers on the Commission in the Area of VAT and Transforming the Status of the VAT Committee into a Comitology Committee*, VEG No 093, taxud.c.1(2020)5815334 (29 Sep. 2020), https://www.vatupdate.com/wp-content/uploads/2020/10/VEG-093-VAT-Committee-and-comitology.pdf (last visited 19 Jul. 2021).

32. Case C-144/00, *Criminal proceedings against Matthias Hoffmann*, 14 Nov. 2002, ECLI: EU:C:2002:654, Opinion of AG Geelhoed, para. 72; Case C-401/06, *Commission of the European Communities v Federal Republic of Germany*, 13 Sep. 2007, ECLI:EU:C:2007:520, Opinion of AG Bot, para. 50; Case C-155/12, *Minister Finansów v RR Donnelley Global Turnkey Solutions Poland sp. z o.o.*, 31 Jan. 2013, ECLI:EU:C:2013:57, Opinion of AG Kokott, paras. 46 et seqq.

33. Kokott, *supra* note 29, para. 37; Lamensch, *The Use of Soft Law*, *supra* note 29, at 31; Lamensch, *Soft Law and EU VAT*, *supra* note 29, at 15.

34. *See*, e.g., Case C-593/19, *SK Telecom Co. Ltd. v Finanzamt Graz-Stadt*, 15 Apr. 2021, ECLI: EU:C:2021:281, paras. 48 et seqq.

35. *See* European Commission, *Explanatory Notes VAT Invoicing Rules* (5 Oct. 2011), https://ec.europa.eu/taxation_customs/system/files/2016-09/explanatory_notes_en.pdf (last visited 19 Jul. 2021); European Commission, *Guide to the VAT Mini One Stop Shop*, *supra* note 11; European Commission, *Explanatory Notes on the EU VAT Changes to the Place of Supply of Telecommunications, Broadcasting and Electronic Services That Enter into Force in 2015*, *supra* note 11; European Commission, *Explanatory Notes on EU VAT Place of Supply Rules on Services Connected with Immovable Property That Enter into Force in 2017* (26 Oct. 2015), https://ec.europa.eu/taxation_customs/system/files/2016-09/explanatory_notes_new_en.pdf (last visited 14 Jul. 2021); European Commission, *Explanatory Notes on the EU VAT Changes in Respect*

Commission are not legally binding but should be seen as interpretative guidance and as help for the Member States for transforming the legal amendments uniformly.[36] Therefore, the explanatory notes are published approximately one year before the amendments to the VAT Directive enter into force.[37]

Lastly, the work by the VAT Expert Group should also be mentioned.[38] The VAT Expert Group does not publish legally binding opinions and was established by the European Commission by a decision in 2012.[39] In the VAT Expert Group, persons with the necessary expertise in the field of VAT from business, consumer organisations, or tax trade associations are represented who can contribute to the development and implementation of VAT policy.[40] The group's task is to advise the European Commission on the preparation of legislative acts and other policy initiatives in VAT and to provide information on the practical implementation of legislative acts and other policy initiatives.[41]

---

of *Call-Off Stock Arrangements, Chain Transactions and the Exemption for Intra-Community Supplies of Goods ('2020 Quick Fixes')* (Dec. 2019), https://ec.europa.eu/taxation_customs/sites/default/files/explanatory_notes_2020_quick_fixes_en.pdf (last visited 20 Jun. 2021); European Commission, *Explanatory Notes on the New VAT E-Commerce Rules* (30 Sep. 2020), https://ec.europa.eu/taxation_customs/sites/taxation/files/vatecommerceexplanatory_28102 020_en.pdf (last visited 2 Feb. 2021); European Commission, *Guide to the VAT One Stop Shop* (Mar. 2021), https://ec.europa.eu/taxation_customs/system/files/2021-03/oss_guidelines_en_ 0.pdf (last visited 19 Jul. 2021); *see* for further information on the explanatory notes Kokott, *supra* note 29, paras. 38 et seqq.; Lamensch, *The Use of Soft Law, supra* note 29, at 34 et seqq.; Lamensch, *Soft Law and EU VAT, supra* note 29, at 17 et seqq.; *see* also, critically, on the explanatory notes Ad van Doesum et al., *Fundamentals of EU VAT Law* 20 et seq. (Wolters Kluwer 2020).

36. *See* European Commission, *Explanatory Notes: VAT Invoicing Rules, supra* note 35, at 1; European Commission, *Explanatory Notes: Place of Supply of Telecommunications, Broadcasting and Electronic Services, supra* note 11, at 3; European Commission, *Explanatory Notes: Services Connected with Immovable Property, supra* note 35, at 2; European Commission, *Explanatory Notes: 2020 Quick Fixes, supra* note 35, at 3; European Commission, *Explanatory Notes: VAT E-Commerce Rules, supra* note 35, at 1.

37. *See* European Commission, *Explanatory Notes: VAT Invoicing Rules, supra* note 35, which were published on 5 Oct. 2011 for provisions that entered into force on 1 Jan. 2013; European Commission, *Explanatory Notes: Place of Supply of Telecommunications, Broadcasting and Electronic Services, supra* note 11, which were published on 3 Apr. 2014 for provisions that entered into force on 1 Jan. 2015; European Commission, *Explanatory Notes: Services Connected with Immovable Property, supra* note 35, which were published on 26 Oct. 2015 for provisions that entered into force on 1 Jan. 2017; European Commission, *Explanatory Notes: 2020 Quick Fixes, supra* note 35, which were published on Dec. 2019 for provisions that entered into force on 1 Jan. 2020; European Commission, *Explanatory Notes: VAT E-Commerce Rules, supra* note 35, which were published on 30 Sep. 2020 for provisions that entered into force on 1 Jul. 2021.

38. *See* for further information on the work of the VAT Expert Group Kokott, *supra* note 29, para. 41; Lamensch, *The Use of Soft Law, supra* note 29, at 39 et seqq.; Lamensch, *Soft Law and EU VAT, supra* note 29, at 22 et seqq.

39. Commission Decision of 26 June 2012 Setting up a Group of Experts on Value Added Tax (2012/C 188/02) (28.06.2012).

40. *See* preamble pt. 4 of the *ibid.*

41. *See* Article 2 of the *ibid.*

1.4 METHODOLOGY

1.4.1 The Interpretation of Law

1.4.1.1 Doctrinal Legal Research

This is a work written in the field of law. It uses the methods that are traditional to 'doctrinal legal research'. At a minimum, the method of doctrinal legal research comprises a two-step process, namely, locating the sources of the law and thenceforth interpreting and analysing the text.[42] This research undertakes both steps.

To apply the law to one concrete case, a thought process is necessary which, in methodology, is described as a conclusion.[43] Within this thought process, the applicable law represents the major premise. The minor premise is formed by the detection that a situation can be subsumed under the law. By the conclusion, the proper assessment applicable to the situation is obtained from the law.[44] However, to reach such a conclusion, it is first necessary to determine the applicable legislative provision and to identify to which situations the legislative provision is applicable. Accordingly, in locating the sources of the law, an extensive search of the primary sources of law that are defined as encompassing treaties, legislation, regulation, case law, and constitutions is undertaken.[45]

By relating a situation to a legislative provision, a legal assessment is necessary. For doing so, the legislative provision must be broken down into its elements, and it must be examined whether it is applicable to the situation in question. If this process of equating the situation with the legislative provision was successful, the situation could be subsumed under the legislative provision. Thus, it should be established whether the legislative provision comprises the concrete situation in question.[46] Due to the subsumption of the situation under a legislative provision, the minor premise establishes the syllogism of the application of the law. The conclusion from the major premise, the legislative provision, shows that the legal assessment that the law provides when all elements of the legislative provision are realised should apply to the specific case.[47] However, in order to be able to subsume a situation under an identified legislative provision, the content of the law must first be determined. This is the objective of the interpretation and represents the second step of the process.

---

42. Terry Hutchinson & Nigel Duncan, *Defining and Describing What We Do: Doctrinal Legal Research*, 17 Deakin Law Review 110 (2012).
43. Franz Bydlinski, *Juristische Methodenlehre und Rechtsbegriff* 395 et seqq. (Springer 2011); Karl Larenz, *Methodenlehre der Rechtswissenschaft* 250 et seq. (Springer 1991).
44. Wolfgang Gassner, *Interpretation und Anwendung der Steuergesetze: kritische Analyse der wirtschaftlichen Betrachtungsweise des Steuerrecht* 5 (Orac 1972).
45. Harvard Law School Library, *Legal Research Strategy, Primary Sources for Legal Research*, https://guides.library.harvard.edu/law/researchstrategy/primarysources (last visited 27 Mar. 2020); Emily Carr, *Legal Research: A Guide to Secondary Resources*, https://guides.loc.gov/law-secondary-resources (last visited 24 Jul. 2020).
46. Terry Hutchinson & Nigel Duncan, *supra* note 42, at 111.
47. Franz Bydlinski, *supra* note 43, at 395 et seqq.; Wolfgang Gassner, *supra* note 44, at 7; Karl Larenz, *supra* note 43, at 250 et seq.

Basically, the application of the law is confronted with similar problems in all areas of law – the bridging between a general-abstract legislative provision and a concrete situation. A fundamental uniformity of legal methodology can therefore be assumed which is the so-called classical canon of interpretation.[48] This classical canon of interpretation was developed by jurisprudence but has been codified in some legal systems[49] and includes a textual (or grammatical), contextual, teleological, and historical interpretation.[50] Since this book focuses on VAT law, the relevant provisions of the VAT Directive and the corresponding VAT Implementing Regulation are subject to such an interpretation.

1.4.1.2   *The Different Interpretation Methods*

Every interpretation of a text – and thus also the interpretation of a legal text – begins with the literal sense.[51] The literal sense represents the meaning of an expression or a combination of words in the general language use or, which is particularly relevant in the field of tax law,[52] in the specific language use.[53] The grammatical interpretation thus concludes its content from the wording of the law. To determine the meaning of a legislative provision, however, not only the general or specific language usage of the legislator but also the rules of grammar are used.

The contextual interpretation is based on the fact that legal sentences are not to be read by themselves but are integrated into a structure of regulations. A legal sentence therefore only acquires its full meaning from the context of its parts and in connection with all legal provisions that relate to each other as well as from the context of the entire legal system.[54] This interpretation element explores the meaning of a law within its context.[55]

---

48. *See* Winfried Brugger, *Concretization of Law and Statutory Interpretation*, 11 Tulane European & Civil Law Forum 232 (1996); Bohumila Salachová & Bohumil Vítek, *Interpretation of European Law, Selected Issues*, 61 Acta Universitatis Agriculturae et Silviculturae Mendelianae Brunensis 2717 (2013); both articles refer to Savigny, *see* Friedrich Carl von Savigny, *System des heutigen Römischen Rechts* 212 et seqq. (1840).
49. *See*, e.g., Article 31 of the Vienna Convention on the Law of Treaties (relevant for the interpretation of tax treaties), *see* Sjoerd Douma, *Legal Research in International and EU Tax Law* 22 et seq. (Kluwer 2014); *see* also in the Austrian private law §§ 6 and 7 ABGB, which have also been applied by the Austrian Supreme Administrative Court to tax cases, *see* Wolfgang Gassner, *supra* note 44, at 126.
50. United States, Congressional Research Service, *Statutory Interpretation: General Principles and Recent Trends*, https://www.everycrsreport.com/reports/97-589.html#_Toc407006254 (last visited 27 Mar. 2020); Winfried Brugger, *supra* note 48, at 232 et seqq.
51. *See* Karl Larenz, *supra* note 43, at 320 et seq.; Michael Potacs, *Rechtstheorie* 169 et seq. (facultas 2019).
52. *See* Wolfgang Gassner, *supra* note 44, at 12.
53. *See* Winfried Brugger, *supra* note 48, at 236 et seq.; Karl Larenz, *supra* note 43, at 324 et seq.
54. *See* Winfried Brugger, *supra* note 48, at 238 et seq.
55. *See* the extensive discussion of Karl Larenz, *supra* note 43, at 310 et seq.

The historical interpretation is based on the history of the law's origin that deals with the search for the problem-relevant intention of the historical legislator.[56] The interpretation material consists of all revealing indications of the will or intention of the legislator who enacted the legislative provision to be interpreted.[57] To get an insight into the intention of the legislator, the legal status prior to the enactment of the provision to be interpreted is particularly informative since a comparison often makes it possible to identify what, or if anything at all, should be modified. However, the comparison of the enacted provision with the legal literature available at the time and the comparison of the eventually enacted provision with previous drafts are also informative. In a subspecies of the historical interpretation, the historical-teleological interpretation, the aim is to find out why – i.e., for what rationale or for what purpose – the legislative provision was introduced.[58]

The purpose of a legislative provision expressed in the law is explored by teleological interpretation.[59] It starts out from the legislator's objective and takes the legislator's objective further thus developing the *ratio legis*.[60] The teleological-systematic interpretation aims to avoid contradictions in the law. The aim is to put the purpose and the valuation basis of other, systematically insightful legislative provisions in relation to the concrete legislative provision to be interpreted. In the interpretation, attention must be paid to ensure that the valuation and corresponding objective of the other systematically insightful regulation can also be interpreted into the law in question. Therefore, the fundamental principle of equality according to which the equal is to be treated equally and the unequal is to be treated unequally is simultaneously acknowledged.[61] This element plays a decisive role, particularly in the context of interpretation in conformity with EU law and constitutional law.

For any interpretation, all of the described elements must be taken into account. In principle, none of the elements can be excluded from the outset, but they should rather work together. In general, the literal element plays a special role since the legal text is the basis for the interpretation, and the latter must therefore begin with the interpretation of the meaning of the words. However, the weighting of the interpretation methods for the interpretation in EU law is slightly different from that in national law or public law.[62] Since EU legislation is published in 24 different languages and no

---

56. Winfried Brugger, *supra* note 48, at 240; for the distinction between 'intentionalism' and 'purposivis', *see*, e.g., Jonathan R. Siegel, *The Inexorable Radicalization of Textualism*, 158 University of Pennsylvania Law Review 117 (2009).
57. The most informative are usually the historical materials that include all written statements on the origin of the law such as the different commentaries and evaluations by the European Commission and the European Parliament during the legislative process.
58. *See* Karl Larenz, *supra* note 43, at 328 et seq.; Michael Potacs, *Rechtstheorie*, *supra* note 51, at 196 et seqq.
59. *See* Winfried Brugger, *supra* note 48, at 242.
60. *See* Wolfgang Gassner, *Interpretation und Anwendung der Steuergesetze: kritische Analyse der wirtschaftlichen Betrachtungsweise des Steuerrecht*, *supra* note 44, at 12 et seq.; Michael Potacs, *supra* note 51, at 183 et seqq.
61. *See* Karl Larenz, *supra* note 43, at 339 et seq.
62. Bohumila Salachová & Bohumil Vítek, *Interpretation of European Law, Selected Issues*, 61 Acta Universitatis Agriculturae et Silviculturae Mendelianae Brunensis, *supra* note 48, at 2718.

language version has priority over another, an unambiguous grammatical interpretation is not always possible in EU law.[63] In EU law, therefore, the systematic and teleological interpretation plays a more significant role in achieving a more uniform result. In *Cilfit*, the CJEU stated that 'every provision of Community law must be placed in its context and interpreted in the light of the provisions of Community law as a whole, regard being had to the objectives thereof and to its state of evolution at the date on which the provision in question is to be applied'.[64] Within the application of the systematic and theological interpretation, it was brought forward in literature that reference to a comparative interpretation of the laws of the Member States can be repeatedly recognised, especially when the CJEU interpreted general principles common to the Member States.[65] Furthermore, the historical interpretation can also be used in EU law, although it is difficult to determine the will of the EU legislator. EU legislation is the result of a political compromise in which the concerned Member States may have pursued different objectives.[66]

Moreover, the wording of the law not only is the starting point for determining the meaning but also defines the limits of the interpretation. Only in the case of an unintended 'gap in the legislation'[67] can one go beyond the literal meaning of a legislative provision. The instrument of analogy then extends the scope of application of a legislative provision to cases that are not regulated by this legislative provision.[68] The conclusion by analogy is diametrically opposed to the appeal from the contrary, also called the *argumentum a contrario*. The appeal from the contrary concludes that the legal consequence ordered in a legal provision should only be applied under the factual preconditions of this provision; i.e., it should by no means be extended to further cases not covered by the legislative provision. Whether a conclusion by analogy or by appeal from the contrary is required in a concrete context is determined by the purpose of the provision.[69]

---

63. Case C-283/81, *Srl CILFIT and Lanificio di Gavardo SpA v Ministry of Health*, 6 Oct. 1982, ECLI:EU:C:1982:335, para. 18; José A. Gutiérrez-Fons & Koen Lenaerts, *To Say What the Law of the EU Is: Methods of Interpretation and the European Court of Justice*, 20 Columbia Journal of European Law 8 (2014); Bohumila Salachová & Bohumil Vítek, *supra* note 48, at 2718.
64. Case C-283/81, *CILFIT v Ministero della Sanità*, 6 Oct. 1982, ECLI:EU:C:1982:335, 20.
65. *See* the extensive discussion on the importance of comparative law in the CJEU's interpretation in Miguel Poiares Maduro, *Interpretation of European Law: Judicial Adjudication in a Context of Constitutional Pluralism*, 1 European Journal of Legal Studies 140 et seqq. (2007); *see also* Bohumila Salachová & Bohumil Vítek, *supra* note 48, at 2719.
66. *See* Hannes Rösler, *Interpretation of EU Law*, in *Max Planck Encyclopedia of European Private Law* 979 (Jürgen Basedow et al. eds., Oxford University Press 2012).
67. For further explanations, *see* Franz Bydlinski & Peter Bydlinski, *Grundzüge der juristischen Methodenlehre* 85 et seqq. (facultas 2018); Karl Larenz, *Methodenlehre der Rechtswissenschaft*, *supra* note 43, at 370 et seq.; *see* also Wolfgang Schön, *Die Analogie im Europäischen (Privat-)Recht*, in *Privatrechtsdogmatik im 21. Jahrhundert: Festschrift für Claus-Wilhelm Canaris zum 80. Geburtstag* 147 et seqq. (Marietta Auer et al. eds., De Gruyter 2017), who discusses the 'gap in legislation' and analogy on a European level in detail.
68. Terry Hutchinson & Nigel Duncan, *Defining and Describing What We Do: Doctrinal Legal Research*, 17 Deakin Law Review, *supra* note 42, at 111.
69. Winfried Brugger, *Concretization of Law and Statutory Interpretation*, 11 Tulane European & Civil Law Forum, *supra* note 48, at 231; Bydlinski & Bydlinski, *supra* note 67, at 91.

1.4.1.3 Peculiarities in the Interpretation of EU Law

Additionally, it is important to bear in mind that EU law is an independent regulatory system and has supremacy over the national law of the Member States.[70] The VAT Directive establishes a common VAT system within the EU that should lead to the application of uniform definitions among the different Member States.[71] Since the EU has introduced the VAT system with the legal instrument of a directive, the Member States have an obligation to implement the VAT Directive into national law.[72] Although directives, in general, do not have a direct effect, the CJEU has held that national courts and (tax) administrations must interpret the national law in light of EU law if possible.[73] To achieve the goal of a non-conflicting interpretation in the Member States, the CJEU has repeatedly emphasised that no reference to national legal systems is permissible.[74] Such a reference would stand in the way of a uniform application of the VAT Directive in all EU Member States. In the case of uncertainties arising in proceedings before a national court, a question for a preliminary ruling may be referred to the CJEU since only the CJEU can decide on the interpretation of EU law.[75] With the guidance from the decisions by the CJEU, the national courts should also apply the methods of interpretation recognised by the national law to interpret the national VAT acts in conformity with the wording and purpose of the VAT Directive.[76] Thus, CJEU judgments have a major impact on the application of the VAT Directive and Member States' domestic VAT law.

1.4.2 Materials

In this book, the legislative provisions for digital platforms introduced by the e-commerce package will be examined by applying the legal methods described and

---

70. Case C-6/64, *Flaminio Costa v E.N.E.L.*, 15 Jul. 1964, ECLI:EU:C:1964:66, 593 et seq.; *see* also, on the discussion of the absolute supremacy versus relative supremacy of EU law: Paul P. Craig & Gráinne De Búrca, *EU Law: Text, Cases, and Materials, supra* note 23, at 304 et seq.; Robert Schütze, *European Union Law* 196 et seqq. (Oxford University Press 2021).
71. Case C-320/88, *Staatssecretaris van Financiën v Shipping and Forwarding Enterprise Safe BV*, 8 Feb. 1990, ECLI:EU:C:1990:61, para. 8; Case C-305/01, *Finanzamt Groß-Gerau v MKG-Kraftfahrzeuge-Factoring GmbH*, 26 Jun. 2003, ECLI:EU:C:2003:377, para. 38; *see* also, e.g., Bohumila Salachová & Bohumil Vítek, *Interpretation of European Law, Selected Issues*, 61 Acta Universitatis Agriculturae et Silviculturae Mendelianae Brunensis, *supra* note 48, at 2718.
72. *See* Article 288 (3) of the TFEU; *see* also Paul P. Craig & Gráinne De Búrca, *supra* note 23, at 139; Schütze, *supra* note 70, at 169.
73. Case C-14/83, *Sabine von Colson and Elisabeth Kamann v Land Nordrhein-Westfalen*, 10 Apr. 1984, ECLI:EU:C:1984:153, para. 36; Schütze, *supra* note 70, at 177 et seqq.
74. Case C-320/88, *Staatssecretaris van Financiën v Shipping and Forwarding Enterprise Safe*, 8 Feb. 1990, ECLI:EU:C:1990:61, para. 8.
75. *See* Article 267 of the Consolidated Version of the Treaty on the Functioning of the European Union, OJ C 326 (2012).
76. Joined Cases C-397/01 to C-403/01, *Bernhard Pfeiffer (C-397/01), Wilhelm Roith (C-398/01), Albert Süß (C-399/01), Michael Winter (C-400/01), Klaus Nestvogel (C-401/01), Roswitha Zeller (C-402/01) and Matthias Döbele (C-403/01) v Deutsches Rotes Kreuz, Kreisverband Waldshut eV*, 5 Oct. 2004, ECLI:EU:C:2004:584, paras. 113 et seqq.; *see* also Hannes Rösler, *Interpretation of EU Law, in Max Planck Encyclopedia of European Private Law, supra* note 66, at 980 et seq.

taking into account the relevant case law, literature, and administrative practice on this subject. In order to meet the requirements of a scientific work, a complete survey of the literature, judicature, and administrative practice that has already been written on the individual subject areas is necessary. In addition to the complete coverage of international literature, contributions from national, notably German and Austrian, literature will also be consulted when appropriate.

The concrete procurement of the necessary documents and information is carried out by means of relevant monographs, commentaries, contributions in anthologies, administrative instructions, articles in professional journals, judgments, as well as the respective legal texts with their associated materials.

1.5   STRUCTURE OF THIS BOOK

1.5.1   Research Questions and Outline

This book hypothesises an increased role for platforms in the VAT collection throughout the EU in light of the recent developments. Therefore, a proper design and implementation of the new rules introduced with the e-commerce package by the Member States is necessary to achieve the goals set out by the European Commission, i.e., to make the VAT system more fraud-resistant, simplify compliance obligations, enforce the principle of neutrality, and reduce distortion of competition.[77]

As this book concentrates on the VAT treatment of the supply of goods through digital platforms, the underlying general research question is as follows:

How are digital platforms that enable supplies of goods through their interfaces treated for VAT purposes under EU VAT law?

This comprehensive research question can be clustered into three areas that are also reflected in the outline. Each section raises certain, more specific research questions.

Section two will discuss the background of the implemented changes. This section analyses the qualification of the supply over platforms before the legislative changes of the e-commerce package were implemented. This is essential since, although the e-commerce package is influencing the VAT treatment of platforms, the e-commerce package does not cover all supplies facilitated by platforms. Therefore, this section focuses on the following research questions. Which role do platforms play within the sale of goods or services from a VAT perspective? Are they to be qualified as agents or intermediaries? Does the platform carry out one single supply, i.e., the supply of the good or service offered on the platform, or does it carry out two distinct supplies? Moreover, the reasons for the changes and the approaches by the OECD and the EU will be explained.

---

77. *See* European Commission, *Proposal for a Council Directive Amending Directive 2006/112/EC and Directive 2009/132/EC as Regards Certain Value Added Tax Obligations for Supplies of Services and Distance Sales of Goods*, COM(2016) 757 final, *supra* note 1, at 2 et seq.

In the following sections, the VAT treatment of platforms under the new rules will be discussed. Consequently, section three will provide an in-depth analysis of the deemed supplier rule in Article 14a of the VAT Directive. It will concentrate on the following research question. What is the scope of the newly implemented rule? Thereby, the personal scope and the substantive scope of Article 14a of the VAT Directive will be discussed.

Only if all requirements of Article 14a of the VAT Directive were fulfilled would the platform become the deemed supplier and fictitiously be included in the supply chain for VAT purposes, which will be discussed in section 4 of this book. The underlying research questions of this section will be: What are the legal consequences of Article 14a of the VAT Directive for the underlying supplier, the platform, and the customer? A critical analysis will be conducted on the deemed supply and the legal consequences such as the applicable place of supply rules, the time of the chargeable event, the determination of the taxable amount, the applicable exemptions and rates, the input VAT deduction, and the invoicing obligations. These topics will be discussed for the supply between the underlying supplier and the platform as well as between the platform and final customers. Additionally, this section will also analyse the platform's record-keeping obligations and the potential application of compliance simplification mechanisms. The final part of section 4 will provide a legal and practical analysis on the question of returned goods and subsequent discounts.

Lastly, section 5 will analyse a potential infringement of the principle of equality and neutrality. Since Article 14a of the VAT Directive has a rather narrow scope of applicability, the underlying question is whether these limitations are in line with the principle of equality and the principle of neutrality. Several carefully chosen examples will be discussed, and a detailed analysis of a possible infringement of the principle of equality and neutrality is undertaken.

1.5.2   Delimitations

As the supplies through e-commerce channels have a wide reach and cover several, constantly further developing areas of VAT law, this book is based on several delimitations. The focus of this book is the amendment of the VAT Directive with the e-commerce package and the impact it has on the supply of goods through digital platforms. The most relevant legal amendment for this book is the introduction of Article 14a of the VAT Directive. Therefore, a number of delimitations are already provided by the scope of Article 14a of the VAT Directive:

- As the title of this book already suggests, this work is based on the investigation of the supply of goods through platforms. When necessary, relevant provisions on the supply of services will also be investigated, but the focus of this book remains on the supply of goods.
- The book is based on situations in which the underlying supplier and the platform qualify as taxable persons, and the customers generally qualify as

consumers. Thereby, other business models such as sharing economy plat-forms[78] or platforms where consumers act as underlying suppliers are not in the scope of this book. Furthermore, B2B transactions are not analysed in depth in this work.

Additionally, specific further legal discussions and amendments to the law will not be covered by this book such as the generally introduced record-keeping obliga-tions when the platform did not become the deemed supplier according to Article 242a of the VAT Directive, national joint and several liability provisions for platforms based on Article 205 of the VAT Directive, the record-keeping obligations for payment service providers,[79] the DAC 7,[80] discussions on split payments,[81] and an in-depth analysis of customs law. As this book still tries to give a thorough and full insight into the supply of goods through e-commerce platforms, certain aspects of other areas of (VAT) law and questionable issues thereof may be chosen and discussed, but a full legal analysis of the delimitated topics is omitted in this book.

---

78. The European Commission defines the term 'collaborative economy', which is an interchange-able term for sharing economy, as 'Business models where activities are facilitated by collabo-rative platforms that create an open marketplace for the temporary usage of goods or services often provided by private individuals. The collaborative economy involves three categories of actors: (i) service providers who share assets, resources, time and/or skills – these can be private individuals offering services on an occasional basis ("peers") or service providers acting in their professional capacity ("professional services providers"); (ii) users of these; and (iii) interme-diaries that connect – via an online platform – providers with users and that facilitate transactions between them ("collaborative platforms"). Collaborative economy transactions generally do not involve a change of ownership and can be carried out for profit or not-for-profit.' *See* European Commission, *Communication from the Commission to the European Parliament, the Council, the European Economic and Social Committee of the Regions – A European Agenda for the Collaborative Economy,* COM(2016) 356 final 3 (2016), https://eur-lex .europa.eu/legal-content/EN/TXT/PDF/?uri = CELEX:52016DC0356&from = EN (last visited 2 Feb. 2021).

79. *See* Council Directive (EU) 2020/284 of 18 February 2020 Amending Directive 2006/112/EC as Regards Introducing Certain Requirements for Payment Service Providers, OJ L 62 (2020); Council Regulation (EU) 2020/283 of 18 February 2020 Amending Regulation (EU) No 904/2010 as Regards Measures to Strengthen Administrative Cooperation in Order to Combat VAT Fraud, OJ L 62 (2020); *see* also the discussions in literature on these legal amendments, Mariken van Hilten & Giorgio Beretta, *The New VAT Record Keeping and Reporting Obligations for Payment Service Providers,* 31 International VAT Monitor (2020); Madeleine Merkx & Anne Janssen, *A New Weapon in the Fight Against E-Commerce VAT Fraud: Information from Payment Service Providers,* 30 International VAT Monitor (2019).

80. *See* Council Directive (EU) 2021/514 of 22 March 2021 Amending Directive 2011/16/EU on Administrative Cooperation in the Field of Taxation, OJ L 104 (2021).

81. *See,* e.g., the discussions by Charlène A Herbain & Alain Thilmany, *Split Payment: The Validity of a Not so New Alternative Vat Collection Method,* British Tax Review (2018); Bartosz Gryziak, *Split Payment Across the European Union – Review and Analysis,* 31 International VAT Monitor (2020).

CHAPTER 2
Background on the E-Commerce Package

2.1 DESCRIPTION OF THE BUSINESS MODEL OF DIGITAL PLATFORMS

2.1.1 General Remarks on Digital Platforms

Although, 20 years ago, it was impossible to imagine buying many goods and services over the Internet, this is our reality nowadays. In addition to local stores, companies often offer their goods and services online. Especially for SMEs, however, it is often not feasible to set up an 'own' online store. Therefore, the business model of platforms is particularly relevant for SMEs. The idea behind digital platforms has a long tradition. Traditional marketplaces still exist in the form of bazaars or malls. In their physical as well as in their digital manifestation, marketplaces have the benefit of offering a platform to connect suppliers of goods or services and customers. The change we see today is that the physical infrastructure is no longer necessary, and the traditional marketplaces are often replaced or at least supplemented by a presence on the Internet, e.g., online marketplaces or digital platforms. Today, almost any good and service can be purchased via the Internet.

Depending on the kind of goods or services a platform offers, different types of platforms can be identified:[82]

- Product platforms offer goods for sale.
- Service platforms offer services for sale.
- Sharing economy platforms offer services mainly provided by customers. Examples for sharing economy services are accommodation or transportation

---

82. For an overview of the different platforms with examples of companies, *see* Aleksandra Bal, *Managing EU VAT Risks for Platform Business Models*, 72 Bulletin for International Taxation, s. 2.1 Table 1 (2018).

services. Sharing economy platforms can be offered against a monetary consideration, as a barter transaction, or without any payment.[83]

– Communication platforms offer communication services. These can be services such as video calls, phone calls or online messengers for the transmission of written messages.
– Social media platforms offer a social community in the form of a network, i.e., to exchange information with each other, to create and spread media content individually, in a defined community, or openly in society.
– Development platforms provide, e.g., an app store for users to download apps to their computers or mobile devices.
– Search platforms act as a search engine throughout the Internet and provide the person doing the search with a list of results.

Although the platforms can be clustered into different kinds of platforms, especially platforms that connect suppliers and customers, i.e., e-commerce platforms, service platforms, sharing economy platforms, and development platforms, share a similar structure in which three parties are involved: the platform itself, the seller or service provider, and the customer.[84] Thereby, the platform provides a matching mechanism to match sellers with (potential) customers.[85]

The following three sections will give a more detailed overview on the main parties involved in a transaction through a platform: the platform,[86] the suppliers,[87] and the customers. As this book has a focus on the supply of goods, the following sections will elaborate on the functioning of platforms and benefits for the different actors using online platforms following the example of platforms through which goods are offered.

2.1.2   The Role of Platforms

2.1.2.1   *The Functioning and Involvement in the Supply of Goods by Platforms*

Generally, it should be noted that product platforms often operate two kinds of businesses. On the one hand, they use their platform as their own online store. In this case, the platform itself would appear as the supplier supplying its own goods and

---

83. European Commission, *Communication from the Commission to the European Parliament, the Council, the European Economic and Social Committee of the Regions – A European Agenda for the Collaborative Economy*, supra note 78, at 3.
84. For an overview of the different actors from an organisational perspective, *see*, e.g., Marshall W. Van Alstyne et al., *Pipelines, Platforms, and the New Rules of Strategy*, Harvard Business Review (4 Jan. 2016), https://hbr.org/2016/04/pipelines-platforms-and-the-new-rules-of-strategy (last visited 31 Jul. 2020).
85. *See*, e.g., OECD, *Unpacking E-Commerce* 9 (6 Jun. 2019), https://www.oecd-ilibrary.org/docserver/23561431-en.pdf?expires = 1649151696&id = id&accname = ocid177428&checksum = 458D5AEFA55FEF35AC0944FC4A300A4C (last visited 5 Apr. 2022).
86. In this book also referred to as marketplace, intermediary, or electronic interface.
87. In this book also referred to as underlying supplier.

would not be considered as being an intermediary. On the other hand, the platform may function as an intermediary. In the latter case, the platform provides the infrastructure for the other involved parties, the suppliers and customers. In this sense, platforms make a digital marketplace or web store available so the suppliers are able to publish information about their goods online.[88]

To use the platform service, suppliers normally have to sign up with the relevant platform and describe their goods. Depending on the platform where the supply is offered, the price may either be suggested by the platform or set by the supplier. When all of the necessary information is inserted into the digital mask of the platform, the offer from the supplier is published online.

After the publication of the offer on the platform, the platform matches interested customers with the supplier.[89] If there was a customer who wanted to buy the offered goods, there would be two possibilities for the purchase to be performed. The platform may have: (i) implemented a messaging system within its digital structure where the customer can contact the supplier and the further details of the transaction, i.e., mode of transport and payment, are discussed. This option is often used when private persons sell their goods via a platform. In this case, the payment is mostly organised privately between the customer and the supplier in either a cash payment when the purchased goods are picked up or by a bank transfer from the customer to the supplier. The (ii) possibility to finalise the transaction is that the platform itself has implemented an automated system via which the mode of transportation and the payment process are set by either the platform or the underlying supplier. In this case, the platform may also be involved in the payment process. The customer can enter the necessary paying details on the platform, and the payable amount is deducted from the chosen payment method, e.g., bank transfer, credit card, or PayPal. If the platform was involved in the payment process, then the platform would forward the purchase price to the supplier after deducting the provision for the sale. Depending on the platform, the platform may also receive a provision or fee from the customer for the use of the platform.

Once a good is purchased via the platform, the transport must be organised. For this, transport suppliers generally have three options:

1. Suppliers may organise the transport themselves.[90] This is the most independent choice for suppliers, but it follows that the suppliers must be capable of storing the goods themselves. When an order is made by a customer, the supplier has to organise the transport from the storage facility to the customer. The benefit of this transportation option is that the supplier can respond to special requests by the customers since the goods are in the supplier's storage facilities. Additionally, the supplier knows at what time, from which warehouse, and which good is transported to the customer.

---

88. Efraim Turban et al., *Electronic Commerce 2018: A Managerial and Social Networks Perspective* 47 (Springer 2018).
89. *Ibid.*
90. Amiya K. Chakravarty, *Supply Chain Transformation: Evolving with Emerging Business Paradigms* 151 (Springer 2014).

2. Suppliers can introduce the so-called drop shipping.[91] In this case, the suppliers do not own the goods yet but instead order them themselves from a producer when the customer orders the goods via the platform. Typically, the goods will be sent from the producer directly to the customer. Thus, drop shipping would generally fulfil the requirements of a VAT chain transaction. The benefit of this option is that the suppliers do not incur any storage costs. One downside of this distribution option is that the customers may have to wait a longer time for the goods to be delivered.

3. Suppliers may outsource the distribution to e-commerce fulfilment service providers.[92] These e-commerce fulfilment services may be offered by the platforms themselves or by third parties. The benefit of this option is that the suppliers pay for a full service: The e-commerce fulfilment service provider stores and packs the goods, organises the transportation, and also performs a quality control in the case of returns.[93] One disadvantage of this option is that the supplier is dependent on the information by the platform concerning the location of the good.

Whichever transportation system the suppliers implement depends strongly on the company size and economic capabilities of the supplier in question, e.g., private suppliers selling their goods via platforms will more likely organise the transport themselves.

Some platforms, especially big marketplaces, have extended their services to offer storage and transportation services.[94] In these cases, suppliers may store their goods in the warehouses of the company offering the platform. When an order is received by the platform, the demand can be met with the goods that are already stored in the warehouse. In these cases, the platform often also provides the service of transport for the purchased goods to the customer. For this transportation service, some of the marketplaces have introduced their own postal delivery services. In a last step, some platforms also offer a customer service for questions concerning the goods or the delivery, complaints, returns, and warranty cases.

2.1.2.2 *The Benefit for Platforms*

The platform has a big competitive advantage compared to other web shops run by one supplier, i.e., the data that the platform is able to collect. Since a variety of goods are offered on the platform, it receives an immense amount of data from suppliers that includes different price ranges and qualities of a product. At the same time, the

---

91. *Ibid.* at 157.
92. *Ibid.* at 158.
93. *Ibid.*
94. Turban et al., *supra* note 88, at 47.

platform also collects sales data from the customers.[95] This guarantees that the platform can use personalised marketing strategies to increase sales.[96]

2.1.3 The Benefit for Suppliers

Especially smaller local companies and private persons make use of the new possibilities of the Internet. Often, SMEs only have limited resources, and it is not feasible for them to set up their own online store. In this case, platforms offer the possibility to set up an online presence without the need to introduce an individual online shop. By using this service, SMEs can expand their customer base not just by having a higher visibility but also by their geographical reach. In 2022, already 22 % of EU enterprises offered their goods and services on platforms and/or in their own web shops.[97] Whereas companies often use a platform to increase their geographical reach, private suppliers mainly use platforms to sell second-hand goods that are their private property.

2.1.4 The Benefit for Customers

Similarly, as the supplier can be private sellers or companies, the customers buying the goods via the platform may be consumers or businesses. When a customer buys goods online, the customer enjoys several advantages.

First of all, the customer can stay at home or in the office and only needs to access the marketplace online to be able to look at an immense variety of goods.

Second, the offered goods often cover different quality and price ranges. A comparison of the different goods is made accessible since marketplaces often provide for a comparison feature for the different products and, additionally, an online feedback report of the good. Within this feedback service, the rating and description are published by other customers which may also influence the choice of prospective customers.

The third benefit for customers ordering online is the home delivery and return policy. Many marketplaces offer a very timely one-day delivery. At the same time, consumers have, based on EU law, a 14-day return right for online purchases.[98] Within these 14 days, consumers do not have to indicate any reason for returning the goods. Many platforms have extended the returns time frame and have extended this policy

---

95. *See* further on how data can create competitive advantages, e.g., Andrei Hagiu & Julian Wright, *When Data Creates Competitive Advantage*, Harvard Business Review (2020), https://hbr.org/2020/01/when-data-creates-competitive-advantage (last visited 5 Apr. 2022).
96. *See* generally on target-marketing, e.g., Gerrit Heinemann, *Der Neue Online-Handel* 273 et seq. (Springer Gabler 2021).
97. Eurostat, *E-Commerce Sales*, https://ec.europa.eu/eurostat/web/products-eurostat-news/-/ddn-20211228-1 (last visited 21 Feb. 2022).
98. *See* Article 9 of Directive 2011/83/EU of the European Parliament and of the Council of 25 October 2011 on Consumer Rights, Amending Council Directive 93/13/Eec and Directive 1999/44/EC of the European Parliament and of the Council and Repealing Council Directive 85/577/EEC and Directive 97/7/EC of the European Parliament and of the Council Text with EEA Relevance, OJ L 304/64 (2011).

also to business customers. This return right combined with the liberal return and warranty policy of some marketplaces gives customers more confidence to purchase goods online.

2.2 THE (PREVIOUS) VAT TREATMENT OF THE SUPPLY OF GOODS THROUGH PLATFORMS

2.2.1 The Different VAT Supplies in E-Commerce

After having set out the functioning of platforms, the question arises of how the different actions by the parties involved qualify from a VAT perspective. Thereby, this section will concentrate on the legal qualification before the implementation of the EU VAT e-commerce package that came into force in July 2021. When goods are sold via platforms, the VAT treatment of supplies through platforms raises specific questions that, up until today, remain mostly unanswered. The biggest difficulty is the application of the VAT Directive and the principles set out therein that were introduced for a 'brick and mortar' economy to the new system of the digital economy.[99]

Figure 2.1   Overview of the Different Supplies of an Order via a Platform

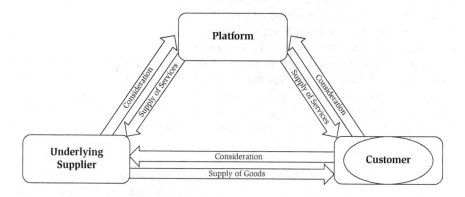

In general, one supply of goods through a platform can be separated into three supplies (*see* Figure 2.1 for a graphical illustration of the different supplies): First, the supply of the good from the underlying supplier to the customer; second, the supply of the platform service from the platform to the underlying supplier of the good; and, third, the supply of the platform service to the customer. Thereby, depending on the business model of the platform, the platform may charge both the underlying supplier and the customer or only one of the two for its services. The qualification of these three supplies encounters different difficulties and specific issues concerning their VAT

---

99. *See*, e.g., the criticism by Francesco Cannas et al., *A New Legal Framework Towards a Definitive EU VAT System: Online Hosting Platforms and E-Books Reveal Unsolved Problems on the Horizon*, 46 Intertax (2018).

treatment. The following sections will discuss certain issues that arise from this challenge of applying the traditional VAT system to these new commerce forms.[100]

In a preliminary section 2, schemes of the VAT Directive will be discussed that may alter the VAT qualification of the supply chain. First is the question of whether the supplies that the customer receives (the supply of the good from the underlying supplier and the supply of the service by the platform) are, in fact, two distinct supplies or should qualify as one composite supply. The second section will examine whether the platform acts as an undisclosed agent. These preliminary qualifications have an impact on the further VAT treatment of supplies. The affirmation of one of these two preliminary qualifications would affect all three highlighted supplies. After this discussion, the following three sections will discuss in detail the question of how the three identified supplies should be treated for VAT purposes if the two preliminary questions were denied.[101]

2.2.2 Alternations in the Supply Chain for VAT Purposes?

2.2.2.1 *The Supply Through Platforms: A Composite Supply?*

2.2.2.1.1 *General Remarks on the Supply Through Platforms*

One difficulty of supplying goods through platforms is deciding whether the supply that the customer receives (the service from the platform and the good from the underlying supplier) should be considered as one single supply or whether the supply should be separated into two supplies. If the supply was separated, the customer would receive two supplies, i.e., on the one hand, the supply of the good by the underlying supplier and, on the other hand, the service of the platform for providing the infrastructure of the platform if the customer paid a fee for the platform service. The following section will discuss the CJEU's case law on the definition and criteria of a composite supply.

2.2.2.1.2 *The CJEU's Definition, Criteria and Consequences of the Composite Supply*

2.2.2.1.2.1 The General Rule

The VAT Directive does not provide a clear definition of what is part of one supply and how many different supplies of goods or services can still qualify as one single supply. Therefore, the CJEU was repeatedly referred to in this matter. Already in 1999, the CJEU developed the general rule that every supply must be regarded as separated and

---

100. As this book focuses on the supply of goods, the following legal qualifications will concentrate on the qualification of e-commerce platforms selling goods; for a detailed analysis for certain issues arising from the sharing economy, *see* Giorgio Beretta, *European VAT and the Sharing Economy, supra* note 13; certain legal issues from the sharing economy also arise with the legal qualification of the supply of goods via platforms.
101. *See* also Figure 1: Overview of the Different Supplies of an Order via a Platform.

distinct for VAT purposes.[102] In the earlier cases, the CJEU derived this principle from Article 2 (1) of the Sixth VAT Directive which stipulates that 'the supply of goods or services [is] effected for consideration within the territory of the country by a taxable person acting as such'.[103] Neither AG Fennelly[104] nor the CJEU explained how they came to the conclusion to base the general rule that every supply must be regarded as separate and distinct on Article 2 (1) of the Sixth VAT Directive. The CJEU might have derived this conclusion from the question referred to in the preliminary ruling by the House of Lords which already referred to Article 2 (1) of the Sixth VAT Directive.[105] The House of Lords likely formulated the preliminary question by referring to Article 2 (1) of the Sixth VAT Directive as the United Kingdom has implemented Article 2 (1) of the Sixth VAT Directive in section 2 (1) of the UK Value Added Tax Act 1983.[106] According to section 2 (1) of the Value Added Tax Act 1983, the scope of the VAT is 'a taxable supply made by a taxable person in the course or furtherance of any business carried on by him'. The wording of the national implementation referring to 'a taxable supply' would allow the interpretation of the general rule that every supply must be treated separate and distinct. Seemingly, the CJEU based the derivation of the general single supply rule on Article 2 (1) of the Sixth VAT Directive without further questioning.

With the introduction of the VAT Directive, the content of Article 2 (1) of the Sixth VAT Directive was implemented in Article 1 (2) second indent of the VAT Directive. Article 1 (2) second indent of the VAT Directive stipulates that the VAT is levied 'on each transaction'. By referring to 'each transaction', the legislator indicated that every supply must be evaluated separately on its own. In later CJEU cases, the Court referred to Article 1 (2) second indent of the VAT Directive when stating that every supply must be regarded as separate and distinct which therefore serves as the basis for the 'principle of singularity'.[107] Since the development of this general rule in CPP,[108] it has evolved into established case law.[109]

---

102. Case C-349/96, *Card Protection Plan Ltd (CPP) v Commissioners of Customs & Excise*, 25 Feb. 1999, ECLI:EU:C:1999:93, para. 29; *see* also in general on the CJEU's composite supply doctrine: Oskar Henkow, *Defining the Tax Object in Composite Supplies in European VAT*, 2 World Journal of VAT/GST Law (2013); Howard Liebman & Olivier Rousselle, *VAT Treatment of Composite Supplies*, 17 International VAT Monitor (2006).

103. Case C-349/96, *CPP*, 25 Feb. 1999, ECLI:EU:C:1999:93, para. 29; Case C-41/04, *Levob Verzekeringen BV and OV Bank NV v Staatssecretaris van Financiën*, 27 Oct. 2005, ECLI: EU:C:2005:649, para. 20.

104. Case C-349/96, *Card Protection Plan Ltd (CPP) v Commissioners of Customs & Excise*, 11 Jun. 1998, ECLI:EU:C:1998:281, Opinion of AG Fennelly.

105. Case C-349/96, *CPP*, 25 Feb. 1999, ECLI:EU:C:1999:93, para. 12.

106. Value Added Tax Act 1983.

107. Case C-392/11, *Field Fisher Waterhouse LLP v Commissioners for Her Majesty's Revenue and Customs*, 27 Sep. 2012, ECLI:EU:C:2012:597, para. 14; Case C-224/11, *BGZ Leasing sp. z o.o. v Dyrektor Izby Skarbowej w Warszawie*, 17 Jan. 2013, ECLI:EU:C:2013:15, para. 29; Case C-42/14, *Minister Finansów v Wojskowa Agencja Mieszkaniowa w Warszawie*, 16 Apr. 2015, ECLI:EU:C:2015:229, para. 30; *see* also Cristina Trenta, *Rethinking EU VAT for P2P Distribution* 111 (Kluwer Law International 2015); Giorgio Beretta, *European VAT and the Sharing Economy*, *supra* note 13, at 151 Trenta and Beretta both refer to the established rule by CJEU as the 'principle of singularity'.

108. Case C-349/96, *CPP*, 25 Feb. 1999, ECLI:EU:C:1999:93.

109. Case C-41/04, *Levob Verzekeringen BV and OV Bank NV*, 27 Oct. 2005, ECLI:EU:C:2005:649, para. 20; Case C-242/08, *Swiss Re Germany Holding GmbH v Finanzamt München für*

Nevertheless, the CJEU has developed two exceptions from this general 'principle of singularity': the exception of indivisible economic supplies and the exception of ancillary supplies. The legal consequence of these two exceptions is that several distinct supplies are treated as one single supply.

2.2.2.1.2.2   The Exception of Indivisible Economic Supplies

The first exception from the single supply rule is applicable to supplies that are 'so closely linked that they form, objectively, a single, indivisible economic supply, which it would be artificial to split'.[110] If a single supply was artificially split, the distortion of the functioning of the VAT system might be the consequence.[111] Since the theoretical explanation of this exception is abstract and CJEU case law does not provide a further detailed explanation on what is considered to be an objectively single, indivisible economic supply, the following examples will show the extent of this exception.

In *Don Bosco Onroerend Goed*,[112] the CJEU had to decide whether the sale of a plot of land and the demolishing of the buildings thereon was one single supply or two distinct supplies. In this specific case, the plot of land was purchased to build new construction and, therefore, the already existing buildings had to be demolished. The demolishing of the buildings started on the same day that the plot of land was transferred to the buyer.[113] As the CJEU emphasised, the economic purpose of the buyer of the plot was to purchase land for construction.[114] Since the purchased land only became economically useful for the buyer together with the demolition of the buildings, the CJEU held that this supply was one composite supply.[115] The CJEU concluded that the VAT exemption of Article 13 B (g) of the Sixth VAT Directive that covers the supply of buildings or parts thereof was not applicable to the transaction in question.[116] The decision on the applicability of the exemption in Article 13 B (h) of the Sixth VAT Directive that covers the supply of land that has not yet been built on was

---

Körperschaften, 22 Oct. 2009, ECLI:EU:C:2009:647, para. 51; Case C-111/05, *Aktiebolaget NN v Skatteverket*, 29 Mar. 2007, ECLI:EU:C:2007:195, para. 22; Case C-453/05, *Volker Ludwig v Finanzamt Luckenwalde*, 21 Jun. 2007, ECLI:EU:C:2007:369, para. 17; Case C-425/06, *Ministero dell'Economia e delle Finanze v Part Service Srl*, 21 Feb. 2008, ECLI:EU:C:2008:108, para. 50; Case C-461/08, *Don Bosco Onroerend Goed BV v Staatssecretaris van Financiën*, 19 Nov. 2009, ECLI:EU:C:2009:722, para. 35; Case C-276/09, *Everything Everywhere Ltd v Commissioners for Her Majesty's Revenue and Customs*, 2 Dec. 2010, ECLI:EU:C:2010:730, para. 21; Case C-117/11, *Purple Parking Ltd and Airparks Services Ltd v The Commissioners for Her Majesty's Revenue & Customs*, 19 Jan. 2012, ECLI:EU:C:2012:29, para. 26; Case C-392/11, *Field Fisher Waterhouse*, 27 Sep. 2012, ECLI:EU:C:2012:597, para. 15.

110. Case C-349/96, *CPP*, 25 Feb. 1999, ECLI:EU:C:1999:93, para. 29; Case C-41/04, *Levob Verzekeringen and OV Bank*, 27 Oct. 2005, ECLI:EU:C:2005:649, para. 22; *see* the critical discussion whether the CJEU follows a subjective or objective approach by Giorgio Beretta, *supra* note 13, at 151 et seqq.
111. Case C-349/96, *CPP*, 25 Feb. 1999, ECLI:EU:C:1999:93, para. 29; Case C-41/04, *Levob Verzekeringen and OV Bank*, 27 Oct. 2005, ECLI:EU:C:2005:649, para. 20.
112. Case C-461/08, *Don Bosco Onroerend Goed*, 19 Nov. 2009, ECLI:EU:C:2009:722.
113. *Ibid.* paras. 13 et seqq.
114. *Ibid.* para. 39.
115. *Ibid.*
116. *Ibid.* para. 41.

left for the national court to take.[117] The CJEU, though, reminded the national court that the purpose of the exemption in Article 13 B (h) of the Sixth VAT Directive is to exempt only plots of land without buildings and is not supposed to cover the buildings.[118]

The CJEU's decision in *Deutsche Bank*[119] and *Blackrock Investment Management*,[120] both cases in the area of financial services, were decided with a similar argument. *Deutsche Bank* concerned the provision of a service package consisting of, on the one hand, analysing and monitoring assets of a client and, on the other hand, purchasing and selling the assets of that same client. The CJEU decided in this case that the average client investor buying this service wished to receive the combination of the service although, in general, the two services may also be provided separately.[121] Therefore, both services were so closely linked that they formed a single supply.[122] Similarly, the CJEU held in *Blackrock Investment Management* that the supply of a service package for portfolio management was also considered to be one single supply although the service package was used for the management of special VAT exempt funds and other non-VAT exempt funds.[123] The CJEU emphasised that the fact that customers used the supply for two different kinds of portfolio management should not lead to the conclusion that the supplies were distinct and that, in this given case, no principal and ancillary could be distinguished because the supplies were of equal importance.[124] In *Blackrock Investment Management* as well as *Deutsche Bank*, the main question was whether the single supply was an exempt supply.[125] In both cases, the CJEU concluded that the exemption was not applicable. In general, exemptions must be interpreted strictly as they constitute an exception to the general rule.[126]

---

117. *Ibid.* para. 42.
118. *Ibid.* para. 43; with reference to Case C-468/93, *Gemeente Emmen v Belastingdienst Grote Ondernemingen*, 28 Mar. 1996, ECLI:EU:C:1996:139, para. 20.
119. Case C-44/11, *Finanzamt Frankfurt am Main V-Höchst v Deutsche Bank AG*, 19 Jul. 2012, ECLI:EU:C:2012:484.
120. Case C-231/19, *Blackrock Investment Management (UK) Limited v Commissioners for Her Majesty's Revenue and Customs*, 2 Jul. 2020, ECLI:EU:C:2020:513.
121. Case C-44/11, *Deutsche Bank*, 19 Jul. 2012, ECLI:EU:C:2012:484, paras. 24 et seqq.
122. *Ibid.* para. 28.
123. Case C-231/19, *Blackrock Investment Management (UK)*, 2 Jul. 2020, ECLI:EU:C:2020:513, para. 40.
124. *Ibid.* paras. 32 et seqq.
125. In Case C-44/11, *Deutsche Bank*, 19 Jul. 2012, ECLI:EU:C:2012:484, the CJEU dealt with the applicability of Articles 135 (1) (f) and 135 (1) (g) of the VAT Directive; in Case C-231/19, *Blackrock Investment Management (UK)*, 2 Jul. 2020, ECLI:EU:C:2020:513 the CJEU dealt with the applicability of Article 135 (1) (g) of the VAT Directive.
126. Case C-44/11, *Deutsche Bank*, 19 Jul. 2012, ECLI:EU:C:2012:484, para. 42; Case C-231/19, *Blackrock Investment Management (UK)*, 2 Jul. 2020, ECLI:EU:C:2020:513, para. 45; similarly, the CJEU has decided that, if a complex composite supply exists of supplies for which different VAT rates would be applicable, the standard rate is applicable to the whole complex supply, *see* Case C-432/15, *Odvolací finanční ředitelství v Pavlína Baštová*, 10 Nov. 2016, ECLI: EU:C:2016:855, para. 75; *see* also, for a graphic overview of the legal consequences of the indivisible economic supply in Frank Nellen & Ad van Doesum, *Taxable Amount & VAT Rates, in CJEU – Recent Developments in Value Added Tax 2018*, 218 (Michael Lang et al. eds., Linde Verlag 2019).

In the described cases, the various components of the supplied good or service were equally important for the supply.[127] Therefore, both supplies were indispensable for carrying out the composite supply.[128] This equal importance made the differentiation difficult for which legal rules should be followed for the composite supply in question.

All of the described examples discussed the question of whether a VAT exemption was applicable to the supply in question. In this sense, no definite conclusion can be drawn on how the CJEU distinguishes which part of the supply defines the VAT treatment of the composite supply. The judgments are in line with the general rule developed by the CJEU to interpret exemptions strictly as they are an exception to the general rule that a VAT should be levied on all supplies.[129] From the CJEU case law, it seems likely that, for the application of an exemption to a composite supply subsumed under this exception, all supplies must fulfil the requirements of an exemption for the exemption to be applied.

The CJEU has not yet had to decide many cases where a composite supply consisted of a good and a service in which both components are equally important besides the discussed *Don Bosco* case. If the composite supply was supplied between two taxable persons from one Member State to another, the place of supply would depend on the classification of the supply. If, on the one hand, the supply was qualified as a supply of goods, the supplier would have to declare an intra-Community supply of the Member State of dispatch and the recipient would have to declare the correspondent intra-Community acquisition in the Member State of arrival. If, on the other hand, the supply was qualified as a supply of services, the reverse-charge mechanism according to Article 196 of the VAT Directive would be applicable.

The CJEU has dealt with such a situation in *Aktiebolaget NN*.[130] In this case, the Swedish company Aktiebolaget NN fixed and buried fibre optic cables in the ground of the Member State of the purchaser of the cable. After a testing period of 30 days in which eventual faults were repaired, Aktiebolaget NN transferred the ownership of the cable to the purchaser. The CJEU referred in this case to the abstract qualifications of an indivisible economic supply and came to the conclusion that this supply was a single transaction for VAT purposes.[131] In a second step, the CJEU though held that 'it is vital to identify the predominant elements of that supply'.[132] From this point onwards, the CJEU referred to the second exception and tried to determine which part

---

127. Case C-44/11, *Deutsche Bank*, 19 Jul. 2012, ECLI:EU:C:2012:484, para. 27.
128. *Ibid.*
129. *See*, e.g., Case C-348/87, *Stichting Uitvoering Financiële Acties v Staatssecretaris van Financiën*, 15 Jun. 1989, ECLI:EU:C:1989:246, para. 13; Case C-281/91, *Muys' en De Winter's Bouw- en Aannemingsbedrijf BV v Staatssecretaris van Financiën*, 27 Oct. 1993, ECLI:EU:C:1993:855, para. 13; Case C-2/95, *Sparekassernes Datacenter (SDC) v Skatteministeriet*, 5 Jun. 1997, ECLI:EU:C:1997:278, para. 20; Case C-461/08, *Don Bosco Onroerend Goed*, 19 Nov. 2009, ECLI:EU:C:2009:722, para. 25; Case C-44/11, *Deutsche Bank*, 19 Jul. 2012, ECLI:EU:C:2012:484, para. 42; Case C-231/19, *Blackrock Investment Management (UK)*, 2 Jul. 2020, ECLI:EU:C:2020:513, para. 22.
130. Case C-111/05, *Aktiebolaget NN*, 29 Mar. 2007, ECLI:EU:C:2007:195.
131. *Ibid.* paras. 24 et seqq.
132. *Ibid.* para. 27.

of the supply was ancillary to the other.[133] The CJEU came to the conclusion that, in the given case, the predominant part of the transaction was the supply of the cable and, therefore, this composite supply should have qualified as a supply of goods.[134] Although the CJEU applied the second exception of the composite supply rule to distinguish whether the composite supply was a supply of goods or services, the Court first based its general conclusion that this transaction was a composite supply on the first exception.[135] This mixture of applications of the first and second exception leaves room for interpretation. Since the qualification and explanation of why the supply in question was to be regarded as a composite supply were not based on an in-depth analysis, it could be argued that this case should actually be categorised under the second exception, i.e., the ancillary supply rule. It is likely that the CJEU used the ancillary supply doctrine to resolve this case since it seemed rather clear that the customer purchased the fibre optic cables and that the subsequent testing service was rather ancillary with the purpose of checking that the fibre optic cables fulfil all technical functions. Following from this line of thought, the Court should not have qualified the supply as being a composite indivisible economic supply as this exception requires that both supplies are equally important for the composite supply.

After all, relevant for deciding whether a supply is an indivisible economic supply is to determine the essential features of the transaction from the view of a 'typical customer'.[136]

2.2.2.1.2.3   The Exception of Ancillary Supplies

The second exception would be applied if one supply was ancillary to the other. The main question within this exception is when the line can be drawn for a supply to still be considered ancillary and when is it considered as being so distinct to be its own. For this differentiation, the CJEU held that a 'service must be regarded as ancillary to a principal service if it does not constitute for customers an aim in itself, but a means of better enjoying the principal service supplied'.[137]

---

133. A similar mixture where the CJEU tested both exceptions in parallel can be found in Case C-392/11, *Field Fisher Waterhouse*, 27 Sep. 2012, ECLI:EU:C:2012:597, paras. 22 et seqq., where the CJEU refers to both exceptions continuously and does not seem to provide the national court with guidance regarding which of the exceptions should be applicable in the given case.

134. Case C-111/05, *Aktiebolaget NN*, 29 Mar. 2007, ECLI:EU:C:2007:195, para. 40.

135. This confusion of which exception of the composite supply rule should be applied in the case *Aktiebolaget N* can also be found in literature; *see* Giorgio Beretta, *European VAT and the Sharing Economy*, *supra* note 13, at 152, who discusses the case Aktiebolaget NN in the section of the exception of indivisible economic supplies; whereas Oskar Henkow, *Defining the Tax Object in Composite Supplies in European VAT*, 2 World Journal of VAT/GST Law, *supra* note 102, at 192 discusses the case *Aktiebolaget NN* in the section of the exception of ancillary supplies.

136. *See*, e.g., Case C-44/11, *Deutsche Bank*, 19 Jul. 2012, ECLI:EU:C:2012:484, para. 21. For further information on these two determining factors, *see* s. 2.2.2.1.2.4 The Determination of a Single Versus a Composite Supply and VAT Consequences thereof.

137. Case C-349/96, *CPP*, 25 Feb. 1999, ECLI:EU:C:1999:93, para. 30; Case C-453/05, *Ludwig*, 21 Jun. 2007, ECLI:EU:C:2007:369, para. 18; *see* also Joined Cases C-308/96 and C-94/97,

In this sense, the CJEU held in *Everything Everywhere*[138] that additional charges invoiced by a supplier of telecommunication services to its customers for the processing of the payment were ancillary to the supplied telecommunication services. In this case, Everything Everywhere provided its customers with telecommunication services. The payment of these services could be processed through different possibilities. Whereas the direct bank transfer and the payment via a direct debit mandate were free of charge, Everything Everywhere imposed an additional charge for the use of other payment options.[139] The CJEU emphasised in this case that the provided payment processing did not constitute an aim itself to the customer for purchasing the telecommunication service, but it was intrinsically linked to the supply of the service.[140] Since, in this case, the customers did not intend to purchase two distinct supplies, the payment services were, in the view of the customers, ancillary to the principal service, i.e., the provision of telecommunication services.[141]

Similarly, the CJEU held in *Levob*[142] that the supply of a previously developed, basic software recorded on a carrier that was further customised to the needs of the specific customer was one single supply. The CJEU emphasised the importance of the economic purpose of the transaction in this ruling.[143] The customers of the software could not have received the desired benefit from the software without its further customisation. Therefore, the importance of the customisation and the extent, duration and cost of the customisation were relevant for distinguishing which of the supplies was predominant.[144] In *Levob*, the CJEU held that, in the given case, the principal supply and therefore the predominant supply was not the sale of the good, i.e., the previously developed software on a carrier, but the sale of the service of the customisation of the software.[145]

Once it is determined that a supply is a composite supply in the form of one being ancillary to the other, it should be distinguished which supply is the principal supply and which supply is the ancillary supply. When in doubt, the CJEU refers to a combination of qualitative criteria and quantitative criteria.[146] This could also be seen in the described case of *Levob*: The qualitative criterion is reflected in the benefit for the customer for receiving the adapted and personalised software, whereas the quantitative criteria are reflected in the extended duration and cost of the customisation. The

---

Commissioners of Customs and Excise v T.P. Madgett, R.M. Baldwin and The Howden Court Hotel, 22 Oct. 1998, ECLI:EU:C:1998:496, para. 24.

138. Case C-276/09, *Everything Everywhere*, 2 Dec. 2010, ECLI:EU:C:2010:730.
139. *Ibid.* para. 10.
140. *Ibid.* paras. 27 et seq.
141. *Ibid.* para. 30.
142. Case C-41/04, *Levob Verzekeringen BV and OV Bank NV*, 27 Oct. 2005, ECLI:EU:C:2005:649.
143. *Ibid.* para. 24.
144. *Ibid.* para. 28.
145. *Ibid.* para. 29.
146. Joined Cases C-497/09, C-499/09, C-501/09 C-502/09, *Finanzamt Burgdorf v Manfred Bog (C-497/09), CinemaxX Entertainment GmbH & Co. KG v Finanzamt Hamburg-Barmbek-Uhlenhorst (C-499/09), Lothar Lohmeyer v Finanzamt Minden (C-501/09) and Fleischerei Nier GmbH & Co. KG v Finanzamt Detmold (C-502/09)*, 10 Mar. 2011, ECLI:EU:C:2011:135, para. 62; Case C-18/12, *Město Žamberk v Finanční ředitelství v Hradci Králové, now Odvolací finanční ředitelství*, 21 Feb. 2013, ECLI:EU:C:2013:95, para. 33.

determination of which supply serves as the ancillary and which supply is the principle supply is highly relevant since the VAT treatment of the ancillary supply follows the VAT treatment of the principal supply[147] regarding the applicable rates, exemptions, place of supply rules, chargeability, and even the liability for payment of the VAT.

After all, relevant for deciding whether the transaction in question is a composite supply based on one supply being ancillary to the other is the determination of the essential features of the transaction from the view of a 'typical customer'.[148]

2.2.2.1.2.4 The Determination of a Single Versus a Composite Supply and VAT Consequences Thereof

Both discussed exceptions are based on the underlying idea that, although the concerned supplies could qualify as separate supplies based on the 'principle of singularity',[149] these separate supplies are dependent on each other and are therefore treated as one composite single supply.[150] However, the line between when a supply is considered to be a single supply and when it is considered to be a composite supply is blurred. In the end, the CJEU often provides the national courts with guidance on the qualification as a single supply or a composite supply but leaves the final decision mostly to the national courts.

For determining whether the supply is one single supply, the CJEU considers the 'essential features' of the transaction and highlights that all circumstances under which the transaction takes place should be evaluated.[151] As already discussed, in both exceptions, the economic use of the supply is of utmost importance for determining whether the supply consists of several distinct supplies or of one composite supply.[152] With this very general statement, the CJEU used the following criteria to determine whether the supply consists of several distinct supplies or of one composite supply:

---

147. *See*, e.g., Case C-349/96, *CPP*, 25 Feb. 1999, ECLI:EU:C:1999:93, para. 30; Case C-34/99, *Commissioners of Customs & Excise v Primback Ltd*, 15 May 2001, ECLI:EU:C:2001:271, para. 45; Case C-41/04, *Levob Verzekeringen and OV Bank*, 27 Oct. 2005, ECLI:EU:C:2005:649, para. 21.
148. *See*, e.g., Case C-41/04, *Levob Verzekeringen and OV Bank*, 27 Oct. 2005, ECLI:EU:C:2005:649, para. 20; Case C-276/09, *Everything Everywhere*, 2 Dec. 2010, ECLI:EU:C:2010:730, para. 26. For further information on these two determining factors, *see* s. 2.2.2.1.2.4 The Determination of a Single Versus a Composite Supply and VAT Consequences thereof.
149. *See* s. 2.2.2.1.2.1 The General Rule.
150. Case C-425/06, *Part Service*, 21 Feb. 2008, ECLI:EU:C:2008:108, para. 51; Case C-392/11, *Field Fisher Waterhouse*, 27 Sep. 2012, ECLI:EU:C:2012:597, para. 15.
151. Case C-349/96, *CPP*, 25 Feb. 1999, ECLI:EU:C:1999:93, para. 29; Case C-41/04, *Levob Verzekeringen and OV Bank*, 27 Oct. 2005, ECLI:EU:C:2005:649, para. 20; Case C-276/09, *Everything Everywhere*, 2 Dec. 2010, ECLI:EU:C:2010:730, para. 26; Case C-117/11, *Purple Parking Ltd and Airparks Services*, 19 Jan. 2012, ECLI:EU:C:2012:29, para. 29; Case C-392/11, *Field Fisher Waterhouse*, 27 Sep. 2012, ECLI:EU:C:2012:597, para. 19.
152. *See* s. 2.2.2.1.2.2 The Exception of Indivisible Economic Supplies with reference to Case C-461/08, *Don Bosco Onroerend Goed*, 19 Nov. 2009, ECLI:EU:C:2009:722, para. 39 and s. 2.2.2.1.2.3. The Exception of Ancillary Supplies with reference to Case C-41/04, *Levob Verzekeringen BV and OV Bank NV*, 27 Oct. 2005, ECLI:EU:C:2005:649, para. 24.

- The contractual structure or general conditions of the transaction.[153]
- The fact that the two supplies are, by their nature, closely linked.[154]
- The invoicing and pricing of the supply in question.[155] The invoicing of the supply in question might be an indication that the supply should be treated as one single (composite) supply if the supplier charged its customers with one single price.[156] Ultimately, the agreed price is a reflection of the interests of the parties involved in the transaction.[157] If the charge attributable to the different elements of a supply could not be easily factored out, this would speak in favour of a single supply because splitting the charge would be artificial.[158]
- To the fact that, in principle, also third parties could supply the goods or services.[159] The possibility that the good or service might be supplied by a third party is inherent to the concept of a composite supply.[160] If other suppliers could not supply the good or service in question, it would be likely that the supply is one single supply without the need to apply any exception of the composite supply rules.

After all, the CJEU held for all determining factors described above that they are, by themselves, not decisive for the decision of whether the supply is to be treated as one (composite) supply or several distinct supplies.[161] The CJEU consequently assesses the existence of a single service in a consideration of the overall circumstances.

---

153. Case C-425/06, *Part Service*, 21 Feb. 2008, ECLI:EU:C:2008:108, para. 54; Case C-224/11, *BGZ Leasing*, 17 Jan. 2013, ECLI:EU:C:2013:15, paras. 46 et seq.
154. The CJEU referred to this criteria especially in connection with insurance services which, by their nature, are closely linked to the goods for which the insurance is applicable for; *see*, e.g., Case C-224/11, *BGZ Leasing*, 17 Jan. 2013, ECLI:EU:C:2013:15, para. 36; Case C-584/13, *Directeur général des finances publiques v Mapfre asistencia compañia internacional de seguros y reaseguros SA and Mapfre warranty SpA v Directeur général des finances publiques*, 16 Jul. 2015, ECLI:EU:C:2015:488, para. 51.
155. Case C-349/96, *CPP*, 25 Feb. 1999, ECLI:EU:C:1999:93, para. 31; Case C-276/09, *Everything Everywhere*, 2 Dec. 2010, ECLI:EU:C:2010:730, para. 29; Case C-117/11, *Purple Parking and Airparks Services*, 19 Jan. 2012, ECLI:EU:C:2012:29, para. 34.
156. Case C-349/96, *CPP*, 25 Feb. 1999, ECLI:EU:C:1999:93, para. 31; Case C-276/09, *Everything Everywhere*, 2 Dec. 2010, ECLI:EU:C:2010:730, para. 29; Case C-117/11, *Purple Parking and Airparks Services*, 19 Jan. 2012, ECLI:EU:C:2012:29, para. 34; Case C-224/11, *BGZ Leasing*, 17 Jan. 2013, ECLI:EU:C:2013:15, para. 44.
157. Case C-117/11, *Purple Parking and Airparks Services*, 19 Jan. 2012, ECLI:EU:C:2012:29, para. 35.
158. Case C-581/19, *Frenetikexito – Unipessoal Lda v Autoridade Tributária e Aduaneira*, 22 Oct. 2020, ECLI:EU:C:2020:855, Opinion of AG Kokott, para. 33.
159. Case C-392/11, *Field Fisher Waterhouse*, 27 Sep. 2012, ECLI:EU:C:2012:597, 26.
160. *Ibid.* para. 26.
161. Already in the earlier cases, the CJEU held that 'the single price may suggest that there is a single service', *see* Case C-349/96, *CPP*, 25 Feb. 1999, ECLI:EU:C:1999:93, para. 31; in the later cases, the CJEU explicitly stated that, by themselves, the pricing, the close nature of the supplies and the possibility of third parties supplying the goods or services are not decisive or sufficient; *see* Case C-276/09, *Everything Everywhere*, 2 Dec. 2010, ECLI: EU:C:2010:730, para. 30; Case C-117/11, *Purple Parking and Airparks Services*, 19 Jan. 2012, ECLI:EU:C:2012:29, para. 34; Case C-392/11, *Field Fisher Waterhouse*, 27 Sep. 2012, ECLI:EU:C:2012:597, para. 26; Case C-224/11, *BGZ Leasing*, 17 Jan. 2013, ECLI:EU:C:2013:15, paras 36+47; Case C-584/13, *Directeur Mapfre asistencia and Mapfre warranty*, 16 Jul. 2015, ECLI:EU:C:2015:488, para. 51.

Furthermore, the CJEU held that the decision of whether the supply is one single supply or two distinct supplies should be envisaged by 'a typical customer'.[162] Although the CJEU referred to the 'typical customer' in many cases,[163] the CJEU has not yet given a detailed definition of the 'typical customer'. A certain objectiveness can be assumed though as the CJEU has emphasised that the specific intention of certain customers cannot be taken into account because this subjective approach would not ensure legal certainty.[164]

After all, for the decision of whether a supply is one composite supply or should qualify as two single supplies, the specific circumstances of the cases must be considered from the eyes of a typical customer. Therefore, the two measures of the determination of the specific circumstances of the transaction and the impression of the typical customer should be tested concurrently and complement each other.[165] Despite some similarities in the CJEU case law, the CJEU takes a case-by-case decision and applies and evaluates which different circumstances are to be applied depending on the specific facts of the case. Thus, it is difficult to draw a clear line of which circumstances in which situations should outweigh the others. The one common denominator is reflected in the view of the *typical customer*. However, even with this common denominator, the general guidance and provided definitions by the CJEU are rather scarce.

The question of whether a supply is a composite supply or is split up into independent supplies is highly relevant for the VAT treatment of the transaction. If the transaction was considered as one composite supply, all components of the composite supply would receive one VAT treatment. As already discussed, ancillary parts follow the VAT treatment of the principal part of the supply, whereas the VAT treatment for the exception of an indivisible economic supply might be more difficult to determine.[166] Therefore, the distinction of a single or composite supply might impact the applicable rates, exemptions, place of supply rules, chargeability, and even the liability for payment of the VAT.[167]

---

162. Case C-349/96, *CPP*, 25 Feb. 1999, ECLI:EU:C:1999:93, para. 29; Case C-41/04, *Levob Verzekeringen BV and OV Bank NV*, 27 Oct. 2005, ECLI:EU:C:2005:649, para. 20; Case C-276/09, *Everything Everywhere*, 2 Dec. 2010, ECLI:EU:C:2010:730, para. 26; Case C-44/11, *Deutsche Bank*, 19 Jul. 2012, ECLI:EU:C:2012:484, para. 21; Case C-463/16, *Stadion Amsterdam CV v Staatssecretaris van Financiën*, 18 Jan. 2018, ECLI:EU:C:2018:22, para. 30.

163. Case C-349/96, *CPP*, 25 Feb. 1999, ECLI:EU:C:1999:93, para. 29; Case C-41/04, *Levob Verzekeringen and OV Bank*, 27 Oct. 2005, ECLI:EU:C:2005:649, para. 20; Case C-111/05, *Aktiebolaget NN*, 29 Mar. 2007, ECLI:EU:C:2007:195, para. 23; Case C-453/05, *Ludwig*, 21 Jun. 2007, ECLI:EU:C:2007:369, para. 23; Case C-276/09, *Everything Everywhere*, 2 Dec. 2010, ECLI:EU:C:2010:730, para. 26; Case C-117/11, *Purple Parking and Airparks Services*, 19 Jan. 2012, ECLI:EU:C:2012:29, para. 30; Case C-44/11, *Deutsche Bank*, 19 Jul. 2012, ECLI:EU:C:2012:484, para. 21; Case C-463/16, *Stadion Amsterdam*, 18 Jan. 2018, ECLI:EU:C:2018:22, para. 30.

164. Case C-18/12, *Město Žamberk*, 21 Feb. 2013, ECLI:EU:C:2013:95, para. 36; *see also* Oskar Henkow, *Defining the Tax Object in Composite Supplies in European VAT*, 2 World Journal of VAT/GST Law, *supra* note 102, at 199.

165. Oskar Henkow, *supra* note 102, at 199.

166. *See* s. 2.2.2.1.2.2 The Exception of Indivisible Economic Supplies and 2.2.2.1.2.3 The Exception of Ancillary Supplies.

167. Ben Terra & Julie Kajus, *Introduction to European VAT*, s. 10.4.1.1 (IBFD 2021).

2.2.2.1.3   Can Two Suppliers Supply One Composite Supply?

After the two exceptions of the composite supply have been discussed, this section will focus on the question of whether two suppliers are able to supply one composite supply. The background for this question is that, often, one supplier sells a full package to a customer. For the supplier to be able to provide this package of goods or services to the customer, the suppliers themselves purchase the relevant goods and services from other sub-suppliers. In many cases, the sub-suppliers deliver the goods or services to the customer. Therefore, the question arises whether the composite supply rules, either being ancillary supplies or indivisible economic supplies, are also applicable when two or more suppliers supply the different components of a composite supply.

The CJEU's case law has not yet explicitly addressed this issue. In some cases, the supply in question was provided by different suppliers which did not seem to influence the CJEU case law on the composite supply rules. Accordingly, the CJEU held in *Madgett und Baldwin*[168] that, if 'bought in' transportation services from third parties remained ancillary to the accommodation services provided by the supplier, these 'bought in' services would be part of the composite supply.[169] Also, in *Bookit*,[170] the CJEU did not deny the applicability of the ancillary composite supply rules just because the services were provided to the customers by two taxable persons. In the *Bookit* case, the CJEU had to decide whether payment services were ancillary services to the purchase of cinema tickets.[171] The final assessment on whether the payment services were ancillary to the ticket sale was left to the national court.[172]

Similar judgments can also be seen with the first discussed exception, i.e., the composite supply of indivisible economic supplies. In the *Wojskowa Agencja Mieszkaniowa w Warszawie*[173] case, the CJEU had to decide whether the letting of immovable property with additional services such as water, heating, and electricity could qualify as one single composite supply by the landlord. In this case, the CJEU left the final decision again to the national court, but the fact that additional services were supplied by third party suppliers and the landlord of the customers simply passed on the costs to the tenants should not have any effect on the test of whether the supply was a composite or two single supplies by the landlord.[174]

---

168. Joined Cases C-308/96 and C-94/97, *Madgett and Baldwin*, 22 Oct. 1998, ECLI:EU:C:1998:496.
169. *Ibid.* paras 25 et seq.
170. Case C-607/14, *Bookit, Ltd v Commissioners for Her Majesty's Revenue and Customs*, 26 May 2016, ECLI:EU:C:2016:355.
171. *Ibid.* para. 11; thereby, the cinema tickets were purchased from Bookit's mother company for which Bookit acted as an agent.
172. *Ibid.* para. 27.
173. Case C-42/14, *Wojskowa Agencja Mieszkaniowa w Warszawie*, 16 Apr. 2015, ECLI: EU:C:2015:229.
174. *Ibid.* paras 21 + 46; to this extent, *see* also Case C-425/06, *Part Service*, 21 Feb. 2008, ECLI:EU:C:2008:108, paras 54 et seqq.; also in this case, the CJEU held that the national court should assess whether the supply in question, although provided by two different suppliers, is one composite supply. The main focus of this case was not the composite supply but testing whether the contractual structure was abusive.

Finally, in the *Mapfre asistencia und Mapfre warranty*[175] case, the CJEU explicitly gave regard to a service being supplied by different suppliers. The case revolved around a second-hand motor vehicle dealer who offered, additionally to the purchase of a motor vehicle, a warranty covering the repair of mechanical breakdowns.[176] The CJEU held that it is 'subject to determination by the referring court ... [whether] those two transactions, provided, moreover, by two different suppliers, constitute an indivisible economic supply which it would be artificial to split'.[177] In the *Mapfre asistencia und Mapfre warranty* case, the CJEU emphasised that the supply by two suppliers might be an indication of the supply not being so closely linked that they should be regarded as one composite supply. At the same time, the CJEU did not explicitly state that if two suppliers supplied different components of a supply, the exceptions for the composite supply would not be applicable.

Furthermore, in literature, it has been discussed that the qualification of a single supply by different suppliers depends on how much influence the customer has on the choice and timing of the supply from the third party.[178] If the customer did not have any influence on the part of the supply by the sub-supplier, the supply could be qualified as a composite supply.[179] Most important is, yet again, the qualification of the supply as a composite supply from the eyes of the 'typical customer'. The circumstance that a supply can theoretically also be provided to the customer by a third party is not by itself decisive of whether the supply is a composite supply.[180] Similarly, this section and the analysed CJEU case law show that a composite supply can also likely be supplied by different suppliers. After all, from these cases, it can be derived that the CJEU does not disregard the composite supply rules when two suppliers are providing the customer with the different elements of the composite supply.

2.2.2.1.4   The Qualification of the Sale of Goods Through Platforms

After the discussion of the CJEU's case law and therefore the theoretical basis of the composite supply rules, the question arises of how the supply of goods via platforms should be qualified from a VAT point of view. When suppliers sell their goods on online marketplaces, the customer receives, on one side, the goods from the underlying supplier and, on the other side, also the services provided by the online platform, e.g., the providing and maintenance of the homepage, the display and maintenance of the ratings from other customers, and the customer service of the platform. As determined, the fact that these supplies are provided by different suppliers should not have an

---

175. Case C-584/13, *Mapfre asistencia and Mapfre warranty*, 16 Jul. 2015, ECLI:EU:C:2015:488.
176. *Ibid.* para. 11.
177. *Ibid.* para. 57.
178. Stefanie Baur-Rückert, *Die Einheitlichkeit des Umsatzes im Mehrwertsteuerrecht* 235 (Nomos 2018).
179. Selina Siller & Annika Streicher, *Online Beherbungsplattformen: Leistung des Vermieters und Leistung der Plattform als einheitliche Leistung?*, taxlex, *supra* note 17, at 17.
180. *See*, on this already s. 2.2.2.1.2.4 The Determination of a Single Versus a Composite Supply and VAT Consequences thereof.

influence on the composite supply rules.[181] In general, for the supplies to be considered as one composite supply, two supplies must exist. In the case at hand, the first supply would be the supply of the good from the underlying supplier to the customer for consideration. The second supply would be the service supplied from the platform to the customer if the service was provided for consideration.[182] Therefore, the question arises whether these two supplies may qualify as one composite supply.

For the application of the first exception of the composite supply rules, the two supplies must be so closely linked that it would be artificial to split them from the view of a 'typical customer'. The customer should purchase the composite supply because both elements together have an economic use to him. In this sense, the different components of the supply are of equal use to the customer. When looking at the purchase of goods via platforms, a typical customer would likely not qualify the supplies (the supply of the good and the supply of the platform service) being of equal use since the typical customer would buy the good via the platform to receive the good. The services of the platform only lead to a simplification of the purchasing process: The choice of goods is well displayed, and the comparison of different goods simplifies the decision-making process of the customer. Furthermore, the customer service and the simple and clear return policies of many e-commerce platforms further result in a facilitation to return goods. It seems that the main aim of the customer visiting a platform is to purchase a desired good. Therefore, the two supplies can probably not be qualified as indivisible economic supplies. Nevertheless, the additional services offered by the platform may be qualified as improving the enjoyment of the purchased good. In this sense, the second exception may be applicable. Thus, the purchase of the goods would qualify as the principle supply, whereas the supply of the service from the platform would qualify as the ancillary supply. Therefore, it may be argued that the two supplies could qualify as one composite supply.

Since the CJEU follows a case-by-case analysis for the determination of whether the supply is one composite supply or two single supplies, a closer look must be taken at the construction of the platform, in particular:[183]

- at the contractual structure and general conditions of the transaction;[184] and
- at the invoicing and pricing of the supply in question.[185]

---

181. *See* s. 2.2.2.1.3 Can Two Suppliers Supply One Composite Supply?.
182. For a more detailed discussion on whether the supply of the service from the platform to the customer is a taxable transaction under the VAT Directive and to what extent a payment for the provided service is relevant, *see* s. 2.2.5.2 The Necessity for Consideration.
183. In the previous section, also the fact that the two supplies are, by their nature, closely linked has been mentioned as a determining factor; *see* s. 2.2.2.1.2.4 The Determination of a Single Versus a Composite Supply and VAT Consequences thereof. In the case of platforms offering the supply of goods, this natural close link between the supply of the good and the supply of the platform service can likely be denied.
184. Case C-425/06, *Part Service*, 21 Feb. 2008, ECLI:EU:C:2008:108, para. 54; Case C-224/11, *BGZ Leasing*, 17 Jan. 2013, ECLI:EU:C:2013:15, paras 46 et seq.
185. Case C-349/96, *CPP*, 25 Feb. 1999, ECLI:EU:C:1999:93, para. 31; Case C-276/09, *Everything Everywhere*, 2 Dec. 2010, ECLI:EU:C:2010:730, para. 29; Case C-117/11, *Purple Parking Ltd and Airparks Services*, 19 Jan. 2012, ECLI:EU:C:2012:29, para. 34.

Each of these elements should be evaluated from the view of a typical customer.

In many cases, the underlying supplier is publicly displayed on the platform.[186] When a customer is interested in a good, this customer can see who is the underlying supplier. Often, platforms also provide a link to the underlying supplier's profile with the name and seat of establishment, VAT identification number, and the ratings of other customers who already bought goods from the aforementioned supplier. Although the platform has a general power of attorney of being able to conclude the contract with the customers in many cases, the contract for purchasing the good is, in most cases, concluded between the underlying supplier and the customer.

The invoicing and pricing often depend on the platform. There are several options. The platform and the underlying supplier may invoice their services separately. In this case, the customer would receive two separate invoices, i.e., one for the supply of the good from the underlying supplier and the other for the supply of the service from the platform. The other option is the provision of one invoice for both supplies. In this case, the invoice would most likely be issued by the platform, but both services would likely be indicated separately on the invoice.

The conducting of the contract and the invoicing of the supply may hint that the supplies should be considered as two distinct supplies from the view of a typical customer. On the one hand, the platform supplies the service of providing the platform infrastructure including the discussed benefits thereof and, on the other hand, the underlying supplier supplies the desired good. Based on this analysis, the two supplies of many platforms should qualify as two distinct supplies and thus the VAT treatment of each supply must be determined independently. Nevertheless, if one were to argue that the supplies should be one composite supply,[187] the VAT treatment of the ancillary service would follow the VAT treatment of the main supply, i.e., the supply of the goods. This might have an impact not only on the place of supply but also on the rate applicable to the composite supply or possible applicable exemptions. The impact of the legal consequences of the qualification as one composite supply can be clarified with the following example: A Hungarian supplier offers goods on a platform. A customer established in Germany purchases a good from the Hungarian supplier on the platform. The German customer pays a monthly fee for the usage of the platform and indicates the Italian address of the customer's holiday house (B2C transaction) as a delivery address. Thus, the delivery of the good would qualify as a distance sale of goods, and the place of supply would be in Italy[188] under the assumption that the Hungarian supplier has surpassed the applicable distance selling threshold.[189] The platform service would, in this case, be the ancillary supply, and thus the place of

---

186. *See* also the remarks on the qualification of the platform acting as an undisclosed agent in s. 2.2.2.2.4 Does a Platform Act as an Undisclosed Agent?.
187. This might especially be the case if, e.g., the platform models further develop or if the typical customer further develops. These factors might lead to the different outcome with the result that the two supplies should be considered as one composite supply.
188. According to Article 33 (1) (a) of the VAT Directive prior to 30 Jun. 2021 and according to Article 33 (a) of the VAT Directive as of Jul. 1, 2021.
189. *See*, for further information on the applicable place of supply rules before the introduction of the e-commerce package as well as the applicable distance selling thresholds until 30. Jun. 2021, s. 2.2.3.2 Intra-Community B2C Supplies Prior to the Introduction of the E-Commerce

supply would follow the supply of the good, i.e., the place of supply for the supply would also be Italy.[190] Thus, the platform as well as underlying supplier must VAT register in Italy or could, as of 1 July 2021, declare these supplies through the applicable IOSS or EU-OSS.[191]

2.2.2.1.5   *Interim Conclusion*

After all, the final decision of whether the supply of the good and platform service qualify as one composite supply or two distinct supplies must be taken with case-by-case analyses. Thereby, especially different characteristics of the platform to be analysed should be taken into consideration. The result of whether the supplies in question are two single supplies or one composite supply depends on exactly those characteristics. It is not possible to provide a general conclusion of whether the supply through platforms is a composite supply based on EU law and the CJEU's interpretation thereof. However, for many platforms represented on the market, good arguments can be found to deny the application of the composite supply rules, i.e., the contractual structure, the invoicing, as well as the pricing of the supplies.

2.2.2.2   **The Supply Through Platforms: A Supply Through an Undisclosed Agent?**

2.2.2.2.1   *General Remarks on the Role of Platforms and on the Undisclosed Agent Scheme*

From a VAT point of view, the supply of goods from underlying suppliers to customers via platforms raises the question of who is supplying the goods. In general, it could be assumed that the underlying supplier is the person supplying the goods to the customer. Nevertheless, the VAT Directive provides certain exceptions to this assumption. When a customer buys the goods from an underlying supplier via a platform, it could be questioned from a VAT point of view whether the platform acts as an agent. The EU VAT system distinguishes between two agents, i.e., the undisclosed and the disclosed agent. This section elaborates the concept and legal consequences of the undisclosed agent.[192] Also, the characteristics of platforms selling goods will be analysed to evaluate whether the platform acts as an undisclosed agent.

The legal basis for the undisclosed agent of the supply of goods can be found in Article 14 (2) (c) of the VAT Directive which stipulates that 'the following shall be regarded as a supply of goods: ... c) the transfer of goods pursuant to a contract under

---

Package; *see* for the implementation of the EUR 10,000 threshold as of Jul. 1, 2021 s. 2.3.2.2.1 The First Legislative Changes of the E-Commerce Package in 2017.

190. *See,* for the discussion of the qualification of the supply of the platform service and the applicable place of supply before the entering into force of the e-commerce package, s. 2.2.5.3 The Determination of the Place of Supply.

191. *See,* for further information on the IOSS and the EU-OSS, s. 4.11 Special Schemes of the OSS.

192. For an analysis of the disclosed agent scheme, *see* s. 2.2.5.3.2 Does the Platform Act as a Disclosed Agent According to Article 46 of the VAT Directive?.

which commission is payable on purchase or sale'. As the wording of Article 14 (2) (c) of the VAT Directive referring to the payment of a commission might raise interpretational questions,[193] the CJEU has provided guidance on its interpretation. The CJEU stated that a 'contract under which commission is payable constitutes, in principle, an agreement by which an intermediary undertakes to carry out in his own name one or more legal transactions on behalf of a third party'.[194] From this CJEU interpretation, it can be derived that an undisclosed agent must fulfil three requirements: The agent must act in his own name, on behalf of a third party, and the undisclosed agent must take part in the supply. All three conditions must be fulfilled cumulatively.

Similar to the CJEU's interpretation of Article 14 (2) (c) of the VAT Directive, the EU legislator defines the supply of services by undisclosed agents in Article 28 of the VAT Directive as:

> Where a taxable person acting in his own name but on behalf of another person takes part in a supply of services, he shall be deemed to have received and supplied those services himself.

In addition to the requirements for an undisclosed agent for the supply of goods, Article 28 of the VAT Directive also describes the legal consequence of qualifying as an undisclosed agent for the supply of services. As a result of fulfilling the requirements of an undisclosed agent, the supply would fictitiously be treated as if the intermediary had received the service from the principal and supplied the service to the customer himself. Thus, the VAT treatment deviates from the contractual agreement between the involved parties.

Despite the different terminology of Article 14 (2) (c) and Article 28 of the VAT Directive, the CJEU has confirmed that both articles pursue a similar purpose and result in the same legal consequence.[195] The main argument for this reasoning is a systematic argument. The CJEU emphasised that Article 14 (2) (c) of the VAT Directive as well as Article 28 of the VAT Directive are both stipulated under Title IV ('taxable transactions') of the VAT Directive.[196] Thus, the undisclosed agent must fulfil the same requirements independently whether the supply in question concerns goods or services.[197] Also, the legal consequences do not differ between undisclosed agents who

---

193. *See* the critical discussion of Article 14 (2) (c) of the VAT Directive by Stan Beelen, *Is a Generalized Reverse Charge Mechanism the Obvious Remedy Against VAT Fraud?*, in *VAT in an EU and International Perspective: Essays in Honour of Han Kogels* (Henk van Arendonk, et al. eds., IBFD 2011); *see* also Ben Terra & Julie Kajus, *Introduction to European VAT, supra* note 167, ch. 10.2.1.4, who suggest reading Article 14 (2) (c) of the VAT Directive as follows: 'where a taxable person acting in his own name but on behalf of another takes part in a supply of goods, he must be considered to have received and supplied those goods'.
194. Case C-526/13, *UAB 'Fast Bunkering Klaipeda' v Valstybine mokesčių inspekcija prie Lietuvos Respublikos finansų ministerijos*, 3 Sep. 2015, ECLI:EU:C:2015:536, para. 33.
195. Case C-274/15, *European Commission v Grand Duchy of Luxembourg*, 4 May 2017, ECLI: EU:C:2017:333, para. 88.
196. *Ibid.*; Case C-734/19, *ITH Comercial Timişoara SRL v Agenţia Naţională de Administrare Fiscală – Direcţia Generală Regională a*, 12 Nov. 2020, ECLI:EU:C:2020:919, para. 50.
197. *See* the more detailed discussion on the requirements for the undisclosed agent scheme in s. 2.2.2.2.2 The Requirements for an Undisclosed Agent.

supply services and undisclosed agents who supply goods.[198] Similarly and since most judgments were rendered on the applicability of the undisclosed agent scheme for the supply of services, the interpretational aid provided by the CJEU for Article 28 of the VAT Directive should also be applicable when interpreting Article 14 (2) (c) of the VAT Directive. In the following sections, the three requirements for the applicability of Article 14 (2) (c) of the VAT Directive and the legal consequences thereof will be further discussed. In a final section, the platform acting as an undisclosed agent will be analysed.

2.2.2.2.2 *The Requirements for an Undisclosed Agent*

2.2.2.2.2.1 The Requirement of Acting in the Own Name

As a first requirement, an undisclosed agent must be acting in its own name. The CJEU discussed this criterion in depth when interpreting Article 6 (4) of the Sixth VAT Directive[199] in the *Henfling and Others*[200] case. The case revolved around a Belgian company, TFB, whose business was taking horseracing bets in Belgium and other Member States. For serving the local markets, TFB used local agents who were responsible for collecting the stakes, registering the bets, issuing the betting slips, and paying out the winnings to the bettors.[201] The preliminary question that was addressed was whether the local agents, so-called buralistes, were considered as being undisclosed agents and therefore whether the VAT exemption for betting in Article 13 (B) (f) of the Sixth VAT Directive[202] would be applicable to the supply of betting services by the buralistes.

For the decision, whether an agent acts in his own name, 'all the details of the case, and in particular the nature of the contractual obligations of the trader concerned towards its customers',[203] should be considered by the national court. This statement emphasises that the contractual obligation is of importance for determining whether the agent acts in his own name. This reference might lead to different interpretations throughout the different Member States as contracts are, in general, interpreted based on national law.[204] One of the goals of the VAT Directive is to establish a common VAT system within the EU. Therefore, the application of expressions from the VAT Directive

---

198. *See* the more detailed discussion on the legal consequences of the undisclosed agent scheme in s. 2.2.2.2.3 Legal Consequence of the Qualification as an Undisclosed Agent.
199. Sixth Council Directive 77/388/EEC of 17 May 1977 on the Harmonization of the Laws of the Member States Relating to Turnover Taxes – Common System of Value Added Tax: Uniform Basis of Assessment, OJ L 145 (1977); the wording of Article 6 (4) of the Sixth VAT Directive is comparable to Article 28 of the VAT Directive.
200. Case C-464/10, *Belgian State v Pierre Henfling and Others*, 14 Jul. 2011, ECLI:EU:C:2011:489.
201. *Ibid.* para. 13.
202. Stipulated in Article 135 (1) (i) of the VAT Directive.
203. Case C-464/10, *Henfling and Others*, 14 Jul. 2011, ECLI:EU:C:2011:489, para. 40.
204. *See* already Stan Beelen, *Is a Generalized Reverse Charge Mechanism the Obvious Remedy Against VAT Fraud?*, in *VAT in an EU and International Perspective: Essays in Honour of Han Kogels*, *supra* note 193, who discusses the different interpretation of contracts in common and civil law systems.

should be based on uniform definitions among the different Member States, and no reference to national legal systems is permissible.[205] To fulfil these general principles in the case at hand, the CJEU limited the evaluation of the contractual obligation so that national provisions may not extend the legal fiction of (today's) Article 28 of the VAT Directive beyond the criteria stipulated in the VAT Directive; i.e., the national provisions implementing Article 28 of the VAT Directive must be interpreted in conformity with EU law and cannot be affected by national interpretations based on national contract law.[206]

Further, the CJEU held that several factors should be taken into account:

> In that regard, account must be taken, in particular, of whether or not the exercise of their activity requires possession of authorisation by the public authorities, of the fact that the betting slips issued by the 'buralistes' mention TFB's name, that the customers agree, according to the wording of those betting slips, to be subject to the regulations of that company, that the business run by the 'buralistes' carry the sign of TFB, which is the owner of those businesses, and, before the facts in the main proceedings, whether or not the 'buralistes' acted as agents.[207]

The first criterion, the possession of a public authorisation for the selling of bets, is a rather specific criterion in this case. The other four stated criteria are more general and might also be relevant to any other case. The remaining criteria, especially the display of the intermediary's (TFB's) name, the acceptance of the customers to the terms and conditions of TFB, the display of TFB's company sign by the buralistes, and the note on whether the buralistes acted as agents for TFB can qualify as rather general guidance. Especially, the CJEU seems to emphasise with these criteria the importance of the impression that the customer receives when purchasing the services or goods in question. The contract between the intermediary and the underlying supplier does not seem to be decisive.

A similar emphasis on the importance of the appearance of a taxable person to the contracting party can also be observed in another line of CJEU case law in which the CJEU had to decide which taxable person was actually the contracting party.[208] In these cases, the CJEU had to decide on requirements for carrying out an independent economic activity which is, according to Article 9 (1) of the VAT Directive, one requirement for qualifying as a taxable person. One of the criterion to be fulfilled for carrying out an economic activity is performing the activity in one's own name.[209] In

---

205. *See*, e.g., Case C-320/88, *Staatssecretaris van Financiën v Shipping and Forwarding Enterprise Safe*, 8 Feb. 1990, ECLI:EU:C:1990:61, para. 8.
206. Case C-464/10, *Henfling and Others*, 14 Jul. 2011, ECLI:EU:C:2011:489, para. 43; Case C-520/10, *Lebara Ltd v Commissioners for Her Majesty's Revenue & Customs*, 8 Dec. 2011, ECLI:EU:C:2011:818, Opinion of AG Jääskinen, para. 73; *see* also Pernille Rendahl, *EU VAT and Double Taxation: A Fine Line between Interpretation and Application*, Intertax 452 (2013).
207. Case C-464/10, *Henfling and Others*, 14 Jul. 2011, ECLI:EU:C:2011:489, para. 43.
208. Case C-340/15, *Christine Nigl and Others v Finanzamt Waldviertel*, 12 Oct. 2016, ECLI: EU:C:2016:764, paras 25 et seqq.; Case C-312/19, *Valstybine mokesčių inspekcija (Contrat d'activité commune)*, 16 Sep. 2020, ECLI:EU:C:2020:711, paras 37 et seqq.
209. Case C-340/15, *Nigl and Others*, 12 Oct. 2016, ECLI:EU:C:2016:764, para. 28; Case C-312/19, *Valstybine mokesčių inspekcija (Contrat d'activité commune)*, 16 Sep. 2020, ECLI: EU:C:2020:711, para. 41.

this sense, the CJEU held that just the joint marketing of a product could not lead to the conclusion that several taxable persons become a single association of persons (and therefore one taxable person for VAT reasons) if each taxable person had independent contact with its suppliers, the public (tax) authorities, and its customers.[210] Similarly, in a more recent case, the CJEU held that, even though a partnership agreed that one member may act in the name of both parties if that person did not mention the partner's identity or the partnership in general when engaging in business transactions, the contracting parties could not be aware that the person was acting in the name of the partnership or even that a partner existed.[211] Therefore, the CJEU held that the taxable person who concluded the contract and did not disclose the partner and their partnership was acting in his own name and on his own behalf.[212]

Also, the German Federal Tax Court (Bundesfinanzhof – BFH) followed a similar approach in the so-called retail cases.[213] The German Federal Tax Court held that, if a customer bought goods in a physical shop, this customer could assume that the person selling the goods in this shop acted in its own name.[214] Only if the employee in the shop told or showed the customer that: (i) the employee was acting in somebody else's name other than the shop and (ii) the customer explicitly or implicitly accepted the acting in somebody else's name, then the supply could qualify as a supply by a disclosed agent.[215] The German Federal Tax Court has also extended the principles of these retail cases and the requirements thereof for acting in somebody else's name to services supplied over the Internet.[216]

In the discussed judgments, the CJEU and the German Federal Tax Court concentrated on the external relationship, so the impression the customer receives from the taxable person or the intermediary supplying the goods or the services in question. The internal relationship between the intermediary and the underlying supplier should not influence the criterion of acting in its own name, as the customer normally does not have any insights into the internal relationship between the intermediary and the underlying supplier.

---

210. Case C-340/15, *Nigl and Others*, 12 Oct. 2016, ECLI:EU:C:2016:764, para. 34.
211. Case C-312/19, *Valstybinė mokesčių inspekcija (Contrat d'activité commune)*, 16 Sep. 2020, ECLI:EU:C:2020:711, para. 43.
212. *Ibid.* para. 44.
213. Direct translation from German of the so-called Ladenrechtsprechung.
214. BFH 4 Sep. 1970, V R 80/66, para. 9; 14 May 1970, V R 77/66, para. 8; 16 Dec. 1987, X R 32/82, para. 26.
215. BFH, 4 Sep. 1970 – V R 80/66, para. 9 (n. v.); 14 May 1970 – V R 77/66, para. 8 (n. v.); 16 Dec. 1987 – X R 32/82, para. 26 (n. v.).
216. BFH 15 May 2012, XI R 16/10, paras 26 et seqq.; *see also* Selina Siller & Annika Streicher, *Online-Beherbungsplattformen: Zwischen elektronisch erbrachter Dienstleistung und Margen-besteuerung*, taxlex, *supra* note 17, at 49, who discuss the application of the principles set out in the retail cases to accommodation sharing economy platforms; *see also* David R. Dietsch & Timm Stelzer, *Die Digitalisierung der Ladenrechtsprechung des BFH – Vermittlungsleistungen im Internetzeitalter*, 9 MwStR (2021); Matthias Luther et al., *Wer schuldet die Umsatzsteuer bei Umsätzen über Internetplattformen?*, DStR (2021), who discuss the BFH judgments in detail.

2.2.2.2.2.2   The Requirement of Acting on Behalf of Somebody Else

Whereas the first requirement of acting in its own name has been quite extensively discussed in the CJEU case *Henfling and Others*, the CJEU seemed to assume in that same case that the requirement of acting on behalf of somebody else was fulfilled without any further evaluation on this requirement.[217] As AG Jääskinen pointed out in his opinion in the *Lebara* case, acting on behalf of somebody else means that the underlying supplier is carrying the economic risk of the transaction.[218] The case *Lebara* revolved around a phone company that sold phone cards for third country calls to local distributors. These local distributors would market the phone cards and sell them to local customers. Once a customer bought a phone card, the distributors contacted Lebara to activate the phone card; seemingly, the distributor would only pay for the phone card upon the sale of the phone card from the distributor to the local customer.[219] Therefore, AG Jääskinen concluded that the distributors acted economically on behalf of Lebara.[220] It seems that AG Jääskinen based the conclusion that Lebara was carrying the economic risk of this transaction on the fact that the local distributors would only pay the consideration for the phone cards once they sold them to the customer. If the phone card was not sold at all, the distributor would not carry any economic risk from this supply. Whereas AG Jääskinen's preferred solution to this case was the application of the undisclosed agent scheme in Article 6 (4) of the Sixth VAT Directive,[221] the CJEU did not follow this approach but already stated in the facts of the case that the local distributors were acting in their own name and on their own behalf, i.e., not as Lebara's agents.[222] Thus, compared to the AG Jääskinen, the CJEU did not seem to have doubted that the requirement of acting on behalf of somebody else was not fulfilled in the *Lebara* case.

In addition, a systematic interpretation can support the argument that the carrying of the economic risk might be an indication of acting on behalf of somebody else. In the VAT Directive, Article 36a (3) defines the intermediary operator for a chain transaction as 'a supplier within the chain ... who dispatches or transports the goods either himself or through a third party acting on his behalf'. In the Explanatory Notes on the so-called quick fixes, the European Commission argues that the intermediary operator generally would not lose its position as an intermediary operator if he arranged the dispatch or transportation of the goods through another taxable person in

---

217. Case C-464/10, *Henfling and Others*, 14 Jul. 2011, ECLI:EU:C:2011:489, para. 32.
218. Case C-520/10, *Lebara Ltd*, 8 Dec. 2011, ECLI:EU:C:2011:818, Opinion of AG Jääskinen, para. 75.
219. *Ibid.* para. 16; seemingly, the facts of the case at this point were not clear, as stated by AG Jääskinen in footnote 13 of his opinion; this might have also caused the CJEU to not follow AG Jääskinen's primary conclusion to this case.
220. *Ibid.* para. 75.
221. *Ibid.* para. 82. Article 6 (4) of the Sixth VAT Directive is the equivalent of Article 28 of the VAT Directive.
222. Case C-520/10, *Lebara Ltd v Commissioners for Her Majesty's Revenue & Customs*, 3 May 2012, ECLI:EU:C:2012:264, para. 14.

the same chain.[223] Nevertheless, to qualify as the intermediary operator in the chain transaction, the taxable person arranging the dispatch or transport by the other taxable person in the chain must still carry the risk of accidental loss of the goods during the transport.[224] Thus, also the European Commission seems to review the question of who carries the risk for a transaction when determining whether somebody acts on behalf of somebody else.

Moreover, the CJEU held that a statutory obligation of the underlying supplier might cause an intermediary to act on behalf of somebody else.[225] In the *Amărăşti Land Investment* case, the CJEU had to decide, among other questions, whether Amărăşti Land Investment was acting as an undisclosed agent according to Article 28 of the VAT Directive. Amărăşti Land Investment purchased land from vendors in a two-step procedure. First, the potential vendors promised Amărăşti Land Investment to sell the land to them and, second, after the completion of administrative formalities, the parties signed the contracts.[226] For being able to fulfil the administrative formalities, Amărăşti Land Investment received services from lawyers, notaries, and other companies, in particular for the registration in the so-called Land Register.[227] The CJEU held that it was undisputed that Amărăşti Land Investment acted in its own name[228] but evaluated the second requirement more closely. In this sense, the CJEU held that the registration in the 'Land Register' in Romania was a legal obligation by the vendor.[229] Since Amărăşti Land Investment took the necessary formal steps for the vendor to fulfil this obligation, Amărăşti Land Investment was acting on behalf of the vendor and, subsequently, the CJEU qualified Amărăşti Land Investment as an undisclosed agent within the meaning of Article 28 of the VAT Directive.[230]

In the case that there is no statutory obligation for the intermediary to act on behalf of somebody else, such an obligation can be agreed upon by a contract between the underlying supplier and the intermediary. Although the CJEU already clarified in the case *Fast Bunkering Klaipėda* that a 'contract under which commission is payable

---

223. *See* European Commission, *Explanatory Notes on the EU VAT Changes in Respect of Call-Off Stock Arrangements, Chain Transactions and the Exemption for Intra-Community Supplies of Goods ('2020 Quick Fixes')*, *supra* note 35, at 53.
224. *See ibid.*
225. Case C-707/18, *Amărăşti Land Investment SRL v Direcţia Generală Regională a Finanţelor Publice Timişoara and Administraţia Judeţeană a Finanţelor Publice Timiş*, 19 Dec. 2019, ECLI:EU:C:2019:1136, para. 40; Case C-501/19, *UCMR – ADA Asociaţia pentru Drepturi de Autor a Compozitorilor v Pro Management Insolv IPURL, en qualité de liquidateur de Asociaţia Culturală 'Suflet de Român'*, 21 Jan. 2021, ECLI:EU:C:2021:50, paras 44 et seq.
226. Case C-707/18, *Amărăşti Land Investment*, 19 Dec. 2019, ECLI:EU:C:2019:1136, para. 16.
227. *Ibid.* para. 18.
228. *Ibid.* para. 39.
229. *Ibid.* paras 31 + 40.
230. *Ibid.* paras 41 + 43; similarly, the CJEU has decided in a recent case that a collecting agency is also acting as an undisclosed agent. In this case, the collecting agency was based on the national law. The agency was the only agency allowed and obligated to collectively represent artists in the collecting of the copyright in musical works for the public broadcasting at concerts, events, or artistic performances. The CJEU came to the conclusion that, when remuneration was due, the collection society would collect the remuneration in its own name but on behalf of the artist; *see* Case C-501/19, *UCMR – ADA*, 21 Jan. 2021, ECLI:EU:C:2021:50, paras 44 et seqq.

constitutes, in principle, an agreement …',[231] the establishment of such a contract was further explained in additional recent case law. Thereby, the CJEU held that, although the VAT Directive does not specify the form (written or oral) in which the contract must have been concluded, Article 14 (2) (a) of the VAT Directive explicitly stipulates that, 'pursuant to a contract', a commission is payable.[232] Compared to this clear referral to a contract in Article 14 (2) (a) of the VAT Directive, Article 28 of the VAT Directive does not indicate that a contract or an agreement must be in place. Nevertheless, the CJEU affirms the necessity of concluding a contract also in Article 28 of the VAT Directive since the intermediary must act 'on behalf of another person'. To be able to act 'on behalf of another person', the CJEU argues that there must be a (written or oral) agreement between the intermediary and the underlying supplier.[233]

From these explanations by the CJEU and AG Jääskinen, it can be derived that the criterion of acting on behalf of somebody would be fulfilled if the intermediary did not carry the economic risk of the transaction. Although the intermediary is acting in the name of the underlying supplier, the underlying supplier carries the economic risk of the transaction. Moreover, the CJEU also held that, if the intermediary carried out the formal steps to fulfil a legal obligation of another person acting in its own name that can be based on a statutory or a contractual obligation, the requirement of acting on behalf of somebody else would be fulfilled.

2.2.2.2.2.3   The Requirement of Taking Part in the Supply

The third requirement to qualify as an undisclosed agent is that the intermediary must take part in the supply. This means that the intermediary must be involved in the supply chain between the underlying supplier and the customer.[234] Thereby, the question arises on how far the intermediary can amend a supply to still fulfil the requirement of taking part in the supply (chain).

The CJEU has already emphasised in the *Henfling and Others* case that the 'provision creates the legal fiction of two identical supplies of services provided consecutively'.[235] Thereby, the CJEU seems to have implied that the goods or services cannot be amended or adapted by the intermediary for qualifying as an undisclosed agent.[236] In additional recent case law, this necessity of providing identical supplies was confirmed by the CJEU for a transaction to qualify as a supply through an undisclosed agent; i.e., the goods or services the undisclosed agent (fictitiously)

---

231. Case C-526/13, *Fast Bunkering Klaipeda*, 3 Sep. 2015, ECLI:EU:C:2015:536, para. 33.
232. Case C-734/19, *ITH Comercial Timişoara*, 12 Nov. 2020, ECLI:EU:C:2020:919, para. 52.
233. *Ibid.*
234. Giorgio Beretta, *European VAT and the Sharing Economy, supra* note 13, at 287 et seq.
235. Case C-464/10, *Henfling and Others*, 14 Jul. 2011, ECLI:EU:C:2011:489, para. 35.
236. *See* also the German and Austrian case law in which the national courts decided that, if the intermediary amends the supply of goods or services so the intermediary adds an economic value to the supply, the supply cannot be qualified as a supply through an undisclosed agent; *see* BFH 15 May 1994, XI R 107/92, para. 19; *see* VwGH 29 Jul. 2010, 2008/15/0272, 50; *see* also Selina Siller & Annika Streicher, *Online-Beherbungsplattformen: Zwischen elektronisch erbrachter Dienstleistung und Margenbesteuerung*, taxlex, *supra* note 17, at 50, who analyse these national cases into depth.

purchases must be identical to the goods or services the undisclosed agent (fictitiously) sells to the customer.[237]

2.2.2.2.3 Legal Consequence of the Qualification as an Undisclosed Agent

2.2.2.2.3.1 The Legal Fiction of the Qualification as an Undisclosed Agent

In the case that an intermediary fulfils all criteria, the intermediary acts in his own name but on behalf of somebody else, the intermediary qualifies as an undisclosed agent according to Articles 14 (2) (c) or 28 of the VAT Directive. The consequence of qualifying as an undisclosed agent is the legal fiction of the undisclosed agent being deemed to have received and supplied the services or goods himself.[238] Although solely Article 28 of the VAT Directive explicitly stipulated the legal consequences, the CJEU has confirmed that the same legal consequences should be applied to the legal consequence for the supply of goods through an undisclosed agent (Article 14 [2] [c] of the VAT Directive).[239] The CJEU further described the consequence of fulfilling the criteria of acting as an undisclosed agent as follows:

> Accordingly, that provision creates the legal fiction of two identical supplies of services provided consecutively. Under that fiction, the operator, who takes part in the supply of services and who constitutes the commission agent, is considered to have, firstly, received the services in question from the operator on behalf of whom it acts, who constitutes the principal, before providing, secondly, those services to the client himself.[240]

Therefore, a legal relationship is fictitiously concluded between the customer and the undisclosed agent, on the one hand, and the undisclosed agent and the underlying supplier, on the other hand (*see* Figure 2.2 for a graphical illustration of this legal relationship).[241] As the undisclosed agent for goods (Article 14 [2] [c] of the VAT Directive) and for services (Article 28 of the VAT Directive) is stipulated in the section 'taxable transaction' of the VAT Directive, it follows that also the legal relationship between both the undisclosed agent and the person on behalf of whom the intermediary is acting must be taxable and thus subject to a VAT (or VAT exempt) according to the CJEU.[242]

---

237. *See* Case C-734/19, *ITH Comercial Timişoara*, 12 Nov. 2020, ECLI:EU:C:2020:919, paras 51 + 54; in the German version of this judgment, the CJEU uses the term 'Gleichartigkeit' which means similarity whereas, in the French version, the CJEU uses the term 'identité' which means identical. Also, in the English version, the CJEU uses the term 'identical'.
238. *See* Article 28 of the VAT Directive.
239. Case C-274/15, *Commission v Luxembourg*, 4 May 2017, ECLI:EU:C:2017:333, para. 88.
240. *Ibid.* para. 86; Case C-464/10, *Henfling and Others*, 14 Jul. 2011, ECLI:EU:C:2011:489, para. 35.
241. Case C-464/10, *Henfling and Others*, 14 Jul. 2011, ECLI:EU:C:2011:489, para. 33.
242. *See*, similarly, *ibid.* para. 36; *see*, on the interpretation of this case also Pernille Rendahl, *EU VAT and Double Taxation: A Fine Line between Interpretation and Application*, Intertax, *supra* note 206, at 453 who subsumes that the CJEU implies that consideration is necessary for the supply; *see* more explicitly Case C-274/15, *Commission v Luxembourg*, 4 May 2017, ECLI: EU:C:2017:333, para. 87; Case C-707/18, *Amărăşti Land Investment*, 19 Dec. 2019, ECLI: :EU:C:2019:1136, para. 38.

Figure 2.2   Overview of the Supply Chain for the Undisclosed Agent Scheme

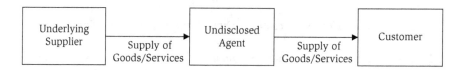

The invoicing is synchronised with the money flow because of the fictitious reclassification into two supplies which might be a benefit from the accounting perspective of the respective parties.[243] However, one disadvantage of the application of the undisclosed scheme may be that the transaction might be qualified differently from a VAT perspective than from the contractual perspective of the transaction. From a VAT point of view, due to the application of Article 14 (2) (c) or 28 of the VAT Directive, two separate supplies must be identified. At the same time, the contractual basis that is relevant for the underlying contract law might be one agreement between the underlying supplier and the customer.[244]

2.2.2.2.3.2   VAT Consequences of the Legal Fiction

In a first instance, it should be reviewed when the fictitious transaction is fulfilled, as this may also have an impact on the applicable taxable transaction and place of supply rule.[245] Thereby, especially the timing of when the supply from the supplier to the undisclosed agent qualifies as a taxable transaction is questionable and has been widely discussed in German and Austrian literature with opposing opinions.[246] This question arises especially when the goods are delivered from the underlying supplier to the undisclosed agent before being sold to the customer. If the supply was delivered from the supplier to the undisclosed agent and, e.g., stored by the undisclosed agent until a customer for the goods was found, then it is questionable whether the transport from the underlying supplier to the undisclosed agent would already qualify as a supply of goods in the meaning of Article 14 (1) of the VAT Directive.

    Some authors argue that the undisclosed agent receives the power to dispose of the goods as an owner already when the goods are transported from the underlying supplier to the undisclosed agent.[247] Following this opinion, the supply of goods from

---

243. Sophie Claessens & Tom Corbett, *Intermediated Delivery and Third-Party Billing: Implication for the Operation of VAT Systems Around the World, in VAT/GST in a Global Digital Economy* 67 (Michael Lang & Ine Lejeune eds., Wolters Kluwer 2015).

244. *Ibid.*; Christian Amand, *EU Value Added Tax: The Directive on Vouchers in the Light of the General Value Added Tax Rules*, 45 Intertax 158 (2017).

245. For a comprehensive overview of the VAT implications, *see* also s. 4 Legal Consequences of the Applicability of Article 14a of the VAT Directive where the VAT consequences on the legal fiction of Article 14a of the VAT Directive will be discussed in detail.

246. *See*, for a detailed overview of the opposing opinions, Norbert Bramerdorfer, *Das Kommissionsgeschäft in der Umsatzsteuer* 120 et seqq. (LexisNexis 2012).

247. Markus Achatz, *Kommissionsgeschäfte und Konsignationsgeschäfte im Unionsrecht, in Reihengeschäfte bei der Umsatzsteuer* 44 (Markus Achatz & Michael Tumpel eds., Linde Verlag 2014); Hans-Hermann Heidner, *Umsatzsteuerliche Behandlung von Kommissionsgeschäften*, 50

the underlying supplier to the undisclosed agent would take place at the time of the delivery of the goods to the undisclosed agent. Nevertheless, at this moment, the taxable amount is not yet determinable because the goods are not yet sold to the final customer. Following this approach, the underlying supplier would have to retroactively fulfil its declaration obligations once the supply to the customer has been finalised since only at this moment can the taxable amount be determined.[248]

Other authors argue that the right to dispose of the goods as the owner has not yet been transferred at the moment of the dispatch or transportation of the goods from the underlying supplier to the undisclosed agent.[249] Although the undisclosed agent receives the goods physically, the undisclosed agent cannot yet dispose of the goods as an owner. Thus, the dispatch or transport of the goods from the underlying supplier to the undisclosed agent cannot be considered as a supply of goods. The supply of goods would only (fictitiously) be fulfilled once the undisclosed agent supplies the goods to the final customer. Since the fiction of the undisclosed agent scheme is only triggered when the undisclosed agent has sold the good to the customer, it is convincing that also the (fictitious) taxable transaction from the supplier to the undisclosed agent should only be affirmed at this moment. If the underlying supplier supplied the goods to another Member State to, e.g., be stored in the warehouse of the undisclosed agent, this transport would trigger an intra-Community transfer according to Article 17 (1) of the VAT Directive. The supply from the underlying supplier to the undisclosed agent, which would follow the general place of supply rules, would only be triggered when the undisclosed agent sells the goods to the customers. If the goods were dispatched from, e.g., the warehouse of the undisclosed agent to the customer in another Member State, then this supply would qualify as a chain transaction.[250]

Similarly, the supply would also qualify as a chain transaction if the goods were delivered directly from the underlying supplier to the final customer (from the first to the last in the chain)[251] which is likely to be the more common case for e-commerce platforms. The consequence of the transaction qualifying as a chain transaction is that the supply with the transport should be determined for the further VAT treatment of the

Umsatzsteuer-Rundschau 519 et seqq. (2001); Wolfgang Schön, *Die Kommission im Umsatzsteuerrecht*, 37 Umsatzsteuer-Rundschau 1 et seqq. (1988).

248. Bramerdorfer, *supra* note 246, at 122 et seqq.; Martin Robisch & Johann Bunjes, *§ 3 Lieferung, sonstige Leistung*, Umsatzsteuergesetz: Kommentar, para. 172 (Johann Bunjes et al. eds., C.H. Beck 2021).

249. *See*, e.g., Otto Sölch et al., *§ 3 Lieferung, sonstige Leistung*, Umsatzsteuergesetz, para. 81 (Otto Sölch & Karl Ringleb eds., C.H. Beck 2021); Bramerdorfer, *supra* note 246, at 122 et seqq.; Franz-J. Giesberts, *Eigentumsübertragung, Verschaffung der Verfügungsmacht und Lieferung*, 25 Umsatzsteuer-Rundschau 61 et seqq. (1976).

250. For further information on the legal qualification of chain transactions, *see* s. 4.3.2 Preliminary Discussion: Chain Transaction.

251. Richard Kettisch, *Reihengeschäfte in der Umsatzsteuer* 269 et seqq. (Verlag Österreich Berliner Wissenschafts-Verlag 2017); Richard Kettisch, *Treibstofflieferungen im Kommissionsgeschäft*, 54 Österreichische Steuerzeitung 56 (2018). One example of when a supply of goods via an undisclosed agent would not be considered as a chain transaction is the supply of immovable property because immovable goods cannot be transported.

two transactions.[252] As a result, in cross-border situations, there will be different places of supplies applicable to the two supplies identified, i.e., the supply from the underlying supplier to the undisclosed agent as well as the supply from the undisclosed agent to the customer.

Second, the qualification of a supply with the involvement of an undisclosed agent will influence the taxable amount. According to Article 73 of the VAT Directive, the taxable amount includes everything that is obtained by the supplier.[253] Therefore, the commission service that the undisclosed agent receives either from the underlying supplier or from the customer is part of the supply of the good or the service provided to the customer. Thus, the commission should not qualify as a separate consideration, e.g., by the underlying supplier or customer, for the intermediation services.[254]

Lastly, the CJEU explicitly held that, since the undisclosed agent provides the identical supply as that which the undisclosed agent received, also the VAT rates and the exemptions depend on the qualification of the supply.[255] The VAT qualification of the underlying operation also decides whether the supply of the undisclosed agent to the final customer is exempt or taxed and which rate is applicable.[256] Therefore, the input VAT deduction on related costs for the undisclosed agent as well as the underlying supplier depends on whether the supply is exempt.[257]

2.2.2.2.4   Does a Platform Act as an Undisclosed Agent?

Several authors evaluated whether a platform qualifies as an undisclosed agent. The authors thereby concentrated on sharing economy platforms[258] and intermediation services for cryptocurrencies.[259] These two intermediation platforms have in common that the supply provided was a service but not a good like in the case of e-commerce platforms offering goods. However, certain parallels can be derived from these

---

252. For further explanations on the chain transaction, the requirements for distinguishing the supply with transport from the supply without transport, and the legal consequences, *see* s. 4.3.2 Preliminary Discussion: Chain Transaction.
253. For further explanations on the taxable amount, *see* s. 4.5 Taxable Amount.
254. *See*, for a detailed discussion of the taxable amount and the VAT treatment of the commission, s. 4.5.5 The Inclusion of Commission Retained by the Platform in the Taxable Amount.
255. Case C-464/10, *Henfling and Others*, 14 Jul. 2011, ECLI:EU:C:2011:489, para. 36.
256. For further explanations on the applicable exemptions and rates, *see* s. 4.6 Applicable Rates and Exemptions.
257. For further explanations on the input VAT deduction, *see* s. 4.8 Input VAT Deduction.
258. Giorgio Beretta, *European VAT and the Sharing Economy*, *supra* note 13, at 249 et seqq.; Selina Siller & Annika Streicher, *Online-Beherbungsplattformen: Zwischen elektronisch erbrachter Dienstleistung und Margenbesteuerung*, taxlex, *supra* note 17, at 49 et seqq.; Lily Zechner, *Ist Uber auch aus Sicht des Umsatzsteuerrechts Beförderungsdienstleister?*, 29 SWI, *supra* note 17, at 525 et seqq.; Lily Zechner, *How to Treat the Ride-Hailing Company Uber for VAT Purposes*, 30 International VAT Monitor, *supra* note 17, at 262 et seq.; Lily Zechner, *Internetplattformen und umsatzsteuerrechtliche Leistungszurechnung am Beispiel Airbnb*, ÖStZ, *supra* note 17, at 303 et seqq.
259. Tina Ehrke-Rabel & Lily Zechner, *VAT Treatment of Cryptocurrency Intermediation Services*, 48 Intertax 504 et seq. (2020); Lily Zechner, *Kryptowährungen: Sind Wechselstuben, Handelsplätze und Walletanbieter umsatzsteuerpflichtig?*, taxlex 395 et seqq. (2017).

previous discussions of platforms in literature that refuse the applicability of the undisclosed agent scheme of the investigated platforms.

As described, for a platform to qualify as an undisclosed agent, the platform must act in its own name as a first requirement.[260] According to this criterion, it is relevant how the typical customer conceives the information provided when purchasing goods via the platform. Therefore, one of the issues to take into consideration for the evaluation of whether the platform is acting in its own name is the information the platform publishes with the offer. On most established platform businesses, the underlying supplier is clearly indicated and visible to the customer, e.g., by stating the name of the underlying supplier with a link under which the customer can access further information on the supplier on a special profile. On this profile, the name and seat of establishment of the underlying supplier are indicated as well as the VAT identification number (if available) and further information that the underlying supplier wishes to display. Therefore, the customer can identify the underlying supplier even before ordering the goods from the platform. Furthermore, the platforms often explicitly indicate in the terms and conditions that the underlying suppliers are listing and selling the products that are displayed. In this sense, the platform highlights its role as an intermediary who only facilitates the offering and purchasing of goods. In many cases, it is also explicitly stated that the platform does not buy or sell the goods offered and that the purchasing contract is concluded between the underlying supplier and the customer. Therefore, the customer receives the impression from the general terms and conditions that the underlying supplier is the contract partner for the supply of the goods. Lastly, the invoice is additional information available to the customer to verify whether the platform is acting in its own name. Most platforms are issuing the invoices in the name and on behalf of the underlying supplier. Thus, the information indicated on the invoice refers to the underlying supplier, and the platform only generates and sends the invoice to the customer (in most cases, automatically). Therefore, the overall impression the customer receives from the platform is that the platform is not acting in its own name as the underlying supplier is indicated wherever possible. As a result, it is likely that the first requirement of the platform acting in its own name is not fulfilled.

According to the second requirement, the platform must act on behalf of the underlying supplier. With this requirement, the economic risk carrying should be evaluated. Since the platform only acts as an intermediary and brings the parties together, the goods are not within the power of disposal of the platform. The intermediation services are compensated by the underlying supplier and the consumer; therefore, the platform does not carry any economic risk. As a conclusion, the criterion of acting on behalf of the underlying supplier is likely to be fulfilled by the e-commerce platform models.

In addition, the third criteria of taking part in the supply can be affirmed for platforms selling goods as the platforms provide the technical infrastructure to offer the goods to the customer. Additionally, the platforms do not generally amend the goods

---

260. *See* s. 2.2.2.2.2.1 The Requirement of Acting in the Own Name.

sold by the underlying suppliers through their platform. Thus, the requirement of providing 'identical supplies' would be fulfilled.

Nevertheless, all three criteria must be affirmed cumulatively for the platform to qualify as an undisclosed agent. As, in many cases, the requirement of acting in the platform's own name is not fulfilled, Article 14 (2) (c) of the VAT Directive is generally not applicable to platforms. Thereby, it is important to point out that, for every platform, the evaluation of whether the platform is acting in its own name or on behalf of the underlying supplier should be carried out separately as this is a case-by-case analysis. In this sense, the German courts had to take a position on whether the platform Amazon acts as an undisclosed agent.[261] In this case, the appellant, the underlying supplier, argued that Amazon acted as an undisclosed agent as Amazon was highly involved in the transaction: Amazon was responsible for the delivery of the goods to the customers from Amazon's warehouses where the goods of the appellant were stored. Moreover, the appellant argued that Amazon is making the decision to whom to supply the goods and is also responsible for the debt collection.[262] Due to this extensive impact of Amazon on the supply, the appellant argued that Amazon exceeded the sole function of a fulfilment service provider but was acting as an undisclosed agent.[263] The Tax Court Düsseldorf (Finanzgericht – FG) did not agree with the appellant's legal opinion because the contract for the supply of the goods was concluded between the underlying supplier and the customer based on German civil law.[264] Additionally, Amazon was authorised by a proxy to conclude these contracts with the customer in the name of the underlying supplier. Nevertheless, this proxy could not lead to the conclusion that Amazon was acting as an undisclosed agent because it is within the nature of this proxy that Amazon would conclude contracts with customers and that the underlying supplier may only find out who their contract partner was at a later point in time.[265] Therefore, the Tax Court Düsseldorf declined the applicability of the undisclosed agent scheme.[266] This decision was confirmed in the appeal by the German Federal Tax Court. The German Federal Tax Court based its confirmation not only on the published literature and case law[267] but also on a systematic argument. The German Federal Tax Court brought forward that, since the

---

261. FG Düsseldorf 10 Nov. 2019, 1 K 2693/17 U; BFH 29 Apr. 2020, XI B 113/19.
262. FG Düsseldorf, 10 Nov. 2019 – 1 K 2693/17 U, para. 47.
263. *Ibid.* para. 51.
264. *Ibid.* para. 70.
265. *Ibid.* para. 72.
266. *Ibid.* paras 76 et seq.
267. BFH 29 Apr. 2020, XI B 113/19, paras 19 + 30; with reference to case law: BGH 26 Jul. 2018, I ZR 20/17, paras 3 + 20; Case C-567/18, *Coty Germany GmbH v Amazon Services Europe Sàrl and Others*, 28 Nov. 2019, ECLI:EU:C:2019:1031, Opinion of AG Campos Sánchez-Bordona, paras 56 et seq. + 61 et seq.; notably, both cases are not VAT cases. The German case was a case on copyright law, and the BGH held that the contract is concluded between the underlying supplier and the customer in a supply through the platform Amazon. The CJEU case was on trademarks of the supply through Amazon. The AG shortly discussed the qualification of Amazon as an intermediary (not in terms of agents as stipulated in the VAT Directive), whereas the CJEU did not refer to this qualification; *see* the corresponding decision by the CJEU: Case C-567/18, *Coty Germany GmbH v Amazon Services Europe Sàrl and Others*, 2 Apr. 2020, ECLI:EU:C:2020:267; *see* also the referred literature by the BFH in XI B 113/19 (29 Apr. 2020):

newly introduced Article 14a of the VAT Directive explicitly stipulates a fictitious chain transaction for the supply of goods through platforms, the EU legislator could not assume that every supply through a platform should qualify as a supply through an undisclosed agent (*argumentum e contrario*).[268]

2.2.2.2.5 Interim Conclusion

In conclusion, platforms offering the supply of goods likely fulfil the criterion of acting on behalf of the underlying supplier and the criterion to take part in the supply. Nevertheless, for the qualification as an undisclosed agent, all three legal requirements must be fulfilled. It is likely that the platforms do not fulfil the requirement of acting in their own name. This general statement cannot be applied to any platform without any further review. Depending on how the platform is set up and which information is made available to the consumer, some platforms that do not display the underlying supplier in an obvious manner to the consumer may, after all, fulfil the requirement of acting in their own name. Therefore, these platforms may be considered to act as an undisclosed agent.

2.2.3 The Supply of Goods from the Underlying Supplier to the Customer

2.2.3.1 General Remarks

Since the two preliminary observations of the composite supply and the undisclosed agent scheme are likely to not be applicable in the case of the supply of goods through online platforms, the follow-up question is how the relevant supplies are treated for VAT purposes. In a first step, the supply of the good from the underlying supplier to the customer will be discussed (*see* Figure 2.3 for a graphical illustration of this supply).

Daniel Denker & Matthias Trinks, *Umsatzsteuerfalle Amazon*, Der Umsatz-Steuer-Berater (2017); Robert Hammerl & Andreas Fietz, *Umsatzsteuerrisiken beim 'Versand durch Amazon'*, NWB (2017).

268. BFH, 29 Apr. 2020 – XI B 113/19, paras 31 et seqq. (n. v.).

Figure 2.3   Overview of the Supply Between the Underlying Supplier and the Customer

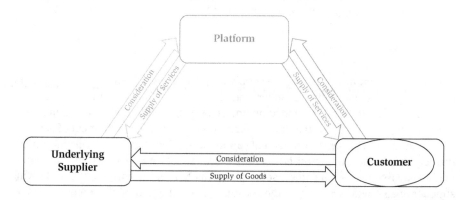

As of 1991, the EU has implemented the so-called distance sale of goods regime for B2C supplies. This distance sale of goods regime has an impact on the place of supply rules. Thus, it is necessary to separate the supplies into B2B supplies and B2C supplies. Thereby, the following sections will explain the applicable rules for B2C supplies as of the pre-implementation of the e-commerce package. As the goods may be delivered from another Member State or a third country, both cases will be discussed. In both cases, however, the prerequisite is that the goods are transported to a place in the EU. This might be the customer's address or another address in the EU indicated by the customer, e.g., if the customer orders a present for a friend. The national supply of a good is taxable in the Member State where the good is supplied, and the corresponding national rate is applicable.[269] Finally, the following sections will concentrate on the place of supply rules,[270] but also other questions will be elaborated when necessary, e.g., the possibility of input VAT deduction.

2.2.3.2   *Intra-Community B2C Supplies Prior to the Introduction of the E-Commerce Package*

In 1991, when the fiscal frontiers within the EU were abolished, the place of supply rule for distance sales of goods within the EU was introduced in Article 28b (B) of the Sixth

---

269. *See* Article 32 first subpara. of the VAT Directive. If the goods are dispatched within one Member State and delivered to the customer (irrelevant whether the customer is a business or consumer) within that same Member State, the place of supply is this Member State. Also, for national supplies, the place of supply rules may be important, especially if Member States apply different VAT rates for the same supply. Examples of this are stipulated in Article 104 of the VAT Directive for Austria and the communes of Jungholz and Mittelberg; Article 105 (2) of the VAT Directive for Portugal and the regions of Azores and Madeira; and Article 120 of the VAT Directive for Greece and the departments of Lesbos, Chios, Samos, the Dodecanese and the Cyclades, and on the islands of Thassos, the Northern Sporades, Samothrace, and Skiros.

270. *See* for a summary of the place of supply rules, e.g., Antonio Vázquez del Rey, *VAT Connecting Factors: Relevance of the Place of Supply*, 43 Intertax (2015).

VAT Directive.[271] This *lex specialis* of the place of supply rule for distance sales of goods within the EU was stipulated in Articles 33-35 of the VAT Directive. The following explanations describe the requirements of Articles 33-35 of the VAT Directive before the entering into force of the e-commerce package.[272]

According to Article 33 (1) of the VAT Directive,[273] the place of supply of a good dispatched or transported from one Member State to another was to be taxed in the place where the dispatch transport ended if the following three requirements were fulfilled. First, the shift in the place of supply was only applicable to a specific group of customers, i.e., non-taxable (legal) persons, farmers eligible for the flat-rate scheme, and taxable persons not entitled to VAT deduction,[274] e.g., because the supplier provided exempt supplies or qualified as a small enterprise. Second, also the kind of good supplied was relevant for the application of the shift in the place of supply as the supplied good could not be a new means of transport,[275] goods supplied after assembly or installation,[276] goods that were subject to excise duties,[277] supplies of second-hand goods, works of art, collectors' items, or antiques.[278] Finally, the transport of the goods must have been organised by the supplier.[279] Taking into consideration the case at hand of a consumer ordering a good via a platform from the underlying supplier and this supplier transported the goods from another Member State to the consumer, it was likely that the requirements of Article 33 (1) of the VAT Directive[280] were fulfilled in many cases considering the described exceptions above.

Even if the supply in question had fulfilled all of the mentioned criteria, the VAT Directive would have provided an additional requirement that the underlying supplier had to fulfil for the shift of the place of supply to be applied. Article 34 of the VAT Directive[281] had stipulated that the change in the place of supply according to Article 33 of the VAT Directive would have been applicable only if the underlying supplier had

---

271. Council Directive of 16 December 1991 Supplementing the Common System of Value Added Tax and Amending Directive 77/388/EEC with a View to the Abolition of Fiscal Frontiers, OJ L 376/1 (1991).
272. *See* also the discussion of the amendments implemented with the e-commerce package as of 1 Jul. 2021 in s. 4.3.4 The Place of Supply Rule for the Supply by the Platform.
273. As of 1 Jul. 2021, the relevant article is Article 33 (a) read in conjunction with Article 14 (4) (1) of the VAT Directive.
274. *See* Article 33 (1) of the VAT Directive with reference to Article 3 (1) of the VAT Directive. As of 1 Jul. 2021, the relevant article is Article 33 (a) read in conjunction with Article 14 (4) (1) with reference to Article 3 (1) of the VAT Directive.
275. *See* Article 33 (1) (b) of the VAT Directive. As of 1 Jul. 2021, the relevant article is Article 33 (a) read in conjunction with Article 14 (1) (b) of the VAT Directive.
276. *See* Article 33 (1) (b) of the VAT Directive. As of 1 Jul. 2021 the relevant article is Article 33 (a) read in conjunction with Article 14 (1) (b) of the VAT Directive.
277. *See* Article 34 (1) (a) of the VAT Directive. As of 1 Jul. 2021, Article 34 of the VAT Directive has been deleted without replacement.
278. *See* Article 35 of the VAT Directive.
279. *See* the detailed discussion on this criterion in Case C-276/18, *KrakVet Marek Batko sp. K. v Nemzeti Adó- és Vámhivatal Fellebbviteli Igazgatósága*, 18 Jun. 2020, ECLI:EU:C:2020:485, paras 54 et seqq.
280. This refers to the article in the VAT Directive before the entering into force of the e-commerce package. As of 1 Jul. 2021, the relevant article is Article 33 (a) read in conjunction with Article 14 (4) (1) of the VAT Directive.
281. As of 1 Jul. 2021, Article 34 of the VAT Directive has been deleted without replacement.

surpassed the threshold of EUR 100,000 (or the equivalent in national currency) in the previous or current calendar year within the Member State of destination.[282] Additionally, Member States could amend the threshold of EUR 100,000 to a threshold of EUR 35,000 or the equivalent in the national currency if a Member State had feared that the threshold of EUR 100,000 would have led to distortion of competition.[283] This national possibility to deviate from the general applicable threshold of EUR 100,000 has led to the implementation of various different distance selling thresholds throughout the EU ranging from approximately EUR 25,304 in Romania to the stipulated threshold of EUR 100,000 in the VAT Directive, in, e.g., Germany, Italy, and France.[284] Moreover, the formulation of 'within that Member State' in Article 34 (1) (b) and (c) of the VAT Directive was to be interpreted as the obligation of the underlying supplier to check whether the threshold was exceeded in each Member State where the underlying supplier was supplying goods. Finally, even if the underlying supplier did not surpass the national threshold, the underlying supplier could opt for the place of supply in the Member State of destination.[285] This option could also be exercised independently for each Member State.

If all of the conditions set out in Articles 33-35 of the VAT Directive were fulfilled, the place of supply would have been the Member State of destination, i.e., the Member State where the dispatch or transport of the goods to the customer ended.[286] Finally, the applicability of Articles 33 and 34 of the VAT Directive resulted in the obligation of the underlying supplier to register for VAT purposes in the Member States in which the underlying supplier surpassed the national distance selling threshold applicable to the distance sale of goods regime or opted into this scheme for being able to fulfil the VAT obligations.[287]

2.2.3.3 *Supplies from Third Countries*

2.2.3.3.1 *The Place of Supply of B2C Imported Goods Prior to the Introduction of the E-Commerce Package*

In many cases, the general place of supply rule for the supply of goods with transport in Article 32 first subparagraph of the VAT Directive will be applicable for the supply

---

282. *See* Article 34 (1) (b) and (c) of the VAT Directive; for the interpretation of Article 34 of the VAT Directive *see*, e.g., Patrick Wille, *The Correct Interpretation of the Thresholds for Distance Sales*, 29 International VAT Monitor (2018). As of 1 Jul. 2021, Article 34 of the VAT Directive was deleted without replacement.
283. *See* Article 34 (2) of the VAT Directive. As of 1 Jul. 2021, Article 34 of the VAT Directive was deleted without replacement.
284. *See*, for an overview of the applicable thresholds throughout the EU as of 1 Jan. 2021, *VAT Thresholds*, https://ec.europa.eu/taxation_customs/system/files/2021-02/vat_in_ec_annexi.pdf (last visited 27 Oct. 2021).
285. *See* Article 34 (4) of the VAT Directive. As of 1 Jul. 2021, Article 34 of the VAT Directive was deleted without replacement.
286. *See*, for the discussion of the intra-Community distance sales of goods as of 1 Jul. 2021, s. 4.3.4.2.1.3.1 Intra-Community Distance Sales of Goods.
287. As of 1 Jul. 2021, this obligation is no longer in place as intra-Community distance sales of goods can be declared via the EU-OSS; *see* s. 4.11 Special Schemes of the OSS.

of imported goods. As the place of supply according to Article 32 first subparagraph of the VAT Directive is the place of the beginning of the dispatch or transport of the goods, this place of supply would be the third country from which the goods are dispatched.

Additionally, the importation of goods is a taxable transaction according to Article 2 (1) (d) of the VAT Directive.[288] The place of supply of this importation is, in general, the Member State within whose territory the goods are located when they enter the EU according to Article 60 of the VAT Directive.[289] If the customer was designated or recognised as being liable to pay the VAT according to Article 201 of the VAT Directive, the customer would have to pay the import VAT. The import VAT is payable either at the express courier or at the postal company or if the customer cleared the goods at customs, then the import VAT would be payable at the competent customs office.

Moreover, in the context of the importation of goods, the VAT Directive provides for an additional special place of supply rules. Article 32 second subparagraph of the VAT Directive shifts the place of supply from the third country into the Member State of importation when three requirements are fulfilled.[290] As a first prerequisite, the place of supply shift only applies when the goods are dispatched or transported from third territories or third countries. Furthermore, the goods in question must be imported by the supplier,[291] and the importer (underlying supplier) must be designated or recognised as being liable to pay the VAT according to Article 201 of the VAT Directive. In the case of an online order of goods from a third country, the dispatch or transportation criterion is likely fulfilled as the goods will be transported from a third country or territory for the supply in the EU. If the importer was the underlying supplier, the remaining question would be whether the importer (underlying supplier) also became liable to pay the import VAT. Based on Article 32 second subparagraph of the VAT Directive, the person liable for the VAT payment is defined in Article 201 of the VAT Directive. Article 201 of the VAT Directive does not stipulate a specified circle of persons who are to be considered to be liable for the VAT payment but leaves this definition to the Member States. One example of a person liable for the VAT payment if stipulated as such in the national law could be the customs declarant according to

---

288. *See,* for further information on the different taxable transactions, s. 4.2 Taxable Transactions.
289. *See* also the deviations from this general rule in Article 61 of the VAT Directive.
290. *See,* for further information on the background of Article 32 second subpara. of the VAT Directive, Ben Terra & Julie Kajus, *Commentary – A Guide to the Recast VAT Directive,* s. 5.2.3.2 (IBFD 2020); and Ben Terra & Julie Kajus, *Introduction to European VAT, supra* note 167, s. 11.2.2.1. *See* also the more detailed discussion of Article 32 second subpara. of the VAT Directive in s. 4.3.4.1.1.2.1 The Shift of the Place of Supply Rule According to Article 32 Second Subparagraph of the VAT Directive.
291. Thomas Bieber, *Der Einfuhrumsatz* 522 (MANZ'sche Verlags- und Universitätsbuchhandlung 2019); from the English language version of the VAT Directive, this requirement is not very clear. The English version only stipulates: 'the place of supply by the importer'. Nevertheless, in the German-language version of the VAT Directive this requirement is stipulated clearer by indicating that '... der Ort der Lieferung, die durch den Importeur bewirkt wird, ...'. Therefore, from the German-language version, it can be derived that the import must be effected by the importer.

Article 77 (3) of the UCC.[292] Whenever the supply in question fulfils all three criteria, then the place of supply shift applies. In this case, the underlying supplier would import the goods into the EU for which the import VAT would become payable. If the importer fulfilled the requirements for the input VAT deduction, the import VAT could be deducted by the importer according to Article 168 (e) of the VAT Directive. Additionally, 'any subsequent supply' is deemed to be taxable in the Member State of importation according to Article 32 second subparagraph of the VAT Directive. Thus, if the goods were sold to a customer in the Member State of importation, the local VAT rate would apply.

Article 32 of the VAT Directive would not be applicable if the good was supplied to another Member State than where the importation was declared. If the customer was a non-taxable (legal) person, e.g., a final consumer, a farmer eligible for the flat-rate scheme, or a taxable person not entitled to a deduction of the VAT, e.g., because the customer provided exempt supplies or qualified as a small enterprise, the VAT Directive would have provided a place of supply shift in Article 33 (2) of the VAT Directive.[293] Article 33 of the VAT Directive derogated Article 32 of the VAT Directive. If the goods were dispatched or transported from a third territory or country and imported by the underlying supplier into a Member State other than the Member State in which the dispatch or transport to the customer ended, the goods should 'be regarded as having been dispatched or transported from the Member State of importation' according to Article 33 (2) of the VAT Directive.[294] The importer would have had to fulfil the importation requirements in the Member State of importation and declare the import VAT in the country of importation. If all of the requirements for the import VAT deduction were fulfilled, then the importer could request the input VAT deduction for the import VAT.[295] Additionally, the place of supply shift stipulated in Article 33 (2) of the VAT Directive[296] would have applied, and, therefore, the place of the dispatch or transportation of the goods would not be the third country but the Member State of importation.[297] The supply from the Member State of importation to the Member State of destination would have been a B2C distance sale of goods.[298]

The special place of supply rules in both Article 32 second subparagraph and Article 33 (2) of the VAT Directive[299] has had the aim to implement the destination principle and charge European VAT on the imported non-EU goods that are supplied

---

292. *See ibid.* at 547 et seqq., who also discussed the implementation in the different Member States with further examples for who can qualify as an importer in the national law.
293. With the entering into force of the e-commerce package as of 1 Jul. 2021, Article 33 (2) of the VAT Directive was amended.
294. With the entering into force of the e-commerce package as of 1 Jul. 2021, Article 33 (2) of the VAT Directive was amended.
295. *See* Article 168 (e) of the VAT Directive.
296. This refers to the article in the VAT Directive before the entering into force of the e-commerce package. Article 33 (2) of the VAT Directive was amended with the e-commerce package.
297. *See* Article 33 (2) of the VAT Directive before entering into force of the e-commerce package. As of 1 Jul. 2021 this article was amended.
298. *See* s. 2.2.3.2 Intra-Community B2C Supplies Prior to the Introduction of the E-Commerce Package.
299. As of 1 Jul. 2021, the relevant article is Article 33 (b) of the VAT Directive.

within the EU.[300] Therefore, the goal of these special place of supply rules is to treat the imported goods with the same European VAT rate as national goods. Thus, the importation of goods should, theoretically, not lead to any distortion of competition.[301]

2.2.3.3.2   The De Minimis VAT Exemption for Imported Goods

Regardless of whether the customer is a business or a consumer and until the entering into force of the e-commerce package as of 1 July 2021, the VAT Directive provided for a VAT exemption of low-valued goods upon importation. The *de minimis* exemption was stipulated in Articles 143 (1) (b) and (c) and Article 23 of Directive 2009/132/EC.[302] According to Article 23 of Directive 2009/132/EC, the importation of goods below EUR 10 was exempt upon admission (obligation for the Member States). Furthermore, the Member States could decide to also exempt the import VAT on goods when the imported goods' total value was more than EUR 10 but did not exceed EUR 22 (option for the Member States).[303] If a Member State had implemented this option, the exact *de minimis* amount in between EUR 10 and EUR 22 could have also been decided by the Member State individually. All Member States had actually implemented a higher threshold than the obligatory EUR 10 threshold but with different applicable thresholds.[304] Therefore, if the imported good in question was below the threshold specified by the Member State of importation, no import VAT would have become due as the import would have been exempt.[305]

2.2.3.4   Interim Conclusion

As the place of supply differs depending on the specific circumstances, it is impossible to generalise the place of supply of the purchases facilitated platforms. A distinction must be made from where the goods are delivered; i.e., the goods could be delivered within the EU or from a third country. This distinction results in different outcomes regarding the place of supply. Finally, also other specific factors must be taken into consideration, particularly the special place of supply rules. In particular, when a good is imported from a third country, the place of supply might be altered depending on who is the importer of the goods. Similarly, in a B2C supply within the EU, it must be closely considered whether the underlying supplier has surpassed the distance selling

---

300. Thomas Bieber, *Der Einfuhrumsatz, supra* note 291, at 521 + 524.
301. *See,* on this, also s. 2.2.3.3.2 The *De Minimis* VAT Exemption for Imported Goods and s. 2.3.2.2.1 The First Legislative Changes of the E-Commerce Package in 2017 on the abolishment of the exemption.
302. Council Directive 2009/132/EC of 19 October 2009 Determining the Scope of Article 143 (b) and (c) of Directive 2006/112/EC as Regards Exemption from Value Added Tax on the Final Importation of Certain Goods, OJ L 292/5 (2009).
303. *See* Article 23 of Directive 2009/132/EC.
304. *See* for an overview of the implemented thresholds, *Buying Online – EU Member States' Rules for VAT on Goods from Outside the EU and other Services,* https://ec.europa.eu/taxation_customs/sites/taxation/files/vat_buying_online.pdf (last visited 16 Nov. 2020).
305. *See,* on the reasons for the abolishment of the exemption, s. 2.3.2.2.1 The First Legislative Changes of the E-Commerce Package in 2017 on the abolishment of the exemption.

threshold in the respective Member State of destination. In the end, the place of supply rules diverging from the general place of supply with transport in Article 32 first subparagraph of the VAT Directive all have the aim to implement the destination principle and therefore ensure that the goods are taxed at the place of consumption and are levelled with the European VAT.[306] It can be questioned whether this aim was fully realised.

2.2.4   The Supply of the Platform Service to the Underlying Supplier

As in most platform structures, the underlying supplier pays a commission and/or a fixed fee for being able to offer and sell goods on the platform; the question arises of how this commission fee is to be treated under the VAT Directive. In general, this supply should qualify as a supply of service for consideration according to Article 2 (1) (c) of the VAT Directive where the consideration is reflected in the commission fee and/or the fixed fee that the underlying supplier pays to the platform (*see* Figure 2.4 for a graphical illustration of this supply).

Figure 2.4   Overview of the Supply Between the Platform and the Underlying Supplier

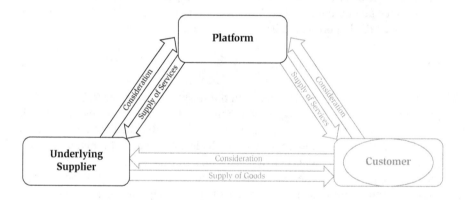

Since the underlying supplier as well as the platforms usually qualify as taxable persons according to Article 9 VAT Directive,[307] the place of supply for this service generally follows the general B2B VAT service rules; the place of supply for the supply of B2B services is stipulated in Article 44 of the VAT Directive. According to Article 44

---

306. *See* also s. 4.3.4 The Place of Supply Rule for the Supply by the Platform for the discussion on the legal consequences of the e-commerce package on the place of supply rules for intra-Community supplies as well as imported supplies through platforms.
307. In general, the underlying supplier could also be a non-taxable person. For simplification reasons, though, this section will focus on the underlying supplier being a taxable person. Nevertheless, the underlying supplier may be a small enterprise according to Article 281 et seqq. of the VAT Directive. In this case, the determination of the place of supply would still follow the general B2B rules; i.e., Article 44 of the VAT Directive would be applicable. The applicability of the small enterprise regime may only influence the input VAT deduction of the underlying supplier being a small trader.

of the VAT Directive, the place of supply depends on the place of establishment of the recipient of the service. In the given case, the underlying supplier would be the recipient of the service provided by the platform.

In certain specific cases, also a special place of supply rule may be applicable, e.g., if the service provided by the platform concerned the sale of an immovable property, the place of supply for the service from the platform to the underlying supplier would follow the special rule stipulated in Article 47 of the VAT Directive. In that specific case, the place of supply would be the place where the immovable property is located. Additionally, the special place of supply rules for disclosed agents in Article 46 of the VAT Directive[308] as well as the special place of supply rule for electronically supplied services in Article 58 of the VAT Directive[309] only apply for supplies to non-taxable persons.

If the underlying supplier was established in the same Member State as the platform, the place of supply would be this Member State, and also the tax rate of the Member State of establishment of both parties involved would be applicable.[310] If the platform and the underlying supplier were established in different Member States, the service would be taxable in the Member State where the underlying supplier is established.[311] In this case, the service is subject to the reverse-charge mechanism according to Article 196 of the VAT Directive. The invoice should be issued without VAT and shall indicate the transfer of the VAT liability to the customer, i.e., the underlying supplier. Additionally, the platform would also have to file a recapitulative statement according to Article 262 (1) (c) of the VAT Directive. Lastly, if the underlying supplier was established in a third country or territory, the place of taxation would be in that third country or territory, and no European VAT would have to be indicated on the invoice from the platform to the underlying supplier.[312]

2.2.5 The Supply of the Platform Service to the Customer

2.2.5.1 General Remarks

The remaining supply of the three-party transaction is the legal VAT qualification of the service supplied from the platform to the consumer (*see* Figure 2.5 for a graphical illustration of this supply). This section will not give a full analysis of all of the possible issues that may arise with the supply of services from the platform to the customer but will instead concentrate on two main issues that raise interesting questions in practice as well as in academia. First, the requirement of consideration will be discussed as this is one requirement for a taxable supply to qualify as such, and it might be questionable

---

308. For further information on the place of supply for disclosed agents, *see* s. 2.2.5.3.2.2 The Legal Consequence of the Qualification as a Disclosed Agent.
309. For further information on the place of supply for electronically supplied services, *see* s. 2.2.5.3.3 Is the Service of the Platform an Electronically Supplied Service?.
310. Depending on the national VAT law, a national reverse-charge mechanism may be applicable to certain services.
311. *See* Article 44 of the VAT Directive.
312. *Ibid.*

whether this criterion is fulfilled in all platform cases. Second, section 2.2.5.3 will concentrate on the place of supply of the transaction and evaluate whether the platform qualifies as a disclosed agent according to Article 46 of the VAT Directive or provides an electronically supplied service according to Article 58 of the VAT Directive to the customer and the consequence this qualification may have on the place of supply of the service.

Figure 2.5   Overview of the Supply Between the Platform and the Customer

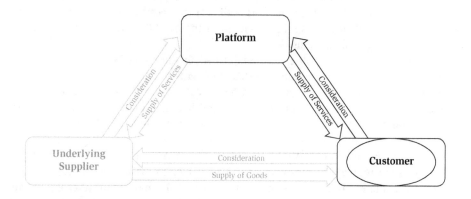

2.2.5.2   *The Necessity for Consideration*

According to Article 2 (1) of the VAT Directive, the supply of goods, the intra-Community acquisition, and the supply of services would be subject to a VAT according to the VAT Directive if they were provided 'for consideration'. Since the VAT Directive only defines the term 'taxable amount' in Article 73 of the VAT Directive as 'the taxable amount shall include everything which constitutes consideration obtained or to be obtained by the supplier, in return for the supply, from the customer or a third party' but does not provide further guidance on the term 'consideration', the CJEU discussed the meaning of the term 'consideration' in several judgments.[313]

Already in 1981, the CJEU took a stand on several questions concerning the definition and requirements of the concept of consideration.[314] First, the CJEU held that anything that is received in return for the supply should be qualified as consideration.[315] Hence, not only cash payments but also payments in kind qualify as consideration.[316] At the same time, it is necessary to calculate the VAT based on the

---

313. *See* also Jasmin Kollmann, *Taxable Supplies and Their Consideration in European VAT: With Selected Examples of the Digital Economy* 65 et seqq. (IBFD 2019) who discusses the term 'for consideration' in depth.

314. Case C-154/80, *Staatssecretaris van Financiën v Association coopérative 'Coöperatieve Aardappelenbewaarplaats GA'*, 5 Feb. 1981, ECLI:EU:C:1981:38.

315. *Ibid.* paras 10 + 13.

316. *See ibid.* para. 10; this statement was explicitly confirmed in Case C-330/95, *Goldsmiths (Jewellers) Ltd v Commissioners of Customs & Excise*, 3 Jul. 1997, ECLI:EU:C:1997:339, paras 23 et seqq.; and in Case C-283/12, *Serebryannay vek EOOD v Direktor na Direktsia 'Obzhalvane i*

taxable amount. Therefore, the consideration must be capable of being expressed in money.[317] Second, the CJEU stated that there must be a direct link between the supply and the consideration that is paid.[318] In subsequent judgments, this direct link test was further developed into the requirement of a legal relationship for a reciprocal performance between the supplier and the customer.[319] Finally, the CJEU held that the value of consideration is not assessed on objective criteria, but it is a subjective value based on the consideration actually received.[320] As the consideration is a subjective value, the value may be below market price or even below the cost price and can still qualify as consideration for VAT purposes.[321] The only strict line on the amount of consideration is drawn in the case when the supply is provided free of charge; i.e., no payment is made.[322] In this case, the requirement of consideration cannot be fulfilled.

Applying these general statements to the service provided by platforms to final customers, a non-unified approach might – yet again – be the case as the qualification depends on the business model of the platform. If the e-commerce platform charged the customer for their services, e.g., in the form of an explicitly indicated service fee on the

---

upravlenie na izpalnenieto' – Varna pri Tsentralno upravlenie na Natsionalna agentsia za prihodite, 26 Sep. 2013, ECLI:EU:C:2013:599, para. 39.

317. Case C-154/80, Staatsecretaris van Financiën v Coöperatieve Aardappelenbewaarplaats, 5 Feb. 1981, ECLI:EU:C:1981:38, para. 13; Case C-33/93, Empire Stores Ltd v Commissioners of Customs and Excise, 2 Jun. 1994, ECLI:EU:C:1994:225, para. 12; Case C-330/95, Goldsmiths v Commissioners of Customs & Excise, 3 Jul. 1997, ECLI:EU:C:1997:339, para. 23; Case C-283/12, Serebryannay vek, 26 Sep. 2013, ECLI:EU:C:2013:599, para. 38.

318. Case C-154/80, Staatsecretaris van Financiën v Coöperatieve Aardappelenbewaarplaats, 5 Feb. 1981, ECLI:EU:C:1981:38, para. 12; see also, for detailed discussion on the requirements of the direct link, Christian Amand, When Is a Link Direct?, 7 International VAT Monitor (1996); Deborah Butler, The Usefulness of the 'Direct Link' Test in Determining Consideration for VAT Purposes, EC Tax Review (2004).

319. Already in Case C-102/86, Apple and Pear Development Council v Commissioners of Customs and Excise, 8 Mar. 1988, ECLI:EU:C:1988:120, para. 15, the CJEU referred to the necessity of an existing relationship between the service provider and the service recipient; in Case C-16/93, R. J. Tolsma v Inspecteur der Omzetbelasting Leeuwarden, 3 Mar. 1994, ECLI:EU:C:1994:80, para. 14, the CJEU then referred to the necessity of a legal relationship between the supplier and the recipient; see also the discussion on the Tolsma v Inspecteur der Omzetbelasting case before the CJEU issued its decision by Ben Terra, Supplies for Consideration, or Must Consideration Be Stipulated?, International VAT Monitor (1993).

320. Case C-154/80, Staatsecretaris van Financiën v Coöperatieve Aardappelenbewaarplaats, 5 Feb. 1981, ECLI:EU:C:1981:38, para. 13; in spite of this general rule, Articles 72 and 80 of the VAT Directive provide for an exception according to which the open market value, i.e., an objective value, is used to determine the taxable amount. Notably, the application of this exception is limited to supplies between connected parties (see Article 80 [1] of the VAT Directive); see also Case C-549/11, Direktor na Direktsia 'Obzhalvane i upravlenie na izpalnenieto' – grad Burgas pri Tsentralno upravlenie na Natsionalnata agentsia za prihodite v Orfey Balgaria EOOD, 19 Dec. 2012, ECLI:EU:C:2012:832, paras 46 et seq., where the CJEU explicitly mentioned that Article 80 of the VAT Directive has the background of preventing tax evasion or avoidance, and, therefore, its applicability is limited to connected parties.

321. Case C-412/03, Hotel Scandic Gåsabäck AB v Riksskatteverket, 23 Nov. 2004, ECLI:EU:C:2004:746, Opinion of AG Colomer, para. 35; this was subsequently confirmed by the CJEU in Case C-412/03, Hotel Scandic Gåsabäck AB v Riksskatteverket, 20 Jan. 2005, ECLI:EU:C:2005:47, para. 22; Case C-285/10, Campsa Estaciones de Servicio SA v Administración del Estado, 9 Jun. 2011, ECLI:EU:C:2011:381, para. 27.

322. Case C-89/81, Staatssecretaris van Financiën v Hong-Kong Trade Development Council, 1 Apr. 1982, ECLI:EU:C:1982:121, para. 19.

invoice, then the requirement of consideration would be fulfilled. The customer and the platform would also fulfil the direct link test as the service fee is directly linked to the intermediation services provided from the platform to the customer. Additionally, the parties would have concluded some kind of contract in which the fee payment is agreed. This contract may, in many cases, be the customer signing up to the platform, thereby indicating the customer's credit card and accepting the general terms and conditions for the usage of the platform. Therefore, both parties have a reciprocal relationship.

The qualification of e-commerce platforms that do not charge any service fee to the customers may result in a different outcome. When there is no consideration exchanged in money, the question arises of whether other goods or services are provided from the customer to the e-commerce platform that could qualify as consideration. With the rise of social media, the question of whether 'free' online services should be taxable has been widely discussed, especially in German literature. Examples of these free online services are not only search engines, social media platforms, and mobile apps but also e-commerce platforms. Although the services are free of monetary charge for the customer, the customer agrees that the platform may use the generated user's data. This data is used by the platform not only to improve the services but also, e.g., for personalised commercials. Therefore, in academia, the question arose whether the data provided by the customer could be qualified as 'consideration' and consequently might lead to a taxable transaction.[323]

---

323. *See* the authors who support that this is a taxable transaction: David Dietsch, *Umsatzsteuerpflicht von kostenlosen sozialen Netzwerken*, MwStR, *supra* note 13, at 868 et seqq.; Tina Ehrke-Rabel et al., *Umsatzsteuer in einer digitalisierten Welt*, *supra* note 13, at 33 et seqq.; Tina Ehrke-Rabel & Sebastian Pfeiffer, *Umsatzsteuerbarer Leistungsaustausch durch 'entgeltlose' digitale Dienstleistungen*, SWK, *supra* note 13, at 532 et seqq.; Nevada Melan & Sebastian Pfeiffer, *Bezahlen mit Rechten, nicht mit Daten: Weitere offene Fragen zur Umsatzsteuerpflicht 'kostenloser' Internetdienste und Smartphone-Apps*, DStR, *supra* note 13, at 1072 et seqq.; Nevada Melan & Bertram Wecke, *Umsatzsteuerpflicht von 'kostenlosen' Internetdiensten und Smartphone-Apps*, DStR, *supra* note 13, at 2267 et seqq.; Nevada Melan & Bertram Wecke, *Einzelfragen der Umsatzsteuerpflicht 'kostenloser' Internetdienste und Smartphone-Apps*, DStR, *supra* note 13, at 2811 et seqq.; Stephan Filtzinger, *Sektorales oder generelles Reverse-Charge? – Reformbedarf bei der Steuerschuldverlagerung*, in *100 Jahre Umsatzsteuer in Deutschland 1918-2018: Festschrift*, *supra* note 13, at 708; Sebastian Pfeiffer, *VAT on 'Free' Electronic Services?*, 27 International VAT Monitor, *supra* note 13, at 158 et seqq.; Sebastian Pfeiffer, *Comment on 'Free' Internet Services*, in *CJEU – Recent Developments in Value Added Tax 2017*, *supra* note 13, at 133 et seqq. *See* the authors, who disagree with this approach: Katharina Artinger, *Taxing Consumption in the Digital Age: Challenges for European VAT*, *supra* note 13, at 212 et seq.; Dietmar Aigner et al., *Digitale Leistungen ohne Geldzahlung im Internet*, SWK, *supra* note 13, at 349 et seqq.; Joachim Englisch, *'Kostenlose' Online-Dienstleistungen: tauschähnlicher Umsatz?*, 66 Umsatzsteuer-Rundschau, *supra* note 13, at 875 et seqq.; Hans-Martin Grambeck, *Keine Umsatzsteuerpflicht bei kostenlosen Internetdiensten und Smartphone-Apps*, DStR, *supra* note 13, at 2026 et seqq.; Nicole Looks & Benjamin Bergau, *Tauschähnlicher Umsatz mit Nutzerdaten – Kein Stück vom Kuchen*, MwStR, *supra* note 13, at 864 et seqq. Michael Tumpel, *Umsatzsteuer bei 'unentgeltlichen' Onlinediensten*, in *Digitalisierung im Konzernsteuerrecht*, *supra* note 13, at 57 et seqq. *See* also the discussion on the question of whether third-party payments by the person to whom the data is sold could be the basis for the consideration: Florian Zawodsky, *Value Added Taxation in the Digital Economy*, British Tax Review, *supra* note 13, at 616 et seqq.; Giorgio Beretta, *European VAT and the Sharing Economy*, *supra* note 13, at 124 et seqq.

Applying this argument to the supply of services by e-commerce platforms to its customers, the customer could 'pay' for the received service by, e.g., signing up to the e-commerce platform (if required) and, with that, providing the e-commerce platform with personal data. Even if the platform's business model did not require the customer to sign up to the e-commerce platform, every visit and search on the platform by the customer and every purchase and review the customer would submit to the platform would provide the platform with more personal data, e.g., with the preferences of the customer regarding which goods are of interest. As discussed in literature, the most difficult criterion in the chain of requirements for a supply to qualify as consideration is the direct link between the service received by the customer and the data that the customer provides to the platform.[324]

If data was accepted as consideration, the taxable amount would have to be determined. Whereas, in many cases, it is possible to determine the monetary value of a barter transaction, e.g., it may be a certain discount that the customer receives for the purchased supply in return of a service,[325] this is more difficult in the case with data as consideration. Some authors argue that there is already a market for data, and thus the monetary value of the taxable amount (the data) can be determined.[326] Nevertheless, this argument can be criticised[327] as this would lead to the determination of the taxable amount based on an objective value, whereas the CJEU has repeatedly held that the taxable amount is generally based on a subjective value.[328] In the case that the opinion is followed that it is impossible to determine the monetary value of data and thus of the barter transaction, the CJEU ruled in the cases *Empire Stores v Commissioners of*

324. Dietmar Aigner et al., *supra* note 13, at 351; Tina Ehrke-Rabel & Sebastian Pfeiffer, *supra* note 13, at 534 et seqq.; Joachim Englisch, *supra* note 13, at 876 et seqq.; Hans-Martin Grambeck, *supra* note 13, at 2029; Nicole Looks & Benjamin Bergau, *supra* note 13, at 870; Nevada Melan & Bertram Wecke, *Umsatzsteuerpflicht von 'kostenlosen' Internetdiensten und Smartphone-Apps*, *supra* note 13, at 2269; Stephan Filtzinger, *supra* note 13, at 707 et seq.; Sebastian Pfeiffer, *VAT on 'Free' Electronic Services?*, *supra* note 13, at 158 et seqq.; Gorka Echevarría Zubeldia, *How VAT-Free Can Free Internet Services Be?*, 30 International VAT Monitor 101 (2019).
325. *See*, e.g., Case C-230/87, *Naturally Yours Cosmetics Limited v Commissioners of Customs and Excise*, 23 Nov. 1988, ECLI:EU:C:1988:508, para. 17; in this case, the CJEU based the monetary value of the barter transaction on the difference between the reduced prices that the consultants paid and the normal wholesale price of the goods.
326. *See*, e.g., Dietmar Aigner et al., *supra* note 13, at 355; David Dietsch, *supra* note 13, at 872 et seq.; Nevada Melan & Bertram Wecke, *Umsatzsteuerpflicht von 'kostenlosen' Internetdiensten und Smartphone-Apps*, *supra* note 13, at 2269.
327. *See*, e.g., Joachim Englisch, *supra* note 13, at 883 et seq.; Tina Ehrke-Rabel & Sebastian Pfeiffer, *supra* note 13, at 533; Sebastian Pfeiffer, *VAT on 'Free' Electronic Services?*, *supra* note 13, at 161 et seq.
328. *See*, e.g., Case C-154/80, *Staatsecretaris van Financiën v Coöperatieve Aardappelenbewaarplaats*, 5 Feb. 1981, ECLI:EU:C:1981:38, para. 13; Case C-230/87, *Naturally Yours Cosmetics Ltd v Commissioners of Customs and Excise*, 23 Nov. 1988, ECLI:EU:C:1988:508, para. 16; in spite of this general rule, Articles 72 and 80 of the VAT Directive provide an exception according to which the open market value, i.e., an objective value, is used to determine the taxable amount. Notably, the application of this exception is limited to supplies between connected parties (*see* Article 80 [1] of the VAT Directive); *see also* Case C-549/11, *Orfey Balgaria*, 19 Dec. 2012, ECLI:EU:C:2012:832, paras 46 et seq., where the CJEU explicitly mentioned that Article 80 of the VAT Directive has the background of preventing tax evasion or avoidance and, therefore, its applicability is limited to connected parties.

Customs and Excise and *Bertelsmann AG v Finanzamt Wiedenbrück* that the cost price of the supply (without any markup) can be used as the taxable basis.[329] Although the CJEU decided in these judgments on the supply of goods, it is likely that the cost price may also be the taxable basis for the supply of services if the monetary value was not determinable. For the supply of services in exchange of data, this cost price may consist of the direct and indirect costs of the e-commerce platform per user, e.g., costs for servers, Internet, and personnel and licence or trademark fees.[330] In practice, the determination of the consideration by an e-commerce platform for each service supply and therefore for each customer purchasing goods through a platform would be a highly complex challenge for the e-commerce platforms.[331] Follow-up questions also arise with the determination of the chargeable event, i.e., when the VAT actually becomes due. This could be, e.g., when the customer signs up to the platform. Nevertheless, a singular chargeable event would likely not fully reflect the costs. If the customer used the platform on a regular basis, then it might be arguable that the VAT also becomes due on a regular basis as the direct and indirect costs of the e-commerce

---

329. Case C-33/93, *Empire Stores Ltd v Commissioners of Customs and Excise*, 2 Jun. 1994, ECLI:EU:C:1994:225, para. 19; Case C-380/99, *Bertelsmann AG v Finanzamt Wiedenbrück*, 3 Jul. 2001, ECLI:EU:C:2001:372, para. 24; *see* also Benjamin Butler, *Non-Monetary Consideration in the Context of VAT: The Status of the Judgment Empire Stores v Commissioners of Customs and Excise in the Light of Later Judgments*, EC Tax Review (2001).

330. Tina Ehrke-Rabel & Sebastian Pfeiffer, *supra* note 13, at 538; Nevada Melan & Sebastian Pfeiffer, *Bezahlen mit Rechten, nicht mit Daten: Weitere offene Fragen zur Umsatzsteuerpflicht 'kostenloser' Internetdienste und Smartphone-Apps*, DStR, *supra* note 13, at 1074; *see* with the deferring opinion that the 'gemeine Wert', i.e., the market value, should be taken as the basis for the determination of the taxable amount; Nevada Melan & Bertram Wecke, *Umsatzsteuerpflicht von 'kostenlosen' Internetdiensten und Smartphone-Apps*, *supra* note 13, at 2269; the application of the market price in a barter transaction, where two services were exchanged was denied by the CJEU in Case C-549/11, *Orfey Balgaria*, 19 Dec. 2012, ECLI:EU:C:2012:832, paras 44 et seq.; *see* also Reuven Avi-Yonah & Nir Fishbien, *The Digital Consumption Tax*, 48 Intertax (2020), who argue that the value of the consideration should be a royalty-like fee derived from the ads and the data collection which is the revenue generated by the platform. The authors, though, discuss the topic of free services in rather general terms and do not seem to limit the scope of their discussion to EU VAT law.

331. Additionally, in the case that the data of the customer qualifies as consideration for a barter transaction, the theoretical follow-up question would be whether the customer also provides the platform with a taxable supply. In the case that the platform provides a B2B supply, this question should be answered in the positive. If the supply is a B2C supply, i.e., the customer is a final consumer, the question arises of whether the final consumer can become a taxable person due to the fact that the customer (continuously) 'sells' data to the e-commerce (and possibly also other online) platforms. As this section concentrates on the platform providing the service to the customer, this follow-up question of whether a consumer qualifies as a taxable person in the case that data is considered to be consideration for VAT purposes will not be dealt with at this point. For discussions in literature on this question *see*, e.g., Giorgio Beretta, *European VAT and the Sharing Economy*, *supra* note 13, at 75 et seqq.; Nevia Čičin-Šain, *Taxing Uber*, in *Uber – Brave New Service or Unfair Competition: Legal Analysis of the Nature of Uber Services*, *supra* note 15, at 187 et seq.; Tina Ehrke-Rabel et al., *Umsatzsteuer in einer digitalisierten Welt*, *supra* note 13, at 58 et seqq.; Ivo Grlica, *How the Sharing Economy Is Challenging the EU VAT System*, 28 International VAT Monitor, *supra* note 15, at 127; Marie Lamensch, *The Scope of the EU VAT System: Traditional Digital Economy Related Questions*, in *CJEU – Recent Developments in Value Added Tax 2017*, *supra* note 15; Katerina Pantazatou, *Taxation of the Sharing Economy in the European Union*, in *The Cambridge Handbook of the Law of the Sharing Economy*, *supra* note 15; Desiree Auer et al., *Umsatzsteuer im Rahmen der digitalen Transformation*, taxlex, *supra* note 15.

platform for a regular user will be higher than the costs for a user who signs up once to the platform and then does not use the platform anymore.

Ultimately, the qualification of the service provided from the e-commerce platform to the customer as a taxable supply depends, upon others, on the question of whether consideration is payable by the customer. If the customer and the platform agreed on a monetary consideration for the services received from the platform, the 'consideration' criterion would undoubtedly be fulfilled. It is more difficult when the consumer does not pay any monetary consideration for the services of the platform. In this case, it could be discussed whether the data that the platform receives from the customer should qualify as consideration and, therefore, the transaction may qualify as a barter transaction. As of today, the national tax authorities do not seem to have followed the approach in literature to qualify data as consideration which may also be the result of the difficulty of establishing the taxable base to calculate the taxable amount if data qualified as consideration. A decisive factor for this approach might also have been the legal opinion of the VAT Committee who denied that the direct link is fulfilled between a consumer giving data to a platform and the service that the consumer receives for the data with the argument that all customers receive the same service from the platform independently on the amount and/or quality of data provided by the customers.[332]

2.2.5.3   *The Determination of the Place of Supply*

2.2.5.3.1   *The General Place of Supply Rules*

The VAT Directive provides different place of supply rules for services depending on the specific circumstances of the case. In general, however, two general place of supply rules for the supply of services can be identified. On the one hand, Article 44 of the VAT Directive stipulates that the place of supply of services to a taxable person shall be the place where that person is established. Therefore, if the customer receiving the platform service was a business and used the platform service, e.g., to order goods for its business, the customer would be a taxable person acting as such. The place of supply of the platform service is thus the place where the customer is established. If the platform and the customer were established in the same Member State, the service would be taxable in that Member State. If the platform and the customer were established in different Member States, then the service would be taxable in the

---

332. VAT Committee, *Question Concerning the Application of EU VAT Provisions, Conditions for There Being a Taxable Transaction When Internet Services Are Provided in Exchange for User Data*, Working Paper No. 958, taxud.c.1(2018)6248826, 5 et seqq. (30 Oct. 2018), https:// circabc.europa.eu/sd/a/ee8603b3-9d86-444f-921c-003e3bee08ce/WP%20958%20-%20Art% 202%20-%20Internet%20services.pdf (last visited 19 Jul. 2021); *see also* Gorka Echevarría Zubeldia, *How VAT-Free Can Free Internet Services Be?*, 30 International VAT Monitor, *supra* note 324.

Member State where the customer was established, and the service would be subject to the reverse-charge mechanism.[333]

On the other hand, Article 45 of the VAT Directive establishes the place of supply of services when the service is supplied to a non-taxable person. According to Article 45 of the VAT Directive, the place of supply to a non-taxable person shall be the place where the supplier has established its business. Therefore, if the person receiving the platform service was a consumer, then the general place supply rule would stipulate that the transaction is taxable at the platform's place of establishment. With this general place of supply rule, the origin principle is, in general, applicable for the supply of services from taxable persons to consumers.

From a systematic point, the heading of section 2 on the place of supply of services being 'General rules' already shows that the VAT Directive also provides other place of supply rules. Section 3 stipulates 'Particular provisions' and therefore for a different place of supply for specific services defined in the VAT Directive. From the headings of these two sections, it could be concluded that section 3 providing the 'Particular provisions' should qualify as *lex specialis* to section 2, the 'General rules'. Also, the CJEU repeatedly held that the general rules do not take precedence over the particular provisions.[334] The general rules should be applied only if a supply did not fall into one of the stipulated particular provisions.[335] Therefore, the CJEU implicitly confirms that the particular provisions are *lege speciales* to the general rules.

---

333. *See* Articles 44 and 196 of the VAT Directive; in general, the same legal consequences apply as those for the supply from the platform service to the underlying supplier as discussed in s. 2.2.4 The Supply of the Platform Service to the Underlying Supplier.

334. *See*, e.g., Case C-327/94, *Jürgen Dudda v Finanzgericht Bergisch Gladbach*, 26 Sep. 1996, ECLI:EU:C:1996:355, para. 21; Case C-167/95, *Maatschap M.J.M. Linthorst, K.G.P. Pouwels en J. Scheren c.s. v Inspecteur der Belastingdienst/Ondernemingen Roermond*, 6 Mar. 1997, ECLI:EU:C:1997:105, para. 11; *Commission of the European Communities v French Republic*, 25 Jan. 2001, ECLI:EU:C:2001:54, para. 41; Case C-108/00, *Syndicat des producteurs indépendants (SPI) v Ministère de l'Economie, des Finances et de l'Industrie*, 15 Mar. 2001, ECLI: EU:C:2001:173, para. 16; Case C-452/03, *RAL (Channel Islands) Ltd and Others v Commissioners of Customs & Excise*, 12 May 2005, ECLI:EU:C:2005:289, para. 24; Case C-114/05, *Ministre de l'Économie, des Finances et de l'Industrie v Gillan Beach Ltd*, 9 Mar. 2006, ECLI:EU:C:2006:169, para. 15; Case C-166/05, *Heger Rudi GmbH v Finanzamt Graz-Stadt*, 7 Sep. 2006, ECLI:EU:C:2006:533, para. 16; these cases all concerned the relationship of Article 9 (1) and Article 9 (2) of the VAT Directive; as the wording and structure of the place of supply rules did not change significantly with the introduction of the VAT Directive, the CJEU also refers to judgments referring to the VAT Directive to this order for determining the place of supply; *see*, e.g., Case C-453/15, *Criminal proceedings against A and B*, 8 Dec. 2016, ECLI:EU:C:2016:933, para. 18.

335. Case C-327/94, *Dudda v Finanzamt Bergisch Gladbach*, 26 Sep. 1996, ECLI:EU:C:1996:355, para. 21; Case C-167/95, *Linthorst, Pouwels en Scheres v Inspecteur der Belastingdienst/Ondernemingen Roermond*, 6 Mar. 1997, ECLI:EU:C:1997:105, para. 11; *Commission v France*, 25 Jan. 2001, ECLI:EU:C:2001:54, para. 41; Case C-108/00, *SPI*, 15 Mar. 2001, ECLI:EU:C:2001:173, para. 16; Case C-452/03, *RAL (Channel Islands) and Others*, 12 May 2005, ECLI:EU:C:2005:289, para. 24; Case C-114/05, *Gillan Beach*, 9 Mar. 2006, ECLI: EU:C:2006:169, para. 15; Case C-166/05, *Heger*, 7 Sep. 2006, ECLI:EU:C:2006:533, para. 16; Case C-155/12, *Minister Finansów v RR Donnelley Global Turnkey Solutions Poland sp. z o.o.*, 27 Jun. 2013, ECLI:EU:C:2013:434, para. 29; Case C-453/15, *A and B*, 8 Dec. 2016, ECLI: EU:C:2016:933, para. 18.

Accordingly, before coming to the conclusion that Articles 44 and 45 of the VAT Directive are applicable to the services provided from the platform to its customers, the applicability of the particular provisions should be discussed. From the particular provisions, especially two may be applicable to the service in question: The supply of services by intermediaries stipulated in Article 46 of the VAT Directive and the supply of telecommunications, broadcasting, and electronic services to non-taxable persons stipulated in Article 58 of the VAT Directive.[336]

2.2.5.3.2 *Does the Platform Act as a Disclosed Agent According to Article 46 of the VAT Directive?*

2.2.5.3.2.1 The Requirements of Acting as a Disclosed Agent

Article 46 of the VAT Directive stipulates a special place of supply when the so-called disclosed agents are the suppliers of the service in question. As the name already suggests, the disclosed agent discloses the name of the underlying supplier to the customer. Therefore, the disclosed agent acts 'in the name and on behalf of another taxable person' as stipulated in Article 46 of the VAT Directive and Articles 30 and 31 of the VAT Implementing Regulation. The difference between the disclosed agent and the undisclosed agent is therefore in the criterion according to which the agent is acting either in his own name which might lead to the conclusion that the intermediary is an undisclosed agent according to Article 14 (2) (c) of the VAT Directive[337] or in the name of the underlying supplier which might lead to the intermediary acting as a disclosed agent. Additionally, a systematic difference between the disclosed and the undisclosed agent is that, whereas the undisclosed agent is stipulated in Title IV ('taxable transactions') of the VAT Directive, the disclosed agent is defined under the place of supply rules in Article 46 of the VAT Directive.

This difference becomes clearer from an analysis of the *United Utilities*[338] case compared to the *Henfling and Others*[339] case. *United Utilities* revolved around Littlewoods organising telephone bookmaking which outsourced a part of their operations to Vertex. Vertex was acting as the call centre for Littlewoods, receiving phone calls and recording the incoming bets based on the conditions dictated by Littlewoods.[340] Hereby, it is important to note that Vertex did not have any discretion on the decision of which bets to accept and, furthermore, Vertex did not disclose their name; the customer would assume that the phone call was taken by Littlewoods.[341] Moreover,

---

336. In theory, also other place of supply rules may be applicable, such as Article 47 of the VAT Directive.
337. For the discussion of the undisclosed agent scheme, *see* s. 2.2.2.2 The Supply Through Platforms: A Supply Through an Undisclosed Agent?.
338. Case C-89/05, *United Utilities plc v Commissioners of Customs & Excise*, 13 Jul. 2006, ECLI:EU:C:2006:469.
339. See for a more detailed discussion on the *Henfling and Others* case, s. 2.2.2.2.2.1 The Requirement of Acting in the Own Name.
340. Case C-89/05, *United Utilities*, 13 Jul. 2006, ECLI:EU:C:2006:469, para. 9.
341. *Ibid.*

Vertex did not bear any financial risk.[342] The question referred to the CJEU in this case was whether the VAT exemption of gambling in Article 13 (B) (f) of the Sixth VAT Directive[343] would be applicable for the services provided from Vertex to Littlewoods. The CJEU denied the applicability of the exemption to these services as the services of the call centre cannot be characterised as a betting transaction.[344] Compared to the *Henfling and Others* case, this case is different based on two factors. First, Vertex did not act independently from Littlewoods as it did not have any discretion on the decision of which bets would be accepted.[345] Second, Vertex accepted the bets on behalf of the organiser Littlewoods.[346] It was clear for the customers from the beginning that the bet was accepted by Littlewoods and not by Vertex; Vertex acted in the name of Littlewoods and not in its own name.[347]

A comparison of these two cases emphasises the difference between an undisclosed and a disclosed agent. Compared to the buralistes in the *Henfling and Others* case, Vertex acted in the name and on behalf of Littlewoods and, therefore, Vertex acted as a disclosed agent.[348] Moreover, the two cases emphasise the importance of the external impression that the customer receives from the intermediary concerning in whose name the intermediary is acting.[349] The qualification of a platform as an undisclosed agent was previously discussed with the outcome that the applicability of Article 14 (2) (c) of the VAT Directive is likely to be denied as the requirement for acting in the own name is likely not fulfilled.[350] At the same time, the requirement for acting on behalf of somebody else was likely to be answered in the affirmative.[351] Therefore, it is likely that the e-commerce platforms offering goods act in the name and on behalf of the underlying supplier and, therefore, the requirements of acting as a disclosed agent according to Article 46 of the VAT Directive might be fulfilled.

Although the two requirements for qualifying as a disclosed agent are likely to be fulfilled in the case of platforms but especially also of e-commerce platforms, the VAT Committee almost unanimously agrees that, if the intermediation services are provided in a digital environment, the platform should additionally fulfil another requirement for acting as a disclosed agent; the intermediary should actively be involved in the intermediation services.[352] The VAT Committee defines this active involvement as

---

342. *Ibid.* para. 10.
343. Stipulated in Article 135 (1) (i) of the VAT Directive.
344. Case C-89/05, *United Utilities*, 13 Jul. 2006, ECLI:EU:C:2006:469, paras 26 + 29.
345. Case C-464/10, *Henfling and Others*, 14 Jul. 2011, ECLI:EU:C:2011:489, para. 32.
346. *Ibid.*
347. Case C-89/05, *United Utilities*, 13 Jul. 2006, ECLI:EU:C:2006:469, para. 9.
348. Pernille Rendahl, *EU VAT and Double Taxation: A Fine Line between Interpretation and Application*, Intertax, *supra* note 206, at 451.
349. See, for further discussion on this, s. 2.2.2.2.2.1 The Requirement of Acting in the Own Name.
350. See s. 2.2.2.2.4 Does a Platform Act as an Undisclosed Agent?.
351. See s. 2.2.2.2.4 Does a Platform Act as an Undisclosed Agent?.
352. VAT Committee, *Guidelines Resulting from Meetings of the VAT Committee, VAT 2015: Interaction Between Electronically Supplied Services and Intermediation Services and Initial Discussion on the Scope of the Concept of Intermediation Services When Taken in a Broader Context*, Guidelines Resulting from the 107th Meeting, taxud.c.1(2017)1402399-914 (8 Jul. 2016), https://ec.europa.eu/taxation_customs/system/files/2021-03/guidelines-vat-committee-meetings_en.pdf (last visited 19 Jul. 2021).

requiring human intervention going beyond the automated supply that is provided.[353] If an intermediation service did not fulfil this active requirement, the supply by the platform should not qualify as a supply through a disclosed agent and, therefore, Article 46 of the VAT Directive is not applicable.[354] Although the VAT Directive does not provide this additional requirement, the VAT Committee seemingly wants to distinguish the place of supply rules of Article 46 and Article 58 of the VAT Directive. [355] In this sense, this additional requirement would qualify the intermediation service as a service through a disclosed agent only when human intervention is needed to provide the intermediation service. If the intermediation service was fully automated, it would qualify as an electronically supplied service according to Article 58 of the VAT Directive.

In literature, this additional requirement has been interpreted as giving preference to the rule for electronically supplied services.[356] Furthermore, the CJEU argues that the purpose of an intermediation service is that the intermediary provides the 'contractual party [with] ... a distinct act of mediation'.[357] Therefore, the intermediation service goes beyond the sole online availability of a platform connecting suppliers and consumers.[358] Thereby, it is worth noting that the cited CJEU judgments do not discuss the disclosed agent scheme but the applicability of certain VAT exemptions to intermediaries.[359] In the judgments, the taxable persons all acted in the name and on

353. *Ibid.*
354. *Ibid.*
355. This additional requirement was also not discussed in the working paper on which the guidelines resulting from the 107th Meeting were based, *see* VAT Committee, *Question Concerning the Application of EU VAT Provisions, VAT 2015: Interaction Between Electronically Supplied Services and Intermediation Services and Initial Discussion on the Scope of the Concept of Intermediation Services When Taken in a Broader Context*, Working Paper No. 906, taxud.c.1(2016)3297911, 7 (6 Jun. 2016), https://circabc.europa.eu/sd/a/ea379e7b-5e2b-421 7-b704-0b13a56de6dc/WP%20906%20-%20Interaction%20between%20electronically%20 supplied%20services%20and%20intermediation%20services.pdf (last visited 19 Jul. 2021) where the VAT Committee argues that, based on Article 46 of the VAT Directive, the intermediation service should follow the place of supply of the underlying supply. If the underlying supply is an electronically provided service, then the intermediation service should also be taxed in the place where the consumer is located. The VAT Committee does not discuss any additional argument for the application of Article 46 of the VAT Directive in the case that the intermediation service is provided via the Internet. For the qualification of the platform service as an electronically supplied service, *see* s. 2.2.5.3.3 Is the Service of the Platform an Electronically Supplied Service?; for further discussion on the supposedly conflict between Article 46 and Article 58 of the VAT Directive, *see* s. 2.2.5.3.4 An Evaluation of the Applicable Place of Supply Rule: Article 46 of the VAT Directive Versus Article 58 of the VAT Directive.
356. Madeleine Merkx, *VAT and E-Services: When Human Intervention Is Minimal*, 29 International VAT Monitor, s. 4.1 (2018).
357. Case C-235/00, *Commissioners of Customs & Excise v CSC Financial Services Ltd*, 13 Dec. 2001, ECLI:EU:C:2001:696, para. 39.
358. *See* Selina Siller & Annika Streicher, *Online-Beherbungsplattformen: Zwischen elektronisch erbrachter Dienstleistung und Margenbesteuerung*, taxlex, *supra* note 17, at 51 et seq.; with additional reference to Case C-235/00, *CSC Financial Services*, 13 Dec. 2001, ECLI: EU:C:2001:696, para. 39; Case C-453/05, *Ludwig*, 21 Jun. 2007, ECLI:EU:C:2007:369, para. 28; Case C-40/15, *Minister Finansów v Aspiro SA*, 17 Mar. 2016, ECLI:EU:C:2016:172, para. 37.
359. Case C-235/00, *CSC Financial Services*, 13 Dec. 2001, ECLI:EU:C:2001:696 was on the applicability of the exemption for transactions and negotiation in shares, interests, debentures and other securities (Article 13B [d] [5] of the Sixth VAT Directive); Case C-453/05, *Ludwig*, 21 Jun.

behalf of the underlying supplier; this fact was not challenged by the CJEU.[360] The case law rather concentrated on the interpretation of the terms 'negotiation'[361] and 'insurance brokers and insurance agents'[362] since the taxable persons needed to fulfil negotiation services or act as insurance brokers or agents for the exemption to be applicable. It seems clear that these terms may require further involvement from the intermediary than simply acting in the name and on behalf of another person. The narrow interpretation of exemptions in general and therefore also of these terms is in line with the CJEU case law.[363] As the terms 'negotiation' and 'insurance brokers and insurance agents' do not seem to be relevant for the applicability of the disclosed agent scheme in Article 46 of the VAT Directive, it seems questionable whether these judgments support the opinion of the VAT Committee that an intermediation service should require a more active involvement from the intermediary, i.e., the platform.[364]

After all, it seems debatable why, for the qualification as a disclosed agent according to Article 46 of the VAT Directive of an online platform, an additional requirement should be fulfilled when this requirement is not stipulated in the VAT Directive. Moreover, a per se negation of the disclosed agent scheme for online platforms that are provided in an automated manner might result in differentiated treatment of online intermediaries compared to offline intermediaries. Such an interpretation resulting in a different treatment of online and offline intermediaries can be in conflict with the principle of neutrality.[365] Therefore, in the case that an e-commerce platform acts in the name and on behalf of the underlying supplier and hence fulfils the legally stipulated requirements, it should qualify as acting as a disclosed agent.

2007, ECLI:EU:C:2007:369 was on the applicability of the exemption for the granting and negotiation of credit (Article 13B [d] [1] of the Sixth VAT Directive); Case C-40/15, *Aspiro*, 17 Mar. 2016, ECLI:EU:C:2016:172 was on the applicability of the exemption for insurance and reinsurance transactions, including related services performed by insurance brokers and insurance agents (Article 135 [1] [a] of the VAT Directive).

360. Whereas, in Case C-235/00, *CSC Financial Services*, 13 Dec. 2001, ECLI:EU:C:2001:696, para. 6, it was explicitly stated that CSC provided services on behalf of financial institutions, in the other two judgments, the CJEU explicitly stated that the intermediary acted in the name and on behalf of another person; *see* Case C-453/05, *Ludwig*, 21 Jun. 2007, ECLI:EU:C:2007:369, paras 6 + 8; Case C-40/15, *Aspiro*, 17 Mar. 2016, ECLI:EU:C:2016:172, para. 11.

361. Case C-235/00, *CSC Financial Services*, 13 Dec. 2001, ECLI:EU:C:2001:696, paras. 37 et seqq.; Case C-453/05, *Ludwig*, 21 Jun. 2007, ECLI:EU:C:2007:369, paras. 38 et seq.

362. Case C-40/15, *Aspiro*, 17 Mar. 2016, ECLI:EU:C:2016:172, paras. 34 et seqq.

363. The CJEU has repeatedly held that exemptions should be interpreted strictly, *see*, e.g., Case C-348/87, *Stichting Uitvoering Financiële Acties v Staatssecretaris van Financiën*, 15 Jun. 1989, ECLI:EU:C:1989:246, para. 13; Case C-281/91, *Muys' en De Winter's Bouw- en Aannemingsbedrijf BV v Staatssecretaris van Financiën*, 27 Oct. 1993, ECLI:EU:C:1993:855, para. 13; Case C-2/95, *Sparekassernes Datacenter (SDC) v Skatteministeriet*, 5 Jun. 1997, ECLI: EU:C:1997:278, para. 20; Case C-453/05, *Ludwig*, 21 Jun. 2007, ECLI:EU:C:2007:369, para. 21; Case C-40/15, *Aspiro*, 17 Mar. 2016, ECLI:EU:C:2016:172, para. 20.

364. Nevertheless, in literature, reference was made to the cases *CSC Financial services, Ludwig* and *Aspiro* to support the interpretation of the VAT committee that an intermediation service should require a more active involvement from the intermediary, i.e., the platform; *see* Selina Siller & Annika Streicher, *Online-Beherbungsplattformen: Zwischen elektronisch erbrachter Dienstleistung und Margenbesteuerung*, taxlex, *supra* note 17, at 51 et seq.

365. For further information on the principle of neutrality, *see* s. 5.2.5.1 Content and Development of the Principle of Neutrality.

2.2.5.3.2.2   The Legal Consequence of the Qualification as a Disclosed Agent

Article 46 of the VAT Directive in connection with Articles 30 and 31 of the VAT Implementing Regulation[366] stipulates a special place of supply rule for the supply of the intermediary to the customer.[367] According to Article 46 of the VAT Directive, the place of supply for services rendered to a non-taxable person as a disclosed agent shall be the place where the underlying transaction is supplied. Notably, this special place of supply is only applicable when the supply is rendered to a non-taxable person, i.e., a consumer. Therefore, if the customer was a consumer, the place of supply of the service from the platform to the consumer would follow the place of supply of the underlying transaction. In the case at hand, it would follow the place of supply for the supply of the good from the underlying supplier to the consumer. As already established, the place of supply depends on whether the good is imported from a third country or territory or whether it is a supply within the EU.[368]

Additionally, the application of the distance selling rules added legal uncertainty for the determination of the place of supply by the disclosed agent prior to the introduction of the e-commerce package. One criterion for the application of the destination principle according to Article 33 (1) of the VAT Directive depended on whether the underlying supplier had surpassed the implemented distance selling threshold of the Member States in question, if the underlying supplier had not surpassed the distance selling threshold, or whether the underlying supplier opted for taxation in the Member State of destination.[369] As the place of supply of the platform service is determined by the place of supply of the underlying transaction, the platform is depending on the information from the underlying supplier. This led to the fact that it was impossible for the platform itself to determine the place of supply for their own transactions without contacting the underlying supplier. Moreover, even though the underlying supplier might have told the platform that the threshold in the Member State of destination was not surpassed yet, and therefore the place of supply was the place of establishment of the underlying supplier, this fact might have changed in the course of the year. In practice, even if the platform had updated the file of underlying suppliers and the necessary information, i.e., in which Member State(s) the underlying suppliers had surpassed the threshold, the platform would have still been dependent on the information from the supplier concerning the threshold surpassing during the

---

366. Council Implementing Regulation (EU) No 282/2011 of 15 March 2011 Laying down Implementing Measures for Directive 2006/112/EC on the Common System of Value Added Tax, OJ L 77/1 (2011).
367. See, on the place of supply of intermediary services, already Case C-68/03, *Staatssecretaris van Financiën v D. Lipjes*, 27 May 2004, ECLI:EU:C:2004:325; and the critical discussion of this case by Michele Iavagnilio, *Intermediary Services – What the ECJ Did Not Say*, 15 International VAT Monitor (2004). It should be noted that this judgment is based on the Sixth Directive. The place of supply rules for disclosed agents in Article 28b (E) of the Sixth Directive were simplified in the VAT Directive.
368. See, for the place of supply rule of the supply of the good from the underlying supplier to the consumer before the introduction of the e-commerce package, s. 2.2.3.3.1 The Place of Supply of B2C Imported Goods.
369. For further information on the distance selling threshold, see s. 2.2.3.2 Intra-Community B2C Supplies Prior to the Introduction of the E-Commerce Package.

year. Therefore, this shift of the place of supply of the platform service depended on the individual circumstances of the underlying supplier. This dependency on information between the platform and the underlying supplier resulted in legal uncertainty for the platform.

A similar dependency on information could be seen when the goods were imported into the EU and the special place of supply rule of Article 33 (2) of the VAT Directive[370] was applicable.[371] First, the platform would have needed to receive the information that the goods were imported into a different Member State than the Member State of destination in this case. Second, the same information necessity concerning the distance selling rules discussed above would apply for the change in place of supply according to Article 33 (2) of the VAT Directive because the supply from the Member State of importation to the Member State of destination would have been a B2C distance sale of goods.[372] Thus, once the platform received the information that the goods were imported in a Member State other than the Member State of destination, then the platform was still confronted with the difficulty of determining the applicable place of supply. In this case, the place of supply could have been the Member State of importation (if the underlying supplier did not surpass the distance selling threshold) or the Member State of destination (if the underlying supplier surpassed the distance selling threshold or opted for taxation in the Member State of destination).

As a result, the place of supply rule would deviate from the general rule in Article 45 of the VAT Directive when a disclosed agent is involved in the supply of goods or services if the customer purchasing the goods was a non-taxable person. Since the disclosed agent scheme does not lead to any legal consequences other than the place of supply shift, each supply must be independently looked at and evaluated for VAT reasons when the supply involves a disclosed agent. In contrast to the application of the undisclosed agent scheme according to Article 14 (2) (c) of the VAT Directive,[373] the disclosed agent is not (fictitiously) included in the supply chain of the supply of the good. Therefore, the supply of the disclosed agent, e.g., would not benefit from a possibly applicable exemption of the supply from the underlying supplier to the customer if the disclosed agent himself did not fulfil the requirements of the exemption himself.[374] Nevertheless, the place of supply shift is a legal consequence that may lead to practical difficulties as the platform's legal qualification of the place of supply depends on the information that the platform receives from the underlying supplier.

---

370. This refers to the article in the VAT Directive before the entering into force of the e-commerce package. Article 33 (2) of the VAT Directive has been amended with the e-commerce package.
371. See, for a detailed discussion of Article 33 (2) of the VAT Directive before entering into force of the e-commerce package, s. 2.2.3.3.1 The Place of Supply of B2C Imported Goods Prior to the Introduction of the E-Commerce Package.
372. See s. 2.2.3.2 Intra-Community B2C Supplies Prior to the Introduction of the E-Commerce Package.
373. See, for the discussions of the legal consequences of the undisclosed agent scheme, s. 2.2.2.2.3 Legal Consequence of the Qualification as an Undisclosed Agent.
374. See also Case C-89/05, *United Utilities*, 13 Jul. 2006, ECLI:EU:C:2006:469.

2.2.5.3.3   Is the Service of the Platform an Electronically Supplied Service?

2.2.5.3.3.1   The Requirements for an Electronically Supplied Service

Article 58 of the VAT Directive stipulates a special place of supply for electronically supplied services. The term 'electronically supplied service' is used in the VAT Directive in the special place of supply rule in Article 58 of the VAT Directive and in the special rule concerning the applicable rate in Article 98 of the VAT Directive.[375] Annex II of the VAT Directive provides an indicative list of electronically supplied services.[376] Since making the platform available to customers cannot be regarded as one of the five services listed in Annex II of the VAT Directive, a final conclusion on whether the services in question are electronically supplied services cannot be drawn from the VAT Directive itself.

Additionally to Annex II of the VAT Directive, Article 7 of the VAT Implementing Regulation provides for a more detailed definition of the term 'electronically supplied services'. Whereas Article 7 (1) of the VAT Implementing Regulation is a general definition of electronically supplied services, Article 7 (2) of the VAT Implementing Regulation stipulates an exemplary (positive) list of services that are considered as electronically supplied services. Article 7 (3) of the VAT Implementing Regulation stipulates a (negative) list of which services are not considered an electronically supplied service. According to the VAT Committee, it should be tested whether the service in question is covered in the list of Article 7 (2) of the VAT Implementing Regulation in a first step.[377]

First, it seems that Article 7 (2) (c) of the VAT Implementing Regulation could cover the service under examination. Article 7 (2) (c) of the VAT Implementing Regulation stipulates that 'services automatically generated from a computer via the Internet ... in response to specific data input by the recipient' are electronically provided services. The scope of this article is rather far-reaching, and the wording could cover any services that are supplied to the customer after the customer provided

---

375. *See* further elaborations on these two legal consequences in s. 2.2.5.3.3.2 The Legal Consequence of an Electronically Supplied Service.
376. The five supplies listed in Annex II of the VAT Directive are: (1) website supply, web hosting, distance maintenance of programmes and equipment; (2) supply of software and updating thereof; (3) supply of images, text, and information and making databases available; (4) supply of music, films and games, including games of chance and gambling games, and of political, cultural, artistic, sporting, scientific, and entertainment broadcasts and events; and (5) supply of distance teaching.
377. *See* VAT Committee, *Guidelines Resulting from Meetings of the VAT Committee: Distance Selling*, Guidelines Resulting from the 104th Meeting, taxud.c.1(2015)4820441-876 (4–5 Jun. 2015), https://ec.europa.eu/taxation_customs/system/files/2021-03/guidelines-vat-commi ttee-meetings_en.pdf (last visited 29 Jul. 2021), where the VAT Committee explicitly states the order for determining whether a service should qualify as an electronically supplied service: 'first check if the service is mentioned in Annex II of the VAT Directive or under Article 7 (2) or Annex I of the VAT Implementing Regulation as being covered by the definition; secondly, if not mentioned there, examine whether the service is mentioned under Article 7 (3) of the VAT Implementing Regulation as not being covered by the definition; finally, if the service cannot be found on any of these lists, verify whether it meets criteria set out under Article 7 (1) of the VAT Implementing Regulation for being covered by the definition'.

the data required to receive the service. It is not quite clear from the wording of Article 7 (2) (c) of the VAT Implementing Regulation which services the legislator had in mind. In theory, the platform service that a consumer receives could as well be subsumed under Article 7 (2) (c) of the VAT Implementing Regulation. The customer chooses the desired good online which is a data input and usually also transmits the delivery and payment data to the platform. In return, the customer receives the platform's service via the Internet. Nevertheless, if Article 7 (2) (c) of the VAT Implementing Regulation was read with such a broad understanding, (almost) any action on the Internet could be subsumed under Article 7 (2) (c) of the VAT Implementing Regulation, including the other listed services in Article 7 (2) of the VAT Implementing Regulation. The data input would be, e.g., required if the customer purchased digitised products as the customer must provide data at least in the form of billing, payment, and delivery information but the supply of digitised products is explicitly listed in Article 7 (2) (a) of the VAT Implementing Regulation. Furthermore, services providing/supporting a presence on the Internet according to Article 7 (2) (b) of the VAT Implementing Regulation also require data from the customer as the service supplier must actually receive the data input about which content should be displayed on the website or webpage. Likewise, for suppliers to sell goods or services via an online marketplace according to Article 7 (2) (d) of the VAT Implementing Regulation, the data on the goods or services and the data on the supplier must be provided for its display on the platform. If the EU legislator had wanted Article 7 (2) (c) of the VAT Implementing Regulation to have such a broad meaning that any data input would result in an electronically supplied service, it would not have been necessary to list the other literae in Article 7 (2) of the VAT Implementing Regulation since the services described in literae (a), (b), and (d) could all be subsumed under Article 7 (2) (c) of the VAT Implementing Regulation. Therefore, a possible conclusion that the services provided by the platform to the customer could fall into the scope of Article 7 (2) (c) of the VAT Implementing Regulation should be taken cautiously. Although the literal interpretation leads to a rather broad scope of Article 7 (2) (c) of the VAT Implementing Regulation, the systematic interpretation might lead to doubts, whether the legislator intended such a broad application.

Additionally, according to Article 7 (2) (d) of the VAT Implementing Regulation, 'the transfer for consideration of the right to put goods or services up for sale on an Internet site operating as an online market on which potential buyers make their bids by an automated procedure and on which the parties are notified of a sale by electronic mail automatically generated from a computer' is an electronically supplied service. Thus, Article 7 (2) (d) of the VAT Implementing Regulation explicitly refers to the supply of services from online markets via the Internet. However, Article 7 (2) (d) of the VAT Implementing Regulation is limited to the service from the platform to the underlying supplier since it explicitly stipulates that the 'the right to put goods or services up for sale on an Internet site' is considered to be an electronically supplied service. Due to this explicit limitation, the supply of the service from the platform to the customer cannot be subsumed under Article 7 (2) (d) of the VAT Implementing Regulation.

As the service from the platform to the customer can only be subsumed with caution under Article 7 (2) of the VAT Implementing Regulation and is also not covered by Article 7 (3) of the VAT Implementing Regulation, in a final step, it could be verified whether the service fulfils the criteria set out in Article 7 (1) of the VAT Implementing Regulation. Article 7 (1) of the VAT Implementing Regulation defines the term 'electronically supplied services' as:

> services which are delivered over the Internet or an electronic network and the nature of which renders their supply essentially automated and involving minimal human intervention, and impossible to ensure in the absence of information technology.

From this legal definition, four criteria can be derived. All four criteria must be fulfilled cumulatively and are of equal importance.[378] First, the provided service must be delivered over the Internet or an electronic network. Since, in the given case, the customer uses the Internet to purchase goods, this criterion can clearly be affirmed. Second, the nature of the service must essentially be automated. With this criterion, the legislator requires that the services are automatically delivered through the use of computers. Due to the automatic process, only little human intervention and little time are required for the supply of the service.[379] As the e-commerce platform is an online platform run via software, this criterion is likely to be fulfilled. This criterion is also very closely linked to the third criterion, i.e., the requirement of minimal human intervention for an electronically supplied service.[380] Minimal human intervention does not mean that no human intervention is allowed to qualify as an electronically supplied service. The initial set-up and regular maintenance of the homepage or the software necessary to supply the service is not detrimental and can be considered as minimal human intervention; the actual regular service delivery, however, should not require human intervention.[381] In general, the service supply from the platform that is based on the search query of the customer, the purchase of the goods by the customer, the return of the goods, and the display of the reviews does not require human intervention. Nevertheless, the offering of customer service could be seen as critical for the requirement of minimal human intervention.[382] In the case of e-commerce plat-forms, a service centre is often implemented by the platform, especially to handle

---

378. *Ibid.*; VAT Committee, *Question Concerning the Application of EU VAT Provisions, VAT 2015: Scope of the Notion of Electronically Supplied Services*, Working Paper No. 843, tax-ud.c.1(2015)694775, 7 (12 Feb. 2015), https://circabc.europa.eu/sd/a/e346e09e-f06e-44cc-8f 39-4334fb99c841/843%20-%20Scope%20of%20notion%20of%20electronically%20supplied %20services.pdf (last visited 19 Jul. 2021).
379. VAT Committee, *supra* note 378, at 5.
380. *Ibid.*
381. *Ibid.*
382. *See* similarly Selina Siller & Annika Streicher, *Online-Beherbungsplattformen: Zwischen elek-tronisch erbrachter Dienstleistung und Margenbesteuerung*, taxlex, *supra* note 17, at 53, who discuss whether the booking of online accommodation services provided from the platform to the customer is an electronically supplied service. The authors discuss that one part of the set-up of the accommodation platform that requires human intervention is the customer service. They conclude that a service centre should not influence the qualification as an electronically supplied service from the accommodation platform to the customer because it is only marginal to the platform service.

returns enquiries. Today, these online return customer services are regularly implemented (at least in a first step) with a Chatbot. Only in the final stage when the Chatbot could not help the customer is the customer connected to the call centre. In this last step, human intervention is undeniably part of the supply. As this customer service, though, is only a marginal part of the service provided and as most customers will likely not even get into contact with the customer service, this human intervention should be qualified as minimal human intervention and should therefore not influence the affirmation of the third criterion. The fourth requirement is the impossibility of ensuring the provision of the service in the absence of information technology. As the considered service is solely provided via the Internet, the Internet is an indispensable medium in this supply. As a result, this criterion can be affirmed, too.

Additionally, Article 7 (2) (d) of the VAT Implementing Regulation also serves as a systematic argument that the supply in question should be seen as an electronically supplied service. According to Article 7 (2) (d) of the VAT Implementing Regulation, 'the transfer for consideration of the right to put goods or services up for sale on an Internet site operating as an online market on which potential buyers make their bids by an automated procedure and on which the parties are notified of a sale by electronic mail automatically generated from a computer' is an electronically supplied service. E-Commerce platforms serve as an intermediary between the underlying supplier and the customer and, therefore, the two supplies, i.e., the supply from the platform to the underlying supplier and the supply from the platform to the customer, are similar in their nature and execution but represent the two necessary ends of the supply chain: the underlying supplier who sells the goods in question and the customer who buys the goods in question – both use the same platform with the same electronically automated system provided by the intermediary, i.e., the platform. It seems that the two supplies of the platform are metaphorically two sides of the same coin, but only one side is explicitly mentioned in Article 7 (2) (d) of the VAT Implementing Regulation to be an electronically supplied service. Thus, also the systematics support that, if the platform service provided to the customer fulfils the criteria of Article 7 (1) of the VAT Implementing Regulation, this service would qualify as an electronically supplied service.[383]

---

383. *See* also the opinion represented by the VAT Committee in VAT Committee, *supra* note 378, at 7, where the VAT Committee explicitly stated that services provided from marketplaces to customers for consideration can be electronically supplied services as long as the criteria in Article 7 (1) of the VAT Implementing Regulation are fulfilled. In this instance, especially the criteria of minimal human intervention and the provision of the service without information technology should be precisely reviewed; *see* also VAT Committee, *Question Concerning the Application of EU VAT Provisions, Services Supplied by Digital Platforms Intervening in Short-Term Leasing or Renting of Immovable Property*, Working Paper No. 990, tax-ud.c.1(2020)1181920 (18 Feb. 2020), https://www.vatupdate.com/wp-content/uploads/2020/06/WP-990-Sharing-economy-platforms-immovable-property.pdf (last visited 19 Jul. 2021); although the content of this working paper was sharing economy platforms providing rentals of immovable property, the VAT Committee explicitly highlights that a variety of different platforms exist. Therefore, a general statement could not be made as to whether platforms offering rentals should be considered as an electronically supplied service. This should also be stressed with e-commerce platforms. If, e.g., a clothing e-commerce platform provides an

2.2.5.3.3.2   The Legal Consequence of an Electronically Supplied Service

Comparable to the application of the disclosed agent scheme, the legal consequence of an electronically supplied service is the change in the place of supply. According to Article 58 (1) (c) of the VAT Directive, the place of supply for electronically supplied services is the place where the consumer is established, has his permanent address, or usually resides.[384] Notably, this deviation from the general supply rules is only applicable for the supply to non-taxable persons. Articles 24 et seqq. of the VAT Implementing Regulation further provide legislative guidance on how to determine the customer's location in the case of establishments in more than one country,[385] presumptions for the location of the customer[386] and the rebuttal of these presumptions, and the evidence necessary for the rebuttal.[387] This should make the determination of the place of establishment, the place of the permanent address, or the usual residence of the consumer clearer to the supplier providing the electronically supplied service.[388] In the case of consumers ordering goods via an e-commerce platform, it is likely that the consumer uses either a computer or a mobile device for ordering the goods online. Therefore, the place of establishment, the place of the permanent address, or the usual residence of the consumer is likely the place where the landline is installed[389] or the place of the used sim card in the case of mobile data use.[390]

This special place of supply rule would have the consequence that the platform has to register in all Member States where it supplies electronically supplied services to consumers. Therefore, the EU legislator introduced the so-called MOSS in 2015 through

---

online style consultation from a human employee of the platform, then it is likely that the platform service will not qualify as an electronically supplied service.

384. *See*, for a summary of the legislative changes in 2015, Hans-Martin Grambeck, *B2C Supplies of Electronic Services from 1 January 2015 from a German Perspective*, 24 International VAT Monitor (2013); Madeleine Merkx, *New Implementing Measures for EU Place-of-Supply Change 2015*, 24 International VAT Monitor (2013); Matthias Weidmann, *The New EU VAT Rules on the Place of Supply of B2C E-Services*, 24 EC Tax Review (2015); Patrick Wille, *New EU VAT Rules for Telecommunications Services from 2015*, 23 International VAT Monitor (2012); Patrick Wille, *New Rules from 2015 Onwards for Telecommunications, Radio and Television Broadcasting, and Electronically Supplied Services*, 26 International VAT Monitor (2015).

385. *See* Article 24 of the VAT Implementing Regulation for the application of Article 58 of the VAT Directive on electronically supplied services.

386. *See* Article 24a and Article 24b of the VAT Implementing Regulation for the application of Article 58 of the VAT Directive on electronically supplied services.

387. *See* Article 24d and Article 24f of the VAT Implementing Regulation for the application of Article 58 of the VAT Directive on electronically supplied services.

388. *See* also European Commission, *Explanatory Notes on the EU VAT Changes to the Place of Supply of Telecommunications, Broadcasting and Electronic Services That Enter into Force in 2015*, *supra* note 11, at 52 et seqq., where the European Commission extensively discusses Articles 24 et seqq. of the VAT Implementing Regulation; *see* also the critical discussion on the parameters for determining the place of establishment, the place of the permanent address, or the usual residence of the consumer by Marie Lamensch, *Unsuitable EU VAT Place of Supply Rules for Electronic Services – Proposal for an Alternative Approach*, 4 World Tax Journal (2012); Marie Lamensch, *The 2015 Rules for Electronically Supplied Services – Compliance Issues*, 26 International VAT Monitor (2015); Marie Lamensch, *European Value Added Tax in the Digital Era: A Critical Analysis and Proposals for Reform*, *supra* note 12, at 92 et seqq.

389. *See* Article 24b (a) of the VAT Implementing Regulation.

390. *See* Article 24b (b) of the VAT Implementing Regulation.

which the supplier, i.e., the platform, must only register in one EU Member State and can comply with the reporting and payment obligations for the electronically supplied services with only one registration in all Member States.[391]

Additionally to this change in the place of supply, Article 98 of the VAT Directive explicitly stipulates that reduced VAT rates are not applicable to electronically supplied services. Therefore, the applicable VAT rate for the electronically supplied service would be the general VAT rate of the country of the place of supply.

2.2.5.3.4 An Evaluation of the Applicable Place of Supply Rule: Article 46 of the VAT Directive Versus Article 58 of the VAT Directive

As the platform service provided to the customer fulfils the criteria to qualify as a service through a disclosed agent[392] as well as an electronically supplied service,[393] the follow-up question is which place of supply rule should, in fact, be applied.[394] In some cases, the place of supply of the disclosed agent scheme and the place of supply of the electronically supplied service will result in the same place of supply, especially when the supply is a supply within the EU, the underlying supplier has surpassed the distance selling threshold in the Member State of destination, and the customer orders the goods to its place of residence. In this case, the supply through a disclosed agent as well as the electronically supplied service leads to taxation where the ordered good is delivered which, in the given case, is also the place of residence of the customer. Nevertheless, there are several constellations when these two place of supply rules lead to taxation in different Member States. One example of such a divergence in the place of supply would be if the customer's usual residence was in Member State 1 from which the customer also ordered the goods, but the goods that the customer ordered were sent to the holiday house in Member State 2. In this case, the application of the place of supply of the disclosed agent scheme in Article 46 of the VAT Directive would lead to taxation in the Member State where the dispatch or transport ends, i.e., Member State 2 (assuming that the underlying supplier has surpassed the national distance selling

---

391. See Articles 369a-369k of the VAT Directive for suppliers who are established in the EU and Articles 358a-369 of the VAT Directive for third country suppliers. Until 1 Jul. 2021, the application of the MOSS was limited to electronically supplied services. As of 1 Jul. 2021, the MOSS was reformed into the OSS, and three different OSS systems were introduced: the Non-EU-OSS, the EU-OSS, and the IOSS. Therefore, as of 1 Jul. 2021, any cross-border B2C services can be declared through the OSS system (Articles 358a-369k of the VAT Directive). See, for further information on the OSS systems, s. 4.11 Special Schemes of the OSS.
392. Article 46 of the VAT Directive; see s. 2.2.5.3.2 Does the Platform Act as a Disclosed Agent According to Article 46 of the VAT Directive?.
393. Article 58 of the VAT Directive, see s. 2.2.5.3.3.1 The Requirements for an Electronically Supplied Service.
394. Literature also picked up this question but could not finally resolve it; see, e.g., Frederek Schuska, Die Abgrenzung von Vermittlungsdienstleistungen zum Eigengeschäft und elektronischen Dienstleistungen, MwStR 308 (2017). In general, it could also be discussed how the general place of supply rule in Article 45 of the VAT Directive should qualify in comparison to the place of supply rule of the disclosed agent and the electronically supplied service place of supply rule. As this has been analysed in s. 2.2.5.3.1 The General Place of Supply Rule already, this section will concentrate on the relationship of the two, more particularly the place of supply rules of Articles 46 and 58 of the VAT Directive.

threshold), whereas the place of supply for the electronically supplied service in Article 58 of the VAT Directive would likely lead to taxation in the Member State of the place of residence of the customer, i.e., Member State 1.[395]

Legal theory provides several maxims being part of the teleological interpretation to resolve such a conflict of norms: the principle of *lex superior*, principle of *lex posterior*, and the principle of *lex specialis*.[396] When applying these principles to the conflict between Articles 46 and 58 of the VAT Directive, the principle of *lex superior derogat legi inferiori*, which stipulates that priority should be given to the higher-ranking norm, is not helping to resolve the conflict as both norms are stipulated in the VAT Directive. Therefore, no higher-ranking law can be identified.

The principle of *lex posterior derogat legi priori* grants priority to the norm that entered into force later in time. Thereby, the principle of *lex posterior* would only be applicable if two colliding norms were incompatible with each other and not if they complemented each other.[397] As Articles 46 and 58 of the VAT Directive are complementary to each other, the principle of *lex posterior derogat legi priori* cannot resolve this conflict either.

Lastly, the principle of *lex specialis derogat legi generali* grants priority to the more specific norm. As already discussed, Articles 46 and 58 of the VAT Directive are *lex specialis* to the general place of supply rule for the B2C supply of services stipulated in Article 45 of the VAT Directive.[398] However, it is questionable whether, within the *lex specialis*, one of the articles can be identified as such and the other as the *lex generalis*, i.e., whether Article 46 of the VAT Directive can be considered as the *lex specialis* to Article 58 of the VAT Directive or vice versa. In this sense, the service of an e-commerce platform represents two main aspects. On the one hand, it is an intermediary service connecting the supplier and the consumer for which the intermediary acts in the name and on behalf of the underlying supplier. On the other hand, this intermediary service is provided through electronic means.

---

395. *See* Article 24b (a) of the VAT Implementing Regulation according to which, if there is a presumption if the electronically supplied service is supplied to a non-taxable person through a fixed land line, then it would be presumed that the place of residency of the non-taxable person is the place where the land line lies. Another example would be when the supply from the underlying supplier to the consumer is a supply within the EU and the underlying supplier did not surpass the registration threshold of the Member State of destination. In this case, the underlying supply would be taxable in the Member State of origin from where the goods are delivered and, therefore, the service of the platform as a disclosed agent would also be taxed in the Member State from where the goods are delivered. At the same time, though, the electronically supplied service's place of supply would be the place where the consumer is established. Therefore, the place of supply rules of the disclosed agent scheme would result in the place from where the goods are delivered (place of origin), whereas the place of supply of the electronically supplied service would result in the place from where the customer most likely orders the goods (place of destination).

396. *See*, e.g., Sjoerd Douma, *Legal Research in International and EU Tax Law, supra* note 49, at 22; *see* also, for the qualification of the principle of *lex specialis* as part of the teleological interpretation Franz Bydlinski, *Juristische Methodenlehre und Rechtsbegriff, supra* note 43, at 465.

397. *See* Karl Riesenhuber, *Europäische Methodenlehre* 211 (De Gruyter 2015).

398. *See* s. 2.2.5.3.1 The General Place of Supply Rules.

In literature, it has been argued that the place of supply of the electronically supplied service is the *lex specialis* to the place of the disclosed agent supply.[399] If this opinion was followed, then the place of supply of the electronically supplied services would precede the 'traditional' place of supply of the disclosed agent.[400] To come to that conclusion, the author compares a classically provided intermediary service to the supply of an electronically supplied intermediary service.[401] As the additional added element of the supply being performed electronically supplied is only fulfilled in the latter case, the author argues that the *lex specialis* is the electronically supplied service.[402] It is not quite clear, though, how the author comes to the conclusion that the electronic providing element of the service precedes over the intermediary aspect of the service.

From a systematic point, the VAT Directive provides the general place of supply in Article 44 of the VAT Directive for B2B supplies and in Article 45 of the VAT Directive for B2C supplies. That these provisions should qualify as the *lex generalis* is also stated in the heading of section 2: 'General rules'. Section 3 provides 'Particular provisions' and therefore for a different place of supply for specific services defined in the VAT Directive. Articles 46 and 56 of the VAT Directive both are in Section 3, the 'Particular provisions'. From the headings of these two sections, it can be concluded that section 3 providing for the 'Particular provisions' should qualify as *lex specialis* to section 2, the 'General rules'. Also the CJEU repeatedly held that the general rules do not take precedence over the particular provisions.[403] Only if a supply did not fall into one of the stipulated particular provisions should the general rules then be applied.[404] Therefore,

399. *See* Tina Ehrke-Rabel, *Aspekte grenzüberschreitenden digitalen Wirtschaftens in der Umsatzsteuer*, in *Digitalisierung im Steuerrecht* 391 et seq. (Johanna Hey ed., Otto Schmidt 2019).
400. *See ibid.*; the author discusses the relationship of the disclosed agent place of supply and the place of supply for electronically supplied services in the example of sharing economy platforms. As the service provided by sharing economy platforms and e-commerce platforms is comparable, it can be assumed that the author's legal qualification could also be applied to e-commerce platforms.
401. *Ibid.* at 392.
402. *Ibid.*
403. *See*, e.g., Case C-327/94, *Dudda v Finanzgericht Bergisch Gladbach*, 26 Sep. 1996, ECLI: EU:C:1996:355, para. 21; Case C-167/95, *Linthorst, Pouwels en Scheres v Inspecteur der Belastingdienst/Ondernemingen Roermond*, 6 Mar. 1997, ECLI:EU:C:1997:105, para. 11; *Commission of the European Communities v French Republic*, 25 Jan. 2001, ECLI:EU:C:2001:54, para. 41; Case C-108/00, *SPI*, 15 Mar. 2001, ECLI:EU:C:2001:173, para. 16; Case C-452/03, *RAL (Channel Islands) Ltd and Others*, 12 May 2005, ECLI:EU:C:2005:289, para. 24; Case C-114/05, *Gillan Beach*, 9 Mar. 2006, ECLI:EU:C:2006:169, para. 15; Case C-166/05, *Heger*, 7 Sep. 2006, ECLI:EU:C:2006:533, para. 16; these cases all concerned the relationship of Article 9 (1) and Article 9 (2) of the VAT Directive; as the wording and structure of the place of supply rules did not change significantly with the introduction of the VAT Directive, the CJEU also refers to judgments referring to the VAT Directive to this order for determining the place of supply; *see*, e.g., Case C-453/15, *A and B*, 8 Dec. 2016, ECLI:EU:C:2016:933, para. 18.
404. Case C-327/94, *Dudda v Finanzamt Bergisch Gladbach*, 26 Sep. 1996, ECLI:EU:C:1996:355, para. 21; Case C-167/95, *Linthorst, Pouwels en Scheres v Inspecteur der Belastingdienst/ Ondernemingen Roermond*, 6 Mar. 1997, ECLI:EU:C:1997:105, para. 11; *Commission v France*, 25 Jan. 2001, ECLI:EU:C:2001:54, para. 41; Case C-108/00, *SPI*, 15 Mar. 2001, ECLI:EU:C:2001:173, para. 16; Case C-452/03, *RAL (Channel Islands) and Others*, 12 May 2005, ECLI:EU:C:2005:289, para. 24; Case C-114/05, *Gillan Beach*, 9 Mar. 2006, ECLI:EU:C:2006:169, para. 15; Case C-166/05, *Heger*, 7 Sep. 2006, ECLI:EU:C:2006:533, para. 16; Case C-155/12, *RR*

the CJEU implicitly confirms that the particular provisions are *lege speciales* to the general rules. Thus, from a systematic point, Articles 46 and 56 of the VAT Directive are both *lege speciales*. Legal theory also provides an explanation when the *lex specialis* rule does not lead to a result. If the two legal bases to be compared did not include one term being wider and one term being narrower but the terms were overlapping, then a solution would only possible with the help of teleological considerations.[405] In the case at hand, the norms are overlapping since the supply of the service by the platform could qualify as a supply by a disclosed agent as well as an electronically supply. Between Article 46 of the VAT Directive and Article 58 of the VAT Directive, no norm can be identified to be wider or narrower. Therefore, the principle of *lex specialis derogat legi generali* arguably does not help to resolve this conflict.

Finally, given that these principles do not seem to lead to a final conclusion of which article should be applied to services provided by e-commerce platforms, the purpose of the place of supply rules should also be taken into consideration. The final shift of place of supply rules, the disclosed agent scheme, and the electronically supplied service was introduced in the same Directive (2008/8).[406] The goal of the severe amendments of the place of supply rules in the Directive (2008/8) was to generally shift the place of supply away from the origin principle to the destination principle since 'the place of taxation should, in principle, be the place where the actual consumption takes place'.[407] With this purpose in mind, it can be argued that precedence should be given to the application of the place of supply of the electronically supplied service as this application would better guarantee the implementation of the destination principle because the disclosed agent scheme results in some cases of taxation in the country of establishment of the underlying supplier instead of the place of residency of the consumer.[408] Additionally, although the principle of taxation at the place of consumption should be the primary place of taxation, this principle should not impose disproportionate administrative burdens on taxable persons.[409] Also, the limitation of administrative burdens would be one benefit for the application of the place of supply of the electronically supplied service as the taxable person may use the MOSS or the applicable OSS to comply with the EU VAT rules.[410] Lastly, also the

---

Donnelley Global Turnkey Solutions Poland, 27 Jun. 2013, ECLI:EU:C:2013:434, para. 29; Case C-453/15, *A and B*, 8 Dec. 2016, ECLI:EU:C:2016:933, para. 18.

405. *See* Reinhold Zippelius, *Juristische Methodenlehre* 32 (Beck 2012).
406. Within this Council Directive (2008/8), several implementation dates were included. Therefore, the place of supply for the disclosed agents came into force earlier (as of 1 Jan. 2010) than the general shift of the place of supply for consumers concerning electronically supplied services (as of 1 Jan. 2015).
407. *See* preamble pt. 3 of the Directive (2008/8).
408. *See* s. 2.2.5.3.2.2 The Legal Consequence of the Qualification as a Disclosed Agent for the discussion of the difficulty with determining the place of supply when applying the disclosed agent scheme.
409. *See* preamble pt. 6 of the Directive (2008/8).
410. The MOSS system was applicable until 30 Jun. 2021 only for electronically supplied services. As of 1 Jul. 2021, the OSS is applicable to all services supplied from one Member State to another which makes this argument of the limitation of the administrative burden negligible as of 1 Jul. 2021. For further information on the different OSSs, *see* s. 4.11 Special Schemes of the OSS.

simplicity argument brought forward by the CJEU should be taken into consideration when evaluating which place of supply should be applicable for the service of e-commerce platforms to consumers.[411] In the *Inter-Mark Group* case, the CJEU denied the application of one particular place of supply rule as the application of this place of supply rule might have led to taxation of the service in several Member States which 'would risk being excessively complex and would thus jeopardise the reliable and correct charging of VAT'.[412] Similarly, also the application of the place of supply of the disclosed agent scheme might lead to a complex determination of the place of supply as the platform relies on the information provided by the underlying supplier. Adopting the simplicity argument from the CJEU to the decision of whether Article 46 or 58 of the VAT Directive should be applied, the simpler and also legally more certain place of supply would be the application of the electronically supplied service in Article 58 of the VAT Directive. Although the general maxims of the teleological interpretation for resolving norm conflicts may not lead to a definite solution to the question about which place of supply rule may be applicable for providing the platform service to the consumer, other teleological arguments can be found that support the conclusion that the place of supply should be determined based on Article 58 of the VAT Directive.

2.2.5.4 Interim Conclusion

The discussion of services of the e-commerce platform provided to the customer points at two issues which should be taken into consideration. First, the general requirement of consideration to qualify as a taxable transaction within the VAT Directive might be doubted for the service from the platform to its customers (depending on the business model) if no consideration was paid for the service by the customer. In this case, literature suggests that the data provided by the customer for the usage of the service of the e-commerce platform may qualify as consideration in VAT terms. If this should be answered in the affirmative, the determination of the taxable base may cause further issues as it would be difficult to determine the value of the data provided by the customer. As of today, it seems that this is a theoretical question since the national tax authorities have not yet followed the approach in literature to qualify personal data as a consideration.

In the case that consideration is paid, a second difficulty is the determination of the applicable place of supply for the service of the e-commerce platform. If the customer was a non-taxable person, the supply of the platform services may fulfil the requirements of two different, particular place of supply rules: the place of supply for disclosed agents in Article 46 of the VAT Directive and the place of supply for electronically supplied services in Article 58 of the VAT Directive. The VAT Committee tried to solve this conflict of the place of supply rules by denying the applicability of the place of supply rule for disclosed agents as, according to the VAT Committee, an additional requirement of active involvement should be fulfilled for Article 46 of the

411. Case C-530/09, *Inter-Mark Group sp. z o.o. sp. komandytowa v Minister Finansów*, 27 Oct. 2011, ECLI:EU:C:2011:697, para. 26.
412. *Ibid.*

VAT Directive to apply. As this additional requirement, though, is not provided in the law and cannot be interpreted from Article 46 of the VAT Directive, the platform service fulfils the requirement of two different particular place of supply provisions. This potential conflict of norms should be resolved by interpretation. The teleological interpretation may lead to the result that the place of supply of electronically supplied services may prevail over the services provided by e-commerce platforms to their final consumers. After all, this qualification would implement the principle of taxation at the place of consumption as, according to Article 58 of the VAT Directive, the place of supply for electronically supplied services is the place of establishment of the consumer.

2.2.6 Conclusion

The VAT treatment of platforms based on the described rules before the introduction of the VAT e-commerce package led to legal uncertainty and open questions. The first legal question concerns observations regarding what kind of supplies are offered and whether the supply of the good by the underlying supplier and the intermediation service by the platform qualify as one composite supply.[413] The second legal question discussed whether the undisclosed agent scheme is applicable.[414] As the affirmation of one of these two observations would influence the VAT chain of supplies, the separate legal analysis for each supply between the three parties involved can only be carried out if these two observations were negated. The undertaken legal analysis has shown that, in many cases, the applicability of the composite supply rule as well as the undisclosed agent scheme must be denied.

A further legal analysis raises many questions since each specific supply in the platform system can be subject to several legal outcomes.[415] Throughout the legal analysis of the different supplies, it can be seen that especially the place of supply rules often lead to legal uncertainty even though the determination of the place of supply is of utmost importance as, according to these rules, the Member States execute their taxation rights. In the case of legal uncertainty concerning the place of supply rules, the different interpretations by the Member States may result in double (non-)taxation. As the CJEU has not yet had a chance to take its stand on the qualification of the supplies through platforms, digital platforms as well as the underlying suppliers have faced legal uncertainties throughout the last years. This legal uncertainty is enhanced by the fact that the legal qualification may depend on contracts and especially on the set-up and publicly available information on the platform. Therefore, an abstract legal qualification for sales through e-commerce platforms is impossible.

---

413. *See* the extensive discussions in s. 2.2.2.1 The Supply Through Platforms: A Composite Supply?.
414. *See* the extensive discussions in s. 2.2.2.2 The Supply Through Platforms: A Supply Through an Undisclosed Agent?.
415. *See* the extensive discussions in s. 2.2.3 The Supply of Goods from the Underlying Supplier to the Customer, s. 2.2.4 The Supply of the Platform Service to the Underlying Supplier and s. 2.2.5 The Supply of the Platform Service to the Customer.

These legal uncertainties are caused by the fact that the European VAT system was introduced for a 'brick and mortar' economy and, since its introduction, only partial legal reforms were implemented to conquer the legal uncertainties evolving from the rapid developments in the digital economy. This shortcoming of the EU VAT system has been recognised by the EU and led to the introduction of the e-commerce package. Although the introduction of Article 14a of the VAT Directive has a fundamental influence on some of the legal consequences discussed, Article 14a of the VAT Directive would only be applicable if specific requirements were fulfilled.[416] Therefore, it must be borne in mind that the VAT rules applicable before the introduction of the VAT e-commerce package are still applicable to supplies of goods through platforms that do not fall into the (rather limited) scope of Article 14a of the VAT Directive. As exposed, the determination of the correct VAT treatment of such supplies is difficult. This difficulty has led the European Commission to announce that a legislative proposal will be published in the future that will also cover other supplies through platforms.[417] This proposal should lead to more legal certainty and clarity for the parties involved.

2.3 THE OECD PROPOSAL AND THE EU E-COMMERCE PACKAGE

2.3.1 The OECD Proposal for the Treatment of Platforms

2.3.1.1 *A Historic Journey on the Development of the OECD Approach on the Platform Economy and VAT*

2.3.1.1.1 *From 1998 until 2017: The Establishment of the Principle of Destination*

The first brick of the evolution of the discussion on platforms and VAT was set as early as 1998 when the ministerial meeting on electronic commerce took place in Ottawa. The OECD recognised early that e-commerce and, in general, the rapid evolvement of the Internet poses taxation questions and therefore agreed on defining five leading principles that should apply to the taxation of e-commerce:

(i) the principle of neutrality: the equal and neutral treatment of e-commerce and traditional commerce and the similar taxation of taxpayers in similar situations carrying out similar transactions;
(ii) the principle of efficiency: the minimisation of compliance costs;

---

416. For the scope of Article 14a of the VAT Directive, *see* s. 4 Legal Consequences of the Applicability of Article 14a of the VAT Directive.
417. European Commission, *Communication from the Commission to the European Parliament and the Council an Action Plan for Fair and Simple Taxation Supporting the Recovery Strategy*, COM/2020/312 final, *supra* note 31, at 15.

(iii) the principles of certainty and simplicity: simple and clear taxation rules make the understanding of taxpayers' obligations easier to anticipate and therefore lead to legal certainty;

(iv) the principles of effectiveness and fairness: taxation systems should minimise tax evasion and avoidance but, at the same time, tax persons with the right amount at the right time;

(v) the principle of flexibility: due to the rapid technological and commercial development, taxation systems should be drafted to be dynamic and flexible in order to be able to adapt to these rapid changes.[418]

Additionally to these five leading principles, the OECD also identified challenges in the implementation of these broad principles. Within these challenges, the OECD explicitly referred to issues on the implementation of consumption taxes and emphasised that digital products should not be qualified as a supply of goods.[419] Moreover, the implementation of the principle of destination according to which taxation should result in the jurisdiction where consumption takes place should be given preference.[420] For the implementation of the principle of destination and the collection of the VAT/GST thereof, countries should consider reverse-charge, self-assessment, or similar mechanisms with the goal, on the one hand, to secure the revenue base and, on the other hand, secure the competitiveness with domestic suppliers.[421] Similarly, also the collection of tax upon importation should be secured and be in line with the systems developed by the WCO.[422] Lastly, the OECD also presented a post-Ottawa agenda process with further guidance for national tax authorities on how to implement the established principles and overcome the defined challenges.[423]

Based on the work of the OECD Ottawa Conference and the therein developed principles, the OECD adopted 'Guidelines on the Definition of the Place of Consumption' in 2001.[424] In the same year, a follow-up report on the implementation of the Ottawa Taxation Framework Conditions was published with an evaluation on the

---

418. OECD, *Electronic Commerce: Taxation Framework Conditions* 4 (1998), https://www.oecd.org/ctp/consumption/1923256.pdf (last visited 9 Dec. 2020); *see* also, for detailed overview on the developments of the OECD approach to the treatment of platforms and VAT: Valentin Bendlinger & Thomas Ecker, *Die Rolle von Plattformen im E-Commerce – Plattformen und ihre umsatzsteuerlichen Pflichten, in Neuerungen bei innergemeinschaftlichen Umsätzen* 172 et seqq. (Markus Achatz et al. eds., Linde Verlag 2020).
419. OECD, *Electronic Commerce: Taxation Framework Conditions, supra* note 418, at 5.
420. *Ibid.*
421. *Ibid.*
422. *Ibid.*
423. *Ibid.* at 6 et seq.
424. OECD, *Consumption Taxation of Cross-Border Services and Intangible Property in the Context of E-Commerce* (1 Feb. 2001), https://www.oecd.org/tax/consumption/2001%20E-Commerce%20Guidelines.pdf (last visited 10 Dec. 2020); OECD, *Taxation and Electronic Commerce: Implementing the Ottawa Taxation Framework Conditions* (1 Jun. 2001), https://www.oecd.org/tax/consumption/Taxation%20and%20eCommerce%202001.pdf (last visited 10 Dec. 2020); in the Appendix I at pp. 44 et seq., the 'Guidelines on the Definition of the Place of Consumption' were included and, at this point, the guidelines were also supplemented by 'Recommended Approaches to the Practical Application of the Guidelines', *see* at pp. 46 et seq.

implementation of the established principles.[425] Throughout this evaluation process, working parties were introduced to evaluate the progress of implementation on each specific tax area.[426] The working party on consumption taxes with a specially introduced subgroup on e-commerce identified two main problematic aspects, i.e., the definition of the place of consumption[427] and the collection mechanism options.[428] Although with B2B supplies, the self-assessment or reverse-charge mechanisms are quite established, the OECD also emphasised that this is not an effective collection mechanism for B2C transactions.[429] Within the evaluation of the collection mechanism options, the option of including intermediaries for digital supplies was brought forward for the first time.[430] The extensive work following the 2001 report was supported by a series of papers by the OECD Committee on Fiscal Affairs, the so-called Consumption Tax Guidance Series. This series was represented by three different papers, with each discussing one aspect of consumption taxation in relation to e-commerce.[431] Additionally, a second follow-up report was published in 2003 in which the OECD first explicitly recognised that the different approaches of the different jurisdictions on taxation of cross-border services and intangibles may lead to a potential for double taxation and unintentional non-taxation.[432]

---

425. OECD, *Taxation and Electronic Commerce: Implementing the Ottawa Taxation Framework Conditions*, supra note 424.
426. *See* especially the reports by the working parties on consumption taxes: Consumption Tax TAG (Technical Advisory Group), *Report by the Consumption Tax Technical Advisory Group (TAG)* (Dec. 2000), http://www.oecd.org/ctp/consumption/1923240.pdf (last visited 11 Dec. 2020); Technology TAG (Technical Advisory Group), *Report by the Technology Technical Advisory Group (TAG)* (Dec. 2000), http://www.oecd.org/ctp/consumption/1923248.pdf (last visited 11 Dec. 2020); Committee on Fiscal Affairs' Working Party No. 9 on Consumption Taxes, *Consumption Tax Aspects of Electronic Commerce* (Feb. 2001), http://www.oecd.org/ctp/consumption/2673667.pdf (last visited 11 Dec. 2020); for a full list of all reports and technical papers by the working groups covering international direct tax issues, consumption tax issues and tax administration issues, *see* OECD, *Taxation Aspects of Electronic Commerce: Publication of Reports and Technical Papers*, http://www.oecd.org/ctp/treaties/ecommercereportsand technicalpapers.htm (last visited 11 Dec. 2020).
427. *See* OECD, *Taxation and Electronic Commerce: Implementing the Ottawa Taxation Framework Conditions*, supra note 424, at 20 for a summary of the analysis and at pp. 24 et seqq. for the full analysis.
428. *See ibid.* at 20 et seq. for a summary of the analysis and at pp. 29 et seqq. for the full analysis.
429. *Ibid.* at 30.
430. *Ibid.* at 32; *see* also Peter Jenkins, *VAT and Electronic Commerce: The Challenges and Opportunities*, 10 International VAT Monitor 5 (1999), who discussed the option to involve banks as VAT withholding intermediaries; *see* similarly the discussion on the extension of the real-time VAT system with the inclusion of financial institutions and payment service providers by Charles Jennings, *The EU VAT System – Time for a New Approach?*, 21 International VAT Monitor 258 (2010).
431. *See* paper no. 1 OECD, *Electronic Commerce – Commentary on Place of Consumption for Business-to-Business Supplies (Business Presence)* (1 Aug. 2003), https://www.oecd.org/ctp/consumption/5592717.pdf (last visited 10 Dec. 2020); *see* paper no. 2 OECD, *Electronic Commerce: Simplified Registration Guidance* (1 Aug. 2003), https://www.oecd.org/ctp/consumption/5590980.pdf (last visited 10 Dec. 2020); *see* paper no. 3 OECD, *Electronic Commerce: Verification of Customer Status and Jurisdiction* (1 Aug. 2003), https://www.oecd.org/ctp/consumption/5574687.pdf (last visited 10 Dec. 2020).
432. OECD, *Implementation of the Ottawa Taxation Framework*, para. 40 (2003), https://www.google.com/url?sa = t&rct = j&q = &esrc = s&source = web&cd = &ved = 2ahUKEwit9q716In5Ah XBDuwKHWD6DG0QFnoECAkQAQ&url = https%3A%2F%2Fwww.oecd.org%2Ftax%2Fad

The follow-up work of the OECD concentrated on the potential double taxation and unintentional non-taxation, which was further evaluated in another report by the OECD in 2004.[433] Within this report, the OECD set the goal to develop a set of framework principles for the application of consumption tax to internationally traded services and intangibles.[434] The ultimate aim of the development of these principles was to develop a 'model framework for applying consumption taxes to international services and intangibles'.[435] The first draft of these principles was published in 2005.[436]

In 2006, the OECD pushed forward the development of international VAT/GST guidelines.[437] The first consultation paper for the preparatory work on the international VAT/GST guidelines yet again focused on the fundamental concepts of applying VAT/GST to cross-border supplies of services and intangibles.[438] In this consultation process, all parties that submitted a comment on the consultation agreed that the destination principle is the preferred place of taxation.[439] In a second consultation paper, examples of complex cross-border transactions were provided.[440] The work throughout these consultations resulted in the first draft of a chapter on the application

---

ministration%2F20499630.pdf&usg=AOvVaw1tqBhIEJI7lj7U8Yb0HzMe (last visited 9 Dec. 2020); these issues were especially pointed out in a report by the Consumption Tax Technical Advisory Group (a Technical Advisory Group consisted of representatives from OECD governments, non-OECD governments and businesses), see OECD, *Implementation Issues for Taxation of Electronic Commerce* (2003), http://www.oecd.org/tax/consumption/5594899.pdf (last visited 11 Dec. 2020).

433. OECD, *Report on the Application of Consumption Taxes to the Trade in International Services and Intangibles* (30 Jun. 2004), http://www.oecd.org/ctp/consumption/2004%20Report.pdf (last visited 11 Dec. 2020).

434. *Ibid.* para. 54.

435. *Ibid.* para. 56.

436. OECD, *The Application of Consumption Taxes to the International Trade in Services and Intangibles – Progress Report and Draft Principles* (30 Jan. 2005), http://www.oecd.org/ctp/consumption/Application%20of%20Consumption%20Taxes%20Progress%20Report%202005.pdf (last visited 11 Dec. 2020).

437. OECD, *International VAT/GST Guidelines* (OECD 2006), http://www.oecd.org/ctp/consumption/36177871.pdf (last visited 11 Dec. 2020); see also the explanation on the VAT/GST Guidelines in OECD, *What Are the OECD International VAT/GST Guidelines?* 3 (Dec. 2010), https://www.internationaltaxreview.com/pdfs/48077011_OECD.pdf (last visited 11 Dec. 2020), where it is explicitly stated that the aim of the introduction of the VAT/GST guidelines is to provide guidance for governments on VAT in general on cross-border trade not only limited to services and intangible property as 'it became increasingly clear that many of the problems surrounding the application of VAT to electronic commerce actually had their roots in the wider area of services and intangibles and that the remaining differences of approaches amongst jurisdictions still had the potential for double taxation and unintended non-taxation'.

438. OECD, *Applying VAT/GST to Cross-Border Trade in Services and Intangibles – Emerging Concepts for Defining Place of Taxation* (Jan. 2008), http://www.oecd.org/ctp/consumption/39874228.pdf (last visited 14 Dec. 2020).

439. OECD, *Applying VAT/GST to Cross-Border Trade in Services and Intangibles – Emerging Concepts for Defining Place of Taxation – Outcome of the First Consultation Document* (Jun. 2008), http://www.oecd.org/ctp/consumption/40931170.pdf (last visited 14 Dec. 2020).

440. OECD, *Applying VAT/GST to Cross-Border Trade in Services and Intangibles Emerging – Concepts for Defining Place of Taxation – Second Consultation Document* (Jun. 2008), http://www.oecd.org/ctp/consumption/40931469.pdf (last visited 14 Dec. 2020).

of VAT/GST on international trade in services and intangibles in the year 2010.[441] After the publication of a first full draft of the VAT/GST Guidelines,[442] a follow-up discussion draft extending the guidelines by two elements was published in the year 2014.[443] These two new elements introduced common principles for the place of B2C supplies of services and intangibles and supporting provisions on how to apply the guidelines in practice.[444] The background for these additional discussion drafts was the publication of the Report on Tax Challenges of the Digital Economy which was prepared within the work of Action 1 of the BEPS Action Plan.[445] The report highlighted the following:

> The collection of VAT in business-to-consumer transactions is a pressing issue that needs to be addressed urgently to protect tax revenue and to level the playing field between foreign suppliers relative to domestic suppliers. Work initiated in this area by the Working Party No. 9 of the OECD Committee on Fiscal Affairs (CFA) shall be completed by the end of 2015, with the Associates in the BEPS Project participating on an equal footing with the OECD member countries, the OECD published the final package of the VAT/GST Guidelines in 2015.[446]

In the final BEPS Action 1 report, also some remarks on VAT issues were included although the report focuses on direct taxation issues of the digital economy.[447] The VAT focus of the Action 1 on VAT in the digital economy was, on the one hand,

---

441. OECD, 'OECD International VAT/GST Guidelines' – 'International Trade in Services and Intangibles' – 'Public Consultation on Draft Guideline for Customer Location' (5 Feb. 2010), http://www.oecd.org/ctp/consumption/44559751.pdf (last visited 14 Dec. 2020).

442. OECD, OECD International VAT/GST Guidelines – Draft Consolidated Version (4 Feb. 2013), http://www.oecd.org/ctp/consumption/ConsolidatedGuidelines20130131.pdf (last visited 14 Dec. 2020).

443. OECD, Discussion Drafts for Public Consultation – International VAT/GST Guidelines – Guidelines on Place of Taxation for Business-to-Consumer – Supplies Of Services and Intangibles – Provisions on Supporting the Guidelines in Practice (18 Dec. 2014), http://www.oecd.org/ctp/consumption/discussion-draft-oecd-international-vat-gst-guidelines.pdf (last visited 14 Dec. 2020); see also the comments on this draft in OECD, Comments Received on Public Discussion Drafts – International VAT/GST Guidelines – Guidelines on Place of Taxation for Business-to-Consumer – Supplies Of Services and Intangibles – Provisions on Supporting the Guidelines in Practice (24 Feb. 2015), http://www.oecd.org/ctp/consumption/03_public-comments-oecd-international-vat-gst-guidelines.pdf (last visited 14 Dec. 2020).

444. OECD, Discussion Drafts for Public Consultation – International VAT/GST Guidelines – Guidelines on Place of Taxation for Business-to-Consumer – Supplies Of Services and Intangibles – Provisions on Supporting the Guidelines in Practice, supra note 443, at 1.

445. OECD, Addressing the Tax Challenges of the Digital Economy – Action 1: 2014 Deliverable (16 Sep. 2014), https://www.oecd-ilibrary.org/docserver/9789264218789-en.pdf?expires = 16079 58732&id = id&accname = ocid177428&checksum = 423372A2CBDB637C4C9A73CC98C1C158 (last visited 14 Dec. 2020); see also the interim report on tax challenges arising from the digital economy which was published in 2018 and evaluated the more recent developments since the publishing of the BEPS Action 1 Final Report from 2015: OECD, Tax Challenges Arising from Digitalisation – Interim Report 2018: Inclusive Framework on BEPS (16 Mar. 2018), https:// www.oecd-ilibrary.org/docserver/9789264293083-en.pdf?expires = 1607599389&id = id&acc name = ocid177428&checksum = 746FC4D50D4B18C97728007D9A84ED5A (last visited 9 Dec. 2020).

446. OECD, Addressing the Tax Challenges of the Digital Economy – Action 1: 2014 Deliverable, supra note 445, at 19 + 159.

447. OECD, Addressing the Tax Challenges of the Digital Economy – Action 1: 2015 Final Report (OECD 5 Oct. 2015), https://www.oecd-ilibrary.org/docserver/9789264241046-en.pdf?expires = 1609863677&id = id&accname = ocid177428&checksum = 0C5F41CC3B2246D3954E6E701F CA6036 (last visited 14 Dec. 2020).

analysing the exemptions and collection options for imports on low-value goods.[448] Due to the increasing online orders of consumers, VAT exemptions on small consignments have resulted in decreased VAT revenues and in competitive advantages for e-commerce stores that may use the VAT exemption on small consignments, whereas traditional sellers have to charge the VAT on their supplies.[449] Therefore, the small-consignment exemption was seen increasingly controversial.[450] Additionally, the OECD presented potential models for the effective collection of import VAT (not customs duties) with explanations of the advantages and disadvantages: the traditional model (the VAT assessment on the border for each consignment),[451] the purchaser collection model,[452] the vendor collection model[453] and the intermediary collection model.[454] On the other hand, the report discusses (remotely delivered) digital B2C supplies and the VAT collection possibilities thereof.[455] The report emphasises the difficulty of making foreign suppliers compliant with national VAT regulations[456] and refers to the collection of the VAT, in this case, to the OECD work on the International VAT/GST Guidelines that were finalised in 2015.[457]

2.3.1.1.2   The Effective Collection of VAT/GST for Digital Services

In 2017, the report 'Mechanisms for the Effective Collection of VAT/GST' was published with the aim to provide recommendations for the collection of cross-border supplies of services and intangibles as suggested in the International VAT/GST Guidelines and in the BEPS Action 1 report.[458] In this report, the destination principle was emphasised again as being the preferred place of taxation,[459] but the report also recognises the difficulty of VAT/GST collection for the supply of services and intangibles when the supplier is a foreign supplier.[460] Whereas supplies of goods physically

---

448. *Ibid.* paras. 310 et seqq. + 322 et seqq.
449. *Ibid.* para. 312.
450. *Ibid.* para. 313.
451. *Ibid.* paras. 326 et seq.
452. *Ibid.* para. 328.
453. *Ibid.* para. 329.
454. *Ibid.* para. 330; with this approach, the OECD explores the possibility of taking into account different intermediaries: postal operators, express carriers, transparent e-commerce platforms, and financial intermediaries.
455. *Ibid.* paras. 314 et seqq. + 335 et seqq.
456. *Ibid.* paras. 317 et seqq.
457. *Ibid.* paras. 335 et seqq.; with reference to OECD, *International VAT/GST Guidelines* (6 Nov. 2015), http://www.oecd.org/ctp/consumption/international-vat-gst-guidelines.pdf (last visited 15 Dec. 2020); *see* also the finalised version in which the Recommendation on the Application of VAT/GST to the International Trade in Services and Intangibles was incorporated into OECD, *International VAT/GST Guidelines* (12 Apr. 2017), https://www.oecd-ilibrary.org/docserver/9789264271401-en.pdf?expires = 1608027058&id = id&accname = ocid177428 &checksum = ACC8441220D1C5B76D60F686C4AA7057 (last visited 9 Dec. 2020).
458. OECD, *Mechanisms for the Effective Collection of VAT/GST When the Supplier Is Not Located in the Jurisdiction of Taxation*, ch. Foreword (2017), http://www.oecd.org/tax/tax-policy/mechanisms-for-the-effective-collection-of-VAT-GST.pdf (last visited 9 Dec. 2020).
459. *Ibid.* para. 13.
460. *Ibid.* para. 26.

cross borders, which facilitated the charging of import VAT and customs duties,[461] the effective collection of VAT on (digital) services cannot be guaranteed by border controls.[462] Therefore, the report highlights possible collection models for the supply of services and intangibles when the supplier is not established in the state of the customer: the collection by the supplier, by the customer, or by the intermediary.[463]

Within these collection models, the OECD recommends the customer collection for B2B supplies which would likely be implemented through a reverse-charge mechanism.[464] For B2C supplies, though, the supplier collection model is the preferred collection method. This collection model should be implemented with a simplified registration and compliance regime to facilitate the supplier's compliance obligations.[465] In addition, the involvement of intermediaries in the collection process is also presented. The OECD does not provide any guidance about who could qualify as an intermediary, but digital platforms are explicitly mentioned in the report as possible intermediaries.[466] The OECD, in the report, distinguishes between two possible approaches to involve intermediaries: the contractual and the deemed supplier approach.[467]

On the one hand, the contractual approach is, as the name already suggests, based on a legal contract between the parties involved, i.e., between the underlying supplier and the digital platform.[468] In this contract, the parties would agree that the platform fulfils the supplier's legal compliance obligations; additionally, the tax authorities would accept the fulfilment of the supplier's compliance obligations by the platform.[469] The OECD emphasised that this contractual approach will only be possible when all necessary information is available to the platform for fulfilling the underlying supplier's compliance obligations.[470] This procurement of the necessary information may be difficult in the case of long distribution chains when multiple suppliers and platforms that are established in different jurisdictions are involved as the underlying contracts between the different parties involved may lead to contradictions.[471]

On the other hand, the OECD suggests a deemed supplier approach according to which the intermediary is deemed to become part of the supply chain for VAT purposes

---

461. *Ibid.* para. 25.
462. *Ibid.* para. 26.
463. *Ibid.* para. 27; these models are reminiscent of the already established collection models for the abolishment of the small-consignment relief in the BEPS Action 1 report, *see* OECD, *Addressing the Tax Challenges of the Digital Economy – Action 1: 2015 Final Report, supra* note 447, paras. 326 et seq.; additionally the OECD also explores the possibility of making use of automated systems in the future but recognises that the technology-based systems are, at the moment of the publication of the report, a facilitation tool for tax collection rather than a full tax collection mechanism by itself; *see* OECD, *Mechanisms for the Effective Collection of VAT/GST When the Supplier Is Not Located in the Jurisdiction of Taxation, supra* note 458, para. 69.
464. OECD, *Mechanisms for the Effective Collection of VAT/GST When the Supplier Is Not Located in the Jurisdiction of Taxation, supra* note 458, paras. 46 et seq.
465. *Ibid.* paras. 33 et seqq.
466. *Ibid.* para. 67.
467. *Ibid.* para. 63.
468. *Ibid.* para. 64.
469. *Ibid.*
470. *Ibid.*
471. *Ibid.* para. 65.

and, therefore, the intermediary is treated fictitiously as the supplier who must legally fulfil the compliance obligations.[472] With this method, the OECD emphasises that only intermediaries who have the corresponding information on the supply can become part of the supply chain, i.e., payment processors, or 'technical intermediaries that only make internet capacity available for carrying content'[473] should be excluded from the deemed supplier approach.[474] As the VAT collection for services sold through intermediaries would be centralised at the intermediaries, the VAT would be collected from fewer suppliers.[475] This also makes the monitoring by the tax authorities easier.[476] Additionally, the report highlights that the intermediaries often have greater capacity and better access to the necessary information for fulfilling the compliance obligations compared to suppliers with little turnover.[477] Although the OECD does not define the term 'intermediary', with this explicit reference to intermediaries having greater capacity available, it seems that the OECD had big digital platforms in mind.[478] The tax authorities as well as businesses have claimed to need further guidance on the potential collection models on online sales; therefore, the report also announced the publishing of a follow-up report on this issue.[479]

2.3.1.2 *The OECD Report on the Role of Digital Platforms in the Collection of VAT/GST on Online Sales*

2.3.1.2.1 *The Inclusion of Intermediaries in the VAT/GST Collection on Online Supplies*

The announced report was published in March 2019 and provides extensive suggestions on how to involve digital platforms in the VAT/GST collection.[480] The report intends to summarise and describe different options on how platforms can be integrated in the collection of the VAT/GST.[481] The background for the urgency of general guidance on the inclusion of intermediaries in the VAT/GST collection was that approximately 57% of online supplies through platforms are supplied by one of the

---

472. *Ibid.* para. 66.
473. *Ibid.*
474. *Ibid.*
475. *Ibid.* para. 67.
476. *Ibid.*
477. *Ibid.*
478. *See* Valentin Bendlinger & Thomas Ecker, *Die Rolle von Plattformen im E-Commerce – Plattformen und ihre umsatzsteuerlichen Pflichten, in Neuerungen bei innergemeinschaftlichen Umsätzen, supra* note 418, at 176; the authors also emphasise that the 'big players' in the platform industry would try to be tax compliant for reputational reasons. Therefore, the VAT collection might be facilitated by the implementation of a deemed supplier approach.
479. OECD, *Mechanisms for the Effective Collection of VAT/GST When the Supplier Is Not Located in the Jurisdiction of Taxation, supra* note 458, para. 62.
480. OECD, *The Role of Digital Platforms in the Collection of VAT/GST on Online Sales, supra* note 8.
481. *Ibid.* at 6.

three biggest platforms.[482] At the same time, the non-compliance rate for goods ordered via an e-commerce channel and transported from outside the EU to EU customers is estimated to account to 65%.[483] The OECD recognises that the *de minimis* exemption may account to a part of this VAT gap, but the OECD also dissuades the removal of the *de minimis* exemption without the introduction of additional measures.[484] These additional measures aim to make the VAT/GST collection more effective by involving platforms in the VAT/GST collection.[485] At the same time, the OECD emphasises that any involvement of the platform in the VAT/GST collection 'should notably be considered in light of effectiveness, efficiency and proportionality and the neutrality principles as promulgated by the [OECD] Guidelines'.[486]

To show how platforms could potentially be included in the VAT/GST collection, the report is divided into three main chapters. The first content-related chapter[487] is on platform liability regimes with a focus on the full liability regime.[488] The third

---

482. *Ibid.* para. 6; with reference to International Post Corporation, *Cross-Border E-Commerce Shopper Survey 2017*, 4 (Jan. 2018), https://www.ipc.be/-/media/documents/public/markets /2018/ipc-cross-border-e-commerce-shopper-survey2017.pdf?la = en&hash = 7FBBDE2919F1B 56DE05BCC71BE486DE283E807AD (last visited 9 Jan. 2021), please note that, according to the report, the referred share is 56%; *see* also the more recent report from the years following: in 2018 a share of 63% on online purchases were ordered from one out of the four biggest e-retailers (Amazon [23%], Alibaba [16%], eBay [14%] and Wish [10%]); *see* International Post Corporation, *Cross-Border E-Commerce Shopper Survey 2018*, 3 et seq. (Jan. 2019), https://www.ipc.be/-/media/documents/public/markets/2019/ipc-cross-border-e-commerce -shopper-survey2018.pdf (last visited 9 Jan. 2021); in 2019, a share of 70% of online purchases were ordered from one out of the four biggest e-retailers (Amazon [25%], Alibaba [20%], eBay [14%] and Wish [11%]); *see* International Post Corporation, *Cross-Border E-Commerce Shopper Survey 2019*, 3 (Jan. 2020), https://www.ipc.be/-/media/documents/public/publications/ipc -shoppers-survey/ipc-cross-border-e-commerce-survey-2019.pdf (last visited 27 Oct. 2021); in 2020, a share of 65% of online purchases were ordered from one out of the four biggest e-retailers (Amazon [26%], AliExpress [19%], eBay [11%] and Wish [9%]); *see* International Post Corporation, *Cross-Border E-Commerce Shopper Survey 2020*, 13 (Jan. 2021), https://www.ipc.be/-/media/documents/public/publications/ipc-shoppers-survey/ipc-cross- border-e-commerce-shopper-survey-2020.pdf (last visited 27 Oct. 2021); in 2021, a share of 62% of online purchases were ordered from one out of the four biggest e-retailers (Amazon [26%], AliExpress [19%], eBay [10%] and Wish [7%]); *see* International Post Corporation, *Cross-Border E-Commerce Shopper Survey 2021*, 12 (Jan. 2022), https://www.ipc.be/-/media/ documents/public/publications/ipc-shoppers-survey/ipc-cross-border-e-commerce-shopper- survey-2021.pdf?la = en&hash = 9303A77CD5B246A6384BE2D1B32BA3F725438985 (last vis-ited 1 Apr. 2022).

483. OECD, *The Role of Digital Platforms in the Collection of VAT/GST on Online Sales*, *supra* note 8, para. 12; with reference to the report by Copenhagen Economics, *see* Bruno Basalisco et al., *E-Commerce Imports into Europe: VAT and Customs Treatment* 6 (4 May 2016), https://www .copenhageneconomics.com/dyn/resources/Publication/publicationPDF/8/348/1462798608 /e-commerce-imports-into-europe_vat-and-customs-treatment.pdf (last visited 9 Jan. 2021); according to this report the VAT loss due to the 65% non-compliance amounts to EUR 1.05 billion.

484. OECD, *The Role of Digital Platforms in the Collection of VAT/GST on Online Sales*, *supra* note 8, paras. 12 et seq.

485. *Ibid.* para. 13.

486. *Ibid.* para. 19.

487. *Ibid.* paras. 31 et seqq.

488. For further discussion on the content of this chapter, *see* s. 2.3.1.2.2 The Platform Becoming Liable for VAT/GST: Platforms' Liability Regimes.

chapter[489] explains possibilities for other involvement of platforms in the VAT/GST collection.[490] The final chapter[491] returns to the discussion on the liability regime, thereby focusing on the joint liability regime and on providing further explanation on supporting measures for the tax authorities in the case that any of the presented possibilities to involve platforms in the VAT/GST collection is nationally implemented.[492]

The OECD emphasises that the report aims to support tax authorities by explaining possible measures to include platforms in the VAT/GST collection with a particular focus on sales that involve the importation of goods[493] but should not be seen as detailed guidelines for national legislators as national legislators are sovereign in the design of their national laws.[494] At the same time, though, the OECD recognises that '[i]nternational consistency will facilitate compliance, lower compliance costs and administrative burdens, and improve the effectiveness of VAT/GST collection'.[495] Therefore, the OECD does not define 'digital platforms' but rather provides a general description of digital platforms:

> [Digital Platforms] can generally be described as the platforms that enable, by electronic means, direct interactions between two or more customers or participant groups (typically buyers and sellers) with two key characteristics: (i) each group of participants ('side') are customers of the platforms in some meaningful way, and (ii) the platform enables a direct interaction between the sides. These platforms are also known as multi-sided platforms.[496]

Moreover, it has been emphasised that platforms in the sharing economy sector were analysed in a separate work stream[497] that was published in April 2021.[498] The explicit exclusion of sharing economy platforms is due to two significant differences compared to e-commerce platforms offering goods. First, the underlying suppliers offering their services via sharing economy platforms are often situated in the

---

489. OECD, *The Role of Digital Platforms in the Collection of VAT/GST on Online Sales*, *supra* note 8, paras. 114 et seqq.
490. For further discussion on the content of this section, *see* s. 2.3.1.2.3 Other Roles for Platforms in the VAT/GST Collection; for the discussion on the platform as a voluntary intermediary *see* s. 2.3.1.2.2 The Platform Becoming Liable for VAT/GST: Platforms' Liability Regimes.
491. OECD, *The Role of Digital Platforms in the Collection of VAT/GST on Online Sales*, *supra* note 8, paras. 155 et seqq.
492. For further discussion on the joint liability regime, *see* s. 2.3.1.2.2 The Platform Becoming Liable for VAT/GST: Platforms' Liability Regimes; the explanation of the supporting measures will not be discussed in any section of this book.
493. OECD, *The Role of Digital Platforms in the Collection of VAT/GST on Online Sales*, *supra* note 8, para. 22.
494. *Ibid.* at 7.
495. *Ibid.*
496. *Ibid.* at 6 + para. 5.
497. *Ibid.* paras. 24 et seqq.; *see also* OECD, *Model Rules for Reporting by Platform Operators with Respect to Sellers in the Sharing and Gig Economy* (2020), http://www.oecd.org/ctp/exchange -of-tax-information/model-rules-for-reporting-by-platform-operators-with-respect-to-sellers-in -the-sharing-and-gig-economy.pdf (last visited 9 Dec. 2020).
498. *See* OECD, *The Impact of the Growth of the Sharing and Gig Economy on VAT/GST Policy and Administration* (19 Apr. 2021), https://read.oecd.org/10.1787/51825505-en?format = pdf (last visited 2 Apr. 2022).

jurisdiction of taxation.[499] Second, sharing economy platforms differ as, in many cases, private persons or entrepreneurs with little turnover are providing the services and, therefore, these underlying suppliers may not fulfil the requirements of being a taxable person.[500] Hence, the OECD concentrates on recommendations for the online supply of goods through platforms and how these platforms can effectively be included in the process for VAT/GST collection.[501]

2.3.1.2.2   The Platform Becoming Liable for VAT/GST: Platforms' Liability Regimes

After these introductory remarks, the second chapter of the OECD report focuses on the possibility of implementing liability regimes on platforms.[502] Thereby, two possibilities are discussed for the introduction of liability regimes, i.e., the full liability regime[503] and other liability regimes, to include platforms in the VAT/GST collection.[504]

Under the full liability regime, the platform would, by law, be included in the transaction of the supply through a platform by acting as the supplier to the customer. The platform would therefore be responsible for complying with the compliance obligations and assessing and remitting the VAT due. The full liability regime would be restricted to the VAT/GST and not influence other relevant legal questions, e.g., obligations due to consumer protection rights such as product liability.[505] The benefit of the full liability regime would, on the one hand, be that tax authorities would face a decrease in taxable persons that have to be monitored; on the other hand, also the costs for the underlying suppliers would be reduced as their VAT/GST obligations would be shifted to the platform.[506] However, the OECD also recognises financial, organisational, and technological burdens that especially platforms with relatively little turnover would face due to the introduction of a full liability regime.[507]

As this burden, though, is not to be underestimated, the OECD report provides further guidance on possibly relevant indicators for designing a full liability regime,

---

499. OECD, *The Role of Digital Platforms in the Collection of VAT/GST on Online Sales, supra* note 8, para. 23; please note that the OECD also recognises that the cross-border element may, in the future, become more relevant for services provided through sharing economy platforms.
500. *Ibid.* para. 25.
501. *Ibid.* paras. 27 et seqq.
502. *Ibid.* paras. 21 et seqq.
503. *Ibid.* paras. 38 et seqq.; *see* also the OECD report from 2017 in which the basis of the content of this 'full liability regime' was already drafted but called the 'deemed supplier approach'; *see* OECD, *Mechanisms for the Effective Collection of VAT/GST When the Supplier Is Not Located in the Jurisdiction of Taxation, supra* note 458, paras. 66 et seqq.
504. OECD, *The Role of Digital Platforms in the Collection of VAT/GST on Online Sales, supra* note 8, paras. 112 et seq. with reference to ch. 3.5 and ch. 4 of the report for further explanations; *see* also the OECD report from 2017 where the voluntary intermediation of platforms was already discussed under the so-called contractual approach *see* OECD, *Mechanisms for the Effective Collection of VAT/GST When the Supplier Is Not Located in the Jurisdiction of Taxation, supra* note 458, paras. 64 et seq.
505. OECD, *The Role of Digital Platforms in the Collection of VAT/GST on Online Sales, supra* note 8, para. 38.
506. *Ibid.* paras 40 + 107.
507. *Ibid.* para. 49.

especially on the functions that digital platforms necessarily need to fulfil for complying with the obligations shifted onto them within the full liability regime.[508] Thereby, the OECD emphasises again that no definition of the term 'platform' is provided due to the potential further evolvement of this term over time.[509] Nevertheless, the OECD recognises two key elements for a platform to become fully liable for the VAT/GST collection. First, as the platform will have to determine the VAT/GST amount, the platform must be able to collect the necessary information for this determination.[510] Second, as the platform must also collect and remit the VAT/GST, the platform must have the means to collect the VAT/GST for this amount.[511] Indirectly, this second requirement refers to the fact that, for the platform to guarantee the collection of VAT/GST from the customer, the platform will have to be involved in the payment process.

Furthermore, the OECD refers to a non-exhaustive list of functions that legislators may consider when implementing a full liability regime (Table 3.1).

Table 3.1   OECD Non-exhaustive List of Platform Functions for the Applicability of the Full VAT/GST Regime[512]

A Non-Exhaustive List of Examples of Functions Considered Relevant for Enlisting Digital Platforms under the Full VAT/GST Liability Regime	
Examples of Functions that May Trigger the Eligibility of Digital Platform for the Full VAT/GST Liability Regime	*Examples of Functions that May Exclude the Digital Platform from Eligibility for the Full VAT/GST Liability Regime*
controlling and/or setting the terms and conditions of the underlying transactions (e.g., price; payment terms; delivery conditions, etc.) and imposing these on participants (buyers, sellers, transporters, etc.);	only carries content (e.g., makes only the Internet network available for carrying content via Wi-Fi, cable, satellite, etc.); or
direct or indirect involvement in the payment processing (either directly or indirectly through arrangements with third parties, collect payments from customers and transmit these payments to sellers less commissions; obtain pre-authorisations or submit payment instructions or information to the platform's own or to a third-party payment platform or to a platform stipulated in the terms and conditions set by platforms);	only processes payments; or

---

508. *Ibid.* paras. 43 et seqq.
509. *Ibid.* para. 43.
510. *Ibid.* para. 45.
511. *Ibid.*
512. *Ibid.* para. 73.

A Non-Exhaustive List of Examples of Functions Considered Relevant for Enlisting Digital Platforms under the Full VAT/GST Liability Regime	
Examples of Functions that May Trigger the Eligibility of Digital Platform for the Full VAT/GST Liability Regime	*Examples of Functions that May Exclude the Digital Platform from Eligibility for the Full VAT/GST Liability Regime*
direct or indirect involvement in the delivery process and/or in the fulfilment of the supply (incl. influencing/controlling the conditions of delivery; sending approval to suppliers and or instructing a third party to commence the delivery; providing order fulfilment services with or without warehousing services);	only advertises offers; or
providing customer support services (returns and/or refunds/assistance with dispute resolution).	only operates as a click-through/shopping referral platform. Such a platform only transfers via software, an Internet link or otherwise a potential customer to the website of a seller, thus enabling the discovery, promotion or listing of goods for sale by a seller. Customer and seller complete the transaction without any direct or indirect involvement of the digital platform in the setting of the terms of the underlying supply or in the payment or delivery process. Where such a platform's fee is, however, calculated on the basis of the final consideration agreed between the customer and the underlying supplier, this may be an indication of an involvement in the underlying transaction that could bring the digital platform within the scope of the regime.

Furthermore, the OECD also evaluates other aspects relevant for the implementation of a full VAT/GST regime.[513] A special focus was put on the supply of goods that are imported from third countries via platforms.[514] The OECD argues that, especially for the importation of low-value goods below the customs' *de minimis* threshold,[515] the

---

513. *Ibid.* paras. 52 et seqq.
514. *Ibid.* paras. 60 et seqq.
515. *See* the stipulation of the *de minimis* standard that is mandatory to be implemented for contracting parties of the Revised Kyoto Convention in WCO, *International Convention on the Simplification and Harmonization of Customs Procedures – Revised Kyoto Convention* (17 Apr. 2008), http://www.wcoomd.org/-/media/wco/public/global/pdf/topics/facilitation/instruments-and-tools/conventions/kyoto-convention/revised-kyoto-convention/body_gen-annex-and-specific-annexes.pdf?la = en (last visited 14 Jan. 2021) Standard 4.13; *see* also the reflection on the principles, among others; also, the *de minimis* threshold due to the steadily increasing amounts of small consignments in WCO, *Guidelines for the Immediate Release of Consignments by Customs* (Jun. 2018), http://www.wcoomd.org/-/media/wco/public/global

full liability regime would support the customs authorities.[516] The customs authorities do not have to intervene in the VAT/GST collection of goods that are below the customs *de minimis* threshold anymore but could use their resources for other key roles since the VAT/GST collection for small consignments ordered through platforms would be secured.[517] Moreover, the OECD also provides further explanations on information needed to operate under the full VAT/GST liability regime,[518] on the collection and payment process[519] and on additional policy design considerations.[520]

Whereas the full liability regime is discussed in great detail in the second chapter of this report, the other liability regimes are only shortly touched upon.[521] The OECD highlights that, in the other liability regimes, the tax authorities would still have to monitor the underlying suppliers because they are still (at least jointly) liable for the VAT.[522] The platform may only become liable under certain circumstances and additionally to the underlying suppliers.[523] The OECD thereby differentiates two variations:

(1) Forward-looking: in the case that the tax authorities find that an underlying supplier is non-compliant, the tax authorities contact the platform and inform the platform about this circumstance.[524] In the case that the platform does not take appropriate action, i.e., securing the compliance or banning the underlying supplier from the platform, the platform may be held jointly liable for the undeclared VAT/GST of the underlying supplier in the future.[525]

(2) Past liability: in the case that the platform should have had a reasonable expectation that the underlying supplier did not fulfil the compliance obligations, the platform may be held jointly liable for the VAT/GST from the past.[526] This approach results in the obligation for platforms to perform due diligence checks on their underlying supplier, the least by reviewing and

---

/pdf/topics/facilitation/instruments-and-tools/tools/immediate-release-guidelines/immedia te-release-guidelines.pdf?db = web (last visited 14 Jan. 2021).

516. OECD, *The Role of Digital Platforms in the Collection of VAT/GST on Online Sales*, *supra* note 8, para. 63.
517. *Ibid.*
518. *Ibid.* paras. 70 et seqq.
519. *Ibid.* paras. 75 et seqq.
520. *Ibid.* paras. 84 et seqq. + 87 et seqq.
521. *Ibid.* paras. 112 et seq. with reference to ch. 3.5 and ch. 4 of the report for further information on the other liability regimes; in literature, it has been argued that the uneven representation of the full liability regime in 73 paragraphs compared to the presentation of the other liability regimes in 2 paragraphs of the second chapter of the OECD report could be interpreted as showing a preference by the OECD for the full liability regime although the report explicitly states that it does not provide any recommendation or preference on any of the presented liability regimes (*see* at para. 34 of the report), *see* Valentin Bendlinger & Thomas Ecker, *Die Rolle von Plattformen im E-Commerce – Plattformen und ihre umsatzsteuerlichen Pflichten*, in *Neuerungen bei innergemeinschaftlichen Umsätzen*, *supra* note 418, at 178 et seq. + 181.
522. OECD, *The Role of Digital Platforms in the Collection of VAT/GST on Online Sales*, *supra* note 8, para. 113.
523. *Ibid.* para. 161.
524. *Ibid.* paras. 163 et seqq.
525. *Ibid.*
526. *Ibid.* paras. 166 et seqq.

verifying the validity of the VAT/GST registration numbers of the underlying suppliers.[527]

Additionally, the OECD explicitly states one possibility to tackle the VAT non-compliance of underlying suppliers who use fulfilment centres for their delivery, i.e., to make the fulfilment centre operators jointly liable for the VAT of goods shipped from their centres.[528] As, in the past, underlying suppliers have often stored goods in third-party fulfilment centres in the destination country to then sell the goods without charging the correct amount of the VAT/GST, fulfilment centres have indirectly supported the fraudulent importation and sale of goods.[529] The OECD recognises, though, that the introduction of a joint liability of fulfilment centre operators may raise proportionality issues within the national law.[530]

Although the joint and several liability variations do not guarantee the securement of the VAT/GST collection, they are instruments that can support the tax authorities with monitoring non-compliant suppliers and may, to some extent, even prevent non-compliant behaviour.[531] Due to the possibility of being held liable for the VAT/GST of the underlying suppliers, platforms have an additional interest that the underlying suppliers who offer goods through the platforms act tax compliant. The OECD, though, also emphasises that the implementation of a joint and several liability variation requires a clear formulation of the criteria in the law under which circumstances the platforms become jointly liable for the VAT/GST to ensure legal certainty.[532] It can be observed that some Member States, e.g., Germany and Austria,[533] have implemented joint liability for platforms if the platform did not become the deemed supplier stipulated in Article 14a of the VAT Directive but was otherwise involved in the supply of goods or services to customers.[534]

2.3.1.2.3   *Other Roles for Platforms in the VAT/GST Collection and Further Supporting Measures for the VAT/GST Collection on Online Sales*

Additionally to the possibility of holding the platform (jointly or directly) liable for the VAT/GST due for the supplies by other taxable persons, the OECD also recognises other roles through which platforms can assist in the VAT/GST collection:[535]

---

527. *Ibid.*
528. *Ibid.* para. 174.
529. *Ibid.* para. 172.
530. *Ibid.* para. 174.
531. *Ibid.* paras 159 + 169.
532. *Ibid.* para. 169.
533. *See* § 25e of the German VAT Act as well as § 27 (1) of the Austrian VAT Act.
534. *See*, for a description of the Austrian joint liability rule and critical discussion, Karoline Spies, *Joint and Several Liability Rules in EU VAT Law*, in *CJEU – Recent Developments in Value Added Tax 2020*, 22 et seqq. (Georg Kofler et al. eds., Linde Verlag 2021).
535. OECD, *The Role of Digital Platforms in the Collection of VAT/GST on Online Sales, supra* note 8, paras. 114 et seqq.

- Information sharing obligations: the platform could be legally obligated to submit (in regular intervals or upon request) information relevant for the tax authorities for the VAT/GST collection.[536] Within the implementation of this obligation, it is important that the law provides a detailed list of which information must be shared[537] and to ensure that platforms have the means to collect the required information.[538]
- Education of the underlying suppliers: especially if underlying suppliers sold their goods in several countries, the different VAT/GST obligations would represent a challenge for them.[539] One option to disseminate the necessary information to underlying suppliers is to introduce an educating obligation to the platform concerning the VAT/GST rules in the specific country to which the underlying supplier is supplying goods.[540]
- Formal cooperation agreements: in this approach, the platform and tax authorities conclude a formal cooperation agreement to exchange information on certain (suspicious) suppliers.[541] Tax authorities as well as platforms may benefit from this agreement as non-compliant underlying suppliers may be identified quickly and necessary steps by the platforms and the tax authorities may be taken.[542] Additionally, the platform may make this cooperation public, so customers and underlying suppliers know that this platform is a 'safe' platform.[543]
- Platforms acting as voluntary intermediaries: if a country decides to implement the voluntary intermediary approach, the basis for this voluntary intermediation would be a contract between the underlying supplier and the platform. This contract could be an explicit agreement, or it could also be a part of the services offered by the platform to its underlying suppliers.[544] The extent of the voluntary involvement of intermediaries could range from the sole support in the calculation of the VAT/GST to the intermediaries taking the full VAT/GST liability.[545] The benefit of this approach for the competent tax authority might be a more efficient and effective VAT/GST collection as only a few platforms would collect or be liable for the VAT/GST compared to thousands of underlying suppliers.[546]

---

536. *Ibid.* paras. 117 et seqq.
537. *See ibid.* at 127 for a suggestion on which information may be relevant for the VAT/GST collection that is likely to be available for platforms.
538. *Ibid.* para. 131.
539. *Ibid.* para. 132.
540. *Ibid.* para. 136.
541. *Ibid.* para. 138.
542. *Ibid.* para. 145.
543. *Ibid.*
544. *Ibid.* para. 154.
545. *Ibid.* para. 147; with reference to OECD, *Mechanisms for the Effective Collection of VAT/GST When the Supplier Is Not Located in the Jurisdiction of Taxation, supra* note 458, paras. 76 et seqq.
546. OECD, *The Role of Digital Platforms in the Collection of VAT/GST on Online Sales, supra* note 8, para. 149.

Whereas the first two chapters had a clear focus on how to include platforms in the VAT/GST collection process, the OECD also explores further possibilities and identifies further measures that tax authorities and legislators should consider for an effective and efficient VAT/GST collection.[547] In this course, the OECD emphasises that the VAT compliance of online sales without the involvement of platforms should not be neglected;[548] a well-working and close cooperation between tax and customs authorities on a domestic level[549] and mutual cooperation and exchange of information on an international level are important.[550] In the final chapters, the OECD highlights the possibility to support the VAT/GST compliance through a risk analysis[551] and reminds that the authorities should remain vigilant against abuse and fraud.[552]

2.3.2 The EU E-Commerce Package for the Treatment of Platforms

2.3.2.1 *A Historic Journey on the Development of the EU Approach on the Platform Economy and VAT*

2.3.2.1.1 *The Early Focus on Electronically Supplied Services and the Implementation of the Principle of Destination*

At the European level, the first discussions on the impact of digitalisation on VAT can be found in the late 1990s. Although, at this point, the Internet was merely used as a tool for information exchange, the Commission was already forward-looking and anticipated that, in the future, the Internet may serve as a digital space through which supplies may be provided. Within the Commission's first communication on the topic of e-commerce and the VAT, the Commission launched a European initiative on electronic commerce with the aim to 'encourage the vigorous growth of electronic commerce in Europe'.[553] Thereby, the Commission highlighted the importance of ensuring a clear and neutral tax environment in order to avoid any market distortion.[554] Furthermore, the Commission also stressed that, although supplies may be provided in a new environment, it is important to secure that the European VAT system remains neutral, simple, and provide for legal certainty.[555] In an interim report following up on

---

547. *Ibid.* paras. 175 et seqq.
548. *Ibid.*
549. *Ibid.* paras. 178 et seqq.
550. *Ibid.* paras. 185 et seqq.
551. *Ibid.* paras. 189 et seqq.
552. *Ibid.* paras. 192 et seq.
553. Commission of the European Communities, *Communication from the Commission to the Council, the European Parliament, the Economic and Social Committee and the Committee of the Regions – A European Initiative in Electronic Commerce*, COM(97) 157 final 1e (18 Apr. 1997), https://eur-lex.europa.eu/legal-content/EN/TXT/PDF/?uri = CELEX:51997DC0157&from = EN (last visited 22 Jan. 2021).
554. *Ibid.* at 19.
555. Commission of the European Communities, *Communication from the Commission to the Council, the European Parliament and the Economic and Social Committee – Electronic Commerce and Indirect Taxation*, COM(1998) 374 final 2 et seq. (17.06.1998), https://eur-lex .europa.eu/legal-content/EN/TXT/PDF/?uri = CELEX:51998DC0374&from = EN (last visited

this book, the European Commission emphasised that, based on the applicable VAT regime at that time, third country suppliers often have a competitive advantage that results in a threat to VAT revenue and also disadvantages European businesses.[556]

Finally, the work of the European Commission led to subsequent legislative adaptions that found an agreement in the Council of the European Union in 2002 and entered into force on 1 July 2003.[557] These changes revolved around amendments to radio and television broadcasting and electronically supplied services and resulted in three revisions of the Sixth VAT Directive: the place of supply for radio and television broadcasting service and electronically supplied services was amended,[558] the introduction of a special registration regime for third country suppliers who provide electronic services in the EU and are neither established nor require a tax registration in the EU,[559] and the introduction of an exemplary list of electronically supplied services in Annex L of the Sixth VAT Directive.[560]

More specifically, the amendments to the place of supply rules resulted in two changes. First, the place of supply of radio and television broadcasting and electronically supplied services to customers (taxable as well as non-taxable persons) established in third countries and to taxable persons established in a Member State other than the service provider was to be the place where the customer was established.[561] Second, when non-taxable persons established in the EU receive electronically supplied services from third country taxable persons, the place of supply would also be the place where the consumer is established.[562] Thereby, the EU implemented the destination principle for electronically supplied services for B2B transactions and for transactions that involve third countries when either the customers or the suppliers are established in a third country.

The background for the implementation of the principle of destination on electronically supplied services in relation to third countries was that the general B2C place of supply rule for services stipulated, at that time, that the place of supply is the

---

22 Jan. 2021); in this Communication, the Commission published six guidelines as a contribution to the Ottawa conference: no new taxes (guideline 1 at pp. 4 et seq.), electronic transmission as services (guideline 2 at p. 5), ensuring neutrality (guideline 3 at pp. 5 et seq.), making compliance easy (guideline 4 at p. 7), ensuring control and enforcement (guideline 5 at pp. 7 et seq.), and facilitating tax administration (guideline 6 at p. 8).

556. European Commission, *Interim Report on the Implications of Electronic Commerce for VAT and Customs*, XXI/98/0359, 7 et seq. (3 Apr. 1998), https://ec.europa.eu/taxation_customs/sites/taxation/files/resources/documents/interim_report_on_electric_commerce_en.pdf (last visited 22 Jan. 2021).

557. *See* Council Directive 2002/38/EC of 7 May 2002 Amending and Amending Temporarily Directive 77/388/EEC as Regards the Value Added Tax Arrangements Applicable to Radio and Television Broadcasting Services and Certain Electronically Supplied Services, OJ L 128/41 (2002); for a discussion on these changes, *see* Luc Hinnekens, *VAT Directive on Electronic Services – Some Open Questions*, 43 European Taxation 279 et seqq. (2003).

558. *See* Article 9 (2) (e) tenth and eleventh indent and Article 9 (2) (f) of the Sixth VAT Directive.

559. *See* especially Article 26c of the Sixth VAT Directive.

560. *See* Annex L of the Sixth VAT Directive. This amendment was further complemented by the introduction of a proper definition of 'electronically supplied services'; *see* Council Regulation (EC) No 1777/2005 of 17 October 2005 Laying down Implementing Measures for Directive 77/388/EEC on the Common System of Value Added Tax, OJ L 288 (2005).

561. *See* Article 9 (2) (e) tenth and eleventh indent of the Sixth VAT Directive.

562. *See* Article 9 (2) (f) of the Sixth VAT Directive.

country where the supplier is established; therefore, the principle of origin was applicable to most services.[563] Due to the fact that electronically supplied services can be supplied from anywhere, even across borders or from third countries, the general B2C place of supply rule may lead to a competitive disadvantage for EU suppliers compared to third country suppliers. Whereas EU suppliers must charge the VAT of the country in which they are established, third country suppliers would charge the same service without the VAT, especially if the third country where the supplier was established has not implemented the principle of origin or has no VAT.[564] With amendments to the place of supply rules towards the principle of destination, the EU tried to abolish this competitive disadvantage for EU suppliers.

Due to this new obligation of third country suppliers to charge the VAT on supplies in the EU, these suppliers would, in general, have to register in all Member States to which they supply the electronic services to fulfil the compliance obligations and remit the VAT due. As this leads to complexity and high compliance costs for suppliers, the EU introduced a special registration scheme with legal amendments effective 1 July 2003. According to this newly introduced simplification scheme, third country suppliers who provide electronic services in the EU and are neither established nor require a tax registration in the EU may register in one Member State, i.e., the Member State of identification.[565] The supplier could fulfil all of the compliance obligations of the different Member States for the supply of electronic services by submitting the VAT return in the Member State of identification by indicating the VAT due and applying the applicable rates of the Member States of destination.[566] Also, the payment was to be transferred to the Member State of identification, and this Member State would then forward the VAT to the Member States where the electronic supplies were actually supplied. In this sense, the predecessor version of the MOSS was introduced in 2003 for third country suppliers.

With a second reform adopted in 2008, further changes were implemented concerning electronically supplied services.[567] Although the legal changes were already

---

563. *See* Article 9 (1) of the Sixth VAT Directive; also today, the principle of origin is the general rule for B2C supplies; *see* Article 45 of the VAT Directive.

564. Economic and Social Committee, *Opinion of the Economic and Social Committee on the Proposal for a Regulation of the European Parliament and of the Council Amending Regulation (EEC) No 218/92 on Administrative Cooperation in the Field of Indirect Taxation (VAT), and the Proposal for a Council Directive Amending Directive No 77/388/EEC as Regards the Value Added Tax Arrangements Applicable to Certain Services Supplied by Electronic Means*, OJ C 116, s. 2.1.3. (20 Apr. 2001), https://eur-lex.europa.eu/legal-content/EN/TXT/PDF/?uri = CELEX:52 000AE1413&from = DE (last visited 23 Jan. 2021); *see* also recital 1 of the Council Directive 2002/38/EC of 7 May 2002 Amending and Amending Temporarily Directive 77/388/EEC as Regards the Value Added Tax Arrangements Applicable to Radio and Television Broadcasting Services and Certain Electronically Supplied Services, OJ L 128/41 (2002).

565. *See* the detailed legal basis for this special scheme in Article 26c of the Sixth VAT Directive.

566. *See* especially Article 26c (5) of the Sixth VAT Directive.

567. Council Directive 2008/8/EC of 12 February 2008 Amending Directive 2006/112/EC as Regards the Place of Supply of Services, OJ L 44/11 (2008); *see* also Council Implementing Regulation (EU) No 282/2011 of 15 March 2011 Laying down Implementing Measures for Directive 2006/112/EC on the Common System of Value Added Tax, OJ L 77/1 (2011); Council Implementing Regulation (EU) No 1042/2013 of 7 October 2013 Amending Implementing Regulation (EU) No 282/2011 as Regards the Place of Supply of Services, OJ L 284 (2013).

introduced with Directive (2008/8) in 2008, the changes concerning the electronically supplied services only entered into force on 1 January 2015.[568]

First, the place of supply rule for electronically supplied services was generally shifted to the place where the consumer is established regardless of whether the electronically supplied service was supplied from a taxable person established in the EU or in a third country.[569] Therefore, the destination principle was implemented for all electronically supplied services. Due to this change and the resulting obligation for suppliers to register in all Member States to which they supply electronic services, EU suppliers would have also faced a considerable increase in compliance costs. Therefore, the previously introduced special registration scheme was extended to all suppliers supplying electronic services to consumers in the EU;[570] with this reform, the MOSS was introduced.[571]

Additionally, the reform nominated an explicit exclusion of the applicability of reduced rates for electronically supplied services.[572] The background for this introduction was that the suppliers need to determine the applicable rates in each Member State for electronic services. Therefore, the legal exclusion of the reduced rates facilitates the determination of the applicable rate in each Member State as the suppliers have the security that the standard rate is applicable to their electronically supplied service.[573]

Finally, in the course of the revision of the VAT Implementing Regulation, further facilitations were introduced for the determination of the place of supply rules for electronically supplied services applicable as of 1 January 2015.[574] In this course, Article 9a of the VAT Implementing Regulation was implemented. Article 9a of the VAT Implementing Regulation represents the first special deemed supplier approach and complements Article 28 of the VAT Directive.[575] According to Article 9a of the VAT

---

568. *See* Article 5 of the Council Directive 2008/8/EC of 12 February 2008 Amending Directive 2006/112/EC as Regards the Place of Supply of Services.
569. *See* Article 58 of the VAT Directive.
570. *See* Article 358 et seqq. of the VAT Directive for suppliers established in third countries and Article 369a et seqq. of the VAT Directive for EU suppliers.
571. *See*, for a critical discussion on MOSS, Marie Lamensch, *Unsuitable EU VAT Place of Supply Rules for Electronic Services – Proposal for an Alternative Approach*, 4 World Tax Journal, *supra* note 388, at 6 et seqq.
572. *See* Article 98 (2) of the VAT Directive; please note that, in 2018 Article 98 (2) of the VAT Directive was amended so that, today, the reduced rate is applicable to electronic books, newspapers, and periodicals; *see* Article 1 (1) of the Council Directive (EU) 2018/1713 of 6 November 2018 Amending Directive 2006/112/EE as Regards Rates of Value Added Tax Applied to Books, Newspapers and Periodicals, OJ L 286 (2018).
573. Marie Lamensch, *European Value Added Tax in the Digital Era: A Critical Analysis and Proposals for Reform*, *supra* note 12, at 158.
574. Council Implementing Regulation (EU) No 1042/2013 of 7 October 2013 Amending Implementing Regulation (EU) No 282/2011 as Regards the Place of Supply of Services, OJ L 284 (2013).
575. For further information on the general deemed supplier approach (i.e., the undisclosed agent scheme) stipulated in Article 14 (2) (c) of the VAT Directive for goods and in Article 28 of the VAT Directive for services, *see* s. 2.2.2.2 The Supply Through Platforms: A Supply Through an Undisclosed Agent?; *see* also the pending case of *Fenix International*, C-695/20, pending, where the First-Tier Tribunal has asked the CJEU whether Article 9a of the VAT Implementing Regulation goes beyond the implementing power stipulated in Article 397 of the VAT Directive as, in the opinion of the referring court, it extends the application of Article 28 of the VAT

Implementing Regulation, taxable persons taking part in electronically supplied services that are supplied through a telecommunications network, an interface, or a portal such as an app store shall be presumed to be acting in their own name but on behalf of the provider of those services within the meaning of Article 28 of the VAT Directive.[576] Therefore, for platforms offering electronically supplied services of underlying suppliers, the legal fiction was introduced that the platform shall be deemed to have received and supplied the electronically supplied services themselves. Only if the underlying supplier was explicitly indicated as the supplier on the invoice was this reflected in the contractual agreements between the parties (i.e., the platform and the underlying supplier), and the platform had no influence on the terms and conditions, the service, and the billing, then this legal fiction should not apply.[577] Article 9a of the VAT Implementing Regulation was the first introduction of a specific deemed supplier approach on an EU level in which platforms are fictitiously considered as having provided the electronically supplied service themselves.

2.3.2.1.2   From the Legal Amendments concerning Electronically Supplied Services to the E-Commerce Package

The first amendments in the VAT Directive and the VAT Implementing Regulation uniformly focused on electronically supplied services. As e-commerce has expanded in the following years, the European Commission decided to set up a Commission Expert Group on Taxation of the Digital Economy.[578] The work of this Expert Group was to monitor and analyse the impact of the digital economy on taxation in general (not limited to the VAT) and to provide possible solutions to address the identified issues.[579] The work resulted in the publication of a report that discussed necessary amendments in the VAT and direct taxation in detail.[580] Therein, the Expert Group suggested that the destination principle should be the primary principle of taxation for remote B2C supplies of goods and services, that the MOSS should be extended for B2C supplies of goods and services, and that the small-consignment exemption for imported goods should be abolished.[581]

Directive; *see* also the discussion of this case by Christian Amand, *Disclosed/Undisclosed Agent in EU VAT: When Is an Intermediary Acting in Its Own Name?*, 32 International VAT Monitor (2021).

576. For further information on the scope of Article 9a of the VAT Implementing Regulation, *see* also s. 5.2.2.2 The Scope of Article 9a of the VAT Implementing Regulation.

577. *See* Article 9a (1) of the VAT Implementing Regulation.

578. European Commission, *Commission Decision of 22.10.2013 Setting up the Commission Expert Group on Taxation of the Digital Economy*, C(2013) 7082 final (22.10.2013), https://ec.europa .eu/taxation_customs/sites/taxation/files/docs/body/com_2013_7082_en.pdf (last visited 24 Jan. 2021).

579. *See ibid.* Article 2.

580. European Commission, *Report of the Commission Expert Group on Taxation of the Digital Economy* (28 May 2014), https://ec.europa.eu/taxation_customs/sites/taxation/files/resour ces/documents/taxation/gen_info/good_governance_matters/digital/report_digital_economy .pdf (last visited 2 Feb. 2021).

581. *Ibid.* at 36 et seqq.

Based on the preparatory work of the Expert Group, the European Commission published a communication and thereby presented a digital single market strategy for Europe. Although this communication focused, in general, on the single market strategy in Europe, one pillar of this strategy had the aim of reducing VAT burdens and obstacles.[582] The European Commission announced the presentation of a legislative proposal in 2016 that should amend the VAT system in respect to four issues:

> (i) extending the current single electronic registration and payment mechanism to intra-EU and 3rd country online sales of tangible goods, (ii) introducing a common EU-wide simplification measure (VAT threshold) to help small start-up e-commerce businesses, (iii) allowing for home country controls including a single audit of cross-border businesses for VAT purposes and (iv) removing the VAT exemption for the importation of small consignments from suppliers in third countries.[583]

2.3.2.2 The EU E-Commerce Package: The Extension of the Principle of Destination

2.3.2.2.1 The First Legislative Changes of the E-Commerce Package in 2017

Following this announcement of the legislative changes, the European Commission presented its proposals in 2016 for the amendments of the VAT Directive,[584] the VAT Implementing Regulation,[585] and the Regulation on Administrative Cooperation and Combating Fraud in the Field of Value Added Tax.[586] One year after the presentation of these proposals, the first part of the so-called e-commerce package was adopted[587] that consisted of three amendments to the VAT Directive and corresponding legal acts.

---

582. European Commission, *Communication from the Commission to the European Parliament, the Council, the European Economic and Social Committee of the Regions – A European Agenda for the Collaborative Economy*, COM(2016) 356 final, *supra* note 78, at 8 et seqq.

583. *Ibid.* at 9.

584. European Commission, *Proposal for a Council Directive Amending Directive 2006/112/EC and Directive 2009/132/EC as Regards Certain Value Added Tax Obligations for Supplies of Services and Distance Sales of Goods*, COM(2016) 757 final, *supra* note 1.

585. European Commission, *Proposal for a Council Implementing Regulation Amending Implementing Regulation (EU) No 282/2011 Laying down Implementing Measures for Directive 2006/112/EC on the Common System of Value Added Tax*, COM(2016) 756 final (1 Dec. 2016), https://ec.europa.eu/transparency/regdoc/rep/1/2016/EN/COM-2016-756-F1-EN-MAIN-PART-1.PDF (last visited 28 Jan. 2021); *see* also the impact assessment European Commission, *Commission Staff Working Document Impact Assessment Accompanying the Document Proposals for a Council Directive, a Council Implementing Regulation and a Council Regulation on Modernising VAT for Cross-Border B2C E-Commerce*, COM(2016) 757 final (1 Dec. 2016), https://ec.europa.eu/transparency/documents-register/api/files/SWD(2016)379_0/de00000000291864?rendition=false (last visited 4 Apr. 2022).

586. European Commission, *Proposal for a Council Regulation Amending Regulation (EU) No 904/2010 on Administrative Cooperation and Combating Fraud in the Field of Value Added Tax*, COM(2016) 755 final (1 Dec. 2016), https://ec.europa.eu/transparency/regdoc/rep/1/2016/EN/COM-2016-755-F1-EN-MAIN.PDF (last visited 28 Jan. 2021).

587. At this point, the e-commerce package consisted of amendments of three different legislative acts: Council Directive (EU) 2017/2455 of 5 December 2017 Amending Directive 2006/112/EC and Directive 2009/132/EC as Regards Certain Value Added Tax Obligations for Supplies of

First, the place of supply rules were revised and adapted. Thereby, three legal amendments were implemented. First, a EUR 10,000 threshold was introduced for the application of the principle of destination on the supply of telecommunication, broadcasting, and electronically supplied services.[588] For this threshold, intra-Community supplies of goods should be taken into consideration as well as cross-border telecommunication, broadcasting, and electronic services if the platform provided such services as well or was the deemed supplier for such services according to Article 9a of the VAT Implementing Regulation.[589] The background for this change was that especially micro-businesses had difficulties complying with the application of the destination principle for all of their supplies of telecommunication, broadcasting, and electronically supplied services.[590] Therefore, due to the legal amendments, only suppliers who surpass the EUR 10,000 threshold must tax their telecommunication, broadcasting, and electronically supplied services in the country of destination. This change is – to some extent – a step back towards the principle of origin for suppliers with relatively little turnover.[591] The second and third legal amendments concerned changes to the place of supply of goods by implementing the principle of destination. On the one hand, the place of supply for intra-Community distance sales of goods is the place where the dispatch or transport to the customer ends.[592] This place of supply for intra-Community distance sales of goods would be, similar to the introduction of the threshold for radio and television broadcasting and electronically supplied services, only applicable if the supplier surpassed the threshold of EUR 10,000.[593] On the other hand, also the place of supply for distance sales of goods imported from third countries is the place where the dispatch or transport to the customer ends.[594] With the implementation of the principle of destination for imported goods, the legislator also

---

Services and Distance Sales of Goods, OJ L 348/7 (2017); Council Implementing Regulation (EU) 2017/2459 of 5 December 2017 Amending Implementing Regulation (EU) No. 282/2011 Laying down Implementing Measures for Directive 2006/112/EC on the Common System of Value Added Tax, OJ L 348/32 (2017); Council Regulation (EU) 2017/2454 of 5 December 2017 Amending Regulation (EU) No. 904/2010 on Administrative Cooperation and Combating Fraud in the Field of Value Added Tax, OJ L 348/1 (2017).

588. *See* Article 58 of the VAT Directive; *see* also, for an extensive summary of these changes, Marta Papis-Almansa, *VAT and Electronic Commerce: The New Rules as a Means for Simplification, Combatting Fraud and Creating a More Level Playing Field?*, 20 ERA Forum, *supra* note 18, at 205 et seqq.

589. *See* Article 59c (1) (c) read in conjunction with Article 59c (1) (b) of the VAT Directive.

590. *See* preamble pt. 3 of the Directive (2017/2455).

591. *See*, for a critical discussion of the introduction of this threshold for the supply of telecommunication, broadcasting, and electronically supplied services, e.g., Aleksandra Bal, *The Changing Landscape of the EU VAT: Digital VAT Package and Definitive VAT System*, 59 European Taxation, *supra* note 18, at 75 et seq.; Valentin Bendlinger & Thomas Ecker, *Die Rolle von Plattformen im E-Commerce – Plattformen und ihre umsatzsteuerlichen Pflichten, in Neuerungen bei innergemeinschaftlichen Umsätzen, supra* note 418, at 195; Marie Lamensch, *European Commission's New Package of Proposals on E-Commerce: A Critical Assessment*, 28 International VAT Monitor 139 et seq. (2017).

592. *See* Article 33 (a) of the VAT Directive; *see* also, for a more extensive summary of the changes and their impact, s. 4.3.4.2 The Place of Supply for Supplies Within the Community.

593. *See* Article 59c of the VAT Directive.

594. *See* Article 33 (b) and (c) of the VAT Directive; *see* also, for a more extensive summary of the changes and their impact, s. 4.3.4.1 The Place of Supply Rules of Imported Distance Sales.

abolished the *de minimis* VAT exemption for small consignments.[595] Thereby, the legislator tried to counteract the distortion of competition from third countries already identified in 1998.[596]

Second, the MOSS system was transformed into the OSS systems. The OSS systems thereby can be separated into three subcategories:[597] the Non-EU-OSS, the EU-OSS, and the IOSS. With the Non-EU-OSS, a possibility was introduced for third country taxable persons to fulfil their compliance obligations for the supply of services in the EU.[598] The Non-EU-OSS is an extension of the MOSS to all kinds of services and is applicable to taxable persons who are not established in the EU. Due to legislative changes, a VAT registration is not excluding taxable persons from the application of the Non-EU-OSS anymore.[599] Through the EU-OSS, three kinds of supplies can be reported: the supply of intra-Community B2C services from suppliers established in the EU, the intra-Community distance sales of goods, and national sales through platforms that are deemed suppliers.[600] Third, distance sales of imported goods with a consignment value of ≤ EUR 150 can be reported via the IOSS.[601]

Lastly, a deemed supplier regime was introduced for platforms. This third significant legal amendment of the VAT Directive came – to some extent – as a surprise as the introduction of Article 14a of the VAT Directive was originally not part of the European Commission's legislative proposals.[602] Nevertheless, the European Parliament proposed a deeming provision in its amendments to the draft act of the VAT Directive for platforms for the importation of low-value goods.[603] Notably, this proposal in the text of the VAT Directive by the European Parliament was limited for platforms that exceed a turnover of one million euros in the current calendar year. The introduction of such a threshold was proposed 'in order to not impose the liability

---

595. *See* Article 3 of the Directive (2017/2455) according to which Title IV of the Directive (2009/132) was deleted; *see*, for further information on the *de minimis* import exemption, s. 2.2.3.3.2 The *De Minimis* VAT Exemption for Imported Goods.
596. *See* European Commission, *Interim Report on the Implications of Electronic Commerce for VAT and Customs*, XXI/98/0359, *supra* note 556, at 24 et seq.
597. *See* European Commission, *Explanatory Notes on the New VAT E-Commerce Rules*, *supra* note 35, at 33; *see* also Valentin Bendlinger & Thomas Ecker, *Die Rolle von Plattformen im E-Commerce – Plattformen und ihre umsatzsteuerlichen Pflichten, in Neuerungen bei innergemeinschaftlichen Umsätzen*, *supra* note 418, at 196 et seq.
598. *See* Articles 358a-369 of the VAT Directive.
599. Please note that the extension of the MOSS for the supply of telecommunication, broadcasting, and electronically supplied services by third country taxable persons registered for VAT purposes in the EU is in force as of 1 Jan. 2019. The further extension of the OSS to all services came into force on 1 Jul. 2021.
600. *See* Articles 369a-369k of the VAT Directive; *see* also, for a more extensive summary of the changes and their impact, s. 4.11 Special Schemes of the OSS.
601. *See* Articles 369l-369x of the VAT Directive; *see* also, for a more extensive summary of the changes and their impact, s. 4.11 Special Schemes of the OSS.
602. European Commission, *Proposal for a Council Directive Amending Directive 2006/112/EC and Directive 2009/132/EC as Regards Certain Value Added Tax Obligations for Supplies of Services and Distance Sales of Goods*, COM(2016) 757 final, *supra* note 1.
603. European Parliament, *Report on the Proposal for a Council Directive Amending Directive 2006/112/EC and Directive 2009/132/EC as Regards Certain Value Added Tax Obligations for Supplies of Services and Distance Sales of Goods*, A8-0307/2017 (16 Oct. 2017), https://www.europarl.europa.eu/RegData/seance_pleniere/textes_deposes/rapports/2017/0307/P8_A(2017)0307_EN.pdf (last visited 5 Apr. 2022).

burden on SMEs or start-ups'.[604] Additionally, also the EU delegations insisted on introducing a provision for electronic interfaces to become liable for collecting the VAT with the aim to improve the effectiveness and efficiency of VAT collection.[605] Based on this insistence, a new text was drafted that was presented at the ECOFIN meeting on 7 November 2017.[606] In this draft, Article 14a of the VAT Directive was included without any exception for SMEs or start-ups, and it received wide support. After further amendments to the text, an agreement could be reached in the 3582nd meeting of the Council of the European Union based on the amended version of the text.[607] However, due to these severe amendments, a statement was prepared to be included in the Council minutes highlighting open questions and detailed implementation issues that were addressed in the second legislative package.[608]

Article 14a of the VAT Directive stipulates that electronic interfaces facilitating the supply of goods may be deemed to have received and supplied the goods themselves if either the supply was a distance sale of goods imported from third countries and the consignment's value does not exceed EUR 150[609] or if the goods were supplied within the Community by a taxable person not established in the EU to non-taxable persons.[610] Additionally to the introduction of the deemed supplier approach for platforms, new record-keeping obligations were introduced. Article 242a of the VAT Directive stipulates an additional reporting obligation for platforms for the supply of goods or services if the platform is not considered the deemed supplier for

---

604. *Ibid.* at 9.

605. Council of the European Union, *Report from the Council of the European Union to the Council*, 13840/17, para. 11 (30 Oct. 2017), https://eur-lex.europa.eu/legal-content/EN/TXT/PDF/?uri =CONSIL:ST_13840_2017_INIT&from=EN (last visited 5 Apr. 2022).

606. Council of the European Union, *supra* note 605.

607. *See* Council of the European Union, *Draft Minutes: 3582nd Meeting of the Council of the European Union (Economic and Financial Affairs), Held in Brussels on 5 December 2017*, 15565/17 (15 Dec. 2017), https://data.consilium.europa.eu/doc/document/ST-15565-2017-ADD-1/en/pdf (last visited 5 Apr. 2022); for the wording of the agreed text, *see* Council of the European Union, *Legislative Acts and Other Instruments: Council Directive Amending Directive 2006/112/EC and Directive 2009/132/EC as Regards Certain Value Added Tax Obligations for Supplies of Services and Distance Sales of Goods*, 14126/17 (28.11.2017), https://www.consilium.europa.eu/media/31929/st14126en17.pdf (last visited 5 Apr. 2022); Council of the European Union, *Legislative Acts and Other Instruments: Council Implementing Regulation Amending Implementing Regulation (EU) No 282/2011 Laying down Implementing Measures for Directive 2006/112/EC on the Common System of Value Added Tax*, 14127/17 (28 Nov. 2017), https://www.consilium.europa.eu/media/31930/st14127en17.pdf (last visited 5 Apr. 2022); Council of the European Union, *Legislative Acts and Other Instruments: Council Regulation Amending Regulation (EU) No 904/2010 on Administrative Cooperation and Combating Fraud in the Field of Value Added Tax*, 14128/17 (28 Nov. 2017), https://www.consilium.europa.eu/media/31931/st14128en17.pdf (last visited 5 Apr. 2017).

608. *See* Council of the European Union, *Draft Minutes: 3582nd Meeting of the Council of the European Union (Economic and Financial Affairs), Held in Brussels on 5 December 2017, supra* note 607. For further information on the second legislative package, *see* s. 2.3.2.2.2 The Second Legislative Changes of the E-Commerce Package in 2019.

609. *See* Article 14a (1) of the VAT Directive; *see* also, for a more extensive summary of the scope and requirements for this deemed supplier regime, s. 3.3.1 Distance Sales of Low-Value Goods Imported from a Third Territory or a Third Country: Article 14a (1) of the VAT Directive.

610. *See* Article 14a (1) of the VAT Directive; *see* also, for a more extensive summary of the scope and requirements for this deemed supplier regime, s. 3.3.2 The Supply of Goods Within the Community: Article 14a (2) of the VAT Directive.

this transaction. According to Article 242a (1) of the VAT Directive, electronic interfaces that facilitate the B2C supply of goods or services to the EU are obligated to keep reports of the facilitated supplies. These records must be kept for 10 years, and the electronic interface must make the records available to the Member States on request.[611] As platforms that fulfil the requirements of Article 14a of the VAT Directive become VAT liable for the facilitated supplies, the general record-keeping obligations are applicable to those platforms.[612]

Most changes from the first legislative package were supposed to enter into force by 1 January 2021.[613] Due to the Covid-19 pandemic, practical implementation difficulties, and challenges brought upon the legislators and tax authorities in the Member States, this entering into force date was postponed by six months.[614] Therefore, the Member States had to implement the changes as of 30 June 2021, and the amendments have been in force since 1 July 2021.

2.3.2.2.2   The Second Legislative Changes of the E-Commerce Package in 2019

The first legislative package from 2017 was complemented by a second legislative package in 2019.[615] Thereby, especially the newly introduced deemed supplier rule in Article 14a of the VAT Directive raised two questions. On the one hand, it was not clear how the term 'facilitate' stipulated in Article 14a and in Article 242a of the VAT Directive should be interpreted;[616] on the other hand, it was also unclear how the chain

---

611. *See* Article 242a (2) of the VAT Directive.
612. *See* especially Article 63c of the VAT Implementing Regulation and Article 242 of the VAT Directive; *see* also, for a more extensive summary of the reporting obligations for platforms as deemed suppliers, s. 4.10 The Platform's Record-Keeping Obligations as a Deemed Supplier.
613. Two of the presented legal amendments already entered into force on 1 Jan. 2019, i.e., the introduction of the uniform threshold for telecommunication, broadcasting, and electronically supplied services and the extension of the MOSS for the supply of telecommunication, broadcasting, and electronically supplied services by third country taxable persons registered for VAT purposes in the EU.
614. *See* Council Decision (EU) 2020/1109 of 20 July 2020 Amending Directives (EU) 2017/2455 and (EU) 2019/1995 as Regards the Dates of Transposition and Application in Response to the Covid-19 Pandemic, OJ L 244 (2020); Council Regulation (EU) 2020/1108 of 20 July 2020 Amending Regulation (EU) 2017/2454 as Regards the Dates of Application in Response to the Covid-19 Pandemic, OJ L 244 (2020); Council Implementing Regulation (EU) 2020/1112 of 20 July 2020 Amending Implementing Regulation (EU) 2019/2026 as Regards the Dates of Application in Response to the Covid-19 Pandemic, OJ L 244 (2020); Commission Implementing Regulation (EU) 2020/1318 of 22 September 2020 Amending Implementing Regulations (EU) 2020/21 and (EU) No 2020/194 as Regards the Dates of Application in Response to the Covid-19 Pandemic, OJ L 309 (2020).
615. *See* already the identified issues with the first legislative package by Council of the European Union, *Draft Minutes: 3582nd Meeting of the Council of the European Union (Economic and Financial Affairs), Held in Brussels on 5 December 2017*, 15565/17, *supra* note 607.
616. *See* the discussions in literature, e.g., Aleksandra Bal, *The Changing Landscape of the EU VAT: Digital VAT Package and Definitive VAT System*, 59 European Taxation, *supra* note 18, at 77; Valentin Bendlinger & Thomas Ecker, *Die Rolle von Plattformen im E-Commerce – Plattformen und ihre umsatzsteuerlichen Pflichten*, in *Neuerungen bei innergemeinschaftlichen Umsätzen*, *supra* note 418, at 200; Marie Lamensch, *Adoption of the E-Commerce VAT Package: The Road Ahead Is Still a Rocky One*, 27 EC Tax Review, *supra* note 18, at 191 et seq.; Marie Lamensch, *Rendering Platforms Liable to Collect and Pay VAT on B2C Imports: A Silver Bullet?*, 29

transaction resulting from the legal fiction of Article 14a of the VAT Directive should be treated.[617] Therefore, the European Commission presented amendments to the VAT Directive and the VAT Implementing Regulation that mainly aimed at supplementing and clarifying the legislative amendments of the legislative changes adopted in 2017.[618] One year after the presentation of these proposals, the second part of the e-commerce package was adopted.[619]

With this second part of the legislative changes, a detailed definition of the term 'to facilitate' was introduced in Article 5b of the VAT Implementing Regulation for the application of Article 14a of the VAT Directive.[620] The stipulated definition is based on a positive list of functions that the platforms must fulfil to facilitate a supply in Article 5b second subparagraph as well as Article 54b second subparagraph of the VAT Implementing Regulation and is complemented by a negative list of functions. If the electronic interface only provided one of the listed functions of this negative list stipulated in Article 5b third subparagraph and Article 54b third subparagraph of the VAT Implementing Regulation, the deemed supplier regime and additional reporting applications would not be applicable. According to these definitions, the platform would facilitate a transaction if the platform fulfilled crucial functions for the transaction to be concluded between the underlying supplier and the customer. Additionally, the amendments also included a legal presumption in Article 5d of the VAT Implementing Regulation according to which the underlying supplier is a taxable person, and the customer is a non-taxable person when Article 14a of the VAT Directive is

International VAT Monitor, *supra* note 18, at 48; Marta Papis-Almansa, *VAT and Electronic Commerce: The New Rules as a Means for Simplification, Combatting Fraud and Creating a More Level Playing Field?*, 20 ERA Forum, *supra* note 18, at 217 et seq.

617. Valentin Bendlinger & Thomas Ecker, *supra* note 418, at 200; Marie Lamensch, *Adoption of the E-Commerce VAT Package: The Road Ahead Is Still a Rocky One*, *supra* note 18, at 191 et seq.; Marta Papis-Almansa, *supra* note 18, at 219 et seq.

618. European Commission, *Proposal for a Council Directive Amending Council Directive 2006/112/EC of 28 November 2006 as Regards Provisions Relating to Distance Sales of Goods and Certain Domestic Supplies of Goods*, COM(2018) 819 final 1 (11.12.2018), https://eur-lex.europa.eu/legal-content/EN/TXT/PDF/?uri = CELEX:52018PC0819&from = EN (last visited 2 Feb. 2021); European Commission, *Proposal for a Council Implementing Regulation Amending Implementing Regulation (EU) No 282/2011 as Regards Supplies of Goods or Services Facilitated by Electronic Interfaces and the Special Schemes for Taxable Persons Supplying Services to Non-Taxable Persons, Making Distance Sales of Goods and Certain Domestic Supplies of Goods*, COM(2018) 821 final 1 (11.12.2018), https://ec.europa.eu/transparency/regdoc/rep/1/2018/EN/COM-2018-821-F1-EN-MAIN-PART-1.PDF (last visited 2 Feb. 2021).

619. Council Directive (EU) 2019/1995 of 21 November 2019 Amending Directive 2006/112/EC as Regards Provisions Relating to Distance Sales of Goods and Certain Domestic Supplies of Goods, OJ L 310/1 (2019); Council Implementing Regulation (EU) 2019/2026 of 21 November 2019 Amending Implementing Regulation (EU) No 282/2011 as Regards Supplies of Goods or Services Facilitated by Electronic Interfaces and the Special Schemes for Taxable Persons Supplying Services to Non-Taxable Persons, Making Distance Sales of Goods and Certain Domestic Supplies of Goods, OJ L 313/14 (2019).

620. *See* also Article 54b of the VAT Implementing Regulation for the application of Article 242a of the VAT Directive. The definitions of when a platform facilitates a supply in Article 5b and Article 54b of the VAT Implementing Regulation have the same wording; *see* also, for more information on the interpretation of the term 'facilitate', s. 3.2.2 The Definition of 'to Facilitate'.

applied.[621] This legal presumption should facilitate the application of Article 14a of the VAT Directive for platforms since the burden of proof for the platform of whether the underlying supplier is a taxable person and the customer is a non-taxable person should be limited.[622]

Furthermore, also clarifications on the legal consequences were introduced. Since the supply in accordance with Article 14a of the VAT Directive qualifies as a chain transaction, clarifications on the determination of the supply with transport were provided and legally nominated in the VAT Directive. According to Article 36b of the VAT Directive, the supply from the platform to the customer is *ex lege* qualified as the supply with transport.[623] Moreover, the VAT exemption in Article 136a of the VAT Directive for the supply from the underlying supplier to the platform was introduced in this second reform.[624] The background for the introduction of Article 136a of the VAT Directive was the prevention of additional administrative burden and the prevention of additional revenue loss due to VAT payments from the platform to the underlying suppliers.[625] Finally, in order to limit the extent of when the platform becomes liable for the VAT payment, a safe harbour rule was introduced with the second legislative amendments in Article 5c of the VAT Implementing Regulation. Under certain circumstances, the platform would not be held liable for the payment of any additional VAT not declared by the platform.[626]

The final amendments in this second legislative revision concerned the record-keeping obligations as stipulated in Article 242a of the VAT Directive. If the platform had become a deemed supplier, then the record-keeping obligations would be stipulated either in Article 63c of the VAT Implementing Regulation or in Article 242 of the VAT Directive. Article 63c of the VAT Implementing Regulation defines the platform's record-keeping obligations if the platform opted to apply the IOSS and/or the EU-OSS.[627] If the deemed supplier did not opt for the application of the IOSS and/or the EU-OSS, then the platform's record-keeping obligations are stipulated in Article 242 of

---

621. *See*, for further information, s. 3.3.4 The Rebuttal Presumption of Article 5d of the VAT Implementing Regulation on the Taxable Status of the Underlying Supplier and the Customer.
622. *See*, for further information, s. 3.3.4 The Rebuttal Presumption of Article 5d of the VAT Implementing Regulation on the Taxable Status of the Underlying Supplier and the Customer.
623. *See*, for more information on the qualification of the supplies as a chain transaction, s. 4.3.2 Preliminary Discussion: Chain Transaction.
624. *See*, for more information on the applicability of the exemption, s. 4.6.2 Applicable Exemptions to the Supply.
625. European Commission, *Proposal for a Council Directive Amending Council Directive 2006/112/EC of 28 November 2006 as Regards Provisions Relating to Distance Sales of Goods and Certain Domestic Supplies of Goods*, COM(2018) 819 final 3 (11.12.2018), https://eur-lex. europa.eu/legal-content/EN/TXT/PDF/?uri = CELEX:52018PC0819&from = EN (last visited 19 Oct. 2021). For further information on the background, *see* s. 4.6.2 Applicable Exemptions to the Supply.
626. *See*, for more information on the requirements for the application of the safe harbour clause and its legal consequences, s. 4.7 The Safe Harbour Clause of Article 5c of the VAT Implementing Regulation.
627. *See* Article 54c (1) (a) of the VAT Implementing Regulation; *see* also, for more information on the reporting obligations for platforms that opted for the IOSS and/or the EU-OSS, s. 4.10.2 The Record-Keeping Obligations According to Article 63c of the VAT Implementing Regulation.

the VAT Directive.[628] Finally, also further clarifications on the necessary record-keeping obligations for platforms that do not fulfil the narrow requirements of Article 14a of the VAT Directive, i.e., do not become the deemed supplier of the transaction but who still facilitate supplies, have been implemented.[629]

The implemented changes of the second legislative package do not, in general, introduce new VAT regimes to the supply in the e-commerce sector. Many of the changes implemented in the second legislative package were introduced in the VAT Implementing Regulation and should therefore clarify the legal amendments of the first legislative package only. Furthermore, the changes to the VAT Directive, such as the *ex lege* determination of the supply with transport in the chain transaction of Article 14a of the VAT Directive and the introduction of the VAT exemption of the supply from the underlying supplier to the platform, should lead to more legal certainty in the application of Article 14a of the VAT Directive.

2.3.3 The OECD Proposal's Influence on the Interpretation of the EU E-Commerce Package

Taking a look at the OECD report on the 'Role of Digital Platforms in the Collection of VAT/GST on Online Sales' and the implementation of the EU e-commerce package, many similarities between the suggested approach by the OECD and the legal implementation by the EU can be found. Within those similarities, especially the abolishment of the import VAT exemption for small consignments and the introduction of a deemed supplier regime for certain supplies of goods are striking. The OECD emphasised the difficulty for legislators to clearly define under which circumstances platforms become, for VAT purposes, part of the supply chain. It seems that the EU legislator faced these difficulties after the introduction of the first legislative part of the e-commerce package and tried to counteract any outstanding questions with the second legislative part of the e-commerce package.

As the EU legislator followed a similar approach as that for the suggestions of the OECD, the question arises to what extent the OECD reports and preparatory documents may have an influence on the interpretation of the EU e-commerce package rules. Therefore, in a first step, it should be evaluated how OECD reports can legally be qualified and whether they have binding force. In general, according to the OECD Convention, there are three options for the OECD to act: taking decisions, making recommendations, and entering into agreements with non-Member States and international organisations.[630] Whereas decisions are legally binding to the OECD members,[631] recommendations are not legally binding[632] but should emphasise a political

---

628. See Article 54c (1) (b) of the VAT Implementing Regulation; *see* also, for more information on the reporting obligations for platforms that did not opt for the IOSS or the EU-OSS, s. 4.10.3 The Record-Keeping Obligations According to Article 242 of the VAT Directive.
629. See Article 54c (2) of the VAT Implementing Regulation.
630. See Article 5 of the *Convention on the Organisation for Economic Co-Operation and Development* (14 Dec. 1960); *see* also, for further background information on the different OECD acts

agreement of the members. In this sense, the VAT/GST Guidelines, for example, qualify as an OECD recommendation.[633] In literature, it has been further argued that recommendations generally qualify as soft law.[634] Compared to the VAT/GST Guidelines, though, the OECD report on the 'Role of Digital Platforms in the Collection of VAT/GST on Online Sales' is not a recommendation but a simple report. Similar to the recommendations, the report shows that there has been political agreement on the issues arising from the platform economy in the e-commerce sector, but the report cannot qualify as having a binding force.

As a follow-up question, it could be evaluated whether the OECD work on the platform economy, in general, and especially the report on the 'Role of Digital Platforms in the Collection of VAT/GST on Online Sales' may have an impact on the interpretation of the EU e-commerce package in the sense that the OECD reports may be considered as being historical material. If the OECD work qualified as historical material, it may be taken into account for the interpretation of the EU e-commerce package. Thereby, it should be noted that the OECD report on the 'Role of Digital Platforms in the Collection of VAT/GST on Online Sales' was only published in March 2019, i.e., after the adoption of the first legislative amendments of the e-commerce package in December 2017 by the EU legislator. Due to this timeline, it is plausible that the preparatory work of the OECD and the involvement of the EU in the OECD work have inspired the EU when drafting the e-commerce package. However, since the publishing of the OECD report was only after the entering into force of the first part of the e-commerce package, the EU preparatory work on the amendments to the e-commerce package could not have been based on the report itself. Another conclusion could be drawn for the second legislative package that was adopted in November 2019, i.e., after the publishing of the OECD report in March 2019. Nevertheless, it should be noted that also the proposal of the amendments to the VAT Directive and the VAT Implementing Regulation were presented in December 2018 by the European

---

Tomáš Zautloukal, *Die rechtliche Bedeutung der OECD-Verrechnungspreisrichtlinien*, in *Verrechnungspreisgestaltung im internationalen Steuerrecht* 96 (Josef Schuch & Ulf Zehetner eds., Linde Verlag 2001).

631. *See* Article 5 (a) of the Convention on the Organisation for Economic Co-Operation and Development.

632. *See* Article 5 (b) of the Convention on the Organisation for Economic Co-Operation and Development.

633. *See* OECD, *International VAT/GST Guidelines*, *supra* note 457, at 4, where it is explicitly stated that the 'Guidelines were incorporated in the Recommendation on the Application of Value Added Tax/Goods and Services Tax to the International Trade in Services and Intangibles'; another example for a recommendation are the Model Tax Conventions and the Commentaries, *see* Thomas Dubut, *The Court of Justice and the OECD Model Tax Conventions or the Uncertainties of the Distinction between Hard Law, Soft Law, and No Law in the European Case Law*, Intertax 4.

634. *See*, on the qualification of the VAT/GST Guidelines as soft law, Kathryn James & Thomas Ecker, *Relevance of the OECD International VAT/GST Guidelines for Non-OECD Countries*, 32 Australian Tax Forum 338 et seqq. (2017); Karoline Spies, *Permanent Establishments in Value Added Tax: The Role of Establishments in International B2B Trade in Services Under VAT/GST Law*, *supra* note 25, at 84 et seqq.; *see* also, on the qualification of the OECD Model Conventions and the Commentaries as a qualification of soft law, Juliane Kokott, *European Court of Justice*, in *Courts and tax treaty Law* (Guglielmo Maisto ed., IBFD 2007); *see* also the critical discussion thereof by Dubut, *supra* note 633.

Commission, i.e., before the publishing of the OECD report. Thus, the wording of the changes in the VAT Directive and in the VAT Implementing Regulation could not have been influenced by the OECD report. In this sense, the OECD report on 'Role of Digital Platforms in the Collection of VAT/GST on Online Sales' is not likely to be considered as historical material for the interpretation of the e-commerce package.[635]

It is not doubted that the work of the OECD had an impact on the drafting of the EU e-commerce package and that, at the same time, the drafting of the e-commerce package by the EU has influenced the work on the OECD report.[636] At the same time, though, the report on the 'Role of Digital Platforms in the Collection of VAT/GST on Online Sales' does not have binding force, and also its interpretational impact on the VAT Directive is questionable. Therefore, the OECD report should not be taken into consideration for interpretational questions about the EU e-commerce package. This lack of influence on the interpretation of the VAT Directive should not diminish the success of the OECD report as it shows the great political unity on the issues arising from the platform economy.

---

635. In general, the impact of the OECD guidelines for the interpretation of EU law has caused discussions in literature; see Karoline Spies, *supra* note 25, at 87 et seq., who discusses the impact of the VAT/GST guidelines on the interpretation of the VAT Directive and argues that the VAT/GST guidelines may have an impact on the interpretation of the VAT Directive for reforms after the publishing of the VAT/GST guidelines; with critical reference to the seemingly conflicting judgments of Case C-138/07, *Belgische Staat v Cobelfret NV*, 12 Feb. 2009, ECLI:EU:C:2009:82, para. 56, where the CJEU explicitly held that the OECD Model Tax Convention does not have binding force for the interpretation of EU law; and Case C-682/15, *Berlioz Investment Fund SA v Directeur de l'administration des contributions directes*, 16 May 2017, ECLI:EU:C:2017:373, para. 67, where the CJEU explicitly took Article 26 of the OECD Model Tax Convention into account for the interpretation of an EU Directive; see also the critical discussion of the *Berlioz Investment Fund* case Michael Lang, *Doppelbesteuerungsabkommen in der Rechtsprechung des EuGH, in Europäisches Steuerrecht: 42. Jahrestagung der Deutschen Steuerjuristischen Gesellschaft e.V., Wien, 18. Und 19. September 2017*, 394 (Michael Lang ed., Otto Schmidt 2018); see also the critical discussion of the *Cobelfret* case by Dubut, *supra* note 633, at 6; see also, for a general analysis of older CJEU case law on the influence of double taxation conventions on EU law, Kokott, *supra* note 634, at 101 et seqq.
636. See also the explicit acknowledgment by the OECD of the work by the EU in OECD, *The Role of Digital Platforms in the Collection of VAT/GST on Online Sales*, *supra* note 8, para. 14.

CHAPTER 3

The Scope of Article 14a of the VAT Directive

3.1   GENERAL REMARKS

Article 14a of the VAT Directive stipulates:

1. Where a taxable person facilitates, through the use of an electronic interface such as a marketplace, platform, portal or similar means, distance sales of goods imported from third territories or third countries in consignments of an intrinsic value not exceeding EUR 150, that taxable person shall be deemed to have received and supplied those goods himself.
2. Where a taxable person facilitates, through the use of an electronic interface such as a marketplace, platform, portal or similar means, the supply of goods within the Community by a taxable person not established within the Community to a non-taxable person, the taxable person who facilitates the supply shall be deemed to have received and supplied those goods himself.

In the subsequent sections, the personal and substantive scopes of the two paragraphs of Article 14a of the VAT Directive will be discussed. Thereby, the personal scope, i.e., the requirements a person must fulfil to be covered by Article 14a of the VAT Directive, is identical in both paragraphs: (i) a taxable person must (ii) facilitate supplies of goods through (iii) the use of an electronic interface. The limitation to taxable persons, the requirements of when a taxable person facilitates supplies, and the 'use of an electronic interface' are discussed in the subsequent chapter under the personal scope.

The substantive scope, i.e., which supplies Article 14a of the VAT Directive is applicable to and who can be the recipient of such supplies, is divided into the two situations described in the two paragraphs of Article 14a of the VAT Directive: distance sales of low-value goods of an intrinsic value not exceeding EUR 150 imported from third territories or counties and the supply of goods to non-taxable persons within the

117

EU. Also, the different requirements of the two paragraphs of the substantive scope will be discussed in the subsequent chapters.

3.2 PERSONAL SCOPE

3.2.1 The Limitation to Taxable Persons

The personal scope of Article 14a of the VAT Directive is clearly limited to taxable persons. The deemed supplier rule of Article 14a of the VAT Directive is only applicable to taxable persons facilitating the supply of goods. According to Article 9 (1) of the VAT Directive, a taxable person is 'any person who, independently, carries out in any place any economic activity, whatever the purpose or results of that activity'.

Based on this definition, taxable persons must fulfil two requirements: they must carry out an economic activity, and this economic activity must be carried out independently. Both terms are further defined in the VAT Directive. According to Article 9 (1) second subparagraph of the VAT Directive, 'any activity of producers, traders or persons supplying services ... shall be regarded as "economic activity"'.[637] Moreover, the exploitation of tangible or intangible property on: (i) a continuing basis with (ii) the purpose to obtain income shall also qualify as an economic activity.[638] E-commerce platforms generally make their website available to bring together suppliers and customers and charge the suppliers and/or the customers a fee for their services. Thus, if the usage of a platform was free for the suppliers and customers and the platform did not generate income, then the requirement of exploiting tangible property to obtain income would likely not be fulfilled. This may be the case if, e.g., a charity platform set up a digital platform and did not charge the suppliers and/or customers a fee for its use. Nevertheless, most e-commerce platforms will fulfil the criterion to exploit their property, i.e., the developed homepage, to 'obtain income'. Also, the criterion that the exploitation of the property has the aim to obtain income on a continuing basis can be affirmed in most cases since a platform would not likely be programmed and put on the Internet if the aim was not to provide its services on a continuing basis. Therefore, e-commerce platforms offering goods in general provide intermediation services that should qualify as fulfilling the criterion of carrying out an economic activity. Finally, taxable persons must also act independently, i.e., persons who are employed and acting within this employment, should not qualify as taxable

---

637. For further detailed information on the term 'economic activity', *see* Ben Terra & Julie Kajus, *Commentary – A Guide to the Recast VAT Directive, supra* note 290, s. 3.2.; Ben Terra & Julie Kajus, *Introduction to European VAT, supra* note 167, s. 9.2.; Ad van Doesum et al., *Fundamentals of EU VAT Law, supra* note 35, at 66 et seqq.
638. *See* Article 9 (1) second subpara. Of the VAT Directive; *see* also Ben Terra & Julie Kajus, *supra* note 290, s. 3.3.; Ben Terra & Julie Kajus, *supra* note 167, s. 9.2.1.; Aleksandra Bal, *European Union – The Vague Concept of 'Taxable Person' in EU VAT Law*, 24 International VAT Monitor, s. 2.5. (2013).

persons.[639] This second criterion is also likely to be fulfilled in the case of e-commerce platforms.

By referring to 'any person' in Article 9 (1) of the VAT Directive, the EU legislator emphasises that individual persons as well as legal persons, independently of their legal form, can qualify as taxable persons as long as they fulfil the criteria of Article 9 (1) of the VAT Directive.[640] Furthermore, the formulation 'any place' highlights that the place where the taxable person is established or resides is irrelevant as long as the taxable person supplies taxable transactions within the EU.[641] Thereby, Article 14a of the VAT Directive is not limited to taxable persons established in the EU. Regardless of whether the platform is established in the EU or in a third country, it might become the deemed supplier if all subsequent requirements were fulfilled.

The notion 'whatever the purpose or results of that activity' refers to two issues. First, a person may qualify as a taxable person in spite of whether profits are procured.[642] Nevertheless, as discussed above, the platform must have the aim of obtaining income.

Second, the principle of neutrality requires that legal as well as illegal transactions are within the scope of the VAT.[643] Therefore, also persons supplying illegal transactions could qualify as taxable persons. The CJEU, though, excluded the collection of VAT and customs duties when there is no legal market for the supplied goods,[644] so for goods that are absolutely precluded and only give rise to penalties under criminal law.[645] In this sense, the CJEU has held that the supply of narcotic

---

639. *See* Article 10 of the VAT Directive; for further detailed information on the term 'independently', *see* Ben Terra & Julie Kajus, *supra* note 290, s. 3.5.; Ben Terra & Julie Kajus, *supra* note 167, s. 9.4.; Ad van Doesum et al., *supra* note 35, at 90 et seqq.

640. Ben Terra & Julie Kajus, *supra* note 167, s. 9.1.1.; Ad van Doesum et al., *supra* note 35, at 62 et seqq.

641. Ben Terra & Julie Kajus, *supra* note 167, s. 9.1.1.; Ad van Doesum et al., *supra* note 35, at 64 et seqq.

642. Ben Terra & Julie Kajus, *supra* note 290, s. 3.2.5.; Ben Terra & Julie Kajus, *supra* note 167, s. 9.1.2.; Ad van Doesum et al., *supra* note 35, at 67 et seq.; Aleksandra Bal, *European Union – The Vague Concept of 'Taxable Person' in EU VAT Law*, *supra* note 638, s. 2.1. + 2.3.

643. Case C-289/86, *Vereniging Happy Family Rustenburgerstraat v Inspecteur der Omzetbelasting*, 5 Jul. 1988, ECLI:EU:C:1988:360, para. 20; Case C-269/86, *W. J. R. Mol v Inspecteur der Invoerrechten en Accijnzen*, 5 Jul. 1988, ECLI:EU:C:1988:359, para. 18; Case C-111/92, *Wilfried Lange v Finanzamt Fürstenfeldbruck*, 2 Aug. 1993, ECLI:EU:C:1993:345, para. 16; Case C-3/97, *Criminal proceedings against John Charles Goodwin and Edward Thomas Unstead*, 28 May 1998, ECLI:EU:C:1998:263, para. 9; Case C-283/95, *Karlheinz Fischer v Finanzamt Donaueschingen*, 11 Jun. 1998, ECLI:EU:C:1998:276, para. 21; Case C-158/98, *Staatssecretaris van Financiën v Coffeeshop 'Siberië' vof*, 29 Jun. 1999, ECLI:EU:C:1999:334, para. 19.

644. Terra & Kajus refer to these goods as 'extra commercium'; *see* Ben Terra & Julie Kajus, *supra* note 167, s. 8.4.1.; *see also* Ad van Doesum et al., *supra* note 35, at 80.

645. *See*, e.g., Case C-294/82, *Senta Einberger v Hauptzollamt Freiburg*, 28 Feb. 1984, ECLI:EU:C:1984:81, paras. 19 et seq.; Case C-269/86, *Mol v Invoerrechten en Accijnzen*, 5 Jul. 1988, ECLI:EU:C:1988:359, para. 15; Case C-289/86, *Happy Family v Inspecteur der Omzetbelasting*, 5 Jul. 1988, ECLI:EU:C:1988:360, para. 17; Case C-343/89, *Max Witzemann v Hauptzollamt München-Mitte*, 6 Dec. 1990, ECLI:EU:C:1990:445, para. 19; Case C-283/95, *Fischer v Finanzamt Donaueschingen*, 11 Jun. 1998, ECLI:EU:C:1998:276, para. 19.

drugs[646] and the importation of counterfeit currency[647] are out of scope of the VAT. Nevertheless, the CJEU also held that, for the illegal export of information systems, the export exemption is applicable[648] and that the organisation of unlawful games of chance is within the scope of the VAT, but the exemption might be applicable.[649] Furthermore, the supply of counterfeit perfumes[650] and the sale of ethyl alcohol are within the scope of the VAT.[651] Lastly, also the renting out of immovable property for the sale of narcotic drugs is within the scope of the VAT as the renting out of immovable property is, in general, a taxable activity.[652] The question arises of whether also e-commerce platforms providing their services for the supply of illegal goods, e.g., narcotic drugs or weapons, can qualify as taxable persons in the meaning of Article 14a of the VAT Directive. As the platform's economic activity is providing intermediary services by offering the technical infrastructure for connecting suppliers and customers, this economic activity should not qualify as an illegal transaction by itself. The supply of intermediary services by the platform for underlying suppliers selling illegal goods is, in this sense, similar to the supply of renting out immovable property for the sale of narcotic drugs.[653] Therefore, platforms providing the technical infrastructure for the supply of illegal goods are also likely to qualify as taxable persons according to Article 14a of the VAT Directive. Whether the platform would actually become the deemed supplier of the supply of the illegal good would, in a second step, have to be tested independently.

Additionally, non-taxable persons who are either persons who do not fulfil the definition of Article 9 (1) of the VAT Directive or a public body acting as such according to Article 13 (1) of the VAT Directive cannot qualify as deemed suppliers as required by Article 14a of the VAT Directive.[654]

Finally, the EU legislator has not included any facilitation for platforms that have not surpassed a certain turnover, i.e., SMEs and start-ups that qualify as taxable

---

646. *See* Case C-294/82, *Einberger v Hauptzollamt Freiburg*, 28 Feb. 1984, ECLI:EU:C:1984:81; Case C-269/86, *Mol v Inspecteur der Invoerrechten en Accijnzen*, 5 Jul. 1988, ECLI:EU:C:1988:359; Case C-289/86, *Happy Family v Inspecteur der Omzetbelasting*, 5 Jul. 1988, ECLI: EU:C:1988:360; the CJEU further held that no customs duties become due for the importation of narcotic drugs, *see* Case C-240/81, *Senta Einberger v Hauptzollamt Freiburg*, 26 Oct. 1982, ECLI:EU:C:1982:364.

647. *See* Case C-343/89, *Witzemann v Hauptzollamt München-Mitte*, 6 Dec. 1990, ECLI: EU:C:1990:445.

648. *See* Case C-111/92, *Lange v Finanzamt Fürstenfeldbruck*, 2 Aug. 1993, ECLI:EU:C:1993:345.

649. *See* Case C-283/95, *Fischer v Finanzamt Donaueschingen*, 11 Jun. 1998, ECLI:EU:C:1998:276.

650. *See* Case C-3/97, *Goodwin and Unstead*, 28 May 1998, ECLI:EU:C:1998:263.

651. *See* Case C-455/98, *Tullihallitus v Kaupo Salumets and others*, 29 Jun. 2000, ECLI: EU:C:2000:352.

652. *See* Case C-158/98, *Coffeeshop 'Siberië'*, 29 Jun. 1999, ECLI:EU:C:1999:334.

653. *See ibid.*

654. *See,* for further information on public bodies as taxable persons, Ben Terra & Julie Kajus, *Commentary – A Guide to the Recast VAT Directive, supra* note 290, s. 3.8.; Ben Terra & Julie Kajus, *Introduction to European VAT, supra* note 167, s. 9.5.; Oskar Henkow, *The VAT/GST Treatment of Public Bodies* (Wolters Kluwer 2013).

persons may also become deemed suppliers based on Article 14a of the VAT Directive.[655] Nevertheless, platforms that are taxable persons but do not surpass a certain turnover may apply the special scheme for small enterprises stipulated in Articles 282-292 of the VAT Directive. Although the special scheme for small enterprises does not influence the qualification of the platform as a taxable person, its applicability may have an impact on the legal consequences of the platform.[656] In the given case of e-commerce platforms, the qualification of the platform as a taxable person should, in general, not pose any further difficulties as the platforms are likely to fulfil all criteria of being a taxable person.

3.2.2 The Definition of 'to Facilitate'

3.2.2.1 The General Definition in Article 5b of the VAT Implementing Regulation

According to Article 14a of the VAT Directive, only taxable persons who facilitate supplies may become a deemed supplier. The term 'to facilitate' has legally been defined in Article 5b of the VAT Implementing Regulation, according to which

> the term 'facilitates' means the use of an electronic interface to allow a customer and a supplier offering goods for sale through the electronic interface to enter into contact which results in a supply of goods through that electronic interface.[657]

This definition allows two possible situations which could be subsumed under the term 'to facilitate'. On the one hand, an underlying supplier may offer goods through an electronic interface, and the customer may purchase these goods. On the other hand, the customer may also make an offer to the supplier for a good that the underlying supplier wishes to auction off through the electronic interface. The pronoun 'which' used in this legal definition emphasises that the facilitation is fulfilled in both described cases under the precondition that the intermediation of the platform actually results in the supply of goods. Therefore, a causality is necessary between the offering of goods on the electronic interface and the supply of the goods. Similarly, the European Commission excludes the possibility that several platforms can become the deemed supplier as the customer, in general, will only proceed with the checkout and payment on one electronic interface.[658] This statement by the European Commission

---

655. Please note that, in a draft version by the European Parliament on the deemed supplier scheme, a turnover of one million euros was required for the platform to become a deemed supplier; *see* European Parliament, *Report on the Proposal for a Council Directive Amending Directive 2006/112/EC and Directive 2009/132/EC as Regards Certain Value Added Tax Obligations for Supplies of Services and Distance Sales of Goods*, A8-0307/2017, *supra* note 603. Such a facilitation for SMEs was not implemented in the final version of Article 14a of the VAT Directive.

656. For further information on the special scheme for small enterprises, *see* s. 4.6.2.2 The Underlying Supplier as a Small Enterprise.

657. *See* Article 5b first subpara. of the VAT Implementing Regulation.

658. European Commission, *Explanatory Notes on the New VAT E-Commerce Rules, supra* note 35, at 21.

finds its support in the text of Article 5b of the VAT Implementing Regulation based on the discussed necessity of the causality between the offering of goods on the electronic interface and the supply of the goods. As the realisation of a supply of goods should be seen independently of the physical delivery of the goods, the physical delivery is not a prerequisite for the affirmation of the facilitation by the platform; i.e., the platform does not have to organise the transport of the goods to fulfil the requirement of 'to facilitate'.[659]

3.2.2.2 *The First Negative List in Article 5b of the VAT Implementing Regulation*

In Article 5b second subparagraph of the VAT Implementing Regulation, a further definition of the term 'to facilitate' was introduced by stipulating a negative list of business activities that the platform may not fulfil to not facilitate a supply. Thereby, the implemented definition in Article 5b second subparagraph of the VAT Implementing Regulation is similar to the guidance provided by the OECD on the functions that legislators may consider when implementing a full liability regime.[660] Article 5b second subparagraph of the VAT Implementing Regulation stipulates:

> However, a taxable person is not facilitating a supply of goods where all of the following conditions are met:
> (a) that taxable person does not set, either directly or indirectly, any of the terms and conditions under which the supply of goods is made;
> (b) that taxable person is not, either directly or indirectly, involved in authorising the charge to the customer in respect of the payment made;
> (c) that taxable person is not, either directly or indirectly, involved in the ordering or delivery of the goods.[661]

By indicating that 'all' of the listed activities must be met, little doubt can be left that the EU legislator meant this list to be read as a cumulative negative list.[662] Therefore, the platform facilitates a supply when only one of the mentioned business activities is undergone by the platform. It is unclear why the EU legislator decided to formulate the list in negative terms since the same result could have been achieved with a positive formulation, i.e., that 'a taxable person is ... facilitating a supply of goods where all of the following conditions are met' and by additionally omitting the 'not' in Article 5b second subparagraph (a)-(c) of the VAT Implementing Regulation. A positive formulation would have made the text of the law easier to understand.

---

659. *Ibid.* at 17.
660. For a more detailed description on the OECD guidance, *see* s. 2.3.1.2.2 The Platform Becoming Liable for VAT/GST: Platforms' Liability Regimes.
661. *See* Article 5b second supara. of the VAT Implementing Regulation.
662. *See* also Marta Papis-Almansa, *VAT and Electronic Commerce: The New Rules as a Means for Simplification, Combatting Fraud and Creating a More Level Playing Field?*, 20 ERA Forum, *supra* note 18, at 217; European Commission, *Explanatory Notes: VAT E-Commerce Rules*, *supra* note 35, at 17.

One similarity in all three literae is that the term 'directly or indirectly' is mentioned.[663] With this wording, the scope of the facilitation of the supply of goods is quite wide as only indirect involvement by the platform is necessary for the platform to facilitate a supply.[664] The aim of such a broad scope was to prevent the artificial splitting of the functions between the underlying supplier and the electronic interface so the platform would not facilitate a supply.[665]

The first mentioned business activity is that the electronic interface sets any terms and conditions. Similar to being indirectly involved with the mentioned business activities, the term 'any' also indicates that the EU legislator wanted the expression 'terms and conditions' to be interpreted broadly.[666] These terms and conditions of the electronic interface must be linked to the supply of good by the underlying supplier. Therefore, if the platform was interfering with setting the price, the delivery, return terms, or the payment terms, then this criterion would be fulfilled.[667] The European Commission further argues that even the setting of the terms and conditions for the use of the electronic interface is sufficient to fulfil Article 5b second subparagraph (a) of the VAT Implementing Regulation.[668] Such a broad interpretation can be seen critically since any platform will have terms and conditions with the customers and the underlying suppliers for the use of the electronic interface. Nevertheless, these terms and conditions may not influence the supply of the goods, but some electronic interfaces may decide to solely cover the use of the interface in their terms and conditions. However, Article 5b second subparagraph (a) of the VAT Implementing Regulation explicitly refers to 'the terms and conditions under which the supply of goods is made'. Therefore, the relevant setting of the terms and conditions by the electronic interface, such as the requirement of when the electronic interface facilitates a supply, should be limited to terms and conditions relevant for the supply of the goods.

Article 5b second subparagraph (b) of the VAT Implementing Regulation stipulates that the electronic interface facilitates a supply when it 'authorises the charge to the customer in respect of the payment made'. Thereby, the actual receiving or collecting of the payment is not necessary by the electronic interface. However, the authorisation of a charge should be fulfilled if the electronic interface decided whether, under which conditions, and at what time the customer pays or is otherwise involved in the authorisation process, e.g., when the electronic interface receives the authorisation message of payment.[669] If the platform was involved in the payment process, the

---

663. Compared to Article 14a of the VAT Directive, Article 9a (1) of the VAT Implementing Regulation does not require 'directly or indirectly' involvement; *see*, for a comparison of these two articles, also Tina Ehrke-Rabel et al., *Umsatzsteuer in einer digitalisierten Welt, supra* note 13, at 133.
664. European Commission, *Explanatory Notes: VAT E-Commerce Rules, supra* note 35, at 18.
665. *Ibid.*
666. *Ibid.*
667. *See* similarly *ibid.* at 18 and with a list of examples at pp. 18 et seq.
668. *Ibid.* at 18.
669. *Ibid.* at 19 and the list of examples at pp. 19 et seq.; *see*, similarly, Article 9a (1) third supara. of the VAT Implementing Regulation, where the taxable person also becomes the deemed supplier when it authorises the charge to the customer; *see* also European Commission, *Explanatory Notes on the EU VAT Changes to the Place of Supply of Telecommunications, Broadcasting and Electronic Services That Enter into Force in 2015, supra* note 11, at 34.

requirement of the authorisation of the charge would likely be fulfilled. The involvement in the payment process by the platform cannot be affirmed, e.g., in the case that the platform does not provide any payment possibilities on the electronic interface, but the payment is transferred directly from the customer to the bank account of the underlying supplier.

The last literae (c) of Article 5b second subparagraph of the VAT Implementing Regulation stipulates that, if a platform was 'involved in the ordering or delivery of the goods', then it would also facilitate a supply. Also, this last function should be interpreted broadly and covers any situation where the electronic interface has, in any way, influence on the ordering or delivery of the goods.[670]

3.2.2.3   *The Carve-Out Negative List in Article 5b of the VAT Implementing Regulation*

Additionally to the previous negative list, Article 5b third subparagraph of the VAT Implementing Regulation provides a second list of functions relevant for the qualification of whether a platform 'facilitates' a supply:

> Article 14a of Directive 2006/112/EC shall not apply to a taxable person who only provides any of the following:
>
> (a) the processing of payments in relation to the supply of goods;
> (b) the listing or advertising of goods;
> (c) the redirecting or transferring of customers to other electronic interfaces where goods are offered for sale, without any further intervention in the supply.

This list is an exclusive list. If a platform only provided one of the indicated functions, it would not qualify as 'facilitating'. Consequently, if the platform provided two or even all three functions, the platform would be facilitating the supply in question. The implementation of this carve-out list is also similar to the OECD's recommendation in its report.[671]

All three literae have in common that the platform, due to its limited access and involvement in the supply, does not receive all of the necessary information for the application of a deemed supplier regime:[672] If the electronic interface solely processed the payment for the supply of goods, e.g., as a payment processing provider, the electronic interface would receive the information that goods have been purchased from one specific website but might not have any knowledge where the goods will be delivered from and to and to what kind of goods the supply is referring. Similarly, an

---

670. *See*, similarly, European Commission, *Explanatory Notes: VAT E-Commerce Rules, supra* note 35, at 20 and with a list of examples at pp. 20 et seq.
671. OECD, *The Role of Digital Platforms in the Collection of VAT/GST on Online Sales, supra* note 8, para. 73. For a more detailed description on the OECD guidance, *see* s. 2.3.1.2.2 The Platform Becoming Liable for VAT/GST: Platforms' Liability Regimes.
672. *See*, similarly, European Commission, *Explanatory Notes: VAT E-Commerce Rules, supra* note 35, at 21.

electronic interface offering advertisements or redirecting customers to other homepages does not even receive the information of whether the advertisement or redirection actually results in the supply of goods. Therefore, in all of those situations, it would be impossible for the electronic interface to fulfil the obligations connected to the deemed supplier regime as the electronic interface does not receive the necessary information.

3.2.2.4   *Criticism on the Definition of 'to Facilitate'*

According to Article 5b third subparagraph (a) of the VAT Implementing Regulation, the sole 'processing of payments' does not make a platform facilitate a supply. Additionally, the platform does not have to be (in)directly involved 'in authorising the charge to the customer'[673] as this is only one of the requirements that can be fulfilled by a platform to become the deemed supplier. Thus, no involvement by the platform in the payment process by neither authorising nor by processing the payment is necessary for the platform to fulfil the requirement of 'to facilitate'.

In literature, it has been criticised that the platform does not have to be involved in the payment process although it becomes the deemed supplier and thus has to pay the VAT due.[674] In the platform business, some platforms are involved in the payment process of the goods supplied through the facilitation by the platform, but some other platforms are not involved in this process. Nevertheless, both platforms can facilitate the supply of goods and thus become the deemed supplier and liable to pay the VAT due. If the platform was not involved in the payment process and the customer transferred the whole amount (consideration for the goods plus the VAT payable) to the underlying supplier, then it would be impossible for the platform to withhold the VAT. In the described circumstances, the full consideration including the VAT would be paid to the underlying supplier instead of to the platform who is the responsible person for paying the VAT that is due to the competent tax authorities. Thus, the platform has to collect the VAT from the underlying supplier.[675] The VAT collection from the underlying supplier is to be based on civil law;[676] i.e., if the underlying supplier did not pay the VAT to the platform, the platform would have to sue the underlying supplier in the course of a civil law procedure. Therefore, platforms are facing a significant increase in compliance efforts and costs but also a negative impact

---

673. *See* Article 5b second subpara. (b) of the VAT Implementing Regulation.
674. *See*, e.g., Marie Lamensch, *Rendering Platforms Liable to Collect and Pay VAT on B2C Imports: A Silver Bullet?*, 29 International VAT Monitor, *supra* note 18, at 48; Marta Papis-Almansa, *VAT and Electronic Commerce: The New Rules as a Means for Simplification, Combatting Fraud and Creating a More Level Playing Field?*, 20 ERA Forum, *supra* note 18, at 219; Stefanie Becker, *Bericht aus Brüssel – Umsetzung der Neuregelungen im E-Commerce ab 1.1.2021*, MwStR, *supra* note 18, at 219; Lukas Franke & Julia Tumpel, *Aus für Mehrwertsteuerbetrug im Onlinehandel?*, SWK, *supra* note 18, at 1357; Stefan Hammerl & Lily Zechner, *SWK-Spezial Plattformhaftung*, *supra* note 18, at 20; Tina Ehrke-Rabel et al., *Umsatzsteuer in einer digitalisierten Welt*, *supra* note 13, at 122.
675. *See*, e.g., Marie Lamensch, *Rendering Platforms Liable to Collect and Pay VAT on B2C Imports: A Silver Bullet?*, *supra* note 18, at 48; Marta Papis-Almansa, *supra* note 18, at 219; Stefanie Becker, *supra* note 18, at 219; also the OECD points this OECD, *The Role of Digital Platforms in the Collection of VAT/GST on Online Sales*, *supra* note 8, at 25.
676. Stefanie Becker, *supra* note 18, at 219.

on their liquidity.[677] In the worst-case scenario, the platform will have to carry the VAT burden. This can be seen as critical since VAT is a tax that should be borne by the final consumers[678] and not by the taxable persons (fictitiously) supplying goods or services. Additionally, it raises the question of the proportionality of Article 14a of the VAT Directive. In fact, the platform should not be disproportionately burdened for being the VAT collector of the Member States.[679] Finally, platforms may have to adapt their business models accordingly in order to minimise the risk of an otherwise threatening final VAT burden.[680]

3.2.3 The Definition of the Use of an Electronic Interface

Furthermore, Article 14a of the VAT Directive stipulates that the facilitation by the taxable supply must be provided 'through the use of an electronic interface such as a marketplace, platform, portal or similar means'. This limitation to the use of electronic interfaces should provide legal certainty that exclusively digital platforms are covered by the scope of Article 14a of the VAT Directive. Traditional marketplaces or other physical sales events such as fairs are excluded from the scope of Article 14a of the VAT Directive.

Moreover, the list of electronic interfaces indicating marketplaces, platforms, portals, or similar means can only be read as an exemplary list. From the inclusion of 'similar means', the EU legislator likely wanted to keep the scope of electronic interfaces broad to account for possible future technological developments. By indicating that the use of similar means is also in the scope of the application of Article 14a of the VAT Directive, the use of devices or software developed in the future and not yet on the market may also be subsumed under Article 14a of the VAT Directive as long as these devices or software are an electronic interface. According to the European

---

677. See, e.g., Marie Lamensch, *Rendering Platforms Liable to Collect and Pay VAT on B2C Imports: A Silver Bullet?, supra* note 18, at 48.

678. The CJEU held, on the one side, that the EU VAT system is intended to tax the final consumer; *see,* e.g., Case C-317/94, *Elida Gibbs Ltd v Commissioners of Customs and Excise,* 24 Oct. 1996, ECLI:EU:C:1996:400, para. 19; Case C-427/98, *Commission of the European Communities v Federal Republic of Germany,* 15 Oct. 2002, ECLI:EU:C:2002:581, para. 29; Joined Cases C-249/12 and C-250/12, *Corina-Hrisi Tulică v Agenţia Naţională de Administrare Fiscală – Direcţia Generală de Soluţionare a Contestaţiilor and Călin Ion Plavoşin v Direcţia Generală a Finanţelor Publice Timiş – Serviciul Soluţionare Contestaţii and Activitatea de Inspecţie Fiscală – Serviciul de Inspecţie Fiscală Timiş,* 7 Nov. 2013, ECLI:EU:C:2013:722, para. 34; on the other side, the CJEU held that the VAT should ultimately be borne by the final consumer, *see,* e.g., Joined Cases C-338/97, C-344/97, C-390/97, *Erna Pelzl and Others v Steiermärkische Landesregierung (C-338/97), Wiener Städtische Allgemeine Versicherungs AG and Others v Tiroler Landesregierung (C-344/97) and STUAG Bau-Aktiengesellschaft v Kärntner Landesregierung (C-390/97),* 8 Jun. 1999, ECLI:EU:C:1999:285, para. 17; Case C-475/03, *Banca popolare di Cremona Soc. coop. arl v Agenzia Entrate Ufficio Cremona,* 3 Oct. 2006, ECLI:EU:C:2006:629, para. 28; Case C-271/06, *Netto Supermarkt GmbH & Co. OHG v Finanzamt Malchin,* 21 Feb. 2008, ECLI:EU:C:2008:105, para. 21.

679. Stefanie Becker, *supra* note 18, at 219. *See,* on the discussion of the proportionality of the broad scope of 'facilitate', s. 5.2.4.2.2.1 The Proportionality in the Strict Sense.

680. *See,* for the discussion of such adaptions in light of the freedom to conduct business, s. 5.3 Discussion of a Possible Infringement of Article 14a of the VAT Directive of the Freedom to Conduct a Business.

Commission, '**Electronic interface** – should be understood as a broad concept which allows two independent systems or a system and the end user to communicate with the help of a device or programme. An electronic interface could encompass a website, portal, gateway, marketplace, application program interface (API), etc.'[681]

3.3   SUBSTANTIVE SCOPE

3.3.1   Distance Sales of Low-Value Goods Imported from a Third Territory or a Third Country: Article 14a (1) of the VAT Directive

3.3.1.1   *The Definition of Distance Sales of Goods Imported from a Third Territory or a Third Country*

3.3.1.1.1   *General Remarks*

According to Article 14a (1) of the VAT Directive, the first situation when a facilitating platform becomes a deemed supplier is for 'distance sales of goods imported from third territories or third countries in consignments of an intrinsic value not exceeding EUR 150'. With the e-commerce package, the importation of distance sales of goods has legally been defined in Article 14 (4) (2) of the VAT Directive:

> (2) 'distance sales of goods imported from third territories or third countries' means supplies of goods dispatched or transported by or on behalf of the supplier, including where the supplier intervenes indirectly in the transport or dispatch of the goods, from a third territory or third country, to a customer in a Member State, where the following conditions are met:
> (a) the supply of goods is carried out for a taxable person, or a non-taxable legal person, whose intra-Community acquisitions of goods are not subject to VAT pursuant to Article 3 (1) or for any other non-taxable person;
> (b) the goods supplied are neither new means of transport nor goods supplied after assembly or installation, with or without a trial run, by or on behalf of the supplier.

Thereby, neither Article 14a (1) of the VAT Directive nor Article 14 (4) (2) (b) of the VAT Directive stipulate that the underlying supplier must be a taxable person. Thus, the taxable status of the underlying supplier is irrelevant for the application of Article 14a (1) of the VAT Directive. From the definition in Article 14 (4) (2) of the VAT Directive, several requirements for the application of Article 14a (1) of the VAT Directive can be derived: (i) the goods must be 'dispatched or transported by or on behalf of the supplier', (ii) the goods must be imported 'from a third territory or a third country', (iii) further criteria on the taxable status of the customer who must be in a

---

681. *See* European Commission, *Explanatory Notes on the New VAT E-Commerce Rules*, *supra* note 35, at 8 et seq.; *see*, very critical on this definition, Sergio Messina, *VAT E-Commerce Package: Customs Bugs in the System? Analysis of the Issues Undermining the New Import VAT Platform Collecting Model*, 13 World Tax Journal, *supra* note 19, at 126 et seq.

Member State are stipulated in Article 14 (4) (2) (a) of the VAT Directive; and finally (iv) requirements on the kind of supplied good according to Article 14 (4) (2) (b) of the VAT Directive. These different requirements will be analysed and interpreted in the subsequent sections.

3.3.1.1.2 The Dispatch or Transportation of Goods by or on Behalf of the Supplier

The first requirement is the dispatch or transportation of goods by or on behalf of the supplier. Although Article 14 (4) (2) of the VAT Directive was newly introduced with the e-commerce package, the term 'goods dispatched or transported by or on behalf of the supplier' is also used in other articles of the VAT Directive.[682] Therefore, the CJEU has already had the chance to discuss the definition and requirements of when goods are dispatched or transported. A clear distinction between 'dispatch' and 'transport' is difficult to find since the dispatch of the goods would naturally result in the transportation of the goods.[683] Nevertheless, the CJEU generally held that the dispatch or transport of goods is to be interpreted as the physical transportation of the goods which would lead to the customer in the Member State receiving the right to dispose of the goods.[684]

Since Article 14 (4) (2) of the VAT Directive was introduced with the e-commerce package, also the stipulation of the sufficiency of an 'indirect' involvement of the supplier in the dispatch or transport of the goods is only applicable as of 1 July 2021. Thereby, in a first step, the transport by or on behalf of the supplier and the indirect involvement in the transport or dispatch by the supplier should be discussed separately. In general, the transport or dispatch by the supplier is fulfilled when the supplier himself transports the goods. The goods may also be transported on behalf of the supplier which means that the supplier organises the transportation of the goods. Therefore, the meaning of transport organisation should be evaluated further. The CJEU had to repeatedly discuss the transport organisation when deciding on the supply with transport in chain transactions. Thereby, the CJEU held that 'an overall assessment of all the circumstances of the case' must be conducted.[685] The European

---

682. The term 'dispatch(ed) and transport(ed)' is used 105 times in the VAT Directive in any cases where the requirements and legal consequences of a supply with transport is stipulated.
683. Case C-276/18, *KrakVet Marek Batko sp. K. v Nemzeti Adó- és Vámhivatal Fellebbviteli Igazgatósága*, 6 Feb. 2020, ECLI:EU:C:2020:81, Opinion of AG Eleanor Sharpston, para. 75; *see* also the discussion in paras. 76 et seqq. on the interpretation of 'dispatch by the supplier' and 'transportation by the supplier'.
684. *See* the discussion of the 'dispatch and transport' by the CJEU on the intra-Community acquisition in Case C-409/04, *The Queen, on the application of Teleos plc and Others v Commissioners of Customs & Excise*, 27 Sep. 2007, ECLI:EU:C:2007:548, para. 42; Case C-414/17, *AREX CZ a.s. v Odvolací finanční ředitelství*, 19 Dec. 2018, ECLI:EU:C:2018:1027, para. 61; Case C-401/18, *Herst s.r.o. v Odvolací finanční ředitelství*, 23 Apr. 2020, ECLI: EU:C:2020:295, para. 34.
685. *See*, e.g., Case C-430/09, *Euro Tyre Holding BV v Staatssecretaris van Financiën*, 16 Dec. 2010, ECLI:EU:C:2010:786, para. 44; Case C-628/16, *Kreuzmayr GmbH v Finanzamt Linz*, 21 Feb. 2018, ECLI:EU:C:2018:84, para. 32; Case C-414/17, *AREX CZ*, 19 Dec. 2018, ECLI: EU:C:2018:1027, para. 72; Case C-401/18, *Herst*, 23 Apr. 2020, ECLI:EU:C:2020:295, para. 43.

Commission argues that mainly the person who contracts the transport with a third party should qualify as the person organising the transport; the payment of the costs for the transport should not be decisive.[686] Additionally, also the risk-carrying during the transportation has been brought forward to be decisive for the transport organisation.[687]

In many cases, the criterion of the transport organisation will not be questionable since, for the application of Article 14 (4) (2) of the VAT Directive, the supplier does not have to organise the transport or dispatch of the goods himself, but indirect involvement is sufficient. Similar to the discussed use of the term 'indirectly' in Article 5b of the VAT Implementing Regulation,[688] again, the use of the term 'indirectly' in this case must lead to a broad interpretation.[689] Thereby, the EU legislator seems to have wanted to exclude circumventions by the suppliers by pushing the transport organisations *pro forma* over to the customer. This aim by the EU legislator can also be seen from the legal definition implemented in Article 5a of the VAT Implementing Regulation which stipulates that the supplier is indirectly involved when:

(a) the supplier subcontracts the dispatch or transport to a third party,
(b) the dispatch or transport is provided by a third party, but the supplier carries (partially) the risk for the delivery,
(c) the supplier invoices the transportation fees to the customer and arranges the delivery by a third party, or
(d) the supplier provides any information to the customer for the delivery of the goods. This last point also included promoting the delivery by a third party or putting the customer into contact with a third party delivery.

Additionally, Article 5a third subparagraph of the VAT Implementing Regulation also stipulates a negative definition when the supplier is not indirectly involved in the supply. This is the case when the customer picks up the goods from the supplier in the third country or when the customer organises the pickup of the goods with a third party without the intervention of the supplier.[690]

---

686. *See* European Commission, *Explanatory Notes on the EU VAT Changes in Respect of Call-Off Stock Arrangements, Chain Transactions and the Exemption for Intra-Community Supplies of Goods ('2020 Quick Fixes')*, *supra* note 35, at 53.
687. Case C-401/18, *Herst s.r.o. v Odvolací finanční ředitelství*, 3 Oct. 2019, ECLI:EU:C:2019:834, Opinion of AG Kokott, paras. 41 et seqq.; *see*, critically, on this aspect European Commission, *Explanatory Notes: 2020 Quick Fixes*, *supra* note 35, at 53.
688. *See* the discussion in s. 3.2.2.2 The First Negative List in Article 5b of the VAT Implementing Regulation.
689. Also, the CJEU has based the interpretation of transport organisation on a rather broad understanding according to which the indirect involvement was already sufficient before this clarification in Article 5b of the VAT Implementing Regulation; *see* Case C-276/18, *KrakVet Marek Batko*, 18 Jun. 2020, ECLI:EU:C:2020:485, paras. 63 et seqq.
690. *See* already with a similar conclusion on the distance selling provisions applicable before 1 July 2021, VAT Committee, *Guidelines Resulting from Meetings of the VAT Committee: Distance Selling*, Guidelines Resulting from the 104th Meeting, taxud.c.1(2015)4820441-876, *supra* note 377.

In a second step, it should be evaluated whether the (indirectly) involved 'supplier' should be the underlying supplier or if the platform should be the (indirectly) involved as it is the (possibly) deemed. According to the civil law contracts, only the underlying supplier has the power of disposal over the goods which is transferred to the customer through the sale of the goods. Therefore, the transportation of the goods can only be organised by either the underlying supplier or by the customer. A third party would only get involved if it was subcontracted by one involved party. In practice, the delivery of the goods is 'organised' by the platform, in many cases. This transport organisation is likely based on subcontracting by the underlying supplier or by the customer. If the underlying supplier was subcontracting the platform with the transportation of the goods, Article 5a (a) of the VAT Implementing Regulation would be fulfilled, and the underlying supplier would be indirectly involved in the dispatch or transport of the goods. Even if the customer was subcontracting the platform with the transportation of the goods, the underlying supplier may still be indirectly involved if the underlying supplier bore at least a partial risk during the transportation.[691] The question of the risk bearing should, in general, also be agreed upon in the sales contract between the underlying supplier and the customer. Therefore, in most practical cases, either Article 5a (a) or Article 5a (b) of the VAT Implementing Regulation should be fulfilled. Even though the platform seems to organise the transport, it was subcontracted by the underlying supplier and/or the underlying supplier carries the risk during the transportation of the goods. In these cases, the underlying supplier would be indirectly involved in the transport, and the underlying supplier would fulfil the condition of being involved in the dispatch or transport of the goods according to Article 14 (4) (2) of the VAT Directive.[692]

Furthermore, this interpretation can also be supported with a systematic argument, i.e., only when the underlying supplier is (indirectly) involved in the dispatch or transport would the supply then qualify as a 'distance sales of goods imported from third territories or third countries'. The fulfilment of the requirements of Article 14 (4) (2) of the VAT Directive therefore triggers the deeming provision in Article 14a (1) of the VAT Directive.[693] Thus, the requirements of Article 14 (4) (2) of the VAT Directive must be fulfilled by the underlying supplier for the deeming provision to become applicable and not by the platform.

Although, at first sight, the usage of 'supplier' in Article 14 (4) (2) of the VAT Directive could cause interpretational questions of whether the underlying supplier or the platform must fulfil the therein stipulated requirements, with the systematic-logical interpretation, it becomes clear that only the (indirect) involvement by the underlying

---

691. See Article 5a (b) of the VAT Implementing Regulation.

692. See, contrary, Sergio Messina, VAT E-Commerce Package: Customs Bugs in the System? Analysis of the Issues Undermining the New Import VAT Platform Collecting Model, 13 World Tax Journal, supra note 19, at 132; the author argues that in cases where the platform, i.e., the deemed supplier, is responsible for the transportation, the platform instead of the underlying supplier would be (indirectly) organising the transportation. Thus, the author raises doubts of the applicability of Article 14a (1) of the VAT Directive in cases where the platform is involved in the transport organisation.

693. See, similarly, ibid. for the full argumentation, pp. 127 et seqq.

supplier can be relevant for the applicability of Article 14 (4) (2) of the VAT Directive. The background for the seemingly unclear wording might be that Article 14 (4) (2) of the VAT Directive is applicable to any case of distance sales imported from third territories or third countries independently of the involvement of a platform. Therefore, it is likely that the EU legislator purposely chose the wording 'supplier' as, in most cases, it is clear who is the supplier of the transaction.[694] If the national legislators decided to include a definition of 'distance sales of goods imported from third territories or third countries' in their national law, special attention could be given to the raised unclearness in Article 14a (1) read in conjunction with Article 14 (4) (2) of the VAT Directive whether the underlying supplier or the platform as the deemed supplier has to be indirectly involved in the dispatch or transport of the goods. A clearer wording in the national law could eliminate the described doubts.

3.3.1.1.3 The Importation from Third Territories and Third Countries

Second, the definition of Article 14 (4) (2) of the VAT Directive is limited to imports from third territories and third countries.[695] Third territories are territories that are part of one Member State but are excluded from the application of the VAT Directive.[696] Third countries are any countries to which the TFEU is not applicable and, thus, the VAT Directive is also not applicable in third countries.[697] From this general definition, the VAT Directive provides exceptions of third countries to which the VAT Directive is applicable.[698] National supplies and intra-Community supplies are therefore explicitly excluded from the application of Article 14 (4) (2) of the VAT Directive.

3.3.1.1.4 The Requirements of Article 14 (4) (2) (a) of the VAT Directive on the VAT Status of the Recipient of the Goods

Furthermore, according to Article 14 (4) (2) (a) of the VAT Directive, a supply can only qualify as a 'distance sales of goods imported from third territories or third countries'

---

694. See contrary *ibid.*
695. For a full list of the status and the applicability of the VAT Directive to specific areas or territories, *see* European Commission, *Territorial Status of EU Countries and Certain Territories*, https://ec.europa.eu/taxation_customs/territorial-status-eu-countries-and-certain-territories_en (last visited 27 Jul. 2021).
696. *See* Article 5 (3) read in conjunction with Article 6 of the VAT Directive; in Article 6 of the VAT Directive, the following third territories are listed: Mount Athos; the Canary Islands; the French territories of Guadeloupe, French Guiana, Martinique, Réunion, Saint-Barthélemy, Saint-Martin; the Åland Islands; Campione d'Italia; the Italian waters of Lake Lugano; the Island of Heligoland; the territory of Büsingen; Ceuta; Melilla; and Livigno.
697. *See* Article 5 (4) of the VAT Directive.
698. This is the case for the Principality of Monaco, the Isle of Man and the United Kingdom Sovereign Base Areas of Akrotiri and Dhekelia; *see* Article 7 (1) of the VAT Directive; additionally, the VAT Directive is also applicable to the supply of goods from and to Northern Ireland; *see* Article 7 (1) of the Agreement on the Withdrawal of the United Kingdom of Great Britain and Northern Ireland from the European Union and the European Atomic Energy Community, OJ L 29/7 (2020) read in conjunction with Article 13 (1) of the Protocol on Ireland/Northern Ireland.

when the recipient of the goods is a non-taxable person.[699] Additionally, also taxable or non-taxable legal persons can be the recipients when they fulfil the requirements according to Article 3 (1) of the VAT Directive. Article 3 (1) (a) of the VAT Directive stipulates that such an intra-Community acquisition is not taxable when the 'supply of such goods within territory of the Member State of acquisition would be exempt pursuant to Articles 148 and 151'. Examples for such exempt supplies are the supply of goods that are necessary for vessels[700] and aircraft[701] and the supply of goods and services to certain public institutions, bodies, or similar.[702] Additionally, taxable persons subject to the flat-rate scheme for farmers[703] could also be the recipient of distance sales of goods imported from third territories or third countries if the farmers purchased the goods for their agricultural, forestry, or fisheries business.[704] Moreover, non-taxable legal persons and taxable persons who only carry out the supply of goods and services for non-deductible supplies, e.g., because the customer exclusively provides exempt supplies or qualifies as a small enterprise, may also be the recipients of distance sales of goods imported from third territories or third countries.[705] In this sense, any taxable person exclusively providing exempt supplies that do not allow the input VAT deduction is also covered as recipient by Article 14 (4) (2) of the VAT Directive.[706]

3.3.1.1.5 Limitations to the Supplied Goods According to Article 14 (4) (2) (b) of the VAT Directive

Finally, also the kind of the supplied good is relevant. According to Article 14 (4) (2) (b) of the VAT Directive, 'distance sales of goods imported from third territories or third countries' cannot be goods supplied after assembly or installation or new means of transport, as defined in Article 2 (2) of the VAT Directive. Other restrictions on the kind of goods are not indicated in the VAT Directive.[707]

---

699. For the discussion of the rebuttable presumption on the status of the recipient of the goods in Article 5d (a) of the VAT Implementing Regulation, see s. 3.3.4 The Rebuttal Presumption of Article 5d of the VAT Implementing Regulation.

700. See Article 148 (a)-(d) of the VAT Directive.

701. See Article 148 (e)-(g) of the VAT Directive.

702. See Article 151 of the VAT Directive; examples of this would be the supply of goods or services under diplomatic and consular arrangements (Article 151 [1] [a] of the VAT Directive), the supply of goods or services to the European Community, the European Atomic Energy Community, the European Central Bank, or the European Investment Bank (Article 151 [1] [aa] of the VAT Directive) or to international bodies (Article 151 [1] [b] of the VAT Directive).

703. See Article 295 et seqq. of the VAT Directive.

704. See Article 3 (1) (b) of the VAT Directive.

705. See Article 3 (1) (b) of the VAT Directive.

706. In this case, the activities listed in Articles 132 and 135 of the VAT Directive seem especially relevant.

707. Although Article 14 (4) (2) (b) of the VAT Directive is applicable to products subject to excise duties, the platform cannot use the IOSS to declare 'distance sales of goods imported from third territories or third countries' that are subject to excise duties; see Article 369l of the VAT Directive. For further information on the IOSS, see s. 4.11 Special Schemes of the OSS.

3.3.1.2 The Consignment's Intrinsic Value

3.3.1.2.1 General Remarks

The second criterion of Article 14a (1) of the VAT Directive stipulates that the supplied goods must be 'in consignments of an intrinsic value not exceeding EUR 150'. Background for the implementation of this intrinsic value may have been that a full customs declaration is necessary for consignments exceeding an intrinsic value of EUR 150 and, thus, the risk of the VAT not being paid is reduced for consignments exceeding the EUR 150 threshold.[708]

The intrinsic value of consignments not exceeding EUR 150 is not only used as a determining factor for the applicability of Article 14a (1) of the VAT Directive but also for determining whether the import is exempt from customs duties[709] and whether a supplier may apply the IOSS.[710] In all three articles, the determination of the consignment's intrinsic value is a triggering criterion: Article 14a (1) of the VAT Directive triggers the deemed supplier regime (if the other requirements were also fulfilled), Article 369l et seqq. of the VAT Directive triggers the possibility to apply the IOSS, and Article 23 of the Regulation (2009/1186) triggers the exemption from customs duties. Due to the use of the same words in these articles, it can be argued that the definitions provided in customs law should also be taken into consideration when interpreting the relevant articles in VAT law and vice versa. Thereby, a uniform interpretation of the law could be guaranteed.[711] This is also supported by the EU legislator explicitly linking the requirement of the consignments' intrinsic value to not exceed EUR 150 in Article 14a (1) of the VAT Directive to the fact that a full customs declaration is only necessary when the value exceeds EUR 150.[712] Therefore, the EU legislator seems to have explicitly chosen a correlation between the provisions of the VAT Directive and customs law in order to not cause any contradictions between customs and VAT law.

From the definition of Article 14a (1) of the VAT Directive, three terms must be interpreted: (i) 'consignments', (ii) 'intrinsic value', and (iii) 'not exceeding EUR 150'.

---

708. *See* the explicit justification by the European Parliament for a draft formulation of the deemed supplier provision where it was stated that a 'full customs declaration is compulsory for imports of goods of more than 150€, thereby reducing the risk of VAT not paid'. European Parliament, *Report on the Proposal for a Council Directive Amending Directive 2006/112/EC and Directive 2009/132/EC as Regards Certain Value Added Tax Obligations for Supplies of Services and Distance Sales of Goods*, A8-0307/2017, *supra* note 603, at 9.

709. *See* Article 23 of the Council Regulation (EC) No 1186/2009 of 16 November 2009 Setting up a Community System of Reliefs from Customs Duty, OJ L 324 (2009).

710. *See* Article 369l et seqq. of the VAT Directive; for further information on the IOSS, *see* s. 4.11 Special Schemes of the OSS.

711. *See*, similarly, also the CJEU holding that to guarantee the sound functioning and uniform interpretation of the VAT system, the same terms in the VAT Directive should not be interpreted differently just because they are used in different provisions of the VAT Directive in Case C-242/08, *Swiss Re Germany Holding*, 22 Oct. 2009, ECLI:EU:C:2009:647, para. 31; *see*, by analogy, also Case C-695/19, *Rádio Popular – Electrodomésticos, SA v Autoridade Tributária e Aduaneira*, 8 Jul. 2021, ECLI:EU:C:2021:549, para. 46.

712. *See* preamble pt. 7 of the Council Directive (EU) 2017/2455 of 5 December 2017 Amending Directive 2006/112/EC and Directive 2009/132/EC as Regards Certain Value Added Tax Obligations for Supplies of Services and Distance Sales of Goods, OJ L 348/7 (2017).

The three different requirements and the additional aspect of the wrong valuation of the goods will be analysed in the subsequent sections.

3.3.1.2.2   The Interpretation of 'Consignments'

The term 'consignments' has not been explicitly defined by the EU legislator in the course of the e-commerce package. Therefore, the interpretative question arises about how broadly the term 'consignments' can be interpreted. If a supplier splits up the delivery of the goods into several parcels, should this qualify as one consignment? If the supplier delivered several orders in one parcel, should this qualify as one consignment? If the underlying supplier transported several orders to the EU in one parcel and split them up in the EU to deliver to different customers, should this qualify as one consignment?

Several definitions of the word 'consignment' can be found in EU customs-related laws or agreements.[713] All of these definitions define 'consignment' as:

'consignment' means products which are either:

(a) sent simultaneously from one exporter to one consignee; or
(b) covered by a single transport document covering their shipment from the exporter to the consignee or, in the absence of such document, by a single invoice.[714]

According to this legal definition, two criteria are required that may be fulfilled alternatively: the simultaneous dispatch or the same transport document (or invoice) for the goods.[715] From this definition, it follows that, when one of the two requirements is fulfilled, the transportation of the goods qualifies as one consignment. If several parcels were sent at the same time and thus several transportation documents are issued, requirement (a) would be fulfilled due to the simultaneous transportation of the

---

713. See, on the discussion of whether the customs law is applicable for interpreting Article 14a (1) of the VAT Directive, s. 3.3.1.2.1 General Remarks.
714. See, e.g., Article 37 (19) of the Commission Delegated Regulation (EU) 2015/2446 of 28 July 2015 Supplementing Regulation (EU) No 952/2013 of the European Parliament and of the Council as Regards Detailed Rules Concerning Certain Provisions of the Union Customs Code, OJ L 343 (2015), where the definition of 'consignment' is explicitly limited to the application of section 2 of the UCC-DA, the preferential origin; Article 1 (k) of the Council Regulation (EC) No 82/2001 of 5 December 2000 Concerning the Definition of the Concept of 'Originating Products' and Methods of Administrative Cooperation in Trade Between the Customs Territory of the Community and Ceuta and Melilla, OJ L 20 (2001); Annex VI Article 1 (n) of the Council Decision 2013/755/EU of 25 November 2013 on the Association of the Overseas Countries and Territories with the European Union, OJ L 344 (2013).
715. There are several conventions that try to uniform the international transportation of goods via sea, road and air; see, e.g., United Nations Convention on Contracts for the International Carriage of Goods Wholly or Partly by Sea (2008), available at https://uncitral.un.org/sites/uncitral.un.org/files/media-documents/uncitral/en/rotterdam-rules-e.pdf (visited 13 Aug. 2021); Convention on the Contract for the International Carriage of Goods by Road (CMR) (19 May 1956), available at https://treaties.un.org/doc/Treaties/1961/07/19610702%2001-56%20AM/Ch_XI_B_11.pdf (visited 13 Aug. 2021); Convention for the Unification of Certain Rules for International Carriage by Air (1999), available at https://www.iata.org/contentassets/fb1137ff561a4819a2d38f3db7308758/mc99-full-text.pdf (visited 13 Aug. 2021).

goods. Similarly, if several orders were put together and covered by only one transport document (or invoice in the absence of the transport document), then requirement (b) would be fulfilled.[716] In both described cases, the parcel(s) would qualify as one consignment.

The European Commission has interpreted the term 'consignments' and introduced a definition thereof. From the chosen wording of the European Commission's interpretation, the definition could be inspired by the aforementioned legal definitions. The European Commission interprets consignments in the Explanatory Notes as 'goods packed together and dispatched simultaneously by the same supplier or underlying supplier to the same consignee and covered by the same transport contract'.[717] According to this definition, the European Commission seems to require three criteria to be fulfilled cumulatively: (i) goods must be packed together, (ii) dispatched simultaneously, and (iii) covered by the same transport contract. In the third criterion, the European Commission refers to the term 'transport contract' whereas the definition in customs law refers to 'transport document'. The reference to 'transport contract' is wider than the reference to 'transport document' since a transport contract can cover several deliveries whereas the transport document is a document issued for the specific transport of one parcel.[718] Nevertheless, since the European Commission also argues that the goods must be (i) packed together assumingly in one parcel, and the goods must be delivered with one transport document. The diverging interpretation by the European Commission may have been based on a practicability argument for the involved parties and the customs authorities as the fulfilling of all three criteria makes the checks easier. If the aforementioned alternative definition was applied, the underlying supplier and platform would face the difficulty that several packages could be dispatched simultaneously. Thus, also several transport documents would be available. Nevertheless, since the packages would have been dispatched simultaneously from one exporter to one consignee, this transportation should qualify as one consignment because requirement (a) would be fulfilled. Thereby, close communication between the taxable person organising the transport (underlying supplier or

---

716. This requirement seems to be especially relevant for big deliveries. If, e.g., one supplier dispatches five containers on one boat, then one transportation contract should be sufficient for this delivery. In this case, the five containers would qualify as one consignment. In general, though, especially with smaller parcels, each parcel should have a separate transport document.

717. European Commission, *Explanatory Notes on the New VAT E-Commerce Rules*, *supra* note 35, at 8 + 71; *see* also similarly European Commission, *Importation and Exportation of Low Value Consignments – VAT E-Commerce Package 'Guidance for Member States and Trade'* 11, https://ec.europa.eu/taxation_customs/system/files/2021-06/guidance_on_import_and_export_of_low_value_consignments_en.pdf (last visited 1 Aug. 2021). It should be noted that the European Commission provides extensive guidance on the IOSS scheme and the requirements thereof. As the applicability of the IOSS scheme and the deemed supplier regime is based on the same wording, the explanations by the European Commission for the IOSS scheme should also serve as interpretational guidance on the deemed supplier provision for determining the meaning of 'in consignments of an intrinsic value not exceeding EUR 150'.

718. Several conventions try to uniform international transportation and thereby also the transportation contracts and documents for the transport of goods via sea, road, and air; *see*, e.g., *Rotterdam Rules*; *Convention on the Contract for the International Carriage of Goods by Road (CMR)*; *Convention for the Unification of Certain Rules for International Carriage by Air*.

platform) and the other involved party would be necessary to find out how many packages would be delivered simultaneously. Thus, the parties would have to add up the value of the different transportation documents (or alternatively invoices) to decide whether Article 14a (1) of the VAT Directive is applicable. In practice, this may cause difficulties for the involved parties (underlying supplier and platform) as a more thorough check and communication between the parties would be necessary. Therefore, due to practicability reasons, the definition of the European Commission seems more convincing for the determination of a consignment within the scope of Article 14a (1) of the VAT Directive.

In many cases, both requirements will be fulfilled as the underlying supplier (or platform) would send the order to the customer including the corresponding transport documents and invoice. Thereby, the general rule is that each parcel that is sent to the customer should qualify as one consignment. The qualification as one consignment becomes more difficult when several goods are ordered in one order or when several orders of goods are placed by the same customer. According to the described legal definition, one single parcel would be considered as one consignment as the goods in that parcel are sent simultaneously under one transport document from the underlying supplier to the customer. Therefore, when one customer orders several goods separately and the underlying supplier (or platform)[719] dispatches all of the goods in one parcel, then this delivery would also qualify as one consignment.[720] The aggregation of shipments has the benefit that the transport costs may be reduced. Nevertheless, although the singular products may not exceed the intrinsic value of EUR 150 due to the aggregation of the goods into one parcel, the intrinsic value of EUR 150 may be exceeded. The result of exceeding the intrinsic value is that the platform is not becoming the deemed supplier for the importation of these goods and, additionally, the underlying supplier cannot use the IOSS for the importation of the goods since, also for the application of the IOSS, the intrinsic value of the consignment must not exceed EUR 150.[721] Thus, if the platform was responsible for the transportation of the goods, the aggregation of orders could be one possibility for the platform to deliberately exceed the EUR 150 threshold and thus not become the deemed supplier. Additionally, a well-established information flow is necessary between the platform and the underlying supplier in order to know whether the platform is becoming the deemed supplier or whether the underlying supplier is the supplier of the goods depending on the bundling of the goods.

Another way of bundling supplies would be to aggregate supplies for several customers into one consignment for the release of free circulation in the EU and to separate the different parcels in the EU for the final delivery to the customers. This

---

719. Whether the underlying supplier or the platform is responsible for the transportation of the goods depends on the contractual relationship between the underlying supplier and the platform.

720. See, similarly, European Commission, *Explanatory Notes: VAT E-Commerce Rules*, supra note 35, at 72 et seq.; European Commission, *Importation and Exportation of Low Value Consignments*, supra note 717, at 47 et seq.

721. See also further the discussions on the application of the IOSS in s. 4.11.2.2 The Introduction of IOSS.

question has already been discussed by the CJEU in the case *Har Vaessen Douane Service*[722] where the CJEU had to determine whether the import duty exemption was applicable for grouped consignments of goods, when the combined value exceeds the intrinsic value, but the individual consignments fall below the intrinsic value. The CJEU decided that the exemption of import duties is applicable when the consignments are individually addressed to the customers.[723] Thus, if the recipient was already indicated on the singular parcels of the consignment, then the consignment could qualify as several consignments with each consisting of the parcel to be sent to the customer.[724]

Finally, the underlying supplier (or platform) may also split up an order by a customer into different consignments. There are several reasons for suppliers splitting up consignments:

- The supplier might not have one ordered item in stock and would therefore deliver the out-of-stock item at a later time.
- The goods of the supplier may be stored in different warehouses (maybe even in different countries), and, therefore, the order is split up into different consignments.
- The underlying supplier may intentionally split up the order, so the singular consignments have an intrinsic value of less than EUR 150; which would generally result in the platform becoming the deemed supplier and the import duty exemption being applicable when the import is declared via the IOSS.[725]

The European Commission argues in the case of splitting up the ordered goods into different consignments that the intrinsic value should be calculated based on the order value, i.e., based on the whole amount of the order independently of how many consignments the goods are delivered.[726] To base the intrinsic value on the order and not on the consignment itself might facilitate the classification by the platform regarding whether it becomes the deemed supplier since the information of the orders placed on the platform should be available to the platform. Nevertheless, such an interpretation can be seen critically as the word 'consignment' would be reinterpreted into 'order'. Such a reinterpretation would be appropriate if the supplier split up the order artificially to circumvent the payment of import duties and/or to trigger the platform liability according to Article 14a (1) of the VAT Directive.[727] In other cases of

---

722. Case C-7/08, *Har Vaessen Douane Service BV v Staatssecretaris van Financiën*, 2 Jul. 2009, ECLI:EU:C:2009:417.
723. *See ibid.* para. 49.
724. *See* also European Commission, *Importation and Exportation of Low Value Consignments*, *supra* note 717, at 48.
725. In general, the decision of how to deliver the goods is a decision not solely made based on the best VAT and customs treatment but also influenced by other important factors. In the described case, splitting up the deliveries would result in, e.g., significantly higher transportation costs.
726. European Commission, *Explanatory Notes on the New VAT E-Commerce Rules*, *supra* note 35, at 73.
727. *Ibid.*; European Commission, *Importation and Exportation of Low Value Consignments*, *supra* note 717, at 48.

splitting up the order, such an interpretation would lead to a not uniform interpretation: as discussed, the bundling of orders to the same customer should qualify as one consignment. If the term 'consignment' was reinterpreted as 'order', as suggested by the European Commission, then also, in the case of bundling the delivery of goods, the intrinsic value should be determined based on each order separately and not based on the (bundled) consignment. Therefore, the general rule for splitting up orders should also be that the intrinsic value of each consignment should be evaluated separately.

After all, the underlying supplier (or platform) dispatching the goods would have some flexibility on the transportation to the customer, especially in the case when more than one singular good is delivered to the customer. The goods may be ordered in one order or in multiple orders. Due to the bundling or splitting up of the goods, the underlying supplier (or platform) can decide whether the requirement of Article 14a (1) of the VAT Directive would be fulfilled. This would cause legal uncertainty for the platform if the platform was not involved with the dispatch of the goods since the platform would be dependent on the information of the shipments provided by the underlying supplier. The dependence of this information from the platform is due to the wording of Article 14a (1) of the VAT Directive referring to 'consignments' instead of order. The EU legislator seems to have chosen this word to provide a facilitation of interpretation because the consignments' intrinsic value is also relevant for the question of the application of the IOSS and the import duties exemption. Thereby, the EU legislator disregarded the possible lack of practical information on the consignments by the platform.[728]

To counteract this information deficit in cases where the platform (or deemed supplier) is not involved in the dispatch of the goods, the platform should indicate in the contract with the underlying suppliers and in the corresponding terms and conditions that the parties can assume that each order is considered to be one consignment. Additionally, an information obligation should be implemented between the parties in order to inform the other party when several orders were bundled or one order was split up. On the one hand, such a stipulation could raise awareness of the underlying suppliers for the discussed issue of bundling or splitting up the goods. On the other hand, the platform would have a right for damages based on civil law if the underlying supplier disregarded this contractual agreement. In many cases, the platform would have the knowledge of the intrinsic value of the good since the platform often administers the orders, and the underlying supplier should also have the knowledge of the order as the underlying supplier must fulfil the order. Based on the order by the customer, the platform and underlying supplier could determine whether the platform became the deemed supplier or whether the underlying supplier is the supplier of the goods.

An alternative approach by the EU legislator could have been to base the application of Article 14a (1) of the VAT Directive on the order of the customer. Instead of the word 'consignment', the EU legislator could have used the word 'order'. This way, the verification by the platform (or underlying supplier) on whether the platform

---

728. Vice versa, also the underlying supplier may suffer from such an information lack if the platform was responsible for the transportation of the goods.

became the deemed supplier would have been facilitated. Nevertheless, basing the application of Article 14a (1) of the VAT Directive on the intrinsic value of the order might have caused further confusion with the application of the IOSS and the exemption of the customs duties which would still be based on the intrinsic value of the consignment. This would especially cause difficulties when a customer places several orders, each with a value of lower than EUR 150. In this case (and if all of the other requirements were fulfilled), the platform would become the deemed supplier of all transactions. Assuming that the underlying supplier would bundle the orders into one consignment for shipping it to the customer, the intrinsic value of the consignment would be higher than EUR 150. As for the use of the IOSS, the word 'consignments' would still be the point of reference, the platform could not use the IOSS, and also custom duties would become payable.[729] After all, the platform (or the underlying supplier) would still have to rely on the information about how the consignment has been dispatched by the underlying supplier (or platform) to know how the goods should be correctly imported into the EU. Thus, the change from 'consignment' to 'order' in Article 14a (1) of the VAT Directive would not merely result in the first indicated facilitation.

Finally, it could also be discussed whether, in the corresponding Article 369l of the VAT Directive (the scope of the application of the IOSS) as well as in Article 143a of the UCC-DA (the exemption of the customs duties), 'consignment' should have been exchanged with the word 'order' so the discussed discrepancies would not arise. Thereby, it should be noted that the application of the IOSS as well as the exemption of customs duties have a simplification character that is not only applicable to the platform as a deemed supplier but to any supplier fulfilling the criteria. For any other suppliers, the discussed information deficit is not relevant. Additionally, the amending of the word 'consignment' to 'order' could raise practical problems for the checks by the customs authorities since the customs authorities must be provided with the 'order' to be able to review the value of the 'order'. Without a copy of the 'order', the customs authorities would not be able to determine whether the 'order' by the customer would exceed the threshold of EUR 150. Additionally, the amendment of 'consignment' to 'order' could result in suppliers implementing technical amendments to their checkout process in order to not allow any orders above EUR 150. If a customer's order exceeded EUR 150, a second order would have to be placed by the customer. Thus, the amendment from 'consignment' to 'order' could lead to circumventions by suppliers with the aim that all orders have the benefit of being declared via the IOSS as well as being exempt from customs duties.

In conclusion, the interpretation of 'consignment' raises several interpretational questions. The EU legislator did not define 'consignment' in the VAT Directive or VAT Implementing Regulation which leads to legal uncertainties for the platform and the underlying suppliers. The European Commission requires three stipulated require-ments to qualify as one 'consignment': (i) goods must be packed together, (ii) dispatched simultaneously, and (iii) covered by the same transport contract. As

---

729. Due to the bundling of the orders, the intrinsic value of the consignment would be exceeding EUR 150.

discussed, this interpretation by the European Commission is convincing for the specific case of the applicability of Article 14 (1) of the VAT Directive. Moreover, the analysis has shown that, due to the bundling or splitting up of the goods, the underlying supplier (or platform) has some leverage in deciding whether the requirements of Article 14a (1) of the VAT Directive are fulfilled.

3.3.1.2.3 The Interpretation of 'Intrinsic Value'

In the course of the preparation of the e-commerce package, a definition of the term 'intrinsic value' was also introduced in Article 1 (48) of the UCC-DA under the heading 'Definitions':[730]

> (48) 'intrinsic value' means
>
> (a) for commercial goods: the price of the goods themselves when sold for export to the customs territory of the Union, excluding transport and insurance costs, unless they are included in the price and not separately indicated on the invoice, and any other taxes and charges as ascertainable by the customs authorities from any relevant document(s);
> (b) for goods of a non-commercial nature: the price which would have been paid for the goods themselves if they were sold for export to the customs territory of the Union.

The background of the introduction of this definition was the aim of achieving a unified interpretation throughout the different Member States in the EU.[731] The term 'intrinsic value' used in the VAT and customs law has been defined to eliminate confusion about its interpretation.[732]

For the application of Article 14a (1) of the VAT Directive, Article 1 (48) (a) of the UCC-DA is especially relevant as the goods bought through platforms are (usually) commercial goods. Therefore, the relevant price would be the net price of the goods that the customer has ordered. This would generally be a subjective price, i.e., independently calculated from the objective value of the goods. The phrase 'when sold for export to the territory of the customs territory of the Union' also stipulates the relevant moment in time of determining the intrinsic value, i.e., the moment when the customer orders the goods and thus the contract between the underlying supplier and the customer is concluded. Diverging from this interpretation, the European Commission seems to interpret the term 'when sold for export to the territory of the customs territory of the Union' as 'at the time of supply (i.e., at the time when the payment by

---

730. Article 1 (48) of the UCC-DA was introduced with the Commission Delegated Regulation (EU) 2020/877 of 3 April 2020 Amending and Correcting Delegated Regulation (EU) 2015/2446 Supplementing Regulation (EU) No 952/2013, and Amending Delegated Regulation (EU) 2016/341 Supplementing Regulation (EU) No 952/2013, Laying down the Union Customs Code, OJ L 203 (2020).
731. See preamble pt. 4 of the ibid.; see also European Commission, Importation and Exportation of Low Value Consignments, supra note 717, at 10.
732. See, on the discussion of whether the UCC-DA is applicable for interpreting Article 14a (1) of the VAT Directive, s. 3.3.1.2.1 General Remarks.

the customer was accepted)'.[733] Thus, the European Commission seems to define the term 'when sold for export to the territory of the customs territory of the Union' in light of article 66a of the VAT Directive, according to which the chargeable event and chargeability are at 'the time when the payment has been accepted'.[734] This interpretation by the European Commission is not convincing since Article 66a of the VAT Directive is one legal consequence of the application of Article 14a of the VAT Directive. Thus, Article 66a of the VAT Directive cannot serve for determining the scope of Article 14a of the VAT Directive. In practice, the customs authority will see the price from the accompanying documents which, in general, would be the invoice accompanying the goods.[735]

Thereby, the intrinsic value is limited to the amount that the customer is paying for the goods excluding any additional costs. According to the definition of Article 1 (48) (a) of the UCC-DA, transport costs and insurance costs must be excluded from the value for determining the application of Article 14a (1) of the VAT Directive when they are explicitly indicated on the invoice. Similarly, also other additional costs such as tooling costs or costs for licence fees must be excluded from the intrinsic value when they are explicitly indicated on the invoice since they do not form part of the price of the goods.[736] Therefore, it is up to the person issuing the invoice to either include or exclude additional costs in the indicated price. This decision may have far-reaching consequences: depending on this decision, the supply in question may be excluded from or included in the deemed supplier regime of Article 14a (1) of the VAT Directive. Additionally, also taxes and charges applied to the imported goods are not part of the intrinsic value. This exclusion only becomes effective when the taxes and charges are indicated on the necessary documents and are therefore verifiable by the competent customs authority.

The legal definition of the 'intrinsic value' has an impact on the application of the deemed supplier regime, the application of the IOSS, and the application of the exemption from customs duties as all of these articles refer to the 'intrinsic value'. Additionally, also other articles in customs law refer to the 'intrinsic value'.[737] Nevertheless, the definition of the 'intrinsic value' is relevant neither for determining the transaction value according to customs law, based on which the customs duties are calculated,[738] nor for determining the consideration according to VAT law.[739]

---

733. European Commission, *Explanatory Notes on the New VAT E-Commerce Rules, supra* note 35, at 70; European Commission, *Importation and Exportation of Low Value Consignments, supra* note 717, at 46.
734. For further information on the chargeable event, *see* 4.4.2 Derogation of the General Rules: Article 66a of the VAT Directive.
735. European Commission, *Explanatory Notes: VAT E-Commerce Rules, supra* note 35, at 70; European Commission, *Importation and Exportation of Low Value Consignments, supra* note 717, at 45. For further information on the invoicing requirements, *see* 4.9 Invoicing Obligations.
736. *See* European Commission, *Explanatory Notes: VAT E-Commerce Rules, supra* note 35, at 55; European Commission, *Importation and Exportation of Low Value Consignments, supra* note 717, at 47 et seq.
737. *See*, e.g., Articles 106 (4), 137 (2) (g), 141 (5) of the UCC-DA; Article 183 (1) (b) of the UCC-IR.
738. *See* Article 70 of the UCC.
739. *See* Article 73 of the VAT Directive.

3.3.1.2.4   The Interpretation of 'Not Exceeding EUR 150'

The value limit of EUR 150 is also derived from customs law and was chosen because imports of a so-called negligible value, i.e., with an intrinsic value of up to EUR 150, are exempt from customs duties and, therefore, a simplified customs declaration is sufficient for the importation of low-value goods.[740] If the value of the good(s) was indicated in euros, the decision of whether the consignment's intrinsic value was not exceeding EUR 150 should be rather simple. Nevertheless, as the goods are imported from third countries, the intrinsic value may be indicated in different currencies than euros. Thus, it is questionable how the intrinsic value is determined in currencies other than euros.

Thereby, the VAT Directive is clearly stating that the intrinsic value should not exceed EUR 150. As Article 14a (1) of the VAT Directive explicitly refers to EUR 150, the local currency should be converted into euros. The moment when the intrinsic value should be determined has already been discussed in the previous section as the moment when the customer orders the goods, and thus the contract between the underlying supplier and the customer is concluded.[741] Thus, the local currency should be converted into euros at this time. It is recommended that the person organising the transportation and issuing the invoice, i.e., either the underlying supplier or the platform, indicates the converted amount in euros on the invoice accompanying the goods.[742] If the converted amount was not indicated on the transportation document or invoice, it would not be possible for the customs authorities to determine whether the intrinsic value of the consignment has exceeded the threshold of EUR 150. Thus, the customs authorities have to convert the amount indicated on the invoice in the foreign currency at the time that the goods enter the EU customs territory. Due to postponing the conversion, the result might be that the converted amount exceeds EUR 150. In this case, the European Commission argues that it should be possible to provide proof that, at the time of the sale for export to the customs territory of the Union, the converted

---

740. *See* preamble pt. 7 of the Council Directive (EU) 2017/2455 of 5 December 2017 Amending Directive 2006/112/EC and Directive 2009/132/EC as Regards Certain Value Added Tax Obligations for Supplies of Services and Distance Sales of Goods, OJ L 348/7 (2017), where the EU legislator explicitly refers to the customs background for the introduction of the intrinsic value of EUR 150; *see*, for the simplified customs declaration, Article 143a of the Commission Delegated Regulation (EU) 2015/2446 of 28 July 2015 Supplementing Regulation (EU) No 952/2013 of the European Parliament and of the Council as Regards Detailed Rules Concerning Certain Provisions of the Union Customs Code, OJ L 343 (2015); this article was introduced by the Commission Delegated Regulation (EU) 2019/1143 of 14 March 2019 Amending Delegated Regulation (EU) 2015/2446 as Regards the Declaration of Certain Low-Value Consignments, OJ L 203 (2019); read in conjunction with the exemption of low-value consignments in Article 23 of the Council Regulation (EC) No 1186/2009 of 16 November 2009 Setting up a Community System of Reliefs from Customs Duty, OJ L 324 (2009).
741. *See* s. 3.3.1.2.3 The Interpretation of 'Intrinsic Value'.
742. *See* similarly European Commission, *Explanatory Notes on the New VAT E-Commerce Rules*, *supra* note 35, at 70 et seq.; European Commission, *Importation and Exportation of Low Value Consignments – VAT E-Commerce Package 'Guidance for Member States and Trade'*, *supra* note 717, at 46 et seq.

value did not exceed EUR 150.[743] If such proof could be provided to the customs authorities, the requirement of the consignment not exceeding EUR 150 should be considered to be fulfilled even though the converted amount was not indicated on the transportation document or invoice.

3.3.2 The Supply of Goods Within the Community: Article 14a (2) of the VAT Directive

3.3.2.1 *The Definition of Supply of Goods Within the Community*

The first criterion from Article 14a (2) of the VAT Directive refers to the place from where and to where the goods are supplied. Two possibilities can be subsumed under the wording 'within the Community'. First is the cross-border supply from one Member State to another. At first sight, readers might conclude that, similar to the application of Article 14a (1) of the VAT Directive, for the application of Article 14a (2) of the VAT Directive, reference is also made to 'intra-Community distance sales of goods' as defined in Article 14 (4) (1) of the VAT Directive. This assumption, though, is not correct. Article 14a (2) of the VAT Directive simply refers to the supply of goods 'within the Community'. In Article 14a (2) of the VAT Directive, no reference can be found to 'intra-Community distance sales of goods'. Therefore, the criteria of Article 14 (4) (1) of the VAT Directive do not have to be investigated as a requirement for the application of Article 14a (2) of the VAT Directive.[744] For the application of Article 14a (2) of the VAT Directive, the goods should be dispatched or transported from one Member State to another; importations from and exportations to third countries are excluded from this legal definition.

Second, also national sales of goods can qualify as a supply of goods within the Community according to Article 14a (2) of the VAT Directive. This is the case when the goods are dispatched and delivered within the same Member State.

Finally, Article 14a (2) of the VAT Directive does not provide any restrictions on the kind of goods for which the platform can become the deemed supplier.

3.3.2.2 *The Requirements for Underlying Suppliers and the Customers*

According to the second and third criteria stipulated in Article 14a (2) of the VAT Directive, the underlying supplier must be a taxable person not established in the EU, and the customer must be a non-taxable person. The residency of the non-taxable

---

743. *See* European Commission, *Explanatory Notes: VAT E-Commerce Rules, supra* note 35, at 70 et seq.; European Commission, *Importation and Exportation of Low Value Consignments, supra* note 717, at 46 et seq.

744. Nevertheless, the requirements of Article 14 (4) (1) of the VAT Directive will be fulfilled in many cases when the platform facilitates a supply from one Member State to another according to Article 14a (2) of the VAT Directive. The requirements of Article 14 (4) (1) of the VAT Directive are further discussed in s. 4.3.4.2.1.3.1.1 The Special Place of Supply Rule for Intra-Community Distance Sales of Goods.

person in the EU is not a requirement for the application of Article 14a (2) of the VAT Directive.

Therefore, Article 14a (2) of the VAT Directive is limited to supplies where the underlying supplier fulfils the criteria as a taxable person.[745] Additionally, this taxable person cannot be established in the EU according to Article 14a (2) of the VAT Directive. This restriction to the underlying supplier's place of establishment can be seen as an indication that especially suppliers established in third countries did not fulfil their legal VAT obligations in the EU since one of the reasons for the introduction of the deemed supplier regime by platforms was to ensure the effective and efficient VAT collection on all supplies in the EU.[746] A taxable person is not established in the EU when the establishment of that person is in a third country or third territory.[747] According to Article 10 (1) of the VAT Implementing Regulation, the place of establishment is the 'place where the functions of the business's central administration are carried out'.[748] Thereby, the place where the general management makes essential decisions takes precedence over the place where the registered office is located and over the place where the management meets.[749] Solely a postal address is not sufficient for the requirement of a taxable person being established in a certain place.[750]

Although Article 14a (2) of the VAT Directive does not provide any further explanations of whether a fixed establishment in the EU would already qualify as 'being established', the term 'taxable person not established within the Community' is defined in Article 358a of the VAT Directive as well as Article 369l of the VAT Directive. Article 358a of the VAT Directive defines the scope of application of the non-EU-OSS, and Article 369l of the VAT Directive defines the scope of application of the IOSS and stipulates that a taxable person not established within the Community cannot have a fixed establishment in the Community. To guarantee a uniform interpretation and application of the VAT Directive, this definition should also be applied when interpreting Article 14a (2) of the VAT Directive. Thus, the underlying supplier cannot have a

---

745. *See*, for the further explanations on the requirements for a taxable person, s. 3.2.1 The Limitation to Taxable Persons; *see* also s. 3.3.4 The Rebuttal Presumption of Article 5d of the VAT Implementing Regulation.
746. *See* preamble pt. 7 of the Council Directive (EU) 2017/2455 of 5 December 2017 Amending Directive 2006/112/EC and Directive 2009/132/EC as Regards Certain Value Added Tax Obligations for Supplies of Services and Distance Sales of Goods, OJ L 348/7 (2017).
747. *See*, for more information on the definition of third countries and territories, s. 3.3.1.1.3 The Importation from Third Territories and Third Countries.
748. Although Articles 10 et seqq. of the VAT Implementing Regulation are referring to the application of Article 44 et seq. of the VAT Directive, the term 'to be established' should be interpreted uniformly in the VAT Directive. Therefore, the definitions from the VAT Implementing Regulation should also be applicable to the application of Article 14 (2) of the VAT Directive; *see*, similarly, also the CJEU holding that, to guarantee the sound functioning and uniform interpretation of the VAT system, the same terms in the VAT Directive should not be interpreted differently just because they are used in different provisions of the VAT Directive in Case C-242/08, *Swiss Re Germany Holding*, 22 Oct. 2009, ECLI:EU:C:2009:647, para. 31; *see* by analogy also Case C-695/19, *Rádio Popular*, 8 Jul. 2021, ECLI:EU:C:2021:549, para. 46.
749. *See* Article 10 (2) of the VAT Implementing Regulation.
750. *See* Article 10 (3) of the VAT Implementing Regulation.

fixed establishment in the EU for Article 14a (2) of the VAT Directive to apply.[751] A fixed establishment is generally a place beside the place of establishment where a sufficient degree of permanence and a suitable structure in terms of human and technical resources is provided.[752] One example for a fixed establishment by the underlying supplier in the EU might be a warehouse when the underlying supplier fulfils the criteria of having a sufficient degree of permanence and a suitable structure in terms of human and technical resources.[753] Whether a warehouse of the underlying supplier fulfils these criteria is a case-by-case analysis. As the knowledge on the place of (fixed) establishment by the underlying supplier is necessary for the platform to determine whether Article 14a (2) of the VAT Directive is applicable, the platform should request this information when an underlying supplier is signing up on the platform to offer goods. Furthermore, the platform should update the master data on the underlying suppliers regularly.

Additionally, Article 14a (2) of the VAT Directive explicitly limits the supply of goods within the Community to the supply to non-taxable persons. In practice, the platform should therefore know whether the underlying supplier and the recipient of the goods is a taxable person or a non-taxable person.[754]

---

751. European Commission, *Explanatory Notes on the New VAT E-Commerce Rules, supra* note 35, at 10.

752. This definition was developed and repeatedly confirmed by the CJEU in its case, *see* Case C-168/84, *Gunter Berkholz v Finanzamt Hamburg-Mitte-Altstadt*, 4 Jul. 1985, ECLI: EU:C:1985:299, para. 18; Case C-231/94, *Faaborg-Gelting Linien A/S v Finanzamt Flensburg*, 2 May 1996, ECLI:EU:C:1996:184, para. 17; Case C-260/95, *Commissioners of Customs and Excise v DFDS A/S*, 20 Feb. 1997, ECLI:EU:C:1997:77, para. 20; Case C-190/95, *ARO Lease BV v Inspecteur van de Belastingdienst Grote Ondernemingen te Amsterdam*, 17 Jul. 1997, ECLI: EU:C:1997:374, para. 15; Case C-390/96, *Lease Plan Luxembourg SA v Belgian State*, 7 May 1998, ECLI:EU:C:1998:206, para. 24; Case C-73/06, *Planzer Luxembourg Sàrl v Bundeszentralamt für Steuern*, 28 Jun. 2007, ECLI:EU:C:2007:397, para. 54; Case C-605/12, *Welmory sp. z o.o. v Dyrektor Izby Skarbowej w Gdańsku*, 16 Oct. 2014, ECLI:EU:C:2014:2298, para. 58; Case C-931/19, *Titanium Ltd v Finanzamt Österreich*, 3 Jun. 2021, ECLI:EU:C:2021:446, para. 42. The CJEU has focused on the notion of fixed establishments when investigating the place of supply of services. Nevertheless, to guarantee a uniform application of the term 'fixed establishment' also for the supply of goods, the mentioned criteria should be fulfilled; for a detailed discussion on fixed establishments, *see* Karoline Spies, *Permanent Establishments in Value Added Tax: The Role of Establishments in International B2B Trade in Services Under VAT/GST Law, supra* note 25.

753. *See,* e.g., VAT Committee, *Implementation of the Quick Fixes Package: Council Directive (EU) 2018/1910 and Council Implementing Regulation (EU) 2018/1912*, Working Paper No. 968, taxud.c.1(2019)3533969, 4 et seqq. (15 May 2019), https://www.google.com/url?sa=t&rct=j&q=&esrc=s&source=web&cd=&cad=rja&uact=8&ved=2ahUKEwijt9fXhZH3AhXGt6Q KHWDDDjwQFnoECAwQAQ&url=https%3A%2F%2Fcircabc.europa.eu%2Fsd%2Fa%2F8e 08ca08-307d-4f28-b14e-c980f9eaecab%2FWP%2520968%2520New%2520legislation%2520-%2520Quick%2520fixes%2520package.pdf&usg=AOvVaw3JpwFYT7BM5VehXK5uJ7tC (last visited 13 Apr. 2022); Karoline Spies, *supra* note 25, at 266.

754. *See also* s. 3.3.4 The Rebuttal Presumption of Article 5d of the VAT Implementing Regulation.

3.3.3 Differences in the Substantive Scope of Article 14a (1) of the VAT Directive and Article 14a (2) of the VAT Directive

The previous sections have shown that the substantive scope of Article 14a (1) of the VAT Directive and Article 14a (2) of the VAT Directive diverge in many instances. Table 3.2 should highlight the differences between the substantive scope of Article 14a (1) of the VAT Directive and Article 14a (2) of the VAT Directive.

Table 3.2 Overview of the Differences in the Substantive Scope of Article 14a (1) of the VAT Directive and Article 14a (2) of the VAT Directive

	Article 14a (1) of the VAT Directive	Article 14a (2) of the VAT Directive
Movement of Goods	Dispatch or transportation of goods by or on behalf of the supplier	No dispatch or transportation necessary
Third Country Element	Importation from third territories and third countries	Underlying supplier cannot be established in the EU
Limitations to the Supplied Goods	Goods supplied after assembly or installation or new means of transport are excluded	No restrictions
Value of the Supplied Goods	Intrinsic value of the consignment not exceeding EUR 150	No restrictions
VAT Status of the Underlying Supplier	Taxable or non-taxable person	Taxable person
VAT Status of the Recipient of the Goods	Non-taxable person and taxable person or non-taxable legal person, whose intra-Community acquisitions of goods are not subject to VAT pursuant to Article 3 (1) of the VAT Directive	Non-taxable person

This table shows that, for some requirements, Article 14a (1) of the VAT Directive is narrower than Article 14a (2) of the VAT Directive, e.g., taking into consideration the kind of supplied good and the value of the good. In other instances, Article 14a (2) of the VAT Directive is narrower than Article 14a (1) of the VAT Directive, e.g., taking into consideration the taxable status of the recipient of the customer and the taxable status of the underlying supplier.

3.3.4 The Rebuttal Presumption of Article 5d of the VAT Implementing Regulation on the Taxable Status of the Underlying Supplier and the Customer

As discussed in the previous sections, the taxable status of the customer is relevant for the application of Article 14a (1) and (2) of the VAT Directive,[755] and the taxable status of the underlying supplier is relevant for the application of Article 14a (2) of the VAT Directive.[756] Since the taxable status of the underlying supplier and customer is often difficult to determine and to prove in e-commerce, Article 5d of the VAT Implementing Regulation provides a rebuttable presumption of the taxable status of the underlying supplier and the recipient of the goods. According to Article 5d of the VAT Implementing Regulation, the underlying supplier is presumed to be a taxable person, and the customer is presumed to be a non-taxable person. This rebuttal presumption is applicable to Article 14a (1) and (2) of the VAT Directive.

In general, it is therefore, by law, presumed that the supply of goods is provided from a taxable person (the underlying supplier) to a non-taxable person (the customer). The background for the introduction of this rebuttable presumption is that the administrative burden of proof by the electronic interface facilitating the supply is reduced.[757] Thereby, the platform can rely on the presumption as long as no contrary information is available to the platform. If the platform received the information from underlying suppliers that they are non-taxable persons, the platform should qualify these underlying suppliers as non-taxable persons since Article 5d of the VAT Implementing Regulation explicitly stipulates that the rebuttal presumption is only applicable '[u]nless [the deemed supplier] has information to the contrary'.[758] Similarly, if the platform received the information that the consumer is a taxable person, the platform should qualify the consumer as a taxable person. According to the European Commission in the Explanatory Notes, the mere absence of the VAT identification number or tax number cannot be interpreted as the underlying supplier not qualifying as a taxable person.[759] This is understandable as not all taxable persons receive a VAT identification number, and, in some countries, even natural persons may receive a tax number.[760] Thus, the sole qualification of the taxable status based on the VAT identification number or tax number should be seen as critical.

---

755. *See* s. 3.3.1.1.4 The Requirements of Article 14 (4) (2) (a) of the VAT Directive on the VAT Status of the Recipient of the Goods and s. 3.3.2.2 The Requirements for Underlying Suppliers and the Customers.

756. *See* s. 3.3.2.2 The Requirements for Underlying Suppliers and the Customers.

757. *See* preamble pt. 8 of the Council Implementing Regulation (EU) 2019/2026 of 21 November 2019 Amending Implementing Regulation (EU) No 282/2011 as Regards Supplies of Goods or Services Facilitated by Electronic Interfaces and the Special Schemes for Taxable Persons Supplying Services to Non-Taxable Persons, Making Distance Sales of Goods and Certain Domestic Supplies of Goods, OJ L 313/14 (2019).

758. *See*, similarly, European Commission, *Explanatory Notes on the New VAT E-Commerce Rules*, *supra* note 35, at 26.

759. *See*, similarly, also *ibid*.

760. In Austria, for example, a taxable person must explicitly indicate in the VAT registration why a VAT identification number is necessary and any natural person who is employed, i.e., not a taxable person in VAT terms, has a tax number.

One practical issue might arise due to the general wording of Article 5d (b) of the VAT Implementing Regulation when testing the taxable status of the recipient of the goods for the application of Article 14a (1) of the VAT Directive. As discussed, the recipient according to Article 14a (1) read in conjunction with Article 14 (4) (2) of the VAT Directive is not only limited to non-taxable persons. Also, the supply to certain taxable persons may lead to the applicability of the deemed supplier regime.[761] The rebuttable presumption of Article 5d (b) of the VAT Implementing Regulation only stipulates that 'the person buying those goods [shall be regarded] as a non-taxable person'. Therefore, Article 14a (1) of the VAT Directive may still be fulfilled if the taxable person provided non-taxable supplies according to Article 3 (1) of the VAT Directive if the taxable person was subject to the flat-rate scheme for farmers or if the taxable person only carried out the supply of goods and services for non-deductible supplies. Thus, if recipients informed the platform that they are taxable persons, the platform should additionally question whether the taxable person is such a special taxable person to which the deemed supplier regime also applies.

Due to this rebuttable presumption, the platforms can rely on the underlying suppliers being taxable persons and the customers being non-taxable persons as long as no other information is provided to them. Article 5d of the VAT Implementing Regulation should thereby lead to legal certainty for the platform when reviewing whether the platform becomes the deemed supplier for a transaction.

3.4 CONCLUSION ON THE SCOPE OF ARTICLE 14A OF THE VAT DIRECTIVE

The previous sections have discussed in detail the personal and substantive scope of Article 14a of the VAT Directive. Thereby, the personal scope of both paragraphs of Article 14a of the VAT Directive is based on three criteria that can be uniformly interpreted: the platform must be: (i) a taxable person (ii) facilitating the supply of goods (iii) through the use of an electronic interface. From these three criteria, the criterion of qualifying as a taxable person seems to be the most uncritical for e-commerce platforms to fulfil. The broad definition of when a platform facilitates a supply can lead to questions and legal uncertainties for platforms. Thereby, especially the fact that the platform does not have to be included in the payment process to become the deemed supplier should be criticised since this leads to a significant increase in compliance efforts and costs and might have a negative impact on their liquidity if the platform did not receive the VAT due from the underlying supplier or the customer. Finally, also the broad wording of 'electronic interface' may raise practical questions, i.e., when does a new technological development qualify as an electronic interface and thus fall into the scope of Article 14a of the VAT Directive? Finally, Article 14a of the VAT Directive does not provide any restrictions on the place of establishment

---

761. *See* s. 3.3.1.1.4 The Requirements of Article 14 (4) (2) (a) of the VAT Directive on the VAT Status of the Recipient of the Goods.

of the platform. Thus, platforms established in the EU as well as in third territories or countries can become deemed suppliers according to Article 14a of the VAT Directive.

Once it is determined that the electronic interface facilitates the supply of goods, the substantive scope of Article 14a of the VAT Directive must be tested (*see* Figure 3.1 for a graphical illustration of this test).

Figure 3.1   Simplified Decision Tree of the Substantive Scope of Article 14a of the VAT Directive

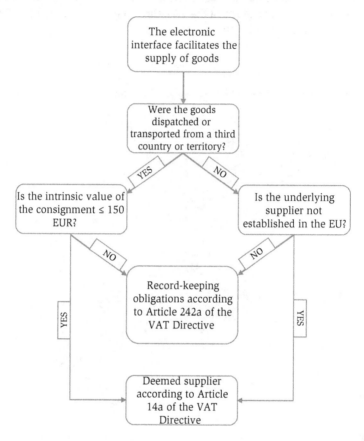

The analysis of the substantive scope showed that both paragraphs of Article 14a of the VAT Directive have some similarities: a third country element should be identified, and, additionally in both cases, the deemed supplier regime is applicable to supplies to non-taxable persons. Nevertheless, a closer analysis also highlighted the differences between paragraph (1) and paragraph (2) of Article 14a of the VAT Directive. Whereas Article 14a (1) of the VAT Directive requires the dispatch or transportation of the goods by or on behalf of the supplier, Article 14a (2) of the VAT Directive does not require any dispatch or transportation. Thus, the platform could also become the supplier, e.g., for the sale of immovable property if the other requirements of Article 14a (2) of the VAT Directive are fulfilled. Furthermore, Article 14a (2) of the VAT Directive is not restricted to the supply of specific goods, whereas Article 14a (1) of the VAT Directive does not apply for goods supplied after assembly or installation as well as new means of transport. In addition, the intrinsic value of the consignment not exceeding EUR 150 is only relevant for the application of the deemed supplier regime according to Article 14a (1) of the VAT Directive. Additionally, Article 14a (2) of the VAT Directive is only applicable to supplies to non-taxable persons, whereas the platform also becomes the deemed supplier for imported goods when the recipient of the goods is a taxable person or non-taxable legal person whose intra-Community acquisitions of goods are not subject to VAT pursuant to Article 3 (1) of the VAT Directive.[762] Finally, differentiation between the two paragraphs could be identified based on the taxable status of the underlying supplier. Article 14a (2) of the VAT Directive is only applicable when the underlying supplier is a taxable person, whereas, for the application of Article 14a (1) of the VAT Directive, the taxable status of the underlying supplier is irrelevant.

Finally, the analysis has also shown that especially Article 14a (1) of the VAT Directive leads to interpretational questions. These interpretational difficulties may be caused by a lack of definitions in the VAT Directive or Implementing Regulation as well as the interconnection between VAT and customs law. For the interpretation of Article 14a (1) of the VAT Directive as well as Article 14a (2) of the VAT Directive, the clarifications implemented based on the second legislative changes were inevitable. However, some questions remain open to interpretation and may cause legal uncertainty for the platforms and the underlying suppliers when deciding whether the deemed supplier regime is applicable, e.g., the definition of a 'consignment'. The quite complicated cross-referencing between the VAT Directive, the VAT Implementing Regulation, and the relevant provisions in customs law causes further difficulties to the application of Article 14a of the VAT Directive.

---

762. *See* the discussion of these taxable persons in s. 3.3.1.1.4 The Requirements of Article 14 (4) (2) (a) of the VAT Directive on the VAT Status of the Recipient of the Goods.

CHAPTER 4

Legal Consequences of the Applicability of Article 14a of the VAT Directive

4.1   GENERAL REMARKS ON THE DEEMED SUPPLIER REGIME

The result of a platform facilitating the supply of goods by fulfilling all of the discussed requirements is that the platform 'shall be deemed to have received and supplied those goods himself'.[763] The deeming provision leads to the platform fictitiously becoming part of the supply chain; i.e., the goods are fictitiously sold from the underlying supplier to the platform and then from the platform to the customer. This fiction is solely applicable to the VAT treatment of the supplies and does not influence contract law. Contractually, the underlying supplier is still the supplier of the goods.

This deemed supplier regime has an impact on many VAT qualifications. Due to Article 14a of the VAT Directive, the requirements for a chain transaction are fulfilled which has an impact on the applicable place of supply rules. Thereby, not only the legal consequences of the transaction between the platform and the consumer but also the transaction between the underlying supplier and the platform must be investigated. Due to the deemed supplier regime, the platform becomes liable for the VAT payment. This results in the platform needing to determine the time of the chargeable event, the taxable amount, and the applicable exemptions and rates. Additionally, the question also arises whether the platform has to invoice the supply to the customer, whether it has to keep certain records, and whether the platform is allowed to deduct the input VAT. As the platform would also have to file the VAT returns and pay the VAT due, the newly introduced compliance simplification mechanisms (OSS) and, for the application of Article 14a (1) of the VAT Directive, newly introduced accompanying customs measures are of importance. All of these legal consequences will be discussed in the forthcoming chapters. Additionally, also the practical question on returns of goods and warranties will be analysed.

---

763. *See* Article 14a of the VAT Directive.

4.2   TAXABLE TRANSACTIONS

The VAT Directive stipulates four different taxable transactions that may be subject to VAT:

> The following transactions shall be subject to VAT:
>
> (a) the supply of goods for consideration within the territory of a Member State by a taxable person acting as such;
> (b) the intra-Community acquisition of goods for consideration within the territory of a Member State ...
> (c) the supply of services for consideration within the territory of a Member State by a taxable person acting as such;
> (d) the importation of goods.[764]

For the supplies in the course of the application of Article 14a of the VAT Directive, the main taxable transaction is the supply of goods for consideration. Thereby, Article 14a of the VAT Directive stipulates that the platform 'shall be deemed to have received and supplied those goods himself'. Thus, the supply from the underlying supplier to the platform is a (fictitious) supply of goods for consideration as well as the (fictitious) supply from the platform to the customer.

Moreover, the platform service is also a taxable transaction which can lead to a supply of services. Especially if the parties agreed on the payment of a fixed amount per week, month, or year for the use of the platform, then this should be qualified as a separate service fee for the use of the platform because it is independent of the sales facilitated by the platform.[765] If the parties agreed on a commission-based consideration, then this commission could be considered as being part of the taxable amount for the supply of the good and thus is not a separate taxable transaction.[766]

Additionally, other taxable transactions might be relevant. For the analysis of these additional taxable transactions, it should be distinguished whether Article 14a (1) or 14a (2) of the VAT Directive is applicable. When Article 14a (1) of the VAT Directive is applicable, also the taxable transaction of the importation of the goods is fulfilled. Who carries out the taxable transaction of the importation depends on who is actually importing the goods. The VAT Directive does not stipulate a specified circle of persons who are to be considered importers but leaves this definition to the Member States. One example of an importer if stipulated as such in the national law could be the customs declarant according to Article 77 (3) of the UCC.[767] Thus, the national law of the

---

764. *See* Article 2 (1) of the VAT Directive.
765. *See,* for the discussion of the legal qualification of this supply, s. 2.2.4 The Supply of the Platform Service to the Underlying Supplier as well as s. 2.2.5 The Supply of the Platform Service to the Customer.
766. *See,* for a detailed discussion of the commission of the platform, s. 4.5.5 The Inclusion of Commission Retained by the Platform in the Taxable Amount.
767. *See* Thomas Bieber, *Der Einfuhrumsatz, supra* note 291, at 547 et seqq., who also discussed the implementation in the different Member States with further examples for who can qualify as an importer in the national law.

Member State could stipulate that the platform and/or the customer as well as the underlying supplier could qualify as importers.

If Article 14a (2) of the VAT Directive was applicable and the supply is an intra-Community distance sales of goods according to Article 14 (4) (2) of the VAT Directive, then the transfer according to Article 17 of the VAT Directive should also be analysed. According to Article 17 (1) of the VAT Directive, the 'transfer by a taxable person of goods forming part of his business assets to another Member State shall be treated as a supply of goods for consideration'. Thus, the transfer of the goods by the platform from one Member State to another would generally trigger a deemed supply according to Article 17 (1) of the VAT Directive. However, pursuant to Article 17 (2) (a) of the VAT Directive, no such transfer would be fulfilled if it was a supply according to Article 33 of the VAT Directive which, among others, includes the intra-Community distance sales of goods.[768]

Finally, the intra-Community acquisition may be relevant in the case that a customer purchases new means of transport.[769] The subsequent sections discuss the impact of the taxable transactions for the further legal obligations by the underlying supplier, the platform, as well as the customer.

4.3   PLACE OF SUPPLY RULES

4.3.1   General Remarks

The place of supply rules generally determine which country has the right to tax a taxable transaction. When a taxable transaction is supplied within one Member State from a taxable person established in that Member State to a customer in that same Member State, the place of supply is generally in that Member State.[770] Especially when a transaction is a cross-border transaction, the rules on the place of supply regulate the allocation of taxing rights between the different Member States and thereby should avoid double (non-)taxation.[771]

---

768. *See*, for further information on the place of supply of intra-Community distance sales of goods, s. 4.3.4.2.1.3.1 Intra-Community Distance Sales of Goods; Article 33 of the VAT Directive is stipulating two further places of supplies; *see* the detailed discussions in 4.3.4.1.1.2.2 The Importation of the Goods in a Different Member State than the Member State of where the Dispatch or Transport Ends as well as 4.3.4.1.1.2.3 The Place of Supply when the Platform Applies the IOSS.
769. *See* the discussion of the place of supply in s. 4.3.4.2.2 The Place of Supply of the Intra-Community Acquisition of New Means of Transport.
770. Also, within national supplies the place of supply rules may be important, especially if Member States apply different VAT rates for the same supply. Examples of this are stipulated, e.g., in Article 104 of the VAT Directive for Austria and the communes of Jungholz and Mittelberg, in Article 105 (2) of the VAT Directive for Portugal and the regions of Azores and Madeira and in Article 120 of the VAT Directive for Greece and the departments of Lesbos, Chios, Samos, the Dodecanese and the Cyclades, and on the islands of Thassos, the Northern Sporades, Samothrace and Skiros.
771. Ben Terra & Julie Kajus, *Commentary – A Guide to the Recast VAT Directive*, *supra* note 290, s. 5.1.1.

The place of supply rules for the supply of goods are stipulated in Articles 31-42 of the VAT Directive. Thereby, the allocation of the taxing right depends on whether the supply is with or without transport;[772] whether the consumer is a taxable or non-taxable person;[773] or whether the goods are supplied on a ship, aircraft, or train[774] or through a natural gas system or a heating or cooling network.[775]

Due to the limited scope of Article 14a of the VAT Directive, only certain place of supply rules are relevant for determining which Member State has the right to tax the relevant supplies. The fiction of the inclusion of the platform in the VAT supply chain according to Article 14a of the VAT Directive results in two separate taxable transactions: the first supply from the underlying supplier to the platform and the second supply from the platform to the customer. At the same time, the goods are transported from the underlying supplier or from a warehouse directly to the customer. This is a so-called chain transaction. One example of when a supply of goods facilitated by a platform would not be considered as a chain transaction is the supply of immovable property because immovable goods cannot be transported.[776] Nevertheless, in most cases, supplies facilitated by platforms according to Article 14a of the VAT Directive would qualify as chain transactions. Therefore, the following section will provide background information on chain transactions and a short historical overview of the development of the articles now in force. Additionally, the legal qualification of the supply with transport within the chain transaction fictitiously created due to Article 14a of the VAT Directive will be examined. The sections following this analysis will discuss in detail the allocation of taxing rights for the supply from the underlying supplier to the platform as well as for the supply from the platform to the customer. In a final section, also the place of supply for taxable transactions by the customer are reviewed.

4.3.2 Preliminary Discussion: Chain Transaction

4.3.2.1 The Development of Jurisprudence on Chain Transactions Before the Implementation of the 'Quick Fixes'

Before the introduction of the so-called quick fixes, which entered into force on 1 January 2020,[777] no legal definition for chain transactions was provided in the VAT Directive. Thus, the CJEU was questioned repeatedly on the legal qualification of chain

---

772. *See* Article 31-36 of the VAT Directive.
773. *See* Articles 33-36 and 40-42 of the VAT Directive.
774. *See* Article 37 of the VAT Directive.
775. *See* Article 38-39 of the VAT Directive.
776. As the scope of Article 14a (1) of the VAT Directive requires that the goods are transported (*see* s. 3.3.1.1.2 The Dispatch or Transportation of Goods By or on Behalf of the Supplier), the facilitation of the supply of immovable property is only possible when Article 14a (2) of the VAT Directive is applicable.
777. *See* Council Directive (EU) 2018/1910 of 4 December 2018 Amending Directive 2006/112/EC as Regards the Harmonisation and Simplification of Certain Rules in the Value Added Tax System for the Taxation of Trade Between Member States, OJ L 311 (2018); Council Implementing Regulation (EU) 2018/1912 of 4 December 2018 Amending Implementing Regulation (EU) No 282/2011 as Regards Certain Exemptions for Intra-Community Transactions, OJ L 311 (2018).

transactions, i.e., two or more successive supplies of the same good that are directly transported from the first supplier to the final customer in the chain.[778] All of the CJEU judgments concerned intra-Community chain transactions.[779]

For chain transactions within the EU, the allocation of the supply with and without transport was carried out – in the absence of special provisions – according to the general place of supply rules of the VAT Directive. In a chain transaction, only one supply can be the supply with transport. All other supplies must qualify as the supplier without transport. In the earlier CJEU case law, two possible elements were introduced for the allocation of the supply with transport: (i) if the first acquirer informed the vendor of the intention to transport the goods to another Member State and (ii) appeared under a VAT number different from the country of origin, the supplier of the first supply could assume a supply with transport (exempt intra-Community supply).[780] In later case law, the CJEU seems to neglect these two elements and focused exclusively on the transfer of the right to dispose of the goods.[781]

The CJEU held that the transactions have to follow each other in time because the intermediary operator can only transfer the right to dispose of the goods as an owner to the final customer when the intermediary has received it from his seller.[782] Therefore, the place of supply for the different supplies in the chain must be determined individually. To guarantee a uniform interpretation of the VAT Directive, the transfer of the right to dispose of the goods is not restricted to transfers stipulated in the national law.[783] Whether the acquirer physically transports or receives the object

---

778. *See*, e.g., Case C-245/04, *EMAG Handel Eder OHG v Finanzlandesdirektion für Kärnten*, 6 Apr. 2006, ECLI:EU:C:2006:232; Case C-430/09, *Euro Tyre Holding*, 16 Dec. 2010, ECLI: EU:C:2010:786; Case C-587/10, *Vogtländische Straßen-, Tief- und Rohrleitungsbau GmbH Rodewisch (VSTR) v Finanzamt Plauen*, 27 Sep. 2012, ECLI:EU:C:2012:592; Case C-386/16, 'Toridas' UAB v Valstybine mokesčių inspekcija prie Lietuvos Respublikos finansų ministerijos, 26 Jul. 2017, ECLI:EU:C:2017:599; Case C-628/16, *Kreuzmayr*, 21 Feb. 2018, ECLI::EU:C:2018:84; Case C-414/17, *AREX CZ*, 19 Dec. 2018, ECLI:EU:C:2018:1027; Case C-401/18, *Herst*, 23 Apr. 2020, ECLI:EU:C:2020:295.
779. *See* also the critical discussion on the question of whether the CJEU case law is also applicable to third country chain transactions in Christina Pollak & Draga Turić, *Reihengeschäfte mit Drittstaatsbezug*, taxlex 340 (2021).
780. Case C-430/09, *Euro Tyre Holding*, 16 Dec. 2010, ECLI:EU:C:2010:786, para. 35.
781. *See* Case C-628/16, *Kreuzmayr*, 21 Feb. 2018, ECLI:EU:C:2018:84, paras. 35 et seq.; Case C-414/17, *AREX CZ*, 19 Dec. 2018, ECLI:EU:C:2018:1027, paras. 72 et seqq.; nevertheless, also in the earlier cases, the right to dispose of the goods has been repeatedly emphasised by the CJEU; *see*, e.g., Case C-245/04, *EMAG Handel Eder*, 6 Apr. 2006, ECLI:EU:C:2006:232, para. 38; Case C-430/09, *Euro Tyre Holding*, 16 Dec. 2010, ECLI:EU:C:2010:786, para. 45; Case C-386/16, *Toridas*, 26 Jul. 2017, ECLI:EU:C:2017:599, para. 36.
782. *See* Case C-245/04, *EMAG Handel Eder*, 6 Apr. 2006, ECLI:EU:C:2006:232, para. 38.
783. *See* Case C-414/17, *AREX CZ*, 19 Dec. 2018, ECLI:EU:C:2018:1027, para. 75; *see* also Case C-320/88, *Staatssecretaris van Financiën v Shipping and Forwarding Enterprise Safe*, 8 Feb. 1990, ECLI:EU:C:1990:61, paras 7 et seq.; Case C-291/92, *Finanzamt Uelzen v Dieter Armbrecht*, 4 Oct. 1995, ECLI:EU:C:1995:304, paras. 13 et seq.; Case C-185/01, *Auto Lease Holland BV v Bundesamt für Finanzen*, 6 Feb. 2003, ECLI:EU:C:2003:73, paras. 32 et seq.; Case C-111/05, *Aktiebolaget NN*, 29 Mar. 2007, ECLI:EU:C:2007:195, para. 32; Case C-25/03, *Finanzamt Bergisch Gladbach v HE*, 21 Apr. 2005, ECLI:EU:C:2005:241, para. 64.

is irrelevant for this qualification.[784] Precise criteria as to how the power of disposal is transferred cannot be found in the CJEU case law; according to the CJEU, a comprehensive assessment of all of the particular circumstances of the individual case must be carried out.[785] This legal uncertainty led to different implementations and practical difficulties regarding how to determine the supply with transport in the Member States.

4.3.2.2   *Legal Qualification of the Supply with Transport*

The EU legislator has addressed the legal uncertainty of the allocation of the supply with transport when the transport is organised by the intermediary operator in the so-called quick fixes.[786] The European Commission justified the limitation of the legal qualification of chain transactions when the intermediary operator organises the transport with the argument that it was necessary to have a separate rule for the attribution of the supply with transport when the first supplier or last recipient in the chain organises the transport.[787] Article 36a of the VAT Directive introduced a choice for the intermediary operator[788] when the intermediary operator organises the transport:[789] If the intermediary operator used his VAT number from a Member State other than the Member State of origin, the supply with transport would be attributed to the supply to the intermediary operator.[790] If the intermediary operator used his VAT number from the country of origin, the supply with transport would be allocated to the

---

784. *See* Case C-414/17, *AREX CZ*, 19 Dec. 2018, ECLI:EU:C:2018:1027, para. 75; Case C-123/14, *'Itales' OOD v Direktor na Direktsia 'Obzhalvane i danachno-osiguritelna praktika' Varna pri Tsentralno upravlenie na Natsionalnata agentsia za prihodite*, 15 Jul. 2015, ECLI: EU:C:2015:511, para. 36.

785. *See* Case C-414/17, *AREX CZ*, 19 Dec. 2018, ECLI:EU:C:2018:1027, para. 72; Case C-401/18, *Herst*, 23 Apr. 2020, ECLI:EU:C:2020:295, paras. 41 et seqq.; in contrast to this, AG Kokott, who argues that special regard should be given to determine who and on whose behalf the transport is organised, which is ultimately the person who bears the risk of the accidental loss of the goods during the transport; *see* Case C-401/18, *Herst*, 3 Oct. 2019, ECLI:EU:C:2019:834, Opinion of AG Kokott.

786. *See* Council Directive (EU) 2018/1910 of 4 December 2018 Amending Directive 2006/112/EC as Regards the Harmonisation and Simplification of Certain Rules in the Value Added Tax System for the Taxation of Trade Between Member States, OJ L 311 (2018); Council Implementing Regulation (EU) 2018/1912 of 4 December 2018 Amending Implementing Regulation (EU) No 282/2011 as Regards Certain Exemptions for Intra-Community Transactions, OJ L 311 (2018); *see also* European Commission, *Proposal for a Council Directive Amending Directive 2006/112/EC as Regards Harmonising and Simplifying Certain Rules in the Value Added Tax System and Introducing the Definitive System for the Taxation of Trade Between Member States*, COM(2017) 569 final 13 (04.10.2017), https://ec.europa.eu/transparency/documents-register /api/files/COM(2017)569_0/de00000000189092?rendition = false (last visited 21 Sep. 2021), where the European Commission explains that it is not necessary to have a separate rule for the attribution of the supply with transport if the first supplier of the chain or the customer organises the transport.

787. *See* the explanatory memorandum from the European Commission, *Proposal for a Council Directive Amending Directive 2006/112/EC as Regards Harmonising and Simplifying Certain Rules in the Value Added Tax System and Introducing the Definitive System for the Taxation of Trade Between Member States, supra* note 786, at 12.

788. The term 'intermediary operator' is also defined in Article 36a (3) of the VAT Directive.

789. For examples of the use of this choice, *see* s. 5.2.4.1.5.2.3 The Legal Consequences of the Basic Example: Transport Organised by the Platform.

790. *See* Article 36a (1) of the VAT Directive.

supply by him to the next person in the chain.[791] In this respect, the determination of the transport organisation likely replaces the focus developed by the CJEU on the transfer of the right to dispose of the goods which does not always lead to an unambiguous result.[792] The introduction of this simplification rule should contribute to the avoidance of double (non-)taxation and lead to more legal certainty by standardising chain transactions throughout the Member States.[793]

At the same time, the EU legislator stipulated in Article 36a (4) of the VAT Directive that this allocation of the supply with transport, which is generally applicable, is not applicable to situations covered by Article 14a of the VAT Directive. Article 36a (4) of the VAT Directive was implemented with the 'quick fixes' and has been in force as of 1 January 2020, although Article 14a of the VAT Directive only entered into force on 1 July 2021.[794] Article 36a (4) of the VAT Directive is of an explanatory nature: In the chain transaction triggered by Article 14a of the VAT Directive, the intermediary operator (the platform) cannot be responsible for the transport organisation since the platform is only fictitiously included in the chain. According to civil law contracts, only the underlying supplier has the power of disposal over the goods which is transferred to the customer through the sale of the goods. Even if the platform seemed to organise the transport, it would be subcontracted by the underlying supplier and/or the underlying supplier carries the risk during the transportation of the goods.[795]

Finally, with the implementation of the second legislative package, Article 36b of the VAT Directive was introduced.[796] Systematically, Article 36b of the VAT Directive was introduced under the heading 'Supply of goods with transport' and after Article 36a of the VAT Directive wherein the general rule of chain transactions is stipulated. According to Article 36b of the VAT Directive, the dispatch or transport of the goods is always ascribed to the supply by the platform for deemed supplies according to Article 14a of the VAT Directive.[797] This results in the first supply, the supply from the underlying supplier to the platform, being the supply without transport and the second

---

791. *See* Article 36a (2) of the VAT Directive.
792. *See* Case C-401/18, *Herst*, 23 Apr. 2020, ECLI:EU:C:2020:295, paras. 45 et seq.
793. *See* preamble pt. 6 of the Council Directive (EU) 2018/1910 of 4 December 2018 Amending Directive 2006/112/EC as Regards the Harmonisation and Simplification of Certain Rules in the Value Added Tax System for the Taxation of Trade Between Member States, OJ L 311 (2018).
794. *Ibid.*
795. *See* the detailed discussion in s. 3.3.1.1.2 The Dispatch or Transportation of Goods By or on Behalf of the Supplier. Although the transport organisation was discussed for the scope of Article 14a (1) of the VAT Directive, these explanations are also applicable to Article 14a (2) of the VAT Directive because, also in this case, the platform is only fictitiously included in the chain of supplies.
796. Council Directive (EU) 2019/1995 of 21 November 2019 Amending Directive 2006/112/EC as Regards Provisions Relating to Distance Sales of Goods and Certain Domestic Supplies of Goods, OJ L 310/1 (2019).
797. *See* Article 36b of the VAT Directive, which was introduced by the European Commission, *Proposal for a Council Directive Amending Directive 2006/112/EC as Regards Harmonising and Simplifying Certain Rules in the Value Added Tax System and Introducing the Definitive System for the Taxation of Trade Between Member States*, COM(2017) 569 final, *supra* note 786.

supply, the supply from the platform to the final customer, being the supply with transport (*see* Figure 4.1 for a graphical illustration of this chain transaction).[798]

Figure 4.1   Graphical Illustration of the Fictitious Chain Transaction

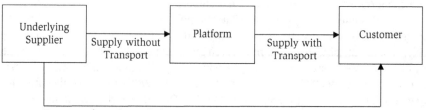

Transport from the Underlying Supplier's Power of Disposal to the Consumer

Whereas the general rule on chain transactions in Article 36a (1) of the VAT Directive is limited to supplies 'from one Member State to another' and therefore is only applicable to EU chain transactions, Article 36b of the VAT Directive refers to supplied goods in accordance with Article 14a of the Directive, and Article 14a (1) of the VAT Directive covers distance sales of goods imported from third territories or third countries.[799] From this wording and the clear determination of the supply with transport for import chain transactions in Article 36b of the VAT Directive, it can be derived that the EU legislator also applies the systematics of having one supply with transport and the other supplies without transport to chain transactions with third countries.[800]

4.3.3   The Place of Supply Rule for the Supply by the Underlying Supplier

Based on the *ex lege* ascription of the supply with transport in Article 36b of the VAT Directive, the supply from the underlying supplier to the platform is the supply without

---

798. For a detailed description of the applicable place of supply rules, *see* s. 4.3.3 The Place of Supply Rule for the Supply by the Underlying Supplier and s. 4.3.4 The Place of Supply Rule for the Supply by the Platform.

799. *See*, for a detailed discussion on the scope of Article 14a (1) of the VAT Directive, s. 3.3.1 Distance Sales of Low-Value Goods Imported from a Third Territory or a Third Country: Article 14a (1) of the VAT Directive.

800. *See* Christina Pollak & Draga Turić, *Reihengeschäfte mit Drittstaatsbezug*, taxlex, *supra* note 779, at 340; also other authors argue that the distinction between the supply with transport and the supply without transport should be applicable to chain transactions with third countries, *see* Thomas Bieber, *Der Einfuhrumsatz*, *supra* note 291, at 629 et seqq. + 857 et seqq.; *Reihengeschäfte in der Umsatzsteuer*, *supra* note 251, at 291; Michael Tumpel, *Reihenlieferungen: EuGH bestätigt österreichische Verwaltungspraxis*, SWK 464 (2006); Michael Tumpel, *Gemeinschaftsrechtliche Vorgaben für Reihenlieferungen*, in *Steuerberatung im Synergiebereich von Praxis und Wissenschaft: Festschrift für Alois Pircher zum 60. Geburtstag* 214 (Peter Pülzl & Alois Pircher eds., Linde Verlag 2007); other authors argue that the import of the goods 'breaks' the chain, *see* Hannes Gurtner & Peter Pichler, *Reihengeschäfte: Offene Fragen zum Urteil des EuGH in der Rs. EMAG*, SWK 795 et seq. (2006).

transport. Also, when the supply concerns immovable property, the supply from the underlying supplier to the platform is a supply without transport. Therefore, Article 31 of the VAT Directive is applicable for all supplies from the underlying supplier to the platform within the application of Article 14a of the VAT Directive.

According to Article 31 of the VAT Directive, the supply shall take 'place where the goods are located at the time when the supply takes place'. Pursuant to Article 14 (1) of the VAT Directive, the supply of goods means that the right to dispose of tangible property as the owner is transferred. Thus, the 'time when the supply takes place' is the time when the right to dispose of the goods is transferred. As the right to dispose of the goods is fictitiously transferred from the underlying supplier to the platform, this moment should be a 'logical second' before the customer receives the right to dispose of the goods.[801] Since the supply from the underlying supplier to the platform is the supply without transport, this is the country of origin. Depending on whether Article 14a (1) or 14a (2) of the VAT Directive is applicable, the place of origin is either in a third country or territory or in a Member State.

In the case of the applicability of Article 14a (1) of the VAT Directive, the place of supply is in a third country. The EU Member States, therefore, do not have any taxing rights for this supply. How the third country treats this supply depends on the national law of the third country. Third countries that have not (yet) implemented a comparable deemed supplier regime might consider the supply by the underlying supplier not as the supply to the platform but as the supply directly to the customer. This would presumably lead to an export in the Member State of origin.

When Article 14a (2) of the VAT Directive is applicable, the country of origin is either a different Member State than the Member State to where the goods are supplied (in the case of an intra-Community distance sales of goods) or the same Member State (in the case of a national supply of the goods or in the case of a supply of immovable property). This means that the taxing right is within the EU. For the underlying suppliers to fulfil their compliance obligations for the fictitious (but VAT exempt[802]) supply of the goods to the platform, they must have a VAT registration in the EU country of origin. Generally, Member States may decide to release certain taxable persons from certain or all VAT obligations according to Article 272 (1) of the VAT Directive; thus, also a release from the obligation to register for the VAT would be possible. Such an option is implemented for several exempt supplies in Article 272 (1) (c) of the VAT Directive. Nevertheless, with the introduction of the e-commerce package,[803] Article 272 (1) (b) of the VAT Directive was amended so that the release of VAT obligations cannot be applied to underlying suppliers who provide exempt supplies according to Article 136a of the VAT Directive. Thus, a VAT registration by the underlying supplier is necessary in the country of origin.

---

801. *See*, on the 'logical second', e.g., Case C-401/18, *Herst*, 3 Oct. 2019, ECLI:EU:C:2019:834, Opinion of AG Kokott, para. 33.
802. *See* for further information on the VAT exemption for the supply from the underlying supplier to the platform s. 4.6.2.1 The Exemption of Article 136a of the VAT Directive.
803. *See* Council Directive (EU) 2019/1995 of 21 November 2019 Amending Directive 2006/112/EC as Regards Provisions Relating to Distance Sales of Goods and Certain Domestic Supplies of Goods, OJ L 310/1 (2019).

4.3.4 The Place of Supply Rule for the Supply by the Platform

4.3.4.1 *The Place of Supply Rules of Imported Distance Sales (Article 14a [1] of the VAT Directive)*

4.3.4.1.1 *The Place of Supply Rules for the Supply of Goods*

4.3.4.1.1.1 The General Place of Supply Rule According to Article 32 First Subparagraph of the VAT Directive

In many cases, the general place of supply rule for the supply of goods with transport in Article 32 first subparagraph of the VAT Directive will be applicable for the supply of imported goods. This general place of supply rule was not amended in the course of implementing the e-commerce package. As the place of supply is the place of the beginning of the dispatch or transport of the goods according to Article 32 first subparagraph of the VAT Directive, this place of supply would be the third country from which the goods are dispatched. Moreover, in the case of importations from third countries, the place of the importation must additionally be determined which will be discussed in a separate section of the place of supply rules.[804]

4.3.4.1.1.2 Deviations from the General Rule of Article 32 First Subparagraph of the VAT Directive

4.3.4.1.1.2.1 The Shift of the Place of Supply Rule According to Article 32 Second Subparagraph of the VAT Directive

Furthermore, the VAT Directive provides a shift of the place of supply rule in Article 32 second subparagraph of the VAT Directive. Also, this shift from the general place of supply rule was not amended in the course of implementing the e-commerce package. According to Article 32 second subparagraph of the VAT Directive, the place of supply shifts from the third country to the Member State of importation when three requirements are fulfilled.[805] As a first prerequisite, the place of supply shift only applies when the goods are dispatched or transported from third territories or third countries. Furthermore, the goods in question must be imported by the supplier,[806] and the

---

804. *See* s. 4.3.4.1.2 The Place of Importation of the Goods.
805. *See* already this discussion in s. 2.2.3.3.1 The Place of Supply of B2C Imported Goods. *See*, for further information on the background of Article 32 second subpara. of the VAT Directive, Ben Terra & Julie Kajus, *Commentary – A Guide to the Recast VAT Directive, supra* note 290, s. 5.2.3.2; and Ben Terra & Julie Kajus, *Introduction to European VAT, supra* note 167, s. 11.2.2.1.
806. Thomas Bieber, *Der Einfuhrumsatz, supra* note 291, at 522; from the English language version of the VAT Directive, this requirement is not very clear. The English version only stipulates: 'the place of supply by the importer'. However, in the German-language version of the VAT Directive, this requirement is stipulated in a clearer manner by indicating that '... der Ort der Lieferung, die durch den Importeur bewirkt wird, ...'. Therefore, from the German-language version, it can be derived that the import must be effected by the importer.

importer (supplier) must be designated or recognised as being liable to pay the import VAT according to Article 201 of the VAT Directive.

Testing these requirements on the platform as a deemed supplier, the first requirement can be affirmed: Article 36b of the VAT Directive stipulates that the supply from the platform to the customer is the supply with transport.[807] Additionally, the goods are dispatched or transported from a third territory or country since this is also one prerequisite for the application of Article 14a (1) of the VAT Directive.[808] The second requirement of the supplier being the importer, in this instance, the platform as the deemed supplier, is a question that depends on the national law of the Member States. The VAT Directive does not stipulate a specified circle of persons who are to be considered importers but leaves this definition to the Member States. One example of an importer, if stipulated as such in the national law, could be the customs declarant according to Article 77 (3) of the UCC.[809] Thus, the national law of the Member State could stipulate that the platform could qualify as the importer. If the platform could act as an importer according to the national law, then this criterion may also be affirmed. Finally, the platform must be liable to pay the import VAT according to Article 201 of the VAT Directive. Article 201 of the VAT Directive does not stipulate a specified circle of persons who are liable to pay the import VAT; instead, the Member States have to define this in their national law. Most Member States define the customer or consignee as liable to pay the import VAT.[810] However, Member States may also determine that the deemed supplier is liable to pay the import VAT. If so, then the shift in the place of supply may be applied according to Article 32 second subparagraph of the VAT Directive.

Article 32 second subparagraph of the VAT Directive has a rather narrow applicability in practice. On the one hand, this is caused by the narrow requirements and the fact that, for Article 32 second subparagraph of the VAT Directive to become applicable, the Member State must indicate the deemed supplier as being the importer and the person to become liable to pay the import VAT. On the other hand, Article 32 second subparagraph of the VAT Directive is often derogated by another special place of supply rule.[811]

Nevertheless, Article 32 second subparagraph of the VAT Directive may be applied in one specific situation: if, e.g., a French customer ordered a good from a third country on a platform, the goods were imported in France, the platform was the customs declarant and thus was the importer based on French law, and the platform became liable to pay the import VAT as the importer according to the French law. In

---

807. *See*, for further information on the ascription of the supply with transport in the chain transaction, s. 4.3.2.2 Legal Qualification of the Supply with Transport.
808. *See*, for the definition of third territories or third countries, s. 3.3.1.1.3 The Importation from Third Territories and Third Countries.
809. *See* Thomas Bieber, *supra* note 291, at 547 et seqq., who also discussed the implementation in the different Member States with further examples of who can qualify as an importer in the national law.
810. European Commission, *Explanatory Notes on the New VAT E-Commerce Rules*, *supra* note 35, at 97.
811. *See*, for explanations on the derogations of Article 32 of the VAT Directive, s. 4.3.4.1.1.2 Deviations from the General Rule of Article 32 first subparagraph of the VAT Directive.

this case, the platform would have to declare and pay the import VAT as the taxable transaction of the importation is fulfilled,[812] and the platform is defined as the person liable to pay the import VAT based on French law. The place of supply for the importation would be the Member State within whose territory the goods are located when they enter the EU; in this case, it would be France.[813] Additionally, the place of supply of the supply to the customer would be shifted to France according to Article 32 second subparagraph of the VAT Directive, and the platform would have to charge the customer the French VAT. Thus, the platform would have to pay the VAT twice: on the one side, the import VAT and, additionally, the French VAT charged to the customer. However, if the platform fulfilled the requirements for the input VAT deduction, the import VAT could be deducted as input VAT by the platform according to Article 168 (e) of the VAT Directive. For declaring the input VAT deduction and the French VAT to the customer, the platform has to be VAT registered in France; the platform cannot declare the VAT through the IOSS when Article 32 second subparagraph of the VAT Directive is applicable.[814]

From a practical point, it is highly important that the parcels are marked in the case that they are already in free circulation in the EU, i.e., when Article 32 second subparagraph of the VAT Directive is applicable.[815] If this was not the case, then the postal carrier delivering the goods to the French customer may not know whether the import VAT was already paid or whether it has not yet been paid and therefore collect the import VAT from the French customer.[816] This would result in the French customer paying the VAT twice: once to the platform and additionally the import VAT to the postal operator. Thus, to avoid this double taxation of the French customer, the postal operators have to explicitly indicate on the consignment whether the parcel is already in free circulation in the EU. Depending on the marking of the parcel, the postal carrier would know if the collection of import VAT from the customer was necessary, i.e., when the consignment is not yet in free circulation. In general, such a label is also necessary when the platform uses the IOSS for the importation of the goods since, in this case, the postal carriers do not have to collect the import VAT from the customers.[817]

---

812. *See,* for the place of supply for the import, s. 4.3.4.1.2 The Place of Importation of the Goods.
813. *See* Article 60 of the VAT Directive. If the platform fulfils the requirements for the input VAT deduction, the import VAT can be deducted by the importer; *see* Article 168 (e) of the VAT Directive.
814. *See,* for the place of supply when the IOSS is applied, s. 4.3.4.1.1.2.3 The Place of Supply when the Platform Applies the IOSS.
815. Similarly, this marking is also important for the cases when the IOSS is applied.
816. For the collection of the import VAT from the French customer, *see* the explanations on the special arrangement in s. 4.12.3 The Simplification Mechanism of Importations for Non-IOSS Suppliers; or alternatively the explanations on the standard import procedure in s. 4.12.4 The Standard Import Procedure.
817. *See,* for the discussion of the place of supply when the IOSS is applied, s. 4.3.4.1.1.2.3 The Place of Supply when the Platform Applies the IOSS.

4.3.4.1.1.2.2 The Importation of the Goods in a Different Member State than the Member State of where the Dispatch or Transport Ends

Another derogation from the general place of supply rule is stipulated in Article 33 (b) of the VAT Directive that was introduced with the first legislative package of the e-commerce package and has been in force as of 1 July 2021.[818] According to Article 33 (b) of the VAT Directive, the place of supply is shifted to the place where the dispatch or transport to the customer ends when two requirements are fulfilled: (i) the supply must be a distance sale of goods imported from third territories or third countries, and (ii) the import was performed in another Member State than where the dispatch or transport ends.

Testing these requirements on the platform as a deemed supplier, the first requirement can be affirmed because the platform only becomes the deemed supplier according to Article 14a (1) of the VAT Directive when the supply is a distance sale of goods imported from third territories or third countries.[819] The second requirement can, in practice, never be fulfilled. Subsequent to the introduction of the e-commerce package, the customs rules were amended and Article 221 (4) of the UCC-IR was introduced.[820] Based on this amendment, only goods covered by the IOSS can be imported into a Member State other than the Member State of final destination.[821] Thus, when goods that are not declared via the IOSS arrive in a Member State different from the Member State of final destination, then they must be put under an external transit arrangement according to Article 226 of the UCC because only the customs authority of the Member State of final destination is allowed to release the goods for free circulation.[822] Once the goods arrive in the Member State of final destination, they will be released for free circulation.[823] Since the second requirement of Article 33 (b) of the VAT Directive would not be fulfilled, the place of supply would follow the previously discussed place of supply rules of Article 32 first subparagraph of the VAT Directive and thus be in the third country.[824] Therefore, the derogation in Article 33 (b) of the VAT Directive is not applicable in practice.

---

818. *See* Council Directive (EU) 2017/2455 of 5 December 2017 Amending Directive 2006/112/EC and Directive 2009/132/EC as Regards Certain Value Added Tax Obligations for Supplies of Services and Distance Sales of Goods, OJ L 348/7 (2017).

819. *See,* for the discussion of the requirements of distance sale of goods imported from third territories or third countries, Article 14 (4) (2) of the VAT Directive; *see* also the explanations in s. 3.3.1.1 The Definition of Distance Sales of Goods Imported from a Third Territory or a Third Country.

820. *See* Commission Implementing Regulation (EU) 2020/893 of 29 June 2020 Amending Implementing Regulation (EU) 2015/2447 Laying down Detailed Rules for Implementing Certain Provisions of Regulation (EU) No 952/2013 of the European Parliament and of the Council Laying down the Union Customs Code, OJ L 206 (2020) 893.

821. *See* Article 221 (4) of the UCC-IR.

822. *See* Article 221 (4) of the UCC-IR.

823. European Commission, *Explanatory Notes on the New VAT E-Commerce Rules, supra* note 35, at 53.

824. *See* s. 4.3.4.1.1.1 The General Place of Supply Rule According to Article 32 first subparagraph of the VAT Directive.

The introduction of Article 221 (4) of the UCC-IR was necessary in order to avoid double taxation, which the following example clarifies:[825] A Belgian non-taxable person orders goods from a platform in Belgium, and the supply fulfils the criteria stipulated in Article 14a (1) of the VAT Directive. The goods are transported to Germany where they would be released for free circulation if Article 221 (4) of the UCC-IR was not implemented. Thus, assuming that the customer is the importer according to German law and would also be the person liable to pay the import VAT based on German law, the customer would have to pay the import VAT in Germany.[826] The customer would not be able to reclaim the import VAT because the customer is a non-taxable person who does not have the right to deduct input VAT. Additionally, Article 33 (b) of the VAT Directive would be triggered since all requirements would be fulfilled. Therefore, the place of the supply of the goods from the platform to the customer would be in Belgium, and the platform would charge the customer with Belgian VAT. Thus, the customer would pay German VAT as well as Belgian VAT. Thus, the supply would be double taxed. With the limitation in Article 221 (4) of the UCC-IR that only the customs authorities from the Member State of destination can release the goods for free circulation, and thus Article 33 (b) of the VAT Directive is not triggered.

It is not clear why the EU legislator has implemented Article 33 (b) of the VAT Directive to then undermine its effect by introducing Article 221 (4) of the UCC-IR. The only practical explanation could be a timing background: the first and second legislative amendments of the e-commerce package were adopted in December 2017[827] and in November 2019.[828] It might have been that the EU legislator did not realise the discussed issue of double taxation at this point but then corrected the unintended double taxation risk by introducing Article 221 (4) of the UCC-IR in the reform adopted in June 2020.[829]

---

825. *See* also the discussion by Ad van Doesum et al., *Fundamentals of EU VAT Law, supra* note 35, at 656.
826. *See,* for the discussion of the place of supply of the importation, s. 4.3.4.1.2 The Place of Importation of the Goods.
827. Council Directive (EU) 2017/2455 of 5 December 2017 Amending Directive 2006/112/EC and Directive 2009/132/EC as Regards Certain Value Added Tax Obligations for Supplies of Services and Distance Sales of Goods, OJ L 348/7 (2017); Council Implementing Regulation (EU) 2017/2459 of 5 December 2017 Amending Implementing Regulation (EU) No. 282/2011 Laying down Implementing Measures for Directive 2006/112/EC on the Common System of Value Added Tax, OJ L 348/32 (2017); Council Regulation (EU) 2017/2454 of 5 December 2017 Amending Regulation (EU) No. 904/2010 on Administrative Cooperation and Combating Fraud in the Field of Value Added Tax, OJ L 348/1 (2017).
828. Council Directive (EU) 2019/1995 of 21 November 2019 Amending Directive 2006/112/EC as Regards Provisions Relating to Distance Sales of Goods and Certain Domestic Supplies of Goods, OJ L 310/1 (2019); Council Implementing Regulation (EU) 2019/2026 of 21 November 2019 Amending Implementing Regulation (EU) No 282/2011 as Regards Supplies of Goods or Services Facilitated by Electronic Interfaces and the Special Schemes for Taxable Persons Supplying Services to Non-Taxable Persons, Making Distance Sales of Goods and Certain Domestic Supplies of Goods, OJ L 313/14 (2019).
829. *See* Commission Implementing Regulation (EU) 2020/893 of 29 June 2020 Amending Implementing Regulation (EU) 2015/2447 Laying down Detailed Rules for Implementing Certain Provisions of Regulation (EU) No 952/2013 of the European Parliament and of the Council Laying down the Union Customs Code, OJ L 206 (2020) 893.

4.3.4.1.1.2.3 The Place of Supply when the Platform Applies the IOSS

A final derogation from the general place of supply rule is stipulated in Article 33 (c) of the VAT Directive. According to Article 33 (c) of the VAT Directive, the place of supply is also shifted to the place where the dispatch or transport to the customer ends when two requirements are fulfilled: (i) the supply must be a distance sale of goods imported from third territories or third countries, and (ii) the platform must declare the import through the use of the IOSS.[830]

Testing these requirements on the platform as a deemed supplier, the first requirement can be affirmed because the platform only becomes the deemed supplier according to Article 14a (1) of the VAT Directive when the supply is a distance sale of goods imported from third territories or third countries.[831] The second requirement is up to the choice of the platform. Since the application of the IOSS is optional, the platform may decide to apply or not apply the IOSS for its distance sale of goods imported from third territories or third countries.[832] If the platform decided to not apply the IOSS (and no other derogation of the place of supply is applicable), then the place of supply would be in the third country.[833] The platform can execute its choice to not apply the IOSS and would thus not become liable to pay the VAT in the EU. Thereby, the platform can undermine the application of Article 14a (1) of the VAT Directive.

If both requirements were fulfilled, then the place of supply shift would apply. As the place of supply according to Article 33 (c) of the VAT Directive is the place where the dispatch or transport of the goods ends, this is the Member State of final destination. Thus, the platform has to charge the VAT to the Member State of destination to the customer.

Additionally, the importation of goods is subject to import VAT according to Article 2 (1) (d) of the VAT Directive. The place of supply of this importation is, in general, the Member State where the goods are located when they enter the EU.[834] To avoid double taxation when the IOSS is applied, Article 143 (ca) of the VAT Directive exempts the importation of distance sale of goods imported from third territories or third countries when the IOSS is used.[835]

---

830. *See,* for further information on the application of the IOSS, s. 4.11 Special Schemes of the OSS.
831. *See,* for the discussion of the requirements of distance sale of goods imported from third territories or third countries, Article 14 (4) (2) of the VAT Directive; *see* also the explanations in s. 3.3.1.1 The Definition of Distance Sales of Goods Imported from a Third Territory or a Third Country.
832. *See* the further explanations in s. 4.11.3.1 Filing the Application to the IOSS and to the EU-OSS.
833. *See* s. 4.3.4.1.1.1 The General Place of Supply Rule According to Article 32 first subparagraph of the VAT Directive.
834. *See* Article 60 of the VAT Directive; *see* also the deviations from this general rule in Article 61 of the VAT Directive; for further information on the place of supply of the importation, *see* s. 4.3.4.1.2 The Place of Importation of the Goods.
835. *See,* for further information on this exemption, s. 4.6.3 Applicable Rates and Exemptions for the Supply of Goods by the Platform.

4.3.4.1.2   The Place of Importation of the Goods

Finally, also the place of supply of the taxable transaction of the importation of goods should be discussed. According to Article 60 of the VAT Directive, the place of supply of this importation is, in general, the Member State where the goods are located when they enter the EU. This place of supply is relevant to most importations when Article 14a (1) of the VAT Directive is applicable: the importation triggered when the platform does not use the IOSS, the importation triggered when the platform uses the IOSS, as well the importation triggered when the place of supply of the good is determined according to Article 32 first subparagraph of the VAT Directive or Article 32 second subparagraph of the VAT Directive.

Additionally, Article 61 of the VAT Directive also provides derogations from the general place of supply rule for the importation of goods in Article 60 of the VAT Directive. According to Article 61 (1) of the VAT Directive, 'where, on entry into the Community, goods which are not in free circulation are placed … under external transit arrangements, the place of importation such goods shall be the Member State' where the goods cease to be covered by this arrangement. As discussed in a previous section, the goods must be placed under an external transit arrangement according to Article 226 of the UCC when the goods are imported into a country other than the Member State of destination and the IOSS is not applied.[836] Thus, in this specific case, the derogation of Article 61 (1) of the VAT Directive would apply, and the Member State of destination would be the place of importation since, in this Member State, the external transit arrangement would be ceased.

Who can qualify as the importer and who is liable to pay the import VAT depends on the national law of the Member State. In practice, the customer will be liable to pay the import VAT in many cases, especially when the general place of supply rule according to Article 32 first subparagraph of the VAT Directive is applicable. The import VAT by the customer is either payable at the express courier or the postal company or, when the customer clears the goods at customs, then at the competent customs office.[837] If the platform applied the IOSS[838] or if Article 32 second subparagraph of the VAT Directive was applicable,[839] then the platform would likely be the importer and liable to pay the import VAT that would be exempt if the IOSS was applicable or the platform would have the right to deduct the input VAT if Article 32 second subparagraph of the VAT Directive was applicable.

---

836. *See* s. 4.3.4.1.1.2.2 The Importation of the Goods in a Different Member State than the Member State of where the Dispatch or Transport Ends.
837. With the e-commerce package, a special arrangement was introduced for the import VAT payment; *see,* for further information, s. 4.12.3 The Simplification Mechanism of Importations for Non-IOSS Suppliers.
838. *See* s. 4.3.4.1.1.2.3 The Place of Supply when the Platform Applies the IOSS.
839. *See* s. 4.3.4.1.1.2.1 The Shift of the Place of Supply Rule According to Article 32 Second Subparagraph of the VAT Directive.

4.3.4.2 *The Place of Supply for Supplies Within the Community (Article 14a [2] of the VAT Directive)*

4.3.4.2.1 *The Place of Supply Rules for the Supply of Goods*

4.3.4.2.1.1 The General Place of Supply Rule According to Article 31 of the VAT Directive

Within the application of Article 14a (2) of the VAT Directive, the supply of immovable property could trigger the general place of supply rule for supplies without transport according to Article 31 of the VAT Directive since immovable property cannot be dispatched or transported. According to Article 31 of the VAT Directive, the supply shall take 'place where the goods are located at the time when the supply takes place'. For the supply of immovable property, this would be the Member State where the immovable property is located.

4.3.4.2.1.2 The General Place of Supply Rule According to Article 32 First Subparagraph of the VAT Directive

The general place of supply rule for the supply of goods with transport in Article 32 first subparagraph of the VAT Directive locates the place of supply to the place where the goods are located when the dispatch or transport to the customer begins; i.e., this would be the place in the EU where the underlying supplier stores the good. Thereby, the principle of origin is implemented. For the determination of the place of supply within the Community, both situations covered by Article 14a (2) of the VAT Directive should be analysed separately.

When the supply is a national supply, then the general rule of the supply with transport is applicable in most cases.[840] In general, the legal consequences for national supplies do not differ within one Member State. Therefore, it would not matter whether the place of supply is at the origin or at the destination, i.e., at the place where the dispatch or transport begins or ends, because the legal consequences would be the same. There is one exception to this general statement:[841] Several Member States apply

---

840. *See* Article 32 first subpara. of the VAT Directive; one exception to this is the supply of installed or assembled goods stipulated in Article 36 of the VAT Directive; for further information on this place of supply, *see* s. 4.3.4.2.1.3.2 The Place of Supply of Installed or Assembled Goods.

841. Additionally, it could be argued that a second exception is third territories. Several parts of Member States are *ex lege* excluded from the application of the VAT Directive *see* Article 5 (3) read in conjunction with Article 6 of the VAT Directive. In Article 6 of the VAT Directive, the following third territories are listed: Mount Athos; the Canary Islands; the French territories of Guadeloupe, French Guiana, Martinique, Réunion, Saint-Barthélemy, Saint-Martin; the Åland Islands; Campione d'Italia; the Italian waters of Lake Lugano; the Island of Heligoland; the territory of Büsingen; Ceuta; Melilla; Livigno. As supplies from such third territories are subsumed under Article 14a (1) of the VAT Directive, the place of supply rules for imported goods would be applicable; *see* s. 4.3.4.1 The Place of Supply Rules of Imported Distance Sales.

different VAT rates for certain regions.[842] This results in customers ordering goods through the facilitation of a platform, e.g., to Madeira, which are delivered from mainland Portugal. They have to pay the VAT rate applicable on the goods from mainland Portugal and not from Madeira since the place of supply is where the dispatch or transport begins, i.e., in mainland Portugal. In this special case, the place of origin is applicable to supplies facilitated by platforms.

When the supply is an intra-Community B2C supply, then the general place of supply rule stipulated in Article 32 first subparagraph of the VAT Directive is applicable to supplies that cannot be subsumed under any deviation from the general place of supply rule according to Article 32 of the VAT Directive.[843] Thus, Article 32 of the VAT Directive is applicable to supplies where the customer picks up the goods since, in this case, Article 33 (b) of the VAT Directive is not applicable. Additionally, the application of the place of supply rule for intra-Community distance sales of goods according to Articles 33 (b) and 35 of the VAT Directive is not applicable to specific kinds of goods.[844] The supply of new means of transport,[845] the supply of second-hand goods, works of art, collectors' items or antiques,[846] and the supply of second-hand means of transport[847] are excluded from the place of supply rule of Article 33 (b) of the VAT Directive and thus follow the general place of supply rule according to Article 32 first subparagraph of the VAT Directive. Additionally, also the supply of goods of micro-platforms follows the general place of supply rule according to Article 32 first subparagraph of the VAT Directive.[848] Therefore, for supplies to which no special place of supply rule is applicable, the principle of origin is still implemented in the VAT Directive.

---

842. Also, within national supplies, the place of supply rules may be important, especially if Member States apply different VAT rates for the same supply. Examples of this are stipulated in Article 104 of the VAT Directive for Austria and the communes of Jungholz and Mittelberg; Article 105 (2) of the VAT Directive for Portugal and the regions of Azores and Madeira; and Article 120 of the VAT Directive for Greece and the departments of Lesbos, Chios, Samos, the Dodecanese and the Cyclades, and on the islands of Thassos, the Northern Sporades, Samothrace and Skiros.

843. See s. 4.3.4.2.1.3 Deviations from the General Place of Supply Rule According to Article 32 of the VAT Directive.

844. See, for further information on the place of supply for intra-Community distance sales of goods, s. 4.3.4.2.1.3 Deviations from the General Place of Supply Rule According to Article 32 of the VAT Directive.

845. The supply of new means of transport in the country of origin is exempt from the VAT according to Article 138 (2) (a) of the VAT Directive. Nevertheless, an intra-Community acquisition must be declared by the customer. For further details on this intra-Community acquisition, see s. 4.3.4.2.2 The Place of Supply of the Intra-Community Acquisition of New Means of Transport.

846. See, for the definition of second-hand goods, works of art, collectors' items or antiques, Article 311 (1) (1)-(4) of the VAT Directive.

847. See, for the definition of second-hand means of transport, Article 327 (3) of the VAT Directive.

848. See, for the definition of micro-platforms and further information on micro-platforms, s. 4.3.4.2.1.3.1.2 The Place of Supply for Supplies Facilitated by Micro-Platform.

4.3.4.2.1.3   Deviations from the General Place of Supply Rule According to
Article 32 of the VAT Directive

4.3.4.2.1.3.1 Intra-Community Distance Sales of Goods

4.3.4.2.1.3.1.1 The Special Place of Supply Rule for Intra-Community Distance Sales of Goods

If the supply is an intra-Community B2C supply of goods, the *lex specialis* place of supply rule stipulated in Article 33 (a) of the VAT Directive may be applicable. According to Article 33 (a) of the VAT Directive, the place of supply for intra-Community distance sales of goods is shifted to the place where the goods are located when the dispatch or transport to the customer ends. With the e-commerce package, the term 'intra-Community distance sales of goods' has legally been defined in Article 14 (4) (1) of the VAT Directive:

(1) 'intra-Community distance sales of goods' means supplies of goods dispatched or transported by or on behalf of the supplier, including where the supplier intervenes indirectly in the transport or dispatch of the goods, from a Member State other than that in which dispatch or transport of the goods to the customer ends, where the following conditions are met:
    (a) the supply of goods is carried out for a taxable person, or a non-taxable legal person, whose intra-Community acquisitions of goods are not subject to VAT pursuant to Article 3 (1) or for any other non-taxable person;
    (b) the goods supplied are neither new means of transport nor goods supplied after assembly or installation, with or without a trial run, by or on behalf of the supplier.

Therefrom, several limitations to the application of the supply shift in Article 33 (a) of the VAT Directive can be derived: (i) the goods must be 'dispatched or transported by or on behalf of the supplier',[849] (ii) the goods must be dispatched or transported from one Member State to another,[850] (iii) criteria on the taxable status of the customer according to Article 14 (4) (1) (a),[851] and (iv) requirements on the kind of supplied good stipulated in Article 14 (4) (1) (b) of the VAT Directive.[852] As the interpretation of most of these terms is uniform with the interpretation of the term 'distance sales of goods imported from third territories or third countries', reference can be made to the previous sections.[853] Many supplies of goods facilitated by

---

849. *See*, on this requirement, the discussed interpretation in s. 3.3.1.1.2 The Dispatch or Transportation of Goods By or on Behalf of the Supplier.
850. This requirement is also one requirement for the application of Article 14a (2) of the VAT Directive; *see* 3.3.2.1 The Definition of Supply of Goods Within the Community.
851. *See*, on this requirement, the discussed interpretation in s. 3.3.1.1.4 The Requirements of Article 14 (4) (2) (a) of the VAT Directive on the VAT Status of the Recipient of the Goods.
852. *See*, on this requirement, the discussed interpretation in s. 3.3.1.1.5 Limitations to the Supplied Goods.
853. *See* s. 3.3.1.1.2 The Dispatch or Transportation of Goods By or on Behalf of the Supplier for the interpretation of (i) 'the dispatch or transportation of goods by or on behalf of the supplier', s. 3.3.2.1 The Definition of Supply of Goods Within the Community, for the interpretation of (ii) the dispatch or transport of the goods from one Member State to another, s. 3.3.1.1.4 The

platforms fulfil the stipulated requirements. As discussed in the previous section,[854] the dispatch or transportation with an indirect involvement of the underlying supplier in the dispatch or transport of the goods will be fulfilled. The second requirement would be fulfilled if the goods were transported from one Member State to another. The third requirement would also be fulfilled because this is one requirement that must have already been fulfilled for the platform to become the deemed supplier according to Article 14 (2) of the VAT Directive. In fact, Article 14 (2) of the VAT Directive is only applicable to non-taxable persons, which is an even narrower scope than the application of Article 33 (a) read in conjunction with Article 14 (4) (1) (a) of the VAT Directive.

Moreover, the kind of good also provides for further restrictions. Additionally to the exclusion of new means of transport and goods supplied after assembly or installation,[855] Article 35 of the VAT Directive excludes supplies of second-hand goods, works of art, collectors' items or antiques,[856] and second-hand means of transport[857] from the applicability of Article 33 of the VAT Directive. Thus, the general place of supply rule according to Article 32 first subparagraph of the VAT Directive is applicable to the supply of new means of transport,[858] second-hand goods, works of art, collectors' items or antiques, and second-hand means of transport. For the supply of goods supplied after assembly or installation, a different deviation of the general place of supply rule is stipulated in Article 36 of the VAT Directive.[859]

When all of the conditions set out in Articles 33 (a) and 35 of the VAT Directive are fulfilled and the platform facilitating the supply is not a micro-platform that opted for the application of Article 33 (a) of the VAT Directive,[860] the place of supply is the Member State of destination, so the Member State where the dispatch or transport of the goods to the customer ends. The applicability of Article 33 (a) of the VAT Directive generally results in the obligation of the platform to register for VAT purposes in the Member States to which the goods are delivered for being able to fulfil the VAT obligations. To circumvent this VAT registration obligation in the different Member States, the platform can use the EU-OSS.[861]

Requirements of Article 14 (4) (2) (a) of the VAT Directive on the VAT Status of the Recipient of the Goods for the discussion of (iii) further criteria on the taxable status of the customer according to Article 14 (4) (1) (a) of the VAT Directive and s. 3.3.1.1.4 The Requirements of Article 14 (4) (2) (a) of the VAT Directive on the VAT Status of the Recipient of the Goods for the discussion of the (iv) requirements on the kind of supplied good according to Article 14 (4) (1) (b) of the VAT Directive.

854. See s. 3.3.1.1.2 The Dispatch or Transportation of Goods By or on Behalf of the Supplier.
855. See Article 33 (a) read in conjunction with Article 14 (4) (1) (a) of the VAT Directive.
856. See, for the definition of second-hand goods, works of art, collectors' items or antiques, Article 311 (1) (1)-(4) of the VAT Directive.
857. See, for the definition of second-hand means of transport, Article 327 (3) of the VAT Directive.
858. Nevertheless, the intra-Community supply of new means of transport would be tax exempt according to Article 138 (2) (a) of the VAT Directive in the country of origin, but the customer would have to declare an intra-Community acquisition in the Member State of destination; see s. 4.3.4.2.2 The Place of Supply of the Intra-Community Acquisition of New Means of Transport.
859. See s. 4.3.4.2.1.3.2 The Place of Supply of Installed or Assembled Goods.
860. See s. 4.3.4.2.1.3.1.2 The Place of Supply for Supplies Facilitated by Micro-Platform.
861. See, for further explanations on the EU-OSS, s. 4.11 Special Schemes of the OSS.

4.3.4.2.1.3.1.2 The Place of Supply for Supplies Facilitated by Micro-Platforms

The exception for micro-platforms was already mentioned repeatedly in the previous sections. In Article 59c of the VAT Directive, the EU legislator included a facilitation for micro-taxable persons who supply intra-Community distance sales of goods and telecommunication, broadcasting, and electronic services. According to this facilitation, the principle of destination stipulated in Article 33 (a) of the VAT Directive is not applicable to taxable persons who fulfil certain criteria.[862] This deviation from the special place of supply rule in Article 33 (a) of the VAT Directive is also applicable to platforms when the platform fulfils the requirements stipulated in Article 59c of the VAT Directive. Thus, these requirements are discussed in this section.

The first requirement stipulates that 'the supplier is established or, in the absence of an establishment, has his permanent address or usually resides only in one Member State'.[863] Based on this criterion, platforms established only in a third country cannot qualify as micro-platforms. Platforms established in only one Member State would fulfil this criterion. Additionally, the question arises of whether a fixed establishment should also qualify as 'being established'. As already discussed, a uniform interpretation of the VAT Directive leads to the conclusion that a fixed establishment should also qualify as 'being established' in a country.[864] Thus, a platform established in a third country could have a fixed establishment in a Member State. If the platform had a fixed establishment in a Member State, then the first criterion would be fulfilled. On the contrary, if a platform was established in a Member State but had a fixed establishment in another Member State, then the first criterion would not be fulfilled since the taxable person can only be established in one Member State. As already discussed, warehouses are only considered to be a fixed establishment when the requirement of a sufficient degree of permanence and a suitable structure in terms of human and technical resources is fulfilled.[865]

The second criterion is that the goods are not supplied to the Member State where the supplier (platform) is established.[866] The European Commission seems to interpret the first and second criteria very narrowly in the Explanatory Notes. It is argued that if a supplier established in the EU (e.g., France) had a warehouse in another Member State (e.g., Germany) and supplied goods from the Member State of establishment as well as from the warehouse to other Member States (neither to the Member State of establishment nor to the Member State of the warehouse, e.g., to Polish and Belgian

---

862. Similarly, also the special place of supply rule for the supply of telecommunication, broadcasting, and electronic services in Article 58 of the VAT Directive is not applicable if the same requirements are fulfilled.
863. *See* Article 59c (1) (a) of the VAT Directive.
864. *See* s. 3.3.2.2 The Requirements for Underlying Suppliers and the Customers.
865. *See* s. 3.3.2.2 The Requirements for Underlying Suppliers and the Customers.
866. *See* Article 59c (1) (b) of the VAT Directive.

customers), the facilitation of Article 59c of the VAT Directive should not be applicable.[867] This conclusion by the European Commission can be seen critically based on the text of the VAT Directive. The conclusion would be correct if the warehouse was to fulfil the requirements of a fixed establishment since, in this case, the supplier would not only be established in one Member State (France) according to Article 59c (1) (a) of the VAT Directive. The conclusion would also be correct if the supplier supplied goods from the warehouse (Germany) to the country of establishment (France) since the goods cannot be dispatched or transported to the Member State of establishment (France) according to Article 59c (1) (b) of the VAT Directive. Nevertheless, based on the described facts by the European Commission, the facilitation of Article 59c of the VAT Directive should be applicable. It is unclear how the European Commission came to the conclusion that Article 59c of the VAT Directive is only applicable when the goods are dispatched or transported from the Member State of establishment.[868]

Finally, the third criterion is that the supplies to other Member States by the platform do not exceed the EUR 10,000 threshold.[869] For determining this threshold, all intra-Community distance sales of goods as well as all cross-border telecommunication, broadcasting, and electronic services to EU consumers must be taken into consideration when the platform provides such services as well or is the deemed supplier for such services according to Article 9a of the VAT Implementing Regulation.[870] Thus, national supplies by the platform are not to be included in the threshold of EUR 10,000. The annual threshold is not a threshold per Member State but for the mentioned supplies to all Member States to which the platform supplies the intra-Community distance sales of goods and the cross-border telecommunication, broadcasting, and electronic services to EU consumers. Additionally, the threshold of EUR 10,000 may not be exceeded in the previous and current calendar year.[871] When the platform exceeds the threshold during a calendar year, Article 33 (a) of the VAT Directive becomes applicable from the moment that the platform has exceeded this threshold.[872] Therefore, especially platforms that have their core business in the Member State of establishment may be able to use the facilitation of Article 59c of the VAT Directive.

Since, in Article 59c (1) (b) of the VAT Directive, the conjunction 'and' is used, these requirements must be fulfilled cumulatively. When the platform does not fulfil one of the discussed requirements, it cannot qualify as a micro-platform. Due to these restrictions and the relatively small threshold of EUR 10,000, the application of Article 59c of the VAT Directive is rather unlikely for platforms.[873] Furthermore, the application of Article 59c of the VAT Directive is optional. Thus, if the platform fulfilled all of

---

867. See European Commission, *Explanatory Notes on the New VAT E-Commerce Rules*, *supra* note 35, at 43; *see*, similarly, the restriction by the European Commission on p. 40, according to which 'the goods must be sent from the Member State of establishment' for Article 59c of the VAT Directive to be applicable.
868. See also the footnote ** in *ibid.* at 40.
869. See Article 59c (1) (c) of the VAT Directive.
870. See Article 59c (1) (c) read in conjunction with Article 59c (1) (b) of the VAT Directive.
871. See Article 59c (1) (c) of the VAT Directive.
872. See Article 59c (2) of the VAT Directive.
873. See, similarly, Christine Weinzierl, *SWK-Spezial E-Commerce Paket 2021*, *supra* note 18, at 108.

the requirements, the micro-platform may still opt for the applicability of Article 33 (a) of the VAT Directive and may thus apply the principle of destination instead.[874]

4.3.4.2.1.3.2 The Place of Supply of Installed or Assembled Goods

The place of supply for the supply of installed or assembled goods is stipulated in Article 36 of the VAT Directive. For the application of Article 36 of the VAT Directive, it is irrelevant whether a trial run of the good is agreed between the parties. The only requirement that must be fulfilled is that the goods must be assembled by the supplier. In this case, the discussion may arise of whether the underlying supplier or the platform should qualify as the supplier indicated in Article 36 first subparagraph of the VAT Directive. For this discussion, reference is made to the previous section;[875] since the VAT Directive requires a uniform interpretation, 'the supplier' referred to in Article 36 of the VAT Directive should be interpreted as the underlying supplier. When the platform facilitates the supply of a good installed or assembled and the underlying supplier is installing or assembling the ordered good, then the place of supply is the place where the goods are installed or assembled.[876] Therefore, Article 36 of the VAT Directive also implements the principle of destination.

4.3.4.2.1.3.3 The Place of Supply of Gas, Electricity and Heat or Cooling Energy

The place of supply for the supply of gas, electricity, and heat or cooling energy is stipulated in Articles 38 and 39 of the VAT Directive.[877] Thereby, the general place of supply depends on the recipient of the gas, electricity, and heat or cooling energy. Article 38 (1) of the VAT Directive is applicable to supplies to taxable dealers as defined in Article 38 (2) of the VAT Directive. Since Article 14a (2) of the VAT Directive is only applicable to supplies to non-taxable persons, the place of supply shift of Article 38 of the VAT Directive is not relevant in this case.

However, Article 39 (1) of the VAT Directive stipulates an alternative place of supply for any supply of 'gas through a natural gas system situated within the territory of the Community or any network connected to such a system, the supply of electricity or the supply of heat or cooling energy through heating or cooling networks'. According to Article 39 (1) of the VAT Directive, the place of supply is where the customer effectively uses or consumes the goods. Additionally, Article 39 (2) of the VAT Directive also stipulates the place of supply for gas, electricity, and heat or cooling energy when the energy is not consumed. In this case, the place of supply for non-taxable persons is the place where the customer has his permanent address or usually resides. Thus, Article 39 of the VAT Directive also implements the principle of destination.

---

874. *See* Article 59c (3) of the VAT Directive.
875. *See*, on this discussion, s. 3.3.1.1.2 The Dispatch or Transportation of Goods By or on Behalf of the Supplier.
876. *See* Article 36 first subpara. of the VAT Directive.
877. Articles 38 and 39 of the VAT Directive are not applicable in the case that Article 14a (1) of the VAT Directive is applied as the supply of gas, electricity, and heat or cooling energy cannot qualify as a consignment; *see*, for the discussion of the term 'consignment', s. 3.3.1.2.2 The Interpretation of 'Consignments'.

4.3.4.2.2 The Place of Supply of the Intra-Community Acquisition of New Means of Transport

Another taxable transaction that the customer might fulfil is the acquisition of a new means of transport when Article 14a (2) of the VAT Directive is applicable. In the previous section, it was already analysed that the place of supply of new means of transport is in the country of origin.[878] At the same time, the acquisition of a new means of transport evokes an intra-Community acquisition according to Article 2 (b) (ii) of the VAT Directive regardless of whether the customer is a taxable or non-taxable person. Pursuant to Article 40 of the VAT Directive, the place of this intra-Community acquisition is the place where the dispatch or transport to the customer ends; thereby, also the principle of destination is implemented. The customer has the obligation to declare the intra-Community acquisition in the country of destination. In order to not double tax the supply of new means of transportation, the supply from the platform to the consumer, which should be taxed in the country of origin, is VAT exempt according to Article 138 (2) (a) of the VAT Directive.

In practice, it will be rare that an underlying supplier established in a third country would supply a new means of transport from a warehouse (that is not a fixed establishment) in the EU through the facilitation of a platform. Thus, the applicability of Article 40 of the VAT Directive seems to be limited. Therefore, the intra-Community acquisition will not be further discussed in the following sections.[879]

4.4 CHARGEABLE EVENT AND CHARGEABILITY OF VAT

4.4.1 General Remarks

The VAT Directive provides harmonised definitions and rules for the chargeable event and the chargeability of the VAT with the aim to ensure the uniform collection of the VAT.[880] Article 62 (1) of the VAT Directive defines the 'chargeable event' as 'the occurrence by virtue of which the legal conditions necessary for VAT to become chargeable are fulfilled'. This is, in other words, the moment when the taxable event is (deemed to be) completed.[881] The moment when the VAT becomes 'chargeable' should be distinguished from the 'chargeable moment'. The chargeability is defined in Article 62 (2) of the VAT Directive as the moment 'when the competent tax authority becomes entitled under the law, at a given moment, to claim the tax from the person liable to pay, even though the time of payment may be deferred'. Therefore, the chargeability

---

878. See s. 4.3.4.2.1.2 The General Place of Supply Rule According to Article 32 First Subparagraph of the VAT Directive.

879. Special provisions relevant for the intra-Community acquisition would be, e.g., Article 68 of the VAT Directive on the chargeable event and chargeability or Article 83 of the VAT Directive on the taxable amount of intra-Community acquisitions.

880. See Case C-169/12, TNT Express Worldwide (Poland) sp. z o.o. v Minister Finansów, 16 May 2013, ECLI:EU:C:2013:314, para. 31; Case C-224/18, Budimex S.A. v Minister Finansów, 2 May 2019, ECLI:EU:C:2019:347, para. 22.

881. Ad van Doesum et al., Fundamentals of EU VAT Law, supra note 35, at 231 et seq.

defines the moment when the competent tax authorities formally become entitled to claim the VAT. The chargeability is not the same moment as when the VAT becomes payable to the competent tax authorities. This is normally the moment when the VAT return becomes due, which can differ between the Member States.[882]

According to the general provision in Article 63 of the VAT Directive, the chargeable event and the chargeability for the supply of goods is the moment when a good is supplied. Furthermore, the subsequent articles provide for derogations from this general provision for successive statements of account or successive payments,[883] continuous supplies of goods and services,[884] payments on accounts,[885] intra-Community acquisitions of goods,[886] and importations of goods.[887] These special derogations will not be further discussed since a special derogation from the general rule is also stipulated for the applicability of Article 14a of the VAT Directive.[888]

4.4.2 Derogation of the General Rules: Article 66a of the VAT Directive

Derogating from the general rule in Article 62 of the VAT Directive, Article 66a of the VAT Directive stipulates as the chargeable event and chargeability 'the time when the payment has been accepted' when Article 14a of the VAT Directive is applied. This derogation is applicable to the supply by the underlying supplier to the platform as well as to the supply by the platform to the customer. The time of the acceptance of the payment is further defined in Article 41a of the VAT Implementing Regulation.

Article 41a of the VAT Implementing Regulation stipulates three different possibilities for the acceptance of the payment:

(1) The receipt of the payment confirmation,
(2) the receipt of the payment authorisation message or
(3) the receipt of a commitment for payment from the customer.

Whichever of these three moments is fulfilled first qualifies as the moment of the acceptance of the payment.[889] The actual payment by the customer is irrelevant.[890] The

---

882. *See* Article 206 read in conjunction with Article 250 of the VAT Directive; *see* also, for platforms using the IOSS and/or the EU-OSS, s. 4.11.4 Declaration and Payment. Also, the CJEU distinguishes between these three moments in time; *see*, e.g., Case C-10/92, *Maurizio Balocchi v Ministero delle Finanze dello Stato*, 20 Oct. 1993, ECLI:EU:C:1993:846, para. 24; Case C-855/19, *G. Sp. z o.o. v Dyrektor Izby Administracji Skarbowej w Bydgoszczy*, 9 Sep. 2021, ECLI:EU:C:2021:714, paras. 26 et seq.; *see* also the detailed descriptions and the criticism of these complicated different definitions by Ad van Doesum et al., *supra* note 35, at 220 et seqq.; the authors additionally discuss the moment of the taxable transaction.
883. *See* Article 64 (1) of the VAT Directive.
884. *See* Article 64 (2) of the VAT Directive.
885. *See* Article 65 of the VAT Directive.
886. *See* Article 68 et seq. of the VAT Directive.
887. *See* Article 70 et seq. of the VAT Directive.
888. *See* the following s. 4.4.2 Derogation of the General Rules: Article 66a of the VAT Directive.
889. *See* Article 41a of the VAT Implementing Regulation.
890. *See* Article 41a of the VAT Implementing Regulation.

indicated information should be available to the platform since the platform must be (in)directly involved in the authorisation process to charge the customer so that Article 14a of the VAT Directive is triggered.[891]

As previously discussed, platforms face a significant increase in compliance efforts and costs but also a negative impact on their liquidity due to the fact that they might not be involved in the payment process and therefore may not have received the VAT although the VAT has already become due as the payment has been accepted.[892] To avoid this negative liquidity effect by the platforms, the EU legislator could have implemented a different definition of the chargeable event and chargeability for the application of Article 14a of the VAT Directive, i.e., the time when the VAT payment was actually received by the platform. Such a definition could have avoided the negative impact on the liquidity of the platform as well as the risk borne by the platform in the case of non-payment or insolvency by the underlying supplier. At the same time, such a derogation would be highly vulnerable to abuse. If the chargeable event and chargeability occurred at the moment of the receipt of the VAT payment by the platform, the platform would not have a lot of incentive to demand the VAT to be paid by the customer (or by the underlying supplier if the customer had already transferred the full amount due including the VAT to the underlying supplier). If the customer or the underlying supplier simply did not pay the VAT to the platform, the chargeable event and the chargeability would not occur, and the platform would not have to pay the VAT to the competent tax authorities. Additionally, the terms of the payment are based on a civil rights agreement between the parties involved and, thus, the VAT payment could be postponed between the parties to a later time. If the chargeable event and the chargeability were defined as the moment when the platform receives the VAT payment, then the parties could choose when the VAT would become chargeable. For this reason, the chargeable event and chargeability are independent of the payment of the VAT in the EU VAT system.[893] Thus, it is consistent within the VAT system that the chargeable event and chargeability for the deemed supplier are independent of the actual payment to the deemed supplier.

4.4.3 The Chargeable Event and Chargeability of the Importation

In addition to the chargeable event and the chargeability of VAT by the underlying supplier and the platform for the supply of the goods for consideration, the chargeable event and the chargeability of the VAT for the importation should also be analysed when Article 14a (1) of the VAT Directive is applicable. For the determination of the chargeable event and the chargeability of the VAT for imports, Articles 70 and 71 of the VAT Directive should be applied. Thereby, Article 70 of the VAT Directive generally

---

891. See Article 5b second subpara. of the VAT Implementing Regulation; for further information on this requirement, see s. 3.2.2.2 The First Negative List in Article 5b of the VAT Implementing Regulation.
892. See the full discussion on this criticism in s. 3.2.2.4 Criticism on the Definition of 'to Facilitate'.
893. One exception of this general rule are advanced payments made on account before the good or service is supplied. In this case, the VAT becomes chargeable on receipt of the payment; see Article 65 of the VAT Directive.

stipulates that the chargeable event and the chargeability occur when the goods are imported.

Additionally, Article 71 of the VAT Directive also provides derogations from the chargeable event and the chargeability of the VAT rule for the importation of goods in Article 70 of the VAT Directive. According to Article 1 (1) of the VAT Directive, '[w]here, on entry into the Community, goods are placed ... under external transit arrangements, the chargeable event shall occur and VAT shall become chargeable only when the goods cease to be covered by those arrangements'. As discussed in a previous section, the goods must be placed under an external transit arrangement according to Article 226 of the UCC when the goods are imported into a country other than the Member State of destination and the IOSS is not applied.[894] Thus, in this specific case, the derogation of Article 71 (1) of the VAT Directive would apply, and the chargeable event and the chargeability would be the moment that the external transit arrangement would be ceased, i.e., the moment when the goods are imported into the Member State of destination.

4.5 TAXABLE AMOUNT

4.5.1 General Remarks

The taxable amount is the basis for the calculation of the VAT. Any supplier (or recipient in the case that the reverse-charge is applicable) has to determine the taxable amount in order to determine the VAT that must be charged to the customer as well as the VAT that has to be declared and paid to the competent tax authorities. Thus, Articles 72-92 of the VAT Directive give guidance on the determination of the taxable amount.

The general rule in Article 73 of the VAT Directive is that the taxable amount includes anything obtained for the supply by the customer or a third party. Therefore, the general rule is a subjective value based on the consideration actually received.[895] Furthermore, Articles 74-80 of the VAT Directive provide specific provisions, e.g., elements that should be included and excluded from the taxable amount,[896] the option

---

894. See s. 4.3.4.1.1.2.2 The Importation of the Goods in a Different Member State than the Member State of where the Dispatch or Transport Ends.
895. See, e.g., Case C-154/80, *Staatsecretaris van Financiën v Coöperatieve Aardappelenbewaarp-laats*, 5 Feb. 1981, ECLI:EU:C:1981:38, para. 13; in spite of this general rule, Articles 72 and 80 of the VAT Directive provide an exception according to which the open market value, i.e., an objective value, is used to determine the taxable amount. Notably, the application of this exception is limited to supplies between connected parties (*see* Article 80 [1] of the VAT Directive); *see* also Case C-549/11, *Orfey Balgaria*, 19 Dec. 2012, ECLI:EU:C:2012:832, paras. 46 et seq., where the CJEU explicitly mentioned that Article 80 of the VAT Directive has the background of preventing tax evasion or avoidance and, therefore, its applicability is limited to connected parties. *See* also the discussion on the subjective value in s. 2.2.5.2 The Necessity for Consideration.
896. *See* Articles 78 and 79 of the VAT Directive; *see*, for further information, s. 4.5.2 The Taxable Amount of the Supply by the Underlying Supplier.

to implement a derogation for the supply of multipurpose vouchers,[897] derogations from the subjective value to an open market value under certain circumstances[898] and specific provisions for deemed supplies,[899] intra-Community acquisitions,[900] and the importation of goods.[901]

The following sections will discuss the taxable amount of the supply by the underlying supplier as well as the taxable amount of the supply by the platform in detail. Furthermore, the taxable amount for the importation will be analysed. In a final section, the payment of a possible commission by the underlying supplier and/or by the customer for the platform services will be examined. In addition, it will be investigated whether a commission should be part of the taxable amount either by the underlying supplier or by the platform.

4.5.2 The Taxable Amount of the Supply by the Underlying Supplier

First of all, it should be noted that the determination of the taxable amount of the supply by the underlying supplier is only relevant when Article 14a (2) of the VAT Directive applies because, in the case of Article 14a (1) of the VAT Directive, the place of supply is in the third country.[902] Only when the place of supply is in a Member State must the taxable amount be determined by the underlying supplier according to EU VAT law.

The combination of Article 73 of the VAT Directive stipulating the general rule for the taxable amount and Articles 78 and 79 of the VAT Directive providing for specific items to be included or excluded from the taxable amount raises the question of the relationship between these articles. According to the CJEU case law, it should be reviewed whether the specific items stipulated in Articles 78 and 79 of the VAT Directive are to be included in or excluded from the taxable amount before the general rule of Article 73 of the VAT Directive applies.[903]

Consequently, in a first step, the underlying supplier should review whether additional costs should be included in the taxable amount according to Article 78 of the

---

897. *See* Article 73a of the VAT Directive.
898. *See* Articles 72 and 80 of the VAT Directive.
899. *See* Articles 74-77 of the VAT Directive.
900. *See* Articles 83 and 84 of the VAT Directive.
901. *See* Articles 85-89 of the VAT Directive; *see,* for further information, s. 4.5.4 The Taxable Amount of the Importation by the Platform or the Customer.
902. *See,* for the place of supply rule, s. 4.3.3 The Place of Supply Rule for the Supply by the Underlying Supplier.
903. Case C-126/88, *Boots Company plc v Commissioners of Customs and Excise,* 27 Mar. 1990, ECLI:EU:C:1990:136, paras. 15 et seq.; Case C-380/99, *Bertelsmann,* 3 Jul. 2001, ECLI: EU:C:2001:372, para. 15; in literature, it is argued that Article 78 of the VAT Directive is the *lex specialis* to Article 73 of the VAT Directive; *see* Ad van Doesum et al., *Fundamentals of EU VAT Law, supra* note 35, at 272; Ad van Doesum & Herman van Kesteren, *Taxes, Duties, Levies and Charges as Part of the Taxable Amount for Value Added Tax,* 26 EC Tax Review (2017). This classification as a *lex specialis* can be criticised because Article 78 of the VAT Directive, by itself, does not stipulate how to determine the taxable amount. Article 78 of the VAT Directive only lists items that should be included in the taxable amount. Thus, Article 73 of the VAT Directive should be applied in conjunction with Article 78 (and Article 79) of the VAT Directive to ensure that anything obtained by the customer is included in the taxable amount.

VAT Directive. Additional expenses are part of the taxable amount 'even though they do not represent any added value and do not constitute the financial consideration for the supply of the goods, [but] they must be directly linked to that supply'.[904] Article 78 of the VAT Directive stipulates that taxes, duties, levies, and charges, as well as incidental expenses such as the commission, packing, transport, and insurance costs are to be included in the taxable amount.

In this instance, the question might arise of whether all taxes, duties, levies, and charges as well as incidental costs incurred can become part of the taxable amount. If, e.g., an underlying supplier offered one price for a car and this price included the payment of the car registration duty, then the car registration duty would not be part of the taxable amount because the car could have also been supplied without the registration, and the registration could have been applied for without purchasing a car.[905] Thus, taxes, duties, levies, and charges as well as incidental expenses can only be included in the taxable amount when they are triggered by the supply.[906] In this sense, one duty that has to be included in the taxable amount is the excise duty when this excise duty is triggered by the supply.

Contrary to these inclusions, Article 79 of the VAT Directive stipulates that price reductions due to early payments, price discounts, and rebates at the time of the supply and amounts received by the supplier as repayment of expenditures incurred in the name and on behalf of the customer and entered in his books in a suspense account shall not be included in the taxable amount.[907]

In a second step, the general rule of Article 73 of the VAT Directive applies. Thus, in addition to the discussed inclusions and exclusions, anything obtained by the underlying supplier for the supply of the good is part of the taxable amount.[908] Instead of Article 73 of the VAT Directive that generally refers to the subjective value agreed between the parties involved, Article 80 of the VAT Directive bases the taxable amount on a market value as defined in Article 72 of the VAT Directive. Article 80 (1) of the

---

904. Case C-98/05, *De Danske Bilimportører v Skatteministeriet*, 1 Jun. 2006, ECLI:EU:C:2006:363, para. 17; with reference to Case C-230/87, *Naturally Yours Cosmetics Limited v Commissioners of Customs and Excise*, 23 Nov. 1988, ECLI:EU:C:1988:508, paras. 11 et seq.; Case C-33/93, *Empire Stores Ltd v Commissioners of Customs and Excise*, 2 Jun. 1994, ECLI:EU:C:1994:225, para. 12; Case C-380/99, *Bertelsmann*, 3 Jul. 2001, ECLI:EU:C:2001:372, paras. 17 et seq.; *see* also similarly Case C-433/09, *European Commission v Republic of Austria*, 22 Dec. 2010, ECLI:EU:C:2010:817, para. 34; Joined Cases C-618/11, C-637/11 and C-659/11, *TVI – Televisão Independente SA v Fazenda Pública*, 5 Dec. 2013, ECLI:EU:C:2013:789, paras 37 + 39; Case C-256/14, *Lisboagás GDL – Sociedade Distribuidora de Gás Natural de Lisboa SA v Autoridade Tributária e Aduaneira*, 11 Jun. 2015, ECLI:EU:C:2015:387, para. 29.
905. Case C-433/09, *Commission v Austria*, 22 Dec. 2010, ECLI:EU:C:2010:817, paras. 19 et seq.; Case C-98/05, *De Danske Bilimportører*, 1 Jun. 2006, ECLI:EU:C:2006:363, para. 40; under certain circumstances, the tax, levy or charge may be part of the taxable amount in Article 73 of the VAT Directive; one example would be Case C-256/14, *Lisboagás GDL*, 11 Jun. 2015, ECLI:EU:C:2015:387 where the CJEU held that the land use taxes paid by the supplier are not to be included based on Article 78 (a) of the VAT Directive but are part of the taxable amount according to Article 73 of the VAT Directive because they are a part of the consideration of the cost of the supply of the property.
906. *See* Ad van Doesum et al., *supra* note 35, at 272.
907. *See*, for further details, also the critical discussions in *ibid.* at 274 et seqq.
908. *See* Article 73 of the VAT Directive.

VAT Directive provides the Member States with the option to implement the open market value 'in respect of the supply of goods or services involving family or other close personal ties, management, ownership, membership, financial or legal ties as defined by the Member State'. Most underlying suppliers and e-commerce platforms would not fulfil the requirement of 'close personal ties' to trigger the determination of the open market value of Article 80 of the VAT Directive.

Thus, in most cases, Article 73 of the VAT Directive should be applicable for determining the taxable amount of the supply from the underlying supplier to the platform which includes anything that the underlying supplier receives for the supply of the good to the platform. In many cases, this would be the final price of the good (excluding the VAT) for which it is offered on the platform and deducted by a possible commission retained by the platform for its services.[909] In practice, underlying suppliers might have difficulties in determining this taxable amount. Depending on the agreement between the underlying supplier and the platform, some platforms have a lot of leeway on the processing of the payments and act very independently from the underlying suppliers. This goes as far as the platform accumulating a deposit from underlying suppliers who newly sign up to the platform. This deposit is aggregated from the actual consideration paid by the customers for the goods when the platform is responsible for the collection of the payment. Especially when underlying suppliers supply their goods with the facilitation of such platforms, the determination of the taxable amount for each supply might be difficult because many platforms do not provide a clear overview in a form of detailed account statements indicating the amounts sold, the commission payable, and the deposit withheld by the platform.

Finally, the determination of the taxable amount of the supply by the underlying supplier is not as relevant since the supply is exempt according to Article 136a of the VAT Directive.[910] Thus, no VAT will become due and payable based on the determination of the taxable amount. Nevertheless, the taxable amount must be indicated on the invoice issued from the underlying supplier to the platform,[911] and it must be included in the VAT return of the underlying supplier.

4.5.3   The Taxable Amount of the Supply of Goods by the Platform

The taxable amount of the supply of goods for consideration by the platform must be determined whenever the place of supply is in the EU. When Article 14a (1) of the VAT Directive is applicable, then the place of supply for the supply of goods is in the EU if the platform uses the IOSS[912] and if Article 32 second subparagraph of the VAT

---

909. See, for the discussion on the inclusion of the commission, s. 4.5.5 The Inclusion of Commission Retained by the Platform in the Taxable Amount.
910. See, for further details on this exemption, s. 4.6.2.1 The Exemption of Article 136a of the VAT Directive.
911. For the invoicing obligation by the underlying supplier, see s. 4.9.2 Invoicing Obligations of the Underlying Supplier.
912. See, for further information, s. 4.3.4.1.1.2.3 The Place of Supply when the Platform Applies the IOSS; for the determination of the taxable amount of the importation see s. 4.5.4 The Taxable Amount of the Importation by the Platform or the Customer.

Directive is applied.[913] When Article 14a (2) of the VAT Directive is applicable, then the place of supply is always in the EU.[914]

For the determination of the taxable amount of the supply of goods for consideration by the platform, reference can be made to the preceding section, i.e., in a first step, the platform will have to review whether any inclusions or exclusions according to Articles 78 and 79 of the VAT Directive apply and, in addition, also apply Article 73 of the VAT Directive.[915] In the determination of the taxable amount by the platform, a possible commission paid by the customer or the underlying supplier would be included in the taxable amount according to Article 78 (a) of the VAT Directive.[916]

4.5.4 The Taxable Amount of the Importation by the Platform or the Customer

In addition to the taxable amounts by the underlying supplier and the platform for the supply of the goods for consideration, the taxable amount for the importation should also be analysed when Article 14a (1) of the VAT Directive is applicable. For the determination of the taxable amount for imports, Article 85 et seqq. of the VAT Directive should be applied. Thereby, Article 85 of the VAT Directive generally stipulates that the taxable amount depends on the value determined for customs purposes. Nevertheless, the subsequent articles also stipulate items that should be included in and excluded from the taxable amount. Similar to the determination of the taxable amount for supplies within the EU, also taxes, duties, levies, and charges as well as incidental expenses such as commission, packing, transport, and insurance costs[917] are to be included in the taxable amount of import supplies.[918] Additionally, price reductions for early payments and price discounts and rebates at the time of the supply should be excluded from the taxable amount.[919] Also, when determining the taxable amount of the importation of goods, a possible commission paid by the customer or the underlying supplier would be included in the taxable amount according to Article 86 (1) (b) of the VAT Directive.[920]

---

913. *See,* for further information, s. 4.3.4.1.1.2.1 The Shift of the Place of Supply Rule According to Article 32 Second Subparagraph of the VAT Directive; for the determination of the taxable amount of the importation, *see* s. 4.5.4 The Taxable Amount of the Importation by the Platform or the Customer.
914. *See* s. 4.3.4.2 The Place of Supply for Supplies Within the Community (Article 14a [2] of the VAT Directive).
915. *See,* for the general rules of determining the taxable amount, s. 4.5.2 The Taxable Amount of the Supply by the Underlying Supplier.
916. *See,* the detailed discussion of the inclusion of the commission, s. 4.5.5 The Inclusion of Commission Retained by the Platform in the Taxable Amount.
917. See Article 86 (1) (b) of the VAT Directive.
918. *See* Article 86 of the VAT Directive.
919. *See* Article 87 of the VAT Directive.
920. *See* the detailed discussion of the inclusion of the commission in s. 4.5.5 The Inclusion of Commission Retained by the Platform in the Taxable Amount.

4.5.5   The Inclusion of Commission Retained by the Platform in the Taxable Amount

The final section on the taxable amount discusses a possible impact of a commission retained by the platform for its services to the underlying suppliers and/or customers on the determination of the taxable amount. In general, platforms charge a commission or a fixed fee to the underlying suppliers and/or customers for their activities. Which kind of payment the platform receives for its services depends on the agreement between the involved parties, i.e., between the underlying supplier and the platform as well as between the platform and the customer. If, on the one side, the parties agree on the payment of a fixed amount per week, month, or year for the use of the platform, then this is to be qualified as a separate service fee for the use of the platform because it is independent of the sales facilitated by the platform.[921] In this case, the fee would be payable even if the underlying supplier did not have any sales in the determined period through the facilitation by the platform and/or the customer did not buy any goods on the platform in the determined period. If, on the other side, the parties agreed on a commission payment, i.e., the platform received a percentage of the remuneration per item sold with the facilitation of the platform, then the question would arise whether the commission should also qualify as a service payment, like the payment of a fixed fee or whether the commission is part of the taxable amount of the supply by the underlying supplier and/or by the platform as the deemed supplier.

To make the following explanations more easily understandable, one example is provided. An underlying supplier wants to earn the amount of EUR 80 for the goods supplied through the facilitation of the platform. The platform charges a commission of 25%, i.e., EUR 20, additionally to the price of EUR 80 to the final consumer. Whether the agreement for the commission due is concluded between the platform and the underlying supplier and/or between the platform and the customer leads to the same economic result: the customer would have to pay EUR 100 (plus VAT). The commission (EUR 20) is: (i) retained by the platform as the platform is responsible for the processing of the payment, and the platform only transfers EUR 80 to the underlying supplier. Alternatively, if the underlying supplier was responsible for the processing of the payment, (ii) the underlying supplier would receive the full amount from the customer (EUR 100 plus VAT) and would have to pay the agreed commission (EUR 20 plus the VAT for the full amount) to the platform. A (iii) possibility would be that the customer pays the commission (EUR 20) to the platform and the price for the goods (EUR 80) to the underlying supplier. The VAT due for the full amount could be transferred either to the platform or the underlying supplier although a direct transfer to the platform would be convenient as, in this case, no further transfer between the platform and the underlying supplier would be necessary.

---

921. *See,* for the discussion of the legal qualification of this supply, s. 2.2.4 The Supply of the Platform Service to the Underlying Supplier as well as s. 2.2.5 The Supply of the Platform Service to the Customer.

The different payment flows depending on whether the platform or the underlying supplier processes the payment also reflect the possible VAT treatments of this example:

(i) the commission is solely part of the taxable amount for the supply by the platform to the customer, and the commission reflects the margin of the platform or

(ii) + (iii) the paid commission is not part of the taxable amount for the supply of the good but qualifies as a separate consideration for the supply of the platform service supplied to the underlying supplier and/or the customer (depending on who the platform concluded the contract with for the commission payment).

Solution (i), i.e., the exclusion of the commission in the taxable amount from the underlying supplier to the platform is the prevailing opinion for the VAT treatment of commissions for undisclosed agents based on Articles 14 (2) (c) and 28 of the VAT Directive in Austria and Germany.[922] However, the Austrian judgment and the Austrian and German commentaries do not further explain how they come to this conclusion. One explanation could be the systematic argument that the undisclosed agent scheme creates a fictitious supply in form of a chain transaction,[923] where the VAT treatment diverts from the contractual basis. This same fiction is created by Article 14a of the VAT Directive. Due to the fiction of Article 14a of the VAT Directive, the platform becomes the deemed supplier of the goods and is part of the supply chain. Therefore, the commission is the margin retained by the platform, and this margin is absorbed in the final price to the customer. The platform does not provide another (different) service to the underlying supplier and/or the customer for VAT purposes which indicates that the commission should be excluded from the taxable amount of the supply from the underlying supplier to the platform. Thus, the application of solution (i) would lead to the systematically (more) correct approach of aligning the fictitious chain transaction of Article 14a of the VAT Directive to the legal consequences of non-fictitious chain

---

922. The national legal commentaries and judgments discuss the taxable amount of the undisclosed agent scheme based on their national law. The cited judgment and commentaries all refer to the undisclosed agent scheme for the supply of services which finds its legal basis in Article 28 of the VAT Directive; *see* the judgment by the Austrian Supreme Administrative Court VwGH 29 Jul. 2010, 2008/15/0272; *see*, e.g., in the Austrian literature Hans Georg Ruppe & Markus Achatz, *zu § 3a UStG*, Umsatzsteuergesetz: Kommentar, para. 16 (Hans Georg Ruppe & Markus Achatz eds., Facultas 2018); Thomas Ecker, *§ 3a*, Umsatzsteuergesetz 485 (Stefan Melhardt & Michael Tumpel eds., Linde Verlag 2021); *see*, e.g., in the German literature Martin Robisch & Johann Bunjes, *§ 3 Lieferung, sonstige Leistung*, Umsatzsteuergesetz: Kommentar, *supra* note 248, para. 296; Alexander Oelmaier, *§ 15 Vorsteuerabzug*, Umsatzsteuergesetz, para. 723 (Otto Sölch & Karl Ringleb eds., C.H. Beck 2021).

923. For further information on the requirements of the undisclosed agent scheme, *see* s. 2.2.2.2 The Supply Through Platforms: A Supply Through an Undisclosed Agent?. Thereby, based on the similar wording and legal consequences of Article 14a of the VAT Directive and Article 28 of the VAT Directive, the VAT treatment of the commission should be treated the same for the undisclosed agent scheme as well as for the deemed supplier in Article 14a of the VAT Directive.

transactions. Thereby, the VAT treatment should be uniformly applied irrespective to whom the customer pays the commission and the price for the goods.

Additionally, the application of solution (i) is also plausible in light of the EU law. Pursuant to Article 78 (b) of the VAT Directive as well as Article 86 (1) (b) of the VAT Directive, any commission paid is part of the taxable amount as it qualifies as an incidental cost. Thus, if solution (i) was followed, the commission should be part of the taxable amount of the supply by the platform to the customer. Moreover, according to the CJEU, the taxable amount must be directly linked to the consideration.[924] This direct link could be affirmed if the underlying supplier and/or the customer had agreed with the platform that the platform receives a commission for each item sold. In this instance, the actual supply of the good to the customer triggers the commission payment, and thus it should qualify as an incidental cost according to Article 78 (b) of the VAT Directive as well as according to Article 86 (1) (b) of the VAT Directive.

On the other side, the application of solutions (ii) and (iii) would reflect the actual contractual relationship between the involved parties. If the deemed supplier rule did not apply, solution (ii) and (iii) would be the correct VAT treatment for the commission.[925] However, it does not seem convincing that the fiction of Article 14a of the VAT Directive is limited to the VAT treatment of the supply of the good and that the commission triggered by this fictitious supply would, yet again, follow the contractual basis agreed between the parties and thus be excluded from the legal consequences of the fictitious chain transaction.

Consequently, the application of solution (i) seems to be the systematically correct solution although it diverts from the contractual agreement of the parties. Regardless of which solution is applied, the commission paid in the course of the application of the undisclosed agent scheme of Articles 14 (2) (c) and 28 of the VAT Directive and in the course of the deemed supplier scheme of Article 14a of the VAT Directive should receive the same VAT treatment because the wording and the legal consequences are similar.

4.6   APPLICABLE RATES AND EXEMPTIONS

4.6.1   General Remarks

Rates and exemptions are highly important in the European VAT system because the rates determine how much tax is payable, and the exemptions are exceptions when no

---

924. Case C-98/05, *De Danske Bilimportører*, 1 Jun. 2006, ECLI:EU:C:2006:363, para. 17; with reference to Case C-230/87, *Naturally Yours Cosmetics Limited v Commissioners of Customs and Excise*, 23 Nov. 1988, ECLI:EU:C:1988:508, paras. 11 et seq.; Case C-33/93, *Empire Stores Ltd v Commissioners of Customs and Excise*, 2 Jun. 1994, ECLI:EU:C:1994:225, para. 12; Case C-380/99, *Bertelsmann*, 3 Jul. 2001, ECLI:EU:C:2001:372, paras. 17 et seq.; *see* also, similarly, Case C-433/09, *Commission v Austria*, 22 Dec. 2010, ECLI:EU:C:2010:817, para. 34; Joined Cases C-618/11, C-637/11 and C-659/11, *TVI*, 5 Dec. 2013, ECLI:EU:C:2013:789, paras 37 + 39; Case C-256/14, *Lisboagás GDL*, 11 Jun. 2015, ECLI:EU:C:2015:387, para. 29.

925. *See*, for further information of the platform service provided to the underlying supplier, s. 2.2.4 The Supply of the Platform Service to the Underlying Supplier.

VAT is payable. Thus, after determining where the transaction is to be taxed and what the taxable amount of the transaction is, the next step for taxable persons would be to determine how high the taxes due are so that the correct amount can be invoiced to the customers.[926]

The rates are probably the least harmonised provisions of the VAT Directive. The VAT Directive provides basic parameters for the rates in Articles 93-101 of the VAT Directive. According to these general parameters, the Member States shall apply one standard rate of a minimum of 15% on the taxable amount[927] which must be the same for the provision of goods and services.[928] Additionally, Member States may introduce one or two reduced VAT rates for the supplies stipulated in Annex III of the VAT Directive except for when these supplies are electronically supplied services.[929] The reduced rate cannot be lower than 5%.[930] Based on these broad parameters provided by the VAT Directive, the Member States have a far-reaching margin on the decision about how high their VAT rates are. The standard rates range from 17% (Luxembourg) to 27% (Hungary), and the reduced rates range from 5%[931] to 18% (Hungary).[932] The different implementations in the Member States will further be extended with the adoption of a reform concerning the VAT rates on 6 April 2022 which is to be implemented in the Member States as of 1 January 2025.[933] Thereby, three reduced VAT rates for the supplies stipulated in Annex III of the VAT Directive and exemptions with the full right to an input VAT deduction can be introduced by the Member States.[934] Two of the three reduced rates cannot be lower than 5%,[935] but a third super-reduced rate can also be lower than 5%.[936] To what extent the Member States will reform the VAT rates based on these changes in the VAT Directive is yet to be awaited.

Compared to rates, the exemptions are better harmonised in the VAT Directive. The VAT exemptions are stipulated in Articles 132-166 of the VAT Directive and can be separated into two different groups of exemptions: on the one side, exemptions with the right to deduct input VAT ('zero-rating')[937] and, on the other side, exemptions without the right to deduct input VAT.[938]

---

926. *See* also the discussion whether invoices have to be issued in s. 4.9 Invoicing Obligations.
927. *See* Article 97 of the VAT Directive.
928. *See* Article 96 of the VAT Directive.
929. *See* Article 98 (3) of the VAT Directive.
930. *See* Article 98 (1) of the VAT Directive.
931. The 5% reduced VAT rate is applicable in Croatia, Italy, Cyprus, Latvia, Lithuania, Hungary, Malta, Poland, Romania and Slovenia.
932. For an overview on the different applicable in the Member States, *see* European Commission, *VAT Rates Applied in the Member States of the European Union*, taxud.c.1(2021) (1 Jan. 2021), https://ec.europa.eu/taxation_customs/system/files/2021-06/vat_rates_en.pdf (last visited 15 Apr. 2022).
933. Council Directive (EU) 2022/542 of 5 April 2022 Amending Directives 2006/112/EC and (EU) 2020/285 as Regards Rates of Value Added Tax, OJ L 107/1 (2022) 542.
934. *See* Article 98 (1) and (2) of the VAT Directive.
935. *See* Article 98 (1) of the VAT Directive.
936. *See* Article 98 (2) of the VAT Directive.
937. *See* Articles 136a-166 read in conjunction with Article 169 (b) read in conjunction with Article 168 of the VAT Directive.
938. *See* Articles 132-137 read in conjunction with Article 169 (b) of the VAT Directive.

Finally, several Member States have special derogations from the general rules concerning applicable rates and exemptions. These derogations can be found in Articles 102-129a of the VAT Directive under the heading 'particular provisions' as well as in Articles 370-393 of the VAT Directive.

The following sections will discuss the rates and exemptions applicable to the supply of goods by the underlying supplier as well as by the platform in detail. Thereby, the general legal basis applicable to both supplies as well as practical issues, such as the application of the exemption for small enterprises, will be analysed. A final chapter will discuss the rates and exemptions applicable to the importation of the goods.

4.6.2 Applicable Exemptions to the Supply from the Underlying Supplier to the Platform

4.6.2.1 *The Exemption of Article 136a of the VAT Directive*

4.6.2.1.1 *General Remarks*

The determination of the tax amount for the supply from the underlying supplier to the platform is rather simple: based on the discussed place of supply rules, the place of supply of the transaction from the underlying supplier to the platform is in the country of origin.[939] Thus, when Article 14a (1) of the VAT Directive is applicable, this country of origin is in a third country and out of scope of the VAT Directive. Only for the applicability of Article 14a (2) of the VAT Directive are the EU rates and exemptions applicable to the supply from the underlying supplier to the platform. According to Article 136a of the VAT Directive, the supply from the underlying supplier to the platform is VAT exempt with the right to deduct the input VAT.[940]

The background for the introduction of Article 136a of the VAT Directive was the prevention of additional administrative burden and the prevention of additional revenue loss due to VAT payments from the platform to the underlying suppliers.[941] The first justification provided by the European Commission for the introduction of the exemption, i.e., the prevention of additional burden, is not quite understandable because the underlying suppliers still have to register for the VAT in the country of origin and declare the exempt supply from the underlying supplier to the platform in the VAT return of the country of origin. In general, Member States may decide to release certain taxable persons from certain or all VAT obligations according to Article 272 (1) of the VAT Directive; thus, also a release from the obligation to register for the VAT would be possible. Such an option is implemented for several exempt supplies in Article 272 (1) (c) of the VAT Directive. Nevertheless, with the introduction of the

---

939. *See* the analysis in s. 4.3.3 The Place of Supply Rule for the Supply by the Underlying Supplier.
940. *See* Article 169 (b) of the VAT Directive.
941. European Commission, *Proposal for a Council Directive Amending Council Directive 2006/112/EC of 28 November 2006 as Regards Provisions Relating to Distance Sales of Goods and Certain Domestic Supplies of Goods*, COM(2018) 819 final, *supra* note 625, at 3.

e-commerce package,[942] Article 272 (1) (b) of the VAT Directive was amended so that the release of VAT obligations cannot be applied to underlying suppliers that provide exempt supplies according to Article 136a of the VAT Directive. Thus, the administrative burden for the underlying supplier is not reduced.

Nevertheless, the exemption in Article 136a of the VAT Directive provides a liquidity benefit for the platform:[943] If the exemption had not been introduced, the platform would have had to pay the VAT to the underlying suppliers and would only receive the input VAT deduction with the filing of the VAT return. Furthermore, the second reason provided by the European Commission is a very relevant point. If the exemption had not been introduced, the VAT payment would have to be made by the platform to the underlying suppliers, and the underlying suppliers would have had to pay the VAT to the competent authorities. As the underlying suppliers are not established in the EU, the risk of VAT loss would not be eliminated if the exemption had not been introduced: due to the non-compliance of the underlying suppliers, the VAT might not have been paid to the competent authorities after all. This would have compromised the aim of the introduction of Article 14a of the VAT Directive, i.e., effective and efficient VAT collection.[944]

4.6.2.1.2 An Evaluation of the Applicable Exemption: Article 136a of the VAT Directive Versus 'Other' Exemptions Stipulated in the VAT Directive

According to the VAT Directive, the supply of the good from the underlying supplier to the platform (or to any other customer) may be an exempt supply. Examples of exemptions that may be applicable to the supply of goods are any exemptions stipulated in Articles 132 and 135 of the VAT Directive as long as the exemption is not limited to the supply of services but (also) applicable to the supply of goods. If, e.g., an underlying supplier established in a third country would sell human breast milk on a platform within the EU and the requirements of Article 14a (2) of the VAT Directive were fulfilled, then the supply would be exempt according to Article 132 (1) (d) of the VAT Directive as well as according to Article 136a of the VAT Directive. Nevertheless, only the exemption of Article 136a of the VAT Directive is an exemption with the right to deduct the input VAT. Thus, the question arises of which exemption should be applicable for the supply from the underlying supplier to the platform if also another exemption could be applied, e.g., Article 136a of the VAT Directive or the 'other' exemption.

---

942. *See* Council Directive (EU) 2019/1995 of 21 November 2019 Amending Directive 2006/112/EC as Regards Provisions Relating to Distance Sales of Goods and Certain Domestic Supplies of Goods, OJ L 310/1 (2019).

943. *See* similarly Marta Papis-Almansa, *VAT and Electronic Commerce: The New Rules as a Means for Simplification, Combatting Fraud and Creating a More Level Playing Field?*, 20 ERA Forum, *supra* note 18, at 220.

944. *See* preamble pt. 7 of the Council Directive (EU) 2017/2455 of 5 December 2017 Amending Directive 2006/112/EC and Directive 2009/132/EC as Regards Certain Value Added Tax Obligations for Supplies of Services and Distance Sales of Goods, OJ L 348/7 (2017).

Similar to the discussed conflict between Articles 46 and 58 of the VAT Directive,[945] also in this conflict of norms, the maxims of *lex superior, lex posterior* and *lex specialis* do not help in resolving the conflict. Since Article 136a of the VAT Directive as well as the 'other' exemption are both stipulated in the VAT Directive, no higher-ranking law can be identified (*lex superior derogat legi inferiori*). Since Article 136a of the VAT Directive and the 'other' exemption complement each other, the principle of *lex posterior derogat legi priori* is not applicable.[946] Additionally, the two legal bases are overlapping, and it is generally not possible to determine whether the 'other' exemption is narrower or wider than Article 136a of the VAT Directive. Therefore, the *lex specialis derogat legi generali* rule also does not lead to a result, and teleological considerations must be applied.[947]

It should be recalled that the background for introducing Article 136a of the VAT Directive was the prevention of additional administrative burden and the prevention of additional revenue loss due to VAT payments from the platform to the underlying suppliers.[948] Additionally, the EU legislator implemented the right for the input VAT deduction when Article 136a of the VAT Directive is applicable, assumingly with the background to not cause any divergences between suppliers supplying goods on platforms and suppliers supplying goods directly to the customers without the intervention of a platform. The customers are, in both cases, charged with the VAT due. If the supply was supplied directly from the supplier to the customer, then the supplier would have to charge the VAT, and, if the supply was facilitated by a platform according to Article 14a (2) of the VAT Directive, then the platform would have to charge the VAT to the customer. Systematically, the underlying supplier should also have the right to deduct the input VAT when Article 14a (2) of the VAT Directive is applicable in order to not miss out on neutralising the incoming VAT. If the EU legislator had excluded the possibility for the underlying supplier to deduct the input VAT, then suppliers would have been treated differently depending on which 'distribution system' (direct supply or supply through a platform) the supplier had chosen. Such a different treatment could be questioned in terms of the principle of neutrality and equality. Therefore, the VAT exemption in Article 136a of the VAT Directive was introduced with the right to deduct the incurred input VAT according to Article 169 (b) of the VAT Directive which can be justified with the argument of the prevention of additional revenue loss as well as the equal treatment of underlying suppliers having the right to the input VAT deduction independently depending on which 'distribution system' (direct supply or supply through platform) is applied.

However, if Article 136a of the VAT Directive was applied to supplies that could be subsumed under another exemption as well, then the underlying supplier would have the right of a full input VAT deduction according to Article 169 (b) of the VAT

---

945. *See* s. 2.2.5.3.4 An Evaluation of the Applicable Place of Supply Rule: Article 46 of the VAT Directive Versus Article 58 of the VAT Directive.
946. *See* Karl Riesenhuber, *Europäische Methodenlehre, supra* note 397, at 211.
947. *See* Reinhold Zippelius, *Juristische Methodenlehre, supra* note 405, at 32.
948. European Commission, *Proposal for a Council Directive Amending Council Directive 2006/112/EC of 28 November 2006 as Regards Provisions Relating to Distance Sales of Goods and Certain Domestic Supplies of Goods*, COM(2018) 819 final, *supra* note 625, at 3.

Directive. Due to this right, the supplier would be in a better position than suppliers that supply their goods directly to the customer without the facilitation of a platform since such suppliers could not apply the exemption of Article 136a of the VAT Directive and thus would also not have the right to the input VAT deduction based on Article 169 (b) of the VAT Directive. Thus, the suppliers would be treated differently depending on which distribution system they use. Suppliers who use the facilitation of a platform to supply the goods would have the right to a full input VAT deduction, whereas suppliers who supply the goods directly to customers would not have the right to deduct the input VAT. This different treatment of the suppliers could be questioned in terms of the principle of neutrality and equality. It can be assumed that the EU legislator did not want to extend the benefit of input VAT deduction to all underlying suppliers but only to underlying suppliers who would also have the right to the input VAT deduction if they had provided the same supply without the facilitation by a platform. Thus, the teleological interpretation would lead to the result that the 'other' exemption should be given priority over Article 169 (b) of the VAT Directive.

4.6.2.2   *The Underlying Supplier as a Small Enterprise*

4.6.2.2.1   *General Remarks*

One practical question is the applicability of the small enterprise scheme for the underlying suppliers. The special scheme for small enterprises is stipulated in Articles 281-294 of the VAT Directive and is optional for Member States to introduce. In fact, not all Member States have introduced this option. The aim of this special scheme is to provide facilitations to small-and medium-sized enterprises.

The first simplification provides a simplified procedure for the charging and collection of the VAT. According to Article 281 of the VAT Directive, Member States may 'apply simplified procedures, such as flat-rate schemes, for charging and collecting VAT provided that they do not lead to a reduction thereof'. The introduction of such a facilitation requires the consulting of the VAT Committee. Additionally, Articles 282-292 of the VAT Directive provide two further possible facilitations: the possibility to introduce an exemption and a graduated relief. Due to territorial limitations of the applicable special scheme for small enterprises, the EU legislator has adopted a reform that becomes applicable as of 1 January 2025.[949]

---

949. *See* Council Directive (EU) 2020/285 of 18 February 2020 Amending Directive 2006/112/EC on the Common System of Value Added Tax as Regards the Special Scheme for Small Enterprises and Regulation (EU) No 904/2010 as Regards the Administrative Cooperation and Exchange of Information for the Purpose of Monitoring the Correct Application of the Special Scheme for Small Enterprises, OJ L 62/13 (2020); for further information on the background of the amendments of the small enterprise scheme, *see* European Commission, *Green Paper: On the Future of VAT Towards a Simpler, More Robust and Efficient Vat System*, COM(2010) 695 final (01.12.2010), https://eur-lex.europa.eu/LexUriServ/LexUriServ.do?uri=COM:2010:0695 :FIN:EN:PDF (last visited 27 Oct. 2021); European Commission, *Commission Staff Working Document Impact Assessment Accompanying the Document Proposal for a Council Directive amending Directive 2006/112/EC on the Common System of Value Added Tax as Regards the Special Scheme for Small Enterprises*, COM(2018) 21 final (18 Jan. 2018), https://ec.europa.eu

The following two sections will investigate the scope of the small enterprise scheme applicable until 31 December 2024 as well as the amended small enterprise scheme applicable from 1 January 2025. A final section will critically review the non-applicability of the small enterprise scheme when Article 14a of the VAT Directive is triggered.

4.6.2.2.2   The Small Enterprises Scheme until 31 December 2024

Articles 282-292 of the VAT Directive provide the possibility of introducing an exemption and a graduated relief. First, taxable persons whose annual turnover is not higher than EUR 5,000 or the equivalent in the national currency can apply the exemption.[950] Second, Member States may introduce graduated VAT relief for taxable persons exceeding the national threshold of the exemption.[951] The application of the exemption is optional for the taxable persons; i.e., they may opt for the normal VAT arrangements.[952] In the case that a taxable person does not opt out of the exemption of the small enterprise scheme, the taxable person may apply the exemption and provide exempt supplies but, at the same time, the input VAT cannot be deducted.[953]

The exemption is further restricted by Article 283 (1) of the VAT Directive. Pursuant to Article 283 (1) of the VAT Directive, transactions carried out on an occasional basis,[954] supplies of new means of transport,[955] and supplies carried out by a taxable person who is not established in the Member State where the VAT is due[956] are excluded from the application of the exemption and the graduated relief. The CJEU has challenged the last exception of the applicability of the small enterprise scheme, i.e., the requirement of establishment in the Member State where the VAT is due. In the *Schmelz*[957] case, the CJEU had to assess whether the territoriality element of this

---

/taxation_customs/system/files/2018-01/18012018_impactassessment_vat_smes_en.pdf (last visited 27 Oct. 2021); European Commission, *Communication from the Commission to the European Parliament, the Council and the European Economic and Social Committee on an Action Plan on VAT*, COM(2016) 148 final (7 Apr. 2016), https://ec.europa.eu/taxation_customs/system/files/2016-10/com_2016_148_en.pdf (last visited 27 Oct. 2021); European Commission, *Proposal for a Council Directive Amending Directive 2006/112/EC on the Common System of Value Added Tax as Regards the Special Scheme for Small Enterprises*, COM(2018) 21 final (18.01.2018), https://eur-lex.europa.eu/legal-content/EN/TXT/PDF/?uri=CELEX:52018 PC0021&from=DE (last visited 27 Oct. 2021).

950. *See* Articles 284, 285 first subpara. and 286 of the VAT Directive; *see* also Article 287 of the VAT Directive, according to which Member States which acceded after 1 Jan. 1978 may apply different thresholds. For an overview of the thresholds in the different Member States, *see VAT Thresholds, supra* note 284.
951. *See* Articles 284 and 285 second subpara. of the VAT Directive.
952. *See* Article 290 of the VAT Directive.
953. *See* Article 289 of the VAT Directive.
954. *See* Article 283 (1) (a) of the VAT Directive; transactions carried out on an occasional basis are defined in Article 12 of the VAT Directive.
955. *See* Article 283 (1) (b) of the VAT Directive; the small enterprise scheme is not applicable to the supply of new means of transport in accordance with Articles 138 (1) and (2) (a) of the VAT Directive.
956. *See* Article 283 (1) (c) of the VAT Directive.
957. Case C-97/09, *Ingrid Schmelz v Finanzamt Waldviertel*, 26 Oct. 2010, ECLI:EU:C:2010:632.

restriction is compatible with the fundamental freedoms and the principle of non-discrimination. The CJEU came to the conclusion that this territoriality restricts the freedom of establishment[958] but justified this restriction with the aim to maintain the effective fiscal supervision and to combat fraud, evasion, and abuse.[959] Thus, the small enterprise scheme applicable until 31 December 2024 is restricted to taxable persons established in the country where the VAT became due.[960]

Applying these general explanations of the small enterprise scheme to the underlying supplier, the small enterprise scheme might only be relevant in the applicability of Article 14a (2) of the VAT Directive because only when Article 14a (2) of the VAT Directive is applicable is the place of supply for the supply by the underlying supplier to the platform in the EU.[961] However, for the application of Article 14a (2) of the VAT Directive, one substantive requirement is that the underlying supplier is not established in the EU.[962] Following the discussed CJEU case law, underlying suppliers cannot apply the special scheme for small enterprises because they are not established in the EU. Thus, the small enterprise scheme is not relevant for the supply of goods from the underlying supplier to the platform.

4.6.2.2.3   The Small Enterprises Scheme as of 1 January 2025

The EU legislator has recognised the setbacks of the territoriality of the small enterprise regime, and thus a reform was adopted.[963] With this reform, the applicable thresholds were clarified and (mostly) unified. Additionally, the territoriality of the small trader regime has been abandoned; i.e., taxable persons supplying goods or services in Member States other than the Member State where they are established may also apply the small enterprise scheme.

---

958. *See* Article 49 of the TFEU.
959. Case C-97/09, *Schmelz*, 26 Oct. 2010, ECLI:EU:C:2010:632, para. 71.
960. *See* also, on the interpretation of 'taxable person who is not established within the territory of the country' Case C-421/10, *Finanzamt Deggendorf v Markus Stoppelkamp*, 6 Oct. 2011, ECLI:EU:C:2011:640.
961. *See* the analysis in s. 4.3.3 The Place of Supply Rule for the Supply by the Underlying Supplier.
962. *See* s. 3.3.2.2 The Requirements for Underlying Suppliers and the Customers.
963. *See* Council Directive (EU) 2020/285 of 18 February 2020 Amending Directive 2006/112/EC on the Common System of Value Added Tax as Regards the Special Scheme for Small Enterprises and Regulation (EU) No 904/2010 as Regards the Administrative Cooperation and Exchange of Information for the Purpose of Monitoring the Correct Application of the Special Scheme for Small Enterprises, OJ L 62/13 (2020); for further information on the background of the amendments of the small enterprise scheme, *see* European Commission, *Green Paper: On the Future of VAT Towards a Simpler, More Robust and Efficient Vat System*, COM(2010) 695 final, *supra* note 949; European Commission, *Commission Staff Working Document Impact Assessment Accompanying the Document Proposal for a Council Directive amending Directive 2006/112/EC on the Common System of Value Added Tax as Regards the Special Scheme for Small Enterprises*, COM(2018) 21 final, *supra* note 949; European Commission, *Communication from the Commission to the European Parliament, the Council and the European Economic and Social Committee on an Action Plan on VAT*, COM(2016) 148 final, *supra* note 949; European Commission, *Proposal for a Council Directive Amending Directive 2006/112/EC on the Common System of Value Added Tax as Regards the Special Scheme for Small Enterprises*, COM(2018) 21 final, *supra* note 949.

For the qualification as a small enterprise, two thresholds must be respected. First, the suppliers may only supply goods and services within the EU of a maximum of EUR 100,000 for the possibility to apply the VAT exemption.[964] Second, when the Member States decide to introduce a national threshold,[965] this national threshold cannot be exceeded by the supplier.[966] If the supplier did not exceed both thresholds, the small enterprise regime may be applicable. Nevertheless, the application of the small enterprise scheme as of 1 January 2025 will still be limited to taxable persons established in the EU.[967] Thus, the underlying supplier cannot benefit from the simplifications of the small enterprise scheme for the supply to the platform.

4.6.2.2.4 Critical Discussion of the Small Enterprises Scheme within the Application of the Deemed Supplier Regime

The possibility for taxable persons established in the EU to apply the small enterprise scheme raises a further issue in the case that the platform becomes the deemed supplier: the final customer does not benefit from the VAT exemption anymore. Taking into consideration the scope of Article 14a of the VAT Directive, this criticism can only arise when Article 14a (1) of the VAT Directive is applicable as only within the applicability of Article 14a (1) of the VAT Directive can the underlying supplier be established in the EU. Additionally, the place of supply must be in the EU. Therefore, the criticism can arise when the underlying supplier would apply the IOSS[968] or when the place of supply is in the EU due to the application of Article 32 second subparagraph of the VAT Directive.[969] Within the application of Article 32 second subparagraph of the VAT Directive, it should be noted that if the Member State of importation has implemented the VAT exemption according to Article 282 of the VAT Directive for small and medium enterprises, then the underlying supplier will not have the right to deduct the import VAT according to Article 289 of the VAT. Thus, the underlying

---

964. *See* Article 284 (2) (a) of the Council Directive (EU) 2020/285 of 18 February 2020 Amending Directive 2006/112/EC on the Common System of Value Added Tax as Regards the Special Scheme for Small Enterprises and Regulation (EU) No 904/2010 as Regards the Administrative Cooperation and Exchange of Information for the Purpose of Monitoring the Correct Application of the Special Scheme for Small Enterprises.
965. The national threshold can be a maximum of EUR 85,000.
966. *See* Article 284 (1) of the Council Directive (EU) 2020/285 of 18 February 2020 Amending Directive 2006/112/EC on the Common System of Value Added Tax as Regards the Special Scheme for Small Enterprises and Regulation (EU) No 904/2010 as Regards the Administrative Cooperation and Exchange of Information for the Purpose of Monitoring the Correct Application of the Special Scheme for Small Enterprises; *see*, for further information on the different thresholds Ad van Doesum et al., *Fundamentals of EU VAT Law, supra* note 35, at 679 et seq.
967. *See* Article 284 (2) of the Council Directive (EU) 2020/285 of 18 February 2020 Amending Directive 2006/112/EC on the Common System of Value Added Tax as Regards the Special Scheme for Small Enterprises and Regulation (EU) No 904/2010 as Regards the Administrative Cooperation and Exchange of Information for the Purpose of Monitoring the Correct Application of the Special Scheme for Small Enterprises.
968. *See* s. 4.3.4.1.1.2.3 The Place of Supply when the Platform Applies the IOSS.
969. *See* s. 4.3.4.1.1.2.1 The Shift of the Place of Supply Rule According to Article 32 Second Subparagraph of the VAT Directive.

supplier could (indirectly) charge the customer for the import VAT by including this import VAT in the price of the good.

However, if the underlying supplier fulfilled the criteria of a small enterprise, then the sales supplied by the underlying supplier without the intervention of a platform would be VAT exempt, and thus no VAT would be charged to the customer if the underlying supplier did not opt out of this exemption. This legal consequence applies irrespective of whether the importation would be VAT exempt according to Article 143 (ca) of the VAT Directive when the IOSS is applied or whether the underlying supplier would pay the import VAT due without the right for the input VAT deduction when Article 32 second subparagraph of the VAT Directive is applied. If the same underlying supplier supplied the same good with the facilitation of a platform and the platform became the deemed supplier, the supply of the same good would not be VAT exempt based on the small enterprise scheme if the platform did not fulfil the requirements of a small enterprise scheme, which is rather unlikely. Thus, the same product supplied by the same underlying supplier may be treated differently when the deemed supplier regime is applied. This might be an incentive for the underlying supplier to not use platforms for the supply of goods. Additionally, this different VAT treatment for the supply of the same good may be questioned in terms of the principle of neutrality and equality.[970]

4.6.3 Applicable Rates and Exemptions for the Supply of Goods by the Platform

4.6.3.1 *The Difficulty of Determination of the Applicable Rate or Exemption*

In the cases where the platform has become the deemed supplier, the first step for determining the applicable VAT rate or exemption is to review where the place of supply is located.[971] Depending on the applicable place of supply, the platform must decide whether the rates or exemptions of the country of origin or the rates or exemptions of the country of destination are applicable.

In determining the applicable rate or exemption, the second step for the platform would be to know which good is actually supplied. For this determination, it might be useful for the platform to request the customs nomenclature of the goods offered for sale by the underlying suppliers. This might help the platform to identify the correct VAT rate or exemption.

In a final step, the VAT rate or exemption in the country of supply must be determined. Due to the different applicable VAT rates in the Member States and the difficulty in determining the correct VAT rate, the European Commission has made

---

970. *See,* for further information on the principle of neutrality, s. 5.2.5.1 Content and Development of the Principle of Neutrality and, on the principle of equality, s. 5.2.3 The Principle of Equality in Article 20 of the CFR.
971. *See* the explanations on the place of supply for the supply by the platform in s. 4.3.4 The Place of Supply Rule for the Supply by the Platform.

available a database in which the different VAT rates of the Member States can be found.[972] The VAT rates indicated on this platform are provided by the tax administrations of the Member States. Thus, there may be delays between national changes to a VAT rate and its publication in the database. There is no (legal) guarantee that the indicated VAT rates are correct, and the information provided on this database is not legally binding.

Additionally, one further practical issue might be the correct display of the price to the customers. As the VAT rates in the EU are not unified, the final price for the good chosen by the customer also depends on the applicable VAT rate. This results in technical challenges for the platform since, for each product, depending on where the goods are delivered, different VAT rates must be programmed in the system and displayed to the customer.

Finally, the platform may, by mistake, have indicated the wrong VAT rate to the customer and thus not have charged enough VAT to the customer. Depending on the information available to the platform, the indication of a too low VAT rate on the invoice might trigger the safe harbour clause in Article 5c of the VAT Implementing Regulation. For the platform not to become liable for the additional VAT, the discussed requirements of the safe harbour clause must be fulfilled.[973]

4.6.3.2 The Platform as a Small Enterprise

The benefit of and the requirements for the application of the small enterprise scheme have already been discussed in a previous section.[974] When the platform fulfils the legal requirements stipulated in Articles 281-294 of the VAT Directive, then the small enterprise regime is applicable to the platform. In practice, the benefit of the small enterprise regime applicable until 31 December 2024 will be very limited for platforms due to the territorial limitations discussed;[975] i.e., only an EU-established platform could apply the small enterprise regime if it was only supplying goods to its Member State of establishment. Nevertheless, especially start-up platforms established in the EU may be able to benefit from the small enterprise regime that is entering into force on 1 January 2025 if they fulfilled the legal requirements.

Additionally, the criticism brought forward for the small enterprise scheme develops into a benefit for the customers when the platform qualifies as a small enterprise:[976] The goods supplied by the platform would be VAT exempt, and thus no VAT would be charged to the customer. If the underlying supplier supplied the same good without the facilitation of a platform and the underlying supplier did not qualify

972. See European Commission, Taxes in Europe Database V3, https://ec.europa.eu/taxation_customs/tedb/taxSearch.html (last visited 19 Oct. 2021).
973. See, for further detailed information on the requirements and legal consequences of the safe harbour clause, s. 4.7 The Safe Harbour Clause of Article 5c of the VAT Implementing Regulation.
974. See s. 4.6.2.2 The Underlying Supplier as a Small Enterprise.
975. See s. 4.6.2.2.2 The Small Enterprises Scheme until 31 December 2024.
976. See, for the discussion of the criticism, s. 4.6.2.2.4 Critical Discussion of the Small Enterprises Scheme within the Application of the Deemed Supplier Regime.

as a small enterprise, then the supply of the same good would not be VAT exempt. Thus, the same product supplied through a platform may benefit from the VAT exemption if the deemed supplier regime was applied.

4.6.4 Applicable Rates and Exemptions Relating to the Importation of the Goods

4.6.4.1 The Exclusive Application of the Standard VAT Rate According to Articles 369y-zb of the VAT Directive when the IOSS Is Not Applied

The first *lex specialis* introduced with the e-commerce package concerning rates and exemptions is the introduction of a simplification mechanism for the import VAT collection when the platform does not use the IOSS.[977] This simplification mechanism must be implemented in all Member States, but it is the customer's decision whether the standard import procedure[978] or the simplification mechanism should be applied. Besides, for this choice by the customer, also some leeway for the Member States has been included: Member States may stipulate in their national law that the standard VAT rate is exclusively applicable according to Article 369za of the VAT Directive when this special arrangement is used for the import VAT collection.

Platforms that supply to Member States that implemented the standard rate for all imports under this special arrangement may face the situation that, depending on which VAT collection mechanism is applicable, the VAT due is different. Thus, if the platform wanted to display the price including the VAT on its website, it might face the difficulty of not knowing which VAT rate is applicable. If the platform applied the IOSS or if the standard import procedure was used, the reduced rate of the Member State of destination may be applicable. If the special arrangement was used, then the standard VAT rate may be applicable for the importation. The customer orders the good on the same platform and receives the same good in all situations. This different application of the standard and reduced rate for the same goods may be questioned by the principle of equality.[979] Thus, the customer should be able to opt for the standard import procedure in order to avail himself of the reduced rate.[980]

---

977. See Articles 369y-zb of the VAT Directive. For further information on this simplification mechanism, see s. 4.12.3 The Simplification Mechanism of Importations for Non-IOSS Suppliers.

978. For further information on the amendments in the standard import procedure due to the introduction of the e-commerce package, see s. 4.12.4 The Standard Import Procedure.

979. See, for further detailed information on the principle of equality, s. 5.2.3 The Principle of Equality in Article 20 of the CFR.

980. See preamble 15 of the Council Directive (EU) 2017/2455 of 5 December 2017 Amending Directive 2006/112/EC and Directive 2009/132/EC as Regards Certain Value Added Tax Obligations for Supplies of Services and Distance Sales of Goods, OJ L 348/7 (2017); European Commission, *Explanatory Notes on the New VAT E-Commerce Rules*, supra note 35, at 80.

4.6.4.2 The Import VAT Exemption According to Article 143 (ca) of the VAT Directive when the IOSS Is Applied: A Highway to Fraud?

The second *lex specialis* introduced with the e-commerce package concerning rates and exemptions is the introduction of Article 143 (ca) of the VAT Directive. According to this provision, the importation of distance sales of goods imported from third territories or third countries is exempt with the aim to avoid double taxation when the IOSS is applied.[981]

The exemption of Article 143 (ca) of the VAT Directive applies when two requirements are fulfilled. The first requirement is that the VAT due 'is to be declared' under the IOSS. Thus, the exemption is applicable when the obligation arises to declare the supply in the IOSS. The actual declaration in the IOSS and payment of the VAT due is not a requirement for Article 143 (ca) of the VAT Directive to apply. It is within the systematics of the IOSS that the exemption can be applied independently of the filing of the IOSS declaration and the payment of the VAT due since the IOSS declaration could be filed and the VAT payment could be paid after the importation of the goods has taken place. The second requirement is the provision of the IOSS identification number to the competent customs office in the Member State of importation, at the latest upon lodging of the import declaration. If both requirements are fulfilled, the importation by the platform is exempt from the payment of the import VAT.

In practice, especially the second requirement, i.e., the provision of the IOSS identification number to the competent customs authorities, will be decisive. It is relevant for the exemption that, on the import declaration, a (valid) IOSS identification number is indicated. In practice, the competent customs authorities should review the IOSS identification number, and the importation will be exempt from the payment of import VAT if the IOSS identification number is valid. This formalistic approach has been criticised in literature as it is vulnerable to fraud:[982] fraudsters may indicate the IOSS identification number of other suppliers or other platforms in the import declaration so that the importation is VAT exempt. Although the IOSS identification number is generally not publicly available, the platform must give the underlying supplier its IOSS identification number when the underlying supplier organises the transport because the IOSS number must be included in the import declaration. Thus, the underlying supplier will have the IOSS identification numbers of all of the platforms that the underlying supplier offers its goods on as long as the requirements of Article 14a (1) of the VAT Directive are fulfilled, and the platform decides to use the IOSS for

---

981. For further information on the IOSS, *see* s. 4.11 Special Schemes of the OSS.
982. *See*, e.g., Marie Lamensch, *Rendering Platforms Liable to Collect and Pay VAT on B2C Imports: A Silver Bullet?*, 29 International VAT Monitor, *supra* note 18, at 48 et seq.; Marie Lamensch et al., *New EU VAT-Related Obligations for E-Commerce Platforms Worldwide: A Qualitative Impact Assessment*, 13 World Tax Journal, *supra* note 18, s. 3.3.4.; Madeleine Merkx, *New VAT Rules for E-Commerce: The Final Countdown Has Begun*, 29 EC Tax Review 203 et seq. (2020); Marta Papis-Almansa, *VAT and Electronic Commerce: The New Rules as a Means for Simplification, Combatting Fraud and Creating a More Level Playing Field?*, 20 ERA Forum, *supra* note 18, at 214.

the importations. Thereby, it seems that fraudsters could easily access the IOSS identification number of the market leading platforms as most e-commerce sales are concentrated on just a handful of platforms.[983] This might lead to suppliers indicating the IOSS identification number of a platform (or of another supplier of whom the IOSS identification number has become public) to the customs authorities to receive the import VAT exemption.

In order to prevent the misuse of the IOSS identification number, the Member States of importation generate monthly reports of all imports for which the IOSS identification number has been used.[984] The Member State of identification[985] reconciles the value of the imports with the transactions reported in the IOSS return.[986] In literature, three weaknesses of this reconciliation have been brought forward by Merkx:[987]

(i) The temporal aspect: under the temporal aspect, the author argues that the chargeable event of the supply facilitated by a platform (the time of the acceptance of the payment[988]) is preceding the time of the actual import. Thus, the supply of the good could be declared in an earlier IOSS return than the moment of the use of the IOSS identification number, i.e., the actual importation of the good.[989]

(ii) The return of goods: when goods are returned, these returns are indicated in the IOSS declaration at the time of the return. Thus, the amount received by the conciliation of the use of the IOSS identification number will be higher than the actual amount declared in the IOSS return.[990]

(iii) The organisation of the transport by the customer: a similar wrong reconciliation might appear if the customer, instead of the underlying supplier or platform, organised the transport. This might be the case when the 'supplier provides any information to the customer for the delivery of the goods'[991] as this provision of information is already sufficient for the underlying supplier

---

983. See Marie Lamensch, *Rendering Platforms Liable to Collect and Pay VAT on B2C Imports: A Silver Bullet?*, *supra* note 18, at 49. in 2021 a share of 62% on online purchases were ordered from one out of the four biggest e-retailers (Amazon [26%], AliExpress [19%], eBay [10%], and Wish [7%]), *see* International Post Corporation, *Cross-Border E-Commerce Shopper Survey 2021*, *supra* note 482, at 12.

984. See European Commission, *Importation and Exportation of Low Value Consignments – VAT E-Commerce Package 'Guidance for Member States and Trade'*, *supra* note 717, at 9; with reference to Article 55 and Annex 21-01, 21-02 and 21-03 of the Commission Implementing Regulation (EU) 2015/2447 of 24 November 2015 Laying down Detailed Rules for Implementing Certain Provisions of Regulation (EU) No 952/2013 of the European Parliament and of the Council Laying down the Union Customs Code, OJ L 343 (2015).

985. See, for explanations on the definition of the Member State of identification, s. 4.11.3.2 The Member State of Identification.

986. See European Commission, *Importation and Exportation of Low Value Consignments*, *supra* note 717, at 9.

987. See Merkx, *supra* note 982, at 204 et seq.

988. See, for further information, s. 4.4.2 Derogation of the General Rules: Article 66a of the VAT Directive.

989. See Merkx, *supra* note 982, at 204.

990. See *ibid.* at 204 et seq.

991. Article 5a (d) of the VAT Implementing Regulation.

to be indirectly involved in the transport.[992] In this case, the transport service provided from the transport company to the customer is a separate service, but, according to Article 86 (1) (b) of the VAT Directive, the transport costs should also be included in the taxable amount for reporting the import VAT. Thus, the amount for which the import VAT exemption would be applied would be different from the amount declared in the IOSS return.[993]

Especially the first issue brought forward is a critical aspect that can have an impact on the reconciliation because the timing makes it difficult to determine the correctness of the reconciliation. In practice, the value of the imports and the transactions reported in the IOSS return will likely deviate from each other due to this aspect.

The second and third arguments brought forward could be criticised. The author argues in the second aspect that the return of goods might cause discrepancies between the amounts declared in the IOSS return and the value of the imports. This is only true when the goods are imported and returned in the same month. In this case, the goods would simply not be reported in the IOSS return, but they would have been imported, and, thus, the value would be indicated as imports to which the exemption applies. Nevertheless, if the goods were returned in a different month than the importation, then the return of the goods would be declared in the current IOSS return. In the current IOSS return, reference must be made to the tax period, the Member State of destination, and the tax amount to which the changes in the taxable amount relate.[994] If the IOSS return was filled in correctly, then the tax authorities could identify the amount for returns, and, thus, the amount for returns could be deducted for the reconciliation to prevent deviations.

Finally, the author highlights a third weakness in the case that a separate agreement is made between the customer and the transport company for the transport of the goods. Generally, the transportation costs should be included for reporting the import VAT pursuant to Article 86 (1) (b) of the VAT Directive which could cause a discrepancy between the amount declared in the IOSS return and the amount of imported goods.[995] Thereby, Article 86 (1) (b) of the VAT Directive focuses on the inclusion of incidental costs. Transport costs are only one example of such incidental costs. Generally, it can be seen critically that the transport costs are included in the taxable amount of the import when the transport is organised and (separately paid) by the customer because, in this case, the transport costs are not incidental costs. This interpretation is also in line with the determination of the consignment's intrinsic value being less than EUR 150, which is one requirement for the platform becoming the deemed supplier as well as the application of the IOSS. The consignment's intrinsic value should be calculated excluding transport costs unless they are included in the

---

992. *See* the detailed discussion on the requirements to be 'indirectly' involved in the transport in s. 3.3.1.1.2 The Dispatch or Transportation of Goods By or on Behalf of the Supplier.
993. *See* Merkx, *supra* note 982, at 205.
994. *See* Article 369g (4) of the VAT Directive (EU-OSS) and Article 369t (2) of the VAT Directive (IOSS); *see also* Article 61 of the VAT Implementing Regulation.
995. *See* Merkx, *supra* note 982, at 205.

price.[996] In the case that the customer organises the transport, the transport costs would not be included in the taxable amount of the supply of the good. Instead, a separate supply of service is provided that should be taxed as a supply of service. However, the transport costs would have to be included in the taxable amount of the (exempt) import according to Article 86 (1) (b) of the VAT Directive. In practice, it is likely that the person filling out the import declaration would only indicate the amount indicated on the invoice accompanying the consignment, and, thus, the transport costs would not be declared upon importation. Moreover, even if the person dispatching the goods, i.e., the underlying supplier or platform, would like to include the transport costs in the import declaration, they would not have the knowledge of the amount that the customer pays for the transportation of the good. Thus, although, in theory, a reconciliation of the amounts declared in the import declaration and the amounts declared in the IOSS return may lead to discrepancies, this is an unlikely result in practice.

Furthermore, the reconciliation of the value of the imports with the transactions reported in the IOSS return is an *ex post* analysis and can only be done when the goods were imported and the IOSS declaration has been filed, i.e., no later than the last day of the month following the declaration period.[997] At the moment that the tax authorities realise that the IOSS identification number has been used by fraudsters, the fraudsters would have likely already moved on to use a different IOSS identification number or disappeared fully. This weakness could be avoided if a double check was implemented by the competent customs authorities. Additionally, to verify the IOSS identification number, a transaction number could be issued for each consignment for which the platform becomes the deemed supplier.[998] The platform would have to generate this transaction number in a system that the customs authorities would have access to which could be verified by the customs authorities additionally to the IOSS identification number. If a consignment arrived at customs without a transaction number but the IOSS identification number of the platform was indicated on the import declaration, this could be a sign that the platform's IOSS identification number has been misused, and the customs authorities could investigate further.

Finally, the impact of the misuse of a platform's IOSS identification on the platform should be discussed. Although the consequences of the misuse of the IOSS identification number have not been addressed in the e-commerce package, it is unlikely that the platform can be held liable for the fraudulent use of its IOSS identification number by other suppliers.[999] The platform does not become the deemed

---

996. *See*, for further information of the consignment's intrinsic value, s. 3.3.1.2 The Consignment's Intrinsic Value.
997. *See* Article 369s first subpara. and Article 369v first subpara. of the VAT Directive.
998. Merkx, *supra* note 982, at 204; with reference to D.B. Middelburg, *Nieuwe Btw-Regels Voor Ingevoerde Goederen*, Weekblad fiscaal recht 4 (2020). In general, the same principle could be applied to importations through the IOSS because fraud through the use of a 'foreign' IOSS identification number is not only limited to the use of the platforms' IOSS identification number but may occur to any taxable person who has an IOSS identification number.
999. *See*, similarly, Marie Lamensch et al., *New EU VAT-Related Obligations for E-Commerce Platforms Worldwide: A Qualitative Impact Assessment*, 13 World Tax Journal, *supra* note 18, s. 3.3.4.

supplier when its IOSS identification number is used fraudulently and should also not be punished for the fraudulent behaviour of other taxable persons. Nevertheless, the European Commission argues that also the platform can take precautionary measures to prevent the misuse of its IOSS identification number. It recommends that the platform sanctions underlying suppliers (e.g., by excluding them from the use of the platform) who misuse their IOSS identification number.[1000] Nevertheless, such sanctions can only be applied to suppliers registered on the platform. If, as discussed above, a supplier, e.g., receives the IOSS identification number through the Internet without even providing the goods on the platform, the platform will not be capable of sanctioning this supplier. In the future, a direct exchange of information should be introduced through which the platforms can indicate their IOSS identification numbers to the customs authorities and would not have to further rely on the diligence of the underlying suppliers.[1001]

In conclusion, the introduction of the VAT exemption in Article 143 (ca) of the VAT Directive was necessary to avoid the double taxation of the goods imported from third territories or countries when the IOSS is used. Nevertheless, the EU legislator should have introduced additional cautious steps to more thoroughly avoid the fraudulent use of the IOSS identification number.

4.7 THE SAFE HARBOUR CLAUSE OF ARTICLE 5C OF THE VAT IMPLEMENTING REGULATION

4.7.1 General Remarks

The previous sections have shown that the platform is often dependent on information provided by the underlying supplier to determine its VAT obligations. The information from the underlying supplier is relevant for the platform, e.g., to decide whether it becomes the deemed supplier, to determine how high the taxable amount is, to determine the correct place of supply, and to determine the correct VAT rate or exemption. Against this background, the EU legislator has introduced Article 5c of the VAT Implementing Regulation which restricts the VAT liability of the deemed supplier when certain requirements are fulfilled. According to Article 5c of the VAT Implementing Regulation, the platform is not liable for VAT amounts exceeding the VAT that it has declared and paid on these supplies when three cumulative conditions are met:[1002]

(1) the platform is dependent on the information provided by the underlying suppliers for the correct declaration and payment of the VAT,
(2) the information provided to the platform was incorrect, and

---

1000. European Commission, *Explanatory Notes on the New VAT E-Commerce Rules, supra* note 35, at 76.
1001. *Ibid.*
1002. By indicating that 'all' of the listed conditions must be met, little doubt can be left that the EU legislator meant this list is to be read as a cumulative list.

(3) the taxable person did not know and reasonably could not have known that the information was incorrect.

Thereby, the burden of proof for triggering the safe harbour clause pursuant to Article 5c of the VAT Implementing Regulation lies on the platform.[1003] The European Commission separates this burden of proof into two parts: First, in collecting the information necessary for the requirement (a) and to thereby (b) prove that the information provided by the underlying supplier has been incorrect and, second, in the (c) proof of 'acting in good faith'.[1004] The proof that the platform should provide will be critically discussed in the following section. Thereby, the discussion of the proofs will not follow the structure applied by the European Commission to discuss (a) and (b) of Article 5c of the VAT Implementing Regulation together, but all three points of proof will be discussed in two separate sections. A final section will analyse the legal consequence resulting from Article 5c of the VAT Directive.

4.7.2 Critical Discussion of the Requirements Stipulated in Article 5c of the VAT Implementing Regulation

4.7.2.1 The Platform's Dependency on the Information Provided by the Underlying Supplier

For providing the first piece of proof, the European Commission indicates specific information in the Explanatory Notes that should be collected from the underlying supplier so the platform can prove that it needed to rely on this (wrong) information:

- Place of establishment of the underlying supplier,
- Description of goods,
- Taxable amount for VAT purposes (based on checkout price),
- 'Ship from' location (based on information available up to the point of checkout),
- Information on returns of goods and cancellations of sale.[1005]

Notably, Article 5c (a) of the VAT Implementing Regulation solely stipulates that the platform must have been 'dependent on the information of the underlying suppliers for the correct declaration and payment of VAT'. The VAT Implementing Regulation does not provide a list of what information the platform should collect and keep in its records in order to apply the safe harbour clause of Article 5c of the VAT Implementing Regulation. Nevertheless, the provided list by the European Commission reflects some of the information that the platform needs to determine whether it will become the

---

1003. European Commission, *Explanatory Notes: VAT E-Commerce Rules, supra* note 35, at 24; Marie Lamensch et al., *supra* note 18, s. 3.3.4.; *see* also critically Tina Ehrke-Rabel et al., *Umsatzsteuer in einer digitalisierten Welt, supra* note 13, at 136.
1004. European Commission, *Explanatory Notes: VAT E-Commerce Rules, supra* note 35, at 24 et seqq.
1005. *Ibid.* at 24.

deemed supplier in the first place and how the supply must be treated for VAT purposes.

The following information is necessary for the platform to decide whether it will become the deemed supplier according to Article 14a (1) of the VAT Directive:

- information on the (in)direct involvement by the underlying supplier in the dispatch or transportation of the goods because Article 14a (1) of the VAT Directive is only applicable when the goods have been dispatched or transported by or on behalf of the supplier;[1006]
- information on the place of origin of the goods because Article 14a (1) of the VAT Directive is only applicable to goods imported from a third territory or country;[1007]
- information on the bundling in one consignment or splitting up in more consignments because Article 14a (1) of the VAT Directive is only applicable to consignments of an intrinsic value of less than EUR 150, and the bundling or splitting up of the goods can influence the intrinsic value of the consignment;[1008]
- information on the intrinsic value of the goods because, for the applicability of Article 14a (1) of the VAT Directive, the intrinsic value of the consignment must be determined;[1009]
- the description of the goods because Article 14a (1) of the VAT Directive is not applicable to all kinds of goods.[1010]

Also, to determine the applicability of Article 14a (2) of the VAT Directive, the platform is dependent on the underlying supplier's information. The underlying supplier must inform the platform on the place of establishment because Article 14a (2) of the VAT Directive is only applicable when the underlying supplier is established in a third territory or country.[1011]

Moreover, the platform also needs the indicated information for being able to fulfil its obligations under the VAT Directive. The platform must have a description of the goods to determine the applicable VAT rate or exemption. The description of the goods is necessary whenever the place of supply is in the EU since, in these cases, the platform must decide which rate or whether an exemption is applicable to the supply to the customer: When Article 14a (1) of the VAT Directive is applicable, then the place of supply for the supply of goods is in the EU if the platform used the IOSS[1012] and if

---

1006. *See* the discussions in s. 3.3.1.1.2 The Dispatch or Transportation of Goods By or on Behalf of the Supplier.
1007. *See* the discussions in s. 3.3.1.1.3 The Importation from Third Territories and Third Countries.
1008. *See* the discussions in s. 3.3.1.2.2 The Interpretation of 'Consignments'.
1009. *See* the discussions in s. 3.3.1.2 The Consignment's Intrinsic Value.
1010. *See* the discussions in s. 3.3.1.1.5 Limitations to the Supplied Goods.
1011. *See* the discussions in s. 3.3.2.2 The Requirements for Underlying Suppliers and the Customers.
1012. *See*, for further information, s. 4.3.4.1.1.2.3 The Place of Supply when the Platform Applies the IOSS; for the determination of the taxable amount of the importation *see* s. 4.5.4 The Taxable Amount of the Importation by the Platform or the Customer.

Article 32 second subparagraph of the VAT Directive was applied.[1013] When Article 14a (2) of the VAT Directive is applicable, then the place of supply is always in the EU.[1014]

Additionally, the deemed supplier pursuant to Article 14a (2) of the VAT Directive must receive information from the underlying supplier to decide where the place of supply is. The place of supply depends on the kind of supplied good, e.g., when immovable property is supplied, then the place of supply is where the immovable property is located.[1015] When the supply concerns new means of transport, the supply of second-hand goods, works of art, collectors' items or antiques, or the supply of second-hand means of transport, then the place of supply is the place of origin instead of the place of destination.[1016] Additionally, in the cases where the place of supply is the place of origin, the platform would require information of the dispatch location of the goods.

Finally, the European Commission also lists that the platform should be informed about returns and cancellations.[1017] This is very practical information that the platform should enquire about because, if the platform was not informed about the return of goods, the platform would not reduce the taxable amount in its returns and thus pay too much VAT. Nevertheless, returns do not lead to an underpayment of the VAT but rather to an overpayment of the VAT by the platform. According to the wording of Article 5c of the VAT Directive, the platform 'shall not be held liable for the payment of VAT in excess of the VAT which he declared and paid' and, thus, Article 5c of the VAT Directive is only applicable to VAT underpayments by the platform. Although the information on returns is necessary in order to not overpay the VAT, it is not relevant information for the application of Article 5c of the VAT Implementing Regulation.

The difficult part of the proof will be that the platform is dependent on the information provided by the underlying supplier. This dependency of the platform highly depends on how much the platform is involved in setting the price of the goods, organising the transport, and being responsible for the returns. In general, it can be assumed that the more the platform is involved in these processes, the less the platform will depend on the information of the supplier as it would accumulate this information itself. The dependency on the information could be proven by showing that the platform could not receive the necessary information from its own homepage and was not involved in the payment and delivery process. In this case, there must have been some kind of communication between the underlying supplier and the platform for the platform to receive the necessary information.

1013. *See,* for further information, s. 4.3.4.1.1.2.1 The Shift of the Place of Supply Rule According to Article 32 Second Subparagraph of the VAT Directive; for the determination of the taxable amount of the importation *see* s. 4.5.4 The Taxable Amount of the Importation by the Platform or the Customer.
1014. *See* s. 4.3.4.2 The Place of Supply for Supplies Within the Community (Article 14a [2] of the VAT Directive).
1015. *See* s. 4.3.4.2.1.1 The General Place of Supply Rule According to Article 31 of the VAT Directive.
1016. *See* s. 4.3.4.2.1.2 The General Place of Supply Rule According to Article 32 First Subparagraph of the VAT Directive.
1017. European Commission, *Explanatory Notes on the New VAT E-Commerce Rules, supra* note 35, at 24.

4.7.2.2 The Proof of Incorrect Information Provided to the Platform

The second criterion according to Article 5c (b) of the VAT Directive is the proof that the information provided to the platform was erroneous. In practice, it is difficult for the platform to detect that the information provided by the underlying supplier was incorrect. Since the platform is dependent on the information of the underlying supplier,[1018] the platform would only receive the information that the provided information was erroneous if the underlying supplier provided the platform with this information.

Thus, the platform would likely only find out that it should have declared VAT or did not declare enough VAT when the competent authority confronts the platform. In this case, the platform would have to provide the tax authorities with the information that it received from the underlying supplier and collected as discussed in the previous section.[1019] If the information provided to the platform was erroneous and thus did not reflect the reality, then the proof of Article 5c (b) of the VAT Directive would be fulfilled.

4.7.2.3 The Proof of Acting in Good Faith

The second piece of proof that the platform must provide is that it 'did not know or could not have known that the information provided by the underlying supplier to the platform is incorrect'.[1020] This formulation leads to the first criticism concerning this criterion: the EU legislator has chosen a negative formulation in Article 5c (c) of the VAT Implementing Regulation by referring to 'did not know' or 'should not have known'. In this sense, it is questionable how a platform can provide proof for something that it did not know or should not have known. Instead of this negative formulation, the EU legislator could have chosen a positive formulation, e.g., that the platform was acting in good faith.

Nevertheless, it is likely that, by interpretation, this negative proof can be provided by proving that the platform acted in good faith. Such an interpretation finds its support in the CJEU case law. It seems that the third requirement for the application of Article 5c of the VAT Implementing Regulation is derived from the CJEU case law on tax evasion and fraud. The CJEU held that 'it is not contrary to European Union law to require an operator to act in good faith and to take every step which could reasonably be asked of it to satisfy itself that the transaction which it is carrying out does not result in its participation in tax fraud'[1021] and, thus, the CJEU substituted the negative

---

1018. *See* s. 4.7.2.1 The Platform's Dependency on the Information Provided by the Underlying Supplier.
1019. *See* s. 4.7.2.1 The Platform's Dependency on the Information Provided by the Underlying Supplier.
1020. *See* Article 5c (c) of the VAT Implementing Regulation.
1021. Case C-273/11, *Mecsek-Gabona Kft v Nemzeti Adó- és Vámhivatal Dél-dunántúli Regionális Adó Főigazgatósága*, 6 Sep. 2012, ECLI:EU:C:2012:547, para. 48; the origin for this can be found in Joined Cases C-354/03, C-355/03, C-484/03, *Optigen Ltd (C-354/03), Fulcrum Electronics Ltd (C-355/03) and Bond House Systems Ltd (C-484/03) v Commissioners of*

requirements of 'did not know' or 'should not have known' into a positive requirement of 'acting in good faith'. From this rather general statement on 'acting in good faith', the further question arises of what 'every step which could reasonably be asked' of the CJEU case law on tax evasion and fraud means. This statement is to be analysed on a case-by-case basis. Which steps are still within the 'commercial care'[1022] of a platform and which steps might exceed the commercial care highly depends on the platform and its means.

The European Commission argues that platform operators could communicate the importance of providing the platforms with the necessary data to the underlying suppliers.[1023] Furthermore, the European Commission suggests that the platforms set up for the (automatic) collection of information on the supplies facilitated and random or – if the necessary resources were available – fully automated verification of the information provided by the underlying suppliers.[1024] Additionally, the platform should also take into consideration 'readily available data on the goods from internal and external sources'.[1025] Thereby, the European Commission does not further explain to which internal and external sources it refers. These wide-reaching statements by the European Commission have (understandably) been criticised in literature.[1026] To fulfil such data collection, verification and the indicated further internal and external research on the underlying suppliers and on the goods provided by the underlying suppliers is practically not feasible for platforms that already have to conquer the additional administrative and cost burden from the changes due to the e-commerce package.

Instead of this very broad criterion, the EU legislator could have included a more specific definition of which proof the platform must provide to show that it 'acted in good faith'. Such further legal provisions could have limited the legal uncertainty that platforms face due to the wide wording of Article 5c of the VAT Implementing Regulation. Nevertheless, a further general definition might have been difficult to

Customs & Excise, 12 Jan. 2006, ECLI:EU:C:2006:16, para. 52; and was in later judgments repeatedly confirmed, see, e.g., Case C-384/04, Commissioners of Customs & Excise and Attorney General v Federation of Technological Industries and Others, 11 May 2006, ECLI-:EU:C:2006:309, para. 33; Joined Cases C-439/04 and C-440/04, Axel Kittel v Belgian State (C-439/04) and Belgian State v Recolta Recycling SPRL (C-440/04), 6 Jul. 2006, ECLI-:EU:C:2006:446, para. 51; Case C-409/04, Teleos and Others, 27 Sep. 2007, ECLI-:EU:C:2007:548, para. 65; Case C-271/06, Netto Supermarkt, 21 Feb. 2008, ECLI-:EU:C:2008:105, para. 24; Case C-499/10, Vlaamse Oliemaatschappij NV v FOD Financiën, 21 Dec. 2011, ECLI:EU:C:2011:871, para. 25; Case C-80/11, Mahagében Kft v Nemzeti Adó- és Vámhivatal Dél-dunántúli Regionális Adó Főigazgatósága (C-80/11) and Péter Dávid v Nemzeti Adó- és Vámhivatal Észak-alföldi Regionális Adó Főigazgatósága (C-142/11), 21 Jun. 2012, ECLI:EU:C:2012:373, paras. 53 et seq.; Case C-324/11, Gábor Tóth v Nemzeti Adó- és Vámhivatal Észak-magyarországi Regionális Adó Főigazgatósága, 6 Sep. 2012, ECLI-:EU:C:2012:549, para. 42; Case C-26/16, Santogal M-Comércio e Reparação de Automóveis Lda v Autoridade Tributária e Aduaneira, 14 Jun. 2017, ECLI:EU:C:2017:453, paras. 71 et seq.
1022. See Case C-271/06, Netto Supermarkt, 21 Feb. 2008, ECLI:EU:C:2008:105, para. 27.
1023. European Commission, Explanatory Notes on the New VAT E-Commerce Rules, supra note 35, at 25.
1024. Ibid.
1025. Ibid. at 25 et seq.
1026. Marie Lamensch et al., New EU VAT-Related Obligations for E-Commerce Platforms World-wide: A Qualitative Impact Assessment, 13 World Tax Journal, supra note 18, s. 3.3.4.

adopt as a small platform has different possibilities and features available than some of the platform market leaders. Thus, the broad wording of Article 5c of the VAT Implementing Regulation will lead to a case-by-case analysis where smaller platforms will likely have to implement fewer measures to show that they 'acted in good faith' compared to bigger platforms. It remains questionable how the national tax authorities and courts will interpret this proof and how often the safe harbour clause will actually be applied.

4.7.3 The Legal Consequences of Article 5c of the VAT Implementing Regulation

Article 5c of the VAT Implementing Regulation covers two situations: (i) the platform did not know that it became the deemed supplier for a transaction and thus did not declare the VAT due for that transaction, and (ii) the platform declared less VAT than it should have correctly declared. When the discussed proof can be provided by the platform, then the platform does not become liable for the (additional) VAT due. In this context, it is questionable who is liable for the (additional) VAT. Since the VAT liability has been transferred to the platform, the underlying supplier is not liable for the payment of the VAT anymore. Thus, such additional VAT does not seem to be paid by anyone, according to the VAT Directive.

Nevertheless, the Member States may determine, based on Article 205 of the VAT Directive, that, in this case, the underlying supplier should become liable for the additional VAT due. According to Article 205 of the VAT Directive, 'Member States may provide that a person other than the person liable for payment of VAT is to be held jointly and severally liable for payment of VAT.' Thus, Member States may nominate an additional person liable for the VAT payment additionally to the person liable for the VAT payment according to Articles 193-200 and 202-204 of the VAT Directive.[1027] To exercise the choice to hold the underlying supplier liable for the additional VAT, the Member States would have to include such a rule in their national law.

4.8 INPUT VAT DEDUCTION

4.8.1 General Remarks

The right of an input VAT deduction is one of the cornerstones of the VAT system. The background for the right of an input VAT deduction is the basic idea that the EU VAT

1027. AG Kokott refers to this liability as a 'secondary liability'; *see* Case C-4/20, *'ALTI' OOD v Direktor na Direktsia 'Obzhalvane i danachno-osiguritelna praktika' Plovdiv pri Tsentralno upravlenie na Natsionalnata agentsia za prihodite*, 14 Jan. 2021, ECLI:EU:C:2021:12, Opinion of AG Kokott, para. 28.

system is based on: the taxation of final consumption.[1028] Nevertheless, since the output is taxed at each stage of production and not only at the sale to the final consumers, input VAT must be refunded to the taxable persons supplying goods or services.[1029] The VAT deduction system relieves taxable persons from carrying the VAT burden under the condition that the taxable person carries out taxable transactions. According to the settled CJEU case law:

> the deduction system is meant to relieve the trader entirely of the burden of the VAT payable or paid in the course of all his economic activities. The common system of value-added tax therefore ensures that all economic activities, whatever their purpose or results, provided that they are themselves subject to VAT, are taxed in a wholly neutral way.[1030]

The general right for an input VAT deduction is stipulated in Article 168 of the VAT Directive. Pursuant to Article 168 of the VAT Directive, a taxable person is allowed to deduct the input VAT from the VAT that the taxable person is liable to pay when the purchased goods or services are used for taxed transactions. From the limitation of Article 168 of the VAT Directive, it can already be derived that the input VAT deduction is not possible when the taxable person provides exempt output supplies.[1031] In general, the input VAT deduction arises at the time that the deductible VAT becomes chargeable.[1032] From this general rule, Article 167a of the VAT Directive provides the option for Member States to divert. When Member States have implemented Article 167a of the VAT Directive, the VAT only becomes chargeable in accordance with Article 66 (b) of the VAT Directive when the VAT for the goods or services has been paid to the supplier. The following sections will discuss the input VAT deduction that is applicable to the underlying supplier as well as to the platform.

1028. The CJEU held, on the one side, that the EU VAT system is intended to tax the final consumer; see, e.g., Case C-317/94, *Elida Gibbs Ltd v Commissioners of Customs and Excise*, 24 Oct. 1996, ECLI:EU:C:1996:400, para. 19; Case C-427/98, *Commission v Germany*, 15 Oct. 2002, ECLI:EU:C:2002:581, para. 29; Joined Cases C-249/12 and C-250/12, *Tulică and Plavoşin*, 7 Nov. 2013, ECLI:EU:C:2013:722, para. 34; on the other side, the CJEU held that the VAT should ultimately be borne by the final consumer; see, e.g., Joined Cases C-338/97, C-344/97, C-390/97, *Pelzl and Others*, 8 Jun. 1999, ECLI:EU:C:1999:285, para. 17; Case C-475/03, *Banca popolare di Cremona*, 3 Oct. 2006, ECLI:EU:C:2006:629, para. 28; Case C-271/06, *Netto Supermarkt*, 21 Feb. 2008, ECLI:EU:C:2008:105, para. 21.
1029. See, e.g., Liam Ebrill et al., *The Modern VAT* 16 et seqq. (International Monetary Fund 2001).
1030. Case C-268/83, *D.A. Rompelman and E.A. Rompelman-Van Deelen v Minister van Financiën*, 14 Feb. 1985, ECLI:EU:C:1985:74, para. 19; this was repeatedly confirmed by the CJEU; see, e.g., Case C-37/95, *Belgische Staat v Ghent Coal Terminal NV*, 15 Jan. 1998, ECLI:EU:C:1998:1, para. 15; Joined Cases C-110/98 to C-147/98, *Gabalfrisa SL and Others v Agencia Estatal de Administración Tributaria (AEAT)*, 21 Mar. 2000, ECLI:EU:C:2000:145, para. 44; Case C-98/98, *Commissioners of Customs and Excise v Midland Bank plc.*, 8 Jun. 2000, ECLI:EU:C:2000:300, para. 19; Case C-408/98, *Abbey National plc v Commissioners of Customs & Excise*, 22 Feb. 2001, ECLI:EU:C:2001:110, para. 24; Case C-488/07, *Royal Bank of Scotland plc v The Commissioners of Her Majesty's Revenue & Customs*, 18 Dec. 2008, ECLI:EU:C:2008:750, para. 15.
1031. From this general rule, there are exceptions when the input VAT deduction is possible, although the output transactions are VAT exempt; see Article 169 (b) and (c) of the VAT Directive.
1032. See Article 167 of the VAT Directive.

4.8.2 Input VAT Deduction by the Underlying Supplier

The supply from the underlying supplier to the platform is an exempt supply.[1033] Nevertheless, pursuant to Article 169 (b) of the VAT Directive, the applicable exemption of Article 136a of the VAT Directive is an exemption with the right to deduct the input VAT. Thus, the underlying supplier generally has the right to fully deduct the input VAT.

However, as discussed in a previous section,[1034] this right to the input VAT deduction is only applicable when the supply from the underlying supplier to the platform is exempt according to Article 169 (b) of the VAT Directive. If another exemption was applicable for the supply from the underlying supplier to the platform and this exemption was an exemption without the right to deduct the input VAT, then the underlying supplier would not have the right to deduct the incurred input VAT.

4.8.3 Input VAT Deduction by the Platform

For the input VAT deduction by the platform, the general rule of Article 168 of the VAT Directive is applicable. In general, the platform can deduct any input VAT from costs related to its taxable activity, e.g., administrative costs to uphold the functioning of the platform, IT costs, costs for customer service, and others. Since the incoming supply from the underlying supplier to the platform is VAT exempt, no input VAT will be deductible from this transaction.

According to Article 168 of the VAT Directive, the input VAT deduction is limited to taxed supplies. Thus, the platform's input VAT deduction depends on whether the platform facilitates solely the supply of taxed goods or also the supply of exempt goods. When the platform provides exempt as well as taxed (deemed) supplies, the right to an input VAT deduction depends on whether the platform can link the incoming costs to particular transactions or whether the incoming costs are general costs. If the incoming transactions could be directly linked to a particular outgoing transaction[1035] and this outgoing transaction was taxed then the platform would have the right to fully deduct the input VAT; if the outgoing transaction was exempt, then the platform would not have the right of the input VAT deduction. Nevertheless, in practice, the incoming transactions that can be directly linked to the outgoing transactions would be the exempt supplies from the underlying suppliers to the platform. Thus, no input VAT deduction would be possible from these incoming transactions as no VAT was paid. Additionally, the platform may incur incoming general costs that are not attributable to a specific outgoing transaction. In this case, the platform would only be allowed to partially deduct the input VAT in accordance with Articles 173-175 of the VAT Directive; the platform would have to determine a pro rata for the input VAT deduction

---

1033. *See* Article 136a of the VAT Directive; for further information on this exemption, *see* s. 4.6.2.1 The Exemption of Article 136a of the VAT Directive.
1034. *See* s. 4.6.2.1.2 An Evaluation of the Applicable Exemption: Article 136a of the VAT Directive Versus 'Other' Exemptions Stipulated in the VAT Directive.
1035. *See*, e.g., Case C-98/98, *Midland Bank*, 8 Jun. 2000, ECLI:EU:C:2000:300, para. 24.

of the general costs.[1036] This results in the platform possibly not being able to deduct all incurred input VAT in the case that the (deemed) supplied goods are VAT exempt. The partial input VAT deduction can result in the platform not only incurring higher administrative costs from becoming the deemed supplier but additional higher costs for only being able to partially deduct the input VAT.

Finally, one procedural aspect should be discussed. When the platform opts to use the facilitation of the IOSS or EU-OSS,[1037] the discussed input VAT deduction pursuant to Article 168 of the VAT Directive cannot be applied for if the platform was not registered for the VAT in the country where the input VAT was incurred.[1038] For the platform to declare the input deduction, the refund must be made in accordance with Directive 2008/9/EC[1039] (platforms established in the EU) or in accordance with Directive 86/560/EEC[1040] (platforms established in third territories or countries).

4.9   INVOICING OBLIGATIONS

4.9.1   General Remarks

The invoice has an important function in the VAT system. On the one side, it is, from a general perspective, the document where the different goods or services purchased are indicated and the applicable VAT rate can be identified. On the other side, the invoice is necessary to recover the input VAT in a B2B context which is one of the cornerstones of the EU VAT system.[1041] Thereby, the format of the invoice is not relevant, and the competent authorities shall accept paper invoices as well as electronic invoices.[1042] Furthermore, the VAT Directive provides detailed descriptions of the content for invoices in Article 226 of the VAT Directive.

The following sections will discuss the invoicing obligations for both supplies: on the one hand, the supply from the underlying supplier to the platform and, on the other hand, the supply from the platform to the customers.

1036. For further information on the pro rata, *see*, e.g., Ad van Doesum et al., *Fundamentals of EU VAT Law*, *supra* note 35, at 442 et seqq.
1037. For further information on the IOSS and/or the EU-OSS, *see* s. 4.11 Special Schemes of the OSS.
1038. *See* Article 369j of the VAT Directive (EU-OSS) and Article 369w of the VAT Directive (IOSS).
1039. Council Directive 2008/9/EC of 12 February 2008 Laying down Detailed Rules for the Refund of Value Added Tax, Provided for in Directive 2006/112/EC, to Taxable Persons Not Established in the Member State of Refund but Established in Another Member State, OJ L 044 (2008).
1040. Thirteenth Council Directive 86/560/EEC of 17 November 1986 on the Harmonization of the Laws of the Member States Relating to Turnover Taxes – Arrangements for the Refund of Value Added Tax to Taxable Persons Not Established in Community Territory, OJ L 326 (1986) 560.
1041. *See*, on the VAT input deduction, the previous s. 4.8 Input VAT Deduction.
1042. *See* Article 218 of the VAT Directive; *see* also Article 217 of the VAT Directive for the definition of an 'electronic invoice'.

4.9.2 Invoicing Obligations of the Underlying Supplier

According to Article 219a (1) of the VAT Directive, the applicable invoicing rules depend on the place of supply of the taxable transaction. Since, for the fictitious supply from the underlying supplier to the platform, different places of supply are possible; also, the invoicing rules depend on whether Article 14a (1) of the VAT Directive or Article 14a (2) of the VAT Directive is applicable.[1043] When Article 14a (1) of the VAT Directive is applicable, then the place of supply is in the third country from where the goods are imported. Therefore, in the EU, no invoicing obligations arise for the underlying supplier for the transaction to the platform.

When Article 14a (2) of the VAT Directive is applicable, the place of supply is in the EU – either in the same EU Member State to where the goods are supplied or in the country from where the goods were stored and are transported to the final consumer. As this is a B2B transaction, the underlying supplier has an obligation to issue an invoice to the platform.[1044] Thereby, the invoice must fulfil the national requirements as stipulated in the law where the supply takes place. Since the supply from the underlying supplier to the platform is exempt from the VAT,[1045] Articles 220 (2) and 221 (3) of the VAT Directive provide for the possibility that Member States may exclude certain exempt supplies from the obligation to issue an invoice. However, the exemption of Article 136a of the VAT Directive is not mentioned in Article 220 (2) of the VAT Directive nor in Article 221 (3) of the VAT Directive. Thus, the underlying supplier must issue an invoice to the platform for the fictitious sale of the goods in case of Article 14a (2) of the VAT Directive when Article 136a of the VAT Directive is applicable.[1046] If another exemption was applicable to the supply from the underlying supplier to the platform,[1047] then the underlying supplier would not have an obligation to issue an invoice according to Article 221 (3) of the VAT Directive as long as the supply would be exempt based on Articles 132 or 135 (1) (h) to (l) of the VAT Directive.

Additionally, depending on the contractual relationship between the underlying supplier and the platform, the underlying supplier may issue an invoice to the customer on the amount payable for the goods as well. It should be noted that, from a VAT point of view, no such obligation exists for the underlying supplier. Thus, this invoice does

---

1043. *See,* for the determination of the place of supply, sec 4.3 Place of Supply Rules.
1044. *See* Article 220 (1) (1) of the VAT Directive.
1045. *See,* for the discussion of applicable exemptions, s. 4.6 Applicable Rates and Exemptions.
1046. This obligation to issue an invoice is also in line with the general possibility for Member States to release certain taxable persons from some or all VAT obligations. Such an option is implemented for several exempt supplies; *see* Article 272 (1) (c) of the VAT Directive. Nevertheless, with the introduction of the e-commerce package, Article 272 (1) (b) of the VAT Directive was amended so that the release of VAT obligations cannot be applied to underlying suppliers that provide exempt sales according to Article 136a of the VAT Directive; *see,* for this amendment, Council Directive (EU) 2019/1995 of 21 November 2019 Amending Directive 2006/112/EC as Regards Provisions Relating to Distance Sales of Goods and Certain Domestic Supplies of Goods, OJ L 310/1 (2019).
1047. *See,* for the discussion of the relationship of the exemption stipulated in Article 136a of the VAT Directive and 'other' exemptions, s. 4.6.2.1.2 An Evaluation of the Applicable Exemption: Article 136a of the VAT Directive Versus 'Other' Exemptions Stipulated in the VAT Directive.

not have to fulfil the requirements for invoices stipulated in the VAT Directive. Nevertheless, if the contractual relationship between the underlying supplier and the platform did not provide for the single invoicing of the full price (price for the goods plus the VAT) by the platform to the customer, the underlying supplier may decide to issue an invoice to the customer indicating the amount payable by the customer (price of the goods).

4.9.3   Invoicing Obligations of the Platform

According to Article 220 (1) (1) of the VAT Directive, an invoicing obligation exists only for the supply of goods and services to other taxable persons or to non-taxable legal persons. Thus, the VAT Directive does not provide for an invoicing obligation for B2C transactions.[1048] Therefore, a differentiation must be made of whether the platform became the deemed supplier according to Article 14a (1) of the VAT Directive or according to Article 14a (2) of the VAT Directive. If the platform became the deemed supplier according to Article 14a (1) of the VAT Directive, the customer may be taxable or non-taxable legal persons if the intra-Community acquisition by the taxable or non-taxable legal person was not taxable according to Article 3 (1) of the VAT Directive.[1049] In this case, the platform has an obligation to issue an invoice.

When the customer of platforms according to Article 14 (2) of the VAT Directive is a non-taxable person, the VAT Directive stipulates in Article 220 (1) (2) of the VAT Directive that the platform must issue an invoice for the supply of intra-Community distance sales of goods when the platform does not use the EU-OSS. Otherwise, the VAT Directive generally does not stipulate an obligation to issue an invoice when Article 14 (1) or (2) of the VAT Directive is applied. However, Member States may introduce the obligation to issue an invoice also for B2C supplies in their national law according to Article 221 (1) of the VAT Directive. Thus, the platform must determine the applicable law to find out whether it has an obligation to issue an invoice and which invoice requirements the invoice must fulfil.

The answer to these two questions depends on the country of the place of supply.[1050] When that country has introduced the obligation to issue invoices for B2C supplies of goods, then the platform must issue an invoice. As the review of the different invoicing obligations in all 27 Member States may lead to different results on whether an invoice must be issued and which details must be indicated on the invoice, one further facilitation is provided for suppliers that use the IOSS and/or the EU-OSS to

---

1048. *See* Article 220 (1) (1) of the VAT Directive according to which the invoicing obligation exists only for the supply of goods and services to other taxable persons or to non-taxable legal persons.

1049. *See* s. 3.3.1.1.4 The Requirements of Article 14 (4) (2) (a) of the VAT Directive on the VAT Status of the Recipient of the Goods.

1050. *See* Article 219a (1) of the VAT Directive; for the determination of the place of supply; *see* s. 4.3 Place of Supply Rules.

declare their supplies.[1051] According to Article 219a (2) (b) of the VAT Directive, for taxable persons who make use of the IOSS and/or the EU-OSS, the invoicing rules of the Member State of identification apply.[1052] In general, these explanations are equally applicable to Article 14a (1) of the VAT Directive and Article 14a (2) of the VAT Directive.

Nevertheless, for the application of Article 14a (2) of the VAT Directive, one additional special 'facilitation' was introduced. When the supply is an intra-Community distance sales of goods according to Article 33 (a) of the VAT Directive and the platform uses the EU-OSS to declare its supplies, no invoice must be issued at all according to Article 220 (1) (2) of the VAT Directive *e contrario*. The aim of the EU legislator for introducing this 'general exemption' to disregard the obligation of issuing an invoice was the reduction of the burden on businesses applying the EU-OSS for declaring their intra-Community distance sales of goods.[1053] However, when the platform issues an invoice, although it is not obligated to do so, this invoice must follow the invoicing formalities of the Member State of identification according to Article 219a (2) (b) of the VAT Directive.[1054] Additionally, the national law of the Member State could divert from this facilitation and could implement the obligation to issue an invoice also for intra-Community distance sales of goods declared via the EU-OSS according to Article 221 (1) of the VAT Directive. Thus, although the EU legislator seemed to have wanted to facilitate the invoicing for intra-Community distance sales of goods declared via the EU-OSS, this facilitation is not obligatory, and Member States can divert from it. Therefore, the national law of the Member State of identification must be reviewed for the decision of whether the platform must issue an invoice.

Moreover, the 'facilitation' of Article 220 (1) (2) of the VAT Directive is only applicable to the supply of intra-Community distance sales of goods. Thus, the platform must also ensure national deliveries pursuant to Article 14a (2) of the VAT Directive of whether the Member State of identification requires the issuing of an invoice and, if so, an invoice must be issued for the national supply of goods facilitated through platforms. It is not clear why the EU legislator has not extended the 'facilitation' stipulated in Article 220 (1) (2) of the VAT Directive to national supplies by platforms declared in the EU-OSS. This cascade of different rules and invoicing obligations is graphically displayed in the following decision tree (*see* Figure 4.2).

1051. Article 219a (2) (b) of the VAT Directive not only is limited to the IOSS and EU-OSS but also includes supplies that can be declared in the case of the Non-EU-OSS which is not applicable to deemed suppliers according to Article 14a of the VAT Directive.

1052. For further information on the Member State of identification, *see* s. 4.11.3.2 The Member State of Identification.

1053. *See* Council Directive (EU) 2017/2455 of 5 December 2017 Amending Directive 2006/112/EC and Directive 2009/132/EC as Regards Certain Value Added Tax Obligations for Supplies of Services and Distance Sales of Goods, OJ L 348/7 (2017) preamble 9 of the.

1054. *See*, similarly, European Commission, *Explanatory Notes on the New VAT E-Commerce Rules*, *supra* note 35, at 15 + 41.

Figure 4.2   Simplified Decision Tree of the Invoicing Obligations for Supplies Facilitated by Platforms

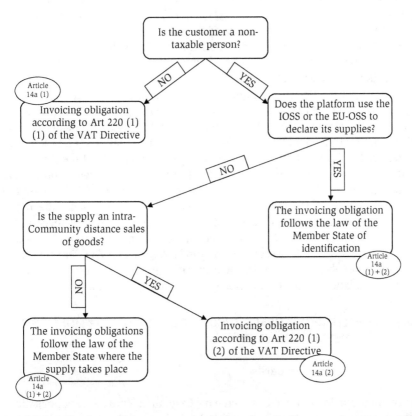

Additionally, it could be reviewed whether the platform can issue a simplified invoice according to Article 220a of the VAT Directive if the platform had an obligation to issue an invoice. According to Article 220a (1) of the VAT Directive, the issuance of a simplified invoice is possible when the amount of the invoice is not higher than EUR 100 or the equivalent of the national currency and when the invoice is a document in accordance with Article 219 of the VAT Directive. Moreover, the issuance of a simplified invoice is restricted to certain situations according to Article 220a (2) of the VAT Directive: The supply cannot be an intra-Community distance sales of goods for which the platform does not apply the EU-OSS.[1055] Additionally, the platform must be a taxable person established in the same Member State where the VAT is due.[1056] Thus,

---

1055. *See* Article 220a (2) of the VAT Directive with reference to Article 220 (1) (2) of the VAT Directive.
1056. Additionally, Article 220a (2) of the VAT Directive also stipulated that a simplified invoice can be issued if the person receiving the supplied good or service is liable for the payment of the VAT due. Generally, the VAT Directive does not apply such a reverse-charge mechanism when Article 14a of the VAT Directive is applied.

platforms established in a third territory or country as well as platforms established in a different Member State than where the good is supplied are not allowed to issue a simplified invoice. Due to these restrictions based on the place of establishment of the supplier, the application of Article 220a (1) of the VAT Directive is rather limited when Article 14a of the VAT Directive is applied.

One further, rather practical, question arises from the discussed difficulty by the platforms to apply the correct VAT rate.[1057] It might happen that a platform issues an invoice indicating the wrong VAT amount on the invoice to the customer, e.g., because the platform applied the standard rate, although a reduced rate is applicable. According to Article 203 of the VAT Directive, the VAT shall become payable if a person indicated the VAT on the invoice. Thus, the question arises of whether the platform becomes liable for the VAT payment due to the indication of the wrong (too high) VAT rate on the invoice. The background for the introduction of Article 203 of the VAT Directive was to prevent the risk of revenue loss due to the input VAT deduction by taxable persons and, thus, it seems to relate to B2B transactions only.[1058] In the case of B2C supplies, the question of whether the VAT becomes payable solely due to the indication of the VAT amount on the invoice even though there is no risk of revenue loss is currently pending at the CJEU.[1059] The follow-up question of the necessity for invoice corrections when the VAT according to Article 203 of the VAT Directive became payable has also been raised to the CJEU. The decision on these issues will also influence the platforms' correction process and administrative burden.

4.10 THE PLATFORM'S RECORD-KEEPING OBLIGATIONS AS A DEEMED SUPPLIER

4.10.1 General Remarks

With the introduction of the e-commerce package, the record-keeping obligations for platforms were amended. Several quite detailed record-keeping obligations were introduced. Thereby, the VAT Directive distinguishes between the record-keeping obligations when the platform becomes the deemed supplier for the supplies it facilitated or when it does not become the deemed supplier. If the platform does not become the deemed supplier,[1060] the record-keeping obligations follow Article 242a of the VAT Directive. As this part of the work concentrates on the legal consequences of Article 14a of the VAT Directive, Article 242a of the VAT Directive will not be further

---

1057. *See,* on this discussion, s. 4.6.3 Applicable Rates and Exemptions for the Supply of Goods by the Platform.

1058. Case C-138/12, *Rusedespred OOD v Direktor na Direktsia 'Obzhalvane I upravlenie na izpalnenieto' – Varna pri Tsentralno upravlenie na Natsionalnata agentsia za prihodite,* 11 Apr. 2013, ECLI:EU:C:2013:233, para. 24; Case C-48/20, *UAB 'P' v Dyrektor Izby Skarbowej w B,* 18 Mar. 2021, ECLI:EU:C:2021:215, para. 27.

1059. *Finanzamt Österreich,* C-378/21, pending; *see* also the discussion on the pending questions by Annika Streicher, *Rechnungsberichtigung bei Kleinbetragsrechnungen,* ecolex (2021).

1060. I.e., the platform did not become a deemed supplier based on Article 14a of the VAT Directive or based on Article 9a of the VAT Implementing Regulation.

discussed. If the platform became the deemed supplier, two different record-keeping obligations may be applicable for the supply which depend on whether the platform decides to apply the IOSS and/or the EU-OSS or not.[1061]

The following sections will discuss the record-keeping obligations for the underlying supplier and the platform. The focus is set on the record-keeping obligations of the platforms, but also the record-keeping obligations of the underlying supplier will be analysed. Thereby, the following sections will discuss the record-keeping obligations when the platform opted in to the IOSS and/or the EU-OSS as well as the general record-keeping obligations that are applicable when the platform does not use the OSS. Since the supply from the underlying supplier to the platform is a general B2B supply, the final section on the general record-keeping obligations is also relevant for the supply from the underlying supplier to the platform when Article 14 (2) of the VAT Directive is applied.

4.10.2 The Record-Keeping Obligations According to Article 63c of the VAT Implementing Regulation

Based on Articles 369k and 369x of the VAT Directive, taxable persons that have opted for the application of the IOSS and the EU-OSS must keep 'sufficiently detailed' records of their transactions covered by the IOSS and the EU-OSS.[1062] The EU legislator further defines which records must be kept in order to qualify as 'sufficiently detailed' in Article 63c of the VAT Implementing Regulation:

- the Member State of consumption to which the goods are supplied;[1063]
- the description and quantity of goods supplied;[1064]
- the date of the supply of the goods or services;[1065]
- the taxable amount indicating the currency used;[1066]
- any subsequent increase or reduction of the taxable amount;[1067]
- the VAT rate applied;[1068]
- the amount of VAT payable indicating the currency used;[1069]

1061. *See* Article 54c (1) of the VAT Implementing Regulation.
1062. In Article 54c (1) (a) of the VAT Implementing Regulation, explicit reference is made to platforms becoming the deemed suppliers having the obligations to keep records based on Article 63c of the VAT Directive if the IOSS and/or the EU-OSS is applied.
1063. *See* Article 63c (1) (a) of the VAT Implementing Regulation (EU-OSS) and Article 63c (2) (a) of the VAT Implementing Regulation (IOSS).
1064. *See* Article 63c (1) (b) of the VAT Implementing Regulation (EU-OSS) and Article 63c (2) (b) of the VAT Implementing Regulation (IOSS).
1065. *See* Article 63c (1) (c) of the VAT Implementing Regulation (EU-OSS) and Article 63c (2) (c) of the VAT Implementing Regulation (IOSS).
1066. *See* Article 63c (1) (d) of the VAT Implementing Regulation (EU-OSS) and Article 63c (2) (d) of the VAT Implementing Regulation (IOSS).
1067. *See* Article 63c (1) (e) of the VAT Implementing Regulation (EU-OSS) and Article 63c (2) (e) of the VAT Implementing Regulation (IOSS).
1068. *See* Article 63c (1) (f) of the VAT Implementing Regulation (EU-OSS) and Article 63c (2) (f) of the VAT Implementing Regulation (IOSS).
1069. *See* Article 63c (1) (g) of the VAT Implementing Regulation (EU-OSS) and Article 63c (2) (g) of the VAT Implementing Regulation (IOSS).

- the date and amount of payments received;[1070]
- where an invoice is issued, the information contained on the invoice;[1071]
- the information used to determine the place where the dispatch or the transport of the goods to the customer begins and ends;[1072] and
- proof of possible returns of goods, including the taxable amount and the VAT rate applied.[1073]

Additionally, when the platform applies the EU-OSS, any payments on account received before the supply of the goods or services must be recorded[1074] and, when the platform applies IOSS, additional information must be recorded:

- the order number or unique transaction number[1075] and
- the unique consignment number when the platform is directly involved in the delivery.[1076]

The records must be made available electronically to the Member State of identification upon request and the Member State of consumption, and they must be kept for 10 years following the year when the transaction was carried out.[1077] The records should enable the tax authorities of the Member State of consumption to verify whether the filed VAT return is correct.[1078] Furthermore, the platform may be excluded from the application of the IOSS and the EU-OSS if the requested records were not provided within one month after the subsequent reminder.[1079]

4.10.3   The Record-Keeping Obligations According to Article 242 of the VAT Directive

When the platform does not apply the IOSS and/or the EU-OSS, the platform must follow the record-keeping obligations according to Article 242 of the VAT Directive.[1080] Pursuant to Article 242 of the VAT Directive, 'every taxable person shall keep accounts in sufficient detail for VAT to be applied and its application checked by the tax

---

1070. See Article 63c (1) (h) of the VAT Implementing Regulation (EU-OSS) and Article 63c (2) (h) of the VAT Implementing Regulation (IOSS).
1071. See Article 63c (1) (j) of the VAT Implementing Regulation (EU-OSS) and Article 63c (2) (i) of the VAT Implementing Regulation (IOSS).
1072. See Article 63c (1) (k) of the VAT Implementing Regulation (EU-OSS) and Article 63c (2) (j) of the VAT Implementing Regulation (IOSS).
1073. See Article 63c (1) (l) of the VAT Implementing Regulation (EU-OSS) and Article 63c (2) (k) of the VAT Implementing Regulation (IOSS).
1074. See Article 63c (1) (i) of the VAT Implementing Regulation.
1075. See Article 63c (2) (l) of the VAT Implementing Regulation.
1076. See Article 63c (2) (m) of the VAT Implementing Regulation.
1077. See Article 369k (2) of the VAT Directive (EU-OSS) and Article 369x (2) of the VAT Directive (IOSS).
1078. See Article 369k (1) of the VAT Directive (EU-OSS) and Article 369x (1) of the VAT Directive (IOSS).
1079. See Article 58b (2) (c) and 63c (3) of the VAT Implementing Regulation; for further information on the exclusion from the IOSS and the EU-OSS, see s. 4.11.5 Deregistration and Exclusion from the IOSS and the EU-OSS.
1080. See Article 54c (1) (b) of the VAT Implementing Regulation.

authorities'. As Article 242 of the VAT Directive refers to 'every taxable person', the underlying suppliers must also keep records based on Article 242 of the VAT Directive. Neither the VAT Directive nor the VAT Implementing Regulation provide further instructions regarding which information must be kept, how long this information must be kept and if, how, and when the information should be provided to the competent tax authorities. It is up to the discretion of the Member State to stipulate the further details of this reporting obligation.[1081]

4.11 SPECIAL SCHEMES OF THE OSS

4.11.1 General Remarks

With the introduction of the e-commerce package, a broad reform of simplification measures was introduced. The MOSS introduced in 2015 was extended, and three different OSSs were introduced. Depending on which kind of supplies a taxable person provides and where the taxable person is established, one (or more) of the OSSs may be applicable for fulfilling the VAT obligations in the countries of destination. All three OSSs have in common that their applicability is limited to supplies to non-taxable persons as well as to supplies to non-taxable legal persons and to taxable persons who only carry out the supply of goods and services for non-deductible supplies.[1082] Therefore, in the deemed supplier regime, only the platform as the deemed supplier may apply the OSS.

The motivation for the introduction of the OSS is the limitation of the administrative burden and the simplification of administrative obligations for taxable persons.[1083] When a taxable person decides to apply an OSS, a VAT registration in different Member States of destination can be avoided since all supplies that fall into the scope of reporting of the OSS can be reported in the OSS of the Member State of identification.[1084] The application of the OSS is optional. However, when the platform opts to use the OSS, then all supplies within the scope of the OSS must be declared via the OSS.[1085] Additional benefits are the submission of the return and payment of the total declared

---

1081. *See*, similarly, also Ad van Doesum et al., *Fundamentals of EU VAT Law*, *supra* note 35, at 675.
1082. The Non-EU-OSS in Article 359 of the VAT Directive and the EU-OSS in Article 369b (a) read in conjunction with Article 14 (4) (1) and Article 14a (2) of the VAT Directive (intra-Community distance sales of goods by a platform) and in Article 369b (b) read in conjunction with Article 14a (2) of the VAT Directive (national supplies by a platform) are limited to supplies to non-taxable persons. In general, the EU-OSS is also applicable to supplies to non-taxable legal persons and to supplies to taxable persons who only carry out the supply of goods and services for non-deductible supplies, but Article 14a (2) of the VAT Directive is limited to supplies to non-taxable persons.
1083. *See* preamble pt. 7 and pt. 17 of the Council Directive (EU) 2017/2455 of 5 December 2017 Amending Directive 2006/112/EC and Directive 2009/132/EC as Regards Certain Value Added Tax Obligations for Supplies of Services and Distance Sales of Goods, OJ L 348/7 (2017).
1084. *See* European Commission, *Explanatory Notes on the New VAT E-Commerce Rules*, *supra* note 35, at 33.
1085. *See* Article 359 of the VAT Directive (Non-EU-OSS), Article 369b second subpara. Of the VAT Directive (EU-OSS), and Article 369m (1) second subpara. of the VAT Directive (IOSS).

amounts in the Member State of identification and simplifications due to being in contact with only one tax authority and language of one Member State.[1086]

Although, with the e-commerce reform, three different OSSs were introduced, only two of the OSSs are applicable for the supplies of goods through platforms: the EU-OSS and the IOSS. The third OSS, the Non-EU-OSS, only covers the supply of services from third country suppliers, which is not regulated by Article 14a of the VAT Directive.[1087] The following sections will discuss the application, requirements and legal consequences of the EU-OSS and the IOSS by platforms. Furthermore, the legal consequences may also alter when a platform decides to use the EU-OSS or the IOSS. These different legal consequences have been indicated in the previous sections already, where the corresponding legal consequence of the deemed supplier regime was discussed. In a final section, the simplification mechanism of importations for non-IOSS suppliers will be critically analysed.

4.11.2   The Scope of the EU-OSS and the IOSS

4.11.2.1   *The Extension of the MOSS to Intra-Community Distance Sales and to National Supplies by Platforms*

The EU-OSS is stipulated in Articles 369a-369k of the VAT Directive and in Articles 57a-63c of the VAT Implementing Regulation. The scope of application of the EU-OSS is limited to taxable persons carrying out intra-Community distance sales of goods, the national supply of goods when the deemed supplier regime according to Article 14a (2) of the VAT Directive is applicable, and the cross-border supply of services to non-taxable persons within the Community that is not relevant for the application of Article 14a of the VAT Directive.[1088] According to this scope, platforms facilitating the supply of goods within the Community according to Article 14a (2) of the VAT Directive can use the EU-OSS to fulfil their VAT obligations in the EU.[1089]

4.11.2.2   *The Introduction of IOSS*

The IOSS is stipulated in Articles 369l-369x of the VAT Directive and in Articles 57a-63c of the VAT Implementing Regulation. The scope of application of the IOSS is limited to distance sales of goods imported from third territories or third countries in consignments of an intrinsic value not exceeding EUR 150 but excluding goods subject to excise duty.[1090]

1086. *See* European Commission, *Explanatory Notes: VAT E-Commerce Rules, supra* note 35, at 33.
1087. *See* Articles 358a-369 of the VAT Directive and Articles 57a-63c of the VAT Implementing Regulation.
1088. *See* Article 369b of the VAT Directive.
1089. *See* Article 369b (a) read in conjunction with Article 14 (4) (1) and Article 14a (2) of the VAT Directive and Article 369b (b) read in conjunction with Article 14a (2) of the VAT Directive.
1090. *See* Article 369l first subpara. of the VAT Directive; for the definition of distance sales of goods imported from third territories or third countries, *see* s. 3.3.1.1 The Definition of Distance

Concerning the taxable person using the IOSS (the platform), restrictions can be found in Article 369m (1) of the VAT Directive. Taxable persons established in the EU and taxable persons established in a third country with which the EU has concluded a mutual assistance agreement may apply the IOSS without any further restrictions.[1091] Up until the finalisation of this book, the EU has only concluded such an agreement with Norway.[1092] Additionally, the question arises of whether a fixed establishment should also qualify as 'being established'. As already discussed, a uniform interpretation of the VAT Directive leads to the conclusion that a fixed establishment should also qualify as 'being established' in a country.[1093] Furthermore, warehouses are only considered to be a fixed establishment when the requirement of a sufficient degree of permanence and a suitable structure in terms of human and technical resources is fulfilled.[1094]

Taxable persons established in a third country with whom the EU has not concluded a mutual assistance agreement and who do not have a fixed establishment in the EU must be represented by an intermediary established in the EU in order to use the IOSS.[1095] According to this scope, all platforms facilitating the supply of distance sales of goods imported from third territories or third countries according to Article 14a (1) of the VAT Directive can use the IOSS to fulfil their VAT obligations in the EU.[1096] Nevertheless, platforms that are established in a third country other than Norway and do not have a fixed establishment in the EU must be represented by an intermediary established in the EU to use the IOSS.

4.11.3 Registration to the IOSS and the EU-OSS

4.11.3.1 Filing the Application to the IOSS and to the EU-OSS

Taxable persons are not obligated to make use of the IOSS or the EU-OSS since the application of any OSS is optional.[1097] When a taxable person decides to use the simplification scheme(s), it is necessary to register with the tax office in the competent or chosen Member State, i.e., the so-called Member State of identification.[1098] After

---

Sales of Goods Imported from a Third Territory or a Third Country and, for the discussion of the consignments' intrinsic value, *see* s. 3.3.1.2 The Consignment's Intrinsic Value.

1091. *See* Article 369m (1) (a) and (c) of the VAT Directive.
1092. *See* Agreement Between the European Union and the Kingdom of Norway on Administrative Cooperation, Combating Fraud and Recovery of Claims in the Field of Value Added Tax, OJ L 195 (2018).
1093. *See* s. 3.3.2.2 The Requirements for Underlying Suppliers and the Customers.
1094. *See* s. 3.3.2.2 The Requirements for Underlying Suppliers and the Customers.
1095. *See* Article 369m (1) (b) of the VAT Directive; for the definition of the intermediary *see* Article 369l (2) of the VAT Directive.
1096. *See* Article 369m (1) read in conjunction with Article 14 (4) (2) and Article 14a (1) of the VAT Directive.
1097. The VAT Directive states that 'Member States shall permit ...', which means that the application of the IOSS as well as the EU-OSS is facultative; *see* Article 369b of the VAT Directive (EU-OSS) and Article 369m (1) of the VAT Directive (IOSS).
1098. *See,* for further information on the determination of the Member State of identification, s. 4.11.3.2 The Member State of Identification.

informing or applying at the Member State of identification, the EU-OSS is generally applicable from the first day of the following quarter after the filing of the application[1099] except for when the first supplies that are covered by the EU-OSS are provided before the next quarter. In this case, the taxable person may inform the tax authorities of the Member State of identification before the tenth of the month following this first supply; then, the EU-OSS can be applied by the taxable person starting with the commencement of the supplies.[1100] Compared to this, the IOSS can only be applied from the day that the IOSS identification number is received by the taxable person or by its intermediary.[1101] Furthermore, due to the different scope of the IOSS and the EU-OSS, a platform may have to apply for the IOSS as well as for the EU-OSS if the platform provided intra-Community distance sales, national supplies, as well as imported distance sales.

With the registration to the IOSS and/or the EU-OSS, the following information must be provided to the Member State of identification (Table 4.1).[1102]

Table 4.1   *Overview of the Information Necessary for IOSS and EU-OSS Registration*

Registration Information	IOSS	EU-OSS
Individual VAT identification number allocated by the Member State of identification in accordance with Article 369d of the VAT Directive	✓	✓
If the taxable person is represented by an intermediary, the individual identification number of that intermediary	✓	×
VAT identification number or national tax number	✓	×
Company name	✓	×
Trading name(s) of the company if different from the company name	✓	✓
Full postal address of the company	✓	✓
Country in which the taxable person has his place of business if not in the Union	✓	✓
E-mail address of the taxable person	✓	✓
Website(s) of the taxable person	✓	(✓)
Contact name	✓	✓
Telephone number	✓	✓

1099. *See* Article 57d (1) first subpara. of the VAT Implementing Regulation.
1100. *See* Article 57d (1) second subpara. of the VAT Implementing Regulation.
1101. *See* Article 57d (2) of the VAT Implementing Regulation.
1102. *See* Annex I of the Commission Implementing Regulation (EU) 2020/194 of 12 February 2020 Laying down Detailed Rules for the Application of Council Regulation (EU) No 904/2010 as Regards the Special Schemes for Taxable Persons Supplying Services to Non-Taxable Persons, Making Distance Sales of Goods and Certain Domestic Supplies of Goods, OJ L 40/114 (2020); column C provides the application information for the EU-OSS, and column D provides the application information for the IOSS; *see* also, for the application of the IOSS, Article 369p of the VAT Directive.

Registration Information	IOSS	EU-OSS
IBAN number	✓	✓
Individual VAT identification number(s) or if not available tax reference number(s) allocated by the Member State(s) in which the taxable person has a fixed establishment(s) other than the Member State of identification	✓	✓
Full postal address and trading name of fixed establishments in Member States other than the Member State of identification	✓	✓
VAT identification number(s) allocated by Member State(s) as a non-established taxable person	×	✓
Electronic declaration that the taxable person is not established within the Union	×	✓
Indicator of whether the taxable person is an electronic interface according to Article 14a (2) of the VAT Directive	×	✓
Date of commencement of the use of the scheme	✓	✓
Date of request by the taxable person (or the intermediary acting on his behalf) to be registered under the scheme	✓	✓
Date of registration decision by the Member State of identification	✓	✓
Indicator of whether the taxable person is a VAT group	×	✓
Individual VAT identification number(s) allocated by the Member State of identification in accordance with Articles 362, 369d or 369q of the VAT Directive if the taxable person has previously used or is currently using one of these schemes	✓	✓

✓ = necessary information; (✓) = the information must be provided, if available; × = not necessary information

The formalities and actual registration format and systems are to be implemented in the national law of the Member States. Thereby, the VAT Directive only stipulates that the communication concerning the IOSS and the EU-OSS should be electronic.[1103] When a taxable person applies for the IOSS, the Member State of identification issues the IOSS identification number to the taxable person (the platform) or its intermediary.[1104] With the successful registration for the IOSS/EU-OSS, taxable persons must declare the mentioned supplies through the IOSS/EU-OSS; a VAT registration in the different Member States of destination is not necessary anymore.[1105]

1103. *See* Article 369c of the VAT Directive (EU-OSS) and Article 369o of the VAT Directive (IOSS).
1104. *See* Article 369q of the VAT Directive; the use of the IOSS identification number for applying the import VAT exemption s. 4.6.3 Applicable Rates and Exemptions for the Supply of Goods by the Platform; for the registration to the EU-OSS, the taxable person should not receive a new tax number but the tax number already allocated to the taxable person by the Member State of identification shall be used; *see* Article 369d first subpara. of the VAT Directive.
1105. *See* Article 369c of the VAT Directive (EU-OSS) and Article 369o of the VAT Directive (IOSS).

4.11.3.2　The Member State of Identification

The so-called Member State of identification depends on the establishment of the taxable person. When the taxable person is established in the EU or is a third country supplier with a fixed establishment in the EU, then the Member State of (fixed) establishment is the Member State of identification.[1106] If the taxable person was a third country supplier and has more than one fixed establishment in the EU, the taxable person may choose the Member State of identification.[1107]

Similarly, third country suppliers without any fixed establishments in the EU may choose the Member State of identification.[1108] Thereby, two further restraints apply: for the use of the EU-OSS, third country suppliers without any fixed establishment in the EU may only choose one Member State as the Member State of identification from which the dispatch or transport of the goods begins.[1109]

For the application of IOSS, third country suppliers without a fixed establishment in the EU must be represented by an intermediary who is established in the EU.[1110] When an intermediary is appointed, the Member State of identification depends on the establishment of the intermediary. When the intermediary is established in one Member State or is a third country intermediary with one fixed establishment in one Member State, then this Member State is the Member State of identification.[1111] When the intermediary is not established in the EU but has more fixed establishments in the EU, then the intermediary can choose the Member State of identification.[1112] Although the VAT Directive stipulates that third country suppliers may choose the Member State of identification for the IOSS,[1113] this choice is actually executed by the choice of the intermediary. The platform may choose the intermediary based on which Member State the intermediary is established since some legal consequences depend on the national law of the Member State identification; e.g., Member States could decide that no invoice must be issued for supplies to non-taxable persons when the IOSS is applied.[1114] Thus, a platform established in a third country could choose an intermediary established in a country that has implemented such a facilitation to be able to use

---

1106. *See* Article 369d (2) first subpara. of the VAT Directive (EU-OSS) and Article 369l (3) (b) and (c) of the VAT Directive (IOSS).
1107. *See* Article 369a (2) second subpara. of the VAT Directive (EU-OSS) and Article 369l (3) (b) of the VAT Directive (IOSS).
1108. *See* Article 369l (3) (a) of the VAT Directive.
1109. *See* Article 369a (2) second subpara. of the VAT Directive.
1110. *See* Article 369m (1) (b) and Article 369l (3) (d) of the VAT Directive. Any other taxable person may also appoint an intermediary but, for third country suppliers without a fixed establishment in the EU, the appointment of an intermediary is a requirement for applying the IOSS. The intermediary is responsible to fulfil the VAT obligations and is liable to pay the VAT for the taxable person; *see* Article 369l (2) of the VAT Directive.
1111. *See* Article 369l (3) (d) of the VAT Directive.
1112. *See* Article 369l (3) (e) of the VAT Directive.
1113. *See* Article 369l (3) (a) of the VAT Directive.
1114. *See* the discussion in s. 4.9.3 Invoicing Obligations of the Platform.

this facilitation. Finally, also platforms established in the EU can appoint an intermediary who becomes liable for the VAT payment and who fulfils the reporting obligations according to the IOSS.[1115] Nevertheless, the appointment of an intermediary by a platform established in the EU does not have an influence on the Member State of identification.[1116]

Whenever the taxable person chooses the Member State of identification, the taxable person is bound to this choice for the calendar year of the filing of the application and the two following calendar years.[1117]

4.11.4   Declaration and Payment

Once a taxable person is registered for the IOSS and /or the EU-OSS, any transaction to which the IOSS or the EU-OSS applies must be declared via the IOSS or the EU-OSS.[1118] The taxable person cannot choose to apply the IOSS or EU-OSS in certain Member States and to follow the general reporting rules in other Member States. Thus, the IOSS and EU-OSS are based on an 'all in or all out' principle.

The taxable person must submit the OSS return no later than the last day of the month following the declaration period and also transfer the VAT due to the competent tax authority of the Member State of identification.[1119] The declaration period for the EU-OSS is the calendar quarter,[1120] whereas, for the IOSS, it is the calendar month.[1121] Even when a taxable person has not made any IOSS or EU-OSS transactions in a declaration period, a nil-return must be filed.[1122] When the taxable person (or intermediary) fails to submit the VAT return or to transfer the outstanding VAT amount, the Member State of identification must issue an electronic reminder on the tenth day after the VAT return should have been submitted or the payment should have been made.[1123]

In the IOSS and the EU-OSS returns, the following information must be included:

– the VAT identification number or the IOSS identification number,[1124]
– and separated for each Member State in which VAT is due:

1115. *See* Article 369l (2) of the VAT Directive.
1116. *See* Article 369l (3) (c) of the VAT Directive.
1117. *See* Article 369a (2) second and third subpara. of the VAT Directive (EU-OSS) and Article 369l (2) second subpara. of the VAT Directive (IOSS).
1118. *See* Article 369b second subpara. of the VAT Directive (EU-OSS) and Article 369m (1) second subpara. of the VAT Directive (IOSS).
1119. *See* Article 369f and Article 369i first subpara. of the VAT Directive (EU-OSS) and Article 369s first subpara. and Article 369v first subpara. of the VAT Directive (IOSS).
1120. *See* Article 369f of the VAT Directive.
1121. *See* Article 369s first subpara. of the VAT Directive.
1122. *See* Article 369f of the VAT Directive (EU-OSS) and Article 369s first subpara. of the VAT Directive (IOSS), *see* also Article 59a of the VAT Implementing Regulation.
1123. *See* Article 60a first subpara. and Article 63a first subpara. of the VAT Implementing Regulation; *see* also, on the exclusion of the IOSS and the EU-OSS due to the repeating failure of the reporting and payment obligations; s. 4.11.5 Deregistration and Exclusion from the IOSS and the EU-OSS.
1124. *See* Article 369g (1) of the VAT Directive (EU-OSS) and Article 369t (1) of the VAT Directive (IOSS).

- the total value exclusive of VAT,
- the applicable VAT rate,
- the total amount per rate, and
- the total amount of VAT due.[1125]

Furthermore, Article 369g (2) of the VAT Directive stipulates additional information that should be included in the EU-OSS return: when the dispatch or transport commences in another Member State than the Member State of identification, the platform should also indicate its VAT identification number of the Member State from where the goods are dispatched or transported.[1126] For supplies facilitated by platforms, this additional information should be indicated for intra-Community distance sales as well as national sales according to Article 14a (2) of the VAT Directive.[1127] Although the VAT Directive stipulates it as additional necessary information, this information must only be provided to the Member State of identification 'if available'.[1128] The same additional requirement has also been included in the VAT Directive for any other taxable person, i.e., not electronic interfaces facilitating supplies making use of the EU-OSS but without the simplification that this information must only be included 'if available'.[1129]

It is questionable why the EU legislator stipulated that only for supplies facilitated by platforms must the information be provided 'if available'. In general, the platform does not have to be VAT registered in the country of origin. As discussed, the fictitious (exempt) supply from the underlying supplier to the platform is the supply without transport at the place of origin, i.e., the Member State from where the goods are dispatched or transported.[1130] If the platform did not have any additional taxable activity (except the deemed supplies) in this place of origin, then no VAT registration would be necessary in the country of origin. Therefore, the platform might not even have a VAT identification number of the country of origin.

Similarly, other taxable persons may also use the EU-OSS but might not be registered in the Member State of origin. One example would be a taxable person who is established in Austria and also applied for the EU-OSS in Austria. The taxable person also has a warehouse in Germany (not a fixed establishment) for which the taxable person only purchases goods from German suppliers. The goods from the warehouse are only supplied to consumers in other Member States (not Germany). These supplies are declared through the EU-OSS, and the input VAT deduction is claimed through the VAT refund process.[1131] In this situation, the taxable person is not obligated to register

---

1125. *See* Article 369g (1) of the VAT Directive (EU-OSS) and Article 369t (1) of the VAT Directive (IOSS).
1126. *See* Article 369g (2) third subpara. of the VAT Directive.
1127. *See* Article 369g (2) (b) of the VAT Directive.
1128. *See* Article 369g (2) third subpara. of the VAT Directive.
1129. *See* Article 369g (2) second subpara. of the VAT Directive.
1130. *See* the discussion on the place of supply in s. 4.3.3 The Place of Supply Rule for the Supply by the Underlying Supplier.
1131. *See* Article 469j of the VAT Directive.

for the VAT in Germany.[1132] Although platforms and other taxable persons do not have an obligation to register in the country of origin, these two suppliers require a different set of information when using the EU-OSS. The platform must only provide the VAT identification number of the country of origin when the country of origin is not the Member State of identification if that information is 'available', whereas, for other suppliers, the indication of the VAT identification number is obligatory. The reason for this differentiation is unclear.

Finally, the declaration and the payment should be made in euros.[1133] If the currency of the Member State of identification was not euros, then the national law of the Member State of identification may stipulate that the VAT return should be made in the national currency.[1134] Conversions due to supplies to Member States with different currencies than the currency that the VAT return must be declared in should be converted on the last date of the tax period applying the conversion rate published by the European Central Bank.[1135]

4.11.5   Deregistration and Exclusion from the IOSS and the EU-OSS

The VAT Directive stipulates several reasons for the exclusion of taxable persons from the IOSS and the EU-OSS. First, the taxable person (or intermediary) has an obligation to inform the Member State of identification in the case that the taxable activity to which the IOSS or the EU-OSS is applicable is ceased or if the taxable person no longer meets the conditions necessary for the application of the IOSS or the EU-OSS.[1136] This information is to be provided, at the latest, on the tenth day of the month following the cessation or the non-fulfilment of the requirements and results in the exclusion of the taxable person from the IOSS or the EU-OSS.[1137] Furthermore, the Member State of identification may also exclude the taxable person from the IOSS and/or the EU-OSS if it assumes otherwise that the taxable activity was ceased.[1138] This may be the case when the taxable person has not made any supplies covered by the IOSS or the EU-OSS

1132. As soon as the taxable person supplies the goods from the German warehouse to German customers or if the taxable person purchases the goods from other Member States and transports them to Germany for the storage in the warehouse, a VAT registration in Germany would be necessary.
1133. *See* Article 369h (1) of the VAT Directive (EU-OSS) and Article 369u (1) of the VAT Directive (IOSS).
1134. *See* Article 369h (1) of the VAT Directive (EU-OSS) and Article 369u (1) of the VAT Directive (IOSS).
1135. *See* Article 369h (1) and (2) of the VAT Directive (EU-OSS) and Article 369u (1) and (2) of the VAT Directive (IOSS).
1136. *See* Article 369c of the VAT Directive (EU-OSS) and Article 369o of the VAT Directive (IOSS); *see* also Article 57h (1) (a) and (b) of the VAT Implementing Regulation.
1137. *See* Article 369e (a) and (c) of the VAT Directive (EU-OSS) and Article 369r (1) (a) and (c) and (3) (a) and (c) of the VAT Directive (IOSS); *see* also Article 57h (1) of the VAT Implementing Regulation.
1138. *See* Article 369e (b) of the VAT Directive (EU-OSS) and Article 369r (1) (b) and (3) (b) of the VAT Directive (IOSS); if the taxable person no longer meets the requirements, the taxable person (or its intermediary) should also inform the Member State of identification, at the latest, on the tenth day of the month; *see* Article 57h (1) of the VAT Implementing Regulation.

within two years.[1139] One further reason to exclude a taxable person from the IOSS is when the appointed intermediary informs the Member State of identification that the intermediary does not represent the taxable person anymore.[1140]

Additionally, the taxable person should also be allowed to inform the Member State of identification in the case that it simply wants to deregister from the IOSS or the EU-OSS. As the use of the IOSS as well as the EU-OSS is voluntary, this decision by the taxable person should also lead to the exclusion from the IOSS and/or the EU-OSS, although the VAT Directive does not explicitly provide a legal basis for this case.

Finally, the taxable person may also be excluded from the IOSS and/or the EU-OSS if the taxable person repeatedly failed to comply with the rules of the IOSS and/or the EU-OSS.[1141] The VAT Implementing Regulation stipulates three reasons that lead to an exclusion due to the failure to comply with the rules. Thereby, the EU legislator used the term 'at least in the following cases'.[1142] Thus, the list stipulated in Article 58b (2) of the VAT Implementing Regulation is a non-exhaustive list, and the Member States may determine further reasons that lead to an exclusion from the IOSS and/or the EU-OSS:

- The taxable person (or intermediary) does not file three consecutive VAT returns in due time. For the exclusion from the IOSS and/or the EU-OSS, all three VAT returns have not been submitted within 10 days after the reminder was issued to the taxable person (or intermediary).[1143]
- The taxable person (or intermediary) does not pay the VAT due in due time for three consecutive VAT periods. For the exclusion from the IOSS and/or the EU-OSS, the payments for the three VAT periods have not been transferred within 10 days after the reminder was issued to the taxable person (or intermediary).[1144] The exclusion of the IOSS and the EU-OSS is not possible when the remaining unpaid amount does not exceed EUR 100.[1145]
- The taxable person (or intermediary) does not provide the Member State of identification upon request with the electronically kept records according to Articles 369k and 369x of the VAT Directive[1146] within one month after the subsequent reminder.[1147]

An additional consequence of a taxable person being excluded from the IOSS or the EU-OSS due to the failure to comply with the rules is that the taxable person is

---

1139. *See* Article 58a of the VAT Implementing Regulation.
1140. *See* Article 369r (3) (d) of the VAT Directive.
1141. *See* Article 369e (d) of the VAT Directive (EU-OSS) and Article 369r (1) (d) and (3) (e) of the VAT Directive (IOSS).
1142. *See* Article 58b (2) of the VAT Implementing Regulation.
1143. *See* Article 58b (2) (a) of the VAT Implementing Regulation.
1144. *See* Article 58b (2) (b) of the VAT Implementing Regulation.
1145. *See* Article 58b (2) (b) of the VAT Implementing Regulation.
1146. *See,* for further information on the record-keeping obligations for platforms applying the EU-OSS or the IOSS, s. 4.10.2 The Record-Keeping Obligations According to Article 63c of the VAT Implementing Regulation.
1147. *See* Article 58b (2) (c) of the VAT Implementing Regulation.

excluded from the use of all OSSs in any Member State for two years following its exclusion.[1148]

The exclusion becomes effective on the first day of the quarter (EU-OSS) or of the month (IOSS) following the day that the exclusion was sent to the taxable person.[1149] If a taxable person was excluded from the IOSS due to the failure to comply with the IOSS rules, then this exclusion would become effective from the day following the day that the decision on the exclusion was sent to the taxable person,[1150] and the IOSS identification number would also become invalid on that day.[1151]

4.12   ACCOMPANYING CUSTOMS MEASURES

4.12.1   General Remarks

With the introduction of the e-commerce package, specific customs measures were also amended. First of all, the small import VAT consignment exemption for imports of EUR 22 or below as determined by the Member States was abandoned.[1152] The background for this abolishment was a tremendous loss of VAT due to two reasons. On the one hand, suppliers declared consignments wrongly and acted fraudulently.[1153] On the other hand, even if suppliers had declared the consignments correctly because the price was EUR 22 or below, the exemption would still lead to a distortion of competition since EU suppliers who did not import their goods would have to charge VAT to the customers for the same low-value goods.[1154] The abolishment of the *de minimis* VAT exemption results in (import) VAT becoming due on all importation of goods. Even though the import VAT is exempt according to Article 143 (ca) of the VAT Directive when the supplier declares the supply on the IOSS,[1155] the place of supply is in the

---

1148. *See* Article 58b (1) first subpara. of the VAT Implementing Regulation; this strict consequence is not applicable in the case that the intermediary fails to comply with the IOSS or the EU-OSS rules; *see* Article 58b (1) second subpara. of the VAT Implementing Regulation.

1149. *See* Article 58 (2) and (3) of the VAT Implementing Regulation; in the case that the exclusion is due to the change of the place of business or the place of fixed establishment, then the exclusion is effective from the day of that change; *see* Article 58 (2) and (3) (a) of the VAT Implementing Regulation.

1150. *See* Article 58 (3) (b) of the VAT Implementing Regulation.

1151. *See* Article 58 (4) of the VAT Implementing Regulation; if the taxable person is deregistered due to another reason, then the IOSS identification number can still be used to supply the goods invoiced before the exclusion of IOSS. The IOSS identification number will become invalid, at the latest, two months after exclusion from the IOSS.

1152. *See* Article 3 of the Directive (2017/2455) according to which Title IV of the Directive (2009/132) was deleted; *see*, for further information on the *de minimis* import exemption, s. 2.2.3.3.2 The *De Minimis* VAT Exemption for Imported Goods.

1153. *See* the study conducted by EY on behalf of the European Commission: European Commission, *Assessment of the Application and Impact of the VAT Exemption for Importation of Small Consignments*, Specific Contract No 7 TAXUD/2013/DE/334 Based on Framework Contract No Taxud/2012/CC/117, Final Report, *supra* note 2, at 70.

1154. *See* European Commission, *Interim Report on the Implications of Electronic Commerce for VAT and Customs*, XXI/98/0359, *supra* note 556, at 24 et seq.

1155. *See*, for further information on the import VAT exemption, s. 4.6.4.2 The Import VAT Exemption According to Article 143 (ca) of the VAT Directive when the IOSS Is Applied: A Highway to Fraud?.

Member State of destination.[1156] Thus, the supplier still has the obligation to declare and pay the VAT for the supply of goods declared on the IOSS.

Additionally, in customs law, further facilitation measures for imports of a value below EUR 150 were implemented. A super-reduced data set was introduced to facilitate the customs declaration in Article 143a of the UCC-DA. This customs declaration for low-value consignments is applicable to all imports when the consignment value is below EUR 150, irrespectively which customs procedure is used to declare the importation.[1157] Moreover, the introduction of the IOSS and of another simplification mechanism (when the platform does not apply the IOSS) have an influence on customs procedures and required amendments in the customs law.

The implications of the introduction of the IOSS on customs law and the additional special arrangement will be discussed in the following sections. To complete the picture, the general customs procedure for import supplies for when the platform became the deemed supplier will be shortly analysed.

4.12.2   The Application of the IOSS and Corresponding Customs Measures

The IOSS procedure has been discussed in previous sections from a VAT point of view, including the formal requirements and the procedural aspects.[1158] However, the application of the IOSS also has an influence on the customs procedure.

The IOSS identification number of the platform must be included in the import declaration as this is one requirement for the import VAT exemption according to Article 143 (ca) of the VAT Directive to apply.[1159] The customs authorities check the validity of the IOSS identification number, and, when the IOSS identification number proves to be valid, then the consignment is exempt from import VAT.[1160] In order to prevent the misuse of the IOSS identification number, Member States generate monthly reports of all imports for which the IOSS identification number has been used.[1161] The Member State of identification[1162] reconciles the value of the imports with the

---

1156. See s. 4.3.4.1.1.2.3 The Place of Supply when the Platform Applies the IOSS.
1157. See Article 143a of the UCC-DA; for further detailed information on the reduced data set, see also European Commission, *Importation and Exportation of Low Value Consignments – VAT E-Commerce Package 'Guidance for Member States and Trade'*, supra note 717, at 24 et seqq.
1158. See s. 4.11 Special Schemes of the OSS.
1159. See, for further information on the import VAT exemption, s. 4.6.4.2 The Import VAT Exemption According to Article 143 (ca) of the VAT Directive when the IOSS Is Applied: A Highway to Fraud?.
1160. See, for further information on this exemption, s. 4.6.3 Applicable Rates and Exemptions for the Supply of Goods by the Platform.
1161. See European Commission, *Importation and Exportation of Low Value Consignments*, supra note 717, at 9; with reference to Article 55 and Annex 21-01, 21-02 and 21-03 of the Commission Implementing Regulation (EU) 2015/2447 of 24 November 2015 Laying down Detailed Rules for Implementing Certain Provisions of Regulation (EU) No 952/2013 of the European Parliament and of the Council Laying down the Union Customs Code, OJ L 343 (2015).
1162. See, for explanations on the definition of the Member State of identification, s. 4.11.3.2 The Member State of Identification.

transactions reported in the IOSS return.[1163] From this reconciliation, divergences may arise if, e.g., underlying suppliers used the IOSS identification number of the platform also for direct supplies to their customers in order to be able to use the exemption of import VAT.[1164]

Furthermore, customs authorities have to ensure the correct taxation of distance sales of goods imported from third territories or third countries when applying the IOSS. Thus, the customs authorities provide validation checks in order to review whether the amount indicated on the import documentation is correct and reflects the price the customer paid for the consignment.[1165] Generally, the customs authorities could do such checks by comparing the amount indicated on the import documentation as well as the amount indicated on the invoice accompanying the import documents. If no such invoice was enclosed or the customs authorities doubt that the accompanying information and invoice was incorrect, further enquiries to the platform would be necessary for the customs authority to validate the amount indicated on the import document, e.g., proof of payment by the customer.

Divergences between the amount declared in the import documentation and the amount actually paid by the customer are, from a customs point of view, uncritical as long as the amount is still below the EUR 150 threshold since, in this case, the import VAT exemption according to Article 143 (ca) of the VAT Directive still applies. Nevertheless, undervaluation would lead to the conclusion that the IOSS was not applicable, and the import VAT would not have been exempt.

Undervaluation means that, on the import declaration, an amount below EUR 150 was indicated whereas the actual supply of the good exceeded EUR 150. The reason for the undervaluation of consignments in the platform economy is mainly the fraudulent behaviour of the underlying supplier: The underlying supplier may, e.g., deliver multiple goods in one consignment. In this case, the total value of the consignment should be taken as a reference point.[1166] Similarly, the underlying supplier could also generally indicate a lower amount in the import declaration than the amount that the underlying supplier charged to the customer. Both situations could evolve if the underlying supplier organised the transport and did not inform the platform about the correct circumstances, i.e., that several orders were delivered in one consignment or that the actual price of the goods exceeded EUR 150.[1167] In both cases, the underlying supplier could undervalue the goods so that no import VAT and

---

1163. *See* European Commission, *Importation and Exportation of Low Value Consignments*, *supra* note 717, at 9.
1164. Marie Lamensch, *Rendering Platforms Liable to Collect and Pay VAT on B2C Imports: A Silver Bullet?*, 29 International VAT Monitor, *supra* note 18, at 48 et seq.; Madeleine Merkx, *The Wizard of OSS: Effective Collection of VAT in Cross-Border E-Commerce* 53 (Stichting NLFiscaal 2020). *See* also the discussion on the impact of such a misuse of the IOSS identification number in s. 4.6.3 Applicable Rates and Exemptions for the Supply of Goods by the Platform.
1165. *See* Article 140 of the UCC-IA.
1166. *See* European Commission, *Explanatory Notes on the New VAT E-Commerce Rules*, *supra* note 35, at 71 et seqq. *See* also, on the discussion of the definition of 'consignment', s. 3.3.1.2.2 The Interpretation of 'Consignments'.
1167. *See*, on the importance of good communication between the person organising the transport (underlying supplier or platform) and the other involved party, s. 3.3.1.2.2 The Interpretation of 'Consignments'.

customs duties become due in the case that the customs authorities do not notice this undervaluation. This undervaluation would likely make the products sold by the underlying supplier more competitive compared to the sale of other suppliers since the VAT declared by the platform via the IOSS would be based on a lower amount than the VAT that should have actually been declared. Generally, the platform does not become the deemed supplier according to Article 14a (1) of the VAT Directive in this case since the consignment's value would exceed EUR 150, and thus Article 14a (1) of the VAT Directive would not be triggered.[1168] Nevertheless, if the platform did not know the actual value of the consignment, then the platform could believe that it became the deemed supplier. Thus, an additional benefit for the underlying supplier would be that the underlying supplier would not declare and pay the VAT as the platform would assume that it became the deemed supplier according to Article 14a (1) of the VAT Directive and would pay the VAT due (assumingly based on the undervalued amount).

Theoretically, also the platform could undervalue the imported goods. Nevertheless, in practice, an undervaluation is unlikely when the platform organises the transport. The platform only becomes the deemed supplier when the intrinsic value of the consignment of EUR 150 is not exceeded. Thus, the platform would not have any benefit from undervaluing the supply of goods of an intrinsic value of more than EUR 150 since the platform would not even become liable for the VAT in this case.

If the checks by the customs authority showed that a supply was undervalued and that the intrinsic value exceeded EUR 150, the customs authorities of the country of importation would collect the import VAT and customs duty although the importation was originally declared via the IOSS.[1169] Therefore, the standard import procedure would be applied.[1170] If the customer accepted the delivery of the goods and paid the additional import VAT charged by the customs authority, the customer should request the already paid VAT from the platform as the charging of the VAT by the (deemed) supplier was incorrect.[1171] The platform should correct the IOSS declaration in the case that the supply has already been declared in the IOSS declaration or should not declare this undervalued supply in its IOSS declaration if the IOSS declaration had not yet been filed since the IOSS is not applicable to supplies of more than EUR 150.

1168. *See* s. 3.3.1.2 The Consignment's Intrinsic Value.
1169. *See* European Commission, *Explanatory Notes: VAT E-Commerce Rules*, *supra* note 35, at 69; European Commission, *Importation and Exportation of Low Value Consignments – VAT E-Commerce Package 'Guidance for Member States and Trade'*, *supra* note 717, at 44.
1170. *See*, for further information on the standard import procedure, s. 4.12.4 The Standard Import Procedure.
1171. *See* European Commission, *Explanatory Notes: VAT E-Commerce Rules*, *supra* note 35, at 69; European Commission, *Importation and Exportation of Low Value Consignments*, *supra* note 717, at 44. Similarly, the customer should also be able to request the full payment (the consideration for the supply and paid VAT) if the customer rejects the acceptance of the goods.

4.12.3   The Simplification Mechanism of Importations for Non-IOSS Suppliers

In the case that a platform decides to not apply the IOSS,[1172] the VAT Directive provides an additional simplification mechanism in Articles 369y-zb of the VAT Directive. This alternative simplified procedure was introduced to facilitate the collection of import VAT by a deferred payment mechanism.

The substantive scope of application of this secondary simplification mechanism is the same as for the application of IOSS: it is applicable to the importation of goods in consignments of an intrinsic value not exceeding EUR 150.[1173] This special arrangement is limited to imports, where the goods are imported to the Member State where the dispatch or transport ends.[1174]

Since, in this case, the platform does not collect the VAT due but the customer is responsible for the payment of the import VAT according to Article 369z (1) (a) of the VAT Directive, the mechanism provided for in Articles 369y-zb of the VAT Directive facilitates the import VAT collection from the customer. Thereby, 'the person presenting the goods to customs on behalf of the person for whom the goods are destined' can use the special arrangements to declare and pay the import VAT due according to Article 369y of the VAT Directive. Article 63d second subparagraph of the VAT Implementing Regulation further stipulates that the condition of 'presenting the goods to customs on behalf of the person for whom the goods are destined'[1175] is fulfilled if the 'person presenting the goods to customs declares his intention to make use of the special arrangement and to collect the VAT from the person for whom the goods are destined'. In practice, the persons presenting the goods to the customs authority on behalf of the customers are postal operators, express carriers, or customs agents.[1176] Thereby, Article 369y states that the Member State of importation 'shall permit' the application of this special arrangement which means that the person presenting the goods to the customs authority on behalf of the customers is not obligated to use this special arrangement.

If the person presenting the goods to the customs authorities wanted to apply this special arrangement, then the person should 'collect the VAT from the person for whom the goods are destined and effect the payment of such VAT' according to Article 369z (1) (b) of the VAT Directive. Thus, the person presenting the goods to the customs authorities collects the VAT from the customer and makes the VAT payment to the competent authorities.

1172. *See* Article 369y of the VAT Directive.
1173. *See* Article 369y of the VAT Directive; goods subject to excise duties are explicitly excluded from the application of this special scheme except for perfume and toilet water; *see* Article 24 of the Council Regulation (EC) No 1186/2009 of 16 November 2009 Setting up a Community System of Reliefs from Customs Duty, OJ L 324 (2009).
1174. *See* Article 369y of the VAT Directive; *see* also Article 221 (4) of the UCC-IR.
1175. *See* Article 369y of the VAT Directive.
1176. *See* European Commission, *Explanatory Notes: VAT E-Commerce Rules, supra* note 35, at 79; European Commission, *Importation and Exportation of Low Value Consignments, supra* note 717, at 51.

With this facilitation for the customer, obligations for the persons presenting the goods to the customs authority on behalf of the customers arise. That person must: (i) declare the collected VAT electronically, (ii) pay the VAT to the authorities, and (iii) keep records of the transactions according to Article 369zb of the VAT Directive. Thus, to fulfil the (i) requirement, a separate monthly declaration must be filed electronically in addition to the general VAT and potential OSS declarations of the person presenting the goods to the customs authority on behalf of the customer.[1177] Additionally, it should be noted that only the 'VAT collected under this special arrangement' must be reported according to Article 369zb (1) of the VAT Directive. Thereby, the EU legislator has implemented a safety mechanism for the persons presenting the goods to the customs authority on behalf of the customers in the case that the customers do not accept the goods and thus do not pay the VAT due. Implicitly, this also highlights that the customer does not have an obligation to accept the goods. In the case of non-acceptance of the consignment by the customer, the person presenting the goods to customs does not become liable to pay the import VAT.[1178] With this specification, the burden of refund procedures of the persons presenting the goods to the customs authority on behalf of the customers can be limited when the customer is not accepting the consignment.[1179]

According to the (ii) requirement, the persons presenting the goods to the customs authority on behalf of the customers must pay the VAT to the authorities. The VAT payment becomes due on a monthly basis according to Article 369zb (2) of the VAT Directive. The moment of payment is stipulated in the national law of the Member State of destination and follows the due date of the import duty.[1180]

The (iii) requirement stipulates a record-keeping obligation of the persons presenting the goods to the customs authority on behalf of the customers. The records must be kept for the time stipulated in the national law of the Member States according to Article 369zb (3) of the VAT Directive and must be made available electronically to the authorities upon request. Finally, the records should be so detailed that the authorities can verify that the VAT declared is correct.[1181]

Additionally, to this framework that the Member States have to implement, Member States may implement a further facilitation for the persons collecting the import VAT: Member States may stipulate in their national law that the standard VAT rate is exclusively applicable when this special arrangement is used for the import VAT collection.[1182] The reason for this optional facilitation is probably the difficulty for the person presenting the consignment at customs to know the correct VAT rate.[1183]

1177. *See* Article 369zb (1) of the VAT Directive.
1178. *See* Article 369zb (1) of the VAT Directive; *see*, similarly, European Commission, *Explanatory Notes: VAT E-Commerce Rules, supra* note 35, at 80.
1179. *See* European Commission, *Importation and Exportation of Low Value Consignments, supra* note 717, at 51.
1180. *See* Article 369zb (2) of the VAT Directive.
1181. *See* Article 369zb (3) of the VAT Directive.
1182. *See* Article 369za of the VAT Directive.
1183. *See* European Commission, *Explanatory Notes: VAT E-Commerce Rules, supra* note 35, at 80; European Commission, *Importation and Exportation of Low Value Consignments, supra* note 717, at 51.

However, this option may be questioned by the principle of equality: In Member States that implemented the standard rate for all imports under this special arrangement, the VAT collection mechanism decides which VAT rate is applicable. When the standard import procedure is used for the import, then the reduced import VAT rate may be applicable. If the special arrangement was used, then the standard import VAT rate would be applicable. Nevertheless, the customer would, in both cases, receive the same good. As this different application of the standard and reduced rate for the same goods raise issues with the principle of equality,[1184] the customer should be able to opt for the standard import procedure to avail himself of the reduced rate.[1185] This option is not explicitly stipulated in the VAT Directive but, since the exclusive application of the standard VAT rate is optional,[1186] the special arrangement should not be applied when the customer wishes to use the standard import procedure. In this case, the customer would have to decline the delivery based on the special arrangement by communicating this declination to the person presenting the goods to the customs authority on behalf of the customer. The import declaration would have to be amended, and the standard VAT collection mechanism would be applied.[1187] In practice, it could be questioned whether the customers even know which rate is applicable to the good purchased. Furthermore, even if customers were aware of the applicable VAT rates, many customers likely would not know that there is the option to also apply the standard import procedure. This results in the option rather being theoretically applicable than being used by the customers.

4.12.4 The Standard Import Procedure

The general customs procedure for import supplies when the platform became the deemed supplier is applicable in the case that the platform does not apply the IOSS and, also, the special arrangement is not applicable, e.g., if the customer declined the acceptance of the goods based on the special arrangements or if the postal carrier in question did not offer the delivery based on the special arrangements. As no amendments were implemented with the introduction of the e-commerce package, this procedure will only be shortly described.

For the application of the standard import procedure, the goods must be imported to the country of destination, i.e., the country from where the customer ordered the goods.[1188] In general, the import VAT collection is within the responsibility of the national customs authorities and, therefore, other customs authorities may not apply

---

1184. *See*, for further detailed information on the principle of equality, s. 5.2.3 The Principle of Equality in Article 20 of the CFR.
1185. *See* preamble 15 of the Council Directive (EU) 2017/2455 of 5 December 2017 Amending Directive 2006/112/EC and Directive 2009/132/EC as Regards Certain Value Added Tax Obligations for Supplies of Services and Distance Sales of Goods, OJ L 348/7 (2017); European Commission, *Explanatory Notes: VAT E-Commerce Rules*, *supra* note 35, at 80.
1186. *See* Article 369y of the VAT Directive where it is stipulated that 'the Member State of importation shall permit ...'.
1187. European Commission, *Explanatory Notes: VAT E-Commerce Rules*, *supra* note 35, at 80.
1188. *See* Article 221 (4) of the UCC-IR.

the VAT rate of other Member States and collect the import VAT for goods that are further delivered to another Member State.[1189] The import VAT must be paid by the person determined in the national law of importation in accordance with Article 201 of the VAT Directive;[1190] many Member States define the customer or consignee as liable to pay the import VAT.[1191]

4.13 OVERVIEW OF THE LEGAL CONSEQUENCES OF ARTICLE 14A OF THE VAT DIRECTIVE

The previous sections have shown that different legal consequences can be applicable for the deemed transactions of Article 14a of the VAT Directive. A first distinction in the legal consequences is due to the different scope of paragraphs (1) and (2) of Article 14a of the VAT Directive. Additionally, the different scope also triggers different taxable transactions to become applicable, i.e., the importation and/or the supply of the good. Thus, the legal consequences also depend on which taxable transaction is evaluated. Finally, the EU legislator has introduced several facilitations when the IOSS or the EU-OSS is applied. Thus, the choice by the platform to apply the IOSS or EU-OSS can also alter the legal consequences. Table 4.2 is a summary of the legal consequences of Article 14a of the VAT Directive which tries to display the differences and alternations of the legal consequences.

1189. European Commission, *Importation and Exportation of Low Value Consignments – VAT E-Commerce Package 'Guidance for Member States and Trade'*, *supra* note 717, at 54.
1190. *Ibid.* at 55.
1191. European Commission, *Explanatory Notes: VAT E-Commerce Rules*, *supra* note 35, at 97.

Table 4.2   Simplified Overview of the Legal Consequences of Article 14a of the VAT Directive

Place of Supply	Article 14a (1)				Article 14a (2)	
	Import		Supply		Underlying Supplier to Platform	Platform to Customer
	IOSS	Non-IOSS	IOSS	Non-IOSS		
	Article 60: place of importation (but exempt)	Article 60: place of importation if the goods are imported in country of destination → EU Member State of destination Article 61: place where the external transit arrangement ceases if goods are imported in another Member State EU Member State of destination	Article 31: place of origin → third country Article 33 (c): place of destination → EU Member State of destination	Article 32 first subpara: place of origin → third country Article 32 second subpara: place of final destination EU Member State of destination	Article 31: place of origin → EU Member State of origin	Article 31: Immovable property → place of property Article 32 first subpara: supply by Micro Platforms, supply of second-hand goods, works of art, collectors' items or antiques and the supply of second-hand means of transport → EU Member State of origin Article 33 (a): intra-Community distance sales of goods → EU Member State of destination Article 36: assembled goods place of instalment/assembly of the goods Article 39: supply of gas, electricity and heat or cooling energy → place of consumption or (secondary) place of residence

237

	Article 14a (1)				Article 14a (2)	
	Import		**Supply**			
	IOSS	**Non-IOSS**	**IOSS**	**Non-IOSS**		
Chargeable Event	Article 70: when goods are imported	Article 70: when goods are imported — Article 71: when the goods are ceased to leave the external transit arrangement	*	Article 66a: when the payment was accepted	**Underlying Supplier to Platform** — Article 66a: when the payment was accepted	**Platform to Customer** — Article 66a: when the payment was accepted
Taxable Amount	Articles 85 + 86: consideration incl. charges and incidental costs (commission)		*	Articles 73 + 78: consideration incl. charges and incidental costs (incl. platform margin)	**Underlying Supplier to Platform** — Article 73 + 78: consideration incl. charges and incidental costs (excl. platform margin)	**Platform to Customer** — Articles 73 + 78: consideration incl. charges and incidental costs (incl. platform margin)
Rates & Exemptions	Article 143 (ca): exempt	Article 369za: standard VAT rate if imported under simplified import mechanism or otherwise depending on imported good: standard/reduced rate or exempt	*	Article 282: SME exemption or otherwise depending on supplied good: standard/reduced rate or exempt	**Underlying Supplier to Platform** — Article 136a: exempt or exempt based on other exemption (e.g., Article 132 or 135)	**Platform to Customer** — depending on supplied good: standard/reduced rate or exempt

	Article 14a (1)				Article 14a (2)	
Invoicing Obligation	**Import**		**Supply**		**Underlying Supplier**	**Platform**
	IOSS	**Non-IOSS**	**IOSS**	**Non-IOSS**	Article 219a (1): obligation to issue invoice; criteria follow Member State of origin	
		**	*			EU-OSS: invoicing obligation follows the law of the Member State of identification
			Supply to taxable person: invoicing obligation according to Article 220 (1); criteria follow the law of the Member State of identification	Supply to taxable person: invoicing obligation according to Article 220 (1); criteria follow the law of the Member State where the supply takes place		Intra-Community distance sales of goods but non-application of EU-OSS: invoicing obligation according to Article 220 (1) (2)
			Supply to non-taxable person: invoicing obligation follows the law of the Member State of identification	Supply to non-taxable person: invoicing obligation follows the law of the Member State where the supply takes place		National supply of goods but non-application of EU-OSS: invoicing obligation follows the law of the Member State where the supply takes place

239

	Article 14a (1)				Article 14a (2)	
Record-Keeping Obligations	**Import**		**Supply**		**Underlying Supplier**	**Platform**
	IOSS	**Non-IOSS**	**IOSS**	**Non-IOSS**		
		**	Article 242: general record-keeping obligation			
			Article 369x: detailed record-keeping obligation	Article 242: general record-keeping obligation		EU-OSS: detailed record-keeping obligation (Article 369k)
						Non-application of EU-OSS: Article 242: general record-keeping obligation

*not necessary, since place of supply in third country; ** not required

240

4.14   THE RETURN OF GOODS AND WARRANTY CASES

4.14.1   General Remarks

As in any business sector, some delivered goods may have a defect also in e-commerce. In such cases, the customers may claim a warranty for the defected goods. Generally, the supplier has several possibilities on how to rectify the defect. The supplier could repair the good, the supplier could exchange the good, the supplier could offer the customer a subsequent discount, could gift the good to the customer, or the contract could be reversed, i.e., the good is returned to the supplier, and the customer receives the money paid for the good. Additionally, consumers have the right to return the ordered goods within 14 days in e-commerce.[1192] Within these 14 days, consumers do not have to indicate any reason for returning the goods. In e-commerce, approximately 30% of the goods purchased are returned.[1193]

The following sections will discuss the VAT implications for warranty cases and the return of goods. Although the platform is becoming part of the VAT chain and is the deemed supplier for the supply of the goods, many warranty cases mainly have an impact on the VAT obligations of the underlying supplier being the actual supplier of the goods. The fiction of Article 14a of the VAT Directive should not be extended to other transactions that are not covered by Article 14a of the VAT Directive. In fact, the discussion of the platform's legal rights and obligations can be limited to cases for which the good is returned, when a subsequent discount is offered, or when the good is gifted to the customer since, only in these cases would the original taxable transaction, the supply of the good for which the platform became the deemed supplier, be affected, and the platform would have the right to amend the taxable amount. In the case of the exchange of the good and the repair of the good, the original taxable transactions of the supply of the good are not amended, and thus no legal consequences arise for the platform.

The legal obligations, rights, and consequences resulting from warranty cases; the gifting of goods, returns, and subsequent discounts for underlying suppliers; and the platform will be discussed in the following sections.

1192. *See* Article 9 of Directive 2011/83/EU of the European Parliament and of the Council of 25 October 2011 on Consumer Rights, Amending Council Directive 93/13/Eec and Directive 1999/44/EC of the European Parliament and of the Council and Repealing Council Directive 85/577/EEC and Directive 97/7/EC of the European Parliament and of the Council Text with EEA Relevance, OJ L 304/64 (2011).

1193. *See*, e.g., Marie Lamensch, *Rendering Platforms Liable to Collect and Pay VAT on B2C Imports: A Silver Bullet?*, 29 International VAT Monitor, *supra* note 18, at 48; Lionel Valdellon, *Must-Know Ecommerce Return Rate Statistics and Trends in 2021*, https://clevertap.com/blog /ecommerce-return-rate-statistics/ (last visited 1 Oct. 2021); other sources estimate the returns between 15-40% for online purchases; *see* Courtney Reagan, *That Sweater You Don't Like Is a Trillion-Dollar Problem for Retailers. These Companies Want to Fix It*, https://www .cnbc.com/2019/01/10/growing-online-sales-means-more-returns-and-trash-for-landfills.html (last visited 1 Oct. 2021); additionally, the return rate may also depend on the country; *see* Fran Whittaker-Wood, *What Country Has the Highest Online Shopping Return Rate?*, https:/ /www.paymentsjournal.com/highest-online-shopping-return-rate/ (last visited 1 Oct. 2021).

4.14.2   The Return of Goods and Subsequent Discounts

4.14.2.1   *General Remarks*

The third and fourth possibilities for the underlying supplier to fulfil the warranty obligation is to offer the customer a subsequent discount or to reverse the contract which would also be the case if the customer returned the goods out of free will, i.e., without the product having a defect. Both options have in common that the taxable amount can be reduced. Thereby, this reduction of the taxable amount not only has an impact on the underlying supplier but also on the platform. Additionally, in the case of the return of the good, the VAT implications caused by the transport of the good back to the underlying supplier should be discussed. The legal rights, obligations, and consequences for the underlying supplier will be discussed in the subsequent section, i.e., The Legal Rights, Obligations and Consequences for the Underlying Supplier for the Return of Goods and Subsequent Discounts.

4.14.2.2   *The Legal Rights, Obligations and Consequences for the Underlying Supplier for the Return of Goods and Subsequent Discounts*

4.14.2.2.1   *The Right to Amend the Taxable Amount for the Return of Goods or Subsequent Discounts by the Underlying Supplier*

Returns by customers and subsequent discounts to customers result in the reduction of the taxable amount. Article 90 of the VAT Directive is the fundamental provision for adjustments in the taxable amount. According to Article 90 (1) of the VAT Directive, '[i]n the case of cancellation, refusal or total or partial non-payment or where the price is reduced after the supply takes place, the taxable amount shall be reduced accordingly under conditions which shall be determined by the Member States'. The return of goods would qualify as a 'cancellation', and the subsequent discounts would qualify as reductions of the price after the supply has taken place in the sense of Article 90 (1) of the VAT Directive. Thus, the taxable amount can be reduced based on the details stipulated in the national law where the supply took place, i.e., the country of origin.[1194]

In the case of a return, the taxable amount is reduced to zero. In the case of a subsequent discount, the taxable amount is reduced by the subsequent discount. This amendment in the taxable amount should be declared in the VAT return of the underlying supplier in the month when the return or subsequent discount took place if the national law required a correction also for VAT exempt supplies such as the supply from the underlying supplier to the platform.[1195] If the delivery of the goods and the return thereof were in the same month, then the supply would not have to be declared

---

1194. *See* the analysis in s. 4.3.3 The Place of Supply Rule for the Supply by the Underlying Supplier.
1195. *See* s. 4.6.2.1 The Exemption of Article 136a of the VAT Directive.

in the VAT return. As the underlying supplier provides the supply without transport,[1196] the amendment must be declared in the Member State of origin. Thus, the amendment of the taxable amount pursuant to the VAT Directive only has an impact on the cases of Article 14a (2) of VAT Directive because the country of origin is not in the EU when Article 14a (1) of the VAT Directive is applied. Moreover, it should be noted that the VAT correction of the taxable amount influences the whole supply chain, i.e., the supply from the underlying supplier to the platform as well as the supply from the platform to the customer.[1197]

4.14.2.2.2   The Transportation of the Returned Goods Back to the Underlying Supplier

4.14.2.2.2.1   The Legal Consequences due to the Transport of the Goods Back to the Underlying Supplier to a Third Country

4.14.2.2.2.1.1 Customs Implications of the Export for the Return of the Goods

When the goods are transported to a third country to be returned, then the question arises of how these returns should be treated from a customs perspective. Thereby, customs law provides for a facilitation of the re-exportation of low-value goods, i.e., consignments with values of up to EUR 1,000 according to Article 140 (1) (d) of the UCC-DA.[1198]

According to this simplification, no export custom duties arise for consignments with values of up to EUR 1,000 when the requirements of Article 142 of the UCC-DA are fulfilled. Thereby, especially Article 142 (b) of the UCC-DA should be reviewed. In general, the simplifications of re-exportations from Articles 140 (1) (d) and 141 (4) and (4a) of the UCC-DA do not apply when an application for the repayment of duty or other charges is made.[1199] Generally, the import of the goods supplied within the application of Article 14a (1) of the VAT Directive was exempt from import duties according to Article 23 (1) of the Regulation (2009/1186), thus no duty or other charges became due for the importation of the goods. Therefore, also no application for repayment of duty and other charges can be filed. Therefore, the simplification of re-exportation should generally be applicable to the exportation of the goods as long as the value of the goods does not exceed EUR 10,000. The goods are deemed to be declared for export by their exit from the customs territory of the EU and no further formality must be fulfilled.[1200]

1196. *See* the qualification in s. 4.3.2.2 Legal Qualification of the Supply with Transport.
1197. For the amendment of the taxable amount by the platform, *see* s. 4.14.2.3 The Right to Amend the Taxable Amount for the Return of Goods or Subsequent Discounts by the Platform.
1198. *See* Articles 140 (1) (d), 141 (4), and 142 of the UCC-DA.
1199. *See* Article 142 (b) of the UCC-DA.
1200. *See* Article 141 (4) of the UCC-DA.

4.14.2.2.2.1.2 VAT Implications of the Export for the Return of the Goods

For the export from the EU into a third country, it should be analysed in a first step who is exporting the defect good in question and thus who has the (legal) power of disposal over the goods. If the customer sent the goods to a third country to return the good, it could be argued that the underlying supplier had the power to dispose of the goods. The underlying supplier would rectify the faulty delivery or fulfil its obligation to accept returns within a certain period of time stipulated in the law[1201] or agreed contractually between the underlying supplier and the customer, and thus the underlying supplier would likely carry the risk of loss or accidental damage of the goods during transport. Additionally, the underlying supplier would communicate the address to the customer where the goods should be returned to which can also be interpreted as the underlying supplier having the power to dispose of the goods. Thus, it can be argued that the underlying supplier receives the power to dispose of the goods in the Member State to which the goods were delivered to the customer. The exportation would, in this case, be VAT exempt according to Article 146 of the VAT Directive.

4.14.2.2.2.2 The Transport of the Goods Back to the Underlying Supplier to an EU Member State

4.14.2.2.2.2.1 The Legal Consequences for the Underlying Supplier due to the Transport of the Goods Back to the Underlying Supplier

When the goods are transported within the EU from one Member State to another, this transport from the customer to the underlying supplier must be reviewed in the case of the return of the good. As previously discussed, the underlying supplier receives the power of disposal over the returned goods in the country to which the goods were delivered.[1202] Thus, it should be investigated whether the transport of the goods back to the country of origin triggers an intra-Community transfer according to Article 17 (1) of the VAT Directive by the underlying supplier.[1203]

Thereby, it should be noted that, pursuant to Article 17 (2) (a) of the VAT Directive, no intra-Community transfer is fulfilled when it is a supply according to Article 33 of the VAT Directive which, among others, includes the intra-Community distance sales of goods.[1204] Thus, for the supply of the goods when the supply is an

---

1201. *See* Article 9 of Directive 2011/83/EU of the European Parliament and of the Council of 25 October 2011 on Consumer Rights, Amending Council Directive 93/13/Eec and Directive 1999/44/EC of the European Parliament and of the Council and Repealing Council Directive 85/577/EEC and Directive 97/7/EC of the European Parliament and of the Council Text with EEA Relevance, OJ L 304/64 (2011).

1202. *See* s. 4.14.2.2.2.1.2 VAT Implications of the Export.

1203. For the detailed description of the legal obligations due to the intra-Community transfer, *see* s. 4.14.4 The Repair of Goods.

1204. *See,* for further information on the place of supply of intra-Community distance sales of goods, s. 4.3.4.2.1.3.1 Intra-Community Distance Sales of Goods; Article 33 of the VAT Directive is stipulating two further places of supplies; *see* the detailed discussions in s. 4.3.4.1.1.2.2 The Importation of the Goods in a Different Member State than the Member State of where the Dispatch or Transport Ends as well as 4.3.4.1.1.2.3 The Place of Supply when the Platform Applies the IOSS.

intra-Community distance sales of goods, no additional intra-Community transfer is triggered.

Regarding the returns, the question arises of whether, by interpretation, the exception of Article 17 (2) (a) of the VAT Directive can also be applied to the return of the goods. From a systematic point of view, this should be affirmed. It would not be systematic if, for the supply of the good, Article 17 (2) (a) of the VAT Directive was triggered but, for the return of the good, Article 17 (2) (a) of the VAT Directive was not applied. Additionally, the application of Article 17 (2) (a) of the VAT Directive to returns can also find its support in the systematics of the VAT Directive. The obligation to register for the VAT due to the intra-Community transfer would generally arise for suppliers providing intra-Community distance sales of goods. With the e-commerce package, the facilitation of the EU-OSS has been introduced for declaring those intra-Community distance sales of goods.[1205] Thereby, the main aim of the introduction of the EU-OSS was to circumvent the VAT registration obligation of suppliers in the different Member States throughout the EU. If the return of the goods systematically triggered the obligation to register for the VAT in the Member State of destination, the aim of the EU-OSS would be undermined. Thus, by interpretation, the return of the good should not trigger an intra-Community transfer by the underlying supplier according to Article 17 (1) of the VAT Directive.

This result may differ in one case. One practical issue from the return of goods for underlying suppliers may arise when the goods are not transported back to the country from which they were delivered to the customer. This may be the case when the underlying supplier stores the goods in several warehouses in the EU. Often, the returns are delivered to one specific warehouse in order to perform the quality check there. Furthermore, the return to a third Member State may also be the case, especially when the platform is responsible for the processing of the returns and storage.[1206] If a good was returned and the platform is responsible for the return, then the platform's return centre may be in a different country than the warehouse from which the good was originally delivered. These cases raise the questions of whether and how the movement to the warehouse in a Member State other than the Member State from where the goods were originally delivered must be declared by the underlying supplier in its VAT return. The reduction of the taxable amount (fictitious) from the underlying supplier to the platform is, as discussed in the previous section, also possible in the case that the good is returned to another Member State.[1207]

1205. *See* the discussion of the facilitation of the EU-OSS in s. 4.11 Special Schemes of the OSS.

1206. Such a responsibility can be agreed between the underlying supplier and the platform; *see* the explanations on the different services offered by platforms in s. 2.1.2 The Role of Platforms.

1207. *See* s. 4.14.2.2.1 The Right to Amend the Taxable Amount for the Return of Goods or Subsequent Discounts by the Underlying Supplier.

Figure 4.3   Graphical Overview of the Return of Goods to a Different Member State

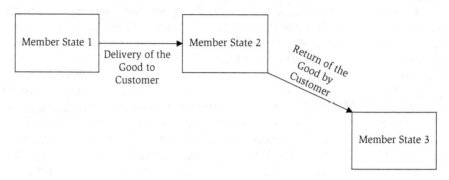

In this case, the return of the goods to a third Member State triggers an intra-Community transfer according to Article 17 (1) of the VAT Directive by the underlying supplier because the underlying supplier (or the platform acting on behalf of the underlying supplier) decides to transport the goods to another Member State.[1208] Due to the applicable exemption for the intra-Community supply[1209] and the input VAT deduction of the intra-Community acquisition,[1210] no VAT should become due for payment from this transaction. Nevertheless, VAT registration of the underlying supplier is necessary in the country of destination (Member State 2 of Figure 4.3) as well as in the country to where the goods are finally returned (Member State 3 of Figure 4.3). Thus, the return of the goods to a third Member State would trigger the VAT registration obligation in the country of destination (Member State 2 of Figure 4.3) as well as in the country to where the goods are finally returned (Member State 3 of Figure 4.3).

Especially big platforms have several return warehouses throughout the EU. When the platform is responsible for the return management, then a close communication between the platform and the underlying supplier is of utmost importance. Only based on this information flow will the underlying supplier know to which warehouse the returns are delivered. This issue of the lack of information of the underlying supplier generally does not arise when the underlying supplier is responsible for the returns and the logistics thereof because the underlying supplier would, in this instance, know which country the returned goods are delivered to and thus should be aware of the VAT obligations arising therefrom.

4.14.2.2.2.2.2 Practical Implications and Critical Discussion of the Intra-Community Transfer

As discussed in the previous section, the affirmation of the intra-Community transfer in the case that the return is sent to a third Member State results in the obligation by the

---

1208. For the detailed description of the legal obligations due to the intra-Community transfer, *see* s. 4.14.4 The Repair of Goods.
1209. *See* Article 138 (1) of the VAT Directive.
1210. *See* Article 168 (c) of the VAT Directive.

underlying supplier to register for the VAT in the Member State of destination and, when the goods are returned to a third Member State, also in that third Member State. This creates a high compliance burden for the underlying suppliers without any VAT payment to the competent tax authorities as the intra-Community supply would be exempt from the VAT in the country of dispatch according to Article 138 (1) of the VAT Directive, and the VAT due of the intra-Community acquisition can be deducted in the same VAT return as input VAT by the underlying supplier.[1211]

The affirmation of an intra-Community transfer when goods are returned results in an increase in the VAT compliance burden. This is not only an issue with B2C transactions but also with B2B transactions. The VAT Committee discussed specific warranty and return cases for B2B transactions already in 1994.[1212] In this meeting, the VAT Committee unanimously agreed that, when the goods are transported to a third Member State, the first refused supply can be disregarded 'if a short time has elapsed between the first dispatch and the supply to a new purchaser'.[1213] According to this statement by the VAT Committee, the original intra-Community supply does not have to be reported; i.e., the supplier should file for correction of the taxable amount if the corresponding return has already been filed. If the return took place in the same VAT period, then no indication in the VAT return of this supply must be made. The return transport of the goods to a third Member State does not trigger any VAT consequences from the Member State of the original delivery (Member State 2 of Figure 4.3) to the third Member State (Member State 3 of Figure 4.3) which also implies that the supplier does not have to register in the country of destination of the original delivery for the intra-Community transfer (Member State 2 of Figure 4.3).[1214] If the goods were transported to a new customer in a third Member State, the supplier would declare an intra-Community supply from the Member State of origin (Member State 1 of Figure 4.3) to the third Member State (Member State 3 of Figure 4.3).[1215]

These facilitations could also be applied to the returns for the previously discussed B2C supplies as the systematics of the VAT system for B2B and B2C supplies are similar. In this case, the only practical difference would be that the underlying supplier would not have to declare an intra-Community supply to the third Member State (Member State 3 of Figure 4.3), but an intra-Community transfer since the customer would be returning the goods to a warehouse instead of forwarding the goods to a different customer of the underlying supplier.[1216]

Although this suggested facilitation by the VAT Committee is practical and eliminates the VAT registration obligation by the underlying supplier in the Member

---

1211. *See* Article 168 (c) of the VAT Directive.
1212. VAT Committee, *Guidelines Resulting from Meetings of the VAT Committee: Tax Arrangements for Defective Goods*, Guidelines Resulting from the 41st Meeting, XXI/711/94 (28 Feb.–1 Mar. 1994), https://ec.europa.eu/taxation_customs/system/files/2021-03/guidelines-vat-committee-meetings_en.pdf (last visited 29 Jul. 2021).
1213. *Ibid.*
1214. *See* also Ben Terra & Julie Kajus, *Commentary – A Guide to the Recast VAT Directive, supra* note 290, s. 4.6.2.1.
1215. *See* also *ibid.*
1216. In practice, the goods are not directly forwarded to new customers but returned to warehouses and, from there, supplied to a new customer.

State of destination (Member State 2 of Figure 4.3), it is incompatible with the provisions of the VAT Directive.[1217] With the e-commerce package, the EU legislator would have had the chance to implement facilitation for suppliers concerning the return of goods to third Member States. However, the introduction of such facilitation was neglected or overseen by the EU legislator.

4.14.2.3 The Right to Amend the Taxable Amount for the Return of Goods or Subsequent Discounts by the Platform

Returns by customers and subsequent discounts to customers result in the reduction of the taxable amount according to Article 90 (1) of the VAT Directive. The amendment in the taxable amount must be declared in the VAT return of the platform in the month when the return or subsequent discount took place and thus also reduces the taxable amount in that month. Based on the reduction of the taxable amount in the corresponding month, the VAT due would also be reduced. In which return the correction of the taxable amount must be declared depends on whether the platform is applying the IOSS and/or the EU-OSS. If the delivery of the goods and the return thereof were in the same month and the supply was declared on the IOSS or the EU-OSS, then the supply would generally not have to be declared in the IOSS/EU-OSS VAT return.[1218] If the IOSS and/or the EU-OSS was not applied, the correction would follow the law of the Member State of destination where the supply had originally been declared. The reduction of the taxable amount also has a reduction of VAT as a consequence.[1219]

If the platform applied the IOSS and/or the EU-OSS and the return or subsequent discount took place in a later period, the changes in the taxable amount could be reported via the IOSS or the EU-OSS within three years after submission of the original declaration.[1220] Corrections must be included in the current IOSS/EU-OSS return and reference must be made to the tax period for the Member State of destination and to the tax amount to which the changes relate.[1221] When the correction concerns a time frame after the three-year period, the VAT Directive or VAT Implementing Regulations do not

---

1217. See similarly Michael Tumpel, *Mehrwertsteuer im innergemeinschaftlichen Warenverkehr: Analyse der Besteuerung des Warenverkehrs im Binnenmarkt nach dem Gemeinschaftsrecht und dem österreichischen Umsatzsteuerrecht* 527 + 529 (Linde Verlag 1997).

1218. Although the term 'amendment' used in Article 369g (4) of the VAT Directive (EU-OSS) and Article 369t (2) of the VAT Directive (IOSS) is not defined in the VAT Directive, it should have the same meaning as the term 'correction'; *see* the convincing argumentation from the VAT Committee, *Scope of the One-Stop-Shop (OSS) with Regard to Intra-Community Distance Sales of Goods, Relevant VAT Return Period and Amendments of Previous Vat Returns,* Working Paper No. 1040, taxud.c.1(2022)1785494, 6 et seqq. (03.03.2022), https://circabc.europa.eu /ui/group/cb1eaff7-eedd-413d-ab88-94f761f9773b/library/c249d43c-df2-4dee-9f66-649c7b 28adec/details (last visited 23 Apr. 2022).

1219. *See,* similarly, Case C-330/95, *Goldsmiths v Commissioners of Customs & Excise,* 3 Jul. 1997, ECLI:EU:C:1997:339, para. 16; Case C-588/10, *Minister Finansów v Kraft Foods Polska SA,* 26 Jan. 2012, ECLI:EU:C:2012:40, para. 27.

1220. *See* Article 369g (4) of the VAT Directive (EU-OSS) and Article 369t (2) of the VAT Directive (IOSS); *see also* Article 61 of the VAT Implementing Regulation.

1221. *See* Article 369g (4) of the VAT Directive (EU-OSS) and Article 369t (2) of the VAT Directive (IOSS); *see also* Article 61 of the VAT Implementing Regulation.

provide any further guidance on how to report such amendments. A possible correction is governed by the national law of the country of destination.[1222] The national law should provide further information on whether and how long corrections of the taxable amount can be declared and how these amendments have to be declared. Thus, after the expiry of the three-year period, the correction likely has to be made via the assessment procedure by declaration in the national VAT return.[1223] To file a national VAT return, a VAT registration by the platform in the country of destination is necessary.

4.14.2.4 Practical Difficulties of Repayments due to Returns and Subsequent Discounts

Returns and subsequent discounts highlight the problem of the discrepancy between the contractual agreement of the supply of the goods (between the underlying supplier and the customer) and the fictitious integration of the platform for the VAT qualification. If goods were returned or a discount is subsequently granted (e.g., due to a defect on the good), the corrected VAT would have to be refunded to the consumer.[1224]

In these cases, it could be problematic that, depending on the business model, the platform is not necessarily involved in the reversal and rebate discussion between the underlying supplier and the customer. Therefore, the platform may not have the necessary information on the reversal of the transaction or for the reduction of the taxable amount. Furthermore, there are two possibilities for the practical processing of the repayment of the full price and the discount: the electronic interface could be responsible for the entire reversal of the transaction and discounts. Thus, the platform would receive the necessary information and refund the (pro rata) purchase price including the VAT (and then forward the proportion of the price for the good to the seller). The other option would be for the consumer to receive two payments: the VAT from the electronic interface and the (pro rata) price for the goods from the underlying supplier. This practical difficulty shows that the smooth implementation of Article 14a of the VAT Directive will, in many cases, require new contractual agreements between the platform and the underlying supplier and might even involve an adaptation of the business model of the platforms.

1222. *See* European Commission, *Guide to the VAT One Stop Shop, supra* note 35, at 40.
1223. *See*, similarly, Christina Pollak, *Die OSS Im Überblick – Umsatzsteuerliche Vereinfachung Oder Undurchsichtige Verkomplizierung?*, 2 AVR 163 (2021).
1224. This section is based on a German publication by the author; *see* Christina Pollak & Karoline Spies, *Die umsatzsteuerlichen Änderungen bei Warenverkäufen über Plattformen: Online-Plattformen als Steuerschuldner*, ecolex, *supra* note 18, at 702 et seq.

4.14.2.5   Interim Conclusion on the Return of Goods and Subsequent Discounts

The return of goods and the offering of subsequent discounts influence the underlying supplier's as well as the platform's legal rights and obligations. Thereby, the underlying supplier as well as the platform can reduce the taxable amount of the VAT or IOSS/EU-OSS return according to Article 90 (1) of the VAT Directive.

Furthermore, the transportation of the goods from the customer to the underlying supplier should be reviewed in the case that the goods are returned. For this transaction, several different possibilities have been discussed in the preceding sections: (i) the return of the goods to a third country, (ii) the return of the goods to the Member State from where the goods were delivered, and (iii) the return of the goods to a different Member State than from where the goods were delivered.

In the (i) case of the transport to a third country, the facilitated re-exportation of low-value goods is possible, and no further customs formalities must be fulfilled by the underlying supplier. If (ii) the goods were returned within the EU, the systematic interpretation has shown that no intra-Community transfer according to Article 17 (1) of the VAT Directive should be triggered for the underlying supplier. The final case, i.e., the return of the goods to a different Member State than from where the goods were delivered, raises difficulties in practice. In this situation, the underlying supplier would have to declare an intra-Community transfer according to Article 17 (1) of the VAT Directive from the Member State which the goods were delivered to the customer to the Member State, which the goods are returned to. This means that the underlying supplier would have to be VAT registered in the country of (original) destination as well as in the country where the goods are finally returned.

4.14.3   The Gifting of the Goods to the Customer

In e-commerce, the underlying supplier might decide to gift the good to the customer if the customer wished to return the good. In this instance, the supplied good remains with the customer but, at the same time, the customer gets back the money for the supply. The background for this choice by the underlying supplier may be that the cost-benefit analysis shows that the return of the good would cause higher costs than giving the good for free to the customer.

From a VAT perspective, the taxable amount declared by the underlying supplier as well as by the platform may be corrected to zero although the customer can keep the good as the customer receives a reimbursement of the payment made. Thus, the correction of the taxable amount discussed in the previous section would also be applicable in this case.[1225] Additionally, it must be reviewed whether the gifting of the goods causes any taxable transaction pursuant to the VAT Directive.

1225. *See,* for the correction possibility by the underlying supplier, s. 4.14.2.2.1 The Right to Amend the Taxable Amount for the Return of Goods or Subsequent Discounts by the Underlying Supplier; *see* also, for the correction necessary by the platform, s. 4.14.2.3 The Right to Amend the Taxable Amount for the Return of Goods or Subsequent Discounts by the Platform.

According to Article 16 first subparagraph of the VAT Directive, the supply of goods by a taxable person forming part of the business assets for the disposal free of charge is equivalent to the supply of goods for consideration. This deemed supply rule only applies when the input VAT was wholly or partially deductible.[1226] Thus, when the underlying supplier decides to gift the good free of charge to the customer, it has to qualify as a supply of goods for consideration if the underlying supplier also declared the input VAT deduction for the supplied good.[1227]

However, the VAT Directive also provides two exceptions to this general rule: on the one hand, gifts of low value and, on the other hand, samples of goods.[1228] Especially the exception of the supply of goods of small value could be applied in the given case. Thereby, the value to be considered as adequately 'small' is different between the Member States. Some Member States do not have a monetary limitation for defining gifts of small value; some other countries have implemented a fixed amount in their national law of practice.[1229] In general, the Member States are free to decide applicable ceilings 'on the basis of their economic prosperity, average prices and average income levels. However, the threshold must not be so low as to make Article 5 (6) of the Sixth VAT Directive meaningless or inapplicable, or so high so as to deviate from what "small value" might be understood to mean in common language'.[1230] Thus, depending on the national law of the Member State of destination, the gift to the customer may qualify as a gift of small value, and, if so, no VAT will be due.

Alternatively, the second exception from the deemed supply of Article 16 second subparagraph of the VAT Directive could also be reviewed, i.e., the supply of samples. Thereby, the CJEU has held that the sample must have 'the essential qualities of the product which they represent'.[1231] In some cases, the sample may differ from the final form of the product, but, in some other cases, the final product is supplied as a sample that depends on the essential qualities of the product.[1232] In general, the value of the

---

1226. *See* Article 16 first subpara. of the VAT Directive.
1227. *See,* for further information on the input VAT deduction by the underlying supplier, s. 4.8.2 Input VAT Deduction by the Underlying Supplier.
1228. *See* Article 16 second subpara. of the VAT Directive.
1229. *See* Ben Terra & Julie Kajus, *Commentary – A Guide to the Recast VAT Directive, supra* note 290, s. 4.6.1; the European Commission provided an overview of the different provisions in the Member States based on an enquiry by a member of the European Parliament; for the enquiry, *see Written Question No 617/89 by Mr Fernand Herman (PPE) to the Commission of the European Communities*, 90/C 39/52 (27 Oct. 1989), https://eur-lex.europa.eu/legal-content/EN/TXT/PDF/?uri = OJ:C:1990:039:FULL&from = GA (last visited 29 Nov. 2021); and for the answer by the European Parliament *see Supplementary Answer given by Mrs Scrivener on Behalf of the Commission*, C 317 (7 Sep. 1992), https://eur-lex.europa.eu/legal-content/EN/TXT/PDF/?uri = OJ:JOC_1992_317_R_0001_01&qid = 1638271319631&from = DE (last visited 30 Nov. 2021); thereby, the specific limits for the Member States at that time are indicated.
1230. Case C-581/08, *EMI Group Ltd v The Commissioners for Her Majesty's Revenue and Customs*, 15 Apr. 2010, ECLI:EU:C:2010:194, Opinion of AG Jääskinen, para. 92; Article 5 (6) of the Sixth VAT Directive is the equivalent provision to Article 16 second subpara. of the VAT Directive.
1231. *See* Case C-581/08, *EMI Group Ltd v The Commissioners for Her Majesty's Revenue and Customs*, 30 Sep. 2010, ECLI:EU:C:2010:559, para. 28.
1232. *See ibid.*

supplied sample is not limited which is in contrast to the presents of small value. Thus, the gifting of the goods supplied to the customer could be considered as a sample.

Nevertheless, this subsumption is not quite convincing. Article 16 second subparagraph of the VAT Directive should be read narrowly because it is an exception to the general rule to tax deemed supplies according to Article 16 first subparagraph of the VAT Directive.[1233] Additionally, the purpose of giving samples is to convince potential buyers of the quality of the goods and to encourage the decision to purchase the good.[1234] In the given case, the customer already purchased the good and decided not to keep the good. Hence, the decision to purchase an (additional) good will likely not be influenced by the underlying supplier gifting the good to the customer, and, as the customer decided to send the goods back, the customer will likely also not further recommend the good to other people. Accordingly, the purpose of the exception from taxation for samples is not fulfilled in the case at hand, and, if the value of the goods exceeded the threshold of the value for gifts of small value, then Article 16 second subparagraph of the VAT Directive should not apply.

Concluding, underlying suppliers should, in a first step review, decide whether the good gifted to the customer exceeds the national threshold of the small value for gifts. If this national threshold was not exceeded, then the gifting of the good would not lead to a deemed supply. If the small value was exceeded, then the gifting of the good would be a deemed supply according to Article 16 first subparagraph of the VAT Directive. Thereby, the CJEU has confirmed that the reason why a taxable person gives out gifts is not relevant; also gifts that support the taxable person's taxable activity qualify as a deemed supply.[1235] Thus, if the national threshold of gifts of small value was exceeded, then the supply would be a national supply in the Member State of destination according to Article 31 of the VAT Directive as the goods would not be transported or dispatched.[1236] Therefore, the underlying supplier would have to register for VAT purposes in that Member State to pay the VAT due. The taxable amount to be declared would be the purchase price of the gifted good or of a similar good or the cost price in the case that the purchase price is not determinable according to Article 74 of the VAT Directive.

4.14.4 The Repair of Goods

4.14.4.1 *General Remarks*

Another possibility for the underlying supplier to remove a defect from a sold product would be to repair the goods. The repair of goods could trigger two possible taxable

---

1233. *See ibid.* paras. 19 et seq.
1234. *See,* similarly, also Case C-581/08, *EMI Group*, 15 Apr. 2010, ECLI:EU:C:2010:194, Opinion of AG Jääskinen, para. 30.
1235. *See* Case C-48/97, *Kuwait Petroleum (GB) Ltd v Commissioners of Customs & Excise*, 27 Apr. 1999, ECLI:EU:C:1999:203, para. 22.
1236. *See,* for the discussion of the place of supply according to Article 31 of the VAT Directive, s. 4.3.3 The Place of Supply Rule for the Supply by the Underlying Supplier as well as s. 4.3.4.2.1.1 The General Place of Supply Rule According to Article 31 of the VAT Directive.

transactions depending on the circumstances of the case: the act of repairing the goods and a possible transport of the goods to another country to enable this repair. The following sections will discuss these taxable transactions and the VAT treatment resulting from the repair of a defected good.

4.14.4.2 The Legal Consequence of the Repair of Goods

The first identifiable transaction is the repair of the good itself. This may qualify as a supply of service by the underlying supplier. Pursuant to Article 2 (1) (c) of the VAT Directive 'the supply of services for consideration ...' shall be subject to the VAT. In the cases of warranty, the underlying supplier repairs the goods free of charge; i.e., the customer would not pay for the repair of the goods. Thus, the repair of the goods would not qualify as a supply of service according to Article 2 (1) (c) of the VAT Directive because no consideration is paid by the customer.[1237]

4.14.4.3 The Legal Consequences of Transporting the Defect Goods from the Member State of Destination to Another Country

4.14.4.3.1 General Remarks

The second identifiable transaction that should be examined would arise if the goods were transported to another country (e.g., the country of origin) for the repair. In this instance, the goods are repaired in that other country and, after the repair, they would be transported back to the customer. In this case, it must be distinguished whether the country to where the goods are transported for the repair is an EU Member State or a third country. If the goods were transported to a third country, then the goods would have to be exported from the EU and reimported into the EU after the repair. The exportation as well as reimportation of the repaired good will be discussed in the subsequent section. Additionally, also the transport from the Member State of destination to another Member State for the repair of the defect goods and the subsequent transport of the repaired goods back to the Member State of destination will be analysed based on the VAT Directive in the subsequent sections.

4.14.4.3.2 Transportation of Defect Goods from the Member State of Destination to a Third Country

4.14.4.3.2.1 Export Implications of the Transportation of Defect Goods

When the goods are transported to a third country for the repair of the goods, then the question arises of how these returns should be treated from a customs perspective. As

---

1237. *See* Article 2 (1) (c) of the VAT Directive.

the exportation of low-value goods has already been discussed in a preceding section, reference can be made to that section.[1238]

4.14.4.3.2.2   Import Implications of the Transportation of Defect Goods

4.14.4.3.2.2.1 The General Import Exemption for Low-Value Consignments

In addition to the exportation, also the reimportation of the repaired goods must be reviewed. According to Article 23 (1) of the Regulation (2009/1186) 'any consignments made up of goods of negligible value dispatched direct from a third country to a consignee in the Community shall be admitted free of import duties'. Thereby, Article 23 (2) of the Regulation (2009/1186) defines 'goods of negligible value' as goods for which the intrinsic value 'does not exceed a total of EUR 150 per consignment'. Article 23 of the Regulation (2009/1186) is applicable to any goods except for alcoholic products, perfumes, toilet waters, tobacco, and tobacco products.[1239] Therefore, the reimportation of the repaired goods would not trigger the payment of import duties if the intrinsic value of the consignment was below EUR 150.

If the consignment's intrinsic value exceeded EUR 150, other possibilities of import release should be reviewed.[1240] In the course of supplies for which the platform became the deemed supplier, this may be the case when the goods were sold according to Article 14a (2) of the VAT Directive. In this case, the deemed supplier regime is not limited to the consignment's intrinsic value of EUR 150, and the goods could be transported to a third country for the repair.

4.14.4.3.2.2.2 The Special Procedure for Outward Processing

Customs law provides special customs procedures in Article 210 of the UCC. Therein, Article 210 (d) of the UCC stipulates the special procedure for outward processing that is a simplification for the repair of goods in a third country. Article 259 (1) of the UCC further defines the outward processing procedure. The outward processing procedure is a customs procedure that allows Union goods to be temporarily exported from the EU customs territory in order to carry out processing operations. The processed products can then be reimported into the EU with full or partial exemption from import duties.[1241] In the articles preceding Article 259 of the UCC (the general provision on outward processing), specific outward processing cases are stipulated. Thereby, Article 160 of the UCC explicitly stipulates the repair is free of charge. Pursuant to Article 260 (1) of the UCC, a total relief of import duties should be granted if 'goods have been repaired free of charge, either because of a contractual or statutory obligation arising from a guarantee or because of a manufacturing or material defect'. Thus, Article 260 (1) of the UCC could generally apply to the repair of goods by the underlying supplier

---

1238. *See* s. 4.14.2.2.2.1.1 Customs Implications of the Export.
1239. *See* Article 24 of the Regulation (2009/1186).
1240. See s. 4.14.4.3.2.2.2 The Special Procedure for Outward Processing as well as s. 4.14.4.3.2.2.3 The Import Duty Relief of Returned Goods According to Article 203 of the UCC.
1241. *See* Article 259 (1) of the UCC.

in a third country. Nevertheless, Article 260 (2) of the UCC limits this relief from import duties to goods that had no defect 'at the time when the goods in question were first released for free circulation'. Thus, the import relief of Article 260 (1) of the UCC could solely become applicable if the goods were functioning when they were originally imported into the EU.

Although the repair of goods could theoretically qualify as outward processing, the special procedures stipulated in Article 210 of the UCC are limited to taxable persons established in the Customs Union according to Article 211 (3) (a) of the UCC. Since one of the requirements for Article 14a (2) of the VAT Directive to apply is that the underlying supplier is not established in the EU,[1242] it is not possible to apply the outward processing procedure for goods originally supplied in accordance with Article 14a (2) of the VAT Directive.

4.14.4.3.2.2.3 The Import Duty Relief of Returned Goods According to Article 203 of the UCC

Another special exception in the customs code is stipulated in Article 203 of the UCC. Thereby, returned goods can also be relieved from import duties. According to Article 203 (1) of the UCC, '[n]on-Union goods which, having originally been exported as Union goods from the customs territory of the Union, are returned to that territory within a period of three years and declared for release for free circulation shall ... be granted relief from import duty'. Generally, it is likely that underlying suppliers repairing the goods fulfil the time limit of reimporting the goods within three years. However, Article 203 (5) of the UCC stipulates that '[t]he relief from import duty shall be granted only if goods are returned in the state in which they were exported'. Furthermore, pursuant to Article 158 (1) of the UCC-DA which further defines Article 203 (5) of the UCC, the goods 'have not received a treatment or handling other than that altering their appearance or necessary to repair them, restore them to good condition or maintain them in good condition'. Thus, the question arises of whether the exportation of defective goods from the EU and the subsequent importation of the repaired goods into the EU could be subsumed under Article 203 of the UCC.

Thereby, the aim of Article 203 (5) of the UCC should be investigated. It seems that the legislator wanted to avoid the arising of import levies in the case that the (same) goods are exported and then reimported into the EU. The further definition in Article 203 (5) of the UCC is necessary if, e.g., a functioning good was exported from the EU into a third country and becomes defect in the third country. The owner could repair the good in the third country and then reimport the fully functioning good. In this case, the value of the exported functioning good would be the same as the reimported functioning good. Thus, the import levy exemption would be justified as the value of the good would not have increased due to the repair in the third country.[1243]

1242. *See,* for the discussion on the establishment of the underlying supplier of the scope of Article 14a (2) of the VAT Directive, sec 3.3.2.2 The Requirements for Underlying Suppliers and the Customers.
1243. *See,* for further examples when Article 203 (4) of the UCC is applicable, Frauke Schulmeister, *Art. 203*, Zollkodex der Union, paras. 7 et seqq. (Peter Witte ed., C.H. Beck 2022).

Nevertheless, it does not seem that the EU legislator wanted to include improvements of the good under this import levy exemption as such improvements would also increase the value of the good and thus the amount of import levies due.[1244]

This (narrow) interpretation of the repairs mentioned in Article 158 (1) of the UCC-DA also finds its support in the systematics of the UCC. As discussed, Article 210 (d) of the UCC stipulates an import relief for the repair of goods with the special procedure for outward processing. If, additionally, the relief of import duties was possible under Article 203 (5) of the UCC read in conjunction with Article 158 (1) of the UCC-DA, then the special procedure for outward processing would not be necessary anymore because any repairs could be relieved from import duties based on Article 203 (5) of the UCC read in conjunction with Article 158 (1) of the UCC-DA. Thus, also in literature, it is argued that the special procedure for outward processing should be given precedence over the relief from import duties based on Article 203 (5) of the UCC.[1245] It does not seem likely that the EU legislator wanted to subsume the same cases under the outward processing as well as the facilitation of return goods.

Hence, the repair of goods in Article 158 (1) of the UCC-DA should be read narrowly, and the repair of goods that were already broken when they are exported to the third country for the repair should not be subsumed under this import relief. Therefore, the goods exported to a third country for repair that cannot be exempt of import duties according to the general relief of low-value consignments can also not be relieved from import duties according to Article 203 of the UCC since the goods are not in the same condition as they were when they were exported.

4.14.4.3.2.3 VAT Implications of the Transportation of Defect Goods

Also, from a VAT point of view, the export of the defective good from the EU and the reimportation of the repaired good into the EU must be analysed. For the export from the EU into a third country, in a first step, it should be analysed who is exporting the defective good in question and thus who has the (legal) power to disposal of the goods. In the case of the repair of the goods in a third country, the power of disposal of the goods has been transferred to the customer, a non-taxable person, when the (faulty) goods were first delivered to the customer. The repair of the defective goods does not mean that the underlying supplier receives the power to dispose of the goods. The customer only sends the goods back to the underlying supplier for the repair. Thus, at the moment of exportation, the customer and not the underlying supplier has the power to dispose of the goods. Since the customer is often a non-taxable person, no VAT implications arise based on the VAT Directive. Even if the customer was a taxable person, which might have been the case if the goods were originally supplied according to Article 14a (1) of the VAT Directive,[1246] the exportation would be exempt from VAT according to Article 146 of the VAT Directive.

1244. *See*, similarly, *ibid.* para. 14.
1245. *Ibid.* para. 9.
1246. *See* s. 3.3.1.1.4 The Requirements of Article 14 (4) (2) (a) of the VAT Directive on the VAT Status of the Recipient of the Goods.

For the importation of the repaired goods, the VAT Directive provides for a specific provision. According to Article 88 of the VAT Directive, Member States have to 'ensure that the tax treatment of the goods for VAT purposes is the same as that which would have been applied had the repair, processing, adaption, making up or re-working been carried out within their territory.' Thus, it is up to the Member States to determine the taxable amount of import VAT for the reimportation. Thereby, it should be noted that if Member States decided to charge import VAT on such a reimportation, the result may be a double taxation because the VAT was already paid on the originally supplied goods (import). If the Member States charged import VAT, this import VAT would likely be paid by the underlying supplier as the repair of the goods is the underlying supplier's contractual compensation for delivering a defective good in the first place. Thus, it should be reviewed whether the underlying supplier has the right to deduct the import VAT paid. According to Article 168 (e) of the VAT Directive, the goods must have been imported for the use of a taxable transaction. Thereby, the CJEU has clarified that a taxable person uses the imported goods for its taxed transaction 'where the cost of the input services is incorporated either in the cost of particular output transactions or in the cost of goods or services supplied by the taxable person as part of his economic activities'.[1247] In the given case, this requirement could be affirmed since the underlying supplier imports the goods to fulfil the contractual obligations of supplying a functioning good to the customer.

However, Member States may also interpret the use for the purpose of taxed transactions stricter. In Austria and Germany, for example, the prevailing opinion is that the person declaring the input VAT deduction of the import VAT must have had the power to dispose of the goods for being able to deduct the import VAT.[1248] As already discussed above, in the given case, the customer has the power to dispose of the goods when the goods are sent to a third country for the repair and thus also in the moment of import. The lack of power of disposal by the underlying supplier could lead to the result that, in such Member States that apply a similar interpretation to the requirements of the input VAT deduction as in Austria and Germany, the underlying supplier would not have the right to deduct the import VAT. This would lead to a double taxation of the good.

1247. Case C-187/14, *Skatteministeriet v DSV Road A/S*, 25 Jun. 2015, ECLI:EU:C:2015:421, para. 49; with reference to Case C-29/08, *Skatteverket v AB SKF*, 29 Oct. 2009, ECLI:EU:C:2009:665, para. 60; Case C-118/11, *Eon Aset Menidjmunt OOD v Direktor na Direktsia 'Obzhalvane I upravlenie na izpalnenieto' – Varna pri Tsentralno upravlenie na Natsionalnata agentsia za prihodite*, 16 Feb. 2012, ECLI:EU:C:2012:97, para. 48; *see* also Case C-621/19, *Finančné riaditel'stvo Slovenskej republiky v Weindel Logistik Service SR spol. s r.o.*, 8 Oct. 2020, ECLI:EU:C:2020:814, paras. 45 et seq.

1248. *See* the Austrian case law VwGH 24 Mar. 2015, 2013/15/0238; 28 Sep. 2016, Ra 2016/16/0052; 18 Oct. 2018, Ro 2017/15/002; *see* also similarly Hans Georg Ruppe & Markus Achatz, *zu § 12 UStG*, Umsatzsteuergesetz: Kommentar, para. 224 (Hans Georg Ruppe & Markus Achatz eds., Facultas 2018); *see* also the German case law BFH 11 Nov. 2015, V R 68/14, paras. 14 et seqq.; and the German literature Hans-Hermann Heidner & Johann Bunjes, *§ 15 Vorsteuerabzug*, Umsatzsteuergesetz: Kommentar, para. 202 (Johann Bunjes et al. eds., C.H. Beck 2021); Alexander Oelmaier, *§ 15 Vorsteuerabzug*, Umsatzsteuergesetz, *supra* note 922, para. 436.

This raises the question of whether the VAT Directive provides an exemption of the import VAT in the case of reimporting a good. Pursuant to Article 143 (1) (e) of the VAT Directive, such an exemption of the import VAT is applicable when goods are reimported by the person who exported them. Thereby, the exemption of the import VAT is the reflection of the already discussed special arrangement for returned goods in Article 203 of the UCC. Similar to customs law, the VAT exemption is also limited to goods that are 'in the state in which they were exported'.[1249] Nevertheless, in the case that the goods are repaired in the third country, the goods that are reimported are not in the state in which they were exported but repaired. Thus, the exemption in Article 143 (1) (e) of the VAT Directive is not applicable to the case of repairs of goods in third countries.

4.14.4.3.3 Transportation of the Defect Goods from the Member State of Destination to another Member State in the EU

When the goods are transported to another Member State in the EU for the repair, it must be investigated who has the power to dispose of the goods. As discussed in the previous section, the customer has the power to dispose of the goods throughout the transport, i.e., the transportation to the Member State of repair and the transportation back from the Member State of repair to the Member State of destination.[1250] As the customer is a non-taxable person, the movements of the goods for repair do not raise any VAT implications.

4.14.4.4 Interim Conclusion on the Repair of Defect Goods

In conclusion, the repair of the goods as a service does not trigger any VAT conse-quences since the criterion of 'for consideration' is not fulfilled to qualify as a taxable transaction. However, the legal qualification of the transport of the repaired good to a third country of another Member State must be reviewed closely.

Whereas the transportation for repairs from one Member State to another does not trigger any taxable transaction, the exportation and reimportation of the goods raise legal uncertainty for underlying suppliers. Especially the risk by the underlying supplier of not being able to deduct the import VAT as well as possible import levies if the importation was not exempt might lead to additional costs for the underlying supplier if the repair was provided for in a third country. Thus, from a VAT and customs point of view, it may be more convenient for the underlying supplier to not offer the customers repairs in third countries but to reverse the transaction.[1251]

1249. *See* Article 143 (1) (e) of the VAT Directive.
1250. *See* s. 4.14.4.3.2.3 VAT Implications of the Transportation of Defect Goods.
1251. *See* s. 4.14.2 The Return of Goods and Subsequent Discounts.

4.14.5   The Exchange of Defect Goods

4.14.5.1   General Remarks

Instead of repairing the goods, the underlying supplier could also exchange the defective good for a new good. Thus, the customer would send the defective good back to the address indicated by the underlying supplier, e.g., the warehouse from where the goods were delivered. The underlying supplier would send the customer a new (functional) good. Thus, two movements can be identified that may have VAT and customs implications: the return of the defective good from the customer to the underlying supplier and the delivery of the new (functional) good from the underlying supplier to the customer. Thereby, the exchange could be an exchange within the EU or an exchange from a third country. Both situations will be discussed in the subsequent sections from customs as well as a VAT law perspective.

4.14.5.2   The Exchange of the Goods from a Third Country

4.14.5.2.1   Customs Implications of the Exchange of the Goods

Similar to the return of the goods in a third country, also the exchange of the goods leads to the export of the defective good and the importation of the new (functioning) good. For the export of the good, reference can be made to the previous section.[1252] Similarly, also the import implications are similar to the previously discussed implications for the repair of the goods in a third country.[1253] If the consignment of the new product imported into the EU did not exceed the intrinsic value of EUR 150, then the import would be exempt from import duties.[1254] If the value of the good exceeded the intrinsic value of EUR 150, then the special customs procedures of outward processing could generally be investigated. Article 261 of the UCC provides one specific provision of outward processing for the exchange of goods: the standard exchange system. Nevertheless, as discussed in the previous section, one requirement for any outward process is that the underlying supplier is established in the EU;[1255] thus, the application of outward processing would not be possible if the underlying supplier established in third countries would reimport the good.

4.14.5.2.2   VAT Implications of the Exchange of the Goods

The exchange of a defective good results in the exportation of the defective good and the importation of a new functioning good. As discussed in the previous section, for the export from the EU into a third country, it should be analysed in a first step who is

---

1252. *See* s. 4.14.2.2.2.1.1 Customs Implications of the Export.
1253. *See* s. 4.14.4.3.2.2 Import Implications of the Transportation of Defect Goods.
1254. *See* Article 23 of the Regulation (2009/1186); for further details, *see* s. 4.14.4.3.2.2.1 The General Import Exemption for Low Value Consignments.
1255. *See* s. 4.14.4.3.2.2.2 The Special Procedure for Outward Processing.

exporting the defective good in question and who has the power to dispose of the goods. Thereby, the VAT implications of exporting a good for exchanging it for another have the same VAT implications as the return of the good to the underlying supplier.[1256] If the customer sent the goods to a third country with the aim to receive another good in exchange, it could be argued that the underlying supplier had the power to dispose of the goods.[1257] Thus, the exportation would be VAT exempt according to Article 146 of the VAT Directive.

On the other side, the importation of the (functioning) good must be analysed. The determination of the import VAT of the new product would follow the general rules for importation.[1258] The previously discussed Article 88 of the VAT Directive would, in this case, not be applicable because the goods are not repaired, processed, adapted, made up, or re-worked.[1259] Nevertheless, also in this case, the assessment of import VAT upon the importation of the good would result in double taxation because the VAT has already been paid on the originally supplied good (import). The assessed import VAT for the delivery of the functioning good would likely be paid by the underlying supplier as the exchange of the goods is the underlying supplier's contractual compensation for delivering a defective good in the first place. Thus, similar to the discussion of the repair of the good in a third country, it should be reviewed also in this case whether the underlying supplier has the right to deduct the import VAT paid.[1260] In the given case, the requirement to use the imported goods for taxed transactions can be affirmed since the underlying supplier imports the goods to fulfil the contractual obligations of supplying a functioning good to the customer.[1261] Whereas, in the previous section, the right to deduct the import VAT might be denied based on the lack of the power of disposal of the underlying supplier,[1262] this criterion can be affirmed in the case of the exchange of the good. In this case, the underlying supplier is transporting the goods into the EU to provide the goods (free of additional charge) to the customer, and thus the underlying supplier also has the right to dispose of the goods upon importation. Therefore, in the case at hand, the underlying supplier should be allowed to deduct the input VAT incurred according to Article 168 (e) of the VAT Directive, and double taxation could therefore be prevented.

4.14.5.3   The Exchange of the Goods Within the EU

The second possibility to exchange the goods would be if the goods were exchanged for goods that are already in the EU. Thus, the defective good would be transported from

---

1256. See s. 4.14.2.2.2.1.2 VAT Implications of the Export for the Return of the Goods.
1257. See s. 4.14.2.2.2.1.2 VAT Implications of the Export for the Return of the Goods.
1258. See s. 4.5.4 The Taxable Amount of the Importation by the Platform or the Customer.
1259. See s. 4.14.4.3.2.3 VAT Implications of the Transportation of Defect Goods.
1260. See also the discussions in s. 4.14.4.3.2.3 VAT Implications of the Transportation of Defect Goods.
1261. This criterion was also affirmed for the repair of the goods; see s. 4.14.4.3.2.3 VAT Implications of the Transportation of Defect Goods.
1262. See s. 4.14.4.3.2.3 VAT Implications of the Transportation of Defect Goods.

the customer to the other Member State where the good would be exchanged. The new good would then be transported to the customer.

As already discussed in a previous section, for the transport of the goods from the country to which the goods were delivered to (Member State 1) another Member State (Member State 2), it can be argued that the underlying supplier receives the power of disposal over the returned goods in Member State 1.[1263] Therefore, this transportation triggers an intra-Community transfer according to Article 17 (1) of the VAT Directive by the underlying supplier. It could be argued that the discussed analogue application of Article 17 (2) (a) of the VAT Directive should also be applied in the case of the exchange of a defective good for a new good.[1264] Nevertheless, in the given case, the original transaction is not reversed, but the good is exchanged. Thus, it can be questioned whether the exception of Article 17 (2) (a) of the VAT Directive can be applied. If this application was denied, then the place of supply for this intra-Community transfer would be pursuant to Article 32 first subparagraph of the VAT Directive, i.e., the location of the beginning of the dispatch or transport of the goods (Member State 1). Nevertheless, since the goods were supplied across the border to another Member State, this supply would be exempt from the VAT in the country of dispatch according to Article 138 (1) of the VAT Directive if the underlying supplier fulfilled the therein mentioned criteria and the underlying supplier files a recapitulative statement in due time and with the requested information.[1265] In this recapitulative statement, the underlying supplier would have to indicate his VAT identification number of the country where the returned goods are delivered. On the other side of this supply, also the intra-Community acquisition by the underlying supplier is a taxable transaction in the Member State of destination (Member State 2) according to Article 2 (1) (b) (i) of the VAT Directive. The place of the intra-Community acquisition is the place where the dispatch or transport ends.[1266] The underlying supplier should be able to deduct the VAT of the intra-Community acquisition as input VAT in the same VAT return as the declaration of the intra-Community acquisition.[1267] Therefore, no VAT should become due for payment from this transaction, but a VAT registration by the underlying supplier would generally be necessary in the country of origin (Member State 1).

However, the question arises as to how high the taxable amount to be declared in the VAT returns and the recapitulative statement should be. According to Article 76 of the VAT Directive, the taxable amount of the goods for transfers of goods should be the 'purchase price of the goods or similar goods'. In the case of goods being defective, the taxable amount would generally be zero because the purchase price for similar goods would be zero.[1268] Hence, although the obligation to declare an intra-Community

---

1263. *See* s. 4.14.5.2.2 VAT Implications of the Exchange of the Goods.
1264. *See* s. 4.14.2.2.2.2.1 The Legal Consequences for the Underlying Supplier due to the Transport of the Goods Back to the Underlying Supplier.
1265. *See* Article 138 (1a) read in conjunction with Articles 262 et seqq. of the VAT Directive.
1266. *See* Article 40 of the VAT Directive.
1267. *See* Article 168 (c) of the VAT Directive.
1268. A different determination of the taxable amount may be the case when, e.g., the goods are antiques or collectibles; in this case, also defective goods may be considered to have a purchase price. However, the exchange of the good will be difficult as antiques or collectibles are unique and thus cannot simply be exchanged in many cases.

transfer arises, the taxable amount would be zero, and thus the transfer generally does not have to be indicated in the VAT returns and the recapitulative statement of the underlying supplier.

The second identified supply, i.e., the supply of the functional good from the underlying supplier to the customer, cannot qualify as a supply of goods by the underlying supplier[1269] since the customer would not pay for the new delivery of the goods in the case of a warranty. Thus, the criterion of 'for consideration' would not be fulfilled.[1270]

4.14.5.4   *Interim Conclusion on the Exchange of the Goods*

The exchange of the goods from third countries can cause legal uncertainty for underlying suppliers. Although the input VAT deduction of the import VAT due can be confirmed, and thus no double taxation arises, the assessing of possible import levies when the importation is not exempt might lead to additional costs for the underlying supplier

The exchange of the good within the EU is not critical due to the determination of the taxable amount of zero for the transport of the defected goods back to the underlying supplier and due to the fact that no consideration is paid for the resupply of the functional good. Thus, no VAT obligation is triggered for the underlying supplier for the exchange of defected goods within the EU.

4.15   CONCLUSION ON THE LEGAL CONSEQUENCES OF ARTICLE 14A OF THE VAT DIRECTIVE

The previous sections have shown that the platform becoming the deemed supplier of the transaction has a major impact on the platform's VAT obligations in the EU. One side of the coin is that, due to the fictitious inclusion in the supply chain, the VAT obligations for platforms are enormously increased since the platforms are treated as if they acquired and supplied the goods themselves. The other side of the coin is the simplification for the underlying suppliers who do not have to collect and pay the VAT due if the platform became the deemed supplier.

The first difficulty that the platform faces regarding the legal consequences is determining the applicable place of supply. Depending on where the goods come from and what kind of goods are supplied, the place of supply may be the place of origin or the place of destination. The determination of the place of supply has an effect on the further VAT treatment of the supplied goods and is thus of utmost importance. This difficulty is followed by the difficulty of the correct determination of the applicable VAT rate and exemption by establishing the invoicing obligation for B2C supplies in the non-harmonised VAT system and by the extensive reporting obligation. Finally, the

---

1269. *See* Article 2 (1) (a) of the VAT Directive.
1270. *See* Article 2 (1) (a) of the VAT Directive.

return of goods can lead to practical difficulties; it especially highlights the consequences of the interplay between the economic reality of the underlying supplier supplying the goods and the fiction created by Article 14a of the VAT Directive of the platform acting as a deemed supplier. All of the discussed difficulties make the business processes of platforms more complicated and costly.

At the same time, the EU legislator seems to have been aware of these immense difficulties for platforms and implemented several facilitations, e.g., the legal stipulation of the supply with transport in Article 36b of the VAT Directive, the amendment of the chargeable event to the time of the payment acceptance in Article 66a of the VAT Directive, the safe harbour clause in Article 5c of the VAT Implementing Regulation, the application of the exemption for the supply from the underlying supplier to the platform in Article 136a of the VAT Directive and, most of all, the introduction of the IOSS and the EU-OSS.

As the full VAT burden of the supply of the good is shifted to the platforms, the 'big winners' of the introduction of Article 14a of the VAT Directive are the tax authorities and the underlying suppliers. The only VAT payment that might have become due in the chain transaction of Article 14a of the VAT Directive for the underlying supplier has been exempt from the VAT according to Article 136a of the VAT Directive by the EU legislator. Nevertheless, it is not quite clear why the EU legislator did not remove the full obligation (or at least provide the Member States with such an option) for underlying suppliers to VAT registration and filing VAT returns as no VAT becomes due from the applicability of Article 14a of the VAT Directive. One disadvantage for underlying suppliers could be that, due to the inclusion of the platform in the VAT transaction chain, the personal exemption of the small enterprise scheme would not be applicable in the case that the platform does not fulfil the requirements of a small enterprise scheme (which is rather unlikely). This legal consequence would increase the price of the good due to the VAT charged from the platform to the customer. Furthermore, the analysis of the return of the goods has shown that further VAT obligations may be triggered for underlying suppliers when the ordered goods are returned. The EU legislator missed the chance with this broad reform on e-commerce to introduce facilitation for the additional registration obligations resulting from the return of goods.

Finally, the analysis of the legal consequences has also shown that the information exchange between the platform and the underlying supplier is of utmost importance. Depending on the platform model, the platform may require information from the underlying supplier to fulfil its VAT obligations. At the same time, the underlying supplier may require information from the platform if the platform is responsible for certain aspects of the supply. Many platforms had to amend their business model in order to guarantee this information flow and to (at least partially) conquer the discussed difficulties arising from the legal consequences of the application of Article 14a of the VAT Directive.

CHAPTER 5

Discussion of a Possible Infringement of Article 14a of the VAT Directive of the Charter of Fundamental Rights of the European Union

5.1 GENERAL REMARKS

The previous sections have discussed in detail the requirements and the wide-ranging legal consequences resulting from the applicability of Article 14a of the VAT Directive. For VAT purposes, the platforms are fictitiously included in the supply chain due to the deemed supplier regime which leads to many additional obligations for the platform. This extension of the legal obligations for platforms raises the question of whether Article 14a of the VAT Directive infringes provisions of the Charter of Fundamental Rights of the European Union.

Article 51 (1) of the CFR stipulates the scope of the Charter of Fundamental Rights of the European Union: 'The provisions of this Charter are addressed to the institutions, bodies, offices and agencies of the Union with due regard for the principle of subsidiarity and to the Member States only when they are implementing Union law.' Thus, for the Charter of Fundamental Rights of the European Union to become applicable 'Union law must be implemented.' In accordance with settled case law, 'the fundamental rights guaranteed in the legal order of the European Union are applicable in all situations governed by EU law'.[1271] Therefore, the VAT Directive can be challenged based on the fundamental rights stipulated in the Charter of Fundamental Rights of the European Union.

1271. Case C-419/14, *WebMindLicenses kft v Nemzeti Adó- és Vámhivatal Kiemelt Adó- és Vám Főigazgatóság*, 17 Dec. 2015, ECLI:EU:C:2015:832, para. 66; with reference to Case C-617/10, *Åklagaren v Hans Åkerberg Fransson*, 26 Feb. 2013, ECLI:EU:C:2013:105, para. 19.

For analysing a possible infringement of Article 14a of the VAT Directive according to the Charter of Fundamental Rights, two fundamental rights can be discussed. First is the principle of equality. Due to the scope of Article 14a of the VAT Directive, it could be discussed whether platforms that facilitate the supply of certain goods and thus become the deemed supplier are treated unequally compared to other platforms. Moreover, the fundamental right to conduct a business could be challenged. As repeatedly discussed, the platform should amend their business procedures to fully comply with their legal obligations due to the application of Article 14a of the VAT Directive. The following sections will discuss Article 14a of the VAT Directive in light of these two fundamental freedoms of the Charter of Fundamental Rights of the European Union.

5.2 DISCUSSION OF A POSSIBLE INFRINGEMENT OF ARTICLE 14A OF THE VAT DIRECTIVE OF THE PRINCIPLE OF EQUALITY

5.2.1 General Remarks

The first fundamental right to be analysed is a possible infringement of the principle of equality stipulated in Article 20 of the CFR. For this analysis, a more detailed overview and recap of the different deemed supplier regimes will initially be provided. This overview is essential for a better understanding of the subsequent examples. The section following will discuss the scope and requirements of Article 20 of the CFR, including an overview of how the CJEU has applied the principle of equality to VAT cases in the past. Additionally, a detailed analysis of Article 14a of the VAT Directive in light of the principle of equality will be carried out. In a final section, the application of the principle of neutrality will be investigated.

5.2.2 The Different Deemed Supplier Regimes

5.2.2.1 The Restrictions of Article 14a of the VAT Directive

As established in the last sections, Article 14a of the VAT Directive has a major impact on the VAT treatment of sales through platforms when these sales fulfil the stipulated requirements. Thereby, both paragraphs of Article 14a of the VAT Directive have three requirements in common:[1272] First, both paragraphs are explicitly limited to the supply of goods.[1273] With this explicit limitation, the EU legislator intended to restrict the applicability of the platform VAT liability regime according to Article 14a of the VAT Directive and to exclude services from this deemed supplier regime. The second is that only supplies to non-taxable persons, to taxable persons, or non-taxable legal persons

---

1272. See already s. 3.4 Conclusion on the Scope of Article 14a of the VAT Directive.
1273. *See,* for further information on the substantive scope of Article 14a of the VAT Directive, s. 3.3 Substantive Scope.

whose intra-Community acquisitions of goods are not subject to the VAT pursuant to Article 3 (1) or for any other non-taxable person are covered by Article 14a (1) of the VAT Directive;[1274] Article 14a (2) of the VAT Directive is generally limited to supplies to non-taxable persons.[1275] Third, a third country context is required, i.e., either the supplier is established in a third country or the supply is a distance sale of goods imported from a third country.[1276]

5.2.2.2 The Scope of Article 9a of the VAT Implementing Regulation

Another deemed supplier regime is stipulated in Article 9a of the VAT Implementing Regulation which the EU legislator introduced as a clarification of Article 28 of the VAT Directive in 2013.[1277] Article 9a of the VAT Implementing Regulation entered into force on 1 January 2015.[1278] Due to this clarification, platforms providing certain services are considered to become a deemed supplier on the basis of Article 28 of the VAT Directive when the stipulated requirements are fulfilled.

It should be noted that Article 9a of the VAT Implementing Regulation is tertiary law that must be in line with primary law as well as secondary law.[1279] According to Article 397 of the VAT Directive, the Council has the power to adopt 'measures necessary to implement' the VAT Directive. Thus, the provisions of the VAT Implementing Regulation should only be clarifications to the VAT Directive. Thereby, it can be questioned whether the EU legislator has exceeded its power according to Article 397 of the VAT by implementing Article 9a of the VAT Implementing Regulation. This question is pending at the CJEU at the moment.[1280] The referring court, the First-Tier Tribunal, raises this doubt arguing that Article 9a of the VAT Directive extends the application of Article 28 of the VAT Directive instead of providing clarifications thereof.

According to Article 9a of the VAT Implementing Regulation, taxable persons taking part in electronically supplied services that are supplied through a telecommunications network, an interface, or a portal such as an app store[1281] shall be presumed

---

1274. *See* s. 3.3.1.1.4 The Requirements of Article 14 (4) (2) (a) of the VAT Directive on the VAT Status of the Recipient of the Goods.
1275. *See* s. 3.3.2.2 The Requirements for Underlying Suppliers and the Customers.
1276. *See,* for further information on the third country requirement, s. 3.3.1.1 The Definition of Distance Sales of Goods Imported from a Third Territory or a Third Country and s. 3.3.2.2 The Requirements for Underlying Suppliers and the Customers.
1277. For a detailed discussion of the general deemed supplier provisions in Article 14 (2) (c) of the VAT Directive for goods and the corresponding Article 28 of the VAT Directive for services, *see* s. 2.2.2.2 The Supply Through Platforms: A Supply Through an Undisclosed Agent?; *See Fenix International*, C-695/20, pending; *see* also the discussion of this case by Christian Amand, *Disclosed/Undisclosed Agent in EU VAT: When Is an Intermediary Acting in Its Own Name?*, 32 International VAT Monitor, *supra* note 575.
1278. Article 9a of VAT Implementing Regulation was amended based on the Council Implementing Regulation (EU) No 1042/2013 of 7 October 2013 Amending Implementing Regulation (EU) No 282/2011 as Regards the Place of Supply of Services, OJ L 284 (2013).
1279. *See* s. 1.3.1 Sources of EU Law.
1280. *See Fenix International*, C-695/20, pending; *see* also the discussion of this case by Christian Amand, *supra* note 575.
1281. In the following, the telecommunications network, interface, or portal such as an app store will be referred to generically as 'platform'.

to be acting in their own name but on behalf of the provider of those services within the meaning of Article 28 of the VAT Directive. Therefore, a deemed supplier regime was introduced for platforms offering electronically supplied services. Additionally, the deemed supplier regime was also introduced for telephone services supplied over the Internet.[1282]

The legal presumption of the platform becoming the deemed supplier can be rebutted when the 'provider is explicitly indicated as the supplier by that taxable person and that is reflected in the contractual arrangements between the parties'.[1283] Thereby, the explicit 'indication as the supplier' would be fulfilled if the electronic service was identified as such and the underlying supplier of the service was indicated on the invoice, bill, or receipt issued.[1284] This indication must be displayed on all invoices, receipts, or bills throughout the supply chain, i.e., from the underlying supplier(s) to the platform and from the platform to the customer.[1285] A rebuttal of the legal presumption of the platform being the service provider would only be possible if the platform only had minimal involvement in the supply of the electronically supplied services or the telephone services supplied over the Internet. Minimal involvement could be affirmed if the platform

- authorised the delivery of the service to the customer, or
- authorised the charge or the delivery to the customer, or
- set the general terms and conditions of the supply.[1286]

If the platform was involved in any of the three mentioned business processes, the platform would have to indicate itself as the supplier of the service; in this case, the platform is not allowed to indicate another person as the supplier.[1287]

Already with the introduction of Article 9a of the VAT Implementing Regulation, an explicit *ex lege* deemed supplier rule was introduced for platforms. Hereby, a special emphasis must be put on the fact that the scope of Article 9a of the VAT Implementing Regulation only covers the provision of *electronically* supplied services and telephone services supplied over the Internet. Other services are not in the scope of the special deemed supplier rule in Article 9a of the VAT Implementing Regulation.

5.2.2.3   *The General Deemed Supplier Regimes in the VAT Directive*

Additionally to the *leges speciales* of Article 14a VAT Directive and the clarification of Article 28a of the VAT Directive in Article 9a of the VAT Implementing Regulation, the VAT Directive also provides for general deemed supplier regimes. The general deemed

---

1282. *See* Article 9a (2) of the VAT Implementing Regulation.
1283. *See* Article 9a (1) first subpara. of the VAT Implementing Regulation; for further information on the rebuttal of the presumption, *see* European Commission, *Explanatory Notes on the EU VAT Changes to the Place of Supply of Telecommunications, Broadcasting and Electronic Services That Enter into Force in 2015, supra* note 11, at 24 et seqq.
1284. *See* Article 9a (1) second supara. of the VAT Implementing Regulation.
1285. *See* Article 9a (1) second supara. of the VAT Implementing Regulation.
1286. *See* Article 9a (1) third supara. of the VAT Implementing Regulation.
1287. *See* Article 9a (1) third supara. of the VAT Implementing Regulation.

supplier regimes are stipulated in Article 14 (2) (c) of the VAT Directive for the supply of goods and in Article 28 of the VAT Directive for the supply of services.[1288] For the deemed supplier regime to be applied, two requirements must be fulfilled:[1289] the 'intermediaries' must act in their own name[1290] and on behalf of a third party.[1291] Both conditions must be fulfilled cumulatively. As a result of fulfilling the requirements, the supply is fictitiously treated as if the intermediary had received the good or service from the principal and supplied the good or service to the customer himself.

5.2.3 The Principle of Equality in Article 20 of the CFR

5.2.3.1 Content of Article 20 of the CFR and the 'Equality Test'

Already before the introduction of Article 20 of the CFR, the general principle of equality was applicable in the EU. In the earlier cases, the CJEU derived the principle of equality from the non-discrimination clauses of the treaty and the traditions of the Member States.[1292] The principle of equality can be found in all Member States' constitutions and was a general principle of EU law already before its enshrinement in Article 20 of the CFR, as repeatedly emphasised by the CJEU.[1293]

1288. *See*, for a detailed analysis of the general deemed supplier regime, also referred to the undisclosed agent, s. 2.2.2.2 The Supply Through Platforms: A Supply Through an Undisclosed Agent?.

1289. *See*, for the applicability of Article 14 (2) (c) of the VAT Directive, Case C-526/13, *Fast Bunkering Klaipeda*, 3 Sep. 2015, ECLI:EU:C:2015:536, para. 33, where the CJEU explicitly stated that a 'contract under which commission is payable constitutes, in principle, an agreement by which an intermediary undertakes to carry out in his own name one or more legal transactions on behalf of a third party'. For the applicability of Article 28 of the VAT Directive, these two requirements are already stipulated in the VAT Directive.

1290. *See*, for a detailed analysis of the criterion of acting in the own name, s. 2.2.2.2.2.1 The Requirement of Acting in the Own Name.

1291. *See*, for a detailed analysis of the criterion of acting on behalf of a third party, s. 2.2.2.2.2.2 The Requirement of Acting on Behalf of Somebody Else.

1292. *See* Case C-117/76, *Albert Ruckdeschel & Co. and Hansa-Lagerhaus Ströh & Co. v Hauptzollamt Hamburg-St. Annen; Diamalt AG v Hauptzollamt Itzehoe*, 19 Oct. 1977, ECLI: EU:C:1977:160, para. 7; Case C-124/76, *SA Moulins & Huileries de Pont-à-Mousson and Société coopérative Providence agricole de la Champagne v Office national interprofessionnel des céréales*, 19 Oct. 1977, ECLI:EU:C:1977:161, para. 16; with reference to the non-discrimination between producers and consumers in Article 40 (3) of the Treaty Establishing the European Economic Community (1957); this evolved into settled case law; *see*, e.g., Case C-201/85, *Marthe Klensch and others v Secrétaire d'État à l'Agriculture et à la Viticulture*, 25 Nov. 1986, ECLI:EU:C:1986:439, para. 9; Case C-84/87, *Marcel Erpelding v Secrétaire d'État à l'Agriculture et à la Viticulture*, 17 May 1988, ECLI:EU:C:1988:245, para. 29; Case C-267/88, *Gustave Wuidart and others v Laiterie coopérative eupenoise société coopérative and others*, 21 Feb. 1990, ECLI:EU:C:1990:79, para. 13.

1293. *See* the *Explanations Relating to the Charter of Fundamental Rights*, OJ C 303, 24 (14.12.2007), https://eur-lex.europa.eu/legal-content/EN/TXT/PDF/?uri = CELEX:32007X1214(01)&from = EN (last visited 29 Mar. 2021); with reference to Case C-283/83, *Firma A. Racke v Hauptzollamt Mainz*, 13 Nov. 1984, ECLI:EU:C:1984:344; Case C-15/95, *EARL de Kerlast v Union régionale de coopératives agricoles (Unicopa) and Coopérative du Trieux*, 17 Apr. 1997, ECLI:EU:C:1997:196; Case C-292/97, *Kjell Karlsson and Others*, 13 Apr. 2000, ECLI:EU:C:20 00:202.

With the entering into force of the CFR[1294] on 1 December 2009, different equality rights were explicitly stipulated under the heading 'Equality before the law' (title III of the CFR).[1295] Article 20 of the CFR is thereby the general principle of equality and states:

Everyone is equal before the law.

The broad principle in Article 20 of the CFR can be applied across all fields of EU law provided that the general condition of Article 51 (1) of the CFR ('implementing Union law') is fulfilled.[1296] According to Article 20 of the CFR as interpreted by the CJEU, 'comparable situations must not be treated differently, and different situations must not be treated equal, unless such treatment is objectively justified'.[1297]

From this general definition of the principle of equality, the two steps from the so-called equality test developed by the CJEU can be distinguished: (i) the comparability test and the (ii) justifications and proportionality test. First: (i) the comparability test, i.e., to test whether an unequal treatment of comparable situations (or an equal treatment of non-comparable situations) exists, should be performed. Therefore, two comparable groups or situations must be identified.[1298] Subsequently, it must be reviewed whether these comparable groups or situations are treated differently (or non-comparable groups or situations are treated equally) according to the law. This can

---

1294. Charter of Fundamental Rights of the European Union, OJ C 326 (2012).
1295. *See* also the explanations and discussions on Article 20 of the CFR in Mark Bell, *Article 20 – Equality Before the Law*, The EU Charter of Fundamental Rights: A Commentary (Steve Peers et al. eds., Nomos Beck Hart 2014); Alfonso Celotto, *Article 20 – Equality Before the Law*, Human Rights in Europe: Commentary on the Charter of Fundamental Rights of the European Union (William B. T. Mock ed., Carolina Academic Press 2010); Jonathan Tomkin, *Equality*, The EU Treaties and the Charter of Fundamental Rights: A Commentary (Manuel Kellerbauer et al. eds., University Press 2019); Hans D. Jarass, *Art. 20 Gleichheit vor dem Gesetz*, Charta der Grundrechte der EU (Hans D. Jarass ed., C.H. Beck 2021); Cornelia Köchler & Laura Pavlidis, *Gleichheit*, Charta der Grundrechte der Europäischen Union: GRC-Kommentar (Michael Holoubek & Georg Lienbacher eds., MANZ'sche Verlags- und Universitätsbuchhandlung 2019). Next to this general equality principle, the subsequent articles of Article 20 of the CFR stipulate the more specific equality rights, i.e., the principle of non-discrimination in Article 21 of the CFR, the right to cultural, religious, and linguistic diversity in Article 22 of the CFR, equality between women and men in Article 23 of the CFR, the rights of the child in Article 24 of the CFR, and the rights of the elderly in Article 25 of the CFR. As the focus in this chapter will be on Article 20 of the CFR, the more specialised equality principles will not be further discussed.
1296. Mark Bell, *supra* note 1295, para. 20.16.
1297. Case C-106/83, *Sermide SpA v Cassa Conguaglio Zucchero and others*, 13 Dec. 1984, ECLI:EU:C:1984:394, para. 28; Case C-44/94, *The Queen v Minister of Agriculture, Fisheries and Food, ex parte National Federation of Fishermen's Organisations and others and Federation of Highlands and Islands Fishermen and others*, 17 Oct. 1995, ECLI:EU:C:1995:325, para. 46; Case C-248/04, *Koninklijke Coöperatie Cosun UA v Minister van Landbouw, Natuur en Voedselkwaliteit*, 26 Oct. 2006, ECLI:EU:C:2006:666, para. 72; Case C-303/05, *Advocaten voor de Wereld VZW v Leden van de Ministerraad*, 3 May 2007, ECLI:EU:C:2007:261, para. 56; Case C-21/10, *Károly Nagy v Mezőgazdasági és Vidékfejlesztési Hivatal*, 21 Jul. 2011, ECLI:EU:C:2011:505, para. 47.
1298. Cornelia Köchler & Laura Pavlidis, *supra* note 1295, para. 22; *see*, critically, on the comparability test, e.g., Aileen McColgan, *Cracking the Comparator Problem: Discrimination, 'Equal' Treatment and the Role of Comparisons*, European Human Rights Law Review (2006).

be seen as a second, separate step of the comparability test.[1299] The identification of two comparable groups or situations is difficult, especially because the CJEU is not very consistent in its judgments of whether a group or situation is comparable to another.[1300] As Kokott & Dobratz argue[1301] – also taking into consideration the case law on fundamental freedoms for which the non-discrimination test contains a similar step – the Court negates the comparability in some judgments when the law itself already stipulates a different treatment,[1302] bases the affirmation of comparability in other cases very generally on the fact that both persons involved want to apply the provision in question,[1303] or skips this step fully and does not even search for comparable situations.[1304] Furthermore, the authors also argue that the extent of the testing of the objective comparability varies.[1305] In some cases, the CJEU simply states that the situations are objectively comparable without further evaluation while,[1306] in other cases, the CJEU extensively discusses the comparability of the situations based on the objective of the law in question.[1307] The establishing of comparable situations by the

---

1299. *See* Cornelia Köchler & Laura Pavlidis, *supra* note 1295, paras. 28 et seq., who discuss the requirement of a disadvantage as an possible additional step in the equality test; with reference to Joined Cases C-17/61 and C-20/61, *Klöckner-Werke AG and Hoesch AG v High Authority of the European Coal and Steel Community*, 13 Jul. 1962, ECLI:EU:C:1962:30, 692 et seq.; and Case C-462/99, *Connect Austria Gesellschaft für Telekommunikation GmbH v Telekom-Control-Kommission, and Mobilkom Austria AG*, 22 May 2003, ECLI:EU:C:2003:297, para. 115; *see* also Case C-351/98, *Kingdom of Spain v Commission of the European Communities*, 26 Sep. 2002, ECLI:EU:C:2002:530, para. 57; *see* similarly Hans D. Jarass, *supra* note 1295, para. 14; *see* also Juliane Kokott & Lars Dobratz, *Der unionsrechtliche allgemeine Gleichheitssatz im Europäischen Steuerrecht, in Grundfragen des europäischen Steuerrechts* 34 (Wolfgang Schön & Caroline Heber eds., Springer 2015), who separate the comparability test into two separate steps: the unequal treatment of two situations and the test of whether these situations are comparable.
1300. *See* Juliane Kokott & Lars Dobratz, *supra* note 1299, at 34.
1301. *Ibid.*
1302. Case C-599/12, *Jetair NV and BTW-eenheid BTWE Travel4you v FOD Financiën*, 13 Mar. 2014, ECLI:EU:C:2014:144, para. 55 (on the principle of equality in VAT law).
1303. Case C-337/08, *X Holding BV v Staatssecretaris van Financiën*, 25 Feb. 2010, ECLI: EU:C:2010:89, para. 24 (on the freedom of establishment).
1304. The following referred cases are fundamental freedom cases. As the CJEU follows a similar test for the application of the fundamental freedoms and the principle of equality, these cases can also be referred to for showing the inconsistency of the CJEU testing the comparability; *see* Case C-414/06, *Lidl Belgium GmbH & Co. KG v Finanzamt Heilbronn*, 15 May 2008, ECLI:EU:C:2008:278, paras. 18 et seqq.; Case C-157/07, *Finanzamt für Körperschaften III in Berlin v Krankenheim Ruhesitz am Wannsee-Seniorenheimstatt GmbH*, 23 Oct. 2008, ECLI: EU:C:2008:588, paras. 2 et seqq.; Case C-350/11, *Argenta Spaarbank NV v Belgische Staat*, 4 Jul. 2013, ECLI:EU:C:2013:447, paras. 18 et seqq.; *see* also Case C-309/06, *Marks & Spencer plc v Commissioners of Customs & Excise*, 10 Apr. 2008, ECLI:EU:C:2008:211, paras. 51 et seq. (on the principle of equality in VAT law) where the CJEU seems to affirm the comparability of the situations without further elaboration.
1305. Juliane Kokott & Lars Dobratz, *supra* note 1299, at 34 et seq.
1306. Case C-371/10, *National Grid Indus BV v Inspecteur van de Belastingdienst Rijnmond/kantoor Rotterdam*, 29 Nov. 2011, ECLI:EU:C:2011:785, para. 38 (on the freedom of establishment).
1307. Case C-322/11, *K*, 7 Nov. 2013, ECLI:EU:C:2013:716, paras. 37 et seqq. (on the free movement of capital); *see* also Case C-390/15, *Proceedings brought by Rzecznik Praw Obywatelskich (RPO)*, 7 Mar. 2017, ECLI:EU:C:2017:174, paras. 43 et seqq. (on the principle of equality in VAT law).

CJEU is a case-by-case decision which makes it highly difficult to extract general criteria from the cases on when the CJEU finds two situations comparable or not.[1308]

Once it is determined that two comparable situations are treated unequally (or two non-comparable situations are treated equally), the second step in the equality test is to review whether the (un)equal treatment is justified.[1309] Thereby, the CJEU has held that a 'difference in treatment is justified if it is based on an objective and reasonable criterion, that is if the difference relates to a legally permitted aim pursued by the legislation in question'.[1310] In this sense, an objective and reasonable criterion could be the 'objectives of general interest recognised by the Union or the need to protect the rights and freedoms of others'.[1311] Considerations of administrative practicability[1312] or the effectiveness of legal provisions[1313] may also be considered as grounds for justification.[1314]

Additionally, after the identification of possible justifications, the proportionality of the provision concerned and the (un)equal treatment should be reviewed.[1315] Thereby, a distinction must be made between this step in the equality test and the principle of proportionality as a general principle of EU law.[1316] For the proportionality test within the equality test, in a first step, it should be reviewed whether the disputed measure is appropriate for achieving the objective pursued.[1317] Additionally, 'the measure chosen must be the least restrictive among the appropriate measures that may

---

1308. Cornelia Köchler & Laura Pavlidis, *Gleichheit*, Charta der Grundrechte der Europäischen Union: GRC-Kommentar, *supra* note 1295, para. 26, with further examples on the inconsistency of the CJEU case law in para. 27; *see* also Mark Bell, *Article 20 – Equality Before the Law*, The EU Charter of Fundamental Rights: A Commentary, *supra* note 1295, paras 20.23 et seqq.

1309. Cornelia Köchler & Laura Pavlidis, *supra* note 1295, para. 22.

1310. *See, e.g.,* Case C-127/07, *Société Arcelor Atlantique et Lorraine and Others v Premier ministre, Ministre de l'Écologie et du Développement durable and Ministre de l'Économie, des Finances et de l'Industrie*, 16 Dec. 2008, ECLI:EU:C:2008:728, para. 47; Case C-101/12, *Herbert Schaible v Land Baden-Württemberg*, 17 Oct. 2013, ECLI:EU:C:2013:661, para. 77; Case C-356/12, *Wolfgang Glatzel v Freistaat Bayern*, 22 May 2014, ECLI:EU:C:2014:350, para. 43; Case C-156/15, *'Private Equity Insurance Group' SIA v 'Swedbank' AS*, 10 Nov. 2016, ECLI:EU:C:2016:851, para. 49.

1311. Article 52 (1) of the CFR; *see* also Case C-540/16, *UAB 'Spika' and Others v Žuvininkystes tarnyba prie Lietuvos Respublikos žemes ukio ministerijos*, 12 Jul. 2018, ECLI:EU:C:2018:565, para. 36, where the CJEU explicitly refers to the basis for the objective justification test in Article 52 (1) of the CFR; *see* also in literature reference is made to Article 52 (1) of the CFR, e.g., in Mark Bell, *supra* note 1295, para. 20.28; Cornelia Köchler & Laura Pavlidis, *supra* note 1295, para. 34; *see* critically Hans D. Jarass, *Art. 20 Gleichheit vor dem Gesetz*, Charta der Grundrechte der EU, *supra* note 1295, para. 15.

1312. Joined Cases C-248/95 and C-249/95, *SAM Schiffahrt GmbH and Heinz Stapf v Bundesrepublik Deutschland*, 17 Jul. 1997, ECLI:EU:C:1997:377, para. 60.

1313. Case C-84/87, *Erpelding v Secrétaire d'État à l'Agriculture and à la Viticulture*, 17 May 1988, ECLI:EU:C:1988:245, para. 30.

1314. Cornelia Köchler & Laura Pavlidis, *supra* note 1295, para. 34.

1315. *See, e.g.,* Case C-127/07, *Arcelor Atlantique and Lorraine and Others*, 16 Dec. 2008, ECLI:EU:C:2008:728, para. 47; Case C-101/12, *Schaible*, 17 Oct. 2013, ECLI:EU:C:2013:661, para. 77; Case C-356/12, *Glatzel*, 22 May 2014, ECLI:EU:C:2014:350, para. 43; Case C-156/15, *Private Equity Insurance Group*, 10 Nov. 2016, ECLI:EU:C:2016:851, para. 49.

1316. For a further discussion on the synergy between the principle of proportionality and the proportionality test of testing the fundamental rights, *see* Bernhard Oreschnik, *Verhältnismäßigkeit und Kontrolldichte* 140 et seqq. (Springer 2019).

1317. Case C-390/15, *RPO*, 7 Mar. 2017, ECLI:EU:C:2017:174, para. 61.

be envisaged and ... the disadvantages caused must not be disproportionate to the objectives pursued'.[1318] Also, in the second step of the equality test, the intensity of testing the justification and proportionality by the CJEU depends highly on the case at hand.[1319] Thereby, it seems that the CJEU tests the principle of equality in some fields of law more profoundly, such as in labour law, than in other fields of law.[1320]

5.2.3.2 The Applicability of Article 20 of the CFR to VAT Law

The applicability of Article 20 of the CFR to VAT law is, to some extent, difficult to grasp as the CJEU has developed a specific principle that is the reflection of the principle of equality in VAT law, i.e., the principle of neutrality.[1321] Therefore, most cases in VAT law are not tested against the principle of equality but against the principle of neutrality.[1322] The CJEU has only decided on a handful of cases testing the principle of equality in VAT law.[1323]

In the literature, a potential violation of the principle of equality in the VAT is divided into two groups.[1324] The first category refers to potential unequal treatment of suppliers supplying comparable supplies.[1325] In this category, a possible infringement of the principle of equality could arise due to

---

1318. *Ibid.* para. 64.

1319. Cornelia Köchler & Laura Pavlidis, *supra* note 1295, para. 44.

1320. Mark Bell, *Article 20 – Equality Before the Law*, The EU Charter of Fundamental Rights: A Commentary, *supra* note 1295, paras 20.29 + 20.33; Cornelia Köchler & Laura Pavlidis, *supra* note 1295, para. 45.

1321. For further discussions on the principle of neutrality, *see* s. 5.2.5 Article 14a of the VAT Directive as a Violation of the Principle of Neutrality?.

1322. *See*, e.g., Case C-309/06, *Marks & Spencer*, 10 Apr. 2008, ECLI:EU:C:2008:211, para. 49; Case C-174/08, *NCC Construction Danmark A/S v Skatteministeriet*, 29 Oct. 2009, ECLI: EU:C:2009:669, para. 41; Case C-259/10, *Commissioners for Her Majesty's Revenue and Customs v The Rank Group plc*, 10 Nov. 2011, ECLI:EU:C:2011:719, para. 61; Case C-480/10, *European Commission v Kingdom of Sweden*, 25 Apr. 2013, ECLI:EU:C:2013:263, para. 17.

1323. *See*, e.g., Case C-36/99, *Idéal tourisme SA v Belgian State*, 13 Jul. 2000, ECLI:EU:C:2000:405; Case C-460/07, *Sandra Puffer v Unabhängiger Finanzsenat, Außenstelle Linz*, 23 Apr. 2009, ECLI:EU:C:2009:254; Case C-462/16, *Finanzamt Bingen-Alzey v Boehringer Ingelheim Pharma GmbH & Co. KG*, 20 Dec. 2017, ECLI:EU:C:2017:1006; Case C-250/11, *Lietuvos geležinkeliai AB v Vilniaus teritorine muitine, Muitines departamentas prie Lietuvos Respublikos finansų ministerijos*, 19 Jul. 2012, ECLI:EU:C:2012:496; Case C-390/15, *RPO*, 7 Mar. 2017, ECLI:EU:C:2017:174; Case C-534/16, *Finančné riaditel'stvo Slovenskej republiky v BB construct s.r.o*, 26 Oct. 2017, ECLI:EU:C:2017:820.

1324. *See* Karina Kim Egholm Elgaard, *The Effect of the Charter of Fundamental Rights of the European Union on Substantive VAT Law*, in *CJEU – Recent Developments in Value Added Tax 2017*, 28 et seqq. (Michael Lang et al. eds., Linde Verlag 2018); Juliane Kokott & Lars Dobratz, *Der unionsrechtliche allgemeine Gleichheitssatz im Europäischen Steuerrecht*, in *Grundfragen des europäischen Steuerrechts*, *supra* note 1299, at 37 et seqq.

1325. *See* Karina Kim Egholm Elgaard, *supra* note 1324, at 28 et seqq.; Juliane Kokott & Lars Dobratz, *supra* note 1299, at 37 et seq.

- the application of different VAT rates to comparable goods and services,[1326]
- the application of VAT exemptions to comparable goods and services, [1327]
- the application of different price reductions based on Article 90 of the VAT Directive to comparable situations,[1328]
- the different incurrence of tax liability between traders who have to pre-finance the VAT due and traders who do not have to pre-finance the VAT due,[1329]
- the different calculation of input tax deduction for comparable persons (e.g., for goods that are used for taxable as well as tax exempt transactions),[1330]
- the limited scope of application of special regimes (e.g., for travel agencies in Article 306 of the VAT Directive) to narrowly defined economic activities or taxable persons,[1331] or
- the requirement to provide securities or additional evidence for only certain traders for the VAT registration.[1332]

In the literature, the stand-still clauses of the VAT Directive might qualify as an infringement of the principle of equality.[1333] Pursuant to Articles 370-374 of the VAT Directive, Member States can decide to tax or exempt the supply of certain goods or services, although such an exemption is not provided for explicitly in the VAT

1326. *See* Case C-390/15, *RPO*, 7 Mar. 2017, ECLI:EU:C:2017:174; *see* also Juliane Kokott & Lars Dobratz, *supra* note 1299, at 37 et seq., who argue that the CJEU has not yet decided cases based on the principle of equality within the application of different rates to comparable goods and services. Thereby, it should be noted that the article by Kokott & Dobratz was published before the issuing of the judgment of the *RPO* case; with reference to Case C-479/13, *European Commission v French Republic*, 5 Mar. 2015, ECLI:EU:C:2015:141; and to Case C-502/13, *European Commission v Grand Duchy of Luxembourg*, 5 Mar. 2015, ECLI:EU:C:2015:143.

1327. *See* Case C-462/16, *Finanzamt Bingen-Alzey v Boehringer Ingelheim Pharma GmbH & Co. KG*, 11 Jul. 2017, ECLI:EU:C:2017:534, Opinion of AG Tanchev where AG Tanchev based the equality test on Article 20 of the CFR; the CJEU adapted the equality test, without referring to Article 20 of the CFR; *see* Case C-462/16, *Boehringer Ingelheim Pharma*, 20 Dec. 2017, ECLI:EU:C:2017:1006; *see* also the discussion of this AG Tanchev's opinion in Georg Kofler, *Europäischer Grundrechtsschutz im Steuerrecht, in Europäisches Steuerrecht* 151 et seqq. (Michael Lang ed., Otto Schmidt 2018); *see* also Juliane Kokott & Lars Dobratz, *supra* note 1299, at 37, who argue that the CJEU has not yet decided cases based on the principle of equality within the application of exemptions. This statement is still true today as the CJEU did not refer to the principle of equality in its judgment but only AG Tanchev.

1328. *See* Case C-246/16, *Enzo Di Maura v Agenzia delle Entrate – Direzione Provinciale di Siracusa*, 8 Jun. 2017, ECLI:EU:C:2017:440, Opinion of AG Kokott, paras. 56 et seqq.; the CJEU did not take the principle of equality into consideration, *see* Case C-246/16, *Enzo Di Maura v Agenzia delle Entrate – Direzione Provinciale di Siracusa*, 23 Nov. 2017, ECLI:EU:C:2017:887.

1329. *See* Case C-264/14, *Skatteverket v David Hedqvist*, 16 Jul. 2015, ECLI:EU:C:2015:498, Opinion of AG Kokott, para. 41; the CJEU did not take the principle of equality into consideration; *see* Case C-264/14, *Skatteverket v David Hedqvist*, 22 Oct. 2015, ECLI:EU:C:2015:718.

1330. *See* Case C-460/07, *Puffer*, 23 Apr. 2009, ECLI:EU:C:2009:254, paras. 52 et seqq.

1331. *See* Case C-599/12, *Jetair and BTWE Travel4you*, 13 Mar. 2014, ECLI:EU:C:2014:144, paras. 53 et seqq.

1332. *See* Case C-534/16, *BB construct*, 26 Oct. 2017, ECLI:EU:C:2017:820, paras. 43 et seqq.

1333. *See* Karina Kim Egholm Elgaard, *The Effect of the Charter of Fundamental Rights of the European Union on Substantive VAT Law, in CJEU – Recent Developments in Value Added Tax 2017*, *supra* note 1324, at 28 et seqq.; Juliane Kokott & Lars Dobratz, *Der unionsrechtliche allgemeine Gleichheitssatz im Europäischen Steuerrecht, in Grundfragen des europäischen Steuerrechts*, *supra* note 1299, at 37 et seqq.

Directive.[1334] The application of these derogations in the VAT Directive is provided for in the relevant heading to Article 370-374 of the VAT Directive under '[d]erogations applying until the adoption of definitive arrangements'. The different VAT treatment of supplies of goods and services depending on the Member State in which the supply is subject to the VAT can be seen as a violation of the principle of equality.[1335] Although unequal treatment due to transitional arrangements in the case of gradual harmonisation of EU law is, in principle, accepted by the CJEU,[1336] the existence of the 'transitional arrangements' in the VAT Directive for more than 40 years can be viewed critically according to the principle of equality.

A deeper analysis of the *RPO* case provides information on how far the application of Article 20 of the CFR extends and how much leeway the EU legislator has when introducing VAT provisions. In the *RPO* case, the CJEU addressed the question of whether the non-application of the reduced VAT rate for books stipulated in Article 98 (2) read in conjunction with point 6 of Annex III of the VAT Directive[1337] to electronic publications violates Article 20 of the CFR. The CJEU affirmed the comparability of the supply of printed books and electronic books.[1338] However, the different treatment of publications and e-publications can be justified by the principle of legal certainty and the objective of facilitating the administration of VAT and is also proportionate.[1339] In this regard, the CJEU emphasised that 'when the EU legislature adopts a tax measure, it is called upon to make political, economic and social choices, and to rank divergent interests or to undertake complex assessments. Consequently, it should, in that context, be accorded a broad discretion, so that judicial review of compliance with the conditions set out in the previous paragraph of this judgment must be limited to review

---

1334. Juliane Kokott & Lars Dobratz, *supra* note 1299, at 38; Karina Kim Egholm Elgaard, *supra* note 1324, at 31 et seqq.

1335. Juliane Kokott & Lars Dobratz, *supra* note 1299, at 38 et seq.; Joined Cases C-144/13, C-154/13, C-160/13, *VDP Dental Laboratory NV v Staatssecretaris van Financiën and Staatssecretaris van Financiën v X BV and Nobel Biocare Nederland BV*, 4 Sep. 2014, ECLI:EU:C:2014:2163, Opinion of AG Kokott, paras. 84 et seq.; *see* also the discussion of this AG Kokott's opinion in Karina Kim Egholm Elgaard, *The Impact of the Charter of Fundamental Rights of the European Union on VAT Law*, 5 World Journal of VAT/GST Law 87 et seqq. (2016); Karina Kim Egholm Elgaard, *supra* note 1324, at 31 et seqq.; *see* also a similar argumentation by Joachim Englisch, *Gemeinschaftsgrundrechte im harmonisierten Steuerrecht, in Zukunftsfragen des deutschen Steuerrechts* 67 et seqq. (Wolfgang Schön & Karin E.M. Beck eds., Springer 2009).

1336. *See*, e.g., Case C-236/09, *Association Belge des Consommateurs Test-Achats ASBL and Others v Conseil des ministres*, 1 Mar. 2011, ECLI:EU:C:2011:100, para. 23; Joined Cases C-297/10 and C-298/10, *Sabine Hennigs (C-297/10) v Eisenbahn-Bundesamt and Land Berlin (C-298/10) v Alexander Mai*, 8 Sep. 2011, ECLI:EU:C:2011:560, para. 97.

1337. Please note that, after the issuing of the Case C-390/15, *RPO*, 7 Mar. 2017, ECLI:EU:C:2017:174 case, the EU legislator amended the VAT Directive. Due to this amendment, the Member States may also apply the reduced VAT rate to e-publications; *see* Council Directive (EU) 2018/1713 of 6 November 2018 amending Directive 2006/112/EC as regards rates of value added tax applied to books, newspapers and periodicals, OJ L 286 (2018); *see* also the press release Council of the European Union, *Electronic Publications: Council Agrees to Allow Reduced VAT Rates*, https://www.consilium.europa.eu/en/press/press-releases/20 18/10/02/electronic-publications-council-agrees-to-allow-reduced-vat-rates/ (last visited 5 Apr. 2021).

1338. Case C-390/15, *RPO*, 7 Mar. 2017, ECLI:EU:C:2017:174, para. 51.

1339. *Ibid.* paras. 59 et seqq.

as to manifest error'.[1340] Accordingly, the CJEU denied a violation of Article 98 (2) read in conjunction with point 6 of Annex III of the VAT Directive (in the version applicable at that time) against the principle of equality pursuant to Article 20 of the CFR.[1341] Kokott explains the CJEU's reluctance to apply Article 20 of the CFR with respect of the CJEU for the Member States and the separation of powers. On the one hand, Kokott refers to the vertical separation of powers, i.e., the respect of the CJEU for the EU legislator, and, on the other hand, to the horizontal separation of powers between the European Union and the Member States[1342] which is particularly relevant when examining national provisions for their conformity with the principle of equality.

When analysing the CJEU cases, it should be noted that only in the *RPO* case did the CJEU explicitly refer to and examine the violation of Article 20 of the CFR.[1343] In all other cases, an explicit reference to Article 20 of the CFR can only be found in the respective opinions of the Advocate Generals[1344] or the cases were based on the general principle of equality because Article 20 of the CFR was not yet in force.[1345] Moreover, a violation of the general principle of equal treatment has been established only once so far;[1346] in all other rulings, a violation was denied as the situations were not comparable[1347] or justified on the basis of the principle of legal certainty and the objective of facilitating the administration of VAT.[1348]

1340. Case C-390/15, *RPO*, 7 Mar. 2017, ECLI:EU:C:2017:174; with reference to Case C-491/01, *The Queen v Secretary of State for Health, ex parte British American Tobacco (Investments) Ltd and Imperial Tobacco Ltd*, 10 Dec. 2002, ECLI:EU:C:2002:741, para. 123; Case C-203/12, *Billerud Karlsborg AB and Billerud Skärblacka AB v Naturvårdsverket*, 17 Oct. 2013, ECLI: EU:C:2013:664, para. 35.
1341. Case C-390/15, *RPO*, 7 Mar. 2017, ECLI:EU:C:2017:174, para. 71.
1342. *See* the discussion comment by Kokott in Georg Kofler, *Europäischer Grundrechtsschutz im Steuerrecht, in Europäisches Steuerrecht, supra* note 1327, at 191 et seq.
1343. Case C-390/15, *RPO*, 7 Mar. 2017, ECLI:EU:C:2017:174.
1344. *See* Case C-174/11, *Finanzamt Steglitz v Ines Zimmermann*, 19 Jul. 2012, ECLI:EU:C:2012:493, Opinion of AG Mazák, para. 63; Joined Cases C-144/13, C-154/13, C-160/13, *VDP Dental Laboratory and Others*, 4 Sep. 2014, ECLI:EU:C:2014:2163, Opinion of AG Kokott, para. 84; Case C-264/14, *Hedqvist*, 16 Jul. 2015, ECLI:EU:C:2015:498, Opinion of AG Kokott, para. 41; Case C-246/16, *Di Maura*, 8 Jun. 2017, ECLI:EU:C:2017:440, Opinion of AG Kokott, paras 46 + 56; Case C-462/16, *Boehringer Ingelheim Pharma*, 11 Jul. 2017, ECLI:EU:C:2017:534, Opinion of AG Tanchev; AG Tanchev based the equality test on Article 20 of the CFR; the CJEU conducted an equality test but did not refer to Article 20 of the CFR, *see* Case C-462/16, *Boehringer Ingelheim Pharma*, 20 Dec. 2017, ECLI:EU:C:2017:1006.
1345. Case C-460/07, *Puffer*, 23 Apr. 2009, ECLI:EU:C:2009:254; Case C-599/12, *Jetair and BTWE Travel4you*, 13 Mar. 2014, ECLI:EU:C:2014:144.
1346. *See* Case C-309/06, *Marks & Spencer*, 10 Apr. 2008, ECLI:EU:C:2008:211, para. 54.
1347. Case C-460/07, *Puffer*, 23 Apr. 2009, ECLI:EU:C:2009:254, para. 57; Case C-599/12, *Jetair and BTWE Travel4you*, 13 Mar. 2014, ECLI:EU:C:2014:144, para. 55; Case C-534/16, *BB construct*, 26 Oct. 2017, ECLI:EU:C:2017:820, para. 46.
1348. Case C-390/15, *RPO*, 7 Mar. 2017, ECLI:EU:C:2017:174, paras. 59 et seq.

5.2.4 Article 14a VAT Directive as a Violation of the Principle of Equality According to Article 20 of the CFR?

5.2.4.1 *The Comparability Requirement and Identification of Unequal Treatment*

5.2.4.1.1 *Framework for the Identification of Two Comparable Situations*

The first step in the equality test is to define two comparable situations. As established, the CJEU is not very consistent in determining which aspects to consider so that two situations are comparable.[1349] According to the CJEU case law, special regard should be given to the objective of the applicable law;[1350] in this case, the objective of the introduction of the deemed supplier regime in Article 14a of the VAT Directive. Nevertheless, the CJEU also relies on the justification level to substantiate the objective of the introduction of the respective provision.[1351] Therefore, the objective of the provision may also be taken into consideration in the second step of the equality test. To avoid repetitions between the comparability and the justification test, a factual evaluation based on an investigation of the platforms' functions will serve as the basis of the following discussion of the comparable situations. The objective of Article 14a of the VAT Directive will be discussed in detail on the justification level.[1352]

As established, Article 14a of the VAT Directive covers two different situations in which the platform becomes the deemed supplier:[1353] on the one hand, the importation of low-value goods from third countries and, on the other hand, the national or intra-Community supply of goods when the underlying supplier is not established in the EU. Both paragraphs of Article 14a of the VAT Directive have in common that there is a third country element, that the supply is restricted to the supply of goods, and that the facilitated supply is a B2C supply. Additionally, due to the legal consequences of Article 14a of the VAT Directive, all supplies that are facilitated by platforms in the meaning of Article 14a of the VAT Directive should be taxed in the Member State of destination. The scope of Article 14a of the VAT Directive could lead to the understanding that three requirements should be fulfilled by a platform facilitating supplies to possibly qualify as comparable: a third country element should be identified, the

---

1349. *See*, on the discussion of the inconsistency of the CJEU, s. 5.2.3.1 Content of Article 20 of the CFR and the 'Equality Test'.
1350. *See*, e.g., Case C-390/15, *RPO*, 7 Mar. 2017, ECLI:EU:C:2017:174, paras. 43 et seqq.
1351. *See* Case C-390/15, *RPO*, 7 Mar. 2017, ECLI:EU:C:2017:174, where the CJEU referred to the objective of the law on the comparability level in paras. 43 et seqq. In the same judgment, the CJEU also refers to the objective of the law on the justification level, *see* paras. 58 et seqq. *See* also, similarly, in the discussion of the fundamental freedoms and an infringement thereof when levying withholding taxes exclusively from companies not established in the source state. In one case, the CJEU discussed the effective tax collection on the comparability level; *see* Case C-282/07, *Belgian State – SPF Finances v Truck Center SA*, 22 Dec. 2008, ECLI: EU:C:2008:762, para. 48; in another case, the CJEU discussed the effective tax collection as a justification reason; *see* Case C-290/04, *FKP Scorpio Konzertproduktionen GmbH v Finanzamt Hamburg-Eimsbüttel*, 3 Oct. 2006, ECLI:EU:C:2006:630, paras. 35 et seq.
1352. *See* sec 5.2.4.2.1.1 The Objective of the Introduction of Article 14a of the VAT Directive.
1353. *See*, on the substantive scope of Article 14a of the VAT Directive, s. 3.3 Substantive Scope.

platform should facilitate the supply of goods, and the facilitated supply is (generally) a B2C supply.[1354]

However, this understanding is a very narrow interpretation. In fact, if such a narrow understanding was applied for finding comparable situations, it would be likely that no other platform that is not anyhow already fulfilling the criteria of Article 14a of the VAT Directive would qualify as a comparable. Therefore, the focus for the determination of comparable situations should be set on the platform as a taxable person and thereby on the functioning of platforms in general.[1355] If the functioning of the platforms fulfilling the requirements of Article 14a of the VAT Directive was investigated, the determination of comparable elements might also be seen more broadly. The main function of platforms is to offer a digital website for suppliers and customers. Suppliers have the opportunity to offer their goods on the platform, and customers have the chance to purchase goods based on a large(r) choice of different goods.[1356] To fulfil the platform's function, the platform provides services to the underlying supplier and/or customers.[1357] In this sense, the main function of platforms is to act as intermediaries connecting two independent parties by matching suppliers with potential customers. If this broad(er) understanding was used for finding comparable situations to platforms fulfilling the requirements of Article 14a of the VAT Directive, then the three elements stated above, the third country element, the facilitation of the supply of goods, and the facilitation of B2C supplies should not qualify as determining factors on which the comparability should be based.

In the following sections, several platform business models will be described, and it will be investigated whether these platforms may be comparable to a platform facilitating the supply according to Article 14a of the VAT Directive. Thereby, the following situations are only examples and should not be read as a conclusive list of platforms that should be taken into consideration as being comparable. It is likely that, if one of the criteria were not fulfilled (third country element, facilitation of the supply of goods, and facilitation of a B2C supply), the platform may still qualify as comparable as specified in the preceding paragraphs. Thereby, the criterion of being a B2C supply should not be disregarded when finding comparable situations as supplies by non-taxable persons (C2B and C2C supplies) are not taxable under the VAT Directive, and different place of supply rules are applicable to B2B supplies.

To make the situations more vivid, the following initial example of when Article 14a of the VAT Directive is applicable serves as the situation that the other situations will be tested against and compared. If a Russian supplier supplied, e.g., a jacket with a value ≤ EUR 150 from Hungary to an Austrian consumer through the facilitation of a

---

1354. *See* already s. 3.4 Conclusion on the Scope of Article 14a of the VAT Directive and sec 5.2.2.1 The Restrictions of Article 14a of the VAT Directive.
1355. *See*, on the functioning of the platform in general, s. 2.1.2 The Role of Platforms.
1356. *See*, on the general benefits of the suppliers and the customers, s. 2.1.3 The Benefit for Suppliers and s. 2.1.4 The Benefit for Customers.
1357. *See*, on the qualification of the supply of service from the platform to underlying supper, s. 2.2.4 The Supply of the Platform Service to the Underlying Supplier and for the supply of the service from the platform to the customer s. 2.2.5 The Supply of the Platform Service to the Customer.

platform, then the platform facilitating the supply of the jacket would become the deemed supplier according to Article 14a (2) of the VAT Directive. With the applicability of the deemed supplier regime, the platform faces an increasing amount of additional administrative burden due to the additional compliance obligations that also cause additional costs for the platform. These additional administrative burdens and costs could be considered as being a disadvantage for the platform becoming the deemed supplier as sometimes requested by the CJEU for the equality test.[1358]

5.2.4.1.2 Situation 1: The Facilitation of Supplies of EU-Goods by EU Suppliers – Analysis of the Comparability and Identification of Unequal Treatment

The first situation is the facilitation of the supply of goods within the EU by EU suppliers through the facilitation of platforms and thereby amending the initial example slightly. A Hungarian taxable person supplies, e.g., a jacket with a value $\leq$ EUR 150 from Hungary to an Austrian consumer through the facilitation of a platform. In this case, the place of supply is where the goods are located at the time when the dispatch or transport of the goods to the customer ends,[1359] i.e., in Austria. The only element that changed in the given example is the seat of establishment of the supplier. Compared to the initial example where the supplier is established in a third country (Russia), in this case, the supplier is established in a Member State (Hungary). As not all requirements of Article 14a (2) of the VAT Directive are fulfilled, the platform does not become the deemed supplier in the given case. Nevertheless, the activity and services provided by the platform have not changed; the only change between the initial example and the first situation is that the underlying suppliers are established in different countries. As the platform provides the same activity in the initial example and in the described situation acting as an intermediary, it can be argued that the two situations are comparable.[1360]

In the given examples, the platform becomes the deemed supplier in only one of the two cases, i.e., only when the supply of goods by a taxable person established in a third country is facilitated (the case when the Russian supplier is supplying the goods) but not when the platform acts as an intermediary for the supply of goods by an EU taxable person (the case when the Hungarian supplier is supplying the goods).[1361] Although the platforms' intermediation activity is comparable in both cases, only the platform facilitating the supply of goods by the third country supplier becomes the

---

1358. *See*, e.g., Joined Cases C-17/61 and C-20/61, *Klöckner-Werke AG and Others v High Authority*, 13 Jul. 1962, ECLI:EU:C:1962:30, 692 et seq.; Case C-351/98, *Spain v Commission*, 26 Sep. 2002, ECLI:EU:C:2002:530, para. 57; Case C-462/99, *Connect Austria*, 22 May 2003, ECLI: EU:C:2003:297, para. 115.
1359. Article 33 (a) of the VAT Directive.
1360. *See*, for the discussion of the framework of the comparability requirement, s. 5.2.4.1.1 Framework for the Identification of Two Comparable Situations.
1361. Assumingly, the platform does not act in its own name and not on behalf of the underlying EU-supplier. Therefore, Article 14 (2) (c) of the VAT Directive is not applicable.

deemed supplier and is therefore liable for the VAT due. Therefore, the two comparable situations are treated differently in the VAT Directive.

5.2.4.1.3 Situation 2: The Facilitation of Supplies of Accommodation Services or Event Tickets – Analysis of the Comparability and Identification of Unequal Treatment

Another example can be found in the facilitation of the supply of certain services. At first sight, the comparison to platforms facilitating services could raise the question of whether the supply of goods and services can even qualify as being comparable as the VAT system, in general, treats the supply of goods and services differently. This difference becomes especially clear when looking at the place of supply: the general place of supply for B2C supplies of goods follows the destination principle; i.e., sold goods should be taxed where the consumer receives the goods.[1362] For the B2C supply of services, the general place of supply rule stipulates that the place of establishment or usual residence of the supplier is the place of supply for services.[1363] The VAT Directive provides for certain exceptions to this general rule, but, in many cases, the place of supply of services would be the place of establishment or usual residence of the supplier.[1364] Therefore, for the B2C supply of services, the principle of origin has been implemented. Another example for the different treatment of goods and services is the application of the reverse-charge system according to Article 196 of the VAT Directive to B2B supply of services whereas the B2B supply of goods is declared via an intra-Community supply and intra-Community acquisition. Although the consequence of the reverse-charge system for the supply of services and the declaration of an intra-Community supply and intra-Community acquisition lead to a similar result, i.e., the taxation in the Member State of destination, different mechanisms are used to achieve this result. Since both mechanisms have the aim to tax consumption, the different implementation on how this result is achieved is not relevant in terms of determining the comparability of the situations.[1365]

Nevertheless, special regard should be given to the place of supply. When deciding on comparable situations, the place of supply of the service should be in the EU. This is for the following reason: if the place of supply of the service was in the EU due to the nature of the service, then the place of supply would stay in the EU regardless of whether the supplier is the underlying supplier or (fictitiously) the platform. If the place of supply was determined based on the general place of supply

---

1362. *See* Articles 33-35 of the VAT Directive.

1363. *See* Article 45 of the VAT Directive.

1364. The OECD explains the difference in the general implementation of the destination of the supply of goods with the facilitation of border controls or fiscal frontiers. Due to these mechanisms, the tracing of the supply of goods is easier than the supply of services; *see* OECD, *Addressing the Tax Challenges of the Digital Economy – Action 1: 2015 Final Report, supra* note 447, at 222; OECD, *Mechanisms for the Effective Collection of VAT/GST When the Supplier Is Not Located in the Jurisdiction of Taxation, supra* note 458, para. 16.

1365. *See,* similarly, Case C-390/15, *RPO*, 7 Mar. 2017, ECLI:EU:C:2017:174, para. 50, where the CJEU highlights that, regardless of a supply qualifying as a supply of goods or services, the aim of the VAT is to tax consumption.

rule for services pursuant to Article 45 of the VAT Directive, then the place of establishment of the (deemed) supplier would determine the place of supply of the service. Thus, the fictitious inclusion of the platform may change the place of supply, e.g., if the platform was established in a third country and if the platform was fictitiously included in the supply, the place of supply would be in that third country whereas, if the platform was not fictitiously included in the supply of the service and if the underlying supplier was established in the EU, the place of supply would be in the EU. Therefore, if the place of supply was determined based on Article 45 of the VAT Directive, then the place of supply could be altered depending on where the (fictitious) supplier was established. If the underlying supplier was established in a third country, but the platform was established in the EU, the place of supply of the service may be pulled into the EU under the condition that the platform was fictitiously involved in the supply.[1366] On the other hand, if the underlying supplier was established in the EU, but the platform was established in a third country, the fictitious inclusion of the platform would lead to the result of EU Member States losing the right to tax because of the place of establishment of the platform in a third country.[1367]

Taking into consideration the discussed special attention to the place of supply rules, two situations could be discussed where special place of supply rules would be applicable so that the place of supply does not depend on the place of establishment of the (fictitious) supplier: a platform facilitating accommodation services or a platform facilitating the sale of event tickets. The following examples illustrate these two supplies. A person established in a third country rents out an apartment in the EU through the facilitation of a platform. According to Article 47 of the VAT Directive, the place of supply of accommodation services is where the immovable property to be rented out is situated. If, e.g., a taxable person established in Russia rented out an apartment in Vienna, the place of supply of this service would be in Austria.

Similarly, a person established in a third country may sell tickets for concerts (or other events) taking place in the EU through the facilitation of a platform. According to Article 54 of the VAT Directive, the place of supply for cultural, artistic, sporting, scientific, educational, entertainment, or similar events is the place where the event actually takes place. If, e.g., a taxable person established in Russia sold concert tickets for a concert in Vienna, the place of supply of this service would be in Austria.

According to the current applicable rules, a platform facilitating such accommodation services or the sale of event tickets in the EU would generally not become the deemed supplier for the transaction.[1368] The taxable person renting out the apartment

---

1366. In this case, the place of establishment of the platform (EU) would be relevant for determining the place of supply according to Article 45 of the VAT Directive. The EU would not have had the taxing rights if the platform would not have become the deemed supplier because the place of establishment of the underlying supplier is in the given example in the third country.

1367. In this case, the place of establishment of the platform (third country) would be relevant for determining the place of supply according to Article 45 of the VAT Directive. If the platform would not have become the deemed supplier, the taxing rights would have been in the EU since the underlying supplier is established in the EU in the given example.

1368. This statement is based on the assumption that Article 28 of the VAT Directive is not applicable; i.e., the platform does not act in its own name and not on behalf of the lessee. Furthermore, the clarification in Article 9a of the VAT Implementing Regulation would not be

or selling the event tickets would be the contractual partner of the customer not only in light of contract law but also in light of VAT law. The service of the platform would be considered as an intermediation service (likely an electronically supplied service[1369]) provided from the platform to the underlying supplier and/or the customer, but the platform would not qualify as the deemed supplier.[1370] Although the platforms' intermediation activity facilitating the supply of the service is comparable to when the platform facilitates the supply of a good, only the platform facilitating the supply of goods becomes the deemed supplier and is therefore liable for the VAT due.[1371]

It is questionable, though, whether the two platforms involved, i.e., the platform facilitating the accommodation services or the sale of event tickets and the platform facilitating the sale of the jacket, can be considered to be in comparable situations even though the two supplies are not in competition with each other. Thereby, guidance can be found in CJEU case law. The CJEU explicitly held that an 'infringement of the general principle of equal treatment may be established, in matters relating to tax, by other kinds of discrimination which affect traders who are not necessarily in competition with each other but who are nevertheless in a similar situation in other respects'.[1372] In the case *Marks & Spencer,* for example, the CJEU held that taxable persons holding VAT credits and seeking the repayment of their credits from the competent tax authorities are in comparable situations regardless of whether the traders applying for the VAT refund are in competition with each other.[1373] Therefore, the two platforms facilitating the supply of the goods and services do not have to be in competition with each other to be found as being in comparable situations. Concluding, it can be argued that the described platforms are in comparable situations, but only the platform facilitating the supply of goods is becoming a deemed supplier. Therefore, the two comparable situations are treated differently in the VAT Directive.

---

applicable because the provided service is not an electronically supplied service or a telephone service supplied through the Internet, but it is an accommodation service or the service of the sale of event tickets.

1369. *See* s. 2.2.5.3.4 An Evaluation of the Applicable Place of Supply Rule: Article 46 of the VAT Directive Versus Article 58 of the VAT Directive.

1370. *See,* on the services by the platform to the underlying supplier and/or the customer, s. 2.2.4 The Supply of the Platform Service to the Underlying Supplier and s. 2.2.5 The Supply of the Platform Service to the Customer. Although, in these sections, the intermediation service of platforms supplying goods was discussed, these discussions could also apply to platforms supplying services.

1371. *See,* for the discussion of the framework of the comparability requirement, s. 5.2.4.1.1 Framework for the Identification of Two Comparable Situations.

1372. Case C-309/06, *Marks & Spencer,* 10 Apr. 2008, ECLI:EU:C:2008:211, para. 49; Case C-480/10, *Commission v Sweden,* 25 Apr. 2013, ECLI:EU:C:2013:263, para. 17; *see* similarly also Case C-462/16, *Boehringer Ingelheim Pharma,* 11 Jul. 2017, ECLI:EU:C:2017:534, Opinion of AG Tanchev, para. 47.

1373. *See* Case C-309/06, *Marks & Spencer,* 10 Apr. 2008, ECLI:EU:C:2008:211, para. 50.

5.2.4.1.4   Situation 3: The Facilitation of Supplies of Electronically Supplied Services – Analysis of the Comparability and Identification of Unequal Treatment

The third situation is the facilitation of the supply of electronically supplied services through the facilitation of platforms: a platform offers different software from suppliers throughout the world and sets the general terms and conditions for the supplies facilitated through their platform. A Russian taxable person supplies software to a consumer established in Austria through the facilitation of this platform. The supply of standard software for download is explicitly stated in Article 7 (2) (a) of the VAT Implementing Regulation as qualifying as an electronically supplied service. Additionally, for the supply of electronically supplied services, a special place of supply rule is applicable. According to Article 58 (1) (c) of the VAT Directive, the place of supply for electronically supplied B2C services is the place where the non-taxable person is established, so in this case, in Austria. As the platform also sets the terms and conditions for this supply, the platform becomes *ex lege* the deemed supplier of this transaction according to Article 9a of the VAT Implementing Regulation read in conjunction with Article 28 of the VAT Directive. As the platform would facilitate the supply by acting as an intermediary in the initial example as well as in the described situation 3, it can be argued that the two situations are comparable.

In the given examples, the platform becomes the deemed supplier in both cases: the platform facilitating the supply of the electronically supplied services becomes the deemed supplier of the supply of the software according to Article 9a of the VAT Implementing Regulation read in conjunction with Article 28 of the VAT Directive, and the platform facilitating the supply of the jacket from the Russian supplier becomes the deemed supplier according to Article 14a (2) of the VAT Directive. Therefore, the two platforms are in comparable situations, and they are treated in the same way according to the VAT Directive. In this example, Article 14a of the VAT Directive does not lead to a different treatment of the involved platforms.

5.2.4.1.5   Excursus: The Supply of Goods by Platforms

5.2.4.1.5.1   General Remarks on the Excursus

The following excursus will investigate a slightly different case. As discussed, Article 20 of the CFR is applicable to comparable situations that must not be treated differently and different situations that must not be treated equal.[1374] The previous examples have investigated comparable situations that might be treated differently. This excurses will

---

1374. Case C-106/83, *Sermide*, 13 Dec. 1984, ECLI:EU:C:1984:394, para. 28; Case C-44/94, *The Queen v Minister of Agriculture, Fisheries and Food, ex parte Fishermen's Organisations and Others*, 17 Oct. 1995, ECLI:EU:C:1995:325, para. 46; Case C-248/04, *Koninklijke Coöperatie Cosun*, 26 Oct. 2006, ECLI:EU:C:2006:666, para. 72; Case C-303/05, *Advocaten voor de Wereld*, 3 May 2007, ECLI:EU:C:2007:261, para. 56; Case C-21/10, *Nagy*, 21 Jul. 2011, ECLI:EU:C:2011:505, para. 47. *See* the discussions in s. 5.2.3.1 Content of Article 20 of the CFR and the 'Equality Test'.

analyse the second possibility of the application of the principle of equality, i.e., the equal treatment of different situations.

In this example, the platform not only facilitates the supply of a good but buys the goods from the underlying supplier. The goods are delivered from the first party that the platform buys the goods from to the final customer. In this case, the previously determined comparability requirements are not fully fulfilled[1375] because the platform actually buys the goods and not only facilitates the supply of goods through its platform. Therefore, the platform is actually part of the supply chain and not fictitiously included in the supply chain solely for VAT purposes.

5.2.4.1.5.2   Description of the Basic Example

5.2.4.1.5.2.1 The Facts of the Basic Example – Transactions within the EU

In this case, the initial example is amended to the following. A platform supplies a jacket with a value ≤ EUR 150 from Hungary to an Austrian consumer. At the same moment as the customer purchases the jacket through the platform, the Hungarian underlying supplier sells the jacket to the platform.[1376] The jacket is transported from the warehouse of the Hungarian underlying supplier in Hungary directly to the final customer in Austria. Therefore, the requirements of a chain transaction are fulfilled. The same goods are successively supplied and 'are dispatched or transported from one Member State to another Member State directly from the first supplier to the last customer in the chain'.[1377] Thus, the first question of what should be evaluated is which of the two supplies is the supply with transport. There are two options: either the supply from the Hungarian underlying supplier to the platform or the supply from the platform to the Austrian customer. To determine the supply with transport, it should be evaluated who dispatches or transports the goods in question.[1378] From a practical point of view, the transport could either be organised by the Hungarian supplier or the platform. It is rather unrealistic that the customer ordering the goods on the platform would be responsible for organising the transport. The customer orders the goods on the platform, and the platform is also the official seller of the goods, and, therefore, it

---

1375. *See,* for the criteria of the comparability, s. 5.2.4.1.1 Framework for the Identification of Two Comparable Situations.
1376. For the simplicity of this example, a Hungarian underlying supplier was used. This Hungarian underlying supplier could also be interchanged to a Russian underlying supplier as the place of establishment of the underlying supplier is not relevant in this case.
1377. *See* Article 36a of the VAT Directive.
1378. *See* European Commission, *Explanatory Notes on the EU VAT Changes in Respect of Call-Off Stock Arrangements, Chain Transactions and the Exemption for Intra-Community Supplies of Goods ('2020 Quick Fixes'), supra* note 35, at 53, where the European Commission discusses what 'to dispatch or transport' means. In a first step, it should be investigated who organised the transport. This organisation can be made by one party in the chain himself, but that person may also contract other people with the transport of the goods. Thereby, the fact of who actually pays the transport costs should not only be relevant for organising the transport; additionally, according to AG Kokott, also the risk taking of loss or damage of the goods may be taken into consideration for determining who organised the transport; *see* Case C-401/18, *Herst,* 3 Oct. 2019, ECLI:EU:C:2019:834, Opinion of AG Kokott, para. 79.

is likely that the customer does not even know who the underlying supplier is. Depending on who organises the transport, different legal consequences may be applicable.

5.2.4.1.5.2.2 The Legal Consequences of the Basic Example: Transport Organised by the Hungarian Underlying Supplier

The first possibility in the basic example would be that the Hungarian underlying supplier organises the transport of the goods to the Austrian customer (*see* for a graphical illustration of the legal qualification of this chain transaction Figure 5.1). Thus, the first supply from the Hungarian underlying supplier to the platform qualifies as the supply with transport from Hungary to Austria.[1379] The Hungarian underlying supplier would have to declare an intra-Community supply from Hungary to Austria. If the Hungarian underlying supplier fulfilled all requirements, this supply should be VAT exempt.[1380] Additionally, the platform fulfils the requirements of an intra-Community acquisition in Austria.[1381] The platform should be able to deduct the input VAT of this intra-Community acquisition if the legal requirements were fulfilled.[1382]

The second supply from the platform to the Austrian customer would qualify as the supply without transport and therefore is a domestic Austrian sale.[1383] The platform would charge the Austrian customer with Austrian VAT and would pay the Austrian VAT to the Austrian tax authorities. For the fulfilment of the platform's VAT compliance obligations, a VAT registration of the platform in Austria would be necessary.

Figure 5.1   Graphical Illustration of an Intra-Community Chain Transaction: Transport Organisation of the Underlying Supplier

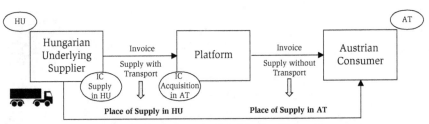

Transport organised by the Hungarian Underlying Supplier from Hungary to Austria

---

1379. *See* Article 32 first subpara. of the VAT Directive.
1380. Article 138 (1) of the VAT Directive; the underlying supplier must also file a recapitulative statement in due time and with the requested information; *see* Article 138 (1a) read in conjunction with Articles 262 et seqq. of the VAT Directive.
1381. The intra-Community acquisition is also a taxable transaction according to Article 2 (1) (b) (i) of the VAT Directive.
1382. *See* Article 168 (c) of the VAT Directive.
1383. *See* Article 31 of the VAT Directive.

5.2.4.1.5.2.3 The Legal Consequences of the Basic Example: Transport Organised by the Platform

The second possibility in the basic example would be that the platform organises the transport of the goods to the Austrian customer (*see* for a graphical illustration of the legal qualification of this chain transaction Figure 5.2). The EU legislator has introduced a simplification mechanism with the introduction of the so-called quick fixes which had to be implemented by the Member States by 1 January 2020.[1384] Thereby, one of these 'quick fixes' was the harmonisation of chain transactions by introducing Article 36a of the VAT Directive. In Article 36a of the VAT Directive, the intermediary operator may choose whether the transaction to him or by him should be treated as the supply with transport, when the intermediary operator organises the transport.[1385] If the intermediary operator used his VAT identification number from another Member State, the supply with transport would be attributed to the supply to him.[1386] If the intermediary operator used his VAT identification number from the country of origin, the moving supply would be allocated to the delivery from him to the following (taxable) person.[1387]

As, in the given case, the intermediary operator (the platform) organises the transport, the platform may influence which supply is the supply with transport by the use of its Hungarian (country of origin) or Austrian (country of destination) VAT identification number. If the platform used its Austrian VAT identification number for the supplies, the first supply from the underlying supplier to the platform would be the supply with transport.[1388] Therefore, the further legal implications are identical to those when the underlying supplier organises the transport.[1389]

1384. Council Directive (EU) 2018/1910 of 4 December 2018 Amending Directive 2006/112/EC as Regards the Harmonisation and Simplification of Certain Rules in the Value Added Tax System for the Taxation of Trade Between Member States, OJ L 311 (2018).
1385. The term 'intermediary operator' is defined in Article 36a (3) of the VAT Directive as 'a supplier within the chain other than the first supplier in the chain who dispatches or transports the goods either himself or through a third party acting on his behalf'.
1386. *See* Article 36a (1) of the VAT Directive.
1387. *See* Article 36a (2) of the VAT Directive.
1388. *See* Article 36a (1) of the VAT Directive.
1389. *See* s. 5.2.4.1.5.2.2 The Legal Consequences of the Basic Example: Transport Organised by the Hungarian Underlying Supplier.

Figure 5.2   Graphical Illustration of an Intra-Community Chain Transaction: Transport Organisation of the Platform by Using the VAT-ID from the Country of Destination

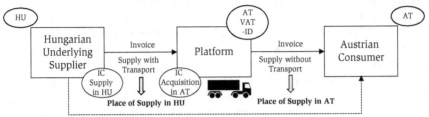

If the platform used its Hungarian VAT identification number for the supplies, the first supply from the Hungarian underlying supplier to the platform would be the supply without transport (*see* for a graphical illustration of the legal qualification of this chain transaction Figure 5.3).[1390] The underlying supplier would have to issue an invoice with Hungarian VAT. The paid VAT by the platform should be deductible as input VAT if all legal requirements were fulfilled.[1391]

The second supply from the platform to the Austrian customer would qualify as the supply with transport from Hungary to Austria.[1392] As the customer in the given case is a consumer, this supply is an intra-Community distance sales of goods. Thus, the place of supply is the place where the dispatch or transport of the goods ends, in the given example case, in Austria.[1393] The platform would charge the Austrian customer with Austrian VAT and would pay the Austrian VAT to the Austrian tax authorities. For the fulfilment of the platform's VAT compliance obligations, the platform may use the EU-OSS.[1394] Alternatively, a VAT registration of the platform in Austria would be necessary.

Figure 5.3   Graphical Illustration of an Intra-Community Chain Transaction: Transport Organisation of the Platform by Using the VAT-ID from the Country of Origin

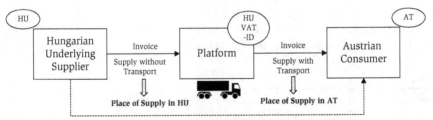

1390. *See* Article 36a (2) of the VAT Directive.
1391. *See* Article 168 (a) of the VAT Directive.
1392. *See* Article 31 of the VAT Directive.
1393. *See* Article 33 (a) of the VAT Directive.
1394. *See,* for more detailed information on the application of the EU-OSS, s. 4.11 Special Schemes of the OSS.

5.2.4.1.5.3   Variant of the Excursus: The Importation of Goods

The previously discussed excursus can be constructed even more complicated if, in the given example, the jacket is not delivered from another Member State but from a third country, e.g., Russia. In this case, the EU chain transaction rules stipulated in Article 36a of the VAT Directive would not be applicable as the scope of Article 36a of the VAT Directive only covers supplies 'from one Member State to another Member State'. When the supply is imported from a third country, the requirement of transport from one Member State to another would not be fulfilled.[1395] Therefore, the choice of the intermediary operator of which supply should be considered the supply with transport is not available to the intermediary operator for import chain transactions. However, Member States have diverted from this strict interpretation of Article 36a of the VAT Directive by the European Commission and have implemented a comparable option for the intermediary operator also in the case of import chain transactions.[1396]

As the VAT treatment of import chain transactions is implemented differently in the Member States, a case-by-case analysis based on the national law of the Member State of destination is necessary for distinguishing the supply with and the supply without transport. The national law and case law should provide further guidance for the elements that are decisive in the domestic law to determine the supply with transport. However, in general, also in the case of import chain transactions, two possibilities can be discussed: either the supply with transport is the first supply (from the underlying supplier to the platform) or the second supply (from the platform to the customer).

If the first supply from the underlying supplier to the platform was the supply with transport, the place of supply of this supply would be in Russia (*see* for a graphical illustration of the legal qualification of this chain transaction Figure 5.4).[1397] The second supply from the platform to the Austrian customer would qualify as the supply without transport and is therefore a domestic Austrian sale.[1398] The platform would charge the Austrian customer with Austrian VAT and would pay the Austrian VAT to the Austrian tax authorities. For the fulfilment of the platform's VAT compliance obligations, a VAT registration of the platform in Austria would be necessary. Thereby, it should be noted that neither the IOSS nor the EU-OSS is applicable for reporting this transaction as the supply from the platform to the Austrian consumer is a national supply in Austria. Thus, this supply does not fulfil the requirement of qualifying as a

---

1395. European Commission, *Explanatory Notes on the EU VAT Changes in Respect of Call-Off Stock Arrangements, Chain Transactions and the Exemption for Intra-Community Supplies of Goods ('2020 Quick Fixes')*, *supra* note 35, at 45.
1396. *See*, e.g., § 3 (6a) of the German VAT Act, where the choice of the intermediary operator has been implemented for import and export chain transactions. Also, Austria has implemented the choice of the intermediary operator for export chain transactions; *see* § 3 (15) of the Austrian VAT. *See* also, critically, on the different implementations of the Member States in Christina Pollak & Draga Turić, *Reihengeschäfte mit Drittstaatsbezug*, taxlex, *supra* note 779, at 338 et seqq.
1397. *See* Article 32 of the VAT Directive.
1398. *See* Article 31 of the VAT Directive.

distance sales of goods imported from third territories or third countries[1399] or the requirement of qualifying as an intra-Community distance sales of goods.[1400] Additionally, the platform did not become the deemed supplier according to Article 14a of the VAT Directive but was the supplier in the described situation. Thus, the exception for platforms as deemed supplier to use the EU-OSS also for national sales is not fulfilled in this variant of the excursus.[1401]

Finally, the importation of the goods in Austria would be a taxable transaction according to Article 2 (1) (d) of the VAT Directive. The import VAT in Austria would be payable by the person who would file the import declaration.[1402] This could be the underlying supplier, the platform, the consumer, or any (in)direct representative. Thereby, it should be noted that only the person with the power of disposal over the goods upon importation has the right to deduct the input VAT of this importation if the legal requirements are fulfilled.[1403] Depending on the agreement between the underlying supplier and the platform, this could be either the underlying supplier or the platform. If a person other than the person having the right to deduct the input VAT has paid the import VAT, this person could request the import VAT payment from the person having the right to deduct the input VAT based on civil law.

Figure 5.4   Graphical Illustration of an Import Chain Transaction: The First Supply Being the Supply with Transport

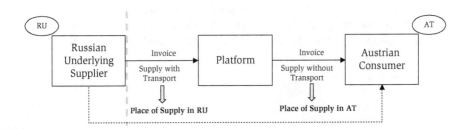

If the first supply from the underlying supplier to the platform was the supply without transport, this supply would be taxable in Russia (*see* for a graphical illustration of the legal qualification of this chain transaction Figure 5.5).[1404] The second supply from the platform to the Austrian customer would qualify as the supply

---

1399. For a detailed discussion of the requirements of distance sales of goods imported from third territories or third countries, *see* s. 3.3.1.1 The Definition of Distance Sales of Goods Imported from a Third Territory or a Third Country.

1400. For a detailed discussion of the requirements of intra-Community distance sales of goods, *see* s. 4.3.4.2.1.3.1 Intra-Community Distance Sales of Goods.

1401. *See* Article 369b (b) of the VAT Directive.

1402. *See* § 26 (1) of the Austrian VAT Act read in conjunction with Article 77 (3) of the UCC.

1403. *See* Article 168 (e) of the VAT Directive; *see*, for further discussions on the criteria in Austria for the input VAT deduction of import VAT, s. 4.14.4.3.2.3 VAT Implications of the Transportation of Defect Goods.

1404. *See* Article 31 of the VAT Directive; the VAT treatment of this supply depends on the national Russian VAT law.

with transport. As the customer in the given case is a consumer, this sale is a distance sale of goods imported from third territories or third countries. Thus, the place of supply would be the place where the dispatch or transport of the goods ends (in the given example case, in Austria) if the platform used the IOSS scheme.[1405] Thereby, the importation would be exempt from the payment of import VAT.[1406] The platform would charge the Austrian customer with Austrian VAT and would pay the Austrian VAT to the Austrian tax authorities via the IOSS.

Alternatively, if a platform did not use the IOSS, the place of supply of the sale of the goods from the platform to the customer could still be in Austria if the platform was the importer of the goods and became liable to pay the import VAT.[1407] The platform would import the goods into the EU and then supply the goods to the customer indicating the local VAT rate.[1408]

If the platform was not the importer of the goods, then the place of supply of the good would be in Russia.[1409] Additionally, the importation of the goods in Austria would be a taxable transaction according to Article 2 (1) (d) of the VAT Directive, generally, in the Member State within whose territory the goods are located when they enter the EU, i.e., in Austria.[1410] The import VAT would be payable by the person who would file the import declaration.[1411] This could (theoretically) be the underlying supplier, the platform, the consumer, or any (in)direct representative. In practice, the Austrian customer would likely file the import declaration and pay the import VAT due. In this case, the import VAT is either payable at the express courier or the postal company or if the customer cleared the goods at customs, then at the competent customs office. As the imported consignment did not exceed EUR 150, the simplification mechanism of importations for non-IOSS suppliers could be applicable.[1412]

1405. *See* Article 33 (c) of the VAT Directive; *see,* for more detailed information on the place of supply when the IOSS is used, s. 4.3.4.1.1.2.3 The Place of Supply when the Platform Applies the IOSS.
1406. *See* 143 (ca) of the VAT Directive.
1407. *See* Article 32 second subpara. of the VAT Directive; for further information, *see* s. 4.3.4.1.1.2.1 The Shift of the Place of Supply Rule According to Article 32 Second Subparagraph of the VAT Directive.
1408. If the importer fulfils the requirements for the input VAT deduction, the import VAT can be deducted by the importer; *see* Article 168 (e) of the VAT Directive.
1409. *See* Article 32 first subpara. of the VAT Directive; for further information, *see* s. 4.3.4.1.1.1 The General Place of Supply Rule According to Article 32 first subparagraph of the VAT Directive.
1410. *See* Article 60 of the VAT Directive.
1411. *See* § 26 (1) of the Austrian VAT Act read in conjunction with Article 77 (3) of the UCC.
1412. *See* the discussion of this simplification mechanism in s. 4.12.3 The Simplification Mechanism of Importations for Non-IOSS Suppliers.

Figure 5.5   Graphical Illustration of an Import Chain Transaction: The Second Supply Being the Supply with Transport

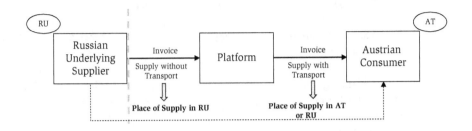

5.2.4.1.5.4   Analysis of the Comparability and Identification of the Equal Treatment

Concerning the comparability of the described cases to the initial example, it can be deduced that the platform in this excursus example is likely not comparable to the platform facilitating supplies according to Article 14a of the VAT Directive because the platform becomes, through the actual supply of the goods from the underlying supplier to the platform, the owner of the goods. Therefore, the platform has the power to dispose of the goods in the excursus examples, and an actual chain transaction exists. The platform does not only facilitate the supply of the good in the excursus but becomes the actual supplier. In the initial example where Article 14a of the VAT Directive is applicable, this chain transaction is only created due to the legal fiction for VAT purposes of the platform being the deemed supplier.[1413] These differences lead to the conclusion that the excursus examples are not in comparable situations to the initial example where the platform became the deemed supplier of the goods.

However, the excursus examples also show that some discussed constellations, especially when the second supply from the platform to the customer is qualified as the supply with transport, have the same legal consequences in the VAT Directive as when the platform becomes the deemed supplier according to Article 14a of the VAT Directive. Therefore, it can be subsumed that, when the supply with transport is allocated to the supply from the platform to consumer (second transaction), then the examples of the excursus and the initial example are treated the same although they are not in comparable situations. This additional variant shows the other way of infringing the principle of equality: treating non-comparable situations alike.

1413. *See* more information on the legal fiction of the chain transaction of Article 14a of the VAT Directive in s. 4.3.2 Preliminary Discussion: Chain Transaction.

5.2.4.2 Possible Justifications and the Proportionality of Article 14a of the VAT Directive

5.2.4.2.1 The Identification of Applicable Justifications

5.2.4.2.1.1 The Objective of the Introduction of Article 14a of the VAT Directive

The second step in the equality test is the review of applicable justifications and the proportionality test. Thereby, the CJEU has repeatedly emphasised, 'when the EU legislature adopts a tax measure, it is called upon to make political, economic and social choices, and to rank divergent interests or to undertake complex assessments'.[1414] Therefore, the EU legislator has a broad discretion in VAT law that limits the justification test by the CJEU to 'manifest errors'.[1415] For determining whether the introduction of Article 14a of the VAT Directive is justified, consideration should be given to the objective and background of the introduction of Article 14a of the VAT Directive.[1416]

According to the EU legislator, the deemed supplier regime was introduced to ensure the effective and efficient collection of the VAT.[1417] Additionally, the e-commerce package of the VAT Directive should make the VAT system more neutral and limit the distortion of competition.[1418] This lack in neutrality and the distortion of competition was based on two factors. The first is the high-non-compliance rate of third country suppliers who simply did not charge the VAT on their supplies in the EU, and second is the application of the small-consignment exemption for import VAT. Therefore, the small-consignment exemption was abolished, and the IOSS was introduced with the aim to facilitate the compliance burden for third country suppliers.[1419] Additionally, the EU legislator has introduced Article 14a of the VAT Directive.[1420] The

---

1414. Case C-390/15, *RPO*, 7 Mar. 2017, ECLI:EU:C:2017:174, para. 54; with reference to Case C-491/01, *British American Tobacco (Investments) and Imperial Tobacco*, 10 Dec. 2002, ECLI:EU:C:2002:741, para. 123; Case C-203/12, *Billerud Karlsborg and Billerud Skärblacka*, 17 Oct. 2013, ECLI:EU:C:2013:664, para. 35; *see* also, similarly, Case C-390/15, *Proceedings brought by Rzecznik Praw Obywatelskich (RPO)*, 8 Sep. 2016, ECLI:EU:C:2016:664, Opinion of AG Kokott, para. 61.
1415. Case C-390/15, *RPO*, 7 Mar. 2017, ECLI:EU:C:2017:174, para. 54; with reference to Case C-491/01, *British American Tobacco (Investments) and Imperial Tobacco*, 10 Dec. 2002, ECLI:EU:C:2002:741, para. 123; Case C-203/12, *Billerud Karlsborg and Billerud Skärblacka*, 17 Oct. 2013, ECLI:EU:C:2013:664, para. 35; *see* also similarly Case C-390/15, *RPO*, 8 Sep. 2016, ECLI:EU:C:2016:664, Opinion of AG Kokott, para. 61.
1416. Case C-390/15, *RPO*, 7 Mar. 2017, ECLI:EU:C:2017:174, paras. 58 et seqq.
1417. *See* preamble pt. 7 of the Council Directive (EU) 2017/2455 of 5 December 2017 Amending Directive 2006/112/EC and Directive 2009/132/EC as Regards Certain Value Added Tax Obligations for Supplies of Services and Distance Sales of Goods, OJ L 348/7 (2017).
1418. *See* European Commission, *Proposal for a Council Directive Amending Directive 2006/112/EC and Directive 2009/132/EC as Regards Certain Value Added Tax Obligations for Supplies of Services and Distance Sales of Goods*, COM(2016) 757 final, *supra* note 1, at 2.
1419. *Ibid.*
1420. At this point, the e-commerce package consisted of amendments of three different legislative acts: Council Directive (EU) 2017/2455 of 5 December 2017 Amending Directive 2006/112/EC

introduction of Article 14a of the VAT Directive also aims at a more neutral VAT system as well as the limitation of competition since the legislator seemingly assumes that the (correct) VAT collection and payment can be improved due to the fictitious inclusion of the platform in the VAT supply chain. With these amendments, the payment of the VAT should be guaranteed, neutrality should be re-established, and the VAT gap incurred in the e-commerce sector should be redeemed.[1421]

Simultaneously, also the administrative burden for the tax authorities, the underlying suppliers, and the consumer should be limited.[1422] The newly introduced EU-OSS and IOSS systems aim at achieving this objective for the platforms as deemed suppliers.[1423] As the platforms become the deemed suppliers for certain transactions, fulfil the compliance obligations, and pay the VAT, the underlying suppliers do not have to be VAT registered in the EU for the supplies for which the platform became the deemed supplier. Thereby, the tax authorities' work is also facilitated because, instead of being confronted with hundreds of suppliers around the globe, many supplies are carried through the platform which, in many cases, is also liable for VAT compliance and payment. As a result, the VAT on imported goods or goods sold via platforms by traders established in third countries was aligned to the VAT treatment of goods sold within the EU by EU traders due to the abolishment of the small-consignment exemption. Additionally, the deemed supplier should guarantee the effective and efficient VAT collection.

The objective of ensuring the effective and efficient collection of the VAT and the limitation of the administrative burden cannot be reasonably doubted to be a legally permitted objective since Article 325 of the TFEU explicitly stipulates that the EU 'shall counter fraud and any other illegal activities affecting the financial interests of the Union'. Based on this objective for the introduction of Article 14a of the VAT Directive, two justification grounds could be found: the effectiveness of legal provisions and the administrative practicability.

5.2.4.2.1.2   The Effectiveness of Legal Provisions as a Justification Ground

One possible justification for Article 14a of the VAT Directive could be the effectiveness of legal provisions and therefore the effectiveness of tax collection.[1424] Article 14a of the

---

and Directive 2009/132/EC as Regards Certain Value Added Tax Obligations for Supplies of Services and Distance Sales of Goods.

1421. *See* preamble pt. 7 of the *ibid.*; according to a study conducted by EY on behalf of the European Commission, the VAT foregone solely due to the low import VAT exemption was estimated to be EUR 535 million in 2013; *see* European Commission, *Assessment of the Application and Impact of the VAT Exemption for Importation of Small Consignments*, Specific Contract No 7 TAXUD/2013/DE/334 Based on Framework Contract No Taxud/2012/CC/117, Final Report, *supra* note 2, at 70.

1422. *See* preamble pt. 7 of the Council Directive (EU) 2017/2455 of 5 December 2017 Amending Directive 2006/112/EC and Directive 2009/132/EC as Regards Certain Value Added Tax Obligations for Supplies of Services and Distance Sales of Goods.

1423. *See*, for a detailed discussion on the IOSS and the EU-OSS, s. 4.11 Special Schemes of the OSS.

1424. *See*, e.g., Case C-84/87, *Erpelding v Secrétaire d'État à l'Agriculture et à la Viticulture*, 17 May 1988, ECLI:EU:C:1988:245, para. 30; *see* also the application of the effectiveness of (direct) tax

VAT Directive was introduced because many suppliers supplying their goods through e-commerce platforms were not compliant with the EU VAT laws. They simply did not fulfil their registration obligations in the country of destination and did not pay the VAT on the goods sold through e-commerce platforms to consumers in the EU. The result was distortion of competition as the goods sold through platforms from third country suppliers would not be charged the VAT compared to national suppliers who would charge the VAT. In many cases, the non-payment of the VAT by the underlying suppliers was likely caused by an information deficit of the underlying suppliers. Additionally, due to the small-consignment exemption, it was difficult for EU tax authorities to receive information of the supplies from third countries. Moreover, if the tax authorities received information of the supply of goods from third country suppliers, the tax authorities could have issued a VAT assessment. Still, the enforcement of this VAT assessment was difficult in practice and would depend on whether the Member States have concluded a mutual assistant agreement with the third country on the collection of the VAT or taxes in general.[1425] Therefore, Article 14a of the VAT Directive should ensure the effectiveness of the VAT collection by including the platforms in the supply chain.

Thereby, the inclusion of the platform in the supply chain according to Article 14a of the VAT Directive seems justifiable with the aim to guarantee the effective VAT collection for taxable transactions in the EU. Thus, the same treatment between platforms that are the deemed suppliers according to Article 14a of the VAT Directive and platforms that supply the goods themselves, i.e., as discussed in the example of the excursus,[1426] seems justifiable.

Against this background, also the comparable situations must be analysed. Thereby, several differences can be found. First, in many cases, the collection of the VAT may be easier in the comparable situations due to the fact that the underlying suppliers are either established in the EU[1427] or have property in the EU in the case of the rental of immovable property.[1428] In the case of immovable property, the VAT due could be collected, as a last resort, by the execution of the immovable property. Additionally, the information deficit of the underlying suppliers may be less. Especially EU suppliers should be aware of the VAT laws as they have several VAT obligations as a taxable person in the EU. Also, in the case of renting out immovable property, the underlying suppliers often have to pay other taxes and fees related to the rental of

---

collection as a justification reason when testing the fundamental freedoms in Case C-290/04, *FKP Scorpio Konzertproduktionen*, 3 Oct. 2006, ECLI:EU:C:2006:630, paras. 35 et seq.; Case C-498/10, *X NV v Staatssecretaris van Financiën*, 18 Oct. 2012, ECLI:EU:C:2012:635, para. 39.

1425. *See,* e.g., Agreement Between the European Union and the Kingdom of Norway on Administrative Cooperation, Combating Fraud and Recovery of Claims in the Field of Value Added Tax, OJ L 195 (2018).

1426. *See,* for description of the excursus, s. 5.2.4.1.5 Excursus: The Supply of Goods by Platforms.

1427. *See,* for the situation of the EU underlying suppliers referred to, s. 5.2.4.1.2 Situation 1: The Facilitation of Supplies of EU-Goods by EU Suppliers – Analysis of the Comparability and Identification of Unequal Treatment.

1428. *See,* for the situation of the EU service providers, s. 5.2.4.1.3 Situation 2: The Facilitation of Supplies of Accommodation Services or Event Tickets – Analysis of the Comparability and Identification of Unequal Treatment.

short-term accommodation in many Member States.[1429] Therefore, the underlying supplier may also receive information on the obligation of paying the VAT due and therefore fulfils the VAT duties.

Whereas the VAT collection from EU suppliers as well as third country suppliers who have immovable property in the EU might be possible, the VAT collection from underlying suppliers providing event tickets could be more difficult. A third country underlying supplier supplying event tickets is neither established in the EU nor has the underlying supplier (immovable) property in the EU. Still, the difference in treatment may be justified as the CJEU has emphasised that the EU legislator may use a step-by-step approach when complex systems are introduced.[1430] The European Commission stated that the role of platforms in the securing of VAT collection will be examined also for the supply of services supplied through platforms, especially having in mind the sharing economy sector.[1431] In this sense, the introduction of Article 14a of the VAT Directive could have only been the first step in implementing a new VAT policy regarding the inclusion of platforms in the VAT supply chain with the aim to simplify, strengthen, and increase neutrality in the internal market.[1432] After all, it seems that the effectiveness of VAT collection may justify the introduction of Article 14a of the VAT Directive.[1433]

5.2.4.2.1.3   The Administrative Practicability as a Justification Ground

Another possible justification could be the administrative practicability of Article 14a of the VAT Directive.[1434] Article 14a of the VAT Directive has the benefit for the underlying suppliers that they do not become liable for the VAT due for the goods that are sold through the e-commerce platforms, but the platforms become liable for the

---

1429. Many countries have a so-called tourism tax that is payable for each night a visitor is staying at the accommodation.
1430. *See*, e.g., Case C-127/07, *Arcelor Atlantique and Lorraine and Others*, 16 Dec. 2008, ECLI: EU:C:2008:728, para. 57; Case C-101/12, *Schaible*, 17 Oct. 2013, ECLI:EU:C:2013:661, para. 91.
1431. European Commission, *Communication from the Commission to the European Parliament and the Council an Action Plan for Fair and Simple Taxation Supporting the Recovery Strategy*, COM/2020/312 final, *supra* note 31, at 15.
1432. *See* a similar argumentation also in Case C-390/15, *RPO*, 7 Mar. 2017, ECLI:EU:C:2017:174, para. 56.
1433. For discussions on the proportionality, *see* s. 5.2.4.2.2 The Proportionality Test.
1434. *See*, e.g., Joined Cases C-248/95 and C-249/95, *SAM Schiffahrt and Stapf v Bundesrepublik Deutschland*, 17 Jul. 1997, ECLI:EU:C:1997:377, para. 60; *see* also the critical discussion of the admissibility of the justification grounds of administrative practicability when applied to fundamental freedoms in Case C-512/13, *C.G. Sopora v Staatssecretaris van Financiën*, 24 Feb. 2015, ECLI:EU:C:2015:108, para. 33; with reference to *F.C. Terhoeve v Inspecteur van de Belastingdienst Particulieren/Ondernemingen buitenland*, 26 Jan. 1999, ECLI:EU:C:1999:22, para. 45, where the CJEU held that administrative considerations cannot justify the derogation from EU law by a Member State; and with references to Case C-110/05, *Commission of the European Communities v Italian Republic*, 10 Feb. 2009, ECLI:EU:C:2009:66, para. 67; Case C-137/09, *Marc Michel Josemans v Burgemeester van Maastricht*, 16 Dec. 2010, ECLI: EU:C:2010:774, para. 82; Case C-400/08, *European Commission v Kingdom of Spain*, 24 Mar. 2011, ECLI:EU:C:2011:172, para. 124, where the CJEU affirmed the introduction of easy manageable and supervisable rules that facilitate the work from the competent authorities.

VAT that is facilitated. Therefore, Article 14a of the VAT Directive has a benefit for tax authorities: tax authorities only have to monitor a limited amount of taxpayers for the supply of goods through e-commerce platforms. In this sense, it could be argued that Article 14a of the VAT Directive is a provision that facilitates the application of the VAT for national tax authorities as the VAT due is more easily collected by the competent authorities.[1435] At the same time, Article 14a of the VAT Directive also benefits the underlying suppliers as the underlying suppliers are not held liable for the VAT on the goods sold through the facilitation of platforms.[1436] The party that faces the higher compliance obligations is the e-commerce platform.

Thereby, the inclusion of the platform in the supply chain according to Article 14a of the VAT Directive does not seem to justify the different (or same in the case of the excursus) treatment.[1437] The reason of administrative practicability could also be applied to other platforms and would also lead to a similar increase of facilitation for the national tax authorities as well as the underlying suppliers. Therefore, the argument of the administrative practicability does not seem to be a ground for justification of the different treatment of platforms that became the deemed supplier according to Article 14a of the VAT Directive and the discussed platforms /suppliers in (non-)comparable situations.

5.2.4.2.2   The Proportionality Test

5.2.4.2.2.1   The Proportionality in the Strict Sense

After having identified one applicable possible justification grounds (the need to ensure the effective VAT collection), the proportionality of the introduction of Article 14a of the VAT Directive should be examined. Thereby, the first step is to investigate whether the measure is appropriate for achieving the objective pursued.[1438] On one side, e-commerce platforms hold, in most cases, the necessary information to determine the correct place of supply and know the amount that is paid for the good sold through their platform and can therefore likely also calculate the VAT due. Furthermore, especially for the big platforms, being compliant with taxes is not only a legal

---

1435. *See* also Case C-390/15, *RPO*, 7 Mar. 2017, ECLI:EU:C:2017:174, para. 60; with reference to Case C-512/13, *Sopora*, 24 Feb. 2015, ECLI:EU:C:2015:108, para. 33.

1436. Although the argument of Article 14a of the VAT Directive benefitting another taxable person by shifting the VAT burden from the underlying suppliers onto the platform may be seen as critical, the CJEU also took into consideration the benefit for other persons and not only the competent authorities; *see* Case C-110/05, *Commission v Italy*, 10 Feb. 2009, ECLI: EU:C:2009:66, para. 67; *see* also the discussion of the shifting of tax obligations from one taxable person to another in Case C-498/10, *X*, 18 Oct. 2012, ECLI:EU:C:2012:635, para. 49.

1437. *See*, for the discussion of the (non-)comparable situations, s. 5.2.4.1.2 Situation 1: The Facilitation of Supplies of EU-Goods by EU Suppliers – Analysis of the Comparability and Identification of Unequal Treatment, s. 5.2.4.1.3 Situation 2: The Facilitation of Supplies of Accommodation Services or Event Tickets – Analysis of the Comparability and Identification of Unequal Treatment and s. 5.2.4.1.5 Excursus: The Supply of Goods by Platforms.

1438. Case C-390/15, *RPO*, 7 Mar. 2017, ECLI:EU:C:2017:174, para. 61.

obligation but also positive marketing for their platform.[1439] Thus, platforms might also be more compliant due to reputational reasons which will facilitate the VAT collection. Therefore, the inclusion of the e-commerce platforms in the VAT collection for sales facilitated through their platforms is likely to achieve the objective of an effective and efficient collection of VAT.

On the other side, in the case that e-commerce platforms do not hold the necessary information to determine the VAT due, the platforms have to amend their business model to receive the necessary information due to the introduction of Article 14a of the VAT Directive. Similarly, platforms may also have to amend their business models if they were not responsible for the process of the payment in order to limit the liquidity burden and the risk of final VAT payment by the platform.[1440] This business model amendment would be necessary if, in the traditional business model of the platform, the payment was instantly transferred from the customer to the underlying supplier. Thus, arguments can be found against the proportionality of Article 14a of the VAT Directive due to the broad definition of 'to facilitate' according to which the platform does not have to be involved in the payment process or payment authorisation to become the deemed supplier.

Furthermore, especially smaller platforms may encounter significant difficulties due to the introduction of Article 14a of the VAT Directive. For smaller platforms, solely the determination of the applicable VAT rate in all 27 different Member States for all of the different goods offered on the platform puts a very high administrative burden on the platform. The difficulty of determining the applicable VAT rate and the corresponding technical programming of the different VAT rates on the digital platform may cause smaller platforms to withdraw sales to some Member States or by certain suppliers if the administrative burden was economically not justifiable for the platform.[1441] This consequence may lead to smaller platforms only facilitating certain supplies to specific countries. Therefore, Article 14a of the VAT Directive may influence the decision of smaller platforms to enter into new markets or to withdraw from markets they were supplying before the introduction of Article 14a of the VAT Directive as well as the decision of who is their underlying supplier.[1442] The European Parliament was aware of this burden for SMEs and start-ups and therefore explicitly limited the application of the deemed supplier regime to platforms that exceed a turnover of one million euros in the current calendar year in its suggested amendments of the provisions relevant for

---

1439. *See* Valentin Bendlinger & Thomas Ecker, *Die Rolle von Plattformen im E-Commerce – Plattformen und ihre umsatzsteuerlichen Pflichten, in Neuerungen bei innergemeinschaftlichen Umsätzen, supra* note 418, at 176.

1440. *See,* for further explanations on the liquidity burden and the risk of VAT payment, in s. 3.2.2.4 Criticism on the Definition of 'to Facilitate'.

1441. *See,* for further explanations on this difficulty, s. 4.6.3 Applicable Rates and Exemptions for the Supply of Goods by the Platform.

1442. Additionally, the impact of Article 14a of the VAT Directive to influence such economic decisions may be questioned based on the freedom to conduct a business according to Article 16 of the CFR; for a discussion of this fundamental right, *see* s. 5.3 Discussion of a Possible Infringement of Article 14a of the VAT Directive of the Freedom to Conduct a Business.

the e-commerce package.[1443] Nevertheless, the EU legislator did not include such a restriction to platforms with a certain turnover in Article 14a of the VAT Directive. Thus, especially for smaller platforms, the proportionality of Article 14a of the VAT Directive may be called into question.[1444]

5.2.4.2.2.2   The Application of Less Restrictive Measures

Additionally, Article 14a of the VAT Directive must be 'the least restrictive among the appropriate measures that may be envisaged [to ensure the effective and efficient VAT collection] and ... the disadvantages caused must not be disproportionate to the objectives pursued'.[1445] Alternatively to the introduction of Article 14a of the VAT Directive, the EU legislator could have tried to counteract the ineffective and inefficient collection of the VAT by relying on exchange information and mutual assistance for the recovery of taxes between the EU and third countries.[1446] If such an agreement was concluded, then the national tax authorities would need to receive information on the underlying suppliers. This information is available to the platforms and, therefore, the recovery of the information could be retrieved from the platforms. Generally, a record-keeping obligation for platforms has already been introduced for the supply of goods that do not fall into the scope of Article 14a of the VAT Directive and for the supply of services supplied through platforms.[1447] In this sense, Article 242a of the VAT Directive could have been applied to all supplies through platforms. In addition to this record-keeping obligation by the platform, the Member States would have to implement a national reporting obligation to receive the information required on the underlying suppliers from the platform in their national law. Additionally, the DAC 7 has to be implemented in the Member States until 1 January 2023 and, thereby, a general reporting obligation for platforms will enter into force.[1448]

However, the extension of Article 242a of the VAT Directive and a reporting obligation of platforms still does not guarantee effective VAT collection. In order to

---

1443. European Parliament, *Report on the Proposal for a Council Directive Amending Directive 2006/112/EC and Directive 2009/132/EC as Regards Certain Value Added Tax Obligations for Supplies of Services and Distance Sales of Goods*, A8-0307/2017, *supra* note 603.

1444. The discussions on the proportionality of Article 14a of the VAT Directive could also be relevant for the discussion of whether the principle of proportionality could be reviewed as a general principle of EU law. For further discussion on the synergy between the principle of proportionality and the proportionality test of testing the fundamental rights, *see* Bernhard Oreschnik, *Verhältnismäßigkeit und Kontrolldichte*, *supra* note 1316, at 140 et seqq.

1445. *See*, e.g., Case C-390/15, *RPO*, 7 Mar. 2017, ECLI:EU:C:2017:174, para. 64.

1446. Such agreements could have a similar scope as the Council Directive 2010/24/EU of 16 March 2010 Concerning Mutual Assistance for the Recovery of Claims Relating to Taxes, Duties and Other Measures, OJ L 84 (2010); and the Council Regulation (EU) 2017/2454 of 5 December 2017 Amending Regulation (EU) No. 904/2010 on Administrative Cooperation and Combating Fraud in the Field of Value Added Tax, OJ L 348/1 (2017); the only country the EU has concluded such an agreement with is Norway; *see* Agreement Between the European Union and the Kingdom of Norway on Administrative Cooperation, Combating Fraud and Recovery of Claims in the Field of Value Added Tax, OJ L 195 (2018).

1447. *See* Article 242a of the VAT Directive.

1448. *See* Council Directive (EU) 2021/514 of 22 March 2021 Amending Directive 2011/16/EU on Administrative Cooperation in the Field of Taxation, OJ L 104 (2021).

ensure effective VAT collection, the platforms would have to submit the collected information on the underlying suppliers and the respective supplies to the national tax authorities. If this data included the correct information, the tax authorities could, in theory, review whether the underlying supplier is registered for VAT purposes in the respective country and whether the underlying supplier has filed for VAT returns and paid the VAT due. If this was not the case, the tax authorities could issue an assessment for the VAT due based on the information received from the platforms. As a last resort, the mutual assistance for the recovery of claims relating to the VAT or taxes could be applied.

Nevertheless, it is questionable whether the introduction of a reporting obligation would lead to the effective and efficient collection of the VAT. First, the described process requires a high man force from the national tax authorities for being able to follow up on the different underlying suppliers. Second, the data provided by the platforms may not be fully reliable. For instance, underlying suppliers may not register under the correct name of the taxable person on the platform but use fictitious names and incorrect addresses of their establishment. As a consequence, the identification of the underlying supplier by the national tax authorities may simply not be possible. Lastly, even if the identification of the underlying suppliers was successful, the EU or the Member States must have concluded an agreement on mutual assistance for the recovery of claims relating to taxes with the respective third country. Additionally, the CJEU has held that the conclusion of mutual assistance agreements cannot replace the collection of taxes by the Member States.[1449] Based on this argument by the CJEU, it can be derived that mutual assistance is not as efficient as the introduction of a tax liability regime for platforms as stipulated in Article 14a of the VAT Directive. Therefore, the sole transmission of information on the underlying suppliers to the tax authorities does not seem to lead to effective and efficient VAT collection.

Another option to make the VAT collection more effective would be to combine the described record-keeping obligations of the platforms with a joint VAT liability of platforms; i.e., if the underlying supplier did not pay the VAT due, the platforms may, under specific circumstances, be held liable for the unpaid VAT.[1450] For the implementation of a joint liability, the EU legislator would have to specify under which circumstances the platform becomes liable for the VAT due additionally to the underlying supplier. These circumstances could refer to the record-keeping obligations of the platform as this obligation for the platform has already been introduced with the introduction of Article 242a of the VAT Directive. Additionally, the collection of

---

1449. Case C-498/10, *X*, 18 Oct. 2012, ECLI:EU:C:2012:635, para. 47.
1450. The introduction of joint liability provisions could raise questions concerning the proportionality of such a provision; *see*, similarly, Karoline Spies, *Joint and Several Liability Rules in EU VAT Law*, in *CJEU – Recent Developments in Value Added Tax 2020*, *supra* note 534, at 1, who discusses the joint liability scheme for platforms implemented in Austria and Germany in light of the principle of proportionality; *see* also, generally, on different implementations of the joint liability in the EU Anne Janssen, *The Problematic Combination of EU Harmonized and Domestic Legislation Regarding VAT Platform Liability*, 32 International VAT Monitor, *supra* note 18, s. 3; *see* also, on the implementation in Germany, Hans-Martin Grambeck, *Electronic Marketplaces May Be Held Liable for German VAT – New Rules Entered into Effect on 1 January 2019*, 30 International VAT Monitor (2019).

information on the underlying suppliers and the supplies facilitated by the platform are within the sphere of the platform. The platform can likely not influence the actual payment of the VAT by the underlying suppliers. Thus, a general VAT liability from the platform in the case that the underlying supplier would not pay the VAT due for the underlying supplier's supplies would not be proportionate. Therefore, additional conditions for the platform being held liable should be introduced. Such additional conditions could be, e.g., that the platform can only be held liable for the VAT not paid by the underlying supplier if the platform did not fulfil (at all or in due time) its record-keeping and reporting obligations.[1451]

Nevertheless, also the introduction of record-keeping obligations by platforms combined with a joint liability regime cannot guarantee a fully effective and efficient VAT collection. If the platform fulfilled its record-keeping obligations duly, then the tax authorities could still encounter the same issues that they encountered with the sole introduction of the record-keeping obligations described before because, in this case, the platform would not be held liable for unpaid VAT that is due.

Although other measures could be envisaged to make the VAT collection more effective and efficient compared to the introduction of Article 14a of the VAT Directive, both suggested approaches do not reach the same efficiency and effectiveness as Article 14a of the VAT Directive. Therefore, it seems that platforms becoming liable for the VAT for sales facilitated through their platforms is not the least restrictive measure that could be applied but the only measure reaching the objective of Article 14a of the VAT Directive, i.e., to make VAT collection effective and efficient.

5.2.4.3   *Interim Conclusion*

The introduction of Article 14a of the VAT Directive has brought an unbalanced system upon platforms. Platforms facilitating the B2C supply of goods having a third country link become the deemed supplier for these transactions whereas platforms facilitating the supply of services (in general) do not become part of the supply chain. This results in much higher costs and administrative burdens for platforms facilitating the supply of goods compared to platforms facilitating the supply of services. These higher costs and the increase in the administrative burden leads to the question of whether Article 14a of the VAT Directive is in accordance with the principle of equal treatment stipulated in Article 20 of the CFR.

The comparability test of the principle of equality to Article 14a of the VAT Directive was based on a factual analysis by concentrating on the main functions of platforms. Based on this framework, several comparable situations could be found and, therefore, the comparability requirement could be affirmed. In the second step of

---

1451. Austria, for example, has introduced the joint liability in the case that a platform does fulfil its record-keeping and reporting obligations in due time. *See* § 18 (11) + (12) read in conjunction with § 27 (1) of the Austrian VAT Act read in conjunction with the Regulation of the Minister of Finance determining record-keeping and due diligence requirements in the area of e-commerce and mail order business ('Sorgfaltspflichten-UStV').

the equality test, one valid justification reason for the introduction of Article 14a of the VAT Directive could be found in effective and efficient VAT collection.

Overall and especially in light of the broad discretion by the EU legislator when introducing VAT provisions, the introduction of Article 14a of the VAT Directive seems generally to be justifiable because Article 14a of the VAT Directive improves effective and efficient VAT collection. Additionally, the introduction of Article 14a of the VAT Directive also seems to be proportionate with two exceptions. The proportionality could be questioned as platforms that are not included in the payment progress also become liable for the VAT payment. Second, the administrative burden introduced with Article 14a of the VAT Directive and thereby also the costs for platforms is especially high for smaller platforms, and no distinction based on the platform size (e.g., based on the amount of turnover) is provided in Article 14a of the VAT Directive. Thus, it may be argued that Article 14a of the VAT Directive is not fulfilling the proportionality requirement for smaller platforms and for platforms that are not included in the payment process.

5.2.5 Article 14a of the VAT Directive as a Violation of the Principle of Neutrality?

5.2.5.1 Content and Development of the Principle of Neutrality

The principle of neutrality is one of the cornerstones of the European VAT system or, as the CJEU describes it, the principle of neutrality 'is a fundamental principle of the common system of VAT established by the relevant Community legislation'.[1452]

1452. Case C-454/98, *Schmeink & Cofreth AG & Co. KG v Finanzamt Borken and Manfred Strobel v Finanzamt Esslingen*, 19 Sep. 2000, ECLI:EU:C:2000:469, para. 59; Case C-25/03, *HE*, 21 Apr. 2005, ECLI:EU:C:2005:241, para. 80; Case C-255/02, *Halifax plc, Leeds Permanent Development Services Ltd and County Wide Property Investments Ltd v Commissioners of Customs & Excise*, 21 Feb. 2006, ECLI:EU:C:2006:121, para. 92; Case C-146/05, *Albert Collée v Finanzamt Limburg an der Lahn*, 27 Sep. 2007, ECLI:EU:C:2007:549, 26; also, in literature, the principle of neutrality has been discussed in detail; *see*, e.g., Charlène Adline Herbain, *VAT Neutrality* (Promoculture-Larcier 2015); Cornelia Zirkl, *Die Neutralität der Umsatzsteuer als europäisches Besteuerungsprinzip* (PL Academic Research 2015); Borbála Kolozs, *Neutrality in VAT*, in *Value Added Tax and Direct Taxation: Similarities and Differences* (Michael Lang et al. eds., IBFD 2009); Ine Lejeune & Jeanine Daou, *VAT Neutrality from an EU Perspective*, in *Improving VAT/GST – Designing a Simple and Fraud-Proof Tax System* (Michael Lang & Ine Lejeune eds., IBFD 2014); Danuše Nerudová & Jan Široký, *The Principle of Neutrality: VAT/GST v Direct Taxation*, in *Value Added Tax and Direct Taxation: Similarities and Differences* (Michael Lang et al. eds., IBFD 2009); Radu Bufan & Aurelian Opre, *The Principle of Tax Neutrality in the Field of Direct and Indirect Taxation*, in *Value Added Tax and Direct Taxation: Similarities and Differences* (Michael Lang et al. eds., IBFD 2009); Frans Vanistendael, *The Role of (Legal) Principles in EU Tax Law*, in *Principles of Law: Function, Status and Impact in EU Tax Law*, *supra* note 23; Christian Amand, *VAT Neutrality: A Principle of EU Law or a Principle of the VAT System?*, 2 World Journal of VAT/GST Law (2015); Oskar Henkow, *Neutrality of VAT for Taxable Persons: A New Approach in European VAT?*, 17 EC Tax Review (2008); Kerrigan, *The Elusiveness of Neutrality – Why Is It So Difficult To Apply VAT to Financial Services?*, 21 International VAT Monitor (2010); Helmut Nieuwenhuis, *Grundsatz der Neutralität der Umsatzsteuer in der Rechtsprechung des EuGH*, 62 Umsatzsteuer-Rundschau (2013); Michael

Although the principle of neutrality is not stipulated in the VAT Directive as such, the EU legislator already referred to it, although only indirectly, in the First Directive.[1453]

In the preamble to the First VAT Directive, the EU legislator emphasised that the First VAT Directive was introduced to eliminate, as much as possible, distortion of competition.[1454] The harmonisation of the VAT should 'result in neutrality in competition, in that within each country similar goods bear the same tax burden, whatever the length of the production and distribution chain'.[1455] Similarly, this was also stipulated in Article 2 of the First VAT Directive in preamble pts four and five of the Sixth VAT Directive and is still stipulated in Article 1 (2) of the VAT Directive. The CJEU has interpreted these legal provisions as all economic activities and all economic operators carrying out the same activities must be treated equally.[1456] In more recent judgments, the CJEU was clearer on these different pillars of the principle of neutrality.[1457] The CJEU has held explicitly that the principle of neutrality has different aspects.[1458] On the one hand is the neutrality of taxation of all economic activities through the input VAT deduction mechanism.[1459] On the other hand is the prohibition to treat similar goods and services that are in competition to each other differently for VAT purposes, especially when exemptions or reduced VAT rates are applied.[1460]

As can already be subsumed from the second pillar, i.e., the prohibition to treat similar goods and services differently for VAT purposes, the second pillar has similarities to the general principle of equality. Therefore, the question of the relationship between the principle of equality and the principle of neutrality arises. In its earlier case law, the CJEU has defined that the principle of equality is the 'corollary' of the principle of neutrality.[1461] In subsequent judgments, the CJEU has clarified 'that the principle of fiscal neutrality was intended to reflect, in matters relating to VAT, the general

---

Ridsdale, *Abuse of Rights, Fiscal Neutrality and VAT*, 14 EC Tax Review (2005); Han Kogels, *Making VAT as Neutral as Possible*, 21 EC Tax Review (2012).

1453. *See* First Council Directive 67/227/EEC of 11 April 1967 on the Harmonisation of Legislation of Member States Concerning Turnover Taxes, OJ 71 (1967); *see* also, on the legislative history of the principle of neutrality, Frans Vanistendael, *supra* note 23, at 368 et seqq.

1454. Preamble of the First Council Directive 67/227/EEC of 11 April 1967 on the Harmonisation of Legislation of Member States Concerning Turnover Taxes.

1455. Preamble of the *ibid.*

1456. Case C-246/04, *Turn- und Sportunion Waldburg v Finanzlandesdirektion für Oberösterreich*, 12 Jan. 2006, ECLI:EU:C:2006:22, para. 32; concerning the equal treatment of all economic activities with reference to Case C-155/94, *Wellcome Trust Ltd v Commissioners of Customs and Excise*, 20 Jun. 1996, ECLI:EU:C:1996:243, para. 38; Case C-381/97, *Belgocodex SA v Belgian State*, 3 Dec. 1998, ECLI:EU:C:1998:589, para. 18; concerning the equal treatment of all economic operators carrying out the same activities with reference to Case C-216/97, *Jennifer Gregg and Mervyn Gregg v Commissioners of Customs and Excise*, 7 Sep. 1999, ECLI:EU:C:1999:390, para. 20.

1457. Also note that, in literature, different categorisations of the principle of neutrality can be found. E.g., Kogels discusses six guidelines of the principle of neutrality; *see* Kogels, *supra* note 1452, at 231 et seq.; *see* also Greggi, who discusses the principle of neutrality from three perspectives: in time, in space, and in business in Marco Greggi, *Neutrality and Proportionality in VAT: Making Sense of an (Apparent) Conflict*, 48 Intertax 124 et seqq. (2020).

1458. Case C-174/11, *Finanzamt Steglitz v Ines Zimmermann*, 15 Nov. 2012, ECLI:EU:C:2012:716, para. 46.

1459. *Ibid.* para. 47.

1460. *Ibid.* para. 48.

1461. Case C-25/03, *HE*, 21 Apr. 2005, ECLI:EU:C:2005:241, para. 72.

principle of equal treatment'.[1462] However, the CJEU further clarified that the principle of neutrality is a secondary law principle and not a general principle of EU law; i.e., it is not primary EU law.[1463] The consequence of this qualification is that the VAT Directive itself cannot infringe the principle of neutrality. If the VAT Directive, as a secondary law act, stipulated a different treatment between comparable services or goods, this different treatment could only be tested against the general principle of equality being primary law.[1464]

Although a different treatment stipulated in the VAT Directive does not infringe the principle of neutrality, the effect of the principle of neutrality must not be underestimated. The principle of neutrality can be applied in two different ways.[1465] The first is as an aid to interpretation.[1466] This interpretative aid of the principle of neutrality applies when interpreting the VAT Directive and therefore allows an examination of the national law and its conformity with the principle of neutrality as secondary EU law prevails over national law.[1467] Second, it also binds the Member States that exercise their discretion when implementing provisions of the VAT Directive into national law.[1468]

1462. *See*, e.g., Case C-309/06, *Marks & Spencer*, 10 Apr. 2008, ECLI:EU:C:2008:211, para. 49; Case C-174/08, *NCC Construction Danmark*, 29 Oct. 2009, ECLI:EU:C:2009:669, para. 41; Case C-259/10, *The Rank Group plc*, 10 Nov. 2011, ECLI:EU:C:2011:719, para. 61; Case C-480/10, *Commission v Sweden*, 25 Apr. 2013, ECLI:EU:C:2013:263, para. 17; *see* also, critically, on this interpretation Joachim Englisch, *Gemeinschaftsgrundrechte im harmonisierten Steuerrecht, in Zukunftsfragen des deutschen Steuerrechts, supra* note 1335, at 59 et seqq.

1463. *See*, e.g., Case C-174/08, *NCC Construction Danmark*, 29 Oct. 2009, ECLI:EU:C:2009:669, para. 42; Case C-44/11, *Deutsche Bank*, 19 Jul. 2012, ECLI:EU:C:2012:484, para. 45; Case C-174/11, *Zimmermann*, 15 Nov. 2012, ECLI:EU:C:2012:716, para. 50; Christian Amand, *VAT Neutrality: A Principle of EU Law or a Principle of the VAT System?*, 2 World Journal of VAT/GST Law, *supra* note 1452, at 168 et seq.

1464. *See*, for the discussion of whether Article 14a of the VAT Directive infringes the principle of equality stipulated in Article 20 of the GRC, s. 5.2.4 Article 14a VAT Directive as a Violation of the Principle of Equality according to Article 20 of the CFR?.

1465. *See* Frans Vanistendael, *The Role of (Legal) Principles in EU Tax Law, in Principles of Law: Function, Status and Impact in EU Tax Law, supra* note 23, at 382 et seqq.; please note that Papis also discusses a third influence of the principle of neutrality on the VAT Directive: The principle of neutrality/equality as a review? In this section, it seems that the author concentrated on the applicability of the principle of equality to the VAT Directive.

1466. *Ibid.*

1467. Lars Dobratz, *EU-Grundrechte und Umsatzsteuerrecht*, 63 Umsatzsteuer-Rundschau 427 et seq. (2014); *see*, e.g., *Ambulanter Pflegedienst Kügler GmbH v Finanzamt für Körperschaften I in Berlin*, 10 Sep. 2002, ECLI:EU:C:2002:473, para. 30; Case C-309/06, *Marks & Spencer*, 10 Apr. 2008, ECLI:EU:C:2008:211, para. 36; Case C-174/08, *NCC Construction Danmark*, 29 Oct. 2009, ECLI:EU:C:2009:669, para. 43; Case C-259/10, *The Rank Group*, 10 Nov. 2011, ECLI:EU:C:2011:719, para. 51; Case C-462/16, *Boehringer Ingelheim Pharma*, 20 Dec. 2017, ECLI:EU:C:2017:1006, para. 46.

1468. Frans Vanistendael, *supra* note 23, at 384 et seq.; Dobratz, *supra* note 1467, at 427; *see*, e.g., Case C-246/04, *Turn- und Sportunion Waldburg*, 12 Jan. 2006, ECLI:EU:C:2006:22, para. 45; Case C-174/11, *Zimmermann*, 15 Nov. 2012, ECLI:EU:C:2012:716, paras. 50 et seqq.; Case C-259/10, *The Rank Group*, 10 Nov. 2011, ECLI:EU:C:2011:719, para. 74.

5.2.5.2 The Applicability of the Principle of Neutrality to Article 14a of the VAT Directive

5.2.5.2.1 The Discussion of Similar Situations According to the Principle of Neutrality

For the test of whether the principle of neutrality is applicable to Article 14a of the VAT Directive, the equality pillar of the principle of neutrality, i.e., the prohibition to treat similar goods and services differently for VAT purposes, is relevant because, in the scope of Article 14a of the VAT Directive, only platforms facilitating the supply of goods become deemed suppliers. According to the CJEU, the respective goods and services must be similar[1469] for the application of the second pillar of the principle of neutrality. Therefore, in a first step, the question arises of which services and goods can and should qualify as similar. The CJEU has provided further guidance on the similarity of goods and services:

> Two supplies of services [or goods] are therefore similar where they have similar characteristics and meet the same needs from the point of view of consumers, the test being whether their use is comparable, and where the differences between them do not have a significant influence on the decision of the average consumer to use one such service or the other.[1470]

An actual competition between the goods and services or distortion of competition because of different treatment is not necessary for goods or services to qualify as similar for purposes of the neutrality principle.[1471] Nevertheless, the suppliers offering the goods or services in question could (theoretically) be competing traders.[1472] The competition between traders seems to be a logical consequence when the respective goods and services offered by the suppliers are identical or similar. Moreover, the CJEU emphasised that the similarity of services or goods may depend on the respective Member State and the Member State's average customer.[1473] Thereby, in the *K Oy* case, the supply of physical publications and the supply of e-publications was discussed. In this specific field, due to the different degree of penetration of new technologies, differences may be found in the Member States. A distinction between the Member States may not be necessary when the accessibility of the goods is comparably widespread in the different Member States. Furthermore, such a distinction between the respective Member States may lead to a different qualification in different Member States which would not truly be in line with a uniform application and interpretation of the VAT Directive.

The similarity requirement seems, at first sight, to be similar to the comparability requirement of Article 20 of the CFR. However, as for the comparability requirement of

---

1469. Case C-259/10, *The Rank Group*, 10 Nov. 2011, ECLI:EU:C:2011:719, para. 44.
1470. *Ibid.*
1471. *Ibid.* para. 36.
1472. Case C-309/06, *Marks & Spencer*, 10 Apr. 2008, ECLI:EU:C:2008:211, paras. 47 et seqq.; Case C-480/10, *Commission v Sweden*, 25 Apr. 2013, ECLI:EU:C:2013:263, para. 17.
1473. Case C-219/13, *K Oy*, 11 Sep. 2014, ECLI:EU:C:2014:2207, para. 30.

Article 20 of the CFR, the goods or services in question do not have to be in competition with each other, and the application of the principle of neutrality requires a more narrow understanding of the similarity criterion. Therefore, also the examples presented for the comparability test of Article 20 of the CFR cannot be used for the application of the principle of neutrality as the supply of a jacket and the supply of renting out an apartment in the EU or the purchase of an event ticket are undoubtedly not similar supplies.[1474] An average customer would not order a jacket instead of renting an apartment or purchasing event tickets. Thus, a different example has to be discussed for demonstration purposes.

Over the last years, many goods were developed that may supersede services that were traditionally performed by people. One example for such goods is the supply of housekeeping robots (e.g., vacuum robots, window cleaning robots, or lawn mowing robots). Thereby, the supply of robots or the leasing of such robots may be compared to the actual supply of housekeeping services.

In the case of a supply of housekeeping robots from a third country through a platform to a consumer in the EU and the value of this robot is ≤ EUR 150, Article 14a of the VAT Directive would be applicable, and the platform would become the deemed supplier.

On the other hand, the lease of housekeeping robots or the physical supply of services of vacuuming, cleaning the windows, or mowing the lawn could also be supplied by a taxable person established in a third country.[1475] Even if the consumer booked the cleaning or gardening or lease services through a platform, the platform would not become liable for the supply of this service. This example is based on the assumption that Article 28 of the VAT Directive is not applicable; i.e., the platform does not act in its own name and not on behalf of the service provider. Furthermore, the clarification in Article 9a of the VAT Implementing Regulation would not be applicable because the provided services are not an electronically supplied service or a telephone service supplied through the Internet, but it is a cleaning or gardening service.

Although, at first sight, the example of housekeeping robots and cleaning and gardening services could seem similar, the example shows several weaknesses. First, it can be questioned whether the described goods (robots) and the cleaning or gardening services are, in fact, similar from the perspective of a consumer. It is likely that, in general, the cleaning or gardening services provide more services than exclusively vacuuming the floors, cleaning the windows or mowing the lawn. In general, also other services might be expected by the consumer and might be agreed upon between the consumer and the service provider when the consumer purchases the cleaning or gardening services. Therefore, the similarity of this example could be questioned. Thereby, it should be noted that the qualification of the similarity might adapt in the future if these robots were further developed and could also provide other services than those described.

1474. *See* s. 5.2.4.1 The Comparability Requirement and Identification of Unequal Treatment.
1475. Although the supply of cleaning and gardening services from third countries to EU Member States might not be possible in all EU Member States, especially when third countries neighbour Member States, such a supply might be possible.

Compared to providing cleaning and gardening services, the criterion of the supply being similar may be affirmed in the case of the lease of housekeeping robots compared to the sale of housekeeping robots as, in this case, the product supplied is the same. The main difference between the sale and the lease of housekeeping robots is the underlying contract and the rights that the customer receives. Nevertheless, the usage of the housekeeping robots should be equal regardless of whether the customer purchases or leases the robots. Therefore, the similarity criterion necessary for the applicability of the principle of neutrality could be affirmed if a housekeeping robot was leased to the customer.

Furthermore, according to the CJEU case law, the principle of neutrality of the second pillar was mainly applied when the application of rates or exemptions for similar goods and services was questioned. In the given case of a platform providing goods or (potentially similar) services, the main legal question is not the applicability of a reduced rate or exemption but the applicability and extension of the deemed supplier regime. The CJEU has not yet been confronted with a similar question and, thus, no similar cases can be discussed at this point.

5.2.5.2.2 The Neutrality-Conform Interpretation of the VAT Directive: Is an Extension of the Deemed Supplier Regimes Possible?

As previously discussed, the principle of neutrality is used as an interpretation aid of the VAT Directive. Thus, an infringement of the neutrality principle could only result in the necessity to interpret the VAT Directive in conformity with the principle of neutrality. Such an interpretation could be attempted, for example, by interpreting Article 14a of the VAT Directive so restrictively that also the supply of the good in question cannot be subsumed under Article 14a of the VAT Directive. Such a restrictive interpretation should be seen critically as Article 14a of the VAT Directive provides specific requirements when it becomes applicable. If the requirements were fulfilled, then Article 14a of the VAT Directive must be applied and, thus, the non-applicability of Article 14a of the VAT Directive, although the requirements are fulfilled, would not be convincing. Another possibility to interpret the VAT Directive in conformity with the principle of neutrality would be, for example, by extending the scope of Article 14a of the VAT Directive or Article 28 of the VAT Directive to comparable situations, which will be discussed in more detail in this section.

Within the traditional interpretation methods, already the literal interpretation raises doubts concerning the extension of the scope. Article 14a of the VAT Directive is explicitly restricted to the supply of goods, and the application of Article 28 of the VAT Directive is explicitly bound to the fulfilment of the two mentioned requirements. Therefore, extending the deemed supplier regime of Article 14a of the VAT Directive to services would be beyond the wording of the VAT Directive. Similarly, interpreting a deemed supplier regime for platforms into Article 28 of the VAT Directive without the platform fulfilling both requirements stipulated in the law would also go beyond the wording of the VAT Directive.

Additionally, one systematic argument can also be found. The introduction of Article 14a of the VAT Directive would have been unnecessary as the general deemed supplier regime for goods stipulated in Article 14 (2) (c) of the VAT Directive could have been applied to the supply of goods facilitated through platforms. Also, in this case, it would not have been necessary to introduce the *lex specialis* for platforms in Article 14a of the VAT Directive if supplies facilitated by platforms could have been subsumed under Article 14 (2) (c) of the VAT Directive without fulfilling the requirements stipulated therein. Therefore, it can be concluded that the general rule of Article 28 of the VAT Directive does not, in general, apply for the supply of services through platforms when the two requirements of acting in its own name and on behalf of the service provider are not fulfilled.

Lastly, also the context and background, especially for the introduction of Article 14a of the VAT Directive, should be investigated as this shows the aim that the EU legislator had in mind when introducing the deemed supplier regime in Article 14a of the VAT Directive. The aim was to guarantee effective and efficient VAT collection in third country cases.[1476] For understanding the full context, the place of supply rules must be taken into consideration. As the general place of supply in B2C supplies of goods follows the destination principle, sold goods should be taxed where the consumer receives the goods.[1477] Therefore, the inclusion of the platforms in the VAT collection by the application of Article 14a of the VAT Directive should guarantee that the VAT is collected and paid in the Member State of destination. The effect of a possible extension of the deemed supplier regime to the supply of services would (partially) be different compared to the supply of goods through platforms. For the B2C supply of services, the general place of supply rule stipulates that the place of establishment or usual residence of the supplier is the place of supply for services.[1478] The VAT Directive provides certain exceptions of this general rule. One exception would be applicable to the supply of cleaning and gardening services as the place of supply for those services is the place where the immovable property is located.[1479] Nevertheless, for the described leasing of housekeeping robots, the general place of supply rule is applicable and, therefore, the place of supply for the leasing services would be the place of establishment or usual residence of the supplier. As the general place of supply rule is linked to the place of establishment or usual residence of the supplier, even if the deemed supplier scheme was applicable, the supply of the leasing of housekeeping robots would not be taxable in the EU if the platform was established

---

1476. *See* preamble pt. 7 of the Council Directive (EU) 2017/2455 of 5 December 2017 Amending Directive 2006/112/EC and Directive 2009/132/EC as Regards Certain Value Added Tax Obligations for Supplies of Services and Distance Sales of Goods, OJ L 348/7 (2017).
1477. *See* Articles 33-35 of the VAT Directive.
1478. *See* Article 45 of the VAT Directive.
1479. *See* Article 47 of the VAT Directive read in conjunction with Article 31a of the VAT Implementing Regulation. The supply of gardening services could be subsumed under Article 31a (2) (e) of the VAT Implementing Regulation, and the supply of cleaning services could be subsumed under Article 31a (2) (k) of the VAT Implementing Regulation. For further information on the place of supply on immovable property, *see* European Commission, *Explanatory Notes on EU VAT Place of Supply Rules on Services Connected with Immovable Property That Enter into Force in 2017, supra* note 35.

in a third country. This issue can generally not be circumvented by introducing a deemed supplier regime for platforms facilitating the supply of services without reforming the place of supply rules and thereby implementing the principle of destination broadly.[1480]

Even if an example was found where platforms would provide goods and services that fulfil the similarity requirement and where the service is taxed based on the destination principle, the literal and systematic interpretation seem to speak against the application of Articles 14a or 28 of the VAT Directive to the supply of services facilitated by platforms. Article 14a of the VAT Directive can only be applied to the supply of goods (if all of the other requirements were also fulfilled) and, for the application of Article 28 of the VAT Directive, the platform should fulfil the requirements of acting in its own name and on behalf of the service provider. Overall, it does not seem possible to reduce the scope of Article 14a of the VAT Directive or to extend the scope of Articles 14a or 28 of the VAT Directive for a general deemed supplier regime for platforms facilitating the supply of services.

5.3 DISCUSSION OF A POSSIBLE INFRINGEMENT OF ARTICLE 14A OF THE VAT DIRECTIVE OF THE FREEDOM TO CONDUCT A BUSINESS

5.3.1 Content of Article 16 of the CFR

The freedom to conduct a business was, similar to the principle of equality, already applicable before Article 16 of the CFR was introduced. The freedom to conduct a business is based on the extensive case law by the CJEU on the freedom to exercise an economic or commercial activity,[1481] on the freedom of contract,[1482] as well as on the recognition of free competition according to Article 119 (1) and (3) of the TFEU.[1483] With the entering into force of the CFR[1484] on 1 December 2009, Article 16 of the CFR was introduced.

> The freedom to conduct a business in accordance with Union law and national laws and practices is recognised.

1480. *See*, already, the discussion on the significant difference in the VAT system of the supply of goods and the supply of services in s. 5.2.4.1.3 Situation 2: The Facilitation of Supplies of Accommodation Services or Event Tickets – Analysis of the Comparability and Identification of Unequal Treatment.
1481. *See*, e.g., Case C-4/73, *J. Nold, Kohlen- und Baustoffgroßhandlung v Commission of the European Communities*, 14 May 1974, ECLI:EU:C:1974:51, para. 14; Case C-230/78, *SpA Eridania-Zuccherifici nazionali and SpA Società Italiana per l'Industria degli Zuccheri v Minister of Agriculture and Forestry, Minister for Industry, Trade and Craft Trades, and SpA Zuccherifici Meridionali*, 27 Sep. 1979, ECLI:EU:C:1979:216, paras 20 + 31.
1482. *See*, e.g., Case C-151/78, *Sukkerfabriken Nykøbing Limiteret v Ministry of Agriculture*, 16 Jan. 1979, ECLI:EU:C:1979:4, para. 19; Case C-240/97, *Kingdom of Spain v Commission of the European Communities*, 5 Oct. 1999, ECLI:EU:C:1999:479, para. 99.
1483. *Explanations Relating to the Charter of Fundamental Rights*, OJ C 303, *supra* note 1293, at 7.
1484. Charter of Fundamental Rights of the European Union, OJ C 326 (2012).

Thereby, the CJEU confirmed that the scope of Article 16 of the CFR is unchanged and applicable to the freedom to exercise an economic or commercial activity as well as the freedom to contract and free competition.[1485] Additionally, the CJEU further held that '[t]he freedom to conduct a business includes, inter alia, the right for any business to be able to freely use, within the limits of its liability for its own acts, the economic, technical and financial resources available to it'.[1486] Moreover, the freedom to conduct a business also covers the freedom to choose with whom a person conducts business as well as the freedom to determine the price for the goods or services offered.[1487] Thus, the scope of Article 16 of the CFR is quite far but is only triggered when a measure infringes the activity of a person and not the substance of a person.[1488] An infringement of the right to conduct business can also be justified provided that the objective of the justification is in accordance with Article 52 (1) of the CFR.[1489]

5.3.2 The Applicability of Article 16 of the CFR to VAT Law

Although there are not many cases in which the CJEU evaluated Article 16 of the CFR for VAT law, the CJEU analysed the freedom to conduct a business in the case *BB Construct*.[1490] In this case, the tax authorities demanded BB Construct to provide a guarantee of EUR 500,000 within 20 days for receiving a VAT registration. The tax authorities justified the demand of such a high guarantee with the fact that the director or associate member of BB Construct was inflicted with the VAT arrears of another company. The referring court asked the CJEU whether the demand of such a guarantee would, upon others, be an infringement of Article 16 of the CFR. The CJEU held that the guarantee amounting to EUR 500,000 is justifiable for ensuring the collection of the VAT and preventing tax evasion. Nevertheless, since the guarantee would likely have caused BB Construct to declare itself insolvent in the case at hand,[1491] the CJEU referred the decision back to the national court that should determine whether a guarantee of

---

1485. *See*, e.g., Case C-283/11, *Sky Österreich GmbH v Österreichischer Rundfunk*, 22 Jan. 2013, ECLI:EU:C:2013:28, para. 42; Case C-534/16, *BB construct*, 26 Oct. 2017, ECLI:EU:C:2017:820, para. 35.
1486. Case C-314/12, *UPC Telekabel Wien GmbH v Constantin Film Verleih GmbH and Wega Filmproduktionsgesellschaft mbH*, 27 Mar. 2014, ECLI:EU:C:2014:192, para. 49; Case C-134/15, *Lidl GmbH & Co. KG v Freistaat Sachsen*, 30 Jun. 2016, ECLI:EU:C:2016:498, para. 27.
1487. Case C-283/11, *Sky Österreich*, 22 Jan. 2013, ECLI:EU:C:2013:28, para. 43; with reference Joined Cases C-90/90 and C-91/90, *Jean Neu and others v Secrétaire d'Etat à l'Agriculture et à la Viticulture*, 10 Jul. 1991, ECLI:EU:C:1991:303, para. 13; Case C-437/04, *Commission of the European Communities v Kingdom of Belgium*, 22 Mar. 2007, ECLI:EU:C:2007:178, para. 51; Case C-213/10, *F-Tex SIA v Lietuvos-Anglijos UAB 'Jadecloud-Vilma'*, 19 Apr. 2012, ECLI:EU:C:2012:215, para. 45.
1488. If a measure intervened with the substance of a person, Article 17 of the CFR should be reviewed; *see*, e.g., Hans D. Jarass, *Art. 17 Eigentumsrecht*, Charta der Grundrechte der EU, para. 4 (Hans D. Jarass ed., C.H. Beck 2021).
1489. *Explanations Relating to the Charter of Fundamental Rights*, OJ C 303, *supra* note 1293, at 7.
1490. Case C-534/16, *BB construct*, 26 Oct. 2017, ECLI:EU:C:2017:820.
1491. *See ibid.* para. 40.

such a high amount is still proportionate for the aim to ensure the correct collection of the VAT and prevent tax evasion or whether it goes beyond what is necessary.[1492]

Additionally, AG Kokott argued in her opinion to the case of *Enzo di Maura* that '[t]he pre-financing of VAT affects the freedom to choose an occupation, to conduct a trade, and the basic right to property (Articles 15, 16 and 17 of the Charter)'[1493] and thus must be proportionate. The case *Enzo di Maura* revolved around the adjustment of the taxable amount because of the insolvency of the customer. This adjustment was denied by the tax authorities with the argument that such an adjustment can only be carried out after the failure of insolvency proceedings that may take up to 10 years in Italy or individual enforcement proceedings.[1494] The CJEU did not apply the freedom to conduct a business or the right to property but based its decision solely on the principle of proportionality.[1495]

Especially the case of *BB Construct* emphasises that the measure reviewed under Article 16 of the CFR must be severe. In the *BB Construct* case, the measure would have caused the taxable person to not only be limited in how and with whom they conduct business but whether they can conduct a business at all.[1496] It is questionable whether the CJEU meant to limit the applicability of Article 16 of the CFR to cases where the conducting of business is impossible. An argument to support this narrow scope of Article 16 of the CFR is the already discussed wide leeway of the EU legislator when introducing VAT provisions.[1497] However, in other areas of law, the CJEU has explicitly indicated that Article 16 of the CFR can also be infringed when a measure limits the freedom to choose with whom a person conducts business.[1498]

5.3.3 Article 14a VAT Directive as a Violation of the Freedom to Conduct a Business According to Article 16 of the CFR?

Article 14a of the VAT Directive raises one critical point which that be an infringement of the freedom to conduct a business. The platforms have to amend their business model and processes for being compliant with Article 14a of the VAT Directive. Due to the obligation to pay the VAT due also for the fictitious supply, the platform must implement internal processes as well as external processes with the suppliers to collect the information required and the VAT due to fulfil its obligation due to Article 14a of the VAT Directive. It is questionable whether the amending of internal and external processes can already be seen as an infringement of the freedom to conduct a business

---

1492. *See ibid.* para. 42.
1493. Case C-246/16, *Di Maura*, 8 Jun. 2017, ECLI:EU:C:2017:440, Opinion of AG Kokott, para. 47.
1494. Case C-246/16, *Di Maura*, 23 Nov. 2017, ECLI:EU:C:2017:887, para. 7.
1495. *Ibid.* paras. 25 et seqq.
1496. *See*, similarly, Annika Streicher, *Cross-Border Juridical VAT Double Taxation in the Framework of European Law* 125 et seq. (2022).
1497. *See*, for this discussion, s. 5.2.3.2 The Applicability of Article 20 of the CFR to VAT Law.
1498. *See*, e.g., Joined Cases C-90/90 and C-91/90, *Neu and Others v Secrétaire d'État à l'Agriculture and à la Viticulture*, 10 Jul. 1991, ECLI:EU:C:1991:303, para. 13; Case C-283/11, *Sky Österreich*, 22 Jan. 2013, ECLI:EU:C:2013:28, para. 43.

as, for any taxable person, there are processes and requirements that taxable person must fulfil for being able to fulfil their VAT obligations.

However, the burden for platforms introduced with Article 14a of the VAT Directive may go as far as to practically hinder platforms from entering new markets or to extend their business model to certain suppliers. A platform could, e.g., be reluctant to offer goods from underlying suppliers established in a third country because such facilitations could trigger Article 14a of the VAT Directive. Thereby, the platform's right to conduct a business may be infringed. An infringement can only be affirmed when the scope of Article 16 of the CFR is not limited to the exclusion of certain taxable persons from an activity but is read broader as discussed in the previous section.

If an infringement of the right to conduct a business was affirmed, then such an infringement could still be justified based on an objective accepted pursuant to Article 52 (1) of the CFR. For the discussion of possible justification grounds and the question of whether such a justification is proportionate, reference is made to the preceding section of Article 20 of the CFR.[1499]

5.4   CONCLUSION

The introduction of Article 14a of the VAT Directive results in much higher costs and administrative burdens for platforms facilitating the supply of goods, especially in comparison to platforms facilitating the supply of services. These higher costs and the increase in administrative burden leads to the question of whether Article 14a of the VAT Directive is in accordance with the principle of equal treatment stipulated in Article 20 of the CFR with the principle of neutrality as well as with the right to conduct a business according to Article 16 of the CFR.

Thereby, it could be shown that the introduction of Article 14a of the VAT Directive could qualify as an infringement of Article 20 of the CFR as well as of Article 16 of the CFR. Nevertheless, one valid justification reason for the introduction of Article 14a of the VAT Directive could be found in effective and efficient VAT collection.

Overall and especially in light of the broad discretion by the EU legislator when introducing VAT provisions, the introduction of Article 14a of the VAT Directive seems to be justifiable because Article 14a of the VAT Directive improves the effective and efficient VAT collection. The analyses has further shown that the introduction of Article 14a of the VAT Directive generally seems to be proportionate. However, two situations have been identified when the proportionality of Article 14a of the VAT Directive can be questioned. The first is the fact that also platforms that are not included in the payment process become liable for the VAT payment. Second is the increase in administrative burden and cost for platforms which is especially high for platforms with little turnover or start-ups. Thereby, the EU legislator did not include any distinction based on the platform size (i.e., based on the amount of turnover) in Article 14a of the VAT Directive. Thus, it may be argued that Article 14a of the VAT

1499. *See* the detailed discussion in s. 5.2.4.2 Possible Justifications and the Proportionality of Article 14a of the VAT Directive.

Directive is not fulfilling the proportionality requirement for smaller platforms and for platforms that are not included in the payment process.

Finally, also the principle of neutrality has been analysed. Although the principle of neutrality is a secondary law principle and thus cannot infringe the VAT Directive, the interpretation of the VAT Directive in light of the principle of neutrality is necessary. Thereby, the first difficulty is finding two similar situations where the supply of goods and services is in competition with each other and both are facilitated by platforms. Even if the discussed example could be regarded as similar, the VAT Directive would not allow the interpretational reduction of Article 14a of the VAT Directive to exclude supplies from the applicability of Article 14a of the VAT Directive when the requirements stipulated therein were fulfilled. Similarly, the interpretational extension of Articles 14a or 28 of the VAT Directive to introduce a deemed supplier regime for all platforms supplying services without the platform fulfilling all legally required criteria would also not be possible.

CHAPTER 6
Conclusions

6.1 THE VAT TREATMENT OF THE SUPPLY OF GOODS BEFORE THE INTRODUCTION OF THE E-COMMERCE PACKAGE

The first part of this book analysed the VAT treatment of platforms before the introduction of the VAT e-commerce package in July 2021 which led to legal uncertainty and a chain of open questions. The first legal question discussed the kind of supplies that are offered by the platform and whether these supplies qualify as one composite supply or several single supplies.[1500] The second question is whether the undisclosed agent scheme of Article 14 (2) (c) of the VAT Directive is applicable.[1501] As the affirmation of one of these two preliminary observations would influence the VAT chain of supplies, the separate legal analysis for each supply between the three parties involved can only be carried out if these two questions could be negated. Thereby, the analysis has shown that a general negation of these questions is not possible as a case-by-case analysis must be conducted. However, for many platforms represented on the market, good arguments can be found to deny the application of the composite supply rules as well as the undisclosed agent scheme.

The further legal analysis raised further questions since each specific supply in the platform system can lead to several legal outcomes.[1502] Throughout the legal analysis of the different supplies, it can be seen that especially the place of supply rules often lead to legal uncertainty even though the determination of the place of supply is of utmost importance as, according to these rules, the Member States execute their taxation rights. In the case of legal uncertainty on the place of supply rules, the different

---

1500. *See* the extensive discussions in s. 2.2.2.1 The Supply Through Platforms: A Composite Supply?.
1501. *See* the extensive discussions in s. 2.2.2.2 The Supply Through Platforms: A Supply through an Undisclosed Agent?.
1502. *See* the extensive discussions in s. 2.2.3 The Supply of Goods from the Underlying Supplier to the Customer, s. 2.2.4 The Supply of the Platform Service to the Underlying Supplier and s. 2.2.5 The Supply of the Platform Service to the Customer.

interpretations by the Member States may result in double (non-)taxation. As the CJEU has not yet had a chance to take its stand on the qualification of the supplies through platforms, digital platforms as well as the underlying suppliers have faced legal uncertainties throughout the last years. This legal uncertainty is enhanced by the fact that the legal qualification may depend on contracts and especially on the set-up and publicly available information on the platform. Therefore, a general legal qualification of sales through e-commerce platforms is impossible.

These legal uncertainties are caused by the fact the European VAT system was introduced for a 'brick and mortar' economy and, since its introduction, only partial legal reforms were implemented to conquer the legal uncertainties revolving from the rapid developments in the digital economy. This shortcoming of the EU VAT system has been recognised by the EU, and it led to the introduction of the e-commerce package. Although the e-commerce package has a fundamental influence on some of the legal consequences discussed, the newly introduced rules are only applicable when specific requirements are fulfilled.[1503] Therefore, it must be born in mind that the VAT rules applicable before the introduction of the VAT e-commerce package are still applicable to supplies of goods through platforms that do not fall into the (rather limited) scope of Article 14a of the VAT Directive. As exposed, the determination of the correct VAT treatment of such supplies is difficult. This difficulty has led the European Commission to announce that a legislative proposal will be published in the future that will also cover other supplies through platforms.[1504] This proposal should lead to more legal certainty and clarity for the parties involved.

6.2   THE SCOPE OF ARTICLE 14A OF THE VAT DIRECTIVE

The sections on the scope of Article 14a of the VAT Directive have discussed the personal and substantive scope of Article 14a of the VAT Directive in detail. Thereby, the personal scope of both paragraphs of Article 14a of the VAT Directive is based on three criteria that can be uniformly interpreted: the platform must be: (i) a taxable person (ii) facilitating the supply of goods (iii) through the use of an electronic interface. From this definition, especially the 'facilitation' of the supply may lead to questions and legal uncertainties for platforms. The place of establishment of the platform is irrelevant for the application of Article 14a of the VAT Directive.

Once it is determined that the electronic interface facilitates the supply of goods, the substantive scope of Article 14a of the VAT Directive must be tested. The analysis of the substantive scope showed that both paragraphs have some similarities: a third country element should be identified and the facilitated supply should be a supply to a non-taxable person. Nevertheless, a closer analysis also highlighted the differences between the two paragraphs. Whereas Article 14a (1) of the VAT Directive requires the

---

1503. For the scope of Article 14a of the VAT Directive, *see* s. 3 The Scope of Article 14a of the VAT Directive.

1504. European Commission, *Communication from the Commission to the European Parliament and the Council an Action Plan for Fair and Simple Taxation Supporting the Recovery Strategy,* COM/2020/312 final, *supra* note 31, at 15.

dispatch or transportation of the goods by or on behalf of the supplier, Article 14a (2) of the VAT Directive does not require any dispatch or transportation. Thus, the platform could also become the supplier, e.g., for the sale of immovable property when the other requirements of Article 14a (2) of the VAT Directive are fulfilled. Furthermore, Article 14a (2) of the VAT Directive is not restricted to the supply of specific goods whereas Article 14a (1) of the VAT Directive does not apply for goods supplied after assembly or installation as well as new means of transport. In addition, the intrinsic value of the consignment not exceeding EUR 150 is only relevant for the application of the deemed supplier regime according to Article 14a (1) of the VAT Directive. Additionally, Article 14a (2) of the VAT Directive is only applicable to supplies to non-taxable persons whereas the platform also becomes the deemed supplier for imported goods when the recipient of the goods is a taxable person or non-taxable legal person whose intra-Community acquisitions of goods are not subject to VAT pursuant to Article 3 (1) of the VAT Directive.[1505] Finally, a differentiation between the two paragraphs could be identified based on the taxable status of the underlying supplier: Article 14a (2) of the VAT Directive is only applicable when the underlying supplier is a taxable person whereas, for the application of Article 14a (1) of the VAT Directive, the taxable status of the underlying supplier is irrelevant.

Finally, the analysis has also shown that, even after the introduction of the second legislative package and the definitions included therein, some questions remain open for interpretation and may cause legal uncertainty for the electronic interfaces and the underlying suppliers when deciding whether the deemed supplier regime is applicable, e.g., the definition of a 'consignment'. The quite complicated cross-referencing between the VAT Directive, the VAT Implementing Regulation, and the relevant provisions in customs law causes further difficulties to the application of Article 14a of the VAT Directive.

6.3 THE LEGAL CONSEQUENCES OF ARTICLE 14A OF THE VAT DIRECTIVE

The sections on the legal consequences of Article 14a of the VAT Directive have shown that the platform becoming the deemed supplier of the transaction has a major impact on the platform's VAT obligations in the EU. One side of the coin is that, due to the fictitious inclusion in the supply chain, the VAT obligations for platforms are enormously increased since the platforms are treated as if they acquired and supplied the goods themselves. The other side of the coin is the simplification for the underlying suppliers who do not have to collect and pay the VAT due if the platform became the deemed supplier.

The first difficulty the platform faces is determining the applicable place of supply. Depending on where the goods come from and what kind of goods are supplied, the place of supply may be the place of origin or the place of destination. The

---

1505. *See* the discussion of these taxable persons in s. 3.3.1.1.4 The Requirements of Article 14 (4) (2) (a) of the VAT Directive on the VAT Status of the Recipient of the Goods.

determination of the place of supply has an effect on the further VAT treatment of the supplied goods and is thus of utmost importance. This difficulty is followed by the difficulty of the correct determination of the applicable VAT rate and exemption by the establishing of the invoicing obligation for B2C supplies in the non-harmonised VAT system and by the extensive reporting obligation when platforms apply the IOSS and/or the EU-OSS. Finally, the return of goods can also lead to practical difficulties; it especially highlights the consequences of the interplay between the economic reality of the underlying supplier supplying the goods and the fiction created by Article 14a of the VAT Directive of the platform acting as a deemed supplier. All of the discussed difficulties make the business processes of platforms more complicated and costly.

At the same time, the EU legislator seems to have been aware of these immense difficulties for platforms and implemented several facilitations, e.g., the legal stipulation of the supply with transport in Article 36b of the VAT Directive, the amendment of the chargeable event to the time of the payment acceptance in Article 66a of the VAT Directive, the safe harbour clause in Article 5c of the VAT Implementing Regulation, the application of the exemption for the supply from the underlying supplier to the platform in Article 136a of the VAT Directive and, most of all, the introduction of the OSS systems.

As the full VAT burden of the supply of the good is shifted to the platforms, the 'big winners' of the introduction of Article 14a of the VAT Directive are the tax authorities and the underlying suppliers. The only VAT payment that might have become due in the chain transaction of Article 14a of the VAT Directive for the underlying supplier has been exempt from VAT according to Article 136a of the VAT Directive by the EU legislator. Nevertheless, it is not quite clear why the EU legislator did not remove the full obligation (or at least provide the Member States with such an option) for underlying suppliers to register for the VAT and file VAT returns although, from the applicability of Article 14a of the VAT Directive, no VAT becomes due. One disadvantage for underlying suppliers could be that, due to the inclusion of the platform in the VAT transaction chain, the personal exemption of the small enterprise scheme would not be applicable in the case that the platform does not fulfil the requirements of a small enterprise scheme (which is rather unlikely). This legal consequence would increase the price of the good by the VAT charged from the platform to the customer. Furthermore, the analysis of the return of the goods has shown that further VAT obligations may be triggered for underlying suppliers when the ordered goods are returned. The EU legislator missed the chance with this broad reform on e-commerce to introduce a facilitation for the additional registration obligations resulting from the return of goods.

Finally, the analysis of the legal consequences has also shown that the information exchange between the platform and the underlying supplier is of utmost importance. Depending on the platform model, the platform may require information from the underlying supplier to fulfil its VAT obligations. At the same time, the underlying supplier may require the information from the platform if the platform was responsible for certain aspects of the supply. Many platforms had to amend their business model in order to guarantee this information flow and to (at least partially) conquer the discussed difficulties arising from the legal consequences of the application of Article 14a of the VAT Directive.

6.4 DISCUSSION OF A POSSIBLE INFRINGEMENT OF ARTICLE 14A OF THE VAT DIRECTIVE OF THE CHARTER OF FUNDAMENTAL RIGHTS OF THE EUROPEAN UNION

The introduction of Article 14a of the VAT Directive results in much higher costs and administrative burdens for platforms facilitating the supply of goods, especially in comparison to platforms facilitating the supply of services. These higher costs and the increase in administrative burden lead to the question of whether Article 14a of the VAT Directive is in accordance with the principle of equal treatment stipulated in Article 20 of the CFR, with the principle of neutrality, as well as with the right to conduct business according to Article 16 of the CFR.

Thereby, it could be shown that the introduction of Article 14a of the VAT Directive could qualify as an infringement of Article 20 of the CFR as well as of Article 16 of the CFR. Nevertheless, one valid justification reason for the introduction of Article 14a of the VAT Directive could be found in effective and efficient VAT collection.

Overall and especially in light of the broad discretion of the EU legislator when introducing VAT provisions, the introduction of Article 14a of the VAT Directive seems to be justifiable because Article 14a of the VAT Directive improves the effective and efficient VAT collection. The analyses have further shown that the introduction of Article 14a of the VAT Directive generally seems to be proportionate. However, two situations have been identified when the proportionality of Article 14a of the VAT Directive can be questioned: First, the fact that also platforms which are not included in the payment progress become liable for the VAT payment; and, second, the increase in administrative burden and cost for platforms which is especially high for platforms with little turnover or start-ups. Thereby, the EU legislator did not include any distinction based on the platform size (i.e., based on the amount of turnover) in Article 14a of the VAT Directive. Thus, it may be argued that Article 14a of the VAT Directive is not fulfilling the proportionality requirement for smaller platforms and for platforms that are not included in the payment process.

Finally, also the principle of neutrality has been analysed. Although the principle of neutrality is a secondary law principle and thus cannot infringe the VAT Directive, the interpretation of the VAT Directive in light of the principle of neutrality is necessary. Thereby, the first difficulty is finding two similar situations where the supply of goods and services is in competition with each other and both are facilitated by platforms. Even if the discussed example could be regarded as similar, the VAT Directive would not allow the interpretational reduction of Article 14a of the VAT Directive to exclude supplies from the applicability of Article 14a of the VAT Directive when the requirements stipulated therein were fulfilled. Similarly, the interpretational extension of Articles 14a or 28 of the VAT Directive to introduce a deemed supplier regime for all platforms supplying services without the platform fulfilling all legally required criteria would also not be possible.

6.5 THE FUTURE OF EFFECTIVE AND EFFICIENT VAT COLLECTION

The introduction of the e-commerce package has the aim to make VAT collection more effective and efficient. Thereby, the principle of destination has been strengthened with the purpose to limit distortion of competition to tax goods bought over the Internet with the same VAT rate as goods bought in traditional stores. The involvement of the platform is the answer of the EU legislator for conquering the non-compliance of many taxable persons (especially taxable persons established in third countries) supplying goods in e-commerce.

Although the EU VAT system is generally based on the principle that taxable persons act as VAT collectors for the competent tax authorities,[1506] the introduction of Article 14a of the VAT Directive has taken the VAT collection obligation by taxable persons to a next level; i.e., it extends the taxable persons' collection obligation to supplies that they did not provide. The platforms only interfere in the supply by providing the electronic interface to conduct the supply. Seemingly, the competent tax authorities could not get the underlying supplier to comply with their VAT obligations, and thus the VAT collection was assigned to the platforms with the introduction of Article 14a of the VAT Directive.

Thereby, the European Commission has already announced that a further extension of the deemed supplier regime to platforms providing the supply of services may, in the future, be implemented.[1507] Similar approaches to make platforms responsible for the VAT/GST collection can also be seen in other countries, e.g., Canada has introduced an obligation for platforms to collect and pay the GST when facilitating the supply of short-term accommodations.[1508] From this further extension of the deemed supplier regime, additional challenges and discussions will arise, e.g., the proportionality of such an extension of the deemed supplier regime.

This book has tried to give an in-depth analysis of the introduction of Article 14a of the VAT Directive and its legal consequences. Thereby, weaknesses in the implementation of Article 14a of the VAT Directive were identified that should be taken into consideration when extending further the existing deemed supplier regime. Nevertheless, this book solely concentrated on the deemed supplier regime of Article 14a of the VAT Directive. Further investigations on other deemed supplier regimes by platforms, e.g., Article 9a of the VAT Implementing Regulation, or Articles 14 (2) (c) and 28 of the

---

1506. *See*, e.g., *Enzo Di Maura v Agenzia delle Entrate – Direzione Provinciale di Siracusa*, ECJ C-246/16, 23 Nov. 2017, para. 23; Case C-127/18, *A-PACK CZ s.r.o. v Odvolací finanční ředitelství*, 8 May 2019, ECLI:EU:C:2019:377, para. 22; Case C-335/19, *E. Sp. z o.o. Sp. k. v Minister Finansów*, 15 Oct. 2020, ECLI:EU:C:2020:829, para. 31; Case C-324/20, *Finanzamt B v X-Beteiligungsgesellschaft mbH*, 28 Oct. 2021, ECLI:EU:C:2021:880, para. 52.

1507. *See* European Commission, *Communication from the Commission to the European Parliament and the Council an Action Plan for Fair and Simple Taxation Supporting the Recovery Strategy*, *supra* note 31, at 15, where the European Commission stated that '[a]lso, the role platforms could have in securing the collection of the tax will be examined.'

1508. An Act to Implement Certain Provisions of the Budget Tabled in Parliament on April 19, 2021 and Other Measures, Second Session, Forty-third Parliament, 69-70 Elizabeth II, 2020-2021, 29 Jun. 2021.

VAT Directive were not the focus of this research. An in-depth analysis of other deemed supplier regimes would lead to a more comprehensive understanding of possible challenges to the extension of the deemed supplier regime to other supplies.

The introduction of Article 14a of the VAT Directive generally raises the question of how far the obligations for the suppliers should go to act as the state's collection mechanism and whether there are any better or easier ways to conquer this issue. In this sense, several other approaches have been brought forward to improve VAT collection and thus to make VAT collection more efficient and effective,[1509] e.g., the introduction of blockchain technology for improving the recording of transactions,[1510] the introduction of mandatory e-invoicing, real-time-reporting and -collecting,[1511] amendments to who collects the VAT (split payments, collection by consumers, etc.),[1512] or the introduction of a general reverse-charge

---

1509. *See,* for a summary of some alternative approaches, Roland Ismer & Magdalena Schwarz, *Combating VAT Fraud through Digital Technologies: A Reform Proposal,* 30 International VAT Monitor (2019).

1510. *See,* e.g., Richard Thompson Ainsworth & Musaad Alwohaibi, *The First Real-Time Blockchain VAT – GCC Solves MTIC Fraud,* Tax Notes International (2017); Richard T. Ainsworth & Andrew Shact, *Blockchain Technology Might Solve VAT Fraud,* 83 Tax Notes International (2016); Richard T Ainsworth et al., *A High-Tech Proposal for the U.K. and Saudi VATs: Fighting Fraud With Mini-Blockchains and VATCoins,* Tax Notes International (2019); Madeleine Merkx, *VAT and Blockchain: Challenges and Opportunities Ahead,* 28 EC Tax Review (2019); Robert Müller, *Building a Blockchain for the EU VAT,* 100 Tax Notes International (2020); Fabrizio Borselli, *VAT Fraud, Cryptocurrencies and a Future for the VAT System,* 30 International VAT Monitor, s. 5.1. (2019); *see also* Robert Müller, *Proposal for an Automated Real-Time VAT Collection Mechanism in B2C E-Commerce Using Blockchain Technology,* 31 International VAT Monitor (2020), who proposes to use the blockchain technology for a real-time VAT collection; *see* also, on the introduction of VATCoins, e.g., Richard T. Ainsworth et al., *VATCoin: Can a Crypto Tax Currency Prevent VAT Fraud?,* 83 Tax Notes International (2016); *A VATCoin Solution to MTIC Fraud: Past Efforts, Present Technology, and the EU's 2017 Proposal,* Tax Notes International (2018).

1511. *See,* e.g., Richard T. Ainsworth & Boryana Madzharova, *Real-Time Collection of the Value-Added Tax: Some Business and Legal Implications,* Boston Univ. School of Law, Law and Economics Research Paper No. 12-51 (2012); Sascha Jafari, *Combining Modern Technology and Real-Time Invoice Reporting to Combat VAT Fraud: No Revolution, but a Technological Evolution,* 31 International VAT Monitor (2020); Sascha Jafari, *Business-Friendly Real-Time Reporting in the European Union – Are We Moving in the Right Direction?,* 32 International VAT Monitor (2021); Müller, *Proposal for an Automated Real-Time VAT Collection Mechanism in B2C E-Commerce Using Blockchain Technology, supra* note 1510; Nicoletta Petrosino, *Are You Ready for the Tax Technology?,* 30 International VAT Monitor (2019).

1512. These might range from the split payments; *see,* e.g., Bartosz Gryziak, *Split Payment Across the European Union – Review and Analysis,* 31 International VAT Monitor, *supra* note 81; Charlène A Herbain & Alain Thilmany, *Split Payment: The Validity of a Not so New Alternative Vat Collection Method,* British Tax Review, *supra* note 81; Charlène Adline Herbain, *VAT Neutrality, supra* note 1452, at 249 et seqq.; Robert C Prätzler, *Split Payments in VAT Systems – Is This the Future?,* 29 International VAT Monitor (2018); *see* also the study conducted by Deloitte on behalf of the European Commission: European Commission, *Analysis of the Impact of the Split Payment Mechanism as an Alternative VAT Collection Method* (Dec. 2017), https://op.europa.eu/en/publication-detail/-/publication/b87224ad-fcce-11e7-b8f5-01aa75 ed71a1/language-en (last visited 29 Nov. 2021); to the customer collecting VAT; *see,* e.g., Marie Lamensch, *Is There Any Future for the Vendor Collection Model in the 21st Century Economy?,* 27 International VAT Monitor (2016); Marie Lamensch & Mack Saraswat, *From Clicks to Compliance: A Data Conduit to Collect VAT,* 28 International VAT Monitor (2017); to the inclusion of financial institutions in the VAT payment; *see,* e.g., Wilhelm G. Schulze & Stephanus P. van Zyl, *The Collection of Value Added Tax on Cross-Border Digital Trade – Part*

mechanism.[1513] Although all of these amendments are likely to reduce the potential of VAT fraud, the introduction of such wide-ranging amendments would require a basic reform of the VAT Directive. Many of the raised open questions and issues are based on the fact that the VAT system was designed and introduced for a 'brick and mortar' economy and not properly reformed although far-reaching technological and economic developments have occurred in the last decades. However, the introduction and development of new technologies open ways to improve VAT collection which should and will play a significant role in the future. Finally, these developments will open new discussions and research possibilities. Thus, it is to say that the future will bring forward new VAT challenges that legislators, academia, and practitioners will have to conquer.

2: VAT Collection by Banks, 47 Comparative and International Law Journal of Southern Africa (2014); *see* also the study conducted by PriceWaterhouseCooper on behalf of the European Commission: European Commission, *Study on the Feasibility of Alternative Methods for Improving and Simplifying the Collection of VAT Through the Means of Modern Technologies and/or Financial Intermediaries* (20 Sep. 2010), https://op.europa.eu/en/publication-detail/ -/publication/e0d6a4f7-9ada-11e6-868c-01aa75ed71a1/language-en (last visited 29 Nov. 2021).

1513. *See*, e.g., Robert F van Brederode & Sebastian Pfeiffer, *Combating Carousel Fraud: The General Reverse Charge VAT*, 26 International VAT Monitor; Marie Lamensch, *Are Reverse Charging and the One-Stop Scheme Efficient Ways to Collect VAT on Digital Supplies*, 1 World Journal of VAT/GST Law (2012); Stan Beelen, *Is a Generalized Reverse Charge Mechanism the Obvious Remedy Against VAT Fraud?*, *in VAT in an EU and International Perspective: Essays in Honour of Han Kogels*, *supra* note 193; Charlène Adline Herbain, *supra* note 1452, at 246 et seqq.; Werner Widmann, *Systembezogene Änderung bei der Umsatzbesteuerung 'Reverse-Charge-Verfahren'*, 55 Umsatzsteuer-Rundschau (2006); Stephan Filtzinger, *Sektorales oder generelles Reverse-Charge? – Reformbedarf bei der Steuerschuldverlagerung*, *in 100 Jahre Umsatzsteuer in Deutschland 1918-2018: Festschrift*, *supra* note 13; *see* also the detailed analysis by Desiree Auer, *Mehrwertsteuerbetrugsbekämpfung in der EU* 141 et seqq. (Linde Verlag 2020).

Bibliography[*]

Monographs

Katharina Artinger, *Taxing Consumption in the Digital Age: Challenges for European VAT* (Nomos 2020).

Desiree Auer, *Mehrwertsteuerbetrugsbekämpfung in der EU* (Linde Verlag 2020).

Stefanie Baur-Rückert, *Die Einheitlichkeit des Umsatzes im Mehrwertsteuerrecht* (Nomos 2018).

Giorgio Beretta, *European VAT and the Sharing Economy* (Kluwer Law International 2019).

Thomas Bieber, *Der Einfuhrumsatz* (MANZ'sche Verlags- und Universitätsbuchhandlung 2019).

Norbert Bramerdorfer, *Das Kommissionsgeschäft in der Umsatzsteuer* (LexisNexis 2012).

Franz Bydlinski, *Juristische Methodenlehre und Rechtsbegriff* (Springer 2011).

Franz Bydlinski & Peter Bydlinski, *Grundzüge der juristischen Methodenlehre* (facultas 2018).

Amiya K. Chakravarty, *Supply Chain Transformation: Evolving with Emerging Business Paradigms* (Springer 2014).

Paul P. Craig & Gráinne De Búrca, *EU Law: Text, Cases, and Materials* (Oxford University Press 7th ed. 2020).

Ad van Doesum et al., *Fundamentals of EU VAT Law* (Wolters Kluwer 2020).

Sjoerd Douma, *Legal Research in International and EU Tax Law* (Kluwer 2014).

Liam Ebrill et al., *The Modern VAT* (International Monetary Fund 2001).

Tina Ehrke-Rabel et al., *Umsatzsteuer in einer digitalisierten Welt* (ifst-Schrift 2020).

Wolfgang Gassner, *Interpretation und Anwendung der Steuergesetze: kritische Analyse der wirtschaftlichen Betrachtungsweise des Steuerrecht* (Orac 1972).

Stefan Hammerl & Lily Zechner, *SWK-Spezial Plattformhaftung* (Linde Verlag 2020).

Gerrit Heinemann, *Der Neue Online-Handel* (Springer Gabler 2021).

Oskar Henkow, *The VAT/GST Treatment of Public Bodies* (Wolters Kluwer 2013).

---

[*] In alphabetical order.

Charlène Adline Herbain, *VAT Neutrality* (Promoculture-Larcier 2015).

Richard Kettisch, *Reihengeschäfte in der Umsatzsteuer* (Verlag Österreich Berliner Wissenschafts-Verlag 2017).

Juliane Kokott, *Das Steuerrecht der Europäischen Union* (C.H. Beck 2018).

Jasmin Kollmann, *Taxable Supplies and Their Consideration in European VAT: With Selected Examples of the Digital Economy* (IBFD 2019).

Marie Lamensch, *European Value Added Tax in the Digital Era: A Critical Analysis and Proposals for Reform* (IBFD 2015).

Karl Larenz, *Methodenlehre der Rechtswissenschaft* (Springer 1991).

Koen Lenaerts & Piet Van Nuffel, *Constitutional Law of the European Union* (Robert Bray ed., Sweet & Maxwell 2005).

Madeleine Merkx, *The Wizard of OSS: Effective Collection of VAT in Cross-Border E-Commerce* (Stichting NLFiscaal 2020).

Bernhard Oreschnik, *Verhältnismäßigkeit und Kontrolldichte* (Springer 2019).

Michael Potacs, *Rechtstheorie* (facultas 2019).

Karl Riesenhuber, *Europäische Methodenlehre* (De Gruyter 2015).

Friedrich Carl von Savigny, *System des heutigen Römischen Rechts* (1840).

Robert Schütze, *European Union Law* (Oxford University Press 2021).

Karoline Spies, *Permanent Establishments in Value Added Tax: The Role of Establishments in International B2B Trade in Services Under VAT/GST Law* (IBFD 2020).

Annika Streicher, *Cross-Border Juridical VAT Double Taxation in the Framework of European Law* (2022).

Rita Szudoczky, *The Sources of EU Law and Their Relationships: Lessons for the Field of Taxation: Primary Law, Secondary Law, Fundamental Freedoms and State Aid Rules* (IBFD 2014).

Ben Terra & Julie Kajus, *Introduction to European VAT* (IBFD 2021).

Cristina Trenta, *Rethinking EU VAT for P2P Distribution* (Kluwer Law International 2015).

Michael Tumpel, *Mehrwertsteuer im innergemeinschaftlichen Warenverkehr: Analyse der Besteuerung des Warenverkehrs im Binnenmarkt nach dem Gemeinschaftsrecht und dem österreichischen Umsatzsteuerrecht* (Linde Verlag 1997).

Efraim Turban et al., *Electronic Commerce 2018: A Managerial and Social Networks Perspective* (Springer 2018).

Christine Weinzierl, *SWK-Spezial E-Commerce Paket 2021* (Linde Verlag 2021).

Reinhold Zippelius, *Juristische Methodenlehre* (Beck 2012).

Cornelia Zirkl, *Die Neutralität der Umsatzsteuer als europäisches Besteuerungsprinzip* (PL Academic Research 2015).

Anthologies and Contributions to Anthologies

Markus Achatz, *Kommissionsgeschäfte und Konsignationsgeschäfte im Unionsrecht*, in *Reihengeschäfte bei der Umsatzsteuer* (Markus Achatz & Michael Tumpel eds., Linde Verlag 2014).

Stan Beelen, *Is a Generalized Reverse Charge Mechanism the Obvious Remedy Against VAT Fraud?*, in *VAT in an EU and International Perspective: Essays in Honour of Han Kogels* (Henk van Arendonk, et al. eds., IBFD 2011).

Valentin Bendlinger & Thomas Ecker, *Die Rolle von Plattformen im E-Commerce – Plattformen und ihre umsatzsteuerlichen Pflichten*, in *Neuerungen bei innergemeinschaftlichen Umsätzen* (Markus Achatz et al. eds., Linde Verlag 2020).

Radu Bufan & Aurelian Opre, *The Principle of Tax Neutrality in the Field of Direct and Indirect Taxation*, in *Value Added Tax and Direct Taxation: Similarities and Differences* (Michael Lang et al. eds., IBFD 2009).

Nevia Čičin-Šain, *Taxing Uber*, in *Uber – Brave New Service or Unfair Competition: Legal Analysis of the Nature of Uber Services* (Jasenko Marin et al. eds., Springer International Publishing 2020).

Sophie Claessens & Tom Corbett, *Intermediated Delivery and Third-Party Billing: Implication for the Operation of VAT Systems Around the World*, in *VAT/GST in a Global Digital Economy* (Michael Lang & Ine Lejeune eds., Wolters Kluwer 2015).

Karina Kim Egholm Elgaard, *The Effect of the Charter of Fundamental Rights of the European Union on Substantive VAT Law*, in *CJEU – Recent Developments in Value Added Tax 2017* (Michael Lang et al. eds., Linde Verlag 2018).

Tina Ehrke-Rabel, *Aspekte grenzüberschreitenden digitalen Wirtschaftens in der Umsatzsteuer*, in *Digitalisierung im Steuerrecht* (Johanna Hey ed., Otto Schmidt 2019).

Joachim Englisch, *Gemeinschaftsgrundrechte im harmonisierten Steuerrecht*, in *Zukunftsfragen des deutschen Steuerrechts* (Wolfgang Schön & Karin E.M. Beck eds., Springer 2009).

Stephan Filtzinger, *Sektorales oder generelles Reverse-Charge? – Reformbedarf bei der Steuerschuldverlagerung*, in *100 Jahre Umsatzsteuer in Deutschland 1918-2018: Festschrift* (UmsatzsteuerForum e.V. ed., Otto Schmidt 2018).

Georg Kofler, *Europäischer Grundrechtsschutz im Steuerrecht*, in *Europäisches Steuerrecht* (Michael Lang ed., Otto Schmidt 2018).

Juliane Kokott, *European Court of Justice*, in *Courts and tax treaty Law* (Guglielmo Maisto ed., IBFD 2007).

Juliane Kokott & Lars Dobratz, *Der unionsrechtliche allgemeine Gleichheitssatz im Europäischen Steuerrecht*, in *Grundfragen des europäischen Steuerrechts* (Wolfgang Schön & Caroline Heber eds., Springer 2015).

Borbála Kolozs, *Neutrality in VAT*, in *Value Added Tax and Direct Taxation: Similarities and Differences* (Michael Lang et al. eds., IBFD 2009).

Marie Lamensch, *Tax Assessment in a Digital Context: A Critical Analysis of the 2015 EU Rules*, in *Value Added Tax and the Digital Economy* (Marie Lamensch et al. eds., Wolters Kluwer 2016).

Marie Lamensch, *The Use of Soft Law by the European VAT Legislator, and What the CJEU Makes of It*, in *CJEU – Recent Developments in Value Added Tax 2015* (Linde Verlag 2016).

Marie Lamensch, *The Scope of the EU VAT System: Traditional Digital Economy Related Questions*, in *CJEU – Recent Developments in Value Added Tax 2017* (Michael Lang et al. eds., Linde Verlag 2018).

Marie Lamensch & Rebecca Millar, *The Role of Marketplaces in Taxing B2C Supplies*, in *CJEU – Recent Developments in Value Added Tax 2018* (Michael Lang et al. eds., Linde Verlag 2019).

Michael Lang, *Doppelbesteuerungsabkommen in der Rechtsprechung des EuGH*, in *Europäisches Steuerrecht: 42. Jahrestagung der Deutschen Steuerjuristischen Gesellschaft e.V., Wien, 18. und 19. September 2017* (Michael Lang ed., Otto Schmidt 2018).

Ine Lejeune & Sophie Claessens, *The VAT One Stop Shop System: An Efficient Way to Collect VAT on Digital Supplies into the EU Consumer Market?*, in *Value Added Tax and the Digital Economy* (Marie Lamensch et al. eds., Wolters Kluwer 2016).

Ine Lejeune & Jeanine Daou, *VAT Neutrality from an EU Perspective*, in *Improving VAT/GST – Designing a Simple and Fraud-Proof Tax System* (Michael Lang & Ine Lejeune eds., IBFD 2014).

Frank Nellen & Ad van Doesum, *Taxable Amount & VAT Rates*, in *CJEU – Recent Developments in Value Added Tax 2018* (Michael Lang et al. eds., Linde Verlag 2019).

Danuše Nerudová & Jan Široký, *The Principle of Neutrality: VAT/GST v Direct Taxation*, in *Value Added Tax and Direct Taxation: Similarities and Differences* (Michael Lang et al. eds., IBFD 2009).

Katerina Pantazatou, *Taxation of the Sharing Economy in the European Union*, in *The Cambridge Handbook of the Law of the Sharing Economy* (Nestor M. Davidson et al. eds., Oxford University Press 2018).

Sebastian Pfeiffer, *Comment on 'Free' Internet Services*, in *CJEU – Recent Developments in Value Added Tax 2017* (Michael Lang et al. eds., Linde Verlag 2018).

Hannes Rösler, *Interpretation of EU Law*, in *Max Planck Encyclopedia of European Private Law* (Jürgen Basedow et al. eds., Oxford University Press 2012).

Wolfgang Schön, *Die Analogie im Europäischen (Privat-)Recht*, in *Privatrechtsdogmatik im 21. Jahrhundert: Festschrift für Claus-Wilhelm Canaris zum 80. Geburtstag* (Marietta Auer et al. eds., De Gruyter 2017).

Karoline Spies, *Joint and Several Liability Rules in EU VAT Law*, in *CJEU – Recent Developments in Value Added Tax 2020* (Georg Kofler et al. eds., Linde Verlag 2021).

Panos Thliveros, *EU OSS & MOSS: A Solution to the Challenges of the Digital Economy?*, in *Taxation in a Global Digital Economy* (Ina Kerschner & Maryte Somare eds., Linde Verlag 2017).

Michael Tumpel, *Gemeinschaftsrechtliche Vorgaben für Reihenlieferungen*, in *Steuerberatung im Synergiebereich von Praxis und Wissenschaft: Festschrift für Alois Pircher zum 60. Geburtstag* (Peter Pülzl & Alois Pircher eds., Linde Verlag 2007).

Michael Tumpel, *Umsatzsteuer bei „unentgeltlichen" Onlinediensten*, in *Digitalisierung im Konzernsteuerrecht* (Sabine Kirchmayr et al. eds., Linde Verlag 2018).

Frans Vanistendael, *The Role of (Legal) Principles in EU Tax Law*, in *Principles of Law: Function, Status and Impact in EU Tax Law* (Cécile Brokelind ed., IBFD 2014).

Tomáš Zautloukal, *Die rechtliche Bedeutung der OECD-Verrechnungspreisrichtlinien*, in *Verrechnungspreisgestaltung im internationalen Steuerrecht* (Josef Schuch & Ulf Zehetner eds., Linde Verlag 2001).

Contributions to Journals

Dietmar Aigner et al., *Digitale Leistungen ohne Geldzahlung im Internet*, SWK (2017).

Richard T. Ainsworth et al., *VATCoin: Can a Crypto Tax Currency Prevent VAT Fraud?*, 83 Tax Notes International (2016).

Richard T Ainsworth et al., *A High-Tech Proposal for the U.K. and Saudi VATs: Fighting Fraud With Mini-Blockchains and VATCoins*, Tax Notes International (2019).

Richard Thompson Ainsworth & Musaad Alwohaibi, *The First Real-Time Blockchain VAT – GCC Solves MTIC Fraud*, Tax Notes International (2017).

Richard T. Ainsworth & Boryana Madzharova, *Real-Time Collection of the Value-Added Tax: Some Business and Legal Implications*, Boston Univ. School of Law, Law and Economics Research Paper No. 12-51 (2012).

Richard T. Ainsworth & Andrew Shact, *Blockchain Technology Might Solve VAT Fraud*, 83 Tax Notes International (2016).

Christian Amand, *When Is a Link Direct?*, 7 International VAT Monitor (1996).

Christian Amand, *VAT Neutrality: A Principle of EU Law or a Principle of the VAT System?*, 2 World Journal of VAT/GST Law (2015).

Christian Amand, *EU Value Added Tax: The Directive on Vouchers in the Light of the General Value Added Tax Rules*, 45 Intertax (2017).

Christian Amand, *Disclosed/Undisclosed Agent in EU VAT: When Is an Intermediary Acting in Its Own Name?*, 32 International VAT Monitor (2021).

Desiree Auer et al., *Umsatzsteuer im Rahmen der digitalen Transformation*, taxlex (2019).

Reuven Avi-Yonah & Nir Fishbien, *The Digital Consumption Tax*, 48 Intertax (2020).

Aleksandra Bal, *European Union – The Vague Concept of 'Taxable Person' in EU VAT Law*, 24 International VAT Monitor (2013).

Aleksandra Bal, *Taxation of Digital Supplies in the European Union and United States – What Can They Learn from Each Other?*, 55 European Taxation (2015).

Aleksandra Bal, *Managing EU VAT Risks for Platform Business Models*, 72 Bulletin for International Taxation (2018).

Aleksandra Bal, *Managing EU VAT Risks for Platform Business Models*, 72 Bulletin for International Taxation (2018).

Aleksandra Bal, *Germany: New VAT Compliance Obligations for Online Platforms*, 28 EC Tax Review (2019).

Aleksandra Bal, *The Changing Landscape of the EU VAT: Digital VAT Package and Definitive VAT System*, 59 European Taxation (2019).

Stefanie Becker, *Bericht aus Brüssel – Umsetzung der Neuregelungen im E-Commerce ab 1.1.2021*, MwStR (2019).

Fabrizio Borselli, *VAT Fraud, Cryptocurrencies and a Future for the VAT System*, 30 International VAT Monitor (2019).

Robert F van Brederode & Sebastian Pfeiffer, *Combating Carousel Fraud: The General Reverse Charge VAT*, 26 International VAT Monitor.

Winfried Brugger, *Concretization of Law and Statutory Interpretation*, 11 Tulane European & Civil Law Forum (1996).

Benjamin Butler, *Non-Monetary Consideration in the Context of VAT: The Status of the Judgment Empire Stores v Commissioners of Customs and Excise in the Light of Later Judgments*, EC Tax Review (2001).

Deborah Butler, *The Usefulness of the 'Direct Link' Test in Determining Consideration for VAT Purposes*, EC Tax Review (2004).

Francesco Cannas et al., *A New Legal Framework Towards a Definitive EU VAT System: Online Hosting Platforms and E-Books Reveal Unsolved Problems on the Horizon*, 46 Intertax (2018).

Stephen Dale & Venise Vincent, *The European Union's Approach to VAT and E-Commerce*, 6 World Journal of VAT/GST Law (2017).

Daniel Denker & Matthias Trinks, *Umsatzsteuerfalle Amazon*, Der Umsatz-Steuer-Berater (2017).

David Dietsch, *Umsatzsteuerpflicht von kostenlosen sozialen Netzwerken*, MwStR (2017).

David R. Dietsch & Timm Stelzer, *Die Digitalisierung der Ladenrechtsprechung des BFH – Vermittlungsleistungen im Internetzeitalter*, 9 MwStR (2021).

Lars Dobratz, *EU-Grundrechte und Umsatzsteuerrecht*, 63 Umsatzsteuer-Rundschau (2014).

Ad van Doesum & Herman van Kesteren, *Taxes, Duties, Levies and Charges as Part of the Taxable Amount for Value Added Tax*, 26 EC Tax Review (2017).

Thomas Dubut, *The Court of Justice and the OECD Model Tax Conventions or the Uncertainties of the Distinction between Hard Law, Soft Law, and No Law in the European Case Law*, Intertax.

Gorka Echevarría Zubeldia, *How VAT-Free Can Free Internet Services Be?*, 30 International VAT Monitor (2019).

Karina Kim Egholm Elgaard, *The Impact of the Charter of Fundamental Rights of the European Union on VAT Law*, 5 World Journal of VAT/GST Law (2016).

Tina Ehrke-Rabel & Sebastian Pfeiffer, *Umsatzsteuerbarer Leistungsaustausch durch „entgeltlose" digitale Dienstleistungen*, SWK (2017).

Tina Ehrke-Rabel & Lily Zechner, *VAT Treatment of Cryptocurrency Intermediation Services*, 48 Intertax (2020).

Joachim Englisch, *‚Kostenlose' Online-Dienstleistungen: tauschähnlicher Umsatz?*, 66 Umsatzsteuer-Rundschau (2017).

Andreas Erdbrügger, *Änderung der EU-Umsatzsteuervorschriften für den E-Commerce ab 2019 bzw. 2021*, DStR (2018).

Lukas Franke & Julia Tumpel, *Aus für Mehrwertsteuerbetrug im Onlinehandel?*, SWK (2018).

Franz-J. Giesberts, *Eigentumsübertragung, Verschaffung der Verfügungsmacht und Lieferung*, 25 Umsatzsteuer-Rundschau (1976).

Hans-Martin Grambeck, *B2C Supplies of Electronic Services from 1 January 2015 from a German Perspective*, 24 International VAT Monitor (2013).

Hans-Martin Grambeck, *Keine Umsatzsteuerpflicht bei kostenlosen Internetdiensten und Smartphone-Apps*, DStR (2015).

Hans-Martin Grambeck, *Electronic Marketplaces May Be Held Liable for German VAT – New Rules Entered into Effect on 1 January 2019*, 30 International VAT Monitor (2019).

Marco Greggi, *Neutrality and Proportionality in VAT: Making Sense of an (Apparent) Conflict*, 48 Intertax (2020).

Ivo Grlica, *How the Sharing Economy Is Challenging the EU VAT System*, 28 International VAT Monitor (2017).

Bartosz Gryziak, *Split Payment Across the European Union – Review and Analysis*, 31 International VAT Monitor (2020).

Hannes Gurtner & Peter Pichler, *Reihengeschäfte: Offene Fragen zum Urteil des EuGH in der Rs. EMAG*, SWK (2006).

José A. Gutiérrez-Fons & Koen Lenaerts, *To Say What the Law of the EU Is: Methods of Interpretation and the European Court of Justice*, 20 Columbia Journal of European Law (2014).

Robert Hammerl & Andreas Fietz, *Umsatzsteuerrisiken beim „Versand durch Amazon"*, NWB (2017).

Hans-Hermann Heidner, *Umsatzsteuerliche Behandlung von Kommissionsgeschäften*, 50 Umsatzsteuer-Rundschau (2001).

Oskar Henkow, *Neutrality of VAT for Taxable Persons: A New Approach in European VAT?*, 17 EC Tax Review (2008).

Oskar Henkow, *Defining the Tax Object in Composite Supplies in European VAT*, 2 World Journal of VAT/GST Law (2013).

Charlène A Herbain & Alain Thilmany, *Split Payment: The Validity of a Not so New Alternative Vat Collection Method*, British Tax Review (2018).

Mariken van Hilten & Giorgio Beretta, *The New VAT Record Keeping and Reporting Obligations for Payment Service Providers*, 31 International VAT Monitor (2020).

Luc Hinnekens, *VAT Directive on Electronic Services – Some Open Questions*, 43 European Taxation (2003).

Terry Hutchinson & Nigel Duncan, *Defining and Describing What We Do: Doctrinal Legal Research*, 17 Deakin Law Review (2012).

Michele Iavagnilio, *Intermediary Services – What the ECJ Did Not Say*, 15 International VAT Monitor (2004).

Roland Ismer & Magdalena Schwarz, *Combating VAT Fraud through Digital Technologies: A Reform Proposal*, 30 International VAT Monitor (2019).

Sascha Jafari, *Combining Modern Technology and Real-Time Invoice Reporting to Combat VAT Fraud: No Revolution, but a Technological Evolution*, 31 International VAT Monitor (2020).

Sascha Jafari, *Business-Friendly Real-Time Reporting in the European Union – Are We Moving in the Right Direction?*, 32 International VAT Monitor (2021).

Kathryn James & Thomas Ecker, *Relevance of the OECD International VAT/GST Guidelines for Non-OECD Countries*, 32 Australian Tax Forum (2017).

Anne Janssen, *The Problematic Combination of EU Harmonized and Domestic Legislation Regarding VAT Platform Liability*, 32 International VAT Monitor (2021).

Peter Jenkins, *VAT and Electronic Commerce: The Challenges and Opportunities*, 10 International VAT Monitor (1999).

Charles Jennings, *The EU VAT System – Time for a New Approach?*, 21 International VAT Monitor (2010).

Kerrigan, *The Elusiveness of Neutrality – Why Is It So Difficult To Apply VAT to Financial Services?*, 21 International VAT Monitor (2010).

Richard Kettisch, *Treibstofflieferungen im Kommissionsgeschäft*, 54 Österreichische Steuerzeitung (2018).

Han Kogels, *Making VAT as Neutral as Possible*, 21 EC Tax Review (2012).

Marie Lamensch, *Are Reverse Charging and the One-Stop Scheme Efficient Ways to Collect VAT on Digital Supplies*, 1 World Journal of VAT/GST Law (2012).

Marie Lamensch, *Unsuitable EU VAT Place of Supply Rules for Electronic Services – Proposal for an Alternative Approach*, 4 World Tax Journal (2012).

Marie Lamensch, *The 2015 Rules for Electronically Supplied Services – Compliance Issues*, 26 International VAT Monitor (2015).

Marie Lamensch, *Is There Any Future for the Vendor Collection Model in the 21st Century Economy?*, 27 International VAT Monitor (2016).

Marie Lamensch, *Soft Law and EU VAT: From Informal to Inclusive Governance?*, 5 World Journal of VAT/GST Law (2016).

Marie Lamensch, *European Commission's New Package of Proposals on E-Commerce: A Critical Assessment*, 28 International VAT Monitor (2017).

Marie Lamensch, *Adoption of the E-Commerce VAT Package: The Road Ahead Is Still a Rocky One*, 27 EC Tax Review (2018).

Marie Lamensch, *Rendering Platforms Liable to Collect and Pay VAT on B2C Imports: A Silver Bullet?*, 29 International VAT Monitor (2018).

Marie Lamensch et al., *New EU VAT-Related Obligations for E-Commerce Platforms Worldwide: A Qualitative Impact Assessment*, 13 World Tax Journal (2021).

Marie Lamensch & Mack Saraswat, *From Clicks to Compliance: A Data Conduit to Collect VAT*, 28 International VAT Monitor (2017).

Howard Liebman & Olivier Rousselle, *VAT Treatment of Composite Supplies*, 17 International VAT Monitor (2006).

Nicole Looks & Benjamin Bergau, *Tauschähnlicher Umsatz mit Nutzerdaten – Kein Stück vom Kuchen*, MwStR (2016).

Matthias Luther et al., *Wer schuldet die Umsatzsteuer bei Umsätzen über Internetplattformen?*, DStR (2021).

Miguel Poiares Maduro, *Interpretation of European Law: Judicial Adjudication in a Context of Constitutional Pluralism*, 1 European Journal of Legal Studies (2007).

Aileen McColgan, *Cracking the Comparator Problem: Discrimination, 'Equal' Treatment and the Role of Comparisons*, European Human Rights Law Review (2006).

Nevada Melan & Sebastian Pfeiffer, *Bezahlen mit Rechten, nicht mit Daten: Weitere offene Fragen zur Umsatzsteuerpflicht „kostenloser" Internetdienste und Smartphone-Apps*, DStR (2017).

Nevada Melan & Bertram Wecke, *Einzelfragen der Umsatzsteuerpflicht „kostenloser" Internetdienste und Smartphone-Apps*, DStR (2015).

Nevada Melan & Bertram Wecke, *Umsatzsteuerpflicht von „kostenlosen" Internetdiensten und Smartphone-Apps*, DStR (2015).

Madeleine Merkx, *New Implementing Measures for EU Place-of-Supply Change 2015*, 24 International VAT Monitor (2013).

Madeleine Merkx, *VAT and E-Services: When Human Intervention Is Minimal*, 29 International VAT Monitor (2018).

Madeleine Merkx, *VAT and Blockchain: Challenges and Opportunities Ahead*, 28 EC Tax Review (2019).

Madeleine Merkx, *New VAT Rules for E-Commerce: The Final Countdown Has Begun*, 29 EC Tax Review (2020).

Madeleine Merkx & Anne Janssen, *A New Weapon in the Fight Against E-Commerce VAT Fraud: Information from Payment Service Providers*, 30 International VAT Monitor (2019).

Sergio Messina, *VAT E-Commerce Package: Customs Bugs in the System? Analysis of the Issues Undermining the New Import VAT Platform Collecting Model*, 13 World Tax Journal (2021).

D.B. Middelburg, *Nieuwe Btw-Regels Voor Ingevoerde Goederen*, Weekblad fiscaal recht (2020).

Robert Müller, *Building a Blockchain for the EU VAT*, 100 Tax Notes International (2020).

Robert Müller, *Proposal for an Automated Real-Time VAT Collection Mechanism in B2C E-Commerce Using Blockchain Technology*, 31 International VAT Monitor (2020).

Helmut Nieuwenhuis, *Grundsatz der Neutralität der Umsatzsteuer in der Rechtsprechung des EuGH*, 62 Umsatzsteuer-Rundschau (2013).

Marta Papis-Almansa, *VAT and Electronic Commerce: The New Rules as a Means for Simplification, Combatting Fraud and Creating a More Level Playing Field?*, 20 ERA Forum (2019).

Nicoletta Petrosino, *Are You Ready for the Tax Technology?*, 30 International VAT Monitor (2019).

Sebastian Pfeiffer, *VAT on 'Free' Electronic Services?*, 27 International VAT Monitor (2016).

Christina Pollak, *Die OSS Im Überblick – Umsatzsteuerliche Vereinfachung Oder Undurchsichtige Verkomplizierung?*, 2 AVR (2021).

Christina Pollak & Karoline Spies, *Die umsatzsteuerlichen Änderungen bei Warenverkäufen über Plattformen: Online-Plattformen als Steuerschuldner*, ecolex (2021).

Christina Pollak & Draga Turić, *Reihengeschäfte mit Drittstaatsbezug*, taxlex (2021).

Steven Pope et al., *Import Value De Minimis Level in Selected Economies as Cause of Undervaluation of Imported Goods*, 8 World Customs Journal (2014).

Robert C Prätzler, *Split Payments in VAT Systems – Is This the Future?*, 29 International VAT Monitor (2018).

Pernille Rendahl, *EU VAT and Double Taxation: A Fine Line between Interpretation and Application*, Intertax (2013).

Michael Ridsdale, *Abuse of Rights, Fiscal Neutrality and VAT*, 14 EC Tax Review (2005).

Bohumila Salachová & Bohumil Vítek, *Interpretation of European Law, Selected Issues*, 61 Acta Universitatis Agriculturae et Silviculturae Mendelianae Brunensis (2013).

Wolfgang Schön, *Die Kommission im Umsatzsteuerrecht*, 37 Umsatzsteuer-Rundschau (1988).

Wilhelm G. Schulze & Stephanus P. van Zyl, *The Collection of Value Added Tax on Cross-Border Digital Trade – Part 2: VAT Collection by Banks*, 47 Comparative and International Law Journal of Southern Africa (2014).

Frederek Schuska, *Die Abgrenzung von Vermittlungsdienstleistungen zum Eigengeschäft und elektronischen Dienstleistungen*, MwStR (2017).

Jonathan R. Siegel, *The Inexorable Radicalization of Textualism*, 158 University of Pennsylvania Law Review (2009).

Selina Siller & Annika Streicher, *Online Beherbungsplattformen: Leistung des Vermieters und Leistung der Plattform als einheitliche Leistung?*, taxlex (2020).

Selina Siller & Annika Streicher, *Online-Beherbungsplattformen: Zwischen elektronisch erbrachter Dienstleistung und Margenbesteuerung*, taxlex (2020).

Jordi Sol, *EU VAT E-Commerce Package – Trust in MOSS and in Electronic Interfaces as Collection Methods*, 32 International VAT Monitor (2021).

Annika Streicher, *Rechnungsberichtigung bei Kleinbetragsrechnungen*, ecolex (2021).

Elvire Tardivon-Lorizon & Amanda Z Quenette, *Indirect Taxation of E-Commerce – Significant Recent Changes in the United States and the European Union*, 29 International VAT Monitor (2018).

Ben Terra, *Supplies for Consideration, or Must Consideration Be Stipulated?*, International VAT Monitor (1993).

Michael Tumpel, *Reihenlieferungen: EuGH bestätigt österreichische Verwaltungspraxis*, SWK (2006).

Antonio Vázquez del Rey, *VAT Connecting Factors: Relevance of the Place of Supply*, 43 Intertax (2015).

Matthias Weidmann, *The New EU VAT Rules on the Place of Supply of B2C E-Services*, 24 EC Tax Review (2015).

Werner Widmann, *Systembezogene Änderung bei der Umsatzbesteuerung „Reverse-Charge-Verfahren"*, 55 Umsatzsteuer-Rundschau (2006).

Patrick Wille, *New EU VAT Rules for Telecommunications Services from 2015*, 23 International VAT Monitor (2012).

Patrick Wille, *New Rules from 2015 Onwards for Telecommunications, Radio and Television Broadcasting, and Electronically Supplied Services*, 26 International VAT Monitor (2015).

Patrick Wille, *The Correct Interpretation of the Thresholds for Distance Sales*, 29 International VAT Monitor (2018).

Patrick Wille, *New VAT Rules on E-Commerce*, 32 International VAT Monitor (2021).

Florian Zawodsky, *Value Added Taxation in the Digital Economy*, British Tax Review (2018).

Lily Zechner, *Kryptowährungen: Sind Wechselstuben, Handelsplätze und Walletanbieter umsatzsteuerpflichtig?*, taxlex (2017).

Lily Zechner, *How to Treat the Ride-Hailing Company Uber for VAT Purposes*, 30 International VAT Monitor (2019).

Lily Zechner, *Ist Uber auch aus Sicht des Umsatzsteuerrechts Beförderungsdienstleister?*, 29 SWI (2019).

Lily Zechner, *Internetplattformen und umsatzsteuerrechtliche Leistungszurechnung am Beispiel Airbnb*, ÖStZ (2020).

A VATCoin Solution to MTIC Fraud: Past Efforts, Present Technology, and the EU's 2017 Proposal, Tax Notes International (2018).

Legal Commentaries

Mark Bell, *Article 20 – Equality Before the Law*, The EU Charter of Fundamental Rights: A Commentary (Steve Peers et al. eds., Nomos Beck Hart 2014).

Alfonso Celotto, *Article 20 – Equality Before the Law*, Human Rights in Europe: Commentary on the Charter of Fundamental Rights of the European Union (William B. T. Mock ed., Carolina Academic Press 2010).

Thomas Ecker, *§ 3a*, Umsatzsteuergesetz (Stefan Melhardt & Michael Tumpel eds., Linde Verlag 2021).

Hans-Hermann Heidner & Johann Bunjes, *§ 15 Vorsteuerabzug*, Umsatzsteuergesetz: Kommentar (Johann Bunjes et al. eds., C.H. Beck 2021).

Hans D. Jarass, *Art. 17 Eigentumsrecht*, Charta der Grundrechte der EU (Hans D. Jarass ed., C.H. Beck 2021).

Hans D. Jarass, *Art. 20 Gleichheit vor dem Gesetz*, Charta der Grundrechte der EU (Hans D. Jarass ed., C.H. Beck 2021).

Cornelia Köchler & Laura Pavlidis, *Gleichheit*, Charta der Grundrechte der Europäischen Union: GRC-Kommentar (Michael Holoubek & Georg Lienbacher eds., MANZ'sche Verlags- und Universitätsbuchhandlung 2019).

Alexander Oelmaier, *§ 15 Vorsteuerabzug*, Umsatzsteuergesetz (Otto Sölch & Karl Ringleb eds., C.H. Beck 2021).

Martin Robisch & Johann Bunjes, *§ 3 Lieferung, sonstige Leistung*, Umsatzsteuergesetz: Kommentar (Johann Bunjes et al. eds., C.H. Beck 2021).

Hans Georg Ruppe & Markus Achatz, *zu § 3a UStG*, Umsatzsteuergesetz: Kommentar (Hans Georg Ruppe & Markus Achatz eds., Facultas 2018).

Hans Georg Ruppe & Markus Achatz, *zu § 12 UStG*, Umsatzsteuergesetz: Kommentar (Hans Georg Ruppe & Markus Achatz eds., Facultas 2018).

Frauke Schulmeister, *Art. 203*, Zollkodex der Union (Peter Witte ed., C.H. Beck 2022).

Otto Sölch et al., *§ 3 Lieferung, sonstige Leistung*, Umsatzsteuergesetz (Otto Sölch & Karl Ringleb eds., C.H. Beck 2021).

Ben Terra & Julie Kajus, *Commentary – A Guide to the Recast VAT Directive* (IBFD 2020).

Jonathan Tomkin, *Equality*, The EU Treaties and the Charter of Fundamental Rights: A Commentary (Manuel Kellerbauer et al. eds., University Press 2019).

Documents and Reports Issued by the EU, OECD and Other Sources

Commission Decision of 26 June 2012 Setting up a Group of Experts on Value Added Tax, (2012/C 188/02) (28.06.2012).

Written Question No 617/89 by Mr Fernand Herman (PPE) to the Commission of the European Communities, 90/C 39/52 (27 October 1989), https://eur-lex.europa.eu/legal-content/EN/TXT/PDF/?uri = OJ:C:1990:039:FULL&from = GA (last visited 29 November 2021).

Supplementary Answer given by Mrs Scrivener on Behalf of the Commission, C 317 (7 September 1992), https://eur-lex.europa.eu/legal-content/EN/TXT/PDF/?uri = OJ:JOC_1992_317_R_0001_01&qid = 1638271319631&from = DE (last visited 30 November 2021).

Explanations Relating to the Charter of Fundamental Rights, OJ C 303 (14.12.2007), https://eur-lex.europa.eu/legal-content/EN/TXT/PDF/?uri = CELEX:32007X121 4(01)&from = EN (last visited 29 March 2021).

Bruno Basalisco et al., *E-Commerce Imports into Europe: VAT and Customs Treatment* (4 May 2016), https://www.copenhageneconomics.com/dyn/resources/Publi cation/publicationPDF/8/348/1462798608/e-commerce-imports-into-europe_ vat-and-customs-treatment.pdf (last visited 9 January 2021).

Commission of the European Communities, *Communication from the Commission to the Council, the European Parliament, the Economic and Social Committee and the Committee of the Regions – A European Initiative in Electronic Commerce*, COM(97) 157 final (18 April 1997), https://eur-lex.europa.eu/legal-content/EN /TXT/PDF/?uri = CELEX:51997DC0157&from = EN (last visited 22 January 2021).

Commission of the European Communities, *Communication from the Commission to the Council, the European Parliament and the Economic and Social Committee – Electronic Commerce and Indirect Taxation*, COM(1998) 374 final (17.06.1998), https://eur-lex.europa.eu/legal-content/EN/TXT/PDF/?uri = CELEX:51998DC0 374&from = EN (last visited 22 January 2021).

Committee on Fiscal Affairs' Working Party No. 9 on Consumption Taxes, *Consumption Tax Aspects of Electronic Commerce* (February 2001), http://www.oecd.org /ctp/consumption/2673667.pdf (last visited 11 December 2020).

Consumption Tax TAG (Technical Advisory Group), *Report by the Consumption Tax Technical Advisory Group (TAG)* (December 2000), http://www.oecd.org/ctp/ consumption/1923240.pdf (last visited 11 December 2020).

Council of the European Union, *Report from the Council of the European Union to the Council*, 13840/17 (30 October 2017), https://eur-lex.europa.eu/legal-content/ EN/TXT/PDF/?uri = CONSIL:ST_13840_2017_INIT&from = EN (last visited 5 April 2022).

Council of the European Union, *Legislative Acts and Other Instruments: Council Implementing Regulation Amending Implementing Regulation (EU) No 282/2011 Laying down Implementing Measures for Directive 2006/112/EC on the Common System of Value Added Tax*, 14127/17 (28 November 2017), https://www. consilium.europa.eu/media/31930/st14127en17.pdf (last visited 5 April 2022).

Council of the European Union, *Legislative Acts and Other Instruments: Council Regulation Amending Regulation (EU) No 904/2010 on Administrative Cooperation and Combating Fraud in the Field of Value Added Tax*, 14128/17 (28 November 2017), https://www.consilium.europa.eu/media/31931/st14128en1 7.pdf (last visited 5 April 2017).

Council of the European Union, *Draft Minutes: 3582nd Meeting of the Council of the European Union (Economic and Financial Affairs), Held in Brussels on 5 December 2017*, 15565/17 (15 December 2017), https://data.consilium.europa.eu/doc/document/ST-15565-2017-ADD-1/en/pdf (last visited 5 April 2022).

Council of the European Union, *Legislative Acts and Other Instruments: Council Directive Amending Directive 2006/112/EC and Directive 2009/132/EC as Regards Certain Value Added Tax Obligations for Supplies of Services and Distance Sales of Goods*, 14126/17 (28.11.2017), https://www.consilium.europa.eu/media/31929/st14126en17.pdf (last visited 5 April 2022).

Economic and Social Committee, *Opinion of the Economic and Social Committee on the Proposal for a Regulation of the European Parliament and of the Council Amending Regulation (EEC) No 218/92 on Administrative Cooperation in the Field of Indirect Taxation (VAT), and the Proposal for a Council Directive Amending Directive No 77/388/EEC as Regards the Value Added Tax Arrangements Applicable to Certain Services Supplied by Electronic Means*, OJ C 116 (20 April 2001), https://eur-lex.europa.eu/legal-content/EN/TXT/PDF/?uri = CELEX:52000AE1413&from = DE (last visited 23 January 2021).

European Commission, *Interim Report on the Implications of Electronic Commerce for VAT and Customs*, XXI/98/0359 (3 April 1998), https://ec.europa.eu/taxation_customs/sites/taxation/files/resources/documents/interim_report_on_electric_commerce_en.pdf (last visited 22 January 2021).

European Commission, *Study on the Feasibility of Alternative Methods for Improving and Simplifying the Collection of VAT Through the Means of Modern Technologies and/or Financial Intermediaries* (20 September 2010), https://op.europa.eu/en/publication-detail/-/publication/e0d6a4f7-9ada-11e6-868c-01aa75ed71a1/language-en (last visited 29 November 2021).

European Commission, *Explanatory Notes VAT Invoicing Rules* (5 October 2011), https://ec.europa.eu/taxation_customs/system/files/2016-09/explanatory_notes_en.pdf (last visited 19 July 2021).

European Commission, *Guide to the VAT Mini One Stop Shop* (23 October 2013), https://ec.europa.eu/taxation_customs/business/vat/telecommunications-broadcasting-electronic-services/sites/default/files/taxud-2013-01228-02-01-en-ori-00-en.pdf (last visited 19 July 2021).

European Commission, *Explanatory Notes on the EU VAT Changes to the Place of Supply of Telecommunications, Broadcasting and Electronic Services That Enter into Force in 2015* (3 April 2014), https://ec.europa.eu/taxation_customs/sites/taxation/files/resources/documents/taxation/vat/how_vat_works/telecom/explanatory_notes_2015_en.pdf (last visited 2 February 2021).

European Commission, *Report of the Commission Expert Group on Taxation of the Digital Economy* (28 May 2014), https://ec.europa.eu/taxation_customs/sites/taxation/files/resources/documents/taxation/gen_info/good_governance_matters/digital/report_digital_economy.pdf (last visited 2 February 2021).

European Commission, *Assessment of the Application and Impact of the VAT Exemption for Importation of Small Consignments*, Specific Contract No 7 TAXUD/2013/DE/334 Based on Framework Contract No Taxud/2012/CC/117,

Final Report (May 2015), https://ec.europa.eu/taxation_customs/sites/taxation /files/docs/body/lvcr-study.pdf (last visited 2 February 2021).

European Commission, *Explanatory Notes on EU VAT Place of Supply Rules on Services Connected with Immovable Property That Enter into Force in 2017* (26 October 2015), https://ec.europa.eu/taxation_customs/system/files/2016-09/explanato ry_notes_new_en.pdf (last visited 14 July 2021).

European Commission, *Communication from the Commission to the European Parliament, the Council, the European Economic and Social Committee of the Regions – a European Agenda for the Collaborative Economy*, COM(2016) 356 final (2016), https://eur-lex.europa.eu/legal-content/EN/TXT/PDF/?uri = CELEX:52016DC0 356&from = EN (last visited 2 February 2021).

European Commission, *Communication from the Commission to the European Parliament, the Council and the European Economic and Social Committee on an Action Plan on VAT*, COM(2016) 148 final (7 April 2016), https://ec.europa.eu/taxation _customs/system/files/2016-10/com_2016_148_en.pdf (last visited 27 October 2021).

European Commission, *Commission Staff Working Document Impact Assessment Accompanying the Document Proposals for a Council Directive, a Council Implementing Regulation and a Council Regulation on Modernising VAT for Cross-Border B2C E-Commerce*, COM(2016) 757 final (1 December 2016), https://ec. europa.eu/transparency/documents-register/api/files/SWD(2016)379_0/de000 00000291864?rendition = false (last visited 4 April 2022).

European Commission, *Proposal for a Council Directive Amending Directive 2006/112/EC and Directive 2009/132/EC as Regards Certain Value Added Tax Obligations for Supplies of Services and Distance Sales of Goods*, COM(2016) 757 final (1 December 2016), https://ec.europa.eu/transparency/regdoc/rep/1/201 6/EN/COM-2016-757-F1-EN-MAIN-PART-1.PDF (last visited 28 January 2021).

European Commission, *Proposal for a Council Implementing Regulation Amending Implementing Regulation (EU) No 282/2011 Laying down Implementing Measures for Directive 2006/112/EC on the Common System of Value Added Tax*, COM(2016) 756 final (1 December 2016), https://ec.europa.eu/transparency/ regdoc/rep/1/2016/EN/COM-2016-756-F1-EN-MAIN-PART-1.PDF (last visited 28 January 2021).

European Commission, *Proposal for a Council Regulation Amending Regulation (EU) No 904/2010 on Administrative Cooperation and Combating Fraud in the Field of Value Added Tax*, COM(2016) 755 final (1 December 2016), https://ec.europa. eu/transparency/regdoc/rep/1/2016/EN/COM-2016-755-F1-EN-MAIN.PDF (last visited 28 January 2021).

European Commission, *Analysis of the Impact of the Split Payment Mechanism as an Alternative VAT Collection Method* (December 2017), https://op.europa.eu/en/ publication-detail/-/publication/b87224ad-fcce-11e7-b8f5-01aa75ed71a1/lang uage-en (last visited 29 November 2021).

European Commission, *Commission Staff Working Document Impact Assessment Accompanying the Document Proposal for a Council Directive amending Directive 2006/112/EC on the Common System of Value Added Tax as Regards the Special*

Scheme for Small Enterprises, COM(2018) 21 final (18 January 2018), https://ec
.europa.eu/taxation_customs/system/files/2018-01/18012018_impactassessme
nt_vat_smes_en.pdf (last visited 27 October 2021).

European Commission, *Explanatory Notes on the EU VAT Changes in Respect of Call-Off Stock Arrangements, Chain Transactions and the Exemption for Intra-Community Supplies of Goods ('2020 Quick Fixes')* (December 2019), https://ec.europa.eu/ taxation_customs/sites/default/files/explanatory_notes_2020_quick_fixes_en. pdf (last visited 20 June 2021).

European Commission, *Explanatory Notes on the New VAT E-Commerce Rules* (30 September 2020), https://ec.europa.eu/taxation_customs/sites/taxation/files/ vatecommerceexplanatory_28102020_en.pdf (last visited 2 February 2021).

European Commission, *VAT Rates Applied in the Member States of the European Union*, taxud.c.1(2021) (1 January 2021), https://ec.europa.eu/taxation_ customs/system/files/2021-06/vat_rates_en.pdf (last visited 15 April 2022).

European Commission, *Guide to the VAT One Stop Shop* (March 2021), https://ec.eu ropa.eu/taxation_customs/system/files/2021-03/oss_guidelines_en_0.pdf (last visited 19 July 2021).

European Commission, *Commission Decision of 22.10.2013 Setting up the Commission Expert Group on Taxation of the Digital Economy*, C(2013) 7082 final (22.10.2013), https://ec.europa.eu/taxation_customs/sites/taxation/files/docs/ body/com_2013_7082_en.pdf (last visited 24 January 2021).

European Commission, *Communication from the Commission to the European Parliament and the Council an Action Plan for Fair and Simple Taxation Supporting the Recovery Strategy*, COM/2020/312 final (15.7.2020), https://eur-lex.europa.eu/ resource.html?uri = cellar:e8467e73-c74b-11ea-adf7-01aa75ed71a1.0003.02/DO C_1&format = PDF (last visited 19 January 2021).

European Commission, *Green Paper: On the Future of VAT Towards a Simpler, More Robust and Efficient Vat System*, COM(2010) 695 final (01.12.2010), https://eur -lex.europa.eu/LexUriServ/LexUriServ.do?uri = COM:2010:0695:FIN:EN:PDF (last visited 27 October 2021).

European Commission, *Importation and Exportation of Low Value Consignments – VAT E-Commerce Package 'Guidance for Member States and Trade'*, https://ec. europa.eu/taxation_customs/system/files/2021-06/guidance_on_import_and_ export_of_low_value_consignments_en.pdf (last visited 1 August 2021).

European Commission, *Proposal for a Council Directive Amending Council Directive 2006/112/EC of 28 November 2006 as Regards Provisions Relating to Distance Sales of Goods and Certain Domestic Supplies of Goods*, COM(2018) 819 final (11.12.2018), https://eur-lex.europa.eu/legal-content/EN/TXT/PDF/?uri = CEL EX:52018PC0819&from = EN (last visited 2 February 2021).

European Commission, *Proposal for a Council Directive Amending Council Directive 2006/112/EC of 28 November 2006 as Regards Provisions Relating to Distance Sales of Goods and Certain Domestic Supplies of Goods*, COM(2018) 819 final (11.12.2018), https://eur-lex.europa.eu/legal-content/EN/TXT/PDF/?uri = CEL EX:52018PC0819&from = EN (last visited 19 October 2021).

European Commission, *Proposal for a Council Directive Amending Directive 2006/112/EC as Regards Harmonising and Simplifying Certain Rules in the Value Added Tax System and Introducing the Definitive System for the Taxation of Trade Between Member States*, COM(2017) 569 final (04.10.2017), https://ec.europa.eu/transparency/documents-register/api/files/COM(2017)569_0/de00000000189092?rendition = false (last visited 21 September 2021).

European Commission, *Proposal for a Council Directive Amending Directive 2006/112/EC on the Common System of Value Added Tax as Regards the Special Scheme for Small Enterprises*, COM(2018) 21 final (18.01.2018), https://eur-lex.europa.eu/legal-content/EN/TXT/PDF/?uri = CELEX:52018PC0021&from = DE (last visited 27 October 2021).

European Commission, *Proposal for a Council Implementing Regulation Amending Implementing Regulation (EU) No 282/2011 as Regards Supplies of Goods or Services Facilitated by Electronic Interfaces and the Special Schemes for Taxable Persons Supplying Services to Non-Taxable Persons, Making Distance Sales of Goods and Certain Domestic Supplies of Goods*, COM(2018) 821 final (11.12.2018), https://ec.europa.eu/transparency/regdoc/rep/1/2018/EN/COM-2018-821-F1-EN-MAIN-PART-1.PDF (last visited 2 February 2021).

European Parliament, *Report on the Proposal for a Council Directive Amending Directive 2006/112/EC and Directive 2009/132/EC as Regards Certain Value Added Tax Obligations for Supplies of Services and Distance Sales of Goods*, A8-0307/2017 (16 October 2017), https://www.europarl.europa.eu/RegData/seance_pleniere/textes_deposes/rapports/2017/0307/P8_A(2017)0307_EN.pdf (last visited 5 April 2022).

International Post Corporation, *Cross-Border E-Commerce Shopper Survey 2017* (January 2018), https://www.ipc.be/-/media/documents/public/markets/2018/ipc-cross-border-e-commerce-shopper-survey2017.pdf?la = en&hash = 7FBBDE2919F1B56DE05BCC71BE486DE283E807AD (last visited 9 January 2021).

International Post Corporation, *Cross-Border E-Commerce Shopper Survey 2018* (January 2019), https://www.ipc.be/-/media/documents/public/markets/2019/ipc-cross-border-e-commerce-shopper-survey2018.pdf (last visited 9 January 2021).

International Post Corporation, *Cross-Border E-Commerce Shopper Survey 2019* (January 2020), https://www.ipc.be/-/media/documents/public/publications/ipc-shoppers-survey/ipc-cross-border-e-commerce-shopper-survey-2019.pdf (last visited 27 October 2021).

International Post Corporation, *Cross-Border E-Commerce Shopper Survey 2020* (January 2021), https://www.ipc.be/-/media/documents/public/publications/ipc-shoppers-survey/ipc-cross-border-e-commerce-shopper-survey-2020.pdf (last visited 27 October 2021).

International Post Corporation, *Cross-Border E-Commerce Shopper Survey 2021* (January 2022), https://www.ipc.be/-/media/documents/public/publications/ipc-shoppers-survey/ipc-cross-border-e-commerce-shopper-survey-2021.pdf?la = en&hash = 9303A77CD5B246A6384BE2D1B32BA3F725438985 (last visited 1 April 2022).

OECD, *Electronic Commerce: Taxation Framework Conditions* (1998), https://www. oecd.org/ctp/consumption/1923256.pdf (last visited 9 December 2020).

OECD, *Consumption Taxation of Cross-Border Services and Intangible Property in the Context of E-Commerce* (1 February 2001), https://www.oecd.org/tax/ consumption/2001%20E-Commerce%20Guidelines.pdf (last visited 10 December 2020).

OECD, *Taxation and Electronic Commerce: Implementing the Ottawa Taxation Framework Conditions* (1 June 2001), https://www.oecd.org/tax/consumption/ Taxation%20and%20eCommerce%202001.pdf (last visited 10 December 2020).

OECD, *Implementation Issues for Taxation of Electronic Commerce* (2003), http://www .oecd.org/tax/consumption/5594899.pdf (last visited 11 December 2020).

OECD, *Implementation of the Ottawa Taxation Framework* (2003), https://www. google.com/url?sa = t&rct = j&q = &esrc = s&source = web&cd = &ved = 2ahUKE wit9q716In5AhXBDuwKHWD6DG0QFnoECAkQAQ&url = https%3A%2F%2 Fwww.oecd.org%2Ftax%2Fadministration%2F20499630.pdf&usg = AOvVaw1 tqBhIEJI7lj7U8Yb0HzMe (last visited 9 December 2020).

OECD, *Electronic Commerce – Commentary on Place of Consumption for Business-to-Business Supplies (Business Presence)* (1 August 2003), https://www.oecd.org/ ctp/consumption/5592717.pdf (last visited 10 December 2020).

OECD, *Electronic Commerce: Simplified Registration Guidance* (1 August 2003), https: //www.oecd.org/ctp/consumption/5590980.pdf (last visited 10 December 2020).

OECD, *Electronic Commerce: Verification of Customer Status and Jurisdiction* (1 August 2003), https://www.oecd.org/ctp/consumption/5574687.pdf (last visited 10 December 2020).

OECD, *Report on the Application of Consumption Taxes to the Trade in International Services and Intangibles* (30 June 2004), http://www.oecd.org/ctp/consumption /2004%20Report.pdf (last visited 11 December 2020).

OECD, *The Application of Consumption Taxes to the International Trade in Services and Intangibles – Progress Report and Draft Principles* (30 January 2005), http://www .oecd.org/ctp/consumption/Application%20of%20Consumption%20Taxes%2 0Progress%20Report%202005.pdf (last visited 11 December 2020).

OECD, *International VAT/GST Guidelines* (OECD 2006), http://www.oecd.org/ctp/ consumption/36177871.pdf (last visited 11 December 2020).

OECD, *Applying VAT/GST to Cross-Border Trade in Services and Intangibles – Emerging Concepts for Defining Place of Taxation* (January 2008), http://www.oecd.org/ ctp/consumption/39874228.pdf (last visited 14 December 2020).

OECD, *Applying VAT/GST to Cross-Border Trade in Services and Intangibles – Emerging Concepts for Defining Place of Taxation – Outcome of the First Consultation Document* (June 2008), http://www.oecd.org/ctp/consumption/40931170.pdf (last visited 14 December 2020).

OECD, *Applying VAT/GST to Cross-Border Trade in Services and Intangibles Emerging – Concepts for Defining Place of Taxation – Second Consultation Document* (June

2008), http://www.oecd.org/ctp/consumption/40931469.pdf (last visited 14 December 2020).

OECD, 'OECD International VAT/GST Guidelines' – 'International Trade in Services and Intangibles' – 'Public Consultation on Draft Guideline for Customer Location' (5 February 2010), http://www.oecd.org/ctp/consumption/44559751.pdf (last visited 14 December 2020).

OECD, What Are the OECD International VAT/GST Guidelines? (December 2010), https://www.internationaltaxreview.com/pdfs/48077011_OECD.pdf (last visited 11 December 2020).

OECD, OECD International VAT/GST Guidelines – Draft Consolidated Version (4 February 2013), http://www.oecd.org/ctp/consumption/ConsolidatedGuidelines20130131.pdf (last visited 14 December 2020).

OECD, Addressing the Tax Challenges of the Digital Economy – Action 1: 2014 Deliverable (16 September 2014), https://www.oecd-ilibrary.org/docserver/9789264218789-en.pdf?expires = 1607958732&id = id&accname = ocid177428&checksum = 423372A2CBDB637C4C9A73CC98C1C158 (last visited 14 December 2020).

OECD, Discussion Drafts for Public Consultation – International VAT/GST Guidelines – Guidelines on Place of Taxation for Business-to-Consumer – Supplies Of Services and Intangibles – Provisions on Supporting the Guidelines in Practice (18 December 2014), http://www.oecd.org/ctp/consumption/discussion-draft-oecd-international-vat-gst-guidelines.pdf (last visited 14 December 2020).

OECD, Comments Received on Public Discussion Drafts – International VAT/GST Guidelines – Guidelines on Place of Taxation for Business-to-Consumer – Supplies Of Services and Intangibles – Provisions on Supporting the Guidelines in Practice (24 February 2015), http://www.oecd.org/ctp/consumption/03_public-comments-oecd-international-vat-gst-guidelines.pdf (last visited 14 December 2020).

OECD, Addressing the Tax Challenges of the Digital Economy – Action 1: 2015 Final Report (OECD 5 October 2015), https://www.oecd-ilibrary.org/docserver/9789264241046-en.pdf?expires = 1609863677&id = id&accname = ocid177428&checksum = 0C5F41CC3B2246D3954E6E701FCA6036 (last visited 14 December 2020).

OECD, International VAT/GST Guidelines (6 November 2015), http://www.oecd.org/ctp/consumption/international-vat-gst-guidelines.pdf (last visited 15 December 2020).

OECD, Mechanisms for the Effective Collection of VAT/GST When the Supplier Is Not Located in the Jurisdiction of Taxation (2017), http://www.oecd.org/tax/tax-policy/mechanisms-for-the-effective-collection-of-VAT-GST.pdf (last visited 9 December 2020).

OECD, International VAT/GST Guidelines (12 April 2017), https://www.oecd-ilibrary.org/docserver/9789264271401-en.pdf?expires = 1608027058&id = id&accname = ocid177428&checksum = ACC8441220D1C5B76D60F686C4AA7057 (last visited 9 December 2020).

OECD, *Tax Challenges Arising from Digitalisation – Interim Report 2018: Inclusive Framework on BEPS* (16 March 2018), https://www.oecd-ilibrary.org/docserver /9789264293083-en.pdf?expires = 1607599389&id = id&accname = ocid177428& checksum = 746FC4D50D4B18C97728007D9A84ED5A (last visited 9 December 2020).

OECD, *The Role of Digital Platforms in the Collection of VAT/GST on Online Sales* (March 2019), http://www.oecd.org/tax/consumption/the-role-of-digital-platforms-in-the-collection-of-vat-gst-on-online-sales.pdf (last visited 24 July 2020).

OECD, *Unpacking E-Commerce* (6 June 2019), https://www.oecd-ilibrary.org/ docserver/23561431-en.pdf?expires = 1649151696&id = id&accname = ocid1774 28&checksum = 458D5AEFA55FEF35AC0944FC4A300A4C (last visited 5 April 2022).

OECD, *Model Rules for Reporting by Platform Operators with Respect to Sellers in the Sharing and Gig Economy* (2020), http://www.oecd.org/ctp/exchange-of-tax-information/model-rules-for-reporting-by-platform-operators-with-respect-to-sellers-in-the-sharing-and-gig-economy.pdf (last visited 9 December 2020).

OECD, *The Impact of the Growth of the Sharing and Gig Economy on VAT/GST Policy and Administration* (19 April 2021), https://read.oecd.org/10.1787/51825505-en?format = pdf (last visited 2 April 2022).

Technology TAG (Technical Advisory Group), *Report by the Technology Technical Advisory Group (TAG)* (December 2000), http://www.oecd.org/ctp/ consumption/1923248.pdf (last visited 11 December 2020).

VAT Committee, *Guidelines Resulting from Meetings of the VAT Committee: Tax Arrangements for Defective Goods*, Guidelines Resulting from the 41st Meeting, XXI/711/94 (28 February–1 March 1994), https://ec.europa.eu/taxation_ customs/system/files/2021-03/guidelines-vat-committee-meetings_en.pdf (last visited 29 July 2021).

VAT Committee, *VAT Treatment of Crowdfunding*, Working Paper No. 836, tax-ud.c.1(2015)576037 (6 February 2015), https://circabc.europa.eu/sd/a/c9b4bb 6f-3313-4c5d-8b4c-c8bbaf0c175a/836%20-%20VAT%20treatment%20of%20 Crowd%20funding.pdf (last visited 19 July 2021).

VAT Committee, *Question Concerning the Application of EU VAT Provisions, VAT 2015: Scope of the Notion of Electronically Supplied Services*, Working Paper No. 843, taxud.c.1(2015)694775 (12 February 2015), https://circabc.europa.eu/sd/a /e346e09e-f06e-44cc-8f39-4334fb99c841/843%20-%20Scope%20of%20notion %20of%20electronically%20supplied%20services.pdf (last visited 19 July 2021).

VAT Committee, *Guidelines Resulting from Meetings of the VAT Committee: Distance Selling*, Guidelines Resulting from the 104th Meeting, taxud.c.1(2015)482 0441-876 (4-5 June 2015), https://ec.europa.eu/taxation_customs/system/files/ 2021-03/guidelines-vat-committee-meetings_en.pdf (last visited 29 July 2021).

VAT Committee, *VAT Treatment of Sharing Economy*, Working Paper No. 878, taxud.c.1(2015)4370160 (22 September 2015), https://circabc.europa.eu/sd/a/878e0591-80c9-4c58-baf3-b9fda1094338/878%20-%20VAT%20treatment%20of%20sharing%20economy.pdf (last visited 19 July 2021).

VAT Committee, *Question Concerning the Application of EU VAT Provisions, VAT 2015: Interaction Between Electronically Supplied Services and Intermediation Services and Initial Discussion on the Scope of the Concept of Intermediation Services When Taken in a Broader Context*, Working Paper No. 906, taxud.c.1(2016)3297911 (6 June 2016), https://circabc.europa.eu/sd/a/ea379e7b-5e2b-4217-b704-0b13a56de6dc/WP%20906%20-%20Interaction%20between%20electronically%20supplied%20services%20and%20intermediation%20services.pdf (last visited 19 July 2021).

VAT Committee, *Guidelines Resulting from Meetings of the VAT Committee, VAT 2015: Interaction Between Electronically Supplied Services and Intermediation Services and Initial Discussion on the Scope of the Concept of Intermediation Services When Taken in a Broader Context*, Guidelines Resulting from the 107th Meeting, taxud.c.1(2017)1402399-914 (8 July 2016), https://ec.europa.eu/taxation_customs/system/files/2021-03/guidelines-vat-committee-meetings_en.pdf (last visited 19 July 2021).

VAT Committee, *Question Concerning the Application of EU VAT Provisions, Conditions for There Being a Taxable Transaction When Internet Services Are Provided in Exchange for User Data*, Working Paper No. 958, taxud.c.1(2018)6248826 (30 October 2018), https://circabc.europa.eu/sd/a/ee8603b3-9d86-444f-921c-003e3bee08ce/WP%20958%20-%20Art%202%20-%20Internet%20services.pdf (last visited 19 July 2021).

VAT Committee, Implementation of the Quick Fixes Package: Council Directive (EU) 2018/1910 and Council Implementing Regulation (EU) 2018/1912, Working Paper No. 968, taxud.c.1(2019)3533969 (15 May 2019), https://www.google.com/url?sa=t&rct=j&q=&esrc=s&source=web&cd=&cad=rja&uact=8&ved=2ahUKEwijt9fXhZH3AhXGt6QKHWDDDjwQFnoECAwQAQ&url=https%3A%2F%2Fcircabc.europa.eu%2Fsd%2Fa%2F8e08ca08-307d-4f28-b14e-c980f9eaecab%2FWP%2520968%2520New%2520legislation%2520-%2520Quick%2520fixes%2520package.pdf&usg=AOvVaw3JpwFYT7BM5VehXK5uJ7tC (last visited 13 April 2022).

VAT Committee, *Question Concerning the Application of EU VAT Provisions, Services Supplied by Digital Platforms Intervening in Short-Term Leasing or Renting of Immovable Property*, Working Paper No. 990, taxud.c.1(2020)1181920 (18 February 2020), https://www.vatupdate.com/wp-content/uploads/2020/06/WP-990-Sharing-economy-platforms-immovable-property.pdf (last visited 19 July 2021).

VAT Committee, *Conferring Implementing Powers on the Commission in the Area of VAT and Transforming the Status of the VAT Committee into a Comitology Committee*, VEG No 093, taxud.c.1(2020)5815334 (29 September 2020), https://www.vatupdate.com/wp-content/uploads/2020/10/VEG-093-VAT-Committee-and-comitology.pdf (last visited 19 July 2021).

VAT Committee, *Scope of the One-Stop-Shop (OSS) with Regard to Intra-Community Distance Sales of Goods, Relevant VAT Return Period and Amendments of Previous Vat Returns*, Working Paper No. 1040, taxud.c.1(2022)1785494 (03.03.2022), https://circabc.europa.eu/ui/group/cb1eaff7-eedd-413d-ab88-94f 761f9773b/library/c249d43c-4df2-4dee-9f66-649c7b28adec/details (last visited 23 April 2022).

WCO, *International Convention on the Simplification and Harmonization of Customs Procedures – Revised Kyoto Convention* (17 April 2008), http://www.wcoomd. org/-/media/wco/public/global/pdf/topics/facilitation/instruments-and-tools/ conventions/kyoto-convention/revised-kyoto-convention/body_gen-annex-and -specific-annexes.pdf?la = en (last visited 14 January 2021).

WCO, *Guidelines for the Immediate Release of Consignments by Customs* (June 2018), http://www.wcoomd.org/-/media/wco/public/global/pdf/topics/facilitation/ instruments-and-tools/tools/immediate-release-guidelines/immediate-release- guidelines.pdf?db = web (last visited 14 January 2021).

Marshall W. Van Alstyne et al., *Pipelines, Platforms, and the New Rules of Strategy*, Harvard Business Review (4 January 2016), https://hbr.org/2016/04/pipelines- platforms-and-the-new-rules-of-strategy (last visited 31 July 2020).

Andrei Hagiu & Julian Wright, *When Data Creates Competitive Advantage*, Harvard Business Review (2020), https://hbr.org/2020/01/when-data-creates-compe titive-advantage (last visited 5 April 2022).

VAT Thresholds, https://ec.europa.eu/taxation_customs/system/files/2021-02/vat_ in_ec_annexi.pdf (last visited 27 October 2021).

Buying Online – EU Member States' Rules for VAT on Goods from Outside the EU and 'other Services, https://ec.europa.eu/taxation_customs/sites/taxation/files/vat_ buying_online.pdf (last visited 16 November 2020).

Emily Carr, *Legal Research: A Guide to Secondary Resources*, https://guides.loc.gov/ law-secondary-resources (last visited 24 July 2020).

Council of the European Union, *Electronic Publications: Council Agrees to Allow Reduced VAT Rates*, https://www.consilium.europa.eu/en/press/press-releases /2018/10/02/electronic-publications-council-agrees-to-allow-reduced-vat-rates/ (last visited 5 April 2021).

European Commission, *Taxes in Europe Database V3*, https://ec.europa.eu/taxation_ customs/tedb/taxSearch.html (last visited 19 October 2021).

European Commission, *Territorial Status of EU Countries and Certain Territories*, https://ec.europa.eu/taxation_customs/territorial-status-eu-countries-and-certa in-territories_en (last visited 27 July 2021).

Eurostat, *E-Commerce Sales*, https://ec.europa.eu/eurostat/web/products-eurostat- news/-/ddn-20211228-1 (last visited 21 February 2022).

Harvard Law School Library, *Legal Research Strategy, Primary Sources for Legal Research*, https://guides.library.harvard.edu/law/researchstrategy/primary sources (last visited 27 March 2020).

OECD, *Taxation Aspects of Electronic Commerce: Publication of Reports and Technical Papers*, http://www.oecd.org/ctp/treaties/ecommercereportsandtechnicalpap ers.htm (last visited 11 December 2020).

Courtney Reagan, *That Sweater You Don't Like Is a Trillion-Dollar Problem for Retailers. These Companies Want to Fix It*, https://www.cnbc.com/2019/01/10/growing-online-sales-means-more-returns-and-trash-for-landfills.html (last visited 1 October 2021).

United States, Congressional Research Service, *Statutory Interpretation: General Principles and Recent Trends*, https://www.everycrsreport.com/reports/97-589.html#_Toc407006254 (last visited 27 March 2020).

Lionel Valdellon, *Must-Know Ecommerce Return Rate Statistics and Trends in 2021*, https://clevertap.com/blog/ecommerce-return-rate-statistics/ (last visited 1 October 2021).

Fran Whittaker-Wood, *What Country Has the Highest Online Shopping Return Rate?*, https://www.paymentsjournal.com/highest-online-shopping-return-rate/ (last visited 1 October 2021).

Table of Cases[*]

---

[*] In chronological order.

343

Opinion of Advocate Generals

Joined Cases C-144/13, C-154/13, C-160/13, *VDP Dental Laboratory NV v Staatssecretaris van Financiën and Staatssecretaris van Financiën v X BV and Nobel Biocare Nederland BV*, 4 Sep. 2014, ECLI:EU:C:2014:2163, Opinion of AG Kokott, 275

Case C-264/14, *Skatteverket v David Hedqvist*, 16 Jul. 2015, ECLI:EU:C:2015:498, Opinion of AG Kokott, 274

Case C-390/15, *Proceedings brought by Rzecznik Praw Obywatelskich (RPO)*, 8 Sep. 2016, ECLI:EU:C:2016:664, Opinion of AG Kokott, 292

Case C-246/16, *Enzo Di Maura v Agenzia delle Entrate – Direzione Provinciale di Siracusa*, 8 Jun. 2017, ECLI:EU:C:2017:440, Opinion of AG Kokott, 274, 276, 310,

Case C-462/16, *Finanzamt Bingen-Alzey v Boehringer Ingelheim Pharma GmbH & Co. KG*, 11 Jul. 2017, ECLI:EU:C:2017:534, Opinion of AG Tanchev, 274

Case C-401/18, *Herst s.r.o. v Odvolací finanční ředitelství*, 3 Oct. 2019, ECLI:EU:C:2019:834, Opinion of AG Kokott, 129, 158, 161, 284

Case C-567/18, *Coty Germany GmbH v Amazon Services Europe Sàrl and Others*, 28 Nov. 2019, ECLI:EU:C:2019:1031, Opinion of AG Campos Sánchez-Bordona, 52

Case C-276/18, *KrakVet Marek Batko sp. K. v Nemzeti Adó- és Vámhivatal Fellebbviteli Igazgatósága*, 6 Feb. 2020, ECLI:EU:C:2020:81, Opinion of AG Eleanor Sharpston, 128

Case C-581/19, *Frenetikexito – Unipessoal Lda v Autoridade Tributária e Aduaneira*, 22 Oct. 2020, ECLI:EU:C:2020:855, Opinion of AG Kokott, 33

Case C-4/20, '*ALTI' OOD v Direktor na Direktsia 'Obzhalvane i danachno-osiguritelna praktika' Plovdiv pri Tsentralno upravlenie na Natsionalnata agentsia za prihodite*, 14 Jan. 2021, ECLI:EU:C:2021:12, Opinion of AG Kokott, 208

Cases of National Courts

VwGH 29 Jul. 2010, 2008/15/0272, 46, 185
VwGH 24 Mar. 2015, 2013/15/0238, 257
VwGH 28 Sep. 2016, Ra 2016/16/0052, 257
VwGH 18 Oct. 2018, Ro 2017/15/002, 257
BFH 14 May 1970, V R 77/66, 43
BFH 4 Sep. 1970, V R 80/66, 43
BFH 16 Dec. 1987, X R 32/82, 43
BFH 15 May 1994, XI R 107/92, 46
BFH 15 May 2012, XI R 16/10, 43
BFH 11 Nov. 2015, V R 68/14, 257
BGH 26 Jul. 2018, I ZR 20/17, 52
BFH 29 Apr. 2020, XI B 113/19, 52
FG Düsseldorf 10 Nov. 2019, 1 K 2693/17 U, 52

Table of Conventions

Table of Legislation and Agreements

359

Index

EUCOTAX Series on European Taxation

(1) Peter HJ Essers, Guido JME de Bont & Eric CCM Kemmeren (eds), *The Compatibility of Anti-Abuse Provisions in Tax Treaties with EC Law*, 1998 (ISBN 90-411-9678-1).

(2) Gerard TK Meussen (ed.), *The Principle of Equality in European Taxation*, 1999 (ISBN 90-411-9693-5).

(3) Michael Lang (ed.), *Tax Treaty Interpretation*, 2001 (ISBN 90-411-9857-1).

(4) Pasquale Pistone, *The Impact of Community Law on Tax Treaties: Issues and Solutions*, 2002 (ISBN 90-411-9860-1).

(5) René Offermanns, *The Entrepreneurship Concept in a European Comparative Tax Law Perspective*, 2002 (ISBN 90-411-9887-3).

(6) Michael Lang & Mario Züger, *Settlement of Disputes in Tax Treaty Law*, 2002 (ISBN 90-411-9904-7).

(7) Carlo Pinto, *Tax Competition and EU Law*, 2003 (ISBN 90-411-9913-6).

(8) Michael Lang, Hans-Jörgen Aigner, Ulrich Scheuerle & Markus Stefaner, *CFC Legislation, Tax Treaties and EC Law*, 2004 (ISBN 90-411-2284-2).

(9) Mattias Dahlberg, *Direct Taxation in Relation to the Freedom of Establishment and the Free Movement of Capital*, 2005 (ISBN 90-411-2363-6).

(10) Michael Lang, Judith Herdin & Ines Hofbauer, *WTO and Direct Taxation*, 2005 (ISBN 90-411-2371-7).

(11) Dennis Weber, *Tax Avoidance and the EC Tray Freedoms: A Study of the Limitations under European Law for the Prevention of Tax Avoidance*, 2005 (ISBN 90-411-2402-0).

(12) Félix Alberto Vega Borrego, *Limitations on Benefits Clauses on Double Taxation Conventions*, 2005 (ISBN 90-411-2370-9).

(13) Michael Lang, Josef Schuch & Claus Staringer, *ECJ-Recent Developments in Direct Taxation*, 2006 (ISBN 90-411-2509-4).

(14) Reuven S. Avi-Yonah, James R. Hines Jr. & Michael Lang, *Comparative Fiscal Federalism. Comparing the European Court of Justice and the US Supreme Court's Tax Jurisprudence*, 2007 (ISBN 978-90-411-2552-1).

(15) Christiana HJI Panayi, *Double Taxation, Tax Treaties, Treaty-Shopping and the European Community*, 2007 (ISBN 978-90-411-2658-0).

(16) Dennis Weber, *The Influence of European Law on Direct Taxation: Recent and Future Developments*, 2007 (ISBN 978-90-411-2667-2).

(17) Michael Lang & Pasquale Pistone, *The EU and Third Countries: Direct Taxation*, 2007 (ISBN 978-90-411-2665-8).

(18) Oskar Henkow, *Financial Activities in European VAT: A Theoretical and Legal Research of the European VAT System and Preferred Treatment of Financial Activities*, 2007 (ISBN 978-90-411-2703-7).

(19) Michael Lang (ed.), *Tax Compliance Costs for Companies in an Enlarged European Community*, 2008 (ISBN 978-90-411-2666-5).

(20) Michael Lang (ed.), *Source versus Residence. Problems Arising from the Allocation of Taxing Rights in Tax Treaty Law and Possible Alternatives*, 2008 (ISBN 978-90-411-2763-1).

(21) Ioanna Mitroyanni, *Integration Approaches to Group Taxation in the European Internal Market*, 2008 (ISBN 978-90-411-2779-2).

(22) Rolf Eicke, *Tax Planning with Holding Companies. Repatriation of US Profits from Europe: Concepts, Strategies, Structures*, 2008 (ISBN978-90-411-2794-5).

(23) Peter Essers et al. (ed.), *The Influence of IAS/IFRS on the CCCTB, Tax Accounting, Disclosure and Corporate Law Accounting Concepts: 'A Clash of Cultures'*, 2008 (ISBN 978-90-411-2819-5).

(24) Tonny Schenk-Geers, *International Exchange of Information and the Protection of Taxpayers*, 2009 (ISBN 978-90-411-3142-3).

(25) Raymond Adema, *UCITS and Taxation: Towards Harmonization of the Taxation of UCITS*, 2009 (ISBN 978-90-411-2839-3).

(26) Michael Lang, Jianwen Liu & Gongliang Tang (eds), *Europe–China Tax Treaties*, 2010 (ISBN 978-90-411-3216-1).

(27) Michael Lang, Pasquale Pistone, Josef Schuch & Claus Staringer (eds), *Procedural Rules in Tax Law in the Context of European Union and Domestic Law*, 2010 (ISBN 978-90-411-3376-2).

(28) Sjaak J.J.M. Jansen, *Fiscal Sovereignty of the Member States in an Internal Market: Past and Future*, 2011 (ISBN 978-90-411-3403-5).

(29) Dennis Weber & Bruno da Silva, *From Marks & Spencer to X Holding: The Future of Cross-Border Group Taxation*, 2011 (ISBN 978-90-411-3399-1).

(30) Claus Bohn Jespersen, *Intermediation of Insurance and Financial Services in European VAT*, 2011 (ISBN 978-90-411-3732-6).

(31) Sabine Heidenbauer, *Charity Crossing Borders: The Fundamental Freedoms' Influence on Charity and Donor Taxation in Europe*, 2011 (ISBN 978-90-411-3813-2).

(32) Michael Lang, et al., *The Future of Indirect Taxation: Recent Trends in VAT and GST Systems around the World*, 2012 (ISBN 978-90-411-3797-5).

(33) Harm van den Broek, *Cross-Border Mergers within the EU: Proposals to Remove the Remaining Tax Obstacles*, 2012 (ISBN 978-90-411-3824-8).

(34) Michael Lang, et al. (eds), *Tax Treaty Case Law around the Globe – 2011*, 2012 (ISBN 978-90-411-3876-7).

(35) Dennis Weber (ed.), *CCCTB: Selected Issues*, 2012 (ISBN 978-90-411-3872-9).

(36) Daniël Smit, *EU Freedoms, Non-EU Countries and Company Taxation*, 2012 (ISBN 978-90-411-4041-8).

(37) Rita de la Feria, *VAT Exemptions: Consequences and Design Alternatives*, 2013 (ISBN 978-90-411-3276-5).

(38) Karin Simader, *Withholding Taxes and the Fundamental Freedoms*, 2013 (ISBN 978-90-411-4842-1).

(39) Madeleine Merkx, *Establishments in European VAT*, 2013 (ISBN 978-90-411-4554-3).

(40) Carla De Pietro, *Tax Treaty Override*, 2014 (ISBN 978-90-411-5406-4).

(41) G.K. Fibbe & A.J.A. Stevens (eds), *Hybrid Entities and the EU Direct Tax Directives*, 2015 (ISBN 978-90-411-5942-7).

(42) Gerard Staats, *Personal Pensions in the EU*, 2015 (ISBN 978-90-411-5953-3).

(43) Michael Lang & Ine Lejeune (eds), *VAT/GST in a Global Digital Economy*, 2015 (ISBN 978-90-411-5952-6).

(44) Massimo Basilavecchia, Lorenzo del Federico & Pietro Mastellone (eds), *Tax Implications of Environmental Disasters and Pollution*, 2015 (ISBN 978-90-411-5611-2).

(45) Cristina Trenta, *Rethinking EU VAT for P2P Distribution*, 2015 (ISBN 978-90-411-6137-6).

(46) Marie Lamensch, Edoardo Traversa & Servaas van Thiel (eds), *Value Added Tax and the Digital Economy: The 2015 EU Rules and Broader Issues*, 2016 (ISBN 978-90-411-6612-8).

(47) Raffaele Petruzzi, *Transfer Pricing Aspects of Intra-Group Financing*, 2016 (ISBN 978-90-411-6732-3).

(48) Mario Grandinetti (ed.), *Corporate Tax Base in the Light of the IAS/IFRS and EU Directive 2013/34: A Comparative Approach*, 2016 (ISBN 978-90-411-6745-3).

(49) Bruno da Silva, *The Impact of Tax Treaties and EU Law on Group Taxation Regimes*, 2016 (ISBN 978-90-411-6905-1).

(50) Michael Lang, Alfred Storck & Raffaele Petruzzi (eds), *Transfer Pricing in a Post-BEPS World*, 2016 (ISBN 978-90-411-6710-1).

(51) Marta Papis-Almansa, *Insurance in European VAT: Current and Preferred Treatment in the Light of the New Zealand and Australian GST Systems*, 2017 (ISBN 978-90-411-8360-6).

(52) Wolfgang Speckhahn, *Real Estate Investment Trusts In Europe: Europeanising Tax Regimes*, 2017 (ISBN 978-90-411-8360-6).

(53) Frank J.G. Nellen, *Information Asymmetries in EU VAT*, 2017 (ISBN 978-90-411-8837-3).

(54) Erik Ros, *EU Citizenship and Direct Taxation*, 2017 (ISBN 978-90-411-8584-6).

(55) Werner Haslehner, Georg Kofler & Alexander Rust (eds), *EU Tax Law and Policy in the 21st Century*, 2017 (ISBN 978-90-411-8815-1).

(56) Claudia Sanò, *National Legal Presumptions and European Tax Law*, 2018 (ISBN 978-90-411-6613-5).

(57) Christoph Marchgraber, *Double (Non-)Taxation and EU Law*, 2018 (ISBN 978-90-411-9410-7).

(58) Dennis Weber & Jan van de Streek (eds), *The EU Common Consolidated Corporate Tax Base: Critical Analysis*, 2018 (ISBN 978-90-411-9233-2).

(59) Werner Haslehner (ed.), *Investment Fund Taxation: Domestic Law, EU Law, and Double Taxation Treaties*, 2018 (ISBN 978-90-411-9669-9).

(60) Jérôme Monsenego, *Selectivity in State Aid Law and the Methods for the Allocation of the Corporate Tax Base*, 2018 (ISBN 978-90-411-9413-8).

(61) José Manuel Almudí Cid, Jorge A. Ferreras Gutiérrez & Pablo A. Hernández González-Barreda (eds), *Combating Tax Avoidance in the EU: Harmonization and Cooperation in Direct Taxation*, 2019 (ISBN 978-94-035-0154-3).

(62) Werner Haslehner, Georg Kofler & Alexander Rust (eds), *Time and Tax: Issues in International, EU, and Constitutional Law*, 2019 (ISBN 978-94-035-0354-7).

(63) Nathalie Wittock, *Sales Promotion Techniques and VAT in the EU*, 2019 (ISBN 978-94-035-0861-0).

(64) Carla De Pietro (ed.), *New Perspectives on Fiscal State Aid: Legitimacy and Effectiveness of Fiscal State Aid Control*, 2019 (ISBN 978-94-035-1415-4).

(65) Giorgio Beretta, *European VAT and the Sharing Economy*, 2019 (ISBN 978-94-035-1435-2).

(66) Claudio Cipollini, *Special Tax Zones and EU Law: Theory, Implementations, and Future Challenges*, 2020 (ISBN 978-94-035-1885-5).

(67) Gianluigi Bizioli, Mario Grandinetti, Leopoldo Parada, Giuseppe Vanz & Alessandro Vicini Ronchetti (eds), *Corporate Taxation, Group Debt Funding and Base Erosion: New Perspectives on the EU Anti-Tax Avoidance Directive*, 2020 (ISBN 978-94-035-1170-2).

(68) Ronald Hein & Ronald Russo (eds), *Co-operative Compliance and the OECD's International Compliance Assurance Programme*, 2020 (ISBN 978-94-035-1951-7).

(69) Jeffrey Owens & Jonathan Leigh Pemberton, *Cooperative Compliance: A Multi-stakeholder and Sustainable Approach to Taxation*, 2021 (ISBN 978-94-035-3193-9).

(70) Christina Pollak, *Platforms in EU VAT Law: A Legal Analysis of the Supply of Goods*, 2022 (ISBN 978-94-035-1026-2).